Masters and Lords

Masters & Lords

MID-19TH-CENTURY U.S. PLANTERS AND PRUSSIAN JUNKERS

Shearer Davis Bowman

New York   Oxford
OXFORD UNIVERSITY PRESS
1993

Oxford University Press

Oxford   New York   Toronto
Delhi   Bombay   Calcutta   Madras   Karachi
Kuala Lumpur   Singapore   Hong Kong   Tokyo
Nairobi   Dar es Salaam   Cape Town
Melbourne   Auckland   Madrid

and associated companies in
Berlin   Ibadan

Published by Oxford University Press, Inc.,
200 Madison Avenue, New York, New York 10016

Oxford is a registered trademark of Oxford University Press

Library of Congress Cataloging-in-Publication Data
Bowman, Shearer Davis.
Masters and lords : mid-19th-century U.S. planters and Prussian
Junkers / Shearer Davis Bowman.
p. cm.   Includes bibliographical references and index.
ISBN 0-19-505281-1
1. Plantation owners—Southern States—History—19th century.
2. Plantation life—Southern States—History—19th century.
3. Southern States—History—1775-1865.
4. Nobility—Prussia, East (Poland and R.S.F.S.R.)—History—19th century.
5. Prussia, East (Poland and R.S.F.S.R.)—History.   I. Title.
F213.B68   1993
305.5′232′097509034—dc20   92-16398

1 3 5 7 9 8 6 4 2

Printed in the United States of America
on acid-free paper

To Lee,
with love and gratitude

Acknowledgments

NINETEEN YEARS AGO, when I began graduate study at Berkeley, I fancied myself a historian of modern Germany and had not the faintest notion of doing "comparative history." My scholarly interest in the American South was slight at best, despite my having been born and raised in the capital city of the Confederacy by two proud native Virginians. However, living outside the South for the first time awakened a latent curiosity in the region's past of slaves and slaveholders; by my third year at the University of California, their histories had captured my academic imagination. Hoping to combine my growing fascination with the Old South and my continuing interest in things German, I first explored the possibility of comparing planters and Junkers in a seminar taught by Kenneth M. Stampp. The paper I wrote for that seminar proved to be a turning point in my scholarly development, and I will always be grateful to Ken for helping me develop that fledgling essay into the dissertation (completed in 1986) that became the foundation for this book. Like numerous graduate students before me, I learned much from his extraordinary talents as an exacting scholar and friendly critic. I am also much indebted to Gerald D. Feldman, in whose graduate seminar I first did original research with German sources. Jerry has been enthusiastic about this comparative project from its inception, and the final product has been much improved by his insights and suggestions. I regret that *Masters and Lords* was not published before the death of Reinhard Bendix in 1991. His graduate seminar, his published work in historical and political sociology, and his introducing me to Professor Rudolf von Thadden at the University of Göttingen opened important intellectual doors for me. Robert G. Moeller and James Oakes head the list of other friends and teachers at Berkeley who influenced my thinking about this historical comparison.

Most of the research on which this book is based would have been impossible without the assistance provided by staff members at the following archives and libraries: the Alabama Department of Archives and History in Montgomery;

Alderman Library at the University of Virginia, Charlottesville; the Arkansas History Commission in Little Rock; the Barker Texas History Center of the Center for American History at the University of Texas at Austin; the Georgia Historical Society in Savannah; the Library of Congress in Washington, D.C.; Lower Saxony's State and University Library in Göttingen; the Main Library at the University of California, Berkeley; the Memphis Public Library in Memphis, Tennessee; the Mississippi Valley Collection at Memphis State University in Memphis, Tennessee; the Mississippi Department of Archives and History in Jackson; the Perkins Library at Duke University in Durham, North Carolina; the Perry-Castañeda Library at the University of Texas at Austin; the Southern Historical Collection at the University of North Carolina at Chapel Hill; the Swem Library at William and Mary College in Williamsburg, Virginia; the Virginia Historical Society in Richmond; the Virginia State Library in Richmond; and the U.S. Department of Agriculture's National Agricultural Library in Beltsville, Maryland. While working in Göttingen, I received special assistance from Joseph Mooser, Hanna Schissler, and Rudolf von Thadden. Both my parents, Shearer and Carolyn Bowman, and my parents-in-law, Howard and Norma Willey, effectively subsidized my research in the South by allowing me to use their homes, in Richmond and Memphis respectively, as bases of operations from which to visit archives and libraries.

Over the many years devoted to researching and writing this book a number of scholars proferred a helpful variety of recommendations as well as reservations about different aspects of my work on planters and Junkers. Most of these recommendations and reservations came in response to papers prepared for academic conferences. I want to thank the following individuals for comments that encouraged me to pursue, or challenged me to reconsider, some facet of my analysis and argument: Edward L. Ayers, Jean Baker, John B. Boles, Kathleen Conzen, David F. Crew, Daniel W. Crofts, George B. Forgie, George M. Fredrickson, Eugene D. Genovese, William E. Gienapp, Raymond Grew, Steven Hahn, John T. Hubbell, John S. Hughes, Michael P. Johnson, Sidney W. Mintz, William C. McNeil, Allan Peskin, Otto Pflanze, Hans Rosenberg, William K. Scarborough, John T. Schlotterbeck, Charles Sellers, Edgar T. Thompson, Marie Tyler-McGraw, and Jonathan Wiener.

I am also appreciative of the assistance provided by several people at Oxford University Press. Sheldon Meyer and Rachel Toor offered both encouragement to forge ahead and suggestions to make the text more palatable. And it was a pleasure to work with copy editor Stephanie Sakson and assistant editor Karen Wolny.

Scattered portions of this book are drawn from previously published essays. Three of those essays appeared in journals to whose editors I am grateful for the different ways they prodded me to improve my historical vision: "Antebellum Planters and *Vormärz* Junkers in Comparative Perspective," *American Historical*

Review 85 (October 1980); "Conditional Unionism and Slavery in Virginia, 1860–1861: The Case of Dr. Richard Eppes," *Virginia Magazine of History and Biography* 96 (January 1988); and "Abolition and Its Aftermath in the U.S. South, 1860–1900," *Itinerario* 12, no. 2 (1988). Two essays appeared in volumes of conference proceedings edited by Sue Eakin and John Tarver: *Plantations Around the World: Proceedings of the First World Plantation Conference, Baton Rouge, October 2–5, 1984* (Baton Rouge: Louisiana State Univ. Agricultural Center, 1986), which includes "A Comparison of Antebellum Southern Plantations and Contemporaneous East Elbian *Rittergüter*"; and *One World, One Institution: the Plantation. Proceedings of the Second World Plantation Conference, Shreveport, Louisiana, October 6–10, 1986* (Baton Rouge: Louisiana State Univ. Agricultural Center, 1989), which includes "U.S. Plantations and the Development of Capitalism." Most recently, "Honor and Martialism in the U.S. South and Prussian East Elbia during the Mid-Nineteenth Century" appeared in Kees Gispen, ed., *What Made the South Different?* (Jackson and London: Univ. Press of Mississippi, 1990).

The argument is often made in university circles, sometimes to justify the so-called "publish or perish" norm for tenure, that productive scholars make better teachers. Although I would not quarrel with this general assertion, I have also found that teaching classes, from lower-division survey courses to specialized graduate seminars, has served to enrich and enlarge the perspectives I bring to research and writing. For this reason, I find it appropriate to express here appreciation for students who took my classes at Hampden-Sydney College in Virginia from 1981 to 1986 and for those who have taken classes with me at the University of Texas at Austin since 1986. In addition, I am grateful for the opportunity at both institutions to teach classes in European as well as American history, thereby enhancing my capacity to think comparatively about the United States and Europe.

If my sanity and humanity have survived the lengthy and frequently frustrating process of researching and writing this book, much of the credit goes to my children, Kate and Will, and to such grand friends as Tighe and Hugh Antrim, Virginia and Tupper Garden, Harriet Hall and John Hughes, Jane and Jack Louis, Howard Miller, Bob Moeller, and Nancy and Ellis Nelson. However, my most profound and heartfelt thanks go to Lee Willey Bowman, who has lived with and endured this project for as long as I have and to whom *Masters and Lords* is dedicated.

Austin, Texas   S. D. B.
December 1992

Contents

PRUSSIA 1848-49

NORTH SEA

DENMARK

HOLSTEIN

MECKLENBURG

PO

Hamburg

NETHER-

Bremen

LANDS

HANOVER

Saxony

Brande

Berlin

Magdeburg

BELG.

Westphalia

Göttingen

AN

HALT

Elbe R.

Rhine land

KING.

Weimar

NASSAU

GRAND
DUCHY
OF
HESSE

THURINGIAN
STATES

ORE MTNS

LUX.
(NETH.)

Frankfurt
am
Main

Rhine R.

PALATINATE
(BAV.)

BADEN

BAVARIA

FRANCE

WÜRTTEM-
BERG

Hohenzollern

Munich

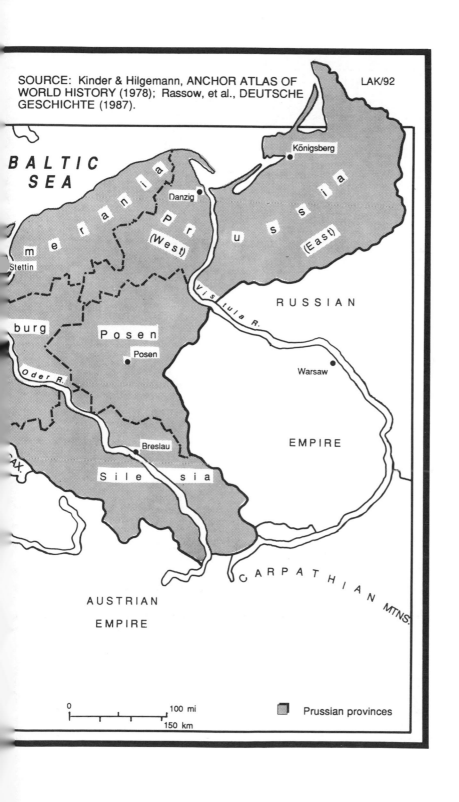

SOURCE: Kinder & Hilgemann, ANCHOR ATLAS OF WORLD HISTORY (1978); Rassow, et al., DEUTSCHE GESCHICHTE (1987).

LAK/92

BALTIC SEA

Königsberg

Danzig

P o m e r a n i a

P r u s s i a
(West)

m e r a n i a

Stettin

P r u s s i a (East)

RUSSIAN

Vistula R.

b u r g

P o s e n

Posen

Oder R.

Warsaw

EMPIRE

Breslau

S i l e s i a

AUSTRIAN

EMPIRE

C A R P A T H I A N MTNS.

0   100 mi
    150 km

Prussian provinces

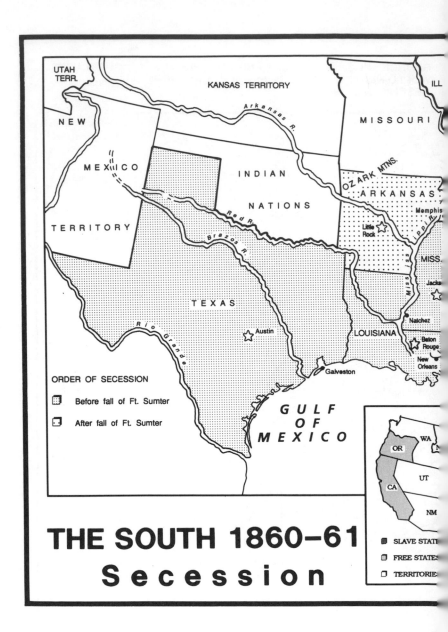

THE SOUTH 1860-61
Secession

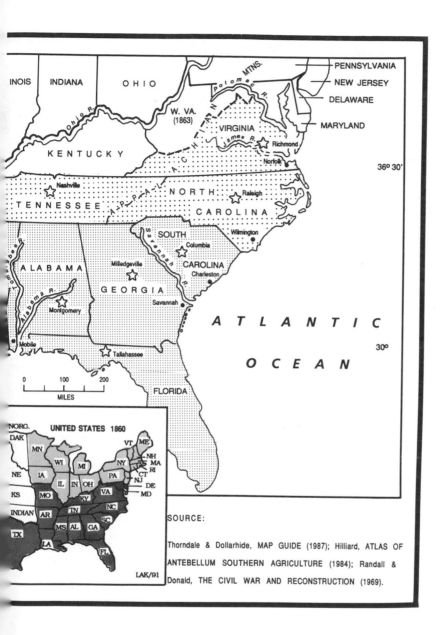

INOIS | INDIANA | OHIO | PENNSYLVANIA
NEW JERSEY
DELAWARE

W. VA.
(1863)

MARYLAND

VIRGINIA

Richmond

Norfolk

36° 30'

KENTUCKY

Nashville

NORTH

Raleigh

TENNESSEE

CAROLINA

SOUTH

Wilmington

Columbia

ALABAMA

Milledgeville

CAROLINA

Charleston

GEORGIA

Savannah

Montgomery

ATLANTIC

Mobile

30°

Tallahassee

OCEAN

0   100   200
MILES

FLORIDA

UNITED STATES 1860

SOURCE:

Thorndale & Dollarhide, MAP GUIDE (1987); Hilliard, ATLAS OF
ANTEBELLUM SOUTHERN AGRICULTURE (1984); Randall &
Donald, THE CIVIL WAR AND RECONSTRUCTION (1969).

LAK/91

Masters and Lords

Introduction

IF WE DEFINE an elite as the "most influential and prestigious" group or class in a society,[1] then two of the most formidable landed elites in modern history were the slaveholding planters of the antebellum U.S. South and the Junker estate owners of Prussian East Elbia during roughly the same era. Indeed, mid-nineteenth-century planters and Junkers constituted perhaps *the* most powerful *regional* landed elites in the history of the Western world, though the South and East Elbia had very different geographic environments, ethnic mixes, and political systems. Far from being superfluous rentiers or sycophantic courtiers, the great majority of planters and Junkers combined a considerable aptitude for profitable estate management with a resolute determination to maintain their influence and prestige as landed upper classes. Even so, they often disagreed among themselves about the most appropriate agricultural method, political strategy, or ideological stance.

It is not surprising that two such powerful and assertive groups have had no dearth of sentimental apologists who remember little but genteel and noble behavior, or of unremitting critics who see only evidence of oppression and ruthlessness. One of Max Weber's comments about the Junkers is equally apropos for the planters: they have been "frequently (and often unjustly) vilified," and "just as frequently (and often unjustly) idolized."[2] Although idolaters and vilifiers can each cite individual examples, neither romantic idolatry nor indignant vilification contribute much to a clear-sighted and fair-minded understanding of the past.[3] In the process of searching for the elusive reality of historical planters and Junkers, we must recognize that the two elites did not constitute monolithic groups with homogenous beliefs and outlooks, and that individual planters and Junkers often displayed the complexities of paradox and inconsistency that seem to characterize most human beings. Nonetheless, what we learn from studying planters and Junkers should illuminate two profound insights into human affairs, the first offered by a nineteenth-century German "radical" and the second by a twentieth-century American "conservative." "Men make their own history, but they do not make it just as they please," wrote Karl Marx in 1852; "they do not make it under circumstances chosen by themselves, but under circumstances directly encountered, given and transmitted from the past."[4] Whereas Marx's statement emphasizes the power of historical tradition in circumscribing human initiative, an observation by Irving Kristol stresses the limitations imposed on individual perception by group membership and identity. "No social group really possesses the imaginative capacity to have a liberal and reformist perspective on itself," observed Kristol in 1968; "individual members of the group may and do—but the group as a whole cannot. Otherwise, the history of human society would be what it is not: an amiable progression of thoughtful self-reformations by classes and institutions."[5]

Simply stated, the overarching goal of this transatlantic juxtaposition is to identify and explore important analogies between planters and Junkers as regional landed elites, and also to isolate and (so far as possible) explain significant differences between their historical milieus. My formulation of this goal owes much to a 1928 essay on the comparative method by French medievalist Marc Bloch, who specified two essential criteria for a fruitful "historical comparison": "a certain similarity or analogy between observed phenomena—that is obvious— and a certain dissimilarity between the environments in which they occur."[6] The analogies between antebellum planters and contemporaneous Junkers derive first and foremost from structural and functional parallels between plantations and Junker estates (*Rittergüter*, literally, "knight's estates") as at the same time commercial agricultural enterprises and authoritarian political communities. Plantations and knight's estates produced generally profitable cash crops—most notably Southern cotton and tobacco, East Elbian wheat and wool—for an international capitalist market then centered in England. And the proprietors of these estates managed their work forces as petty autocrats, even though *Rittergut* laborers ceased to be enserfed as of 1807–10, whereas plantation laborers remained enslaved until the 1860s; for Junker landowners retained inheritable judicial authority over their menial laborers until mid-century, and their police prerogatives survived until the 1870s.[7] Yet plantation masters and *Rittergut* lords inhabited very different geographic, political, and ethnic environments. To cite obvious dissimilarities, the provinces of Prussian East Elbia had no expansive frontier, no republican constitutions, and no slaves of African ancestry, while the states of the U.S. South had no hereditary monarchy, no large standing army, and no legacy of serfdom. Indeed, the differences between the South and East Elbia as historical milieus were of such magnitude that the rationale for their juxtaposition could be summarized simply by borrowing the words that Robert Brentano uses to justify his comparing the Catholic churches of England and Italy during the thirteenth century: the South and East Elbia are each "meant to be seen, for a change, against what it was not. In this sort of profile it has a different look."[8] Philip Morgan offers a similar justification for his three-way comparison of masters and slaves in eighteenth-century Jamaica, South Carolina, and Virginia: "Each looks different in light of the other; and our understanding of each is enlarged by knowledge of the other."[9]

My perspective on planters and Junkers also reflects an interest in some conceptual and social-scientific issues that belong to the broad and diffuse domain of political economy. In particular, to what extent can and should the two landed elites be adjudged "capitalist" and "conservative"? Obviously, how much capitalism or conservatism one finds in the South and East Elbia depends largely on how one defines these contentious terms—a daunting task that I will postpone for subsequent chapters. The significance of these questions is indicated by the fact that at least one of them seems to have engaged the seven other twentieth-century scholars whom I know to have commented in something like systematic fashion on the comparability of nineteenth-century planters and Junkers.[10] Each of these scholars—Dietrich Zwicker,[11] Barrington Moore, Jr.,[12] Eugene D. Genovese,[13] Richard Rubinson,[14] Barbara Jeanne Fields,[15] Steven Hahn,[16] and Edward L. Ayers[17]—offers provocative analysis of our two landed elites. It will become clear in the course of this book that my perspective differs to a greater or lesser extent from each of theirs, although I find myself closest to Barrington Moore's schematic portrait of planters as "Southern Junkers." Chapters 2 and 3 of *Masters and Lords* will evaluate mid-nineteenth century planters and Junkers alike as agrarian entrepreneurs and capitalists, despite very different climatic conditions and social structures in the South and East Elbia. I will also argue, most systematically in Chapter 6, that planters and Junkers each became the font of an authentic and powerful conservatism within the context of the nineteenth-century Western world, even if measured against the standards set by Edmund Burke and his seminal *Reflections on the Revolution in France* (1790). Planters and Junkers were comparably (as distinct from identically) conservative land elites despite their very different political institutions and cultures, whose histories are examined in Chapter 4. In comparing mid-nineteenth-century planters and Junkers as "conservative agrarian capitalists," I can hardly ignore the issues of patriarchy and paternalism. The intricate subtleties subsumed in these two terms are discussed at length in Chapter 5.

— I —

Before proceeding further, I should be more precise about the identity of our two landed elites (preliminary to more detailed group portraits in the first chapter), and also clarify the chronological and geographical boundaries of this study. Most historians of the pre–Civil War South accept the definition of a "planter" as formulated by U.S. census officials in 1860: the owner of twenty or more black slaves. Although I will argue in Chapter 1 for a more expansive and less statistically precise understanding of the term, the twenty-slave definition will suffice for the moment, with the proviso that such a slaveholder was also the proprietor of a rural estate, even if he derived most of his income from another source. The terms Junker and Junkerdom *(Junkertum)* derive from the Middle High German *juncherre,* meaning young lord or nobleman. In the nineteenth century they became generally opprobrious epithets for the supposedly feudal and reactionary proprietors of East Elbian Prussia's legally privileged "knights' estates" *(Rittergüter)* and their many relations in the Prussian officers' corps and royal bureaucracy.[18]

The label East Elbian Prussia warrants some explanation, especially since the political entity of Prussia disappeared from the map of central Europe after Germany's defeat in the Second World War and the country's subsequent dismemberment. In contrast, the states that composed the antebellum South, from Maryland in the east to Texas in the west, can be located on a present-day map of the United States with the same names and borders they had in 1860—with the exception of West Virginia, which seceded from Virginia in 1863. East Elbian Prussia circa 1850 encompassed those six provinces that lay entirely or partly to the east of the Elbe River, which flows roughly northwest into the North Sea from what we know today as Czechoslovakia. The region included most of post-1945 East Germany, northern and western Poland, and the Kaliningrad Oblast of the Soviet Union.

In order to understand planters and Junkers in the 1800s, we need to know something about their prior histories. Hence our analysis will reach back to the Junker elite's emergence in politically fragmented north-central Europe during the sixteenth and seventeenth centuries, and the planter elite's emergence on the Atlantic seaboard under British colonial rule during the seventeenth and eighteenth centuries. Concurrently, there also evolved the systems of unfree or bound labor, serfdom and slavery, that survived until 1807–10 in East Elbia and 1863–65 in the South.[19] But our chronological focus for the South is on the four antebellum, pre–Civil War decades (circa 1820 to 1860), and for East Elbia on the four to five decades following the monarchy's abolition of serfdom. Since people usually reveal the most about themselves during times of stress, anxiety, and conflict, we will pay particular attention to the circumstances, attitudes, and behavior of planters and Junkers during two intense mid-century political crises that offer fine grist for the mills of comparative analysis: the secession crisis of 1860–61 in the United States and the revolutionary crisis of 1848–49 in Prussia. Significantly, both elites confronted these political upheavals from positions of relative economic strength. East Elbian agriculture had recovered by the 1830s from its post-Napoleonic depression, and during the 1840s Junkers enjoyed rising demand for grain as well as a stable market for wool. Across the Atlantic, the 1850s found cotton and tobacco planters alike basking in the economic warmth of the Old South's last boom decade.

In Prussia the aborted "revolution from below" in 1848 represented in part an explosion of tensions and resentments that had been building since the royal bureaucracy's partial "revolution from above" during the Stein-Hardenberg Reform Era of 1807–19. Napoleon's humiliation of the Prussian army and its Junker officers corps at the battles of Jena and Auerstadt in 1806 provided the catalyst of reform, which began when Baron vom Stein's famous October Edict of 1807 announced an end to both serfdom and the titled nobility's legal monopoly on the ownership of knights' estates. The Prussian reform movement began to wane after the final defeat of Napoleonic France in 1814–15, which inaugurated a period of "reaction" and "restoration" throughout Europe. In the states of the German Confederation (1815–66), whose two principal powers were Austria and Prussia, the years from 1815 to 1848 are often referred to as *Vormärz,* the pre-March era, since revolution came to both Vienna and Berlin in mid-March of 1848. In Prussia the revolution brought about the final liquidation of servile "feudal" dues that had survived the Stein-Hardenberg years, as well as the establishment of the first popularly elected assembly in the country's history. Nonetheless, in late 1848 and 1849 the opponents of liberal-democratic constitutionalism regained the upper hand in Prussia, and launched the so-called "Era of Reaction," which lasted until the future Wilhelm I became Prince Regent in 1858. When the prospective "New Era" hailed by constitutional liberals soon foundered on a fundamental conflict between monarchy and parliament over the king's desire for army reorganization and the assembly's insistence on control over military appropriations, a desperate King Wilhelm inadvertently initiated the process of German national unification under Prussian leadership by appointing Junker Otto von Bismarck as minister-president in 1862.

Geographically, I focus on Junkers who lived in the East Elbian territory that Napoleon left to the truncated Kingdom of Prussia under the terms of the Treaty of Tilsit in 1807. This territory included the provinces of Brandenburg, Pomerania, Silesia, and the East and West Prussias (administratively united as the province of Prussia from 1824 to 1878). The Hohenzollern dynasty had acquired most of Brandenburg in the fifteenth and sixteenth centuries, most of East Prussia and Pomerania in seventeenth century, and Silesia and West Prussia in the eighteenth century. After Napoleon's defeat in 1814–15, the Congress of Vienna awarded the Hohenzollern monarchy territory that became four additional provinces. Two lay entirely west of the Elbe River: Westphalia, which Napoleon had incorporated into his Confederation of the Rhine, and the Rhineland, which had been annexed to Revolutionary and Napoleonic France for almost twenty years, and therefore appeared to many Junkers as the seedbed of radicalism in *Vormärz* Prussia. To the east the Hohenzollerns acquired territory that became the provinces of Saxony and Posen. Provincial Saxony, less than half of which lay east of the Elbe River, combined land that had belonged to the Kingdom of Saxony with erstwhile portions of western Brandenburg—the Old Mark and Magdeburg-Halberstadt. Posen encompassed some of the Polish territory that Prussia had originally annexed in 1793–95, and that Napoleon had incorporated into the Grand Duchy of Warsaw. "With a thoroughly progressive Rhineland province closer to liberal France than to its (Prussia's) own conservative eastern region," observes Rudolf von Thadden, "and with 'East Elbia' closely linked—not least through the partition of Poland—with agrarian Eastern Europe, Prussia was torn between a Europe of human rights and a Europe of the old order."[20]

Across the Atlantic the secession crisis of 1860–61 concluded an antebellum era that many historians date from the 1819–20 Missouri controversy over slavery's expansion west of the Mississippi river. Missouri's application to join the federal Union as a slave state sparked what Don Fehrenbacher calls "the first sectional crisis over slavery" and "a new surge in the development of southern consciousness,"[21] spurring many seaboard planters to ponder carefully how the slave states could best protect their region's system of bondage and political influence within the federal Union. During the twenties and thirties debates over the protective tariff and abolitionist agitation, which compounded the white South's anxieties over the dangers of slave violence and rebellion, stoked the fires of North/South sectional conflict; but the question of slavery extension resumed center stage during the 1840s and 1850s, leading to the formation in 1854 of the Republican party as a sectional and explicitly antislavery political organization committed to curbing the expansionistic "Slave Power." In 1860 its presidential candidate, committed to the containment and "ultimate extinction" of slavery, won the White House without receiving a single electoral vote from the slave states. Abraham Lincoln's election—the "Revolution of 1860," according to James McPherson—spurred seven slave states in the Lower South to secede and establish an independent Southern Confederacy, the "Counterrevolution of 1861."[22] The Confederacy's bombardment of Fort Sumter in April and President Lincoln's response of calculated bellicosity led four additional slave states in the Upper South to quit the Union and join the Confederacy. Thus was precipitated what most Northerners in 1861 saw as a war for liberty, the Union, and the Constitution against a rebellion led by the "slaveocracy," and what most white Southerners saw as a war for independence and liberty against abolitionist fanaticism and incipient "Black Republican" tyranny. Although the North's victory in the Civil War destroyed chattel slavery, it did not bring about the expropriation of planter real estate and its redistribution among families of black freedmen. This moderation in the federal government's postwar "Reconstruction" of the South helped make possible the evolution of a decentralized cotton and tobacco plantation system based on sharecropping and tenancy, and the emergence of a reconstituted planter elite composed of both holdovers from the antebellum era and ascendant newcomers.[23]

Our geographic focus is on planters in the eleven slave states of the Deep and Middle South (versus the four slave states of the Border South) that joined the new Confederate States of America in 1861.[24] Four of these seceding states—Virginia, the Carolinas North and South, and Georgia—had participated in the creation of the U.S. Republic in the 1770s and 1780s. Four more—Tennessee, Louisiana, Alabama, and Mississippi—had entered the federal Union during the early national period, between 1790 and 1820. The final three—Arkansas, Florida, and Texas—had joined the United States during the thirties and forties. During the secession crisis of 1860–61 the Border South slave states of Delaware, Maryland, Kentucky, and Missouri remained "loyal" to the Union primarily because of their geographic proximity to, and their strong economic and social ties with, the free states on their northern or eastern borders. Delaware, in which the 1860 census found not a single "planter," was not really a part of the Old South. Maryland, although internally bifurcated between a northerly belt of free-labor counties focused on Baltimore City and a southerly belt of slave-labor plantation counties, might well have quit the Union in 1861 save for the Lincoln administration's pre-emptive strikes against the governor and state legislature at Annapolis in order to prevent the isolation of the national capital behind Confederate lines.[25] Kentuckians and Missourians, like Marylanders, fought their own intrastate civil wars during the early 1860s. Many Border South slaveholders actively supported the Confederate cause, while in the states that seceded many residents of areas with relatively few slaves (most notably the mountainous areas of western Virginian, eastern Tennessee, and western North Carolina) opposed both secession and the Southern Confederacy. Yet their dislike for disunionist planters seldom bespoke a desire to abolish slavery.[26]

Although this book seeks to juxtapose East Elbia and the South as regional societies, the research and analysis frequently focus on the province of Brandenburg and the state of Virginia. This occasional focus can hardly be justified on the grounds that Brandenburg and Virginia were "typical" or representative of their regional societies. Despite the ubiquity of Junkers and knight's estates in Prussia's eastern provinces and an abundance of planters and plantations in every state that joined the Confederacy, East Elbia and the South were both marked by important subregional variations, both among and within provinces and states. For example, Silesia contained many more mountains, Roman Catholics, Slavic Poles, and producers of flax and linen than did Brandenburg. Virginia, unlike Louisiana, contained many mountains, negligible French and Roman Catholic influence, few cotton and no sugar plantations. Nonetheless, the special attention paid to Brandenburg and Virginia can be justified on several grounds. Even as the Mark was the oldest of the Hohenzollern monarchy's East Elbian provinces, so the Old Dominion was the site of England's first permanent settlement in North America. Just as the Junkers of Brandenburg took great pride in the unequaled contributions of the Mark's nobility to the rise of Hohenzollern Prussia, so Virginia planters lauded the leading role played by scions of the Old Dominion in the American Revolution as well as in the establishment and early governance of the United States. Yet each group believed itself to be less powerful and prestigious in 1850 that it had been at the beginning of the century. Junkers in *Vormärz* Brandenburg, like planters in antebellum Virginia, combined a determined resistance to democratic changes in their province's or state's political structure with a notable receptivity to agricultural diversification and improved farming techniques. Moreover, at mid-century the Mark and the Old Dominion were among the most economically diversified of their regions' provinces and states. Brandenburg contained the largest and most industrialized city of East Elbia, Berlin, which also served as the Kingdom of Prussia's capital city. Although the Confederate South's largest city in 1860 was the Mississippi River and Gulf port of New Orleans, the capital of Virginia—Richmond, an inland river city like Berlin—was the region's most industrialized town and became the Confederacy's seat of government in 1861. In short, the landed elites of the Old Dominion and the Mark partook in peculiar and often contradictory blends of prideful historical tradition and accelerating economic change.

— II —

I should acknowledge forthrightly that I am more of a specialist in the history of the Old South than in the history of "Old Prussia" (*Altpreussen*, the predominantly East Elbian heartland of the Hohenzollern monarchy). I originally undertook this historical comparison primarily for what it might reveal about the planter elite, for the fresh perspectives that it might bring to some current debates and controversies in Southern historiography. This bias, if you will, is reflected in the greater breadth of my research on the South than on East Elbia. Whereas my sources on planters include manuscripts found in a number of archives located south of the Mason-Dixon Line, my research on Junkers extends to published documents only, and does not include manuscripts from depositories in recently reunited Germany. The asymmetry in sources may constitute a flaw in my handling of the comparison, making it something less than a thoroughly systematic comparison. I am also well aware that I have not made use of all the myriad printed sources and historical literature that touch in some way on the histories of antebellum planters and contemporaneous Junkers. Even so, the variety of published documents and scholarly studies consulted on both groups seems sufficient to warrant evaluating this book as a legitimate comparative study, one that offers a fresh perspective on each landed elite. The printed sources from East Elbia to which I have devoted the most attention are agricultural periodicals and political proceedings from the 1840s and 1850s, because the historical records for the late antebellum South offer obvious counterparts.[27]

Scholars of U.S. history have at times been charged with cultural and linguistic provincialism. And one can adduce a number of historical factors that explain why many U.S. historians, like many citizens of the United States, have demonstrated a high quantum of nationalist myopia: for example, the new nation's struggle from the Revolution through the War of 1812 to establish for itself an independent existence and identity for itself apart from England, a struggle which promoted a vision of the new country as the world's best hope for a successful experiment in republican government; the combination of geographic isolation with a wealth of natural resources; the country's preoccupation with continental expansion and sectional conflict during the nineteenth century; and the nation's vision of itself during much of the twentieth century, particularly after World War II, as the bastion of democratic capitalism against the totalitarian communism emanating from Soviet Russia. All have contributed to Americans' making what C. Vann Woodward called in 1968 "excessive claims to distinctiveness and uniqueness in their national experience."[28]

Despite the reputed provincialism of Americanists, I doubt that historians of the United States have been, on the whole, any more parochial than, say, historians of Germany or England. Indeed, one could easily argue that since the Second World War history departments in most American universities have been decidedly more cosmopolitan that their European counterparts. This cosmopolitanism has encouraged a number of U.S. historians to undertake international comparative studies of slavery and race relations that have won deserved acclaim among their professional colleagues.[29] Even so, we should remember that history as an institutionalized profession in both the United States and Europe was born during the heyday of nationalism in the nineteenth century.[30] Naturally enough, teaching and research in the discipline have always reflected the national boundaries and loyalties that continue to shape the world in which we live. Considering the rigorous standards of documentation to which most historians pay homage, and the almost bewildering proliferation in recent decades of specialized monographs and journal articles,[31] it is hardly surprising that since the early 1960s few historians on either side of the Atlantic have been prepared or disposed to follow the bold lead of a Robert R. Palmer or Eric Hobsbawm and to explore systematically the ways in which patterns of historical development have simultaneously transcended and been modified by national and transoceanic boundaries in the "modern" Western world.[32] Lest proponents and practitioners of international comparative history succumb to an inflated opinion of their own cause or prowess, however, it should be emphasized that such a comparativist must always strive to minimize the unavoidable trade-off between the investigative thoroughness gained from total immersion in the original documents and scholarly studies of a particular society and culture, and the fresh perspectives and insights that the comparative method can sometimes provide. Furthermore, significant comparative work across national boundaries is well-nigh impracticable without an abundance of secondary literature and edited sources on each of the societies being studied.

— III —

If asked to summarize the most important historical dissimilarity between the United States and Prusso-Germany in the nineteenth century, many scholars would no doubt reiterate the influential argument of political scientist Louis Hartz, as presented in *The Liberal Tradition in America: An Interpretation of American Political Thought Since the Revolution* (1955), and point to the absence of indigenous feudal traditions from U.S. history, including the Old South. To some extent this transatlantic juxtaposition of planters and Junkers is a response to Hartz's insistence that "Any attempt to uncover the nature of an American society without feudalism"—by which he meant "the institutions of the medieval era," like serfdom and a titled nobility—"can only be accomplished by studying it in conjunction with a European society where the feudal structure and the feudal ethos did in fact survive."[33] There is little doubt that something of what Hartz means by "the feudal structure and the feudal ethos" survived in Prussian East Elbia well into the nineteenth century.[34] Although many U.S. historians have agreed with Hartz in seeing the absence of feudalism as the fundamental cause of their country's deep-seated and thoroughgoing "liberalism," and thus of America's historical distinctiveness in relation to Europe,[35] very few have attempted to demonstrate the truth of this proposition through systematic comparative studies of the kind recommended by Hartz.[36]

The dearth of systematic U.S./European comparative studies has been especially regrettable with respect to the Old South, that section of the country for which scholars and literati have advanced the most extreme claims to uniqueness and exceptionalism within the American context, and that section which has seemed most akin to feudal or medieval Europe. "To a far greater degree than the North," observed Allan Nevins, "the South was a land of class stratification and vestigial feudalism."[37] Ever since plantation magnates in colonial Virginia began to think of themselves as transplanted English country gentlemen, occasional friends, foes, and even scholarly interpreters of antebellum planters have suggested their comparability to European landed aristocracies with roots in medieval feudalism. Sociologist Edgar T. Thompson explained that "Titled aristocrats, as opposed to plutocrats, appear to evolve in societies based upon landed estates, and if Southern plantation society developed no genuine titled aristocracy, as the manor did, it did develop a gentry with aristocratic pretensions."[38] Yet historians of the Old South are sharply divided over the degree to which these "aristocratic pretensions" should be taken seriously. At one end of the spectrum we find Eugene Genovese: "The planters, in truth, grew into the closest thing to feudal lords imaginable in a nineteenth-century bourgeois republic." Medieval Europe, by giving birth to "a seigneurial world in which lords and serfs (not slaves) faced each other with reciprocal demands and expectations," had "slowly forged the traditional paternalist ideology to which the southern slave-holders fell heir."[39] At the opposite end of the spectrum stands F. N. Boney: "Overall, the whites of the antebellum South, whether 'aristocrats' or 'rednecks,' lived in a bourgeois world far removed from any kind of Old World seigneurialism or feudalism." Indeed, "the great majority of antebellum upper-class Southerners swam swiftly in the economic mainstream of American life. In the traditional European sense of the world, they were not aristocrats at all but simply very successful American businessmen."[40] Obviously these different evaluations of antebellum planters vis-à-vis European aristocrats fairly cry out for systematic comparative analysis, if only to determine whether businesslike behavior and seigniorial traditions were as incompatible among European aristocracies as both Genovese and Boney seem to imply.

Yet we do not have as yet a satisfactory comparative analysis of planterdom and the English landed gentry, which a good many antebellum Southerners, especially in Virginia, saw as their model. In 1851 Dr. John Peyton Little of Richmond expressed the prevalent notion that during the seventeenth century the Old Dominion had been "settled mainly by the sons of country gentlemen, who brought the love of country life with them across the Atlantic, and infused it into the mass of the population." Consequently, Virginians "have ever preferred that life; and the title of country gentleman, implying the possession of landed estates, has always been deemed more honorable than any other."[41] Lawyer Daniel R. Hundley, a native of Alabama and the son of a transplanted Virginian, wrote in 1860 that "In Virginia, the ancestors of the Southern Gentleman were chiefly English Cavaliers, after whom succeeded the French Huguenots and Scotch Jacobites."[42] Twentieth-century scholars Thomas Jefferson Wertenbaker, Louis Wright, and Bernard Bailyn have discredited the traditional notion that Virginia's colonial gentry derived principally from the wealthy and aristocratic Cavaliers who fled Cromwell's Roundheads after the defeat and execution of Charles I in the 1640s, and have identified the founders of the "First Families of Virginia" as predominantly the younger sons of well-to-do but middle-class families engaged in mercantile business or government service.[43] Nonetheless, Clement Eaton seems warranted in claiming that "a potent force in the development of plantation society was the ideal of the English country gentleman," which was carried west and south by emigrants from the seaboard South, and whose influence was perhaps reinforced during the antebellum era by the popularity of Sir Walter Scott's historical romances.[44] Although the degree to which conscious imitation of the English country gentry was pervasive among the planter elite is open to debate, a systematic comparison of the two landed elites would be a valuable and fascinating contribution to Anglo-American historiography. Chapter 1 of this work will suggest that the landed gentlemen of Georgian and Victorian England actually had less in common with antebellum planters as agrarian busi-

FIGURE 1. Kniephof manor. Otto von Bismarck's residence in Pomerania from 1839 to 1845.

nessmen and managers of labor than did contemporaneous Junkers. Nor did the English gentry, in contrast to planters and Junkers, constitute a distinctively regional elite.

Only recently has an historian of the South—Peter Kolchin, author of *Unfree Labor: American Slavery and Russian Serfdom* (1987)—taken up in systematic and thorough fashion the transatlantic comparison suggested in 1857 by the idiosyncratic Virginian George Fitzhugh, who wrote that "excluding Russia, the South is the only conservative section of civilized Christendom."[45] If we consider that Russian serfdom and Southern slavery emerged under conditions of labor scarcity, during the sixteenth and seventeenth centuries respectively, and that hereditary bondage was abolished in both societies only during the 1860s, then the two systems of unfree labor, the planter and *pomeshchiki* landowning elites, and proslavery thought in the South and proserfdom thought in Russia, are all subjects for fruitful and exciting historical comparison. Nonetheless, mid-nineteenth-century Junkers seem in many ways to have been more analogous to antebellum planters than were contemporaneous *pomeshchiki*. Not only did the Junkers, unlike the Russian landed aristocracy, constitute a distinctively regional landed elite, but the generality of both *Rittergüter* and plantations were a great deal smaller in acreage and population than aristocratic estates in Russia. Furthermore, both the planter and Junker elites seem to have been more involved in the international capitalist market than were Russia's aristocratic landlords. Even though Junkers, like the *pomeshchiki*, had close ties to their country's army and bureaucracy, Junkerdom included a much higher proportion of resident landowners active in local government; and these *Rittergut* owners proved more capable of concerted

FIGURE 2. Bachelor's Hall, renamed Liberty Hall in 1859. Alexander Stephens' Georgia home from 1839 to his death in 1883.

and effective action in opposition to the directives of the monarchical central government.[46] No doubt these differences between Prussian Junkers and Russian *pomeshchiki* help to explain why Kolchin's and my evaluation of planters differ in important respects, since our differing European standards of comparison provide dissimilar perpectives on the Old South. Although *Unfree Labor* sees less "capitalism" and more "paternalism" in the slave South than does *Masters and Lords*, Kolchin and I concur, though for rather different reasons, that proslavery thought in the antebellum South qualifies as a genuinely anti-liberal, conservative ideology.

Having said that Junkers were more analogous to planters than were either English landed gentlemen or Russian *pomeshchiki*, I want to emphasize that successful, constructive use of the comparative method does not require that Bloch's analogous "phenomena" be deemed of greater historical significance than the differences between their "environments." *Masters and Lords* certainly does not contend that the analogies between planters and Junkers as landed elites were more important or more interesting than the dissimilarities between their regional and national environments. As Bloch explained, the comparative historian "selects two or more phenomena which appear at first sight to be analogous and which occur in one or more social milieus. He finds out how these phenomena resemble or differ from one another, traces their evolution, and, as far as possible, explains the similarities."[47] The principal benefit of the comparative method is that it both enables and encourages the historian to see past phenomena not only for what they were but also for what they were not. The analytical interplay of comparison and contrast can yield fresh insights into the history of each phenomenon and society being studied. Henri Pirenne, who aptly defined "the subject of historians' study" as "the development of human societies in space and time," concluded that "the comparative method permits history to appear in its true perspective."[48] More often than not, the "true perspective" fostered by comparative history should involve the isolation and analysis of what Bloch called "the 'originality' of different societies."[49] We cannot understand antebellum planters, or the regional brand of proslavery thought that helped to defend their status and interests, without investigating the Old South's particular blend of racism, republicanism, and westward expansion. Likewise, we cannot comprehend the Junkers, or the Old Prussian thought that helped to defend their interests and stature, without examining East Elbia's particular heritage of monarchism, militarism, and corporatism (or estatism). Thus the comparativist need not repress the two "instincts" which C. Vann Woodward has attributed to every "true historian": "a profound respect for the varied peculiarity of human experience and a jealous regard for the precise integrity of time and space in the remembrance of things past."[50]

1

Landed Autocrats, Gentlemen Farmers, and British Influences

SOME FUNDAMENTAL ANALOGIES between mid-nineteenth century planters and Junkers as landed upper classes can be summarized in the phrases "landed autocrats" and "gentlemen farmers." Exploring these analogies will provide a useful overview of those similar circumstances and characteristics that made proprietors of plantations and knight's estates (*Rittergüter*) comparable landed elites, and will also permit some discussion of significant dissimilarities between their historical environments. In the process it will be helpful to contrast planterdom and Junkerdom with the landed aristocracy (gentry and peerage) of nineteenth-century England, but then to emphasize that England exerted tremendous influence on economic and ideological developments in both the South and East Elbia. Finally, I will emphasize that the comparability of planters and Junkers does not derive from the influence of either regional society upon the other.

— I —

The independence and prestige so esteemed by antebellum planters and contemporaneous Junkers rested fundamentally on their ownership of landed estates that were at the same time economic enterprises and political communities. Plantations and *Rittergüter* raised cash crops for foreign and domestic markets; they could be readily acquired by any individual with the purchase price (after 1807 for knight's estates); and they were farmed by workers legally subordinate to the personal, autocratic authority of individual planters and Junkers. This last analogy holds true even though Prussia's monarchy and bureaucracy decreed the abolition of hereditary bondage throughout East Elbia as of 1810, well over half a century before the same was accomplished throughout the South by the Thirteenth Amendment to the U.S. Constitution (ratified in 1865). The juridical abolition of Prussian serfdom was a more complicated and prolonged process than was the de jure abolition of Southern slavery, primarily because enserfed peasants, unlike chattel slaves, had substantive historical and legal claims upon the parcels of land they farmed in return for dues and services owed to their manorial lords. At the same time, the de facto abolition of bondage in the South, which persisted for many African-Americans in the postbellum guises of debt peonage, statutory segregation, and legal disfranchisement, was far more complicated and prolonged than it would have been had Southern masters and slaves, like lords and serfs in East Elbia, shared the same skin color and ethnic background. The dramatic impact of the black/white dichotomy and anti-Negro racism on the Old South will be a recurring theme of this comparative study. Some perceptive observations on the subject came from the pen of Prussian historian Friedrich von Raumer after he visited the United States in 1844. As a classical liberal who had served under the reformist Chancellor Hardenberg in 1810–11, helping to draft statutes providing for the end of obligations owed by former serfs to their manorial lords, Raumer affirmed in the 1840s "that slavery and serfdom . . . are to be condemned, and that a quiet and suitable dissolution of these relations is possible. " Yet, he added, "this assertion holds good in the first place only for men *of the same stock, of the same race.*" Indeed, "the European abolition of the dependent relations between men of one and the same race was an easy matter, in comparison with the task which Americans have to perform."[1]

In East Elbia the obligations of many former serfs to perform services for their manorial lords remained in force until, in the aftermath of the 1848–49 Revolution, Prussia's newborn parliament finally adopted agrarian legislation in 1850 that provided for the commutation of surviving servile dues, and also established loan banks *(Rentenbanken)* which could advance long-term, low-interest credit that peasants needed to purchase their farms outright. Even so, by the 1830s most *Rittergut* labor was being provided by resident cottagers (often called *Insten*), whom August Meitzen identified as "workers hired on annual contracts."[2] Despite their legal status as "free" men, until mid-century these contractual workers remained subject to much the same species of "feudal" political authority that the Junkers had exercised under serfdom. Meitzen's description of the pre-1848 knight's estate as an "almost completely independent governmental authority *(Herrschaftsverband)*, a state within a state,"[3] reads very much like an antebellum Virginia academic's definition of slavery an "an *imperium in imperio, a government within a government.*"[4] *Rittergut* owners, as administrators or supervisors of police power and lesser justice within their manorial districts, were entitled at times to inflict on their contractual cottagers and servants the sort of physical punishment (for example, with cudgel or whip) that plantation owners could apply at will to their chattel slaves.[5] Of course, how much and what kind of corporal punishment a planter or Junker meted out to his minions varied according to their degree of resistance or recalcitrance as well as the autocrat's personality and disposition, which could manifest themselves in behavior that ran the gamut from callous cruelty to kindly compassion. "The microcosm of the plantation, whatever its macroeconomic performance"—and this statement by Elizabeth Fox-Genovese and Eugene D. Genovese also applies to the Junker estate—"remained a human world, fraught with passions."[6] That masters and lords should strive to avoid outbursts of passion and maintain disciplined equanimity in their dealings with servants was a recurring theme in East Elbian as well as Southern agricultural journals. "Nothing damages the loyalty of the servant and the authority of the manor more," warned a Prussian writer in 1845 who claimed thirty years of manorial experience, "than continuous squabbling along with repeated reprimands and threats."[7]

The plantation, explained South Carolinian Whitemarsh Seabrook in the 1830s, was "a little community" whose subordinate members were the planter's "lawful property," over whom he exercised "executive, legislative, and judicial powers" within the limits set by "the laws of the State."[8] *Rittergut* laborers were not the "lawful property" of their manorial lord, and in absolutist and bureaucratic Prussia "the laws of the State" circumscribed the Junker's personal authority over his free laborers more narrowly than federal and state laws limited the planter's relations with his slaves in the U.S. South.[9] Nevertheless, the autocratic powers exercised by planters and Junkers within the boundaries of their estates were clearly analogous. Max Weber's evaluation of *Rittergüter* is equally appropriate for plantations: they constituted "not only economic entities, but also local centers of political authority" governed by "a political autocrat."[10] What percentage of the population in each regional society was subordinate to the formal authority of Junkers or planters? On the eve of the 1848 Revolution about one-third of East Elbia's population was subject to the local jurisdiction of *Rittergut* proprietors.[11] On the eve of the Civil War slaves composed about one-third of the population in the fifteen slave states, and over half of them belonged to masters owning at least twenty bondsmen (the minimum specified by the 1860 census for classification as a "planter").[12]

To be sure, the legal source of a planter's authority over his slaves was quite different from that of a Junker over his contractual cottagers and servants. The former derived from ownership of Negroes as personal and movable property, as chattel, and not from ownership of any particular tract of land farmed by the slaves. The Junker's manorial authority, be he titled nobleman or untitled commoner, derived from ownership of a *Rittergut*, which entitled him to exercise, either himself or through a personally delegated representative, such powers of local government as lesser justice, police power, and supervision over church and school affairs. While the planter was a master of slaves, the Junker was a *Guts-*

herr, or lord of an estate, whose manorial authority was a holdover from serfdom. As Ernst Rudolf Huber explains, "Serfdom *(Erbuntertänigkeit)* signified no civil-law *(privatrechtlich)* right of property by one man over another as in slavery; instead it rested on the manorial lord's public-law *(offentrechtlich)* powers of sovereignty over the subjects of the estate."[13] Baron vom Stein's Edict of 1807 ended (as of late 1810) the Prussian peasant's hereditary bondage to the knight's estate *(Schollenpflictigkeit)* and the formal obligation of the peasant's children to serve as unmarried servants in the Junker's household *(Gesindezwangsdienst).*[14] Moreover, the legislation of the Stein-Hardenberg era (1807–22) had the effect of attenuating the *Rittergut* owner's de facto authority over those peasants able to become independent farmers; their village and fields were now located outside the boundaries of the knight's estate, though still within the boundaries of the Junker's manorial district *(Gutsbezirk).*[15] While antebellum slaves were in a state of personal bondage to their master, contemporaneous cottagers or servants on a *Rittergut* were legally free individuals, though they did not enjoy equality before the law with their manorial lord. Clearly, slaves constituted a more oppressed class than did *Rittergut* workers, whose marriages were legally acknowledged and who did not have to bear the indignity of being human chattel in a political culture that denigrated their race while glorifying republican freedom and independence. Still, plantations hardly constituted totalitarian institutions; for many slaves and their families found or created opportunities for self-assertive maneuvering and African-American cultural expression.[16]

Although the planter as master wielded more unqualified power over his minions than did the Junker lord, the authority of the *Rittergut* owner over those who lived and labored on his estate remained largely intact between 1807 and the 1848 Revolution. Indeed, during these years the Junker's power over his legally free cottagers and servants seems to have been greater than the power he had wielded over his enserfed peasants prior to Stein's October Edict. According to new regulations for servants who contracted to live in the household of their manorial lords (regulations contained in the *Gesindeordnung* of 1810), the Junker's authority over his domestic servants approximated that of a planter over his chattel slaves.[17] In 1843 the Junker-dominated provincial assembly of Brandenburg declared that the manorial lord's right to inflict corporal punishment on his servants was valuable and even "indispensable."[18] Of course, a Junker did not own and could not sell his servants as chattel. Furthermore, *Gesinde* only came under the sway of a Junker's autocratic authority by agreeing to live and work on the knight's estate, although the paucity of non-agricultural jobs in East Elbia before mid-century acted as an effective form of indirect compulsion.

In short, plantations and knight's estates alike constituted miniature "private law states" within the federal Union and its fifteen slave states, the Kingdom of Prussia and its six eastern provinces.[19] As landed autocrats, planters and Junkers both wielded a kind of private sovereign authority that is incompatible with the democratic nation-state and its concomitant principles of civil and political equality.[20] During the mid-nineteenth century, planters, plantations, and proslavery thought and politics in the South, and Junkers, *Rittergüter,* and "Old Prussian" ideology and politics in East Elbia, constituted the major breakwaters in the United States and the Kingdom of Prussia against what can be termed the liberal or progressive mainstream of Western thought and politics since the American and French Revolutions—that is, against the increasingly popular arguments for, and the gradual and halting movement toward civil and political equality, which in the twentieth century has become a campaign for greater social equality as well.[21] Insofar as antebellum planters and contemporaneous Junkers both sought to defend the autonomy of their "private law states" with political and ideological weapons, they can be adjudged comparably conservative landed elites—an argument to be pursued further in Chapter 6. Between 1861 and 1865 Confederate planters even took up the weapons of war to preserve their landed autocracies, and the Confederacy's military defeat entailed a more thorough collapse of their private law states than any experienced by nineteenth-century Junkers. Although until 1861 monarchical Prussia had a far more powerful national state than did the republican U.S., the Civil War quickly brought a vast expansion of federal power and authority that, as harnessed by antislavery Republicans, abolished slavery in the United States without the sort of financial compensation and piecemeal implementation that had accompanied the earlier process of serf emancipation in Prussia.[22]

Given the power that mid-century plantation and *Rittergut* owners wielded over their laborers, it is no wonder that many apologists for the two elites argued that men of great responsibility and authority had superior virtue and ability as well, and that God had ordained the superior to govern and the weak to submit. According to Karl Ludwig von Haller, a Swiss-German patrician whose multivolume *Restoration of Political Science* (1816–22) exerted a strong influence on Old Prussian ideologues during the *Vormärz* era of 1815–48, "you will find everywhere that those more powerful have nobler, more gracious, and more useful natures."[23] Virginia lawyer, planter, and politician Abel Parker Upshur claimed that the slaveholder's position instilled in him "a more liberal caste of character, more elevated principles, a wider expansion of thought, a deeper and more fervent love, and juster estimate of that liberty by which he is so highly distinguished."[24] Because God had created men with inescapable physical and mental inequalites, wrote Haller, it was a principle of divine and natural law that the weak individual should find in the stronger "a protector, a benefactor." In fact, all social relations appeared to Haller as reciprocal relations of authority and dependence: to the strong and independent belonged "authority and freedom," to the weak and needy "a greater or lesser degree of dependence and servitude."[25] William Harper, a prominent judge and politician in South Carolina, made an analogous argument in 1838: "It is the eternal, unchanging order of nature and God that the being of superior facilities and knowledge, and therefore of superior power, should control and dispose of those who are inferior."[26] Unlike proslavery writers, however, Old Prussian ideologues had no cause to translate the distinction between the superior and the inferior, the weak and the strong, into a racial dichotomy (at least prior to the Junkers' growing dependence on seasonal Polish labor during the last quarter of the nineteenth century). "We believe," explained South Carolina planter David J. McCord, "that God did intend the black man to be inferior, or he would not have made him so. All inequalities of nature are of his doing, and who dares gainsay it?"[27]

That a Prussian nobleman could easily partake in racial prejudice and cultural condescension toward African-Americans is demonstrated by the example of Johann August Heinrich Heros von Borcke (1835–95), author of *Memoirs of the Confederate War for Independence* (1867), which recounts his tenure as a staff officer with General J. E. B. Stuart in 1862–63. Borcke had resigned his commission as a second lieutenant with the Second Brandenburg Regiment of Dragoons in order to fight on behalf of Southern independence, and arrived in Charleston in 1862 on a blockade runner from the Bahamas. Before boarding ship in Nassau, his *Memoirs* relate, Borcke was greatly "amused" by "the negro women." "In all their native hideousness of form and feature, they bedizen their persons with European costumes of every fashion, fabric, and colour, and walk the streets with a solemn dignity that even a Spanish hidalgo might envy."[28] Like most Southern whites, Borcke seems always to have believed what he told a reunion of some 300 former Confederate cavalrymen in Richmond in 1884, that he fought "in defense of right and liberty."[29]

Despite the example of von Borcke and widespread anti-black racism, decidedly negative views of Southern slavery and plantation owners seem to have enjoyed broad currency in Prussia and throughout German-speaking central Europe during the first half of the nineteenth century. Beginning in the late 1700s, Enlightenment intellectuals, most notably Christian Jacob Kraus of Königsberg (a disciple of both Adam Smith and Immanual Kant) and his disciples, drew parallels between Germanic serfdom and American slavery as systems of agrarian servitude, criticizing both systems for their economic inefficiency and social injustice. In the influential *Staats-Lexikon (Encyclopedia of Political Science)*, edited by the liberal academics Karl von Rotteck and Karl Welcker during the 1830s and 1840s, a critic of slavery by the name of F. Murhard argued that "The relationship of the white planter to his black slaves in the New World rests on precisely the same historical foundations as the relationship of the manorial lords in many countries of the Old World to their bondsmen." The writer branded as effectively proslavery all the European thinkers from the school of "restorationist political science" (that is, "Messrs. de Maistre, de Bonald, von Haller") and painted with the same brush the political ideas of the romantic Adam Müller and the entire historical school of law associated with Friedrich Karl von Savigny.

(All these accused authors and their ideas influenced the development of Old Prussian thought to varying degrees.) W. T. Krug, in his polemical *General Handbook of the Philosophical Sciences, Including Literature and History*, published during the 1830s, concluded his discussion of slavery in pointedly comparative fashion: "Thus away with all slavery! It is a scar upon humanity. But away too with its vestiges. For they only perpetuate injustice. See (the entries under) serfdom *(Erbuntertänigkeit)* and bondage *(Leibeigenschaft)*."[30]

In response to such polemics, some "Old Prussian" intellectuals did not shrink from defending slavery in the abstract on historical and religious grounds. In 1828 Heinrich Leo, a Halle academician and member of the "Christian-Germanic" clique around Crown Prince Friedrich Wilhelm, published an essay defending slavery as an institution legitimized by its existence throughout history.[31] The pietistic judge and *Rittergut*-owner Ludwig von Gerlach, in a lecture entitled "Monarchy by Divine Right," declared that "even the authority of the slave owner" was "a divine command and a law justified by God's grace."[32] Yet an Old Prussian ideologue could also evince little empathy or respect for the South's peculiar institution of plantation slavery. Pomeranian pietist Adolf von Thadden-Trieglaff, in an 1842 address criticizing those Junkers who engaged in "petty dealing with knight's estates" and who failed to take seriously the political and "fatherly" *(väterlich)* responsibilities of *Rittergut* ownership, recommended that such a man sell his knight's estate to a responsible proprietor and "acquire a plantation in the part of free North America where even the ladies always carry about whips (for the slaves) instead of fans."[33]

Nonetheless, during the Civil War a good many Junkers demonstrated sympathy for the Confederacy as a bulwark of aristocratic liberty against egalitarian democracy, even if few followed von Borcke's example and crossed the Atlantic to take up arms. Interesting testimony to this sympathy came from Victor Aimé Huber, an idiosyncratic intellectual who had sided with both monarchy and Junkerdom during the 1848 Revolution, but had by 1852 broken with the Junker leadership in protest against what he saw as their lack of respect for monarchical absolutism and their lack of social responsibility for the working classes. Huber noted disparagingly in 1864 that considerable sympathy for the slaveholders' cause could be found "in a significant portion of the so-called conservative movement of our day—even unfortunately, in its specifically religious, Christian elements—chiefly among the higher, aristocratic classes and their spokesmen in the press."[34] Similar evidence is provided by Carl Schurz, a native of the Prussian Rhineland who fled to the United States after his participation in the 1848 Revolution, and became a Republican party leader who served as American ambassador to Spain in 1861–62. There Schurz learned from the Prussian minister to Madrid, Count Galen of Westphalia, that "A large portion of the Prussian aristocracy and many of the army officers sympathized with the rebellious Southern Confederacy. They hated democracy and thus hoped for the collapse of the

U.S. Republic, the strongest and most attractive example of a democracy."[35] At one point King Wilhelm I, in the interests of maintaining Prussia's official neutrality during the Civil War, refused to accept petitions from Prussian officers who wished to serve in the Confederate Army. He also expressed royal disapproval of a dinner given in honor of Confederate officers visiting Berlin.[36]

That some Junkers could be favorably disposed toward the Confederacy is hardly surprising if their knowledge of Southern society derived from such unreliable accounts as a report on American agriculture which appeared in one of East Elbia's leading agricultural journals in 1848. Slaves, wrote the author, "are only on cotton plantations in the South and West, live with their lords, by whom they are well treated, with whom they are on friendly terms *(auf friedlichem Fusse)*, and who consider them as members of the family rather than as slaves."[37] Many planters and Junkers alike tended to see themselves as stern but benevolent patriarchs of extended families that encompassed menials in the slave cabins and cottager quarters as well as gentlefolk in the big house and manor house. And the familial, patriarchal image was a significant component of both proslavery and Old Prussian thought—a topic to be discussed at greater length in Chapter 5. Since the desire or need to extract a profitable return from their estates compelled the preponderance of mid-century plantation and *Rittergut* proprietors to concentrate on promoting the cost-effectiveness of their agricultural operations and tractability of their labor forces, there existed some disparity or inconsistency between managerial practice and familial imagery. In accounting for this disparity we should acknowledge that some planters and Junkers approximated the patriarchal ideal, at least in their interactions with some household servants; and we should also recognize that most planters and Junkers, in evaluating their relationships with minions who worked in the fields, partook of humankind's considerable capacity for rationalization and self-deception. Yet we should also take into account the distinction between the pragmatic outlook of most planters and Junkers and the doctrinaire outlook of many proslavery and Old Prussian intellectuals. The writings of intellectual apologists for the two elites often displayed less interest in the plantation's or *Rittergut*'s success as an agricultural business than in its success at embodying the ideal of a Christian and patriarchal community, one where the survival of hierarchical and deferential social relations allegedly meant less exploitation and more humanity than could exist in the depersonalized and competitive world of urban commerce and industry. To be sure, a doctrinaire intellectual could be highminded or romantic on paper and pragmatic, even sordid in his personal affairs, while the very human desire to see their own behavior and motives cast in a flattering light could dispose pragmatic planters and Junkers to endorse the romantic and patriarchal imagery of doctrinaire intellectuals like William Gilmore Simms and Adam Müller. In fact, antebellum planters were probably more interested in patriarchal and romantic apologetics than were contemporaneous Junkers, because abolitionist and antislavery attacks confronted them with a problem alien to East Elbian Prussia. That formidable problem was reconciling servitude on their estates with the ethos of democracy, individualism, and social mobility that pervaded their national culture. In the words of James H. Kettner, "Negro slavery and the system of racial subordination that accompanied it created profound moral, philosophical, and legal dilemmas in a society committed to the idea that the end of all law, government, and social organization ought to be the maintenance and expansion of liberty."[38] Few planters relished the ideological task of reconciling freedom and servitude in the United States. Most would doubtless have preferred to exclude the subject of slavery from the arena of public debate. All save a minority of secessionist "fire-eaters" feared that continued agitation of the issue might lead to a dissolution of the Union, and they felt uncomfortable and sometimes even embarrassed at having to defend themselves against abolitionist charges that slavery was un-Christian and un-American. They did not enjoy being told that the reality of plantation servitude hardly measured up to the familial image of benevolent patriarchy being disseminated by proslavery writers and speakers, any more than Junkers appreciated the disparaging attacks by their critics on the *Rittergut* owner's frequently callous and exploitative treatment of his servants and cottagers.

But racism and the Old South's quietistic brand of evangelical Protestantism seem to have enabled most planters (though certainly not all) to live with and accept slavery without remorse and soul-searching, if only as a "necessary evil" imposed by God on fallen mankind for the foreseeable future.[39] There is, of course, no way to discover with certainty how many discomforted slaveholders held privately to the fatalistic argument from necessity, any more than we can determine the percentage of masters who believed the "positive good" argument that their peculiar institution was an unabashed divine blessing worthy of indefinite perpetuation.[40] Consider the ambiguous case of John William Burrus, whose father, a Methodist minister, had left Virginia and become a planter in Wilkinson County, Mississippi. In 1836, while a student at Wesleyan College in Connecticut, the younger Burruss wrote to his twenty-four-year-old married sister, Mary McGehee, that he was beset with grave moral misgivings about slavery, and would prefer to pursue a literary career rather than return home to manage the family plantation. His sister responded from Mississippi that "Duty plainly calls you to the station of a 'Planter' & a Planter here is the Master of Slaves. God knows, I would gladly make them freemen if I could. But in his Providence we are called to their care now & of course their government."[41] Her brother did return home, and in 1860 owned fifty-eight slaves in Wilkinson County.[42] The crucial roles played in the justification of black slavery by both religious faith in a benign Creator and racist assumptions are well illustrated in the diary kept by North Carolina native Francis Terry Leak (1803–64), resident in Tippah County, Mississippi, and a wealthy, well educated, genteel man who owned three plantations and approximately 150 slaves on the eve of the Civil War. When his household slave Peter died of influenza in February of 1859, Leak confided to his diary that "Peter was a valuable servant, & a good man—very much attached to my children, who were very much attached to him. We shall miss him very much." Of course, Leak and his family were not so personally attached to the sixty or so slaves who worked under an overseer at his 1500–acre cotton plantation in the Arkansas River bottom land of Pulaski County, Arkansas. After his brother W. F. Leak had written from North Carolina that it was "morally wrong to settle one's negroes" in river bottoms, because slaves often died there in great numbers, Francis Terry Leak responded in late January of 1859 that his Arkansas negroes "enjoy as fine health as they ever did in the uplands." His comments on the morality of Southern slavery deserve to be quoted at length. "I enquired of him if it were not wrong, in any blind mortal, to avow a willingness to sweep out of existence anything that the Creator had made; & if it were not more becoming & reverent to suppose that nothing had been created in vain, & so supposing, humbly to seek to find out the uses of all God's works. I then pointed to the evidences that the (river) bottoms were created for a wise purpose, which were to be found in the peculiar adaption of the soil to the growing of cotton, sugar & corn, which adaption showed that they were designed to be cultivated. I also contended that the peculiar fitness of the negroes' constitution for the cultivation of these rich lands as shown by experience was a clear intimation likewise, that they were designed for that particular labor & c(etera) & c & c." When his brother in North Carolina wrote back that " '10 bales to the hand' had some influence in inducing me to send my hands to the bottom," Leak answered by emphasizing race again: "Ethnologists maintained that the negro differed from the Caucasian in his physical as well as his mental nature; That he belonged to a tropical climate, & could labor & enjoy health where a laboring white man could not live."[43] Of course, no "high-toned" Southern gentleman would engage in such arduous and demeaning labor.

— II —

A snippet of insight into the genteel disdain for vocational manual labor that prevailed among the South's planter elite comes from the travel accounts of Northerner Frederick Law Olmsted. In 1854 the seventeen-year-old son of a planter in the "Yazoo bottoms" of Mississippi told Olmsted that he "never knew a man that was industrious and sassy in this country that didn't get rich, quick, and get niggers to do his work for him."[44] Testimony to a similar disdain for arduous physical labor in East Elbia comes from a Pomeranian agricultural periodical. An army captain and *Rittergut* owner, writing in 1840 about the advantages of the new "Ruchaldo" plow, observed that the plow's designer "still has to battle the stubborn disposition of the common man, because not many lords

(Herren) can or want to plow themselves, and thus the testing of a new plow is left to their people *(Leute)."*[45] These quotations point up the negative social valuation attached to menial labor by members of the planter and Junker elites. This point received somewhat hyperbolic emphasis from a German visitor to the United States in the 1850s, Karl Theodor Griesinger. A radical editor from Baden in southwest Germany, Griesinger was imprisoned there during the 1848 Revolution, and upon being released made a five-year sojourn in America. In his travel account, half of which dealt with the South, Griesinger obviously exploited the subject of "Cotton Barons" as a vehicle for voicing his hostility toward German aristocrats. Nevertheless, at times Griesinger succeeded in delineating some interesting traits which wealthy cotton planters had in common with many Junkers. For example, "He (the planter) certainly does not place the title of count or baron before his name, but he still considers himself the 'exclusive gentleman' and pretends that everyone who is not in the postion of owning a large landed estate and having his bondsmen work the fields for him, simply has no right to consider himself as being on the same level with the planter. The first principle of a Southern planter is precisely 'to let others work for you, because working for oneself is shameful.' "[46] To be sure, in frontier areas of the South aspiring gentlemen often could not and did not consider manual labor as "shameful" as did established gentlemen on the Atlantic seaboard; but the goal of would-be planters on the southwestern frontier was almost invariably to free themselves and their families from the necessity of working in the fields.

As David Castronovo points out in *The English Gentleman* (1987), "the whole notion behind 'the port, charge and countenance of a gentleman' is a conception of prosperity and ease of circumstances attained without manual labor."[47] Peter Laslett reaches a similar conclusion in his study of pre-industrial England: "The primary characteristic of the gentleman was that he never worked with his hands on necessary as opposed to leisurely activities."[48] By this definition planters and Junkers can be termed landed gentlemen, or gentlemen farmers, not in the sense of English landlords living off tenant rents, but in the sense that they did not have to perform *déclassé* manual labor in the fields. The size of their estates and work forces—or perhaps the amount of supplemental income from non-agricultural employment as, say, attorneys or doctors in the South, senior army officers or bureaucrats in East Elbia[49]—was sufficient not only to avoid the necessity of working with their hands but also to employ intermediary personel like foremen and overseers (sometimes called *Inspektoren* in Prussia) to assume the dirty and unpleasant task of serving as full-time, on-the-site supervisors of work in the fields. Although most plantation and *Rittergut* owners were actively engaged in the management of their estates, and were hardly men of indolent luxury, every planter and Junker nevertheless enjoyed some greater or lesser measure of the genteel leisure that was generally esteemed in both the South and East Elbia as a necessary and proper accompaniment of social pre-eminence.[50] Indeed, freedom from arduous manual labor seems to be associated with upper-class status in every society, but especially pre-industrial ones, which lack the abundance of mechanical and electronic devices that have the effect in our own day of blurring somewhat the distinction between "blue collar" and "white collar" jobs.[51]

To inject the English term "gentleman" into a discussion of Prussian history is admittedly problematic, especially since the German language has no precise equivalent.[52] Nor did Prussia ever have a social class like the English gentry, since the law of primogeniture always applied only to the noble estate and not, as in England, to the noble title as well.[53] The frequent social interaction between titled aristocracy and affluent commoners that typified England remained exceptional in Prussia prior to the mid-nineteenth century. Alexis de Tocqueville concluded in the 1850s that England was the only European country "where the caste system had been totally abolished, not merely modified," by the end of the eighteenth century. "Nobility and commoners joined forces in business enterprises, entered the same professions, and—what is still more significant—intermarried."[54] While many younger sons from the English nobility entered the learned professions and a few even turned to business, all the sons of a Prussian noble inherited both noble titles and the accompanying social imperative of entering a vocation (preferably as a *Rittergut* proprietor, army officer, or diplomat) appropriate to noblemen *(Adel),* as distinct from members of the middle class *(Bürgertum).*[55] In post-medieval English history the steady flow of younger aristocratic sons into non-landed occupations, together with the steady flow of wealthy commoners into the ranks of the landed gentry, had the effect, to quote F. M. L. Thompson, of "blurring the distinction between the landed interest and the rest of society."[56] Concurrently, the term "gentleman"—literally and originally denoting a man of gentle birth, one well born into a prominent family—came also to identify any man distinguished by the "character and manners befitting one of gentle birth."[57] The label gentleman, explains John Stuart Mill, "has in every age signified the conduct, character, habits, and outward appearance, in whomsoever found, which belonged or were expected to belong to persons born and educated in a high social position."[58]

In English and even more in American culture during the nineteenth century, the concepts of gentleman and gentility underwent a process that can be termed, after Max Weber, "social democratization," and that had no parallel in Prusso-German culture.[59] In other words, "the English concept of a gentleman *(Gentlemanbegriff)*" became divorced from what Carl Brinkmann calls the "genuinely hierarchical and corporatist *(ständisch)* view of society" that prevailed in Prussia.[60] In England circa 1800, reports Harold Perkin, "There was one horizontal cleavage of great import, that between the 'gentleman' and the 'common people,' but it could scarcely be defined in economic terms. 'All are accounted gentlemen in England who maintain themselves without manual labor,' asserted the most popular eighteenth-century handbook on England, echoing its Elizabethan models."[61]

Whereas the German language has no real equivalent to the English "gentleman," the English language has no real equivalent to the German *Bürgertum* or the French *bourgeoisie;* for "until the nineteenth century at least," says Perkin, "the thing itself did not exist, in the sense of a permanent, self-conscious class in opposition to the landed aristocracy."[62] Nineteenth-century Prussian commoners could not buy their way into the ranks of a landed gentry situated sociologically between the nobility and the middle classes. Purchase of a *Rittergut* perforce made a commoner part and parcel of the legally privileged Junker elite, and generally had the effect of *Feudalisierung,* or "feudalization" of political outlook and social demeanor, on the purchaser and his family.[63]

Despite all the linguistic and historical qualifications that must be made when describing Junkers as landed gentlemen, use of the term in this historical comparison between East Elbia and the South serves the useful purpose of emphasizing that the high social status and prestige attached to freedom from vocational manual labor generally constituted a necessary, though not sufficient, prerequisite for elite status in both East Elbia and the South. It should be stressed that every gentry, or class of gentlemen (and ladies), has paid homage to the cultivated elegance made possible by accumulated wealth and freedom from constant labor. In the inimitable prose of Thorstein Veblen, "Abstention from labor is the conventional evidence of wealth and is therefore the conventional mark of social standing." "Refined tastes, manners, and habits of life are a useful evidence of gentility, because good breeding requires time, application, and expense, and therefore cannot be compassed by those whose time and energy are taken up with work."[64] This is not to say that all or even most planters and Junkers actually manifested "refined tastes, manners, and habits of life."[65] But those most celebrated by their peers were portrayed as having attained the high standards of cultured elegance and personal probity associated with the ideal gentleman. And most planters and Junkers seem to have believed that disinterested and constructive public service was most likely to come from the ranks of those who, in the words of J. R. Pole, "were freed from too many practical, day-to-day pressures and had the leisure for study and reflection and a disposition to take the long view."[66]

Viewing Southern plantation owners as landed gentlemen requires a somewhat unconventional definition of the planter class: that is, those agricultural slaveowners whose holdings in land and slaves were large enough, or whose outside income was high enough, that the job of superintending their slaves' field labor usually fell to white overseers or black foremen.[67] This statistically imprecise definition includes a good many slaveholders, especially among those with non-agricultural sources of income, who owned fewer than the twenty bondsmen specified by census officials in 1860 as the minimum for classification as a "planter."[68] For example, John J. Clendinen of Arkansas, who had moved in 1836 from Harrisburg, Pennsylvania, to Little Rock in order to study law and make his fortune, had by 1844 become a circuit court judge and acquired Oak Lawn farm in Pulaski County, where he owned seventeen slaves in 1860.[69] Even among masters who owned fewer than twenty slaves and lacked genteel supplements to their farming income, we find individuals who employed overseers and sought to become plantation managers.[70] In Conecuh County, Alabama, in 1855, Connecticut-born Sherman G. Forbes farmed part of his 1,060 recently purchased acres with a total of fifteen slaves, eight of them field-hands, working under an overseer's direction.[71] In southeastern Virginia's Southampton County in 1831, the year of Nat Turner's "fierce rebellion," twenty-six-year-old Nathaniel Francis owned 790 acres and employed an overseer for his fifteen slaves, six of them under ten years of age.[72] Other small-scale but ambitious planters, like James Monette of Morehouse Parish in northern Louisiana, managed to withdraw from fieldwork without employing an overseer. During the fall of 1853 Monette had from six to eight male and female pickers working in his cotton fields, and his crop for that year amounted to a respectable fifty bales, or 22,305 pounds. By 1860 he owned twenty-four slaves, thirteen or fourteen of them field-hands, but his cotton crop for that year totaled a disappointing sixty-two bales.[73] Less successful than Monette at realizing the "dream of becoming a planter" was David G. Harris of Spartanburg District in the South Carolina Upcountry, owner of eight non-infant slaves in 1860. Nevertheless, reports the editor of Harris's journals, "Most of the time David acted as manager of farm and labor; sometimes he worked in the fields along side his hands, but he did little work with hoe and mule until Reconstruction forced him back to the soil."[74]

Given my definition of planters as landed gentlemen who might or might not have genteel sources of income in addition to farming with slave labor, it seems problematic to posit an exact number of slaves as the minimum holding for a "planter." Nonetheless, the twenty-slave cutoff, though rather arbitrary, seems to offer the best *statistical* dividing line between the vast majority of lesser slaveholders, who spent a great deal of time in the fields, and the small minority of well-to-do slaveholders who did not. Olmsted, during a visit to Mississippi's "interior cotton districts" in 1854, seems to have anticipated the logic of 1860 census officials when he observed that "Where there are fewer than ten negroes, the owners are frequently seen holding a plow among them; where there are over twenty, a white overseer is usually employed, the owner perhaps directing, but seldom personally superintending the field labor."[75] If we accept the twenty-slave minimum, then the 1860 census counted 47,500 planters, who amounted to about 12 percent of all 395,000 slaveholders. These planters and their immediate families composed 3.2 percent of all white families in the fifteen slave states. In the eleven states that formed the Confederate States of America planter families composed 4.4 percent of all white families.[76] To be sure, these figures are a bit inflated by the failure to take into account the owners of those 5 percent of Southern slaves who worked in "industrial enterprises," and the owners of those

10 percent of slaves who lived in cities, of whom probably two-thirds were "either domestic servants or service tradesmen."[77] Nor do the figures allow for the fact that 1860 census officials made no apparent effort to determine how many slave-holders residing in one county owned additional slaves in other counties or states; thus the aggregate published statistics exaggerate the actual number of slave-holding individuals. In order to illustrate this exaggeration, we can cite the admittedly atypical case of Philip St. George Cocke, son of the aged Jeffersonian John Hartwell Cocke, and a planter whose extensive holdings in both Virginia and Mississippi made him one of the South's wealthiest men.[78] In early 1860 the younger Cocke owned a total of 658 slaves divided among nine distinct plantations in the Old Dominion and the Magnolia State: 283 slaves on three plantations in two different Virginia counties (Powhatan and Brunswick) and 375 slaves on six plantations in two Mississippi counties (Lowndes and Yazoo).[79] Where the published aggregate figures from the 1860 census report four planters, in reality only one existed. Even so, if we make the convenient though debatable assumption that the number of gentlemen-planters who owned fewer than twenty slaves compensates for the inflated number of "planters" reported by the 1860 census, then perhaps the twenty-slave minimum can remain a statistically useful benchmark.

One historian has suggested that the "accurate definition of a planter" should include ownership of a "minimum of between 500 and 1000 acres, of which at least 200 were in cultivation."[80] This acreage standard also seems a bit arbitrary, especially for the tobacco-growing areas of the Upper South and the rice plantations of Georgia and the Carolinas. In 1860, in southside Virginia's Lunenberg County, county magistrate Robert Henderson Allen owned twenty-seven slaves, and at Oral Oaks plantation raised corn, wheat, tobacco, peas, and beans on just under 150 cultivated acres.[81] When, in 1833, Charles Manigault purchased the Georgia estate Gowrie, located on Argyle Island in the lower Savannah River, the plantation included a total of about three hundred acres—"220 acres of improved rice land, eighty acres of uncleared land and fifty slaves."[82] Even in Mississippi, the heartland of the Cotton Kingdom on the eve of the Civil War, cotton planter Charles Whitmore owned about thirty-five slaves and just over 300 acres near Natchez during the 1840s and 1850s.[83]

Landed Junkerdom constituted a smaller, less fluid, and more precisely definable elite than did the South's plantation gentry. This was due in part to the fact that East Elbia did not undergo the dramatic geographic expansion that characterized the slave South during the first half of the nineteenth century, and in part to the fact that *Rittergut* owners enjoyed the sort of exclusive, group-specific, "aristocratic" legal and political privileges that did not distinguish planters from other white citizens in the South. The great majority of knight's estates were legally privileged not only because their owners wielded personal control over local government, but because by law they held a preponderance of seats in the county and provincial assemblies *(Kreistage* und *Landtage).*[84] (The Junkers' dominance of these corporatist representative assemblies will be discussed further in Chapter 4. The *Kreistage* were comparable in some respects to Virginia's planter-dominated county courts, which had constituted the crux of what Charles S. Sydnor calls the plantation gentry's "county oligarchies" since the colonial era.[85] Until the state constitution of 1851 provided for the popular election of justices of the peace, county magistrates were appointed by the governor from a list of nominees submitted by the magistrates then in office, and thus the courts functioned as self-perpepuating "closed corporations."[86]) In addition, *Rittergut* owners in Brandenburg, Pomerania, and provincial Saxony paid no taxes on most of their land until 1861. At mid-century about half of all *Rittergut* land in the Kingdom of Prussia was exempted from land taxes; and even when taxed Junkers enjoyed a lower rate than did peasants.[87] The only comparable sort of outright tax exemption that planters enjoyed on the eve of the Civil War was the exclusion of young slaves (for example, under twelve in Virginia, under fifteen in Alabama) from property taxes. Although the owners of land and slaves bore the brunt of state taxation, planters and lesser slaveholders in all the Southern states succeeded in preventing the extension of *ad valorem* taxes (that is, taxation at full market value) from real estate to slaves. Some states, like South Carolina and Alabama, levied a modest poll or capitation tax on slaves. Others, like Virginia and Texas, applied a lower tax rate to slaves as personal property than was applied to real estate.[88]

According to figures compiled by statistician Georg von Viebahn, *Rittergut* owners and their immediate families, plus the many noble families who did not own knight's estates, amounted to about 168,000 persons, or less than 1 percent (0.95%) of Prussia's total population of 17.7 million in 1858.[89] At this time East Elbia contained approximately 11,500 *Rittergüter,* a figure that had not changed greatly since Prussia's territorial gains in 1814–15 courtesy of the Congress of Vienna, except for the sale of some former royal demesnes as allodial knight's estates.[90] Just as some wealthy Southern slaveholders owned several plantations that might be located in different counties, so did some affluent Junkers, usually members of the old nobility, own several estates that might be situated in different county districts *(Kreise).* An illustrative though hardly typical example is provided by the Brandenburg family von Arnim. In 1856 twenty-eight different von Arnims, among them two women (apparently widows), owned a total of seventy-two *Rittergüter.*[91]

However, the percentage of Junker estates belonging to untitled commoners—as opposed to those with the noble titles *Graf* (count), *Freiherr* (baron), or simply *von* (of or from) in their names—had tripled or quadrupled since 1807, when Baron vom Stein's October Edict had ended the nobility's de jure monopoly on the ownership of knight's estates. By 1856 nearly 45 percent of East Elbian *Rittergüter* belonged to untitled proprietors.[92] The influx of commoners into the ranks of Junkerdom spurred what Reinhard Koselleck calls "the creeping transformation of the landed nobility *(Ritterstand)* into an entrepreneurial class of manorial lords *(Gutsherren)*."[93] In other words, it was only during the first half of the nineteenth century that Junkerdom became what the plantation gentry had always been—a socially mixed elite of landed businessmen.

Prussian statistician K. F. W. Dieterici explained that "The status of a *Rittergut* is independent of the estate's size; it is quite possible for a *Rittergut* owner to sell arable land and fields and to retain for the house and small estate remaining the status of a knight's estate." Dieterici's figures show that at mid-century *Rittergüter* varied in size even more than Southern plantations, ranging from an abnormally small Silesian estate of less than a single acre to an enormous estate in old East Prussia engrossing more than 46,000 acres. However, the overwhelming majority of knight's estates were larger than the 379 acres (600 Prussian *Morgen*) specified by government statisticians as the minimum for a "large landed estate," and the average estate encompassed between 1,300 and 1,400 acres.[94] One observer reported in 1858 that the average *Rittergut* encompassed about 1,660 acres in Brandenburg, 1,600 acres in Pomerania, 1,300 acres in Silesia, and 1,250 acres in provincial Prussia.[95] During the 1840s the most famous of all Junkers, Otto von Bismarck, supervised two different family estates of below-average size, Kniephof in eastern Pomerania and Schönhausen in western Brandenburg. At Schönhausen, where Bismarck had been born and where he took up residence shortly after his father's death in 1845, approximately 1,260 acres were farmed by both a substantial number of contractual laborers and thirty-two smallholders (for example, *Kossäten* and *Büdner*), who continued to perform traditional servile dues until 1852. Kniephof, where Bismarck lived from 1839 to 1845, had no peasants, encompassed about 1,390 acres, marketed potato whiskey, grain, and wool, and could house the families of forty-four contractual laborers *(Insten)* in thatched-roof cottages constructed of timber and mud walls.[96] If Kniephof actually employed forty-four familes it was a relatively labor-intensive operation; for, according to historian Erich Jordan, a *Rittergut* of 1,300 to 1,400 acres would be likely to hire 20 to 22 laboring families (approximately one family for every 100 *Morgen*, or 63 acres), with each family supplying two workers per day.[97] More in line with Jordan's figures was another and smaller estate in eastern Pomerania—Cronsberg (owner unknown), which in the mid-1840s employed fourteen laboring families to farm 803 acres, of which 603 were cropland growing wheat, rye, barley, and oats for the market.[98]

— III —

Some basic analogies between planters and Junkers can be highlighted by contrasting the two elites to the landed aristocracy (gentry and peerage) of nineteenth-century England. Max Weber made some interesting observations along this line in 1919–20. "An aristocrat in the sociological sense," he argued, "is a man whose economic position sets him free for political activities and enables him to live for political functions without living by them; hence he is a receiver of fixed income *(Rentner, rentier)*." By this definition a decided minority of Junkers, and even fewer planters, qualified as aristocrats. "The only country which really possesses such an aristocracy in Europe is England," said Weber. Then he evaluated Junkerdom in terms that can be applied, with slight modifications, to antebellum planterdom: "They are rather a rural middle class with a feudal stamp, coming down from the past, whose members are occupied as agricultural entrepreneurs in the day-to-day struggle of business interests."[99] Yet we should treat skeptically any suggestion that nineteenth-century English landlords lacked the initiative and talents of successful business managers. Although they may have rented out their land, notes J. V. Beckett, "this did not mean that they were passive rent receivers."[100] On the contrary, according to historian David Spring, English landlords were vitally involved in overseeing their estates and clearly displayed such bourgeois qualities as "practicality and prudence." "Of all the qualities associated with aristocracy, these are often the least recognized though they may be the most consistently displayed," suggests Spring. "The truth of the matter may be that English landowners differed little from industrialists, that they were reasonably businesslike in their procedures, that they rationally maximized their incomes."[101] Whether the landed gentlemen of Victorian England were more, less, or equally "businesslike" vis-à-vis the proprietors of Southern plantations or East Elbian *Rittergüter* is a question beyond the scope of the present study. However, we can say definitively that where England's landowning elite comprised predominantly rentiers who let their estates to tenant farmers for rents fixed in advance, most Junkers and planters relied on the more variable and hence riskier profits derived from operating their estates as consolidated enterprises.

In the second place, where English landowners sought and won tariff protection against foreign grain during the era of the Corn Laws (1815–46), most planters and Junkers were staunch free traders,[102] and relied heavily on overseas markets (the English market especially) for disposal of their commodities. Third, planters and Junkers wielded a degree of formal and direct authority over their menials that was absent from the relations of English landlords with their tenants and the day-laborers hired by those tenants. Fourth, unlike English landowners, planters and Junkers composed distinctively regional landed elites.

The regional economies of both the South and East Elbia functioned within the world marketplace—what Eric Hobsbawm has called "the world economy of nineteenth-century capitalism"—as producers of essential agricultural commodities for more urban and industrial areas, particularly England, the world's premier commercial and industrial nation.[103] Beginning in the second half of the eighteenth century, England's growing urban population and textile-based "first" industrial revolution created a profitable international market for producers of wheat, cotton, and wool, and thereby served to enhance the economic vitality of plantation and *Rittergut* agriculture. This economic rejuvenation spurred the rapid expansion of Southern slavery and the gradual eradication of East Elbian serfdom. As will be argued in Chapter 2, this divergence was due primarily to dramatic geographic, demographic, and ethnic differences between the two regions.

Given the powerful economic influence that England exerted on the South and East Elbia, it seems almost fitting that English culture and politics should have provided both Southern proslavery and Old Prussian intellectuals with many of the ideological weapons they used to defend the interests and institutions underlying the planters' and Junkers' prestige and influence as landed elites. The merchant ships that transported Southern cotton and tobacco or East Elbian wheat and wool to England, and recrossed the Atlantic or the North Sea laden with textiles and iron goods, also carried British books and periodicals to readers in America and the German states. Prominent among Britain's literary exports to the South and East Elbia during the first two-thirds of the nineteenth century were the writings of "conservative" authors Edmund Burke (1729–97), Walter Scott (1771–1832), and Thomas Carlyle (1795–1881). Of the three it was Burke, "the political philosopher of the landed interest" in England,[104] and the patron saint of conservative intellectuals in the West since the French Revolution of 1789, who exerted the earliest and the most profound impact on the evolution of conservative ideologies in the South and East Elbia.[105] In the words of Reinhold Aris, "he expressed better than anyone else the desire for stability in society, a desire which lies at the root of all conservative thinking."[106] And this desire can easily reflect an elite's satisfaction with the existing order. Burke's *Reflections on the Revolution in France* (1790)—"this most sacred of conservative texts," says Isaac Kramnick[107]—made a great impact even on Scott and Carlyle, whose first major prose works appeared in 1814 (Scott's *Waverly*) and 1837 (Carlyle's *Sartor Sartoris*). Scott's biographer reports that "above all, the writings of Edmund Burke made him conscious of the power of custom, of deep social, cultural, even ancestral forces, in molding men's minds and hearts."[108] Carlyle declared in his own influential study of the French Revolution that "Great Burke has raised his voice long ago" against the men and ideas of 1789, "eloquently demonstrating that the end of an epoch is come, to all appearances the end of Civilized Time," by which Carlyle meant the time of hierarchy and chivalry romanticized by himself and Burke.[109] George Fitzhugh of Virginia probably relied more heavily than any other notable proslavery or Old Prussian intellectual on Carlyle's tirades against liberal, laissez-faire individualism. Yet in 1857, in an essay on "Southern Thought" where Carlyle's influence was evident, Fitzhugh described Burke as "the most philosophic and farseeing statesman of modern times."[110]

In East Elbia and the South "Burkean ideas" had a notable impact on two extraordinarily capable and highly visible spokesmen for the Junker and planter elites, Ludwig von der Marwitz (1777–1837) of Brandenburg and John C. Calhoun (1782–1850) of South Carolina. According to Richard N. Current, Calhoun's "favorites" were Aristotle and Burke.[111] Charles M. Wiltse reports that the South Carolinian "had high admiration for Burke," but did not cite authorities in either his speeches or his published papers.[112] Nor did the Brandenburg Junker ever cite Burke by name; but Friedrich Meusel tells us that "Marwitz was well acquainted with several of Burke's writings," and his personal library contained both German and French editions of the *Reflections,* marked with marginal notations indicating hearty approval.[113] Both the planter and the Junker found in Burke powerful confirmation of their strong belief in the need for "historical continuity and societal hierarchy."[114]

Although Calhoun and Marwitz did not pay explicit homage to Burke, two of their close associates did: William Harper (1790–1847) and Adam Müller (1779–1829). Furthermore, the careers of Harper and Müller can serve to illustrate that the ranks of proslavery and Old Prussian writers included a number of bright and ambitious men from non-planter and non-Junker family backgrounds—men who won a substantial measure of esteem and influence by employing their intellectual talents in defending the plantation- and *Rittergut*-centered societies of the South and East Elbia. Harper, a native of Antigua (an island in the British West Indies) and the son of a Presbyterian minister who moved to Charleston in 1799, taught school and studied medicine before becoming a lawyer and a state appeals court judge from 1830 to 1835. He also became, says William W. Freehling, "the most skillful dialectician in the nullification movement (of 1828–33) next to Calhoun."[115] During his 1835–47 term as Chancellor of South Carolina, Harper published his widely cited and often republished *Memoir on Slavery* (1837), one of the earliest defenses of Southern slavery as what Calhoun called a "positive good."[116] According to Harper, Edmund Burke was "the greatest political philosopher of modern times." In outlining a course of study in political thought, Harper wrote in 1835 that "above all, I would recommend the speeches and political writings of Burke."[117]

Adam Müller, the son of a minor Berlin bureaucrat, became during the Stein-Hardenberg Reform Era the most outspoken Prussian disciple of both Burke and Friedrich von Gentz, the man who had (in 1793) first translated the *Reflections* into German.[118] After attending the Anglophile University of Göttingen in Hanover until 1801 and then converting to Roman Catholicism in 1805, Müller worked as a tutor and lecturer in the Saxon city of Dresden. Here in 1808 he wrote for the short-lived journal *Phoebus* an essay on scholarly study in which he, much like Harper, insisted that one must "read first the writings of Burke," since they constituted "the greatest school of political wisdom."[119] After establishing his intellectual credentials in 1809 with the publication of *Elements of Statecraft*, he moved to Berlin in search of prestige and power. In 1810, during a series of lectures on Frederick the Great at the new University of Berlin, Müller described Burke as "the last prophet to have come into this disenchanted world."[120] During his two years in Berlin he introduced Ludwig von der Marwitz to some of the ideological concepts and modes of expression that the Junker used in composing petitions of protest from the Brandenburg nobility against Hardenberg's attempt in 1810–11 to subject *Rittergüter* to a land tax.[121] While in Berlin Müller also contributed to Heinrich von Kleist's political newpaper *Berlin Evening Press* (*Berliner Abendblätter*, 1810–11) a number of essays attacking Chancellor Hardenberg's reformist proposals. (The paper's motto was "Read Burke"!) After the Prussian government forced the newpaper to close down in the spring of 1811, Müller left Berlin and eventually took up residence in Vienna, where he found a more secure political position under Friedrich von Gentz.[122]

— IV —

I have emphasized that antebellum planters and contemporaneous Junkers were comparable landed elites primarily because of structural and functional analogies between plantation and *Rittergut* as at the same time authoritarian political communities and commercial agricultural enterprises. To some extent these analogies can be considered "evolutionary," in that they evolved under somewhat comparable sets of historical conditions. To wit, both Prussian East Elbia and the U.S. South originated as colonial lands; both were colonized by immigrants from western Europe who crossed the Elbe River to the east, or the Atlantic to the west, in search of land and opportunity; and hereditary bondage began to take firm hold in these lands during the sixteenth and seventeenth centuries respectively, as the result of complex processes that served the needs of Junkers and nascent planters for "bound" labor forces suited to the production of cash crops on large estates. As Georg Friedrich Knapp put it in 1891, "The modern large-scale business concern of the *Rittergut* began with the forced labor of the unfree, just as the modern plantation business in the colonies began with the forced labor of the unfree; but the planter obtained Negroes in Africa and made them slaves; the *Rittergut* owner did not reach so far, for he took his peasants and made them serfs."[123] Nonetheless, the historical timing of colonization and the ethnic backgrounds of the colonists were quite different for the two regions. Germanic colonization of the Slavic lands east of the Elbe peaked from the twelfth to the fourteenth centuries, and had effectively ended before English colonization of North America even began. "In a little over two centuries, between 1125 and 1346," writes Geoffrey Barraclough, "two-fifths of modern Germany was conquered, colonized, and absorbed."[124] Across the Atlantic, after the colonies of the eastern seaboard had won their independence from England in 1783, voluntary migrants of predominantly English and Scotch-Irish ancestry, and involuntary migrants of African ancestry, streamed into the Trans-Appalachian West; and after the War of 1812 significant numbers began to settle the Trans-Mississippi West. Thus, James Westphall Thompson could state in 1915 that "What the Trans-Allegheny country was to the United States in 1800, that the Trans-Elban *(sic)* country was to the Germans in 1200." [125]

The process of colonization left the nineteenth-century South and East Elbia with very different racial legacies. Germanic colonists and the indigenous Slavs became thoroughly intermixed in most parts of East Elbia within a couple of centuries. In the South (where the indigenous Native American tribes were decimated by Old World diseases prior to military defeat and "removal" from their ancestral lands), the region's European and African settlers continued to live under a caste system even after the Civil War brought an end to chattel slavery. The ranks of landed Junkerdom, even in the heartland provinces of Brandenburg and Pomerania, included a large number of families with Slavic names like von Dziembowski and von Kleist. Old Prussian Junker Hans Hugo von Kleist-Retzow, whose extended family owned a total of fifty-three *Rittergüter* in 1856, became a member of the Prussian House of Lords *(Herrenhaus)*; and in 1866 he told his fellow peers that "I, my family, of Slavic stock, became German." [126] (To be sure, in the nineteenth century the Hohenzollern monarchy feared the enduring strength of Polish nationalist sentiment among the Polish aristocracy, or *szlachta,* in Prussian Poland, especially the province of Posen. [127]) In the Old South a man of known black ancestry could never hope to be accepted in the public arena on equal terms with whites, although there were occasional and anomalous African-American planters. The singular Creole culture of Louisiana tolerated a number of mulatto planters like the fair-skinned Andrew Durnford of St. Rosalie sugar plantation in Plaquemines Parish. [128] In South Carolina the more extraordinary William Ellison, dark-skinned son of a white planter and female slave, parlayed his skills as a maker and repairer of cotton gins first into the purchase of freedom and then into the acquisition and expansion of Wisdom Hall cotton plantation in the Sumter District. [129]

It is important to stress that the comparability of planters and Junkers did not derive from common origins, unless one insists on tracing a thin and fragile line back to the Germanic tribes that settled in western Europe during the first millenium A.D. Nor did it result from the influence of one society on the other. To be sure, there are numerous examples of prominent Southerners being favorably impressed by some aspect of Prussian institutional and military life, as well as examples of upper-class East Elbians being interested in the United States. Historian Horst Dippel has determined that at the end of the eighteenth century many educated Prussians were familiar with and interested in the American Revolution, despite the "prevailing indifference" to questions about the internal life of the new United States, including slavery. [130] During the mid-1800s the lure of Texas could reach beyond the Elbe River to provincial Prussia, where in 1849–50 the anomalous Junker Carl von Rosenberg sold the estate Eckitten in order to carry his family across the Atlantic and Gulf of Mexico from Bremen to Galveston. In southeastern Texas's Fayette County he purchased 800 acres that had been part of the "Nassau Farm" established in 1843 by the so-called *Adelsverein,* a group of princes and noblemen from the western reaches of the German Confederation.[131] In Virginia during the 1830s Governor David Campbell and the House of Delegates expressed formal interest in the Prussian primary school system as a source of ideas applicable to public education in the Old Dominion, although the author of an 1839 report on the subject, cleric and educator Benjamin M. Smith, cautioned that "no one can for a moment suppose that the institutions suitable for a monarchy, *can* apply to a republic."[132] In 1861 Virginia lawyer and politician George Wythe Randolph, who would become the Confederacy's second Secretary of War, saw the Prussian militia system as a model on which to base his state's post-secession militia ordinance.[133] Another proslavery Virginian, Thomas R. Dew, visited the German Confederation as a tourist in the 1820s and occasionally referred to Prussia in his published writings. Nonetheless, there is no evidence to support the old notion that before joining the faculty at William and Mary College in 1826 Dew actually studied at German universities, where he allegedly imbibed many of the anti-Jeffersonian ideas presented in his influential proslavery treatise *Review of the Debate in the Virginia Legislature of 1831–'32* (1832).[134] The most widely known native of East Elbia to make his home in the Old South was Francis Lieber (1807–72) of Berlin, who studied at the Prussian universities of Berlin and Halle before immigrating to America in 1827. Ironically, he had to repress "a growing distaste for slavery" during his tenure as a professor of history and political economy at South Carolina College from 1835 to 1856.[135]

East Elbia did import some raw cotton and considerable tobacco from the Old South, such imports usually being handled by non-Prussian merchants in the old Hanseatic towns of Bremen and Hamburg on the North Sea.[136] Junkers could hardly help but be aware of the important contributions which Southern agriculture made to the international economy. In 1852 Prussia's leading agricultural periodical pointed to the "prominent roll which cotton plays in European industry and as an article of consumption among the most numerous classes of the populace," and reported that per capita consumption of cotton in Prussia had increased more than twenty-fold between 1806 and 1849.[137] Although no cotton could be grown in the climate of East Elbia, an inferior grade of tobacco could be and was. In fact, progressive agriculturists in Brandenburg and Pomerania, like their peers in the Upper South, had learned in the eighteenth century that tobacco, wheat, and clover made for an excellent crop rotation.[138] Nonetheless, most East Elbian tobacco seems to have been raised by peasants rather than Junkers, and was markedly inferior even to the lower grades of American tobacco (that is, the "Maryland" type from Maryland and Ohio, and the "Kentucky" type from Kentucky, Tennessee, and Missouri). Great quantities of these inferior American grades were imported into Prussia for mixture with domestic tobacco during the manufacturing process, while the superior grades of American tobacco (from Virginia and North Carolina) were generally kept in the United States for home manufacture or shipped to England.[139]

In return for its tobacco and cotton, the antebellum South received very little from Prussian East Elbia, even in the way of immigrants. With regard to German immigration to the United States from the 1830s to the 1850s, Maldwyn Allen Jones observes that "the great majority of emigrants," both before and after the 1848 Revolution, "came from the states of the southwest, especially Württemberg, Baden, and Bavaria, where, in contrast to the rest of Germany, small agricultural holdings predominated." Those Prussians who, like Carl Schurz, migrated to America during the several decades before the Civil War came overwhelmingly from the western provinces of the Rhineland and Westphalia, which also contained many "small agricultural holdings."[140] Such seems to have been the case with the well-known Prusso-German settlements in antebellum Texas, including that at New Braunfels, founded under the auspices of the *Adelsverein* in 1845 and situated between Austin and San Antonio in Comal County.[141] In 1860 some 80 percent of Comal's population was of German birth or parentage, making it the most German-American county in the state. Yet on 23 February 1861, 74 percent of the voters in Comal Country endorsed the secession of Texas from the Union.[142]

Frederick Law Olmsted had visited Texas in 1854, and his *A Journey through Texas* (1857) was largely responsible for the traditional belief that German immigrants to Texas brought with them a strong and persistent moral distaste for slavery. It is true that a few abolitionist "forty-eighters" were among the "university-educated liberals" who settled in Texas after the 1848 Revolution.[143] Moreover, a significant number of German settlers in the non-plantation Hill Country west of Austin proved unsympathetic to both slavery and secession, later providing "the largest bloc of immigrant Southern Republicans" during Reconstruction.[144] Nonetheless, despite the antislavery pronouncements of a few outspoken German-Texans, Terry G. Jordan insists that "most Germans were either proslavery or simply 'careless of its existence' "; and Randolph B. Campbell argues that the "proslavery consensus" which characterized political life in antebellum Texas also encompassed most German immigrants.[145] Jordan has quipped that Olmsted's "difficulty in finding Anglo-Americans who did not own slaves was exceeded only by his failure to locate Germans who did." Although their European experience with free labor no doubt made some German settlers reluctant to purchase slaves, "a more important factor was probably their meagre capital resources," which also resulted in their generally buying less land than did American settlers. According to the 1850 census, Austin and Fayette counties, in the plantation belt of southeastern Texas, contained twelve German slaveholders (including one "planter"), about one-tenth of all German farmers.[146]

Otto von Roeder was a judicial official in Prussian Westphalia before coming to Texas in the mid-1830s. He purchased Nassau Farm and its slaves from the bankrupt *Adelsverein* in 1848 for $14,000, but in early 1850 sold the manor house with 800 acres for $1800 to the aforementioned Junker immigrant Carl von Rosenberg. Rosenberg wrote to his brother in May of 1850 that Franz, "my German laborer," and "my Negro Toms," purchased for $800, did the "heaviest" work on the new "Rosenberg-Nassau" farm, "so that the children can rest and recover as they wish." He had also bought a "Negress" and her four-year-old son for $700 to provide his wife Amanda with domestic help; but the woman's "laziness and stupidity" quickly convinced him to sell her. Rosenberg and his son Wilhelm were hardly typical Junkers, for their decision to leave Prussia was due in large part to anti-monarchical, republican sympathies. In Texas, Carl told his brother, they were free from "the imagined rights of princes," and "no officials, no soldiers weigh on their shoulders." In 1860–61 both father and son supported secession, Wilhelm writing that he stood with the people of Texas "in upholding the cardinal principles of self-government laid down in the Declaration of Independence, 4 July 1776."[147] The example of the von Rosenbergs demonstrates that even an immigrant of Junker background could embrace the Old South's peculiar combination of racial slavery and libertarian republicanism.

2

Agrarian Entrepreneurs

THIS CHAPTER WILL present a roughly chronological survey of the economic histories of the planter and Junker elites through the middle decades of the nineteenth century. It will sketch their agrarian evolutions from the time of their emergence as landed entrepreneurs, and the concurrent creation of "bound" labor forces in East Elbia and the South, during the sixteenth and seventeenth centuries respectively. After examining these early centuries we will consider how England's industrial revolution, beginning in the late eighteenth century, gave the agrarian entrepreneurship of planters and Junkers a new lease on life and helped to shape the economic and social landscapes of the Old South and contemporaneous East Elbia, albeit in very different ways. In the process we should not only learn more about Junkerdom and the plantation gentry but also gain a heightened appreciation for the regional, national, and continental varieties of productive modes and social structures that interacted over several centuries of economic development in the Western world.

Although I will not address directly the complex and contentious question of whether planters and Junkers qualified as "capitalists" until Chapter 3, here and now I owe the reader some discussion of the potentially ambiguous terms entrepreneur and entrepreneurship. C. Joseph Pusateri, an historian of American business, has examined the various ways in which the term entrepreneur has been defined in English since it first appeared in a 1755 treatise by an Irishman grown rich as a Paris banker. Pusateri concludes that "what is still the most useful and comprehensive definition of entrepreneurship today" is to be found in a 1949 essay by Arthur C. Cole: "the purposeful activity . . . of an individual or group of individuals, undertaken to initiate, maintain, or aggrandize a profit-oriented business unit for the production or distribution of economic goods and services with pecuniary or other advantage the goal or measure of success."[1] A briefer and simpler definition has come more recently from economic historians Heywood Fleisig and Gavin Wright, who see "the concept of entrepreneurship" as involving "the ability to make unusual amounts of money by using commonly available productive resources."[2] By either the Cole or Fleisig-Wright definition, many planters and Junkers achieved impressive entrepreneurial successes. Even if one insists on stressing the term's twentieth-century connotations of "technical and organizational innovation,"[3] the historical records of the Junker and planter elites offer notable examples of such innovation: for example, the rapid spread of Merino sheep breeding in East Elbia and of short-staple cotton cultivation and cotton gins in the South during the early nineteenth century. Indeed, the sixteenth- and seventeenth-century restructuring of *Rittergüter* as export-oriented estates using bound labor, like the ongoing establishment of Southern plantations from the seventeenth to the nineteenth centuries, can be viewed as organizational innovations that served to increase productive efficiency, despite our twentieth-century inclination to assume that free labor is always more efficient as well as morally superior.[4] Nonetheless, when evaluating planters and Junkers it seems advisable to make the distinction between the "creative entrepreneur" who initiates economic changes and the "adaptive entrepreneur" whose organizational and technical skills are devoted to maintaining the ongoing health of a business operation.[5] The preponderance of plantation and *Rittergut* proprietors clearly functioned as adaptive rather than creative entrepreneurs, as have the great majority of businessmen throughout history. And like twentieth-century industrial entrepreneurs producing iron and steel or automobiles, some planters and Junkers were simply more businesslike than others, more capable of productive efficiency and adaptability. What a British historian has said about English agriculture is equally valid for the South and East Elbia: "Between the best — and the least well-managed estates a great gulf yawned."[6]

— I —

Let us begin this overview by examining two impersonal factors that exerted tremendous influence on the two elites throughout their histories as landed entrepreneurs: geography and climate. The many navigable rivers of East Elbia and the South have for centuries provided both fertile alluvial soils and easy transportation to the Baltic and North seas, the Atlantic Ocean and the Gulf of Mexico. Hence it was feasible for *Rittergut* and plantation owners situated along those navigable rivers to produce profitable cash crops for distant markets long before the spread of scientific agricultural techniques and steam railways in the nineteenth century. The number and importance of the Old South's river systems—the mighty Mississippi in particular—seem to be more widely appreciated than the number and importance of East Elbia's rivers. Yet, as British observers pointed out in 1870, Prussia's 3800 miles of navigable rivers, only 430 of them made steerable by artificial improvements, gave it first place among all European states for length of navigable rivers relative to the country's land area.[7] The four largest Prussian river basins were, in descending order, those of the Oder, the Elbe, the Rhine, and the Vistula (or Weichsel); and of these only the Rhine did not service East Elbia. With the development of river steamboats in the early 1800s, national and international markets began to exert greater influence over larger areas of East Elbia and the South. (The slave states had a much lower population density and a far larger expanse of hilly backcountry than did the provinces of East Elbia, thanks to the Appalachian Mountains east of the Mississippi and the more modest Ozark Highlands west of the Mississippi. Hence the antebellum South retained many substantial non-plantation areas whose economic life was oriented more toward household production and local self-sufficiency rather than toward the growing of cash crops for external markets.[8]) The feasibility of using steamboats on the Mississippi and Ohio rivers for upriver as well as downriver trade was firmly established by the late 1810s; and the steamship came into use on the Oder and Elbe rivers during the twenties.[9] It was during the 1830s that the first railroads appeared in the two regions. The first railroad in the future states of the Confederacy was a 136–mile line between Charleston and Hamburg, South Carolina, that was built with both private and state funds and completed in 1833, when it was the world's longest line. In East Elbia a privately built sixteen-mile railroad between Berlin and Potsdam opened in 1838.[10] Although the pace of rail construction in both regions accelerated rapidly during the 1850s, river transport remained predominant. In Alabama, which produced more cotton in 1850 than any other state, and placed second behind Mississippi in 1860, the Tombigbee and Alabama Rivers constituted what one historian has called the state's "only commercial highway" for most of the antebellum era. Primarily because both streams flowed into Mobile Bay, the port of Mobile shipped more cotton in 1859–1860 than any other Southern port save New Orleans.[11] The province of Prussia (East and West Prussia united), wrote a local author in 1863, contained many "natural waterways" navigable inland for a distance of 46 to 83 miles, the two most important being the Vistula (with the port of Danzig near its mouth) and the Pregel (served by the port of Königsberg). Estates situated along these streams, he explained, enjoyed the advantages of both easy transportation and good soil.[12]

To be sure, there were obvious differences in geography and climate between the South and East Elbia, and these help to explain many dissimilarities between the agricultural histories of plantations and *Rittergüter*. Consider that the South lies between 25 and 40 degrees of north latitude, whereas East Elbia lies between 50 and 55 degrees. Most of the Lower South (including East Texas, but not the southern tip of Florida, which was virtually unsettled in 1860) belongs to what climatologists have termed the "warm-temperate sub-tropical zones," experiences 210 to 300 freeze-free days per year, and receives at least 32 and as much as 64 inches of annual precipitation. East Elbia, in contrast, lies close to the northern limit of the "cool-temperate zones" and "woodland climates," enjoys only

170 to 190 frost-free days annually, and has a yearly average precipitation that varies according to locale from 20 to 40 inches, although mid-twenties is the norm.[13] Where the Lower South is congenial to cotton and even suitable in places for rice and sugar, East Elbia's climate is amenable to the hardier grains and tubers. The fact that the Upper South, with a median growing season of 180 to 210 days, lies at the southern limit of the "cool-temperate zones" helps to explain why nineteenth-century farmers in both the state of Virginia and the province of Brandenburg could raise cereal grains, tobacco, and livestock, although eastern Virginia's relatively mild climate favored the finer grades of tobacco, while rye was better suited to the colder and dryer climate of Brandenburg. As one moved southwest from Virginia to Mississippi, the warming influence of the Gulf Stream was supplanted west of the Appalachian Range by the stronger warming influence of the Gulf of Mexico. Thus, mean winter and summer temperatures in Richmond for the years 1824–27 were 37.2 and 75.4 degrees Fahrenheit, and in Natchez for the period 1836–47 they were 52.2 and 81 degrees.[14] As one moved east and slightly north from Brandenburg to provincial Prussia, the warming influence of the Gulf Stream gradually dissipated before the cooling impact of the Siberian land mass. Hence, during the 1860s the mean winter and summer temperatures for Brandenburg were 31.5 and 64.3 degrees Fahrenheit, and for old East Prussia 25.5 and 61.9 degrees.[15] To the minds of most antebellum Southerners Napoleon Bonaparte's quip about East Prussia's climate could well have applied to all of East Elbia: "six months' winter and six months without summer."[16]

— II —

Junkers and planters initiated their careers as agrarian entrepreneurs during the sixteenth and seventeenth centuries respectively, during the post-medieval blooming of what David Landes has termed "commercial capitalism."[17] During this "age of exploration" and era of "commercial revolution," western Europe extended its mercantile and territorial ambitions overseas, and the center of European economic life shifted from the southern lands of the Mediterranean to the northwest maritime countries bordering the Atlantic Ocean and the North Sea. First the Netherlands and then England were the principal beneficiaries of this shift. They became the commercial, banking, and manufacturing foci of a slowly integrating European economy based on interregional specialization and trade, which in turn became a nascent global economy, "a European centered world economy" involving parts of Africa, Asia, and the Americas.[18] During the generally prosperous and inflationary span of decades sometimes referred to as the long sixteenth century (circa 1480–1620), western Europe's growing population and increasing wealth resulted in food deficits covered partly by grain from the Baltic littoral,[19] and also stimulated popular demand for exotic commodities like sugar and tobacco from the New World, crops that Sidney W. Mintz calls "low-cost, high-energy food substitutes."[20]

Grain shipments from the Baltic, totaling about six million kilograms (that is, more than 13 million pounds) in 1460, stood at 100 million kilograms a century later, and stayed near that level into the early 1600s. Growing west European demand for grain, combined with the increased supplies of silver provided by central European and New World silver mines, sent rye prices at Polish Danzig up nearly 250 percent during the second half of the sixteenth century. Since rye prices at Amsterdam, which received about 80 percent of Danzig's exports circa 1600, remained almost twice their level at Danzig, the grain trade provided substantial profits to all involved, from the East Elbian estate owner to the Dutch merchant.[21] Although economic historians of the sixteenth century have tended to focus on rye shipped from the Baltic ports of Danzig, Stettin, and Königsberg, we should not overlook grain raised on *Rittergüter* in middle and western Brandenburg and floated down the Elbe to the North Sea port of Hamburg. One historian of sixteenth-century Brandenburg has concluded that "The extent of grain production decisively influenced the income of the Junkers."[22] According to Hartmut Harnisch, who has culled statistics from the extant records of two royal demesnes and three Junker estates, Electoral Brandenburg was as involved in the European grain trade as was Poland to the east, and exported enough cereals annually to feed half of Amsterdam's population of 100,000.[23] Junkers in Brandenburg seem to have responded to rising grain prices in much the same fashion as did *Rittergut* owners in Pomerania, described in the 1530s by Thomas Kantzow, a secretary to the Duke of Pomerania at Wolgast. "In earlier years the noblemen were not very industrious and attentive to agriculture," preferring instead to reside at court or to pursue military careers, noted Kantzow; "but this has changed recently, and the nobility *(Adel)* has never been so rich and powerful as now."[24] Nonetheless, because poor seed-to-yield ratios and local consumption permitted Junkers to market at most a third of their grain harvest (in contrast to the export by New World tobacco and sugar planters of virtually their entire crops), the lords of Brandenburg also depended on income from such collateral operations as beer brewing and the raising of sheep for wool.[25]

The European taste for tobacco had been awakened by Spanish growers in the West Indies, and by 1700 smoking tobacco had become, in the words of Ralph Davis, "a solace of the poor in every country."[26] Tobacco shipments from the Chesapeake plantations of Virginia and Maryland, which quickly captured the London market in the seventeenth century, amounted to 20 million pounds in 1700, and in the mid-1730s, after the opening of the French market to English merchants, reached 80 million pounds annually.[27] In 1697 three well-informed Virginians had portrayed nascent planters as follows: "The only Thing whereof they make as much as they can, is Tobacco, there always being a Vent for that at one time of the Year or other; besides that their Want of Cloathes and Household-Furniture, and all their other Necessaries, instigate them to make as much Tobacco as they can, this being the Money of the Country which Answers all Things."[28] A British visitor to the Virginia Tidewater in 1732 said of planters that "all their Care is for Tobacco and Little Else Minded Except Corn,"[29] an observation indicating that Chesapeake planters were well aware of the economic advantages to be derived from plantation self-sufficiency in basic foodstuffs.[30] In 1775, when tobacco exports hit 220 million pounds, two-thirds of the residents in Virginia and Maryland were raising tobacco. The Chesapeake colonies contained one-third of all British colonials on the North American mainland, but accounted for 60 percent of the value of all exports from the thirteen colonies.[31] During the 1770s and 1780s tobacco planters could also be found in inland areas of the newer seaboard colonies of South Carolina and Georgia, as well as in the Natchez District of the lower Mississippi River valley; and in both subregions tobacco plantations served as commercial precursors to the upland cotton plantations first established in the 1790s.[32] Rice cultivation dominated the South Carolina lowcountry by the 1720s, and spread northward along the Cape Fear River of North Carolina in the 1730s and southward into coastal Georgia during the 1750s. Indigo, used in the production of bluish textile dyes, attracted the attention of inland as well as coastal planters with the introduction of a British bounty in 1748. During the years 1768–1772 rice and indigo accounted for fifty-five percent and twenty percent respectively of the value of all exports from the South Carolina lowcountry. Indigo production reached its peak during the 1770s, only to collapse in the 1790s because of competition from the East India Company and the absence of a British bounty.[33] However, the 1790s also brought cotton gins and the beginnings of the expansive Cotton Kingdom, even as the introduction to then Spanish Louisiana of an efficient sugar mill made possible the localized spread of sugarcane plantations.[34]

In responding to favorable international markets for their cash crops, proprietors of plantations in the colonial South and of knight's estates in early modern East Elbia, confronting high land-labor ratios and nonexistent or weak political opposition, instituted or intensified systems of unfree labor that survived into the nineteenth century. Daniel Chirot has called them "agricultural servile labor systems oriented to the market."[35] However, whereas Southern plantations first emerged as commercial by-products of post-medieval European expansion overseas, East Elbian *Rittergüter* were a legacy of the great late-medieval wave of German colonization that swept into the Slavic lands beyond the Elbe River, the eastern frontier of the old Hohenstaufen Reich. (During this late-medieval process of colonizing East Elbia with recruits from western Germany, the feudal lords would keep small parcels of lands for themselves, often cultivating them with landless hirelings, while receiving rents in kind or money from the free peasantry and exercising nominal judicial authority over the peasant villages.[36])

Whereas seventeenth-century Virginia planters imported first indentured servants from Europe and later black slaves from sub-Saharan Africa (usually by way of the West Indies),[37] manorial lords in sixteenth-century Brandenburg exploited their feudal powers of local jurisdiction (judicial and police) in order to expand the size of their demesnes and impose heavier labor services on the peasantry, in the process depriving them of freedom of movement and reducing them to some form of hereditary servitude. These changes, common to most of the territories that would become Prussian East Elbia, created the historical combination of *Gutsherrschaften* and *Gutswirtschaften*—that is, manorial estates where a substantial percentage of the land belonged to the lords, who farmed it with bound labor subordinate to the lords' autocratic political authority.[38] In contradistinction to the *Grundherrschaften* that continued to prevail west of the Elbe River—that is, a more politically and economically decentralized manorial system whereby the peasantry provided aristocratic landlords with rents in kind or money rather than labor services—the eastern *Gutsherrschaft* "depended on the exploitation of peasant labor for the cultivation of the noble's own extensive demesne or 'farmland' (*Vorwerksland*)."[39] Neither the serfs of early modern East Elbia nor slaves in the colonial South submitted to exploitation by their lords and masters without resistance. Their resistence could manifest itself in a variety of comparable ways, for example, shoddy work, the purchase of freedom, running away, and occasionally open revolt, as in the Silesian peasant revolt of 1765–66 and the Stono rebellion of 1740 in South Carolina.[40] Nonetheless, East Elbian peasants could consistently engage in more formal and efficacious protests against Junker encroachments, due to a constellation of historical circumstances that gave serfs recognized powers of communal autonomy and legal resistance unavailable to Southern slaves.[41] A substantial number of East Elbian peasants enjoyed hereditary claims to their farms, and peasant villages could become litigants in the state court. Full peasants and substantial cottagers (*Vollbauern* and *Kossäten*) were themselves taxpayers and later soldiers in whose survival the territorial ruler had a vested interest.[42] These circumstances meant that Junkers simply could not attain as high a degree of autocratic control over the lives of their bound labor force as did planters, with the notable exception of those adolescent peasant children compelled to live and work on *Rittergüter* as manorial servants for three or more years (*Gesindezwangsdienst*).[43]

Although the lords of Brandenburg initiated efforts to reduce the mobility and autonomy of the peasantry in the 1480s, formal decrees effecting what Hartmut Harnisch calls "the legal chaining of the immediate producers to the soil and thereby to the lords" date from the first half of the sixteenth century.[44] By the early seventeenth century peasants without hereditary land tenure in both Electoral Brandenburg and the Duchy of Pomerania were obligated, in the words of a 1616 Pomeranian statute, to perform "unlimited labor services of all sorts *(allerhand ungemessene Frondienste),"* [45] services which the peasants often hired farmhands to perform. Growing western European demand and rising grain prices stimulated the Junkers' interest in enlarging their demesne acreage and in farming their estates more intensively, both of which required larger inputs of labor. Thus, notes F. L. Carsten, "The serfdom of the peasants everywhere developed in proportion to the demand for labour on the demesnes." [46] The various territorial princes, themselves large landowners interested in agricultural profits, and also dependent on the cooperation of the noble-dominated corporatist assemblies for financial credits in times of war, generally sided with the entrepreneurial aristocracy not only in imposing greater restrictions and heavier obligations on the peasantry, but also in breaking the local towns' traditional monopolies on the brewing of beer for sale as well as on handling the trade in cereals, thereby allowing the Junkers more remunerative direct access to foreign merchants. A famous settlement in Brandenburg between the Hohenzollern prince and landed nobility *(Ritterstand)* took the form of a famous compact *(Landtags-Rezess)* concluded in 1653. Because the occupation and devastation of Brandenburg by Swedish troops in the course of the Thirty Years' War had weakened the nobility's resistance to the Great Elector's demands for a standing army, the nobility wanted state assistance in restoring their control over the peasantry after the population decline and the widespread collapse of Junkerdom's manorial authority during the long years of warfare. In return for endorsing the principle of a tax-supported standing army (which numbered 30,000 by the time of the Great Elector's death in 1680), and for implicitly allowing the monarchy a free hand in the conduct of foreign affairs, Junkerdom received royal confirmation of their seigniorial rights and assurances that the state would not act unilaterally to interfere with their *Gutsherrschaften* or alter the tax-exempt status of noble land. [47] It was this 1653 "Recess" that Brandenburg Junkers would regularly cite as the legal basis for their opposition to Chancellor Hardenberg's agrarian and tax reforms of 1810–11. [48]

In seventeenth-century Virginia the emergent planter elite encountered virtually no political opposition in securing bound labor, and even enjoyed unrestricted headright privileges, which awarded fifty acres of land to "the importer of each head, whether that of freeman, indentured servant, relative, or slave into the colony." [49] Indentured servitude, established circa 1618, provided "a workable means of supplying white settlers and cheap labor" for most of the century. [50] By 1625 over one-third of the 1200 Virginia colonists were indentured servants, bound usually to four-year terms of service. From 1625 to 1640, years of tobacco boom and high mortality, an annual average of a thousand white servants arrived in Virginia, and at mid-century such servants amounted to half the colony's population. Because planters became accustomed to employing overseers and whips in supervising the gang labor of white servants, often traded them like property, and developed a fear of rebellious servants, Edmund S. Morgan has concluded that the Old Dominion "developed her plantation system without slaves, and slavery introduced no novelties to methods of production."[51]

For decades after a Dutch ship brought the first "Negroes" to Virginia in 1619, most blacks in the new colony seem to have been considered servants rather than slaves, and some even became property owners and masters of other servants. It was not until the 1660s that enslavement of blacks received formal legal recognition from the General Assembly. A 1682 law subjected all imported Africans to automatic hereditary bondage, and a comprehensive "slave code" was published in 1705.[52] Prior to the 1660s it had been widely assumed that an African's conversion from "heathenism" to Christianity precluded that individual's continued enslavement; but the growing profitability of slave labor, strongly reinforced by culture-bound English views of blackness as evil and Africans as barbaric, led the Virginia legislature to sever the connection between conversion and emancipation in 1667.[53] The growing profitability of slavery during the second half of the seventeenth century seems to have resulted in part from a decline in the colony's mortality rate during the middle decades of the century, so that the expensive investment in a slave for life became a better risk vis-à-vis the cheaper investment in a temporary servant.[54] Although the cost of an indentured servant might still be one-third or one-quarter the cost of a slave, during the first year of his or her four-year indenture a new servant had to learn the techniques of tobacco cultivation, and thus the planter had the services of an experienced servant for only three years. But a slave, once trained, worked for life; and the offspring of a female slave became her master's property. According to nabob William Fitzhugh (1651–1701), a colonist with modest capital resources could afford to buy a plantation with eight to ten slaves, which would yield "a handsom, gentile and sure subsistence"; and Fitzhugh himself had started out just this way.[55] The replacement of indentured servitude with black slavery received an even more powerful impetus from the stabilizing and then declining numbers of indentured servants leaving England from the 1660s to the 1680s, at a time when the available supply of slaves was expanding and the opening of New York and Pennsylvania to English settlement attracted some servants who might otherwise have settled in the Chesapeake colonies of Maryland and Virginia. "Dwindling supplies and spiraling prices for servants joined with ample supplies and a steady, perhaps falling price for slaves to persuade (Chesapeake) planters to draw on Africa for labor," conclude McCusker and Menard.[56] Although there is some question as to exactly when black slaves began to supersede white servants as the principal source of plantation labor,[57] there is no doubt that the Chesapeake region was fast becoming a "slave society" during the early decades of the eighteenth century, and that the region's slave population began to grow through natural increase (versus imports) by the 1730s. By mid-century the Tidewater plantations of the fabled "First Families of Virginia" were farmed almost exclusively by slave labor, as were the lowcountry plantations of South Carolina's grandees.[58]

South Carolina, founded in 1669, had never depended much on indentured servitude for plantation labor, and acquired a "black majority" by 1710. Experienced planters from the Caribbean island of Barbados, "England's first plantation society,"[59] were prominent among the early settlers, and effected a direct transplantation of black slavery from West Indian sugar estates to rice plantations in the Carolina lowcountry. The familiarity of West African Negroes with rice cultivation, as well as their greater inherited resistance to yellow fever and malaria, made possible the rapid growth of rice culture in South Carolina during the early 1700s.[60] Slavery also flourished south of the Savannah River after Georgia (founded in 1733) repealed its prohibition against the institution in 1750–51. In 1773 William Gerard De Brahm (1717–99), who had led a large migration of German settlers to Georgia in the 1750s, and then invested his own money in human property, observed that in dealing with slave labor, "the preventing of Idleness is the Art, from which depends the whole Discipline of the Negroes and the Planter's Success."[61]

Thus, in the words of W. Robert Higgins, "the institution of slave labor was universally accepted in the South in the eighteenth century, and people in all areas and strata of society looked to the possession of Negroes as a reflection of their own status and an avenue for financial advancement."[62] As seaboard society became more settled and hierarchical in the eighteenth century, did the plantation gentry become less entrepreneurial and more aristocratic? Perhaps the question assumes a false dichotomy, since entrepreneurial behavior and aristocratic values are not mutually exclusive. Jack P. Greene explains that "The 'market mentality' so powerfully exhibited by its (the Chesapeake region's) seventeenth-century inhabitants by no means dissipated but coexisted—easily—with rising aspirations for the establishment of a traditional patriarchy." Chesapeake planters continued "to devote themselves to the active and energetic pursuit of profit through the production of tobacco for an international commercial market."[63] Greene's observation suggests that Hans Rosenberg's evaluation of sixteenth-century Junkers is also appropriate for planters in the colonial South: "The historical evidence demonstrates very clearly that . . . a rational, economically acquisitive mentality and conduct of life was quite compatible with the ethics and customs of an aristocratic class."[64] Men like Hartwig von Bredow II, of Friesack in Brandenburg's Havelland district, and William Fitzhugh, builder of a thirteen-room mansion at Bedford in Virginia's Stafford County, were both landed entrepreneurs and gentlemen farmers. Von Bredow, the son and namesake of an entrepreneurial Junker, belonged to one of the oldest noble families in Brandenburg, whereas Fitzhugh, the son of a substantial English woolen-draper, was a first-generation planter who had come to Virginia in the early 1670s with legal training and some money. Both men accumulated land, established new farms *(Vorwerke)* or plantations, sought out new sources of forced labor, made substantial profits from marketing their own produce plus that of peasants or lesser planters and farmers in their neighborhoods, and were active in local politics.[65] They manifested many of those traits of worldly rationality that Max Weber saw as having, in the words of Reinhard Bendix, "a many-sided development peculiar to Western civilization and more or less directly related to the development of capitalism."[66]

— III —

Eighteenth-century England combined a number of attributes that enabled the country to experience "the first industrial revolution":[67] for example, a unified national market, facilitated by the close proximity of most areas in the island country to the seacoast, and by the absence in the southern and midland regions of mountain barriers to overland commerce or canal construction; a rapidly growing population (from the 1740s), and a very high degree of social mobility and fluidity in comparison with the rest of Europe; an expanding overseas trade that obviously benefited from the colonies and the protection provided by the British navy; a government that actively supported the country's commercial and manufacturing interests, to the point of waging war; a highly commercial agricultural sector, and a substantial manufacturing sector, especially in coal and woolens. It seems to have been the growth in foreign and domestic demand that provided the crucial macroeconomic spur to "the fundamental technological breakthrough in the cotton industry that we call the Industrial Revolution."[68] That breakthrough involved the fusion of rollers and spindles in the cotton-spinning mule of the 1780s, which, when linked to steam power, marked the beginnings of a "modern" factory system of production and the birth of industrial capitalism.

From 1784 to 1856, explains Ralph Davis, "British exports, mainly of manufactured goods, though including some raw and semi-processed materials, were exchanged almost entirely for foodstuffs and raw materials."[69] East Elbia and the South quickly became two of England's most important partners in this trading pattern, although the exchange was usually mediated by third parties. Non-Prussian merchants in the old, still independent Hanseatic ports on the North Sea—Bremen and especially Hamburg, which the New Orleans periodical *DeBow's Review* called "the great entrepôt of the nations of Europe"[70]—facilitated a triangular trade between East Elbia, England, and western Germany in much the same way that New York City functioned as a commercial intermediary between the South, the Northeast, and England.[71] (The beginning of regular steamship service across the North Sea between Hull and Hamburg in 1828 expanded Hamburg's intermediary role in Anglo-German trade, just as the transatlantic Black Ball steamship service between Liverpool and New York, begun in the early 1820s, enhanced New York's involvement in Anglo-American trade.[72])

Among Britain's four most important imports during the years 1824–26, the South provided most of the cotton (no. 1), and East Elbia supplied much of the wool (no. 4). For the years 1854–56 cotton and wheat headed the list of English imports; again, England received most of its cotton from the South and much of its wheat from East Elbia.[73]

English and western European dependence on foreign grain had declined markedly during the seventeenth and early eighteenth century, as the rate of population growth had fallen almost to the point of stagnation. Consequently, average annual grain shipments from the Baltic dropped from 68,000 tons for the years 1600–1649, to 56,000 tons for 1650–99, to 32,000 tons during the period 1700–1749. At the same time English farmers were beginning to increase their productivity per acre with new techniques of crop rotation and animal husbandry borrowed from the Dutch, and by the 1720s England was even exporting surplus barley and wheat to Holland, Spain, and Portugal.[74] During the 1600s East Elbia's population and agriculture had suffered greatly from the Thirty Years' War (1618–48) and subsequent conflicts involving Sweden and Poland. The twin ravages of war and disease reduced both the supply of labor and agricultural productivity in a region whose frequency of poor soils and infrequency of improved farming techniques necessitated vast inputs of land and labor in order to produce grain surpluses for export.[75] The labor shortage redounded to the advantage of assertive peasant households and compelled some Junkers to hire more landless laborers *(Einlieger* and *Tagelöhner)* and to maintain plow animals at their own expense. From the late seventeenth century until the death of Frederick the Great in 1786 the increasingly absolutist Hohenzollern monarchy sought to promote autarchy within Brandenburg-Prussia, in part by restricting grain exports. Junker agriculturalists became heavily dependent on the domestic market, while the army officers' corps and civil bureaucracy provided honorable careers for many Junkers and their sons. In Brandenburg both the labor supply and internal demand rose during the eighteenth century as the rural population exceeded its pre-1618 level and Berlin grew from 55,000 in 1709 to 178,000 in 1803. Although the state preferred to purchase cheaper Polish grain for its grain magazines, the expanding domestic market was reserved for *Rittergut* owners and lessees of royal demesnes.[76]

After England's rate of population growth revived during the mid-1700s, the country began to import wheat regularly in the 1760s. Rising prices on the English market caught the attention of East Elbian merchants and Junker landowners, who agitated successfully after the death of Frederick the Great in 1786 for relaxation of restrictions on grain exports.[77] England even imported some grain from the Upper South on the eve of the American Revolution, although the preponderance of Chesapeake grain shipments abroad (amounting to nearly 20 percent of the area's export earnings circa 1770) went to the West Indies and southern Europe.[78] Progressive planters in parts of eastern Maryland and

Virginia's Tidewater and Eastern Shore, suffering from the effects of soil depletion and poor tobacco yields in conjunction with recurring depressions in tobacco prices between 1680 and 1740, had been diversifying their crops and marketing corn and wheat for decades. By doing so they had helped the British Empire meet the demands of monocultural sugar plantations in the West Indies for foodstuffs.[79] Especially after 1760, increasing numbers of Virginia planters, including such notables as George Washington and Robert Carter II of Nomini Hall (son of Robert "King" Carter), reduced their tobacco acreage and turned increasingly to the production of grains for markets outside the Old Dominion. Cultivation of wheat as a money crop accelerated in the Tidewater once the American Revolution, in the words of Louis Morton, "gave a check to the exportation of leaf tobacco from which it never recovered."[80] Although the western spread of tobacco farming helped keep prices low for most of the antebellum era, another boom would come to Chesapeake tobacco growers during the 1850s.[81]

English demand for foreign cereals had much less impact on Upper South planters than on Junkers, who enjoyed the advantage of closer proximity and cheaper transport costs. From 1801 to 1805, as the wars of the French Revolution and Napoleon caused European grain prices to skyrocket,[82] England imported an annual average of 320,000 tons. Of that total one-tenth came from North America, one-fifth from Ireland, and at least one-third from Prussia (which by 1800 included almost all the grain-exporting areas of the recently partitioned Kingdom of Poland).[83] Such figures led Gunther Ipsen to conclude that "the British industrial system found its first partner in Prussia,"[84] which was almost entirely East Elbian prior to 1815. If Prussia was industrializing England's first major supplier of essential agricultural commodities, the southern United States and their cotton were close behind in second place. From a mere 40,000 pounds in 1790 (a few years before the invention of the cotton gin), American cotton exports to Great Britain ballooned to 17.8 million pounds by 1800 and reached 75.3 million pounds in 1820,[85] a year when *Rittergut* owners were suffering badly from the inevitable post-Napoleonic glut of grain on the European market.

— IV —

In East Elbia during the last third of the eighteenth century, an obvious and common response to rising grain prices was simply to purchase more land or bring more land into cultivation. Indeed, the provincial mortgage credit associations *(Landschaften)*—first established by Frederick the Great after the Seven Years' War, and constituting what Eckert Kehr called "the foundations of speculative agrarian capitalism" in Prussia—served to fuel a veritable mania of speculation in *Rittergut* real estate. Such speculation led to widespread overindebtedness and thereby set the stage for many of the bankruptcies and foreclosures that hit Junkerdom first after Napoleon forced Prussia into the French Continental System after 1806, and then during the grave post-1818 depression.[86] A government official in Breslau observed in 1788 that "In Silesia landed estates are traded almost like horses."[87] In Brandenburg between 1800 and 1805 Lieutenant-General Friedrich Wilhelm Karl von Schmettau (1742–1806?) made a net profit of 119,000 *Taler* from the sale of three estates. He puchased another estate in 1805—Hackenau, in the county of Lebus—for 96,000 *Taler* from a von Piper, who made a 100 percent profit himself. Speculator von Schmettau promptly petitioned the king for permission to sell the estate in parcels to peasants, as "this transaction will only then be advantageous to me."[88]

Nonetheless, during the late 1700s some noble *Rittergut* proprietors, at times following the lead of innovative "commoner" lessees of crown and knight's estates, strove to increase their yields-per-acre and income by enclosing open fields and bringing uncultivated land under the plow. They used natural fertilizers like dung and marl, and shifted from the traditional three-field system to "improved" three-field systems which involved planting the fallow with fodder crops like clover.[89] The additional labor necessary to implement these improvements usually came from the ranks of the land-poor or landless, whose increasing numbers reflected the growth of Brandenburg-Prussia's population from 3.5 million circa 1740 to 5.7 million in 1805.[90] Improving Junkers came to rely less on compulsory labor services *(Fronarbeit)* provided by peasant households (especially those with holdings large enough to support two teams of draught animals); instead they made greater use of hired labor *(Lohnarbeit)* rendered by landless men and women who received wages in kind and money (including housing) while living subordinate to the noble landowner's manorial authority. The profitability of such contractual labor was enhanced by the regulations for servants *(Gesindeordnung)* promulgated in 1769, which imposed a legal freeze on the wages paid to manorial servants and farm laborers just as grain prices began to rise. The Junkers' growing reliance on hired labor was often promoted by the peasants themselves, who resisted Junker demands for increased labor services while becoming interested in producing their own marketable surpluses, an interest they could better pursue by commuting some of their compulsory labor services into rents and devoting more attention to their own farms.[91] Junkers who became accustomed to farming their estates with hired labor would not feel mortally threatened by the formal abolition of serfdom after 1806, so long as they received adequate compensation in land or money for their former rights to compulsory services from bound peasants, and so long as their autocratic powers of local jurisdiction remained essentially intact.

Prominent among the agricultural innovators of eighteenth-century East Elbia was Heinrich Adrian Graf von Borcke (1715–88). A university-educated brigadier general who retired from military service in 1761, he took over management of the *Rittergut* Stargord, an estate of 1200 to 1500 acres located on the river Rega in the eastern Pomeranian county *(Kreis)* of Regenwalde.[92] In

1779 he published a pamphlet describing and promoting his principles of estate management, and had the following "motto" printed in isolation on the page opposite the first page of his preface: "Agriculture is a type of management *(Veranstaltung)*, whereby on a given tract of land one can produce the largest possible quantity of those products that are most certain of disposal to the greatest advantage and at the least cost." It is remarkable how much Borcke's motto anticipated the businesslike approach to farming prescribed three decades later by the most influential of Prussian agronomists, Anglophile Albrecht Thaer, in his *Principles of Rational Agriculture* (1809): "Agriculture is a vocation whose purpose is, through the production (sometimes also through the further processing) of vegetable and animal substances, to derive profit or to acquire money."[93] Count von Borcke heartily recommended to his peers in 1779 the writings of English agronomists, although he warned against too much reliance on "book farming" as opposed to practical experience. "Agriculture is different from all other occupations," he maintained, "in that practice must necessarily precede theory." Borcke, the owner of 600 sheep and 170 cattle as of 1777 (about half of them rented out), was an East Elbian pioneer in the cultivation of clover as fodder, and also emphasized that "clover greatly improves the land." He also applied manure and marl liberally to his fields, concluding "that as the soil is constantly improved with more and more dung and marl, the yields of the estate must always increase."[94]

A contemporary landed gentleman across the Atlantic, and perhaps von Borcke's equal as an agronomist, was Landon Carter (1710–78) of Tidewater Virginia. Carter attended William and Mary College briefly, inherited in 1732 at least eight plantations from his father, "King" Carter, and established his seat of residence at Sabine Hall, on the Rappahannock River in Richmond County. Carter read English agronomists like Jethro Tull (1674–1741), and sounded much like von Borcke when stressing the virtues of fertilizing wheat fields with the manure of cattle fed on turnips, lucerne, and alfalfa. "We see the best manure," he wrote in his diary during 1770, "in the dung of animals that feed on grains and vegetables."[95]

Von Borcke noted in 1779 that his agricultural improvements had required a greater expenditure of farm labor. In order to supplement the field labor of his thirteen peasant households and their draft animals, the Count had established at Stargord eight new families of cottagers *(Kossäten)*. Their duties encompassed plough work with oxen owned by the estate, and their wages included a home, a garden plot, fixed allowances of rye and barley *(Deputat)*, a small fractional share in the grain they threshed during the winter months *(Dresche)*, and free grazing rights for a cow, a pig, and a goose. At harvest time additional labor was provided by the families of four less favored cottagers *(Häusler)*, who received no fixed allowances in kind nor permission to maintain a cow, and by twenty-eight male and female farmhands *(Knechte* and *Mägde)*, who received housing and small cash wages. The farmhands' situation points up the anomalous mixture of so-called "feudal" and "capitalist" elements in *Rittergut* labor relations during the late eighteenth century. Most of Stargord's farmhands had married and then "submitted themselves to serfdom *(gaben sich unterthänig),*" perhaps because in so doing they became entitled to a share in the threshed grain and access to common land. "All this could not have happened, if the wages *(Verdienst)* of this place had not been known," declared von Borcke. "If one provides wages, then people will appear." He boasted that the village of Stargord had 170 more residents in 1777 than before the outbreak of the Seven Years' War in 1756, along with twenty-three new family houses. "There are no beggars in Stargord and all have ample subsistence."[96]

Nevertheless, the Count also reported that the village residents resisted some of his agricultural innovations, in particular the enclosure of open fields. Occasionally they ignored repeated warnings to keep their livestock out of enclosed fields, and Borcke determined simply to leave a few dead cows lying on the ground. Furthermore, he considered it essential to have "good tight and locked-up barns" to prevent villagers from pilfering fodder.[97] This is a recommendation that most planters would have easily understood, since they were always concerned to prevent their slaves from raiding the corn bin or the smoke house during the night.[98] Indeed, Landon Carter apparently had greater difficulties with his black bondsmen than did Borcke with his enserfed families. It is well to remember that Borcke's bound workers were not deemed personal property and members of an inferior race who could be sold off the estate and away from relatives. Landon Carter resorted more often to whipping, as when his slaves failed to remove half of the grains from harvested oats during the threshing process in 1757. "They have been severely whipped day by day," he confided to his diary. "They have all encouragement given them, but are such Villains that they will not thresh them cleaner(,) so that I intend to thresh the straw that is left over again." In 1778, after his slaves had mishandled tobacco leaves, the Virginian exclaimed that "Slaves are devils and to make them otherwise than slaves will be to set them free."[99]

Carter's private frustrations of 1778 anticipated the published invectives of a prominent Georgia planter in 1856—Howell Cobb of Houston County, who became president of the state's Cotton Planters' Convention in 1859. According to Georgia historian Ralph B. Flanders, Cobb's *Scriptural Examination of the Institution of Slavery* (1856) was "the best expression of the moral and theological defense of slavery."[100] Although Cobb acknowledged that some "hard masters" committed "illegal excesses" in punishing their slaves, he also insisted that "We have to control a race of human beings who are under the influence of the most depraved and vicious propensities that ever marked the character of the debased; individuals of which race seem to be incapable of redemption, either by kindness or severity."[101] Mid-nineteenth century Junkers simply did not engage in such racist vilification of East Elbia's rural laborers, although they might make condescending comments about the alleged dearth of industry and order among the Slavic rural population in Polish Posen, and although they both denigrated and feared Polish aspirations to national independence.[102] Given the mixture of fear and loathing evident in so much white discourse about blacks in the slave South, plus the overall success that *Rittergut* owners like von Borcke experienced with contractual labor in the 1700s, it is hardly surprising that Junkers could contemplate and confront the abolition of bondage in the early nineteenth century with far less dread than could planters then or half a century later.

— V —

Although East Elbia's knight's estates circa 1800 were hardly a historical legacy of medieval seigniorialism, it was only during the first half of the nineteenth century that landed Junkerdom became a legally open and socially mixed elite— something that the plantation gentry had always been. On the eve of Baron vom Stein's October Edict of 1807 between 10 and 15 percent of all knight's estates had already fallen *sub rosa* into the hands of non-nobles;[103] but it was only after 1807 that any well-to-do commoner—from the ranks of the bureaucracy, officers' corps, urban business classes, lessees of crown and noble estates, even the peasantry—could purchase completely aboveboard a *Rittergut* and the aristocratic privileges attached to it. By the 1848 Revolution over a third of East Elbia's knight's estates belonged to untitled commoners,[104] and we can get a sense of their diversity by focusing on the province of Brandenburg. Johann Heinrich Leberecht Pistorious (1777–1858), a Berlin liquor merchant, acquired the Brandenburg estate Weissensee in 1821 and transformed it into a 1300–acre "model farm" devoted in part to the growing of potatoes for the distilling of whiskey.[105] Wilhelm Ferdinand Eben (b. 1784), a bureaucrat and the son of a bureaucrat, purchased Schlagenthin from a bankrupt Captain von Göllnitz in 1829. In a description of the estate published in 1847, Eben reported raising grain, sheep, and also potatoes for a distillery located on his 2200 acres. When his son Carl Hermann Eben (b. 1811) purchased Schlagenthin and the attached farm *(Vorwerk)* Ebenau in 1850, at a cost of 120,000 *Taler,* his purchase reportedly included some 4200 sheep and 3100 acres, almost 2000 of them under cultivation. In 1853 the younger Eben established a brickworks at Schlagenthin whose reputed output soon reached 400,000 to 500,000 bricks per year.[106]

Johann Wilhelm Noack, an untitled army captain, purchased the estate Schönwalde in 1838 from August Henriette von Kalkreüth, the widow of another nonnoble army officer, a Lieutenant Kuhlwein, whose bureaucrat father had purchased it from Captain Adolf Ferdinand von Winning in 1805. When Captain Noack died in 1851, the estate encompassed over 2400 acres, and was inherited by his son, Lieutenant Gustav Adolph Noack. According to Heinrich Berghaus's

Land Register for the Mark Brandenburg, compiled in the mid-1850s, the elder Noack "was a capable agriculturist, established enclosed fields *(Schlagwirtschaft),* purified the land of the many boulders scattered over it, fertilized the fields with marl, and introduced a better and more appropriate crop rotation."[107]

At mid-century perhaps the most renowned of Brandenburg's untitled Junkers was Johann Gottlieb Koppe (1782–1863), a cottager's son who worked his way up first as the efficient manager of two noble-owned knight's estates and then (from 1827) as the innovative lessee of the crown estate Wollup. Strongly influenced by Albrecht Thaer, Koppe himself published several agronomic treatises, the most famous being *Instruction in Agriculture and Stock-Farming (Der Unterricht im Ackerbau und der Viehzucht),* which first appeared in 1812 and went through nine editions during the author's lifetime. In 1839 Koppe was elected president of the Association of German Agriculturists and Foresters, and in 1842 he received a royal appointment to the Board of Rural Economy *(Landes-Oeconomie-Collegium),* a fifteen-member committee under the Ministry of the Interior and the most prestigious governmental body for agricultural affairs in Prussia. Also in 1842 he purchased two *Rittergüter,* Beesdau and Kienitz, from the son of a Major von Thünen, who had given Koppe his first managerial position at the estate Gräfendorf bei Jüterbog decades before. Koppe operated the two acquisitions with the assistance of his two youngest sons, and from 1849 to 1852 served in the upper house of the new Prussian legislature.[108] During the 1840s, when rapid population growth and the apparent immiseration of the rural lower classes encouraged talk of partitioning large landed estates, he became an outspoken defender of large farms, primarily on the grounds of productivity. His logic seems to have run as follows: because East Elbia's generally poor soils required generous applications of manure in order to produce good yields, and because there were too few large towns in northeastern Germany to make sufficient manure available to a countryside of small farms, adequate supplies of manure for improved agriculture had to come from large herds of livestock, which could be properly maintained only on large estates. Moreover, wrote Koppe from a decidedly upper-class perspective, "The more landed property is partitioned, the fewer people are found who have the means to advance the higher concerns of humanity or to intervene benevolently in a general emergency."[109]

It seems that most nouveaux Junker families, like the famous sons of the Magdeburg tobacco merchant Johann Gottlieb Nathusius (1760–1835) in provincial Saxony, either shared or adopted the sort of elitist social and political views expressed by Koppe.[110] Thus, the fact that many commoners acquired knight's estates during the first half of the nineteenth century was of less historical significance than the pervasive "improving" impact that the free trade in *Rittergüter* had on the character of Junkerdom as a landed elite. A traumatic weeding out of many less capable or committed proprietors occurred during the decade of intense agricultural depression that followed the collapse of grain prices throughout Europe in 1818. By 1825 grain prices had fallen to 28 percent of their 1817 level,[111] and the English market was effectively closed to foreign cereals under the provisions of the protectionist Corn Laws passed by Parliament in 1816. Many noble *Rittergut* owners, carrying heavy debts incurred from expanding production or speculating in land during the boom years of the wars of the French Revolution and Napoleon, declared bankruptcy. More would have gone under without the special financial assistance channeled through the provincial mortgage credit associations *(Landschaften)* by the royal government. The *Landschaften* sequestered bankrupt estates and sold them to the highest bidders, who included many ambitious and capable non-nobles. In East Prussia alone some 230 *Rittergüter,* or about two-fifths of all mortgaged estates, were placed on the auction block between 1823 and 1833.[112]

Depressed conditions also plagued most Southern planters in the older Atlantic seaboard states during the decade following the Panic of 1819. The downturn evoked a fledgling agricultural reform movement whose leading light became Virginian Edmund Ruffin, author of a famous manifesto for marl as an antidote to acidic soils, *Essay on Calcareous Manures,* which appeared in 1833. Eastern Virginians, many of them already suffering from exhausted land and living amidst a plethora of abandoned "old fields,"[113] faced depressed prices for both tobacco and wheat. At the Virginia Constitutional Convention of 1829–30, Charles F. Mercer of Loudoun County (in the northern Piedmont) estimated that total land values in the Commonwealth had fallen by three-fifths since 1817, from $206 million to $80 or $90 million.[114] South Carolina's backcountry cotton planters suffered from both depleted soils and competition from fresher soils to the southwest, as "overproduction of short-staple cotton sent upland-cotton prices plunging 72 percent from 1818 to 1829, compared to a 49 percent drop in the cost of living."[115] Foreclosed seaboard planters, and more prosperous ones as well, frequently took up the option of moving to more fertile and productive soils west of the Appalachians.[116] The Augusta, Georgia, *Courier* for 11 October 1827 carried the report of a traveler from Charleston to St. Louis who "overtook hordes of cotton planters from North Carolina, South Carolina, and Georgia, with large gangs of negroes, bound to Alabama, Mississippi and Louisiana; 'where the cotton land is not worn out.' "[117] Consequently, the economic depression of the 1820s had less of an "improving" impact on the economic behavior of the planter elite as a whole than on that of the Junker elite. When the prices of cotton and slaves rose dramatically in the mid-thirties, and brought "flush times" to Alabama and Mississippi, the westward migration of planters and would-be planters continued and even surged.[118] Until the Civil War, concludes historian Lacy K. Ford, Jr., "the road to the Southwest was the principal avenue of opportunity in the Old South."[119] Twenty-six-year-old Virginia attorney James Davidson, visiting the Old Southwest in 1836, noted in his diary that "Any young man of energy and good character in the South can make a fortune."

Two or three good cotton crops would pay for a nascent planter's "tract of land and his stock of slaves," wrote Davidson. He "was frequently surprised to see rough, common looking men . . . who, I was told, were making one & two hundred bales of Cotton which would bring $10,000 and $20,000." [120] Regardless of how many men actually experienced this kind of fast success, the belief that such quick and easy ascents were possible on the cotton frontier seems to have been almost an article of faith among many white Southerners. And this faith served to limit the impact of the reformist enthusiasm emanating primarily from eastern Virginia, even after the Panic of 1837 helped bring another string of relatively lean years to Southern agriculture.

It is important to realize that throughout the antebellum era, as new territories and states opened up to the west and south, a planter in the older states could expect to make up some of his short-term agricultural losses, or to enhance his income, from long-term increases in the number and value of his slaves. These usually occupied the pre-eminent position, one could say, in the planter's investment portfolio. Some of a planter's human chattel might be hired out, and some might be sent out of the state to work new and potentially more profitable plantations established by their owner's family. Vivid testimony about both these options comes from the published letters of Virginian Elijah Fletcher (1789–1858), who lived in the Piedmont town of Lynchburg and managed Sweetbriar plantation north of town, in Amherst County. In 1849 Fletcher wrote about hiring out slaves to work on the James River and Kanawha Canal: "I have so many youngsters growing up to take the place of the older ones that I can spare them without interrupting the usual course of plantation work. I make it a sort of punishment too to those who do not please me at home." Two years earlier he had reported the return of his eldest son Sidney (b. 1821) from the new state of Florida. "His object was to seek out a site for a sugar Plantation, thinks it well to colonize a portion of our slaves in that region, being rather over stocked with them here, and knowing the culture of that article much more profitable than the products of this country." [121] Of course, a planter could also engage in profit-taking by selling slaves in response to the demand for labor from the newer plantation states. Virginian Edmund Ruffin, after insisting that "very many masters" had "a fixed rule" never to sell a slave except out of financial necessity or frustration with an incorrigible misfit, nevertheless acknowledged in 1833: "That master alone finds productive value in his increase of slaves, who chooses to turn the increase of his capital, at regular intervals, into money at the highest market price!" [122] Exactly how much income planters in the older, slave-exporting states received from out-of-state slave sales is open to debate; but plausible calculations by Herbert Gutman and Richard Sutch "suggest that approximately 10 percent of the total return to slaveowners in the exporting states was derived from this source." [123]

Rittergut owners did not have a frontier or the option of selling human chattel to cushion the blow of low commodity prices and hard times. Noble Junkers who held on to their land usually did so only by adopting for the first time, or by implementing more systematically, the agricultural improvements being trumpeted by Albrecht Thaer and his cohorts throughout northern Germany. The limitations of the historical record make it impossible to determine with any degree of precision what percentage of noble Junkers actually became "improving" farmers during the first half of the nineteenth century. Nonetheless, the numerous descriptions of *Rittergut* operations published in East Elbian agricultural journals, the rising interest in and growing number of agricultural societies *(Vereine),*[124] and the testimony of many contemporaneous observers all indicate that by the 1840s a decided majority of Junker landowners had long since abandoned the traditional three-field system (rye or wheat, barley, and fallow), and were practicing a more diversified agriculture involving systematic fertilization and new crop rotations that could provide fodder crops for larger livestock holdings. Even Otto von Bismarck (1815–98), who would in 1847–48 acquire a reputation as one of Junkerdom's most outspoken political reactionaries, studied soil chemistry at the Eldena Agricultural Institute near Greifswald in the late 1830s, during his mandatory year of military service. In 1839 he and his older brother Bernhard took over the management of the family's three Pomeranian estates: the *Rittergut* Kniephof and the non-privileged farms Külz and Jarchelin, all heavily mortgaged. Living at Kniephof from 1839 through 1845 (when he inherited the Brandenburg estate Schönhausen upon his father's death), he became involved in the Pomeranian Economic Society at Regenswalde and filled his account books with entries about crop yields. In 1844 he wrote an old friend that for five years he had devoted himself "with some success to the improvement of my rotation."[125]

Among the most persistent and renowned titled advocates for "the advancement of Prussia's practical agriculture" was the retired army Captain Carl von Wulffen-Pietzpuhl (1785–1853) of Brandenburg. After attending Thaer's institute at Möglin and traveling in the Netherlands, France, and Switzerland, Wulffen became a tireless and widely cited promoter of manuring, subsoil plowing, and white lupine—a legume whose cultivation he explained in a book (*Anbau der weissen Lupine*) published in 1828, the same year that he inherited Pietzpuhl. Writing in 1845 for Prussia's leading agricultural journal, Berlin's *Annals of Agriculture,* he identifed "the most important aspect of rational agriculture" as "the art of producing the cheapest dung."[126] During the next two years he was quoted reiterating this same point in both the *Journal of the Provincial Agricultural Society for the Mark Brandenburg and Lower Lausitz* and Pomerania's *General Agricultural Monthly:* "the greater or lesser production of manure is always the measuring rod for determining the success of the yield of one or the other method of farming."[127] Men like the nobleman von Wulffen and the commoner Koppe serve to illustrate why present-day scholars of Junkerdom and East Elbian agriculture invariably agree with Theodor Freiherr von der Goltz's 1903 statement, "At the middle of the nineteenth century noble and commoner estate owners composed a unified occupational group *(Berufstand)*, which far surpassed the nobility at the beginning of the century in knowledge and economic efficiency."[128] Let us see what market adjustments accompanied this growth in knowledge and efficiency during the *Vormärz* era (1815–48).

Even after a series of record harvests beginning in 1818 caused the collapse of European grain prices, the demand from England's growing textile mills kept wool prices high. Whereas Parliament, dominated by grain-growing landlords, adopted the protectionist Corn Laws in 1816, England's tariff on imported wool was reduced by three-quarters between 1819 and 1824.[129] Consequently, it was during East Elbia's post-1818 decade of severe economic depression that more and more Junkers turned their attention to sheep-raising.[130] One of the quickest and most successful conversions was achieved (with governmental assistance) in East Prussia by Baron Magnus von Brunneck-Belschwitz, whose wool earnings rose from 400 *Taler* in 1814 to 22,350 *Taler* in 1825.[131] Another titled entrepreneur, Count Karl von Harrach, saw his income from sheep-raising on three Silesia estates increase from 3,466 *Taler* in 1827–28 to over 11,500 *Taler* in 1842–43,[132] by which time grain prices had recovered from their slump of the 1820s. By 1820 Prussia had supplanted Spain as Britain's foremost foreign source of raw wool, and during the *Vormärz* years Junkerdom probably earned more money from wool exports than from grain exports. Between 1838 and 1845 Prussia's three major ports on the Baltic—Danzig, Stettin, and Königsberg—shipped abroad an annual average of eight million *Taler* worth of fine Merino wool and another 16.5 million *Taler* worth of wool from half-Merino sheep. Grain shipments included only six million *Taler* worth of wheat and two million *Taler* worth of rye.[133] (Given the need to feed a growing East Elbian population and the fact that 20 to 25 percent of a normal grain harvest in the early nineteenth century had to be kept as seed for the next planting, during these years Junkers could and did export a much higher percentage of their wool production than of their grain harvest. On the average more than one-third of wool production was exported, but never more than 10 percent of the grain harvest.[134]) Merino sheep from Spain had been introduced to Prussia under government auspices in the late eighteenth century, out of the standard mercantilist (or cameralist) desire to make a country's populace, and especially its army, self-sufficient in clothing. The monarchy had even imposed a prohibition against the export of raw wool that was lifted only in 1810. From 1816 to 1840 the number of sheep in East Elbia more than doubled, from 7.4 million to 18.3 million. In 1840 about one-quarter of the animals were pure-bred Merinos, about one-quarter were inferior native sheep *(Landschafen)*, and one-half were of mixed breed.[135] Exports of wool from the German states to England, overwhelmingly East Elbian in origin, climbed from 3.6 million pounds in 1814 to a peak of 29 million pounds in 1838. At this time the German states supplied about half of England's imported wool, and imports provided about two-fifths of all the wool processed in England.[136]

In 1837 Adolf von Thadden-Trieglaff of Pomerania alluded to classical mythology in characterizing the mood of confidence then prevalent among his fellow Junkers: "The golden fleece is no longer to be sought on the shores of the Black Sea; England and the Netherlands must now ask for it in our markets with hard currency."[137] Such preening brings to mind the more pretentious "King Cotton" mentality that became widespread among Southern planters in the 1850s. By 1860 the South provided over 70 percent of all British cotton imports—that is, 2.58 million of 3.37 million bales, averaging 424 pounds apiece—and receipts for cotton shipped abroad amounted to almost three-fifths of the total value of all American exports.[138] In 1856 the editor of the Montgomery, Alabama, journal *American Cotton Planter,* Dr. Noah Cloud, glorified the South's highly imperishable and easily marketed snowy staple as "alike the civilizer of mankind, the pacificator of nations, and the unerring regulator of Commerce."[139] Two years later South Carolina planter and U.S. Senator James Henry Hammond declared on the floor of the Senate that after three years without deliveries of Southern cotton, "England would topple headlong and carry the whole civilized world with her, save the South."[140] Such "Cotton is King" arrogance received considerable support from English textile interests. In 1860 *DeBow's Review* of New Orleans quoted at length the *London Cotton Reporter* to the effect that "at least 4,000,000 persons in the country are dependent upon the cotton trade for subsistence." Without cotton from "the slave states of America," "our mills would be stopped for want of cotton, employers would be ruined, and famine would stalk abroad among the hundreds and thousands of work-people who are at present fortunately well employed." Even "Railways would cease to pay, and our ships would lie rotting in their ports, should a scarcity of the raw material overtake us."[141]

Contemporary observers obviously did not know what became clear to economic historian Gavin Wright over a century later, that "the textiles industry was on the verge of a cyclical downturn in 1860."[142] In any event, the Civil War years gave the lie to the English journal's dire predictions, although the price of cotton on the London exchange did jump sharply between 1862 and 1864. When the Union naval blockade effectively cut off foreign access to Confederate ports, reducing British imports of American cotton to 1.84 million bales in 1861 and 71,766 bales in 1862, large reserves from the bumper crop of 1860 softened the blockade's immediate impact on textile producers; and stepped-up imports from "an astonishing variety" of countries—India, Brazil, Egypt, the West Indies, even Italy and Angola—helped to counter the deficit.[143] Nor did the "golden fleece" remain long in East Elbia. In 1841 a prescient writer in Pomerania's *General Agricultural Monthly,* responding to a recent fall in wool prices, predicted that "The golden age of sheep-raising is past and will probably never return." [144] During the forties and fifties, as higher quality wool from Australia proceeded to capture the British market, England's imports of German wool fell to one-quarter of their 1838 peak. [145]

Nevertheless, demand for East Elbian grain waxed as the wool market waned, and the decades from the 1840s to the 1870s became a different kind of "golden age" for Junker agriculture. During the late 1820s and 1830s grain prices gradually revived, primarily because intermittent poor harvests and steadily rising demand in England drove grain prices above the import prohibition levels set by the Corn Laws. By the late 1830s, even though English wheat yields-per-acre had increased by at least 15 percent since 1815, England's population growth was outstripping the growth in agricultural productivity to the point that cereal imports had become the norm. [146] According to an agricultural report from provincial Saxony published in 1840, the previous two years had clearly demonstrated "that the greater or lesser demand for grain in England alone determines the price of the same, and especially of wheat in Germany." [147] During the 1830s and 1840s Prussia provided about 30 percent of all British wheat imports, and 80 to 90 percent of all Prussian wheat exports went to England. [148] Shortly after Parliament voted in 1846 to phase out the Corn Laws by 1849, the editor of the Berlin *Annals of Agriculture* rejoiced: "Because of the recently adopted changes in the Corn Laws of England, competition in that market has been made significantly easier for the German agriculturist." [149] When very poor harvests throughout Europe in 1846–47 caused grain prices to skyrocket, exports of Prussian wheat to England rose dramatically even as Prussia imported greater quantities of less costly rye to help feed its own population. According to figures published by government statistician Dieterici in 1851, net Prussian wheat exports doubled between 1846 and 1848, rising from 2.59 million bushels in 1846, to 3.16 million in 1847, and then to 5.16 million bushels for 1848. Net imports of rye jumped from 2.52 million bushels in 1846 to 4.35 million in 1847; then a good harvest in 1848 enabled Prussia to resume its normal status as a net exporter of rye (1.14 million bushels). [150] It may have been true, as an agricultural writer explained in 1849, that in Prussia and the other states of the German Customs Union the popular attachment to rye was so strong that the people preferred it to wheat even when rye and wheat prices were nearly equal. [151] But it did not escape the attention of Junkerdom's critics that some merchants and *Rittergut* owners profited handsomely during the hard times that helped spark the 1848 Revolution. In April of 1847, speaking before the United Diet called into session by King Friedrich Wilhelm IV, finance minister Franz von Duesberg (from Westphalia) reported serious concern that wheat had left Prussia, and was still leaving, "in great quantities." One non-noble delegate from provincial Saxony, a city merchant named Giese, after emphasizing the shortage of grain in towns and villages, advocated the levying of export taxes to discourage grain exports to England and France. "The many thousands of *Wispels* of grain which travel to the seas on all the rivers of Germany, if we still had them, there would be no want." [152]

American grain (versus flour) made its first permanent inroads into the English market during the late 1840s, and during the years 1851–55 Prussia's share of Britain's wheat imports fell to 15 percent. [153] But the growth of urban markets at Berlin and in the Kingdom of Saxony, together with the gradual lowering of internal transport costs due to better roads and new railroad construction, kept domestic grain prices on an upward track. [154] The following comparison of average decennial wheat prices in Prussia and England suggests how the Junkers' domestic market for grain steadily improved vis-à-vis their traditional English market:

	Prussia	England
1821–30	51	111 +
1831–40	58 +	108
1841–50	70 +	100 +
1851–60	88 +	105 +

(Prices in *Silbergroschen* per bushel *(Scheffel)*; 30 *Silbergroschen* = 1 *Taler* = $0.73 circa 1860.) [155]

Yet the collapse of Junkerdom's mid-century agricultural prosperity was already in the making. Due to the steady spread of steamships over the oceans and of railroads inland, cheap grain from America and Russia would begin to flood the European market in the 1870s. Between 1868 and 1880 the cost of sending a ton of wheat from Chicago to Liverpool via New York dropped 75 percent. [156] Although during the early 1860s Prussia and the other states of the German Customs Union *(Zollverein)* still supplied 30 percent of all foreign wheat sold in Britain, the figure fell to 8 percent for the years 1871–75, and to 4 percent in the early 1880s. [157]

— VI —

We have seen that the first half of the nineteenth century witnessed Junkerdom's transmutation into what Hanna Schissler calls "a relatively homogenous class of noble and commoner agrarian capitalists," [158] and that this transformation involved the steady infusion of "scientific" improvements into *Rittergut* agriculture. Accompanying these two changes was an even more momentous transformation in the make-up of the Junkers' labor force; and this change, like the first two, found no real parallel in the very different historical context of the Old South. The "reformist" agrarian legislation promulgated during the ministerial tenures of Baron vom Stein (1806–07) and Prince von Hardenberg (1810–22) encouraged flexible *Rittergut* owners to complete, and compelled refractory ones to initiate, a transition from "bound" labor to a "free" work force. Although the original goal was to create a strong independent peasantry alongside an open and more efficient class of large landowners, in effect the reform legislation placed most of the peasantry at the mercy of their manorial lords without the "mitigating protection" that the royal bureaucracy had previously provided in the interests of maintaining a large reservoir of both tax-payers and foot-soldiers.[159] In the end the Junkers benefited from the land settlements involved in the abolition of serfdom far more than did the majority of ex-serfs and their offspring, who had little choice but to become the employees of either *Rittergut* owners or the minority of peasants who succeeded in establishing independent farms. The combined impact of ongoing population growth and peasant "regulation" is revealed in some figures for East Prussia. There the number of contractual lodgers and cottagers (for example, *Instleute*) and other wage-earning day-laborers increased from 220,000 in 1805 to 580,000 in 1867, while the number of servants *(Gesinde)* grew from 115,000 to 160,000.[160]

Although East Elbia's peasantry became legally free from hereditary servitude as of November 1810, the disposition of their farms and manorial obligations remained unclear. Under the terms of the 1811 "Regulation Edict," the peasant could cede a portion of his land (one-third if his tenure were hereditary, one-half if non-hereditary), or arrange a schedule of commutation payments, in return for gaining clear title to the rest of his farm and ending his obligation to perform labor services for the lord of the *Rittergut*. If this edict had remained in force, the Junkers would soon have confronted a pressing though temporary labor shortage; for most peasants, like most Southern freedmen after the Civil War, wanted above all to become independent family farmers.[161] One nobleman in Pomerania observed that the peasants "carry thousands of stones from the field, in order to gain one-sixth of an acre of land (one-quarter *Magdeburgisch Morgen*). They root out holly, heather, and tree stumps from where they stood hundreds of years. Everywhere one sees self-reliance and no more of that Slavic abasement which formerly characterized the Pomeranian peasant."[162] The peasantry's desire for land and independence ran directly counter to two of the Junkers' fundamental demands during the Stein-Hardenberg era: free disposition over peasant land, and a large supply of manual laborers susceptible to the Junkers' extra-economic powers of compulsion as manorial lords.[163] An oft-cited 1811 petition to the king from *Rittergut* owners in the Pomeranian county of Stolp explained that if all peasants became property owners, not only would Junkers lose the peasants' labor, but the peasants would monopolize the labor of the poorer families living in the villages. "Our estates will become a hell for us, if independent peasant proprietors are our neighbors."[164]

However, the fierceness of the Junkers' counterattack in several provinces, especially Brandenburg and Silesia, together with the final defeat of Napoleon and the passing of Prussia's crisis years, led to Hardenberg's retrogressive "Declaration of 1816." Under the terms of this new decree, which was enforced by commissioners usually sympathetic to the Junkers and whose application varied from province to province, the great majority of former serfs became ineligible for the "regulation" or settlement of their manorial dues and services. Either the unregulatable peasants' landholdings were too small to support a team of plow oxen (that is, were *nicht spannfähig*), and were thus deemed inadequate to constitute an independent farm; or their claims to the land they farmed were deemed legally tenuous, because the extant records did not identify their families as usufructuary tenants since at least the Seven Years' War of 1756–63. Indeed, unregulatable peasants could legally be evicted from their farms and homes, although the Junkers' immediate need for labor and shortage of cash for wages seem to have prevented wholesale evictions.

After the last gasp of genuinely reformist enthusiasm in 1819, the year 1821 brought a new royal edict whose impact on unregulated peasants proved devastating. This edict provided for the partitioning of millions of acres of common land (community forest and pasture) among *Rittergut* owners and regulated peasants only, with the former doing much better than the latter. Indeed, East Elbian Junkers and aristocratic landlords in Prussia's two western provinces gained over four-fifths of the 25 million acres of common land partitioned between 1821 and 1848.[165] Many unregulated peasants, stripped of their traditional rights to collect firewood or graze livestock on the common lands, found it impossible to support themselves on their own small farms while also having to pay taxes to the monarchy and perform services for their former lords. Consequently, they forfeited their lands to their manorial lords, but often continued to live and work on the estate as cottagers and lodgers on annual contracts. During the post-1818 depression some regulated peasants also found it difficult to make ends meet, and sold their farms to Junkers, town dwellers, or larger peasant proprietors.

Exactly how much land the Junkers gained and the peasants lost as a result of Hardenberg's agrarian legislation has long been a matter of speculation and dispute. The available statistics include land settlements resulting from the law of 1850, which finally extended "regulation" to those peasants who had been excluded by the 1816 Declaration, but who had managed to survive the economic vicissitudes of the intervening three decades. (Even though the majority of formerly enserfed families may have lost their land prior to the Revolution of 1848–49, the absolute number of smallholders "emancipated" after 1850 was still much larger than the number of largeholding peasants "regulated" between 1816 and 1850.[166]) Probably the most judicious statistical estimates are summarized by Christof Dipper, who emphasized in 1980 that the Prussian government's official published figures "are not only unreliable, but possibly even falsified in part." According to Dipper, the Prussian peasantry's net loss between 1816 and 1859 was 1.73 million acres (700,000 hectares), or about 8.2 percent of the land they held in 1816, even after their gains in common land are added. These losses included 1.44 million acres via the "regulation" process, 1.11 million acres through voluntary sales, and 741,000 acres through eviction and forfeit. Peasant gains included 1.56 million acres from the division of the common lands and the redistribution of landholdings so as to form consolidated farms *(Separationen)*, but these accretions were much inferior in quantity and value to the crop land handed over to manorial lords through the regulation process.[167] Moreover, many Junkers opted to receive compensation not only in the form of land but in the form of payments in kind and cash, the latter usually invested in additional land or state bonds. In fact, from the 1830s land transfers seem to have been less significant than monetary payments, especially after legislation in 1850 enlarged the ranks of the "regulatable" and at last established credit institutions geared to peasant farmers.[168] August von Miakowski, a professor at Breslau, reported in 1882 that between 1850 and 1857 alone *Rittergut* owners received 74,266,923 *Taler* in payments from peasants.[169]

As Sigmund Neumann aptly put it, the Stein-Hardenberg reforms "resulted less in the freeing of the peasants than in the victory of the large estate" via a de facto enclosure movement.[170] In 1837 a government official wrote in Thaer's *Möglin Agricultural Yearbooks* that new restrictive legislation was needed to prevent "the colossal enlargement of *Rittergüter*." "It is a fact," he declared, that one-fifth of the peasant farms *(Bauernhöfe)* in Pomerania had perished since 1816.[171] In the Saxon administrative region *(Regierungsbezirk)* of Magdeburg between 1816 and 1851, the number of *Rittergüter* declined slightly from 425 to 417, while the total land area belonging to these estates increased by 32 percent, from under 40,000 to more than 52,000 acres.[172] *Rittergut* owners in the Uckermark and Mittelmark sections of Brandenburg enlarged their landholdings by 18 percent between 1800 and 1860, even apart from their gains in common land. Of this 18 percent three-quarters were acquired during the process of "regulation," and one-quarter through purchase.[173] Among the peasant villages adjacent to the von Arnim estate Boitzenburg (the largest *Rittergut* in the Uckermark at mid-century) was Wichmannsdorf. Out of 610 acres of common land attached to this village, the von Arnims received 343 acres after the year 1821; and the total village landholding declined from 2,462 acres before "regulation" to 1,527 acres as of the year 1858.[174]

The Stein-Hardenberg agrarian legislation, by encouraging *Rittergut* owners to consolidate heretofore scattered strips of arable land, both facilitated and spurred the Junkers' adoption of more productive, labor-intensive, and soil restorative systems of crop rotation. Nonetheless, East Elbia's rising agricultural production during the first half of the nineteenth century seems to have derived less from increased yields-per-acre than from greater acreage under cultivation. (We must remember that simply bringing former fallow land into an "improved" three-field system, whereby nitrogen-fixing clover and legumes were planted after two successive cereal crops, served to increase the amount of cultivated land by one-third.) Although Prussia's average yield-per-hectare for grain apparently rose by just over 27 percent between 1805 and 1840 (and by another 12 percent from 1840 to 1863), the amount of cultivated land in East Elbia may have jumped by as much as 130 percent between 1815 and 1849.[175] Much of the new land had to be farmed merely to feed East Elbia's own population, which grew by 76 percent between 1816 and 1858, from not quite 7.4 million to nearly 13 million. At the same time, this rapid population increase provided the inexpensive labor the Junkers needed to bring millions of new acres under the plow, to apply manure and marl, and to cultivate new labor-intensive root crops (especially potatoes, and to a lesser extent sugar beets) at a time when agricultural machine technology was as yet unable to replace human and animal labor on a large scale.[176]

Whereas corn was the starchy staple for plantation slaves, potatoes were the basic food of *Rittergut* laborers. Potato cultivation had spread rapidly in East Elbia since the late 1700s. The land area devoted to potatoes in Prussia increased nine-fold from 1800 to 1860, and East Elbia's ability to export large quantities of wheat and rye even as its own population grew depended largely on the starchy tuber.[177] The potato grows better in poorer soil than does wheat, and an acre planted in potatoes yields four or five times the calories produced by an acre of grain. Yet an acre of land planted in potatoes requires over three times the labor of an acre planted in wheat. Including tubers in a *Rittergut*'s crop rotation helped to break up and aerate the soil, even as potatoes and sugar beets made it feasible for Junkers to establish liquor distilleries or sugar refineries (or both) on their estates as profitable, even essential auxiliary industries *(Nebengewerbe)*. At mid-century the distilling of potato whiskey *(Schnaps)* was far more widespread, and of much greater economic consequence, than was the refining of beet sugar.[178] Without artificial fertilizers like potash, which began to be used in the 1850s, the sugar beet was not so well suited as the potato to the light and sandy soils of the Baltic provinces, as opposed to the more fertile loams of the central provinces,[179] where the sugar beet had become a major crop on some Saxon and Silesian estates during the pre-1848 era. (The *Annals of Agriculture* reported 107 beet sugar factories in all of Prussia in 1847–48, 56 of them in provincial Saxony and 24 in Silesia. The first German beet sugar factory had been established in 1801–02 on the Silesian estate Kunern by Franz Karl Achard, with financial support from the monarchy.[180]) Agronomist and editor Carl Sprengel explained in 1840 that in eastern Pomerania extensive potato cultivation had developed at the same time as extensive sheep breeding, and with the help of technical advances in distilling. There were estates in the area where one-tenth and even one-sixth of the arable grew potatoes.[181] Brandenburg became noted for a system of rotation that Koppe termed *"märkische Koppelwirtschaft"*—that is, rotating fields between grain, pasture, and extensive potato cultivation.[182] The untitled proprietor of the Brandenburg estate Kützkow reported in 1843 that he had operated a distillery for twenty-seven years, and that he fed the slop byproduct (*Schlempe,* distiller's wash) to a herd of 110 to 130 cattle during the fall, winter, and spring months.[183] Some Junkers, like Lieutenant General von der Marwitz at Friedersdorf and Baron von Eckardstein, saw no advantage in feeding *Schlempe* to livestock, while a moralistic pietist like Baron Ernst von Senfft-Pilsach deplored the "moral and physical" consequences of producing too much *Schnaps.*[184] But a great deal of the distilled "poison" was not only consumed in East Elbia but sold to "many countries."[185] During the agricultural crisis of 1846–48 *Rittergut* owners continued their profitable production of Schnaps, which led the Prussian government to submit to the United Diet in April of 1847 a proposal to prohibit the use of potatoes in distilling. Saxon Count Hugo von Gneisenau, who acknowledged that "I represent in fact a region where distilling is a major part of agriculture," spoke against the proposal and emphasized that "The animal fodder in large operations is provided almost exclusively by distiller's wash. . . ." Much the same argument came from Adolph von Werdeck, a government councilor and proprietor of two estates in Brandenburg, who believed that distilleries, because of the importance of distiller's wash to stock-raising, had "elevated our soil to the level which it now occupies in the world." An untitled delegate by the name of Dittrich, from a town in Silesia, conceded the importance of distilleries for production of meat and manure, but argued that potatoes were necessary to feed the poor during the current crisis. Another non-Junker representative, Mehls from Brandenburg, reported that the purchase of potatoes and grain by distillers was the cause of great unrest in his hometown of Landsberg, and opined that landowners operating distilleries could and should graze their herds on pasture until the crisis had passed.[186]

What sort of workers provided the manual labor needed to raise the huge quantities of potatoes raised on Junker estates, as well as to supervise the stall feeding of livestock? Much of it came from the expanding stratum of smallholders *(Kleinstellenbesitzer)* who usually lived on small parcels of inherited or rented peasant land, and who could make a living only by doing part-time or seasonal work on knight's estates and large peasant farms.[187] Junkers often hired these smallholders as extra hands for the harvest or for major agricultural improvements, just as some planters employed Irishmen to undertake potentially dangerous projects like ditching or hired additional slaves to assist at harvest time.[188] Yet at mid-century most field labor on knight's estates was provided by the many kinds of day-laborers who worked on verbal "contracts" and were collectively known at *Gutstagelöhner.* Many Junkers had begun to employ significant numbers of contractual laborers during the eighteenth century, long before the abolition of serfdom, and their numbers grew rapidly during the several decades after the 1807 emancipation edict.[189] The day-laborers' terms of employment and living conditions varied from province to province and even from estate to estate, just as the work schedules and living conditions of Southern slaves varied according to crop regions and preferences of individual planters. Nevertheless, during the pre-1848 years the most common category of day-laborers seem to have been the cottagers or lodgers known as *Insten*.[190] Two and sometimes three members of such a cottager's household were required to work in the Junker's fields from sunrise to sunset six days per week for most of the year. The compensation paid to the cottager family generally included a small house attached to perhaps half an acre of garden land, most of it planted in potatoes. The *Tagelöhner*, "our so-called small people," observed a Captain von Versen in 1841, had become so dependent on the potato that the word was "the first name which the child learns to babble after father and mother."[191] In addition to a home and garden, the cottager also received the right to graze a few animals on the lord's pastureland, and small cash wages during the four to six months of the year when there was no threshing to be done. It is worth noting that many Southern slave familes received analogous supplements along with their living quarters and food rations. Planters often distributed small monetary payments as presents at Christmastime and as rewards for hard work at the conclusion of a successful harvest. Slave families might also receive a patch of garden land and the right to raise a few chickens, perquisites that allowed slaves to improve their diets and that many planters deemed promotive of industry and contentment among their chattel. "A quasi-holding of property," maintained Virginia's Edmund Taylor in a prize-winning essay of 1860, "tends to make them industrious and respectable, adds materially to their comfort, keeps them from wandering about on holidays and at unreasonable hours of the night." Some planters would buy their slaves' surplus produce and spend the money on purchases requested by the industrious slaves.[192]

During the pre-1848 years the East Elbian *Instmann* also received the harvest from a small portion of the Junker's rotating fields—from two to five acres, plowed by the Junker's draught animals (oxen), which were usually tended by servants. The *Instmann* also received a fraction of the Junker's grain (between one-tenth and one-sixteenth) that the cottager threshed with a flail during the winter months. In some respects this arrangement brings to mind the sharecropping system that emerged in the South after the Civil War. Sharecroppers and cottagers alike were legally free individuals. Much like the sharecropping system, "the cottager system assured an adequate supply of labor for a minimal outlay of cash," to quote J. A. Perkins, "in a local economy that was only in the process of becoming monetized."[193] Yet it is important to emphasize that the postbellum plantation was a decentralized or fragmented agricultural operation composed by and large of individual family holdings, whereas the mid-century *Rittergut* consti-tuted a far more centralized estate in which the Junker's fields were worked by supervised labor. The cottager's unwritten annual contract was in fact somewhat akin to the "profit-sharing agreements" that an occasional antebellum planter made with his slaves, although here too the differences seem to outweigh the analogies.[194] In any event, as steam threshing machines came into widespread use on larger East Elbian estates after mid-century,[195] the cottager's share of the threshing was steadily reduced. In addition, as population, grain prices, and agricultural yields continued to rise from 1840 to 1870, more and more Junkers began to lower their real labor costs by altering the cottager's contract so as to substitute a fixed amount of foodstuffs *(Deputat)* for the traditional proportional share in the harvest. During the last quarter of the century, as the spread of sugar-beet cultivation increased the demand for migratory seasonal labor, Junker agriculturalists did away with the cottager's fixed payment-in-kind in favor of cash wages, thereby completely destroying the foundation for what Max Weber saw as the "community of interest *(Interessengemeinshaft)*" that characterized the traditional relationship between *Insten* and estate owner.[196]

In the Old South human labor was never so plentiful or inexpensive as in contemporaneous East Elbia. Despite the increase in the slave population from about one million in 1808 (the end of U.S. involvement in the African slave trade) to nearly four million in 1860,[197] and despite the long-term decline in cotton prices from 36 cents a pound in 1800 to 11.5 cents per pound in 1860, the cost of a prime field-hand rose from about $400 when Jefferson was elected president to as much as $1500 during the year of Lincoln's election. Yet Negro slavery did increase the amount of money that could be profitably invested in plantation agriculture at a time when no other affordable supply of gang laborers seemed available, and when labor-saving machinery for cultivating and picking cotton was many decades away.[198] (Clement Eaton points out that the harvesting of cotton might last from the second half of August until early January. Because the cotton bolls ripened unevenly, it might be necessary to pick over a field at least three times. "This unequal ripening was the most important reason for the failure until the 1930's to develop a successful mechanical picker."[199]) Furthermore, slavery never presented the same obstacles to innovation and profitability in Southern agriculture that serfdom raised up in East Elbia. Slaves, unlike serfs, had neither formal ties to nor substantive claims upon the land, and therefore constituted no hindrance to a planter's free disposition over his real estate or to an economically "rational" concentration of land into larger productive units.[200]

During the antebellum decades a good many wheat planters in Maryland, Virginia, and North Carolina, along with some cotton planters in the older, more soil-depleted parts of South Carolina and Georgia, sought to follow the "improving" advice of Virginian Edmund Ruffin. They subscribed to agronomic journals (like Ruffin's own *Farmers' Register,* whose first number appeared in 1833), and became enthusiastic and successful converts to "scientific" agriculture.[201] Testimony that improved farming techniques had some impact in South Carolina appeared in the *New York Journal of Commerce,* whose report on the cotton crop of 1859 noted that "of all the upland cottons, that from South Carolina shows the most improvement" in appearance and fiber length. Good weather had played a role, noted the *Journal,* but the improvement was due mainly to "the greater care taken in cultivation," and especially "the attention given to manuring and preparing the soil."[202] A different kind of testimony appears in the extant papers of Georgian William McKinley. While supervising the construction of a "Brick House" at his cotton plantation near Milledgeville from 1858 to 1860, McKinley wondered if he could "imitate the lucerne fields of Italy," and proceeded to sow an experimental plot of 1,512 square yards with a "thicking seeding" of lucerne mixed with turnips. "The hope is to sow one acre this year," wrote McKinley in his notebook, "to have the lucerne root well this fall on clear ground, & after turnips are used in the winter, then for it to spring up in March and prevent weeds and crabgrass. The lot shall be immediately top-dressed with three bushels of ashes and 1/3 of a bushel plaster—to be ashed yearly, & watered with liquid manure."[203] In North Carolina's piedmont county of Northampton, in the valley of the Roanoke River, wheat planter Henry King Burgwyn was one of "a few men zealously engaged in the improvement of their farms," and his essay on "Improvement of Worn-Out Lands by the Use of Peas and Clover" was published in the *Report of the Commissioner of Patents* for 1849.[204]

Both Burgwyn and McKinley were exceptionally affluent planters, each owning well in excess of the fifty slaves that some historians have seen as the minimum owned by "the large, or upper-class planters," or "the planter aristocracy."[205] That the "improving" spirit also possessed some small planters is well illustrated in a short essay written by southside Virginia's H. G. Richardson and published in 1852 in Richmond's *Southern Planter* under the title "Management of a Farm in Prince Edward (County)." According to the 1850 census, Richardson owned fourteen slaves; but since only two of them were under twelve years of age, and the oldest only fifty, his effective work force was close to a dozen; and they worked with "no overseer at home." Richardson raised tobacco, wheat, and oats for the market, and at least enough corn to feed his family and slaves. By penning his cattle during the cold winter and hot summer months, and mixing straw, stalks, and chaff with their dung, he produced enough manure over thirty years to enrich more than sixty acres. "For the last five years," reported Richardson, "my land, negroes, teams, & c(etera) including every expenditure, nett me over ten per cent; and my family enjoys a fine living in the bargain." He described himself as a native Virginian who wished "to check the current of emigration rapidly rolling on in pursuit of Western treasures."[206]

Although many such examples could be cited,[207] at mid-century the planter elite as a whole was undoubtedly behind landed Junkerdom in practicing such productive improvements as soil-enhancing crop rotations, stall-feeding of livestock, and systematic fertilization with manure and marl. There seem to have been three fundamental reasons for the planters' relative laggardness. First, without the artificial fertilizers, pesticides, and fungicides that became readily available only in the twentieth century, the plantation South's relatively warm and wet climate created more natural obstacles than did East Elbia's cooler and dryer climate to the widespread development of a diversified and "improving" agriculture that involved forage/fodder crops and penned livestock. Farming in the Lower South, economic historian Julius Rubin has argued, suffered from "a good many of the disadvantages of tropical climates," such as acidic soils leached by heavy annual rainfalls, low yields of fodder crops due to high temperatures, and debilitating diseases caused by animal parasites (like the swine kidney worm) whose eggs and larvae were not killed in the soil by deep winter freezes.[208] Although East Elbian agriculture certainly did not confront any of the liabilities associated with tropical climates, it did suffer from the sort of plant diseases and animal parasites that are encouraged by successive plantings of the same crop, regardless of climate and geography. The potato blight of the 1840s and the spread of nematodes or eelworms in soils where sugar beets were repeatedly planted are prime examples.[209]

A second fundamental reason for East Elbia's head start in improved and diversified agriculture was a population density at least five or six times that of the South. Consequently, in the South fewer mouths had to be fed from the same plot of land. In 1860 the population density in what census officials labeled the "coastal planting states" (South Carolina, Georgia, Florida, Alabama, Mississippi, and Louisiana) was about 15 persons per square mile, and the figure for the "central slave states" (Virginia, North Carolina, Kentucky, Tennessee, Missouri, and Arkansas) was about 21.[210] As of 1858 the Kingdom of Prussia's Baltic provinces of Pomerania, Posen, and Prussia (East and West)—the least populous by far of the monarchy's eight provinces—contained approximately 113 persons per square mile.[211] This contrast can be presented another, simpler way: East Elbia in 1858, with a land area less than that of Louisiana and Mississippi combined, supported a population larger than that of all fifteen slave states in 1860.[212]

Third, fertile land was much more abundant and less costly in the South than in East Elbia, while plantation labor was much scarcer and dearer than *Rittergut* labor. Consequently, as Florida judge Henry Marie Brackenridge observed in 1831, there was little point in suggesting to the typical cotton planter ideas like crop rotation and horizontal plowing, or reducing the size of fields and putting eroding hillsides into permanent pasture; for their "maxim is that land and soil must be worn out in ten or twelve years at any rate, and that soils which require manure are not worth the trouble of cultivation."[213] As Jefferson had noted in the eighteenth century, it was usually cheaper and easier in America to buy a new acre than to manure an old one.[214] In analogous fashion did a writer in the periodical *American Cotton Planter* point in 1857 to the general belief that it was cheaper in a new country to move on and clear new land rather than to improve old land by rest, rotation, and manuring.[215] The same journal's editor said that planters made the right amount of cotton, but cultivated "too many acres of poor washed land to produce it on." The South needed fewer but more fertile acres of cotton, insisted editor Noah Cloud, and more acres for "hogs, mules, corn, and small grains."[216] Granted, a decided majority of mid-century cotton planters seem to have practiced a simple kind of diversified agriculture adequate for raising enough corn and pork so as to make their plantations self-sufficient in basic foodstuffs. During the late 1840s one writer (probably economist Jacob Cardozo) estimated that the planter could expect a net profit of 7 percent on capital invested (with cotton at ten cents a pound), noting that "there is an increase and improvement in the annual value of negroes upon every well regulated cotton farm." Cardozo also stressed that "the great majority of planters raise or support their families from what may be called the offal of a farm, that is, from what is raised on it and is scarcely missed or calculated in its products, which is always the case when the owner lives on it."[217] But a plantation's self-sufficiency in basic foodstuffs did not necessarily indicate an "improving" system of soil preservation and enrichment. In Mississippi, the "Heartland of the Cotton Kingdom" on the eve of the Civil War, a speaker told the Amite County Agricultural Society in 1857 that without a system of plantation management to restore worn-out soils and prevent cultivated fields from deteriorating, the Amite area would soon suffer from the "emigration of its wealthiest citizens" to new, uncleared lands. The typical farmer, he said, "adopts a certain system of cultivation, and pursues it from year to year, without having any thing to rouse his mind to activity, or to lead him to inquire whether there may not be a more excellent way than that which he is pursuing."[218]

Yet it must be remembered that such agricultural practices were not economically "irrational" so long as fresh fields remained accessible and affordable to cotton planters. And Gavin Wright and Randolph B. Campbell have emphasized that the existing slave states still contained an abundant supply of uncultivated cotton land in 1860.[219] Moreover, slavery as a labor system was well suited to the expansive plantation economy's need for a steady supply of gang laborers whose geographical mobility made them highly responsive to constant, sometimes rapid shifts in demand along an advancing cotton frontier.[220] And this labor mobility was made possible by slave exports from the seaboard and border slave states, Virginia ranking first among them. According to Michael Tadman's computations, from 1820 to 1860 the slave-exporting states (Delaware, Maryland, Virginia, the Carolinas, and Kentucky, and, in the 1850s, Georgia and Tennessee; plus the District of Columbia) sent a net total of about one million slaves west and south; and Tadman estimates that at least half and perhaps two-thirds of these slaves were traded, as opposed to accompanying migrating owners.[221] It had become apparent to William and Mary professor Thomas R. Dew by 1832 that Virginia was "in fact, a negro raising State for other States"; and between 1830 and 1860 almost 300,000 slaves, nearly all of the state's natural increase, left the Old Dominion for destinations west and south. "Shut up all outlet into the southern and southwestern states," wrote Edmund Ruffin in 1833, "and the price of slaves in Virginia would sink down to a cypher."[222]

Slaves, as chattel, constituted a lucrative capital investment. Thomas Affleck, of Ingleside plantation in Adams County, Mississippi, highlighted this fact in his widely used *Cotton Plantation Record and Account Book*. Its section on "The Duties of an Overseer" stipulated that the primary component of "a fine crop " was "an increase in the number and a marked increase in the condition and value of the negroes."[223] In 1856 North Carolinian James L. Gaines told the members of the Moore County Agricultural Society that, despite the mounting strength of antislavery sentiment in the North, "we of the South have an advantage in what is termed our peculiar institution. I allude to that of domestic slavery, for capital invested in that kind of property increases faster than in any other way."[224] To be sure, since slave labor was not of much value to a planter without land, real estate was also an object of investment and speculation in the South. A veritable "speculative mania" for buying land as well as slaves took hold in Alabama and Mississippi during the "flush times" of the 1830s.[225] Nor was it extraordinary in the older seaboard states on the eve of the Civil War to find the sort of newspaper advertisement published by the Lynchburg *Virginian* in late 1859: E. W. Hubard, owner of "A Valuable Farm" situated on the Buffalo River in Nelson County and comprising 1,695 acres and 43 slaves ("the larger proportion young men and girls, including one plantation smith, thus constituting an extra likely lot"), wished to sell the estate "solely to change the investment."[226] Moreover, affluent planters throughout the South might sell their land and move with their slaves to more promising or attractive locales. In Alabama the Tuscaloosa *Flag of the Union* announced in 1843 that Parke Jones wanted to resettle in territorial East Florida and offered his plantation in Marengo County to the highest bidder. The estate included 400 acres, 325 of them cleared and cultivated, a peach orchard, a family house with brick chimneys, cabins for 40 to 50 slaves, an overseer's house, a gin house, a bailing screw, and a horse-powered mill.[227]

Given the antebellum South's relatively high land-labor ratio, slaves were generally a better investment than land, and promised nearly the level of lucrative capital gains that the purchase of a *Rittergut* yielded in contemporaneous East Elbia, with its relatively low land-labor ratio. As mentioned earlier in this chapter, speculation in knight's estates had become rife toward the end of the eighteenth century. Ernst Klein estimates that between 1750 and 1805 estate prices jumped by 325 percent in Silesia and by almost 500 percent in Brandenburg.[228] Although many investors went bust during the post-1818 depression, *Rittergut* prices began to climb again during the 1830s. Agronomist Carl Sprengel, editor of the *General Agricultural Monthly*, reported that Pomeranian *Rittergüter* which had sold during the late 1820s for 50,000 *Taler* were bringing 100,000 to 150,000 *Taler* in 1840.[229] An estate owner in old East Prussia cited the case of a *Rittergut* in a neighboring county *(Kreis)* selling in 1834 for 11,000 *Taler,* in 1841 for 24,000 *Taler,* and in 1849 for 44,000 *Taler.*[230] The extent to which the inelastic supply of increasingly expensive knight's estates was bought and sold during the prosperous middle decades of the century was revealed in a study conducted by the Prussian government during the 1860s. The study showed that the 11,777 *Rittergüter* in the eastern provinces had changed proprietors an average of 2.14 times apiece between 1835 and 1864, and that three-fifths of the changes in ownership had resulted from voluntary sales.[231] These statistics lend substance to the following observation by the editor of a Berlin agricultural journal in 1856, in spite of his misplaced nostalgia: "Landed property has lost its former stability, the estates have become articles of trade and often change their owners more than once a year; every new purchaser enters into the operation of his estate with new hopes, readily giving the seller a moderate profit, so that the price of many estates has doubled over several years, while the (actual) value has increased more slowly, and lies no longer in the immovable soil, but in the intelligence of the proprietor."[232]

Most mid-century *Rittergut* and plantation proprietors alike believed that their success as estate owners depended on intangible assets like their managerial skills as well as on the concrete vagaries of nature. At the same time, fundamental differences in their regional environments meant that Southern planters and East Elbian Junkers had markedly different portfolios of tangible capital assets. In the South the actual market value of plantation real estate tended to be much below the market value of the chattel slaves who worked it, whereas in East Elbia, whose formally free labor was not capitalized, the land itself constituted the Junker's principal capital asset. Although these regional differences dictated very dissimilar patterns of agricultural and social development, the dissimilarities do not demonstrate that one elite proved itself more entrepreneurial or capitalist than the other.

3

Contentious Concepts

BECAUSE I TEND to emphasize the importance of differences between the historical environments of the planter and Junker elites, this study seems to fall under the rubric of what sociologists Theda Skocpol and Margaret Somers have termed "contrast-oriented" comparative history. Its practitioners stand "squarely in the middle between the characteristic disciplinary concerns of social scientists and historians"—that is, between an historical focus on the course and logic of events in a particular society during a particular span of time, and a social-scientific preoccupation with concepts, theories, or models whose explanatory power transcends a specific historical context.[1] These different perspectives are highlighted in a review of Skocpol's own *States and Revolutions: A Comparative Study of France, Russia, and China* (1979) by William McNeill, an historian who has composed impressive trans-national studies like *The Rise of the West: A History of the Human Community* (1963) and *The Pursuit of Power: Technology, Armed Force, and Society Since A.D. 1000* (1982) . After complimenting Skocpol for "a clear, concise, and admirably well-crafted book," McNeill took note of her "implicit repudiation of the roll of personalities in affecting the revolutionary processes she analyzes. To allow that sort of variable would, perhaps, spoil the sociology she seeks to discover in human affairs."[2] Yet McNeill would be among the first to emphasize that historians should make use of interpretive models and concepts developed by social scientists, just as the latter must rely on specialized historical monographs in order to test their theoretical generalizations. If used flexibly and sensitively, social-scientific models and concepts can provide analytical frameworks within which historians can seek to evaluate and even accentuate the unpredictable impact of individual personalities and decisions on the course of events.[3]

"Contrast-oriented" comparative history, explain Skocpol and Somers, is devoted primarily to illuminating the different features of the societies being compared, although "usually such contrasts are developed with the aid of references to broad themes or orienting questions or ideal-type concepts."[4] Several such themes, questions, and concepts inform my approach to planters, Junkers, and their regional societies, and they revolve around a number of inevitably ambiguous and controversial terms. Some such as "modernization," "ideology," and "capitalism" will be discussed in this chapter; others, such as "paternalism" and "conservatism," will be saved for subsequent chapters. Attempting to formulate and justify appropriate working definitions for these terms seems to me a necessary and constructive facet of this comparative study. Yet in doing so I run two serious risks, above and beyond the likelihood of irritating scholars whose understanding of these concepts differs from my own.

First, I fail to heed an eloquent warning issued by H. Stuart Hughes: "Historians are by nature wary of precise definition; they hate to be confined within tight terminological boundaries, and they are ever alert to the fallacy of misplaced concreteness; they much prefer to write ordinary words in their common sense usage and then let the reader little by little become aware of how these words have subtly changed their significance through time."[5] Yet a comparativist dealing with linguistic and historical milieus as dissimiliar as the United States and Prusso-Germany in the nineteenth century cannot simply "write ordinary words in their common sense usage," particularly since most readers will be familiar with only one of the milieus being studied. Comparativists must recognize and carefully define potentially ambiguous terms so that their analysis can better illuminate similarities without depreciating differences between the societies being examined. In many instances a definition should be a conceptual "ideal type," which is employed, in Max Weber's words, "to determine the degree of approximation of the historical phenomenon to the theoretically constructed type."[6] An ideal-typical concept should be viewed as a heuristic analytical tool that can help make sense of historical circumstances and developments inevitably more complex that the ideal type itself. As economic historian David S. Landes has explained, "A model is not worthless or anathema because it is not empirically anchored. If well constructed, it offers the scholar an analytical pattern against which to hold the experiences of history and appreciate their elements of uniqueness and uniformity. The value of such a model is thus heuristic rather than informative; it does not *tell* us what happened but helps us to find and understand what happened."[7] To be sure, a model contradicted by empirical evidence must be revised or rejected.

The second risk was identified by Marc Bloch in 1928: "Historians are easily led to believe that 'comparative history' is a chapter of the philosophy of history or of general sociology. It is evident that the empirical historian will never practice either of the two disciplines, although he may, according to his state of mind, grant them admiration or a skeptical smile."[8] In attempting to deal systematically with abstract and contentious concepts like "modernization" or "capitalism," I may serve to reinforce the impression in the minds of many historians that the comparative method necessarily involves a pronounced shift in emphasis away from the thorough, empirical study of a single person, event, or country to a more freewheeling concern with social-scientific models, ahistorical generalizations, and "universal history." Nor is such an apprehension wholly unjustified. Historian Cyril Black, in his ambitious *The Dynamics of Modernization: A Study in Comparative History* (1966), proclaimed that modernization theory made possible "the broadening of the study of history to include mankind as a whole. It was not long ago that historians hesitated to generalize about Europe and concerned themselves only with individual countries. The time has now come to formulate generalizations about the whole of mankind in modern times."[9] No doubt Marc Bloch's "empirical historian" is more skeptical about the value of such a world-historical perspective than about the utility of a more modest comparative venture limited to two case studies—works such as Carl N. Degler's *Neither Black nor White: Slavery and Race Relations in Brazil and the United States* (1971) or Peter Kolchin's *Unfree Labor: American Slavery and Russian Serfdom* (1987). Such bipolar studies have the notable advantage of permitting the historian to undertake fairly extensive research into original public and private documents (so-called "primary sources") from both societies. This is the sort of research that historians tend to see, usually with justification, as a prerequisite for understanding the complexities and inconsistencies inherent in human behavior, attitudes, and institutions—what Jürgen Kocka calls "the complex and changing interdependence of the large variety of factors determining human development."[10]

A more recent enthusiast than Cyril Black for modernization theory is Americanist Walter Hugins, who argued in 1977 that "historians, scholars of American history in particular, have generally fallen behind their colleagues in the other social sciences in developing and applying comparative methodology or models which could illuminate their teaching or open new vistas in their research."[11] In response to Hugins, let us first question his assumption that history is a discipline within the social sciences rather than a taxonomically independent discipline whose "half-scientific, half-artistic nature," in the words of H. Stuart Hughes,[12] bridges the social sciences and the humanities. With respect to comparative methodology, Hugins fails to acknowledge that sociologists, political scientists, and economists do not agree among themselves about the precise meaning or even the validity of "modernization" as a model of historical development. Today modernization theory appears to have been something of a scholarly fad, one whose heyday extended from the late 1950s through the 1960s among American social scientists interested in understanding and guiding the new, "developing" nations of the "Third World." One of the most blistering critiques of the modernization model has come from sociologist Dean C. Tipps. "The popularity of the notion of modernization must be sought not in its precision as a vehicle of scholarly communication," argues Tipps, "but rather in its ability to evoke vague and generalized images which serve to summarize all the various transformations of social life attendant upon the rise of industrialization and the nation-state in the late-eighteenth and nineteenth centuries."[13]

Nonetheless, I have found one approach to modernization theory particularly helpful in understanding the larger nineteenth-century world within which the planter and Junker elites lived. Its most systematic proponent is political sociologist Reinhard Bendix,[14] whom a German historian writing in 1975 included among a "revisionist" group of social scientists striving to correct the "foolhardy simplification" of early modernization theorists with "historical precision."[15] Bendix views modernization as an historical process encompassing the manifold societal changes wrought since the late eighteenth century by the forces of industrialization and democratization. These two forces originated with England's textile-based "first" industrial revolution of 1760–1830 and France's democratic political and social revolution of 1789–94, which Eric Hobsbawm has termed the "dual revolution" of the late eighteenth century.[16] Economically, modernization has involved the accelerating replacement of manual labor and skill by machine technology, and the increasing substitution of inanimate for animal and human sources of energy and raw materials. These changes have in turn increased per capita wealth, promoted the growth and influence of cities, and brought a higher percentage of the population into direct contact with the marketplace as wage laborers or employers, as producers or consumers; and in so doing economic modernization has helped to undermine traditional, hereditary, "ascriptive" foundations of social and political hierarchy. Politically, modernization has involved, to quote Bendix, "the democratization of societies, especially the destruction of inherited privilege and the declaration of equal rights of citizenship," which involves "the simultaneous trends towards equality and a nation-wide political authority."[17] Political modernization has promoted the development of national states whose governments have involved varying blends of parliamentary, bureaucratic, and autocratic authority, all claiming to rule in the name of the "people."[18]

"The term *modernization*," concludes Bendix, "is applied best where nonindustrial ways of life and hierarchic social orders are threatened by industrial ways and egalitarian social norms."[19] Since the origins of the modernization process in the "pioneer" or "advanced" societies of western Europe, the world's "follower" societies have not experienced the onset of modernization in the same ways as did England or France. Many follower societies have responded to industrialization and democratization as outside challenges rather than indigenous developments, and the modernization process has encountered historical conditions very different from those that prevailed in western Europe during the eighteenth and nineteenth centuries. Moreover, even though there seems to be a logical interrelation between the egalitarian principles of civil and political equality and the economic individualism associated with early industrial capitalism,[20] the process of modernization has never advanced systemically. In other words, nations and regions have not industrialized or democratized at the same time and at the same rate of speed. To wit, England became a mature industrial society half a century before Parliament approved universal adult suffrage after the First World War; and France experienced the radical democratic revolution of 1793–94 long before the process of industrialization had made any significant impact on French society.

This approach to modernization admittedly leaves unanswered a number of important questions about the transatlantic world of planters and Junkers. For example, why did England become the first industrial nation, whose demand for foreign cotton, wheat, and wool created such profitable mid-nineteenth-century markets for crops raised in the South and East Elbia? And why in the late eighteenth century did Britain's North American colonies and Bourbon France, both clearly "preindustrial" societies, become hothouses of republican and democratic ideologies? Nonetheless, Bendix's flexible but hardly ahistorical model lends support to the argument that social scientists can offer historians broad, international perspectives with which to expand their scholarly horizons.

— I —

Another social scientific concept that clearly informs my perspective on planters and Junkers is "social class." The concept of social class, if cogently defined and employed both consistently and heuristically, provides an analytical framework that can facilitate our ability to comprehend the structure of a society, and also help to illuminate interconnections between social and economic structures on the one hand and political and intellectual developments on the other. In other words, class analysis can further the successful integration of what Michael Kammen has termed "deep structures" and "manifest events." Focusing on events "tends to put people into the foreground," whereas focusing on structures "calls our attention to large socioeconomic forces." The historian must examine both events and structures in order to achieve "a fully rounded perception of the past."[21]

Of course, it is far easier simply to talk about social classes than to define them clearly. In the words of Edward Pessen, " 'class' and 'social class' are among the trickiest terms in the vocabulary of social scientists."[22] Many scholars seem to have dismissed class analysis for what they see as its deterministic and collectivist overtones. Even those scholars who are enthusiastic proponents of class analysis—whether they endorse a Marxian focus on the position of social groups within an economic system's relations of property and production, or a Weberian attention to the autonomous importance of social prestige and political power in shaping social stratification—have posited a sometimes bewildering variety of criteria for establishing the boundaries between social classes. William

Reddy expresses his exasperation with class analysis by declaring that "Historians have now reached a point where, to use the concept of class coherently, each practitioner must, and most do, redefine it anew."[23] Reddy would doubtless endorse Joseph Schumpeter's statement that a social class is to some extent "a creation of the researcher, (and) owes its existence to his organizing touch." At the same time, Schumpeter insisted that classes are "social entities which we observe but which are not of our making."[24]

My own sociological perspective seems to constitute a blend of Marxian and Weberian influences, and we should remember that Max Weber was both responding to and building upon the invaluable work of Karl Marx. As used here, the term "social class" identifies a group of families and individuals who derive their livelihood or income from similar sources, and who enjoy analogous levels of social prestige and political authority, which together distinguish them from other groups in a stratified society. This is obviously a static and ahistorical formulation that must be fleshed out, made more precise and concrete, for each historical milieu and group under study. And note especially that the definition is *structural* rather than *attitudinal,* and thus permits the simultaneous use of class analysis and "methodological individualism" in evaluating the planter and Junker elites.[25] That is, although planters and Junkers constituted comparable upper classes due to analogies between plantations and *Rittergüter* as regional sources of income and independence, status and authority, my reading of the two elites' historical records does not support the idea that a social class can be defined in attitudinal and behavioral terms—that is, as a group whose members all partake in an integrated, cohesive set of assumptions and ideas that helps to mold their public behavior and declarations into a consistent or predictable pattern. The fact that planters and Junkers each constituted a landed upper class did not prevent significant variations in public values and behavior among members of each elite. This is not to deny that virtually all members of the planter or Junker elites shared a few bedrock assumptions. For example, antebellum planters were fervid republicans who believed that black slavery had to be made secure against what they perceived to be extremist attacks and threats from hostile and irresponsible agitators; but more often than not planters endorsed differing intellectual arguments or political policies against the forces of abolitionist immediatism as well as more moderate antislavery calls for containment of slavery's geographic expansion. Although mid-century Junkers were devoted monarchists who agreed that *Rittergut* owners should maintain an exalted position in Prussian society, they did not pursue the same strategies for combating or mollifying the threatening forces of liberal constitutionalism, political democracy, and German nationalism. The histories of both elites suggest that the ideas and perspectives of those who belong to a particular social class reflect not only their class interests and experiences but their individual peculiarities and proclivities as well as the larger culture to which they belong.

What implications does this structural definition of social class have for the concept of "ideology"? This word, which derives from Greek roots connoting a discourse of ideas, is another tricky term in the lexicon of social scientists. In recent years many scholars have employed a broad cultural definition that clouds the distinction between world-view and ideology.[26] I find it helpful to differentiate between the two, along the lines suggested by Peter Kolchin: a world view is "a generalized social consciousness, a shared outlook on how things were, could be, and should be," in contrast to "an articulated, carefully formulated philosophical position," or ideology.[27] A *conservative ideology* (part of the larger historical phenomenon of conservatism to be discussed further in Chapter 6) is formulated by intellectuals, drawn especially from the ranks of literati and educated professionals, in order to explain or justify a certain societal organization or way of life that is under philosophical and political attack. Yet different apologists for the status quo approach the task of ideological explanation and justification by resort to ideas and principles that can vary in important particulars. Although proslavery thought in the antebellum South and Old Prussian thought in contemporaneous East Elbia clearly constituted conservative ideologies, we must recognize that neither proslavery nor Old Prussian intellectuals endorsed the same homogenous set of ideas and principles. In short, proslavery or Old Prussian ideologues often disagreed among themselves.[28]

Most members of a class become more conscious of their common interests and values when challenged publicly by members of other groups with conflicting, competing values and interests. From the influential perspective of E. P. Thompson, such group conflict is a prerequisite for class as an historical phenomenon; for "class happens when some men, as a result of common experiences (inherited or shared), feel and articulate the identity of their interests as between themselves, and against other men whose interests are different from (and usually opposed to) theirs."[29] Thompson's formulation recalls Karl Marx's distinction between objective class position in a society (class *an sich,* in itself) and the subjective class consciousness (class *für sich,* for itself) which results when the members become aware of their common position and capable of concerted efforts in pursuit or defense of their class interests.[30] "The separate individuals," wrote Marx and Engels in *The German Ideology* (originally composed in 1845–1846), "form a class only insofar as they have to carry on a common battle with another class; otherwise, they are on hostile terms with each other as competitors."[31] This perspective clearly differs from my own, which posits a simpler structural definition of social class and does not insist on a generalized class consciousness borne of intense inter-class conflict as a prerequisite for class analysis. My own outlook accords with Jon Elster's statement that the "concept of class . . . does not presuppose interaction among members of any given class or a consciousness of common interests." Rather, it "presupposes that there is interaction between different classes, by transfer of surplus or commands."[32] In the case of planters and Junkers, members of each landed elite issued "commands" to their dependent laborers largely by virtue of their autocratic control over government on their estates, and in the process extracted a material "surplus" from these same laborers.

According to Marx and Engels, planters and Junkers each constituted a hegemonic "ruling class" in the economic, political, and ideological realms. "The ideas of the ruling class are in every epoch the ruling ideas, i.e., the class which is the ruling material force of society, is at the same time its ruling intellectual force." Following this line of argument, the Southern proslavery or Old Prussian argument that the relationship between owners of large estates and their laboring dependents constituted essentially a familial, patriarchal interaction between stern but beneficent fathers on the one hand and immature but loyal children on the other would seem to be "nothing more than the ideal expression of the dominant material relationships" in Southern or East Elbian society.[33] Of course, Marx and Engels have not been the only historical sociologists to recognize how romantic ideals have often been propounded in defense of material interests. For example, Max Weber shared Marx's "sociological approach to ideas" and saw ideas as "powerless in history unless they are affiliated with material interests," explain Gerth and Mills. Nonetheless, Weber refused to conceive of ideas as " 'mere' reflections" of material or class interest. Instead, "All spheres—intellectual, psychic, political, economic, religious—to some extent follow developments of their own."[34] In order to understand the evolution of proslavery ideas in the Old South and of Old Prussian ideas in East Elbia, we must consider "subjective" individual factors as well as the "objective" class interests of planterdom and Junkerdom. At the same time, the content and thrust of these conservative ideologies can be fully understood only if one keeps the material interests of planters and Junkers as regional landed elites clearly in view. "Where interests are energetically pursued," explained Otto Hintze in 1931, "an ideology develops to give them inspiration, strength, and justification." These ideas and interests compose "a polar system"; "neither can live over the long haul without the other. Each needs the other as its complement."[35]

But who exactly formulates romantic and idealistic ideologies? Marx and Engels pointed perceptively in *The German Ideology* to "a division of mental and material labor" within the ruling class: "one part appears as the thinkers of the class (its active, conceptive ideologists, who make the perfecting of the illusion of the class about itself their chief source of livelihood), while the others' attitude to these ideas and illusions is more passive and receptive, because they are in reality the active members of their class and have less time to make up illusions and ideas about themselves." And "this cleavage can even develop into a certain opposition and hostility between the two parts."[36] In the South and East Elbia individuals like Edmund Ruffin of Virginia and Baron Karl Adolf Alexander von Hertefeld of Brandenburg, who were at the same time progressive agriculturists and forceful ideologues, warn us not to expect too rigid a "division of mental and material labor" within the planter and Junker elites. Nonetheless, the sort of cleavage and opposition that Marx and Engels saw between thinkers and doers does seem to have manifested itself among mid-century planters and Junkers as a fluctuating, often muted tension between doctrinaire intellectuals and the pragmatic majority of plantation and *Rittergut* owners. Although doctrinaires and pragmatists alike desired to preserve the upper-class prestige and influence of the planter or Junker elite, pragmatic planters and Junkers were most interested in concrete, non-abstract ways of promoting familial advantage, economic gain, and political success. Doctrinaire proslavery or Old Prussian ideologues, often religiously inspired, were more committed than the pragmatists to ideals and principles that transcended the existing order, and sometimes expressed impatience and irritation with the status quo for failing to meet the ideal standards set for it. We will see in Chapter 6 that for a variety of reasons rooted in fundamental economic, social, and political differences between the South and East Elbia, the tension between doctrinaires and pragmatists had less impact on antebellum planters than on contemporaneous Junkers.

— II —

Pragmatic planters and Junkers understood quite clearly that a profitable commercial agriculture was essential to their long-run survival as landed upper classes. Yet the spirit of acquisition did sometimes become muted in families which had owned plantations or knight's estates for generations. Scions of such families might feel superior to hard-driving parvenus because they enjoyed acclaimed pedigrees and the status of "honorific leisure" that Thorstein Veblen saw as a byproduct of affluent persons' devotion to non-economic pursuits.[37] In 1848 an unidentified writer (probably economist Jacob Cardozo) in Charleston's *Southern Quarterly Review* made a judicious assessment of the planter elite: in addition to "the capitalists of the South, whose property is invested in land and negroes," and "who are full of energy and constant and devoted attention to business," "there are also among us those who have inherited a large property in slaves, who take their ease but, rest assured, they are but spending what their more active and thoughtful ancestors have acquired, and it will take but a few years for their agents and negroes to consume all they are worth."[38] Aside from the references to slaves, much the same judgment could be applied to Junkerdom. A few plantation and *Rittergut* owners doubtless did fit the stereotypical literary image of the proud and gracious but economically lax and naive country squire, as portrayed humorously by Joseph G. Baldwin in *The Flush Times of Alabama and Mississippi* (1853) in the figure of "Old Major Willis Wormley" from Virginia, and tragically by Gustav Freytag in *Debit and Credit (Soll und Haben)* (1855) in the character of Silesian Baron Oscar Rothsattel.[39] On this score an observation by economists Paul David and Peter Temin about planters is adaptable to Junkers as well. In order to maintain equilibrium in the market for land or slaves, there had to be some "'Cavalier' fops" selling out to "agricultural capitalists."[40]

It should also be emphasized that if a prominent planter or Junker waxed eloquent about the virtues of rural life, his effusions do not necessarily indicate that he was a poor businessman or oblivious to entrepreneurial opportunity. During the 1850s South Carolina patrician Alfred Huger, who served as postmaster of Charleston and owned the lowcountry rice plantation Wateree, complained in his correspondence about "the fools and swindlers" on New York's Wall Street, and described himself as "a 'Plantation Man'" who treasured "the quiet and retirement of Plantation Life." Yet in 1856 Huger could also offer sound advice to the son of an old friend off to settle in the turbulent territory of "Bleeding Kansas." Look for "good land selected where a town is likely to be established, and the facility of reaching the point where crops are to be sold," recommended Huger; in particular, "look always to a water course—the shortest way to market is the shortest way to Wealth."[41] Compare some remarks by Georg Philipp Ludolph von Beckedorff (ennobled in 1840), president of the Pomeranian Economic Society and of Prussia's Board of Rural Economy, the proprietor of the estate Grünhof in eastern Pomerania, and a university-educated man strongly influenced by the "romantic conservatism" of Adam Müller. In the early 1840s Beckedorff described agriculture as "more than a mere business or trade": "It is a lifelong calling *(Lebensberuf)*, a profession *(Stand)*, truly an existence in itself" that involves all the powers and activities of "the whole man." Yet in recent times, he wrote, agriculture had been "lifted out of the realm of traditional empiricism and into the realm of rational management." Every competent estate owner would testify, insisted Beckedorff, that one can make an adquate return on capital invested in the acquisition, operation, and improvement of land.[42]

To evaluate planters and Junkers as businesslike and entrepreneurial elites does not require that we also label them "modern." Recall Reinhard Bendix's formula: "The term *modernization* is best applied where nonindustrial ways of life and hierarchical social orders are threatened by industrial ways and inegalitarian social norms." According to this ideal-typical definition, the two elites can be viewed as frequently hostile to modernization, or anti-modern, in that they were decidedly anti-egalitarian and because they generally opposed those "modernizers" who wished to promote American or Prussian industrialization by means of protective tariffs. However, as many planters and Junkers seem to have understood quite clearly, the predominant short-run threat to their survival as landed elites did not come from industrialization—which was, after all, creating a profitable international market for their cash crops—but from the democratic and egalitarian legacies of the American and French revolutions, which were working

to undermine the traditional character of the plantation and *Rittergut* as hierarchical and authoritarian institutions.[43] Although industrialists and owners of large
landed estates in the nineteenth-century West sometimes pursued different political and economic objectives, the notion of an irrepressible conflict between "pre-
modern" agrarian elites and "modern" industrial elites serves only to obscure
the substantial degree of mutual accommodation that evolved between older and
newer upper classes. One cannot posit a creeping feudalization of the upper
bourgeoisie during the nineteenth century without also acknowledging a substantial embourgeoisment of the landed aristocracy.[44] After the creation of the Prusso-
German Empire during the years 1866–71, most industrialists and Junkers alike
came to support the notoriously plutocratic three-class suffrage as a way of
limiting the political influence of the lower classes. By the 1870s Bismarck had
come to the conclusion, notes Otto Pflanze, "that men of means—whether agrarian,
commercial, industrial, or banking wealth—had a common cause in preserving
the fabric of society." One fruit of his efforts to encourage the emerging fusion
of agrarian and industrial elites was the so-called "marriage of iron and rye"
consummated in the protective tariff of 1879.[45] Across the Atlantic such peaceable cooperation between the business interests of the slave South and the free
North was actively promoted during the antebellum era by such well-known
Southern spokesmen as John C. Calhoun of South Carolina and George Fitzhugh
of Virginia. The major obstacle to its realization was the intensification during
the 1840s and 1850s of sectional political conflicts over the spread of slavery
into the western territories. The population of the free states did not come to
oppose the further extension of slavery and the allegedly aristocratic "Slave Power"
because these seemed incompatible with urban industrialism. Indeed, Eric Foner
has emphasized that in 1860 Lincoln and the Republican party were defending
the interests of a "pre-modern society" based upon "the small shop, the independent farmer, and the village artisan."[46] Lincoln received far more voter support in the rural areas of the North than in the cities, where Northern business
leaders like the cotton manufacturers of Massachusetts and the merchants of
New York City actively sought to downplay sectional antagonisms. The voters
of the North endorsed the antislavery Republican party in 1860 because the
continued spread of slavery and the "Slaveocracy" seemed incompatible with the
preservation of Anglo-Saxon democratic republicanism in America.[47] As Barrington Moore, Jr., has emphasized, "plantation slavery in the United States
grew up as an integral part of industrialism and presented an obstacle to democracy much more than to capitalism."[48]

— III —

Moore, in his seminal *Social Origins of Dictatorship and Democracy: Lord and Peasant in the Making of the Modern World* (1966), offers some brief but tantalizing

comments on the comparability of nineteenth-century planters and Junkers. In the process Moore provides a useful introduction to what Philp Abrams calls "the oldest and most fundamental of all themes in historical sociology," the labyrinthine and disputatious problem of "capitalism."[49] Moore labels planters "Southern Junkers" in order to illuminate his argument that both landed elites represented historical roadblocks on the democratic and capitalist path "from the preindustrial to the modern world."[50] Although he does not acknowledge that anti-Negro racism contributed mightily to both the South's support for slavery and the North's opposition to its expansion, he does recognize that nineteenth-century Junkers, despite the de jure abolition of serfdom in 1807–10, employed "a highly repressive system of labor" comparable to slavery in that each system relied on non-market "political mechanisms" of repressive exploitation.[51] Both planters and Junkers are portrayed as market- and profit-oriented capitalists, though not of Marx's "bourgeois" variety; for "labor-repressive agricultural systems, and plantation slavery in particular, are political obstacles to a particular kind of capitalism, at a particular historical stage: competitive democratic (bourgeois?) capitalism we must call it for lack of a more precise term."[52] However, the North's victory in the Civil War precluded the sort of peaceable anti-democratic alliance between industrial and agrarian elites that took place in Germany, thereby preventing the United States from experiencing "the capitalist and reactionary form" of modernization that fostered twentieth-century fascism. In the United States during the late antebellum period an economic and political alliance developed between the industrial Northeast and the agrarian but free-labor Old Northwest, and this alliance made the Civil War "the last revolutionary offensive on the part of what may be legitimately be called urban or bourgeois capitalist democracy."[53] The starkness of the American-German contrast is diluted a bit by Moore's concession that the incompleteness of the South's postwar Reconstruction did permit the emergence of "tendencies toward a conservative coalition between propertied interests in the North and South," as evidenced in the support that Republican presidential candidate Rutherford Hayes received from "Conservative" white Southerners during the winter of 1876–77.[54]

Since the publication of Moore's ambitious comparative study four other American scholars (but apparently no German scholars) have dealt briefly but substantively with the question of whether planters and Junkers should be adjudged comparably capitalist. The concern with this issue shown by sociologist Richard Rubinson and historians Eugene Genovese, Barbara Jeanne Fields, and Steven Hahn reflects the strong influence exerted on their thinking, as on Barrington Moore's, by the Marxian tradition in historical sociology. According to this tradition, the modern world is not the complex product of industrialization and democratization working as roughly concurrent but to some extent autonomous forces, à la the ongoing process of modernization. Rather, mainstream Marxian scholarship views the key force in the emergence of the modern world as the complex transition from a "feudal" mode of production—that is, one based on decentralized control over the means of production, a restricted market, unfree labor, and local production for use value—to a "capitalist" mode of production, based on a growing concentration in the ownership of the means of production, an expansive market, free wage labor, and production for exchange value. For Moore, Rubinson, Genovese, Fields, and Hahn, therefore, questions about the capitalist character of a particular class are inseparable from larger questions about the class's role in the historical development of capitalism as a socio-economic system. The fact that the five scholars advance varying perspectives on capitalists and capitalism is testimony to the malleability of Marx's intellectual legacy.

In a 1968 essay entitled "Marxian Interpretations of the Slave South," Genovese included a brief critical response to Barrington Moore's assumption that mid-nineteenth century planters and Junkers were comparably capitalist. "In general he exaggerates the prebourgeois character of the post-Napoleonic Junkers and underestimates the prebourgeois qualities of the slaveholders." Whereas the Prussian abolition of serfdom compelled the Junkers to become more and more genuinely capitalist employers of free labor, the inherently precapitalist character of slave labor prevented the planters from moving beyond the "prebourgeois" stage of class development.[55] This candid chastisement of Moore reflected to some degree Genovese's fraternal irritation with a Marxian scholar whose analysis of the slave South's economy was so compatible with the "neo-classical" or "liberal" perspective on "planter capitalism" that Genovese was so determined to discredit in 1960s.[56] The neo-classical view of the slave plantation as a thoroughly capitalist form of agricultural enterprise had received an influential historical formulation at the hands of Lewis Cecil Gray in his monumental *History of Agriculture in the Southern United States to 1860* (1933). "The plantation was a capitalist type of agricultural organization in which a considerable number of unfree laborers were employed under unified direction and control in the production of a staple crop," stated Gray; ". . . the system represented a capitalistic type of agricultural development, since the value of slaves, land, and equipment necessitated the investment of money capital, often of large amount and frequently borrowed, and there was a strong tendency for the planter to assume the attitude of the business man in testing success by a ratio of net money income to capital invested."[57] On the contrary, according to the impressive corpus of Genovese's writings, planters constituted a precapitalist, prebourgeois class for two distinguishable reasons. First, the "paternalistic" character of the Old South's master-slave relationship—"an organic relationship based on reciprocal obligations"[58]—was economically and ideologically antithetical to a genuinely capitalist social order based on free labor and a bourgeois ideology emphasizing personal freedom. Second, the macroeconomic structure of the Old South prevented the region from following a capitalist path of "sustained growth and qualitative development" via "a broad-based industrial revolution,"[59] primarily because a society based on slave labor and production of staple crops for external markets was incapable of generating an internal market demand that could promote a substantial degree of urbanization, industrialization, and agricultural diversification.[60]

A similar Marxian perspective informs Barbara Jeanne Fields's 1985 essay entitled "The Advent of Capitalist Agriculture: The New South in a Bourgeois World," which devotes some attention to comparing and contrasting the paths of capitalist agricultural development followed by Prussia and the U.S. South in the nineteenth century.[61] Fields insists that "the essence of capitalist social relations in agriculture" is to be found in "a rural majority" whose livelihood comes from "performing agricultural labor in exchange for wages." These workers are not slave property, "nor are they compelled by law to work for the landowner," as under serfdom. Instead, "they must sell their labor power—because they own nothing else, and therefore can acquire the necessaries of life only by working for a wage." The Civil War, by abolishing human property, "removed the most important obstacle to the consolidation of capitalist agriculture in the South," argues Fields, and inaugurated "a prolonged period of transition" to fully capitalist social relations. The sharecropping arrangement that quickly emerged on postbellum plantations represented a "a transitional form on the way to capitalist wage labor." Thus "a peculiar brand of capitalism . . . slowly came to life in the South, so peculiar that a number of people deny that the South was headed toward capitalism at all until World War II." Fields concludes that the post-1865 South experienced a more prolonged transition to capitalist agriculture than did East Elbia after the 1807 abolition of serfdom.[62]

Steven Hahn, in a far-reaching comparative essay entitled "Emancipation and the Development of Capitalist Agriculture: The South in Comparative Perspective" (1990), agrees with Fields in viewing free wage labor as the essence of capitalist economic and social relations. "The abolition of slavery and servile labor ended up accelerating the development of capitalist agriculture most everywhere abolition took place."[63] Even so, whereas Fields maintains that East Elbia and the Junkers experienced after 1807 a more rapid and direct conversion to capitalist labor relations than did the South and its planters after 1865, Hahn contends that abolition "propelled the South most quickly and fully" down the road to capitalist agriculture. The South's more rapid transformation reflected the inability of the postbellum planter class to retain the kind of political clout on the national level that post-emancipation Junkers could exploit in monarchical and bureaucratic Prussia. Hahn, though hardly ignoring the persistence of "extra-economic compulsion and repression" on post–Civil War plantations, still emphasizes "the speed and extent to which capitalist relations came to prevail in the countryside." Few freedmen succeeded in acquiring enough land to become subsistence farmers, while the white yeomanry abandoned their antebellum emphasis on household production and subsistence agriculture to raise cotton for the market and fall "into the vortex of newly fashioned market relations." In the process they succumbed to "the predatory advances of merchant capital" by becoming tenants, sharecroppers, and wage earners.[64]

In sharp contrast to Genovese, Fields, and Hahn, a 1978 essay by Richard Rubinson applies the label capitalist to both antebellum planters and contemporaneous Junkers simply by virtue of their participation in the international capitalist economy that emerged in post-medieval Europe during the sixteenth and seventeenth centuries.[65] As a disciple of historical sociologist Immanuel Wallerstein, he views capitalism as distinguished from previous economic systems in history by, in Wallerstein's words, "the orientation of production to capital accumulation via profit realized on a market—this market is, and has been from the beginning, a world market."[66] Wallerstein himself has dealt in some detail with the preindustrial birth of the international capitalist market during the so-called "long" sixteenth century, when eastern Germany and the New World emerged as "peripheral" regions using unfree laborers to produce agricultural commodities for the more diversified and sophisticated "core" economies of northwest Europe, which contained dynamic commercial and manufacturing sectors and employed free labor. During this long sixteenth century Junkerdom and the first plantation owners of the Americas emerged as "agrarian captitalists" using "coerced cash-crop labor" (that is, serfs and slaves).[67] Thus, Wallerstein rejects the more orthodox Marxian assumption that free wage labor is a *sine qua non* of genuinely capitalist enterprise.

Richard Rubinson carries Wallerstein's perspective into the nineteenth century, and examines the economic status of the United States and "Germany" within the industrializing "capitalist world-system" and its international division of labor during the century's middle decades. He maintains that between 1840 and 1880 both countries shifted from the status of semi-peripheral areas, which had nascent industrial sectors but produced mainly foodstuffs and raw materials for a world market dominated by England, to the status of industrializing core states capable of competing with England. The timing of this shift resulted from the transfer of political power within each country away from the heretofore dominant agrarian elite—planters or Junkers—to the newer and more dynamic class of industrialists. These internal political transformations, according to Rubinson, were consequences of the Civil War in the United States and of national unification in Germany. Yet Rubinson also notes, as does Barrington Moore, that during the 1870s each country witnessed the forging of an economic and political coalition between business and propertied interests in all regions. Just as the election of Hayes signified the appearance of "a truly national upper class" in the U.S., so did the "Great Tariff of 1879" symbolize an integrating national elite in the German Empire.[68]

Although Moore, Genovese, Fields, Hahn, and Rubinson disagree over the precise quantum of "capitalist" qualities displayed by mid-nineteenth-century planters and Junkers, all three agree that they did not constitute "feudal" classes, if only because feudal lords, historically, presided over self-sufficient manors and functioned as mounted warriors rather than as entrepreneurial estate managers. Thus Genovese emphasizes that the slave South "rested on a distinct mode of production that was as different from the feudal as from the capitalist." [69] Very different from this socio-economic perspective on feudalism is the political perspective of National Socialist sympathizer Dietrich Zwicker, author of the only German monograph to suggest an overarching framework for comparing planters and Junkers. Zwicker's schematic intellectual biography of John C. Calhoun, published in 1935, relies uncritically on the writings of nineteenth-century German historian Heinrich von Treitschke and early twentieth-century American historian William E. Dodd. It is virtually oblivious to questions about the economic activities of planters and Junkers, and is overly concerned to draw parallels between Calhoun's political and racial ideas and the "revolutionary conservatism" of the Third Reich, as anticipated in the proto-fascist ideas of Moeller van den Bruck. Nonetheless, the biography includes a provocative chapter entitled "Concurrent Ideas in Germany?" Zwicker concludes that "American slave barons," like "Old Prussian Junkers," were "a feudal class whose existence appeared threatened by a levelling democracy." [70] For Zwicker, therefore, "feudal" signified the political opposite of "democratic" rather than the economic opposite of "capitalist." In fact, the Marxian perspective and that of Zwicker each contain a measure of historical truth.

Elizabeth A. R. Brown has made a persuasive argument that "feudalism" is "a construct devised in the seventeenth century and then subsequently used by lawyers, scholars, teachers, and polemicists to refer to phenomena, generally associated more or less closely with the Middle Ages, but always and inevitably phenomena selected by the person employing the term and reflecting the particular viewer's biases, values, and orientations." [71] However much scholars may debate the precise meaning of the term "feudalism," it is clear that the archetypal feudal system, which reached its apogee in parts of western Europe between 1000 and 1300, contained two basic components: first, the fief, or the grant of land which a vassal lord received from his princely overlord in return for homage and military service; and second, the virtually self-sufficient manor with its serfs, who were "bound" for life to parcels of their lord's land, and who enjoyed the land's usufruct and the lord's protection in return for "rent" paid in labor or in kind. [72] Also clear is the absence of such a feudal system from the antebellum South and contemporaneous East Elbia. It is important to emphasize that feudal society entailed specific political and economic structures, whereas a capitalist economy is devoid of any particular political structure, and has been compatible in history with a variety of different political systems, from autocratic to parliamentary. [73] In other words, "feudalism" and "capitalism" are not a pair of consistently antithetical historical concepts, because the former has political as well as economic denotations, and the latter economic denotations only. Furthermore, whereas a feudal society's blend of certain economic and political characteristics gives "feudalism" a static quality, scholars have often associated the concept of capitalism with at least two post-medieval, post-feudal stages of economic change and development: commercial (or mercantile) capitalism from the fifteenth to the eighteenth century, followed by the birth of industrial capitalism in late eighteenth-century England and its subsequent geographical dispersion.[74] Dividing the history of capitalism into commercial and industrial stages suggests that a more accurate ideal-typical antithesis to "feudal" society, with its precapitalist economics and rigidly hierarchical politics, is "modern" society, characterized by industrial modes of production and egalitarian political norms.[75]

Although I concluded earlier that mid-nineteenth-century planters and Junkers can be construed as "pre-modern" landed elites, I believe that historical understanding of the two social classes is better served by evaluating both as "capitalist" rather than as "precapitalist," despite the fact that plantations were farmed by chattel slaves and knight's estates by legally free individuals. Making this assertion obligates me to offer at least an ideal-type definition of capitalism, even though, as Jean Baechler has conceded in *The Origins of Capitalism* (1971), "every definition, because it is arbitrary, is open to debate." Following Baechler's admonition to employ the definition which "allows for the best interpretation of the facts"[76] (at least as I see them), I find that a 1973 formulation by Jürgen Kocka accords well with my understanding of planters, Junkers, and the nineteenth-century Western world in which they lived. Capitalism, says Kocka, is "an economic system that rests predominantly on private property and private disposition over capital, and that facilitates production and exchange of commodities for the purpose of profit." By this essentially neo-classical definition, mid-nineteenth century planters and Junkers clearly qualified as agrarian capitalists. Kocka also states that formally free, contractual, wage-earning workers are a defining characteristic of "modern industrial capitalism" only.[77] On this score it should be noted that the agricultural and industrial sectors did not always present comparable opportunities for economic and social modernization in the nineteenth-century Western world. On the contrary, because of agriculture's far greater dependence on what rural sociologist Susan Archer Mann calls "the unpredictability and capriciousness of nature" (that is, drought and floods, disease and insects), farms seems to have confronted more formidable natural obstacles than did factories to the "predictability and standardization" associated with industrial capitalism and its use of advanced technology operated by wage labor. "It seems clear," concludes Mann, "that the industrial revolutions of the late eighteenth and nineteenth centuries, while sufficient to industrialize industry, were not sufficient to industrialize many spheres of agriculture."[78]

If one identifies only investment for profit and market production as essential components of a capitalist economy, then it is possible to distinguish between "private capitalism," where productive assets are held and managed by individuals and companies, and "state capitalism," where government owns and supervises the means of production. One virtue of Kocka's formulation is that it accords with the general perception of capitalism as based on private property.[79] On this score, it is worth noting that only during the Stein-Hardenberg era of 1807–22, with the end of serfdom and division of common lands, did Junkers receive free economic disposition over all their land. Although the Hohenzollern monarchy had granted the Junkers of Brandenburg-Prussia allodial title to their estates in the early 1700s, it was not until the 1820s that *Rittergut* proprietors gained the sort of unrestricted disposal over their real estate that plantation owners had enjoyed at least since the American Revolution.

Certainly the prime mover behind capitalist development in Western history has been personal and corporate profit realized through private enterprise; and we tend to associate the quality of entrepreneurship more consistently with the behavior of private businessmen than with the actions of public officials. As several astute scholars have suggested, the history of capitalist economic growth in the modern West has been closely linked with a high degree of autonomy for the economic sector from governmental intrusion (high relative to the Chinese experience, for example).[80] At the same time, to be sure, all levels of government have exerted tremendous influence on the course of capitalist development, not only through strictly economic policies but also through military actions or social and political legislation (such as the legal abolition of serfdom and slavery). Eric Hobsbawm, in analyzing the origins of England's industrial revolution, stresses that the government was "willing to wage war and to colonize for the benefit of British manufacturers," and that "war—and especially that very commercially-minded and middle-class organization, the British navy"—also contributed in direct fashion to "technological innovation and industrialization."[81] The state's contributions to economic growth and development can be especially important during a country's nascent industrialization, when private investment capital alone is inadequate to establish the credit institutions and construct the basic transportation systems necessary for the creation of an unified national market. In the United States even more so than in Prussia during the first two-thirds of the nineteenth century, the public sector promoted the development of financial institutions and transport networks that became an infra-structure for the flowering of industrial capitalism.[82] Antebellum planters and contemporaneous Junkers often opposed measures, like protective tariffs, designed to stimulate industrialization in their own countries, and for several logical reasons. They did not relish paying higher prices for finished goods; they feared that protectionism might jeopardize industrial England's receptiveness to their agricultural exports; and they had no desire to compete for national political clout with independent industrial elites—

particularly in Prussia's western provinces or the U.S. Northeast, those regions which seemed to derive the greatest benefit from protectionist measures.

Yet the majority of planters and Junkers were quite willing to enlist or accept government assistance when it promised to serve their own interests as agrarian capitalists. Planters in the James River Valley of Virginia supported state subsidies for construction of the James River and Kanawha Canal, and planters in Louisiana, Mississippi, Arkansas, Alabama, and Florida encouraged the sale of state bonds in order to create capital for banks that would finance purchases of land and slaves. Most South Carolina planters endorsed state subsidies for internal improvements, first canals (in the 1820s) and later railroads (in the 1850s). Georgia's "planter-capitalists" not only approved such governmental subsidies for internal improvements, but favored having the state government itself build and manage the Western and Atlantic Railroad between Atlanta and Chattanooga, completed in 1851.[83] Junkerdom welcomed the financial assistance provided by the mortgage credit banks *(Landschaften)* first established under Frederick the Great in 1769–70; some estate owners employed the available funds to speculate in *Rittergüter* during a time of rising grain prices. Junkers clamored for direct subsidies from the Hohenzollern monarchy during the severe agricultural depression of the 1820s, even as they welcomed government support for road construction. Although Prussian authorities were slower to subsidize railroad construction than were state governments in the United States, *Rittergut* owners in mountainous Upper Silesia (some of whom operated coal mines and iron works on their estates) welcomed the creation in 1842–43 of the Prussian Railway Fund, which was to purchase limited shares of stock (and also guarantee interest payments on all shares) issued by private companies building new railroads like the Upper Silesian Railway (constructed 1842–46). And some Junker delegates at the 1847 United Diet were happy to have the monarchy guarantee loans to finish construction of the Berlin-Danzig-Königsberg Railroad *(Ostbahn)*, finally completed in 1857.[84]

— IV —

Missing from my discussion of capitalism thus far is an international historical dimension that would help explain the roles played by Southern planters and East Elbian Junkers in the complex course of capitalist development since the medieval era. The Wallersteinian view of capitalism as an evolving "world-system" based on international and inter-regional trade between "peripheries" and "cores" helps to fill this void. From the late fifteenth to the eighteenth century the emergence and consolidation of Junkerdom and then planterdom as peripheral landed elites, producing East Elbian grain and Southern tobacco and rice for merchants and consumers in the core states of northwestern Europe, coincided with the evolution of a preindustrial "capitalist world-economy." Regardless of how far back in history one wishes to trace the origins of capitalism, it seems clear that a dramatic quantitative growth of markets and trade dates from the fifteenth century. As Rosenberg and Birdzell emphasize, this expansion owed much to the technology of the three-masted sailing ship, and "ultimately stimulated, and in its turn was further stimulated by, the rise of the factory system."[85] A world-economy that was industrial as well as capitalist began to appear by the early nineteenth century in the wake of England's industrial revolution, and once again plantations and Junker estates played major roles as suppliers of crucial agricultural commodities like cotton, wheat, and wool. William Parker has pointed out that this nineteenth-century world economy "arranged itself with heavy concentrations of industry in Northwestern Europe and the Northeastern United States," largely because almost all the new transportation techniques developed from 1770 to 1870 "promoted the geographical concentration of industry." In regions such as the U.S. South and Prussia East Elbia, production of crops for export plus reductions in the cost of international transport discouraged industrial development.[86] Something of a symbiotic relationship existed between, on the one hand, the landed elites of the antebellum South and contemporaneous East Elbia—preindustrial, "less developed" peripheries— and on the other hand the urban elites of industrial, "developed" core societies, England in particular, which imported unfinished raw materials and exported finished goods as well as surplus capital. Although the South and East Elbia circa 1850 were still peripheral regions with strong ties to England, the archetypal core state, the Northern states and Prussia's western provinces constituted semi-peripheral zones with growing industrial sectors almost capable of challenging Britain in the international arena. The transformations (after 1860) of the United States and the new Prusso-German Empire into powerful core states and rivals of England had political as well as economic dimensions, and required at the least substantial reductions in the political influence of proslavery planters and Old Prussian Junkers at Washington and Berlin. Yet the political opposition to planterdom and Junkerdom embraced much more than merely industrial interests, and hardly embraced all industrialists.

Wallerstein's view of capitalism as an evolving "world-system" does much to illuminate what Hungarian scholar Györky Ranki has called "the dialectic of development and backwardness" as it operated both within and between particular countries.[87] We have briefly seen how the "capitalist world-economy" model aids in clarifying the economic interaction between industrializing England and predominantly agrarian overseas regions like the South and East Elbia. The model also provides an overarching framework that encompasses what economic historians such as Douglass North and Walther Hoffman have told us about the role of regional differences and regional specialization in the economic growth of the United States and Germany during the first two-thirds of the nineteenth century, an era when declining internal transportation costs as well as overseas demand encouraged the South and East Elbia to indulge their comparative advantage as producers of agricultural surpluses. Much as the marketing of Southern cotton and the manufacturing of cotton goods stimulated economic development in the American Northeast during the antebellum decades, so East Elbian agriculture from the 1830s to the 1870s (roughly from the establishment of a toll-free internal market by the Prussian Customs Union to the creation of a Prusso-German national state) supplied much of the inexpensive food and some of the capital inflow from abroad that made industrial development possible in parts of the German Confederation (especially the Kingdom of Saxony and Prussia's western provinces).[88] In other words, it seems that the South and East Elbia, as relatively "backward" peripheries, played an indirect though important functional role during the nineteenth century first in the evolution of the Anglocentric capitalist world-system, and then in the industrialization of the United States and Prusso-Germany and their own emergence as "advanced" core states.

Yet most scholars in the Marxian tradition, and most Weberians as well, believe that genuine capitalism involves more than private property and the pursuit of profit in an evolving world market. They tend to see capitalism as a particular system of social relations, a special "mode of production," under which wage-earning proletarians sell their "labor power" as a market commodity and share with their employers formal equality before the law. Hence "rational" economic factors, as opposed to hereditary and legal group distinctions, dictate class relations.[89] By these criteria, antebellum planters and contemporaneous Junkers were still to a greater or lesser extent "precapitalist," though Junkerdom had progressed farther down the road toward a capitalist mode of production than had the plantation gentry. The inclination to see proletarian labor as necessary and essential to true capitalism often seems to reflect the assumption that a capitalist economy is also an industrializing economy, that Europe only made "the transition to capitalism in the course of the industrial revolution."[90] This assumption seems to stem in part from the fact that both Marx and Weber lived and wrote in Europe during its era of rapid industrialization and proletarianization. Also contributing to the equation of free labor with capitalism has been a tendency to view the English pattern of capitalist development as something of a universal model; and England seems to have been an individualistic, market-oriented, mobile society heavily dependent on hired labor as early as the thirteenth century.[91]

Marx himself was often somewhat vague and ambiguous on the subject of capitalists and capitalist production—he did not use the term "capitalism" in his published works on historical sociology and political economy.[92] This vagueness and ambiguity are evident in his analyses of Negro slavery.[93] In the *Grundrisse: Foundations of the Critique of Political Economy* (written 1857–58), Marx observed: "The fact that we now not only call the plantation owners in America capitalists, but that they are capitalists, is based on their existence as anomalies within a world market based on free labor."[94] His analysis of American slave plantations in *Theories of Surplus Value* (written 1862–63) is even more equivocal: "where commercial speculations figure from the start and production is intended for the world market, the capitalist mode of production exists, although only in a formal sense, since the slavery of Negroes precludes free wage labor, which is the basis of capitalist production. But the business in which slaves are used is conducted by capitalists. The mode of production which they introduce has not arisen out of slavery but is grafted onto it. In this case the same person is capitalist and landowner."[95] On several occasions Marx himself espied a direct link between early industrial capitalism and plantation slavery. In the first volume of *Capital* (1867) he declared that "the veiled slavery of the wage-workers in the (cotton) factories of Europe needed, for its pedestal, slavery pure and simple in the new world."[96] Two decades earlier, in *The Poverty of Philosophy* (1847), Marx had sounded almost like Immanuel Wallerstein: "Direct slavery is just as much the pivot of bourgeois industry as machinery, credits, etc. Without slavery you have no cotton; without cotton you have no modern industry. It is slavery that gave the colonies their value; it is the colonies that created world trade, and it is world trade that is the pre-condition of large-scale industry."[97] These excerpts offer little support for the argument that all capitalists must employ free wage labor. One notable "Marxist" who believed that unfree labor systems have played a direct role in the historical development of capitalism was Friedrich Engels. His essay "The Mark Brandenburg" (1882), composed shortly before Marx's death, discusses the origins of serfdom in East Elbia during the sixteenth century, and concludes that "The capitalist period announced itself in the country districts as the period of agricultural industry on a large scale, based on the corvée labor of serfs."[98]

Capitalism has been too protean a historical phenomenon to be identified with any particular mode of production. Hence I heartily concur with Jean Baechler that "There is no necessary or essential link between the capitalist system and free labor."[99] Still, much astute contemporary scholarship, non-Marxian as well as Marxian, proceeds from the assumption that true capitalism is a mode of production and system of social relations whose essential foundation is free wage labor. Fernard Braudel, doubtless one of the most learned and thoughtful scholars of capitalism's historical development, posits "a wage-earning proletariat" as one prerequisite for "a capitalist system of management and economic rationalization of land."[100] Nonetheless, Braudel has also suggested that the "ambiguous" and perhaps "anachronistic" term capitalism should be reserved for the speculative "high-profit zone" situated over and above "the underlying double layer composed of material life and the coherent market economy." Since the sixteenth century this "high-profit" zone has been centered first at Amsterdam, then London, followed by New York (and most recently Tokyo?)—in each case within the pre-eminent core state of that era.[101] By this standard there have been only a small number of genuine capitalists in history, the planter and Junker elites not among them. Yet Braudel also emphasizes the degree to which capitalism has always been able "to penetrate systems structurally very foreign to it," as it did in East Elbia and the South. He writes that the "second serfdom" of post-medieval eastern Europe, like plantation slavery in the New World, qualified neither as "a feudal system" nor as "a modern capitalist agriculture *on the English model* (my emphasis)": but it and plantation slavery were "all in the service of an international system itself thoroughly and indisputably capitalist."[102]

From my comparative perspective on planters and Junkers, it seems more straightforward and consistent to view capitalist development as involving a "world system" of interdependent "cores" and "peripheries" that evolved from a mercantile capitalist system in the sixteenth century to an industrial capitalist system in the nineteenth. Although capitalist development since the fifteenth century has certainly furthered proletarianization in core areas by promoting greater reliance on free wage labor in conjunction with technological advances, this does not mean that only a free-labor economy qualifies as capitalist. Recalling Jürgen Kocka's hypothesis that legally free workers receiving contractual wages seem to be a definitive characteristic of "modern industrial capitalism" only,[103] perhaps we can modify Kocka's ideal type to state that only core regions and states have relied predominantly on legally free wage labor, and that these more urbanized core states have always acted as the pacesetting elements in the capitalist world economy. As Sidney W. Mintz has explained, the slave plantations in the peripheries of the New World were in fact "brought into being" by "the existence of capitalism with its European free wage-earner sector."[104] Yet this does not mean that core areas and governments could unilaterally impose some consistent form of unfree labor system on peripheral societies, where in fact different groups of workers could be subject to varying blends of market and extra-economic constraints.[105]

— V —

In evaluating planters and Junkers as regional agrarian capitalists, it is important to distinguish clearly between the microeconomic profitability of plantations and knight's estates to their proprietors, and the macroeconomic impact of plantation and *Rittergut* agriculture on the internal development of the South and East Elbia. As Morton Rothstein points out with regard to the Old South, it is one thing to discuss "whether slavery was on the average profitable for individual plantation entrepreneurs," and another to discuss "whether a society which encouraged and protected slavery did not inescapably create institutions and barriers to long-term (and therefore industrial) growth."[106] Slavery and the plantation economy do seem to have slowed the overall rate of industrial and urban growth in the

South vis-à-vis the North, by drawing investment capital into slave-based agriculture and by preventing the growth of a mass market based on working-class consumers. Heywood Fleisig has suggested that slavery, by relaxing the labor constraint that planters would have faced under a free-labor system, may have served to retard industrialization in the South by increasing the amount of money that could be invested profitably in large-scale agriculture.[107] *Rittergut* agriculture seems to have acted as a similar brake on the rate of East Elbian industrialization during the *Vörmarz* era (1815–48); for, in the words of Hanna Schissler, "agriculture itself absorbed labor power, attracted entrepreneurial talent, and required capital."[108] This does not mean that planters and Junkers were markedly less interested in market conditions or profit margins than the "bourgeoisie" (that is, town-dwelling capitalists engaged in commerce, finance, or manufacturing[109]) of the North or western Prussia. It simply means that the South and East Elbia each had, to quote Barrington Moore, "a capitalist civilization but hardly a bourgeois one."[110] In both regions large-scale commodity agriculture could provide the competent agriculturist a comfortable, even handsome rate of return on monies invested, thanks largely to a usually strong international demand for the staple crops produced on antebellum plantations and contemporaneous *Rittergüter* (except during years of intense though temporary economic depression, like the 1840s for most of the South and the 1820s for most of East Elbia). Hence, compared with entrepreneurs in the U.S. Northeast or Prussia's western provinces, planters and Junkers had few incentives to make substantial and risky investments in ventures unrelated to agriculture, though a considerable number did so. East Elbia's far greater population density and more diversified agriculture meant that extractive rural industries for distilling potato whiskey and refining beet sugar could yield considerable profits for *Rittergut* owners; and Junkers in hilly Upper Silesia had been engaged in mining and smelting operations since the eighteenth century.[111] In the Old South dynamic planters, from Southside Virginia to the South Carolina Upcountry to the Natchez District of Mississippi and Louisiana, recognized the advantages of diversified investment portfolios that included holdings in railroads, banks, mines, and even factories. Indeed, the Southern economy achieved a far higher level of industrial development than did the economy of the mid-nineteenth century's second largest slave society, Brazil, even though the percentage of slaves in the South's populaton was twice the figure for Brazil.[112] Nonetheless, it seems that the successful integration of the South and East Elbia into the capitalist world-economy as commodity-producing peripheries actually had the "rational" effect of hindering the processes of economic diversification and industrialization within their regional economies.

To be sure, plantations and *Rittergüter* also yielded substantial non-monetary returns: the prestige and authority that accompanied ownership of a large landed estate and personal control over the lives and labors of other human beings. As

William Parker observes of the Old South, "To that unimaginative and ignorant inertia that causes profits to be reinvested in the lives from which they spring even in highly 'rational' environments, was added the prestige attaching to the ownership of land and slaves in a plantation society."[113] The same sort of prestige attached to the ownership of knight's estates in East Elbia. Hence some observations by J. P. Cooper with regard to English landowners are also relevant to both the planter and Junker elites: "historically men have always accepted lesser returns from land than from other forms of investment, not simply because land is usually a safe investment, but also because they are investing in non-monetary returns. In the case of large landowners, whether bourgeois, seigneurs, gentry, or magnates, they were and still are buying prestige and authority. . . . While this shows that the return on land cannot be measured exclusively in money, it does not necessarily indicate that . . . the landowners . . . were non-capitalist, or pre-capitalist, or that they were excluded from developing a commercialized agriculture by such behavior."[114] Indeed, the stylized image of the "bourgeois capitalist" driven solely by the disciplined ambition to accumulate wealth seems ahistorical. Virtually all entrepreneurs in history, urban as well as rural, industrial as well as agrarian, have been concerned not only with profits but with proving their personal worth and winning a measure of public esteem for themselves and their families.[115]

— VI —

There is one additional comparative concept, closely related to capitalism, that warrants discussion here—the "Prussian road," a term that has attracted a great deal of attention from historians of the nineteenth-century South in recent years.[116] Yet there seems to be considerable confusion about the origin and meaning of the term. Contrary to what appears to be a widespread scholarly assumption, Barrington Moore, Jr., did not use the phrase in *Social Origins of Dictatorship and Democracy* (1966).[117] The first notable scholar of the South to employ the term was Eugene Genovese, who wrote in 1969 of "the Prussian road to capitalism" taken by Germany and Japan.[118] Subsequently two other scholars of the nineteenth-century South, historical sociologist Jonathan Wiener and historian Lewis Nicholas Wynne, used the term "Prussian road" as an important analytical tool in their studies of post–Civil War planters in Alabama and Georgia respectively.[119] Both Wiener and Wynne modify Genovese's formulation of the concept. Although Genovese, Wiener, and Wynne all approach their topics from a Marxian perspective, the reader of their work does not learn that it was Nicolai Lenin who coined the phrase Prussian road (or "Prussian path") over three-quarters of a century ago to describe the capitalist evolution of Junker agriculture in East Elbia during the nineteenth century.[120] Moreover, the meanings which the three Americanists give to the phrase differ significantly from the definition which

Lenin gave it, and hence from the way in which the phrase was used in East German scholarship from the Second World War to the 1980s.[121]

Lenin delineated the concept of the Prussian road most systematically in a 1907 pamphlet entitled "The Agrarian Program of Social Democracy in the First Russian Revolution, 1905–1907."[122] Here he distinguished between "the Prussian path and the American path" as two different types of "bourgeois agrarian evolution." The Prussian path referred to the gradual transformation of East Elbian agriculture, in the aftermath of the Stein-Hardenberg agrarian legislation of 1807–21, from a "feudal landlordism" based on the forced labor of serfs to a "bourgeois, Junker landlordism" based on expropriated and proletarianized workers. Contrariwise, Lenin's American path of "bourgeois agrarian evolution" referred to the experience of the United States, where a large number of small capitalist farms took the place of Prussia's "big landlord economy." Consequently, the "capitalist development" of American agriculture could proceed "more broadly, more freely, and more rapidly as the result of the tremendous growth of the home market and of the rise in the standard of living, the energy, initiative and culture of the whole population." Lenin erroneously believed that after the defeat of the South's "slave-owning landlords" in the Civil War, "Their estates were broken up, and the land was transformed from large feudal estates into small bourgeois farms." (This error, which Lenin derived in part from the analysis of American circumstances presented in 1899 by German Marxist Karl Kautsky in *The Agrarian Question,* was inadvertently encouaged by U.S. census officials. From 1870 to 1900 the census bureau "considered all farming units, whether operated by an owner or a tenant, as separate farms."[123] Not until 1910 did census officials acknowledge that such mistakes were misleading. The plantation system had survived the war, albeit in a transformed state that scholars call the fragmented or decentralized system based on sharecropping and tenancy.) Lenin, believing that antebellum plantations had been broken up and divided among small independent farmers, saw in the postbellum South a positive model for social democratic agrarian policy in Russia, where, he feared, the agrarian reform act sponsored by chief minister Peter Stolypin in 1906 would place Russia on the anti-democratic Prussian road to agrarian capitalism. Instead, Russian social democracy should work for the passage of new agrarian legislation by the Russian parliament, or Duma, newly established during the 1905 revolution. Such new legislation should provide for peasant colonization of dismembered aristocratic estates, and thereby accelerate "the development of capitalism and the growth of the productive forces" in rural Russia. As Alfred G. Meyer has observed, Lenin reads here like "an apologist of pure competition and bourgeois individualism."[124]

After the establishment of Marxism-Leninism as political and academic orthodoxy in the German Democratic Republic (DDR, formally established in 1949), Lenin's concept of the Prussian road became ensconced in East German historical scholarship by the 1960s.[125] German historians write of *der preußische Weg,* which can be translated as Prussian road, or Prussian way, or Prussian path. The Leninist model of the Prussian way obviously fits well with a Marxist focus on the historical transition from a feudal to a capitalist mode of production and social relations. In the English-speaking world the best-known East German historian is doubtless Jürgen Kuczynski (b. 1904), who lived in both the United States and England prior to 1945, and some of whose work has been published in English. In his 1961 study of the German working class from 1789 to 1848, Kuczynski observed that "the Prussian road in agriculture *(der preußische Weg der Landwirtschaft)* signified the slow transformation of "the socage-based economy of the estate owner *(die fronherrliche Gutsbesitzerwirtschaft)"* into a "bourgeois Junker economy." This transformation began in earnest with Hardenberg's 1811 edict specifying how much land a peasant had to cede to his manorial lord in order to gain clear title to the remainder; and after a more pro-Junker declaration was issued in 1816, there followed the expropriation of many peasants and an attendant increase in the size and economic strength of many *Rittergüter.* [126] From the 1960s to the 1980s variations on Kuczynski's Leninist formulation of the Prussian road concept infused the often impressive research conducted by East German scholars into the social, economic, and political history of East Elbia during the nineteenth century.[127] Although East German historians avoided direct criticism of the Leninist gospel, Georg Moll, in a 1982 essay published in the country's leading historical journal, noted in passing that the American path of capitalist agricultural development was not possible in the U.S. South. Yet he did not suggest that the alternative Prussian road model was applicable to Southern history.[128]

DDR scholars devoted a great deal of attention to the question of exactly when in the nineteenth century East Elbian agriculture and landed Junkerdom completed their capitalist and bourgeois transformation and came to the end of the Prussian road. In other words, at what point in time did the Prussian road process reach "a polarization of class forces between agricultural capitalists on the one hand and the mass of landless rural workers on the other"? [129] By the early 1980s most East German scholars seemed to agree that the Revolution of 1848–49, after failing to follow the revolutionary-democratic route proclaimed by Marx and Engels, inaugurated the final phrase of the Prussian road transformation by compelling the Prussian government to promulgate new agrarian laws in 1850. These new laws provided for the commutation of feudal dues still owed by many lesser peasants, to whom this option had been denied by Hardenberg's Declaration of 1816. The legislation also established loan banks *(Rentenbanken)* to advance the long-term, low-interest credit peasants needed to purchase their farms outright, while also assuring estate owners of dependable monetary compensation, which could in turn be used for land purchases, capital improvements, or the payment of wages to day-laborers. As a consequence of the 1850 legislation, by the 1860s East Elbian agriculture had developed "capitalist relations of production" and "capitalist social structure in the villages."[130] Nonetheless, after concluding that virtually all Junker estates had "a capitalist character" by the 1860s, most scholars still agreed with Hans Mottek that "strong feudal residues remained."[131] The Junkers' local police power survived until 1872; the authoritarian ordinance governing relations between manorial lords and their household servants *(Gesindeordnung)*, issued in 1810, continued in force until 1918, as did the right to establish family trust entails *(Fideikommisse)*. The precise termination date for the Prussian road is important to a Marxist-Leninist scholar because it determines the relative feudal or capitalist character of Bismarck's Prusso-German Empire, created between 1866 and 1871. If East Elbian agriculture and the Junker ruling class were more bourgeois-capitalist than aristocratic-feudal by the 1860s (by which time the foundations of an industrial society had also been laid in the German states), then the fundamental character of the Bismarckian *Kaiserreich* was clearly more capitalist than feudal.[132]

Leninist and East German scholarship was no doubt familiar to English historian Eric Hobsbawm, one of the most respected and perhaps the best-known living Marxian historian in the Western world. As Hobsbawm observed in 1975, "There are two major variants of capitalist agriculture, which Lenin called respectively the 'Prussian' and the 'American' way: large estates operated by capitalist landlord-entrepreneurs with hired labour, and independent commercial farms of varying sizes also operating with hired labour where necessary, though on a smaller scale."[133] However, earlier in the same book Hobsbawm introduced a subtle but significant transmutation of the Prussian road concept which parallels the earlier use of the phrase by Eugene Genovese. During the 1850s and 1860s, wrote Hosbawm, "'bourgeois revolution' was a genuine possibility" in the German states, because "the liberal bourgeoisie was strong, conscious of itself as a class and an independent political force." Yet the creation of a unified German state via Bismarck's "revolution from above" between 1862 and 1871 saved the Junkers from being overwhelmed by the bourgeoisie. According to Hosbawm, "The Prussian way to capitalism was through the combination of a bourgeoisie reluctant to make a bourgeois revolution and a Junker state prepared to give them most of what they wanted without a revolution, for the price of preserving the political control of the landed aristocracy and the bureaucratic monarchy."[134] Eugene Genovese had anticipated this reformulation in 1969, when he equated "the Prussian road to capitalism" with "the road of authoritarianism based on a coalition of industrialists and great aristocratic landowners."[135] In other words, Genovese and Hobsbawm adopted the Prussian road label to describe what Barrington Moore, Jr.'s *Social Origins of Dictatorship and Democracy* (1966) had called "the capitalist and reactionary" route from the "preindustrial to the modern world," a route made possible by the sort of peaceable anti-democratic alliance between industrial and agrarian elites that evolved in Germany and Japan.[136]

Despite their differences in terminology, Genovese and Moore agreed that the political mechanisms for such an authoritarian coalition did not exist in the United States; hence the Civil War.

Thus, where Lenin and his East German disciples limited the "Prussian road" epithet to the emergence of a capitalist *Rittergut* agriculture in East Elbia during the first two-thirds of the nineteenth century, Hobsbawm and Genovese expanded the meaning of the phrase to encompass the authoritarian political coalition that emerged in Prusso-Germany during the Bismarckian era. The centrality of this alliance between traditional Junker power and newer industrial wealth to the creation and character of the Second Empire has been stressed since the Second World War by many historians of modern Germany, West German and American as well as East German. As Karl Dietrich Bracher of the University of Bonn put it in 1970, "the foundation stone of the Second Reich" was "the alliance between the feudal nobility and bourgeois capitalism."[137] East German scholars placed great emphasis on Bismarck's success at forcing Prussia's ostensibly liberal bourgeoisie to accept a class compromise *(Klassenkompromiß)* with the Junkers, and often cited the Prussian Assembly's approval of Bismarck's Indemnity Bill in 1866 as evidence of the fundamentally anti-democratic bourgeoisie's capitulation to Bismarck's Bonapartist dictatorship and thereby to Junker dominance.[138] According to DDR scholars, the Prussian way of capitalist development in rural East Elbia played a crucial role in laying the economic and social groundwork for the anti-democratic coalition between agrarian Junkers and industrial bourgeoisie. Yet Hartmut Harnisch, despite his emphasis on the analytical importance of Lenin's Prussian road model, has persuasively argued that it should apply only to questions about change in the agrarian sector, and not to broader questions about the totality of social and political developments during the nineteenth-century transition from feudalism to capitalism.[139]

Although the Genovese-Hobsbawm view of the Prussian road as paved with an authoritarian-Junker-industrialist coalition does not accord with Lenin's original formulation of the concept, the Genovese-Hobsbawm version cannot be faulted for misrepresenting the course of nineteenth-century Prusso-German history. Can the same be said for Jonathan Wiener's use of the term in *Social Origins of the New South: Alabama, 1860–1885* (1978)? Wiener began this study as a student of Barrington Moore, and the book attributes the Prussian road concept to *Social Origins of Dictatorship and Democracy.* According to Wiener, "the 'Prussian Road' to modern society" means "economic development that preserves and intensifies the authoritarian and repressive elements of traditional social relations."[140] This formulation does not appear to be contradicted by the historical record of nineteenth-century Prussia. Even in major industrializing areas of the western provinces Rhineland and Westphalia, something of what historians have termed traditional paternalistic relationships survived and flourished into the twentieth century.[141]

Although Wiener's idea of a Prussian road to modern society seems historically accurate, later in his book he introduces a new twist. In the postbellum South, with "its dominant planter class and its labor-repressive system of agricultural production," planter ideologues promoted an approach to regional economic development that involved "limited industrial development in the context of a planter-dominated, cotton-producing plantation South; in short, the Prussian Road."[142] However, it is misleading to suggest that during the second half of the nineteenth century the Kingdom of Prussia followed a path of "limited industrial development" comparable to that of the postbellum South. The rapidly expanding industrial sector in the Prussian Rhineland, as well as in the Upper Silesian and Berlin-Potsdam districts of East Elbian Prussia, was responsible for the German Empire's becoming the leading industrial state on the European Continent by 1900.[143]

Another misrepresentation of Prusso-German development appears in Lewis Nicholas Wynne's *The Continuity of Cotton: Planter Politics in Georgia, 1865–1892* (1986). Wynne credits Moore, Genovese, and especially Jonathan Wiener for instructing him in the Prussian road model. According to Wynne, the " 'Prussian Road' approach—the regulation of the growth of industry by an agricultural elite—appeared to be the only hope Georgia planters had of remaining a potent force in the affairs of the state." Georgia planters succeeded in using the state's political machinery to limit and control the pace of industrial and urban growth, and the outcome was "the Prussian Road pattern of industrial development—small textile mills in small rural towns."[144] This construction of the Prussian road gives the reader the false impression that landed Junkerdom imposed such a program of decentralized, small-scale industrial and urban development on nineteenth-century Prussia. Consider that the East Elbian metropolis of Berlin, the capital city of both the Kingdom of Prussia and the German Empire, saw its population climb from 430,000 in 1850 to over 1.3 million in 1885, while a handful of joint-stock banks centered in the city acquired "almost undisputed sway over the German capital market."[145] Imperial Berlin was New York City and Washington, D.C. combined.

Perhaps the best-informed and most substantial discussion of the Prussian road concept by a Southern historian is presented in the previously cited 1985 essay "The Advent of Capitalist Agriculture: The New South in a Bourgeois World," by Barbara Jeanne Fields. She recognizes "the 'Prussian road' to capitalist agriculture" as an analytical tool of Leninist origin. Her insistence that there was "a world of difference" between the "authentic Prussian way" and "what took place in the American South" is part and parcel of her argument that post-1865 plantations traveled the road to capitalist agriculture and capitalist social relations far more slowly and haltingly than did post-1807 Junker estates. Unlike planters, Junkers had both the political power and the financial resources "to convert their work forces into a regulation wage-earning proletariat." Prussian's landed elite certainly did not show "any such sign of weakness as the crop-lien credit system of the American South."[146] As this chapter has made clear, my own perspective on the historical development of capitalism is quite different from Fields's. My perspective makes the model of a Prussian road to capitalist agriculture unusable; yet it encourages me to see labor developments in post-emancipation Junker agriculture as a bit more analogous to what emerged in the plantation South after abolition than does Fields.

My own view is that the plantation South before as well as after the Civil War was capitalist, although the cotton and tobacco plantations of the antebellum and postbellum eras presented very different forms of capitalist agriculture.[147] The fundamental difference was that in the Old South slaves constituted not only a form of coerced cash-crop labor but also an extremely valuable capital asset whose market value rose dramatically over the several decades prior to 1860.[148] During the Civil War this capital asset was abolished without the sort of compensation that Junkers had received earlier in the century, in the form of money or real estate, in return for the abolition of their lordship over peasant land and their rights to compulsory labor services. The uncompensated abolition of slavery does much to explain why the postbellum Southern economy was starved for credit. In cotton- and tobacco-growing areas the fragmented plantation system and sharecropping usually emerged as a sort of compromise between cash-poor landlords and landless freedmen for whom working in gangs, under the personal supervision of the landowner or his proxy, was too reminiscent of bondage. Sharecropping, far more than gang labor, accorded with what most freedmen and their families seem to have considered the primary characteristic of freedom—autonomy and independence. To be sure, sharecropping and tenancy (tenancy being the next higher rung on the ladder to landownership) were not universal even in the cotton South, where many planters retained some acreage for their own immediate use and farmed it with hired hands, usually young, unmarried males. Yet sharecroppers and wage hands alike came to be legally defined as hired laborers. According to laws adopted by the Redeemer governments that came to power with the waning of Reconstruction, sharecropping was not a form of tenancy, whereby the tenant had a prior claim on the crop, but instead constituted a form of hired labor, the worker paid in shares of the crop rather than cash wages. To be sure, vagrancy ordinances, anti-enticement statutes, and the crop-lien system hardly seem compatible with the concept of free wage labor.[149] Due in large measure to the postbellum South's shortage of indigenous credit and declining cotton prices on the international market, lien laws often served to reduce freedmen to the status of debt peonage. It is an "unfortunate historical accident," notes Peter Kolchin, "that emancipation preceded the onset of a generation-long period of agricultural deflation and depression that engulfed the Western world."[150] Not until the mid-twentieth century did the decentralized plantation based on sharecropping and tenancy begin to disappear from the cotton South. During the 1930s and 1940s, under the impact of New Deal agricultural programs and then the Second World War, Southern landlords consolidated their fragmented plantations and adopted new labor-saving machinery operated by wage hands, while the wartime demand for industrial labor in the North and West spurred a mass exodus from the South of former sharecroppers and tenants. Even so, not until the 1960s did Afro-Americans still living in the South gain formal civil and political equality with the Euro-American majority.[151]

Let's shift our focus eastward across the Atlantic Ocean to Prussian East Elbia, and in the process quickly survey some of the same ground covered in Chapter 2. By the time agricultural depression engulfed the Western world in the late nineteenth century, the Junkers had had almost seven decades to make the transition from bound to free labor. Moreover, many *Rittergut* owners already had considerable experience with contractual day-laborers when the abolition of servitude on private estates was announced in 1807. Since the 1820s the Junkers had enjoyed generally favorable demand and profitable markets for the produce of their estates: grain and wool (much of which went to England), potato whiskey, and, from mid-century, beet sugar. Yet during these decades the owners of knight's estates did not make a rapid and dramatic shift to proletarian wage labor. On the eve of the 1848 revolution some Junker estates still depended on the compulsory labor services of unregulated peasants, and some hired the part-time labor of semi-subsistence smallholders who needed supplemental income. But most knight's estates relied heavily on the labor of cottagers or lodgers and their families, most commonly known as *Insten,* whose position has been described as "a kind of semi-feudal sharecropping system."[152] Although these cottagers and lodgers worked in coordinated gangs to a far greater extent than did Southern sharecroppers, their payment included lodging, garden land, and small fractional shares of the grain harvest and threshing, payments in kind which were augmented by small cash wages. Between these cottagers and their manorial lords, as between sharecroppers and their planter landlords, there seems to have existed something of what Max Weber and others have called a "community of economic interest," since both parties stood to benefit from high yields and a successful harvest.[153] Yet after mid-century more and more Junker landowners sought to replace the fractional shares in the harvest and threshing with fixed wages in kind, or *Deputat,* thereby reducing the community of economic interest between laborer and lord. As growing numbers of rural East Elbians migrated to urban centers in the westerly provinces or emigrated to the United States, and as the expanding cultivation of sugar beets increased the demand for large numbers of seasonal laborers, Junker landowners turned rapidly in the 1880s to the seasonal employment of low-wage migratory workers from the Polish districts of the Russian and Austro-Hungarian empires. Concurrently, manorial lords replaced the German cottager's *Deputat,* or fixed payment in kind, with cash wages whose level was determined by the wages paid to migratory Polish workers, which in turn encouraged more Germans to leave the countryside, thereby leading to the seasonal importation of more Polish farmhands. "In 1914," according to Frieda Wunderlich, "one-seventh of all German agricultural workers were aliens (433,000); during the summer months the proportion of foreign workers on certain farms was as high as 50 per cent."[154] Insofar as these migrant Polish laborers were subject to physical abuse, deemed racially and culturally inferior, enjoyed no political rights, and were not permitted to change employers during the agricultural season (April to November), the label "free labor" seems as inappropriate for them as for contemporaneous black sharecroppers. It was not until the German revolution of 1918–19 and the Weimar Republic that agricultural workers achieved a civil and political status equal to that of industrial workers.[155]

Because my own perspective on the nature and evolution of capitalism as an economic system renders suspect the Leninist concept of a Prussian road to capitalist agriculture, I do not find it a useful tool of comparative analysis. Nonetheless, I do find it helpful to think of the modernization process as promoting in rapidly industrializing nations such as Germany and the United States the emergence of a formally free labor force composed of wage earners who share civil and political (versus social) equality with their employers. Whereas rural East Elbia acquired such formally free workers no earlier than the 1920s, over a century after the abolition of hereditary bondage, the rural South acquired this kind of labor force during the second third of the twentieth century, no more than a century after the abolition of hereditary servitude. Yet in both regions the long transition period began with what Harold Woodman has called "uncertainty and experimentation,"[156] which included the evolution of loosely analogous sharecropping systems. Moreover, just as *Rittergut* owners and their workers both took initiatives that conributed to the demise of the cottager arrangement during the late nineteenth century, so too did plantation owners and laborers alike take steps that promoted the disappearance of the sharecropped plantation in the cotton South during the middle decades of the twentieth century. Nonetheless, Junkers after World War I, and planters after World War II, resisted the democratic and egalitarian reforms identified with the Weimar Republic and the U.S. civil rights movement. The histories of the planter and Junker elites in the twentieth century will receive further attention in the Epilogue.

4

Planter Republicanism versus Junker Monarchism

DESPITE ANALOGIES BETWEEN plantations and knight's estates as commercial
enterprises and political communities, these estates and their proprietors functioned within very different geographic, demographic, political, and racial milieus.
Although the plantation and *Rittergut* were both hierarchical and authoritarian
institutions, Southern society as a whole was less hierarchical and more fluid,
less authoritarian and more democratic, than was East Elbian society. This chapter will explore these differences and their historical evolution in such a way as
to illuminate *the* crucial distinction between the mid-nineteenth-century planter
and Junker elites: the former's libertarian but racist republicanism versus the
latter's militarist and corporatist monarchism. (A synonym for corporatist is estatist, or *ständisch*; and a good definition of an estate, or *Stand*, is "a legally
defined segment of the population in a society which has distinctive rights and
duties established by law."[1]) We can highlight this critical disjuncture between
the South and East Elbia by juxtaposing some comments from a pair of prominent mid-century politicians, Ernst Gottfried Georg von Bülow-Cummerow (1775–
1851) of Pomerania and Jefferson Finis Davis (1809–89) of Mississippi.

Ernst von Bülow-Cummerow, though a native of Mecklenburg-Schwerin, became what historian Sigmund Neuman calls "the leading agrarian politician and
most successful publicist of the 1840s" in East Elbian Prussia. He did not belong
to the intensely religious "Old Prussian" court clique (the *Kamarilla*) around
Friedrich Wilhelm IV; and his dearth of doctrinaire pietism made him more
representative of landed Junkerdom than a Ludwig von Gerlach or Adolf von
Thadden-Trieglaff.[2] After youthful stints as an officer in the armies of both

Hanover and Mecklenburg-Strelitz, interspersed by a year of university study at Rostock and Jena during the mid-1790s, he moved to eastern Pomerania in 1805.[3] There he purchased and enlarged several estates in the district Regenwalde, endorsing the end of personal servitude and Hardenberg's legislation for "regulating" the labor obligations owed by formerly bound peasants to their manorial lords. A progressive farmer who established a chemical plant and iron forge on his estates, and a founder of the Regenwalde Agricultural Association in 1831, he agitated on behalf of financial support for landowners from the monarchy in the form of agricultural credit and subsidies for railroad construction. During the summer of 1848, as the democratically elected Prussian National Assembly considered proposals to eliminate the tax-exempt status of *Rittergüter* and to abolish the manorial dues still owed by some peasants to their Junker lords, he became chairman of the eleven-member committee which founded the "Association for the Protection of the Interests of Landed Property and the Advancement of the Welfare of All Classes." This association, the first important agrarian interest group in Prussian history, rejected any attack "on property and the sanctity of contracts." When almost four hundred *Rittergut* owners convened in Berlin in mid-August as the organization's "General Assembly," the meeting was promptly and accurately dubbed the "Junker Parliament."[4]

In 1842 Bülow-Cummerow had written that Prussia definitely did not want a "constitutional" monarchy like that of Louis Philippe in France, because a liberal constitution on the French model established elected legislatures *(Kammern)* with formal "delegated authorities." Such a political system was inherently unstable because it rested on theoretical notions of popular sovereignty and "ideal equality and freedom," and in practice promoted the influence of a selfish and unscrupulous monied aristocracy. What was appropriate for Prussia was a "corporatist" or "estatist" monarchy, in which the monarch remained sovereign but received advice from an assembly of socially prominent, legally recognized, and politically mature groups *(Stände Versammlung),* the first and foremost being the owners of landed estates. "From oldest times in Germany have the owners of ground and soil been considered the only persons entitled to vote." A corporatist monarchy offered the best "security for the spiritual and material interests and freedom of the people *(Volk)*" against both bureaucratic tyranny and democratic degradation.[5] In December of 1848, immediately after King Friedrich Wilhelm IV and his ministers had sought to short-circuit the revolution in Prussia by dissolving the National Assembly and promulgating an "imposed constitution," Bülow-Cummerow took issue with the new constitution's acceptance of democratic manhood suffrage, which he saw as promoting the political power of "communist ideas." Instead of either a democratic or a propertied electorate, he favored a Prussian assembly organized so as to represent three principle "interests": first, the landowners; second, businessmen and owners of mobile capital; and third, all those who worked for others, whether with their hands or their minds.[6] But such a corporatist system was not the aim in 1848–49 of the "ultra-liberals" and the "party of revolution *(Umsturzpartei),*" wrote Bülow-Cummerow in 1850. These radicals might have succeeded in permanently imposing a "miserable" French form of democratic constitutionalism on Prussia had it not been for the army: "only the army remained unshaken; loyal and steadfast to the king, it preserved its old calm." Nonetheless, the king and his ministers had compromised with the forces of revolution by condoning a popularly elected lower house in which landowners did not receive privileged representation. Bülow-Cummerow joined with what he called "the conservative party"—at whose head, he stated, stood the large estate owners—in advocating a corporatist form of parliament, "whereby all interests are represented according to their importance and according to the services which they furnish to the whole community." He emphasized "how little the conditions prevailing in Prussia are suited to a representative body *(Volksvertretung)* with an extensive suffrage." The populace's "political stupidity and indolence" were being exploited by subversive radicals and selfish bureaucrats, against whom the falsely maligned *"Junkertum"* sought "to defend themselves against a palpable and purposeless theft of their property"—that is, the abrogation of their long-established tax exemptions, and insufficient monetary compensation for the abolition of surviving servile dues.[7]

Jefferson Davis, a Kentucky native, was chosen the first and only president of the Confederate States of America in 1861, having risen to public prominence in the United States first as a military hero during the Mexican War, and then as senator from Mississippi and Secretary of War. An 1828 graduate of the U.S. Military Academy at West Point, Lieutenant Davis resigned his commission in 1835 and created Brierfield plantation out of Mississippi River bottom land provided by his older brother, mentor, and neighbor Joseph.[8] In 1845, when he owned over seventy slaves, Davis won election to the federal House of Representatives as a Democrat, but the next year, after the U.S. declaration of war on Mexico, resigned his seat to become colonel of a volunteer regiment from Mississippi. He returned to Washington, D.C., as a senator from late 1847 to 1851, when he resigned to make an unsuccessful bid for the governorship of Mississippi. Nonetheless, by this time his outspoken advocacy of slaveholders' constitutional rights in the federal territories against growing free-soil efforts to contain the spread of slavery had elevated him to the stature of what a contemporary termed "the Calhoun of Mississippi."[9] Indeed, after the South Carolinian's death in 1850, Davis became, according to historian Paul Escott, "the chief theoretician of the southern position on slavery."[10] As Franklin Pierce's Secretary of War from 1853 to 1857, and also during his second stint in the Senate from 1857 to 1861, he ardently supported U.S. acquisition of Cuba (where slavery survived until the 1880s) as "essential to our prosperity and security."[11] Yet Davis was no "ultra" secessionist "fire-eater." This moderate stance helps to explain why, in February of 1861, the Montgomery convention of delegates from the seven seceded slave states made him their unanimous choice for the presidency of the new Southern Confederacy.

Like almost all antebellum planters, Jefferson Davis had too much pride in the legacy of libertarian republicanism inherited from the Founding Fathers, and too much racial disdain for the Negro's capacity for self-government,[12] to admit or even recognize the possibility that there could be any significant parallels between the planter elite and an "aristocratical" class like the Junkers. After all, was not the Junker aristocracy an avowed enemy of the sort of nationalist and liberal-democratic revolutions that Southern planters had helped foment in 1776, and that swept over the European continent in 1848? Jefferson Davis invoked the legacy of 1776 in his 18 February 1861 inaugural address in Montgomery, insisting that the seceded states had "merely asserted a right which the Declaration of Independence of 1776 had declared to be inalienable."[13] That is, a people had the inalienable right of revolution against their government when it became destructive of their individual liberties. On the Fourth of July, 1861, the editor of the Memphis *Daily Avalanche* spoke for Davis and most Confederates when he insisted that Southerners should not hesitate to celebrate "this sacred day"; for the Confederacy was fighting "to maintain the principles of liberty as set forth in the Declaration."[14]

Davis made no mention of slavery in his inaugural address, probably because he did not want to identify the new Confederate government explicitly with human servitude in a speech that was designed largely for foreign consumption. However, he did discuss the peculiar institution and its relation to Southern liberties in his special message to the Confederate Congress on 29 April 1861, a fortnight after the fall of Fort Sumter. He opened the speech by announcing that the Confederate Constitution—modeled, it should be noted, after the U. S. Constitution—had been ratified by each of the seven Lower South states that had met in Montgomery to organize a new federation, and that the new Confederate States of America now existed "in its full proportions and upon its own substantial basis of popular will." (By 1860–61 all white adult males could vote in every slave state; Davis's own state of Mississippi had instituted white manhood suffrage in 1832.[15]) Davis then sketched the history of the sectional conflict that had led to secession, and pointed out that in 1860 the United States presidency had been captured by a political party whose "avowed object" was "the total exclusion of the slave States from all participation in the benefits of the public domain acquired by all the States in common"—that is, the federal territories west of the Mississippi River. The achievement of this goal by Lincoln and the Republicans would result in "rendering the property in slaves so insecure as to be comparatively worthless, and thereby annihilating in effect property worth thousands of millions of dollars." Davis stressed that the Republican party's antislavery posture in 1860 had certainly not been justified by the situation of the slaves themselves: "In a moral and social condition they had been elevated from brutal savages into docile, intelligent, and civilized agricultural laborers, and supplied not only with bodily comforts, but with careful religious instruction, under the supervision of a superior race."[16]

The remainder of this chapter will seek to trace the historical evolution of Bülow-Cummerow's militarist and corporatist monarchism on the one hand, and Jefferson Davis's libertarian but racist republicanism on the other. A précis of the argument here might be helpful. Where the Junkers' elitist position had always depended upon their enjoyment of the sort of "aristocratic," group-specific privileges that were inaccessible to antebellum planters, the plantation gentry's position depended upon a rigid caste distinction between black slavery and white freedom that was foreign to Prussia's traditions of hierarchical corporatism. This racial dichotomy, together with the more geographically expansive and therefore more socially fluid character of Southern white society, enabled planters and plantations to enjoy far greater popular legitimacy and approval in the South than did knight's estates and Junkers in East Elbia. Consequently, the planters could preside in the slave states over what has been termed "*Herrenvolk* democracy," that is, political democracy for the master race.[17] However, while the slave states increasingly became a minority section within the U.S. Republic, East Elbia remained the preponderant region within the Prussian monarchy. This preponderance, in conjunction with what Hans-Jürgen Puhle has called Junkerdom's "privileged position next to the bureaucracy and the military in the Prussian power syndicate,"[18] gave the Junkers greater political flexibility and more durable national clout than was available to slaveholding planters.

— I —

The antebellum United States, geographically isolated from the world's formidable military powers, had a frontier moving westward into territory whose indigenous Native American population had been decimated by diseases and military technology brought by colonists from Europe. Since tribal fragmentation and competition among the surviving American Indians further reduced their capacity for effective resistance to U.S. westward expansion, the American Republic could survive and flourish with a diminutive standing army. Congress provided for the organization of decentralized state militias in which many planters received officers' commissions either by gubernatorial appointment or popular election.[19] Almost all antebellum slaveholders shared the fear of the Founding Fathers (themselves influenced by English "radical" or "country" Whig ideology) that a powerful military establishment might seek to establish the sort of tyranny that George III's army had allegedly sought to impose on the colonies during the 1770s. In the words of Virginia's Bill of Rights, "standing armies in times of peace should be avoided as dangerous to liberty," and "in all cases the military should be under strict subordination to, and governed by, the civil power."[20]

The Kingdom of Prussia, with long-settled states along its exposed borders on the north European plain, depended for its survival and growth upon a large standing army. Its officer corps provided necessary employment as well as social prestige to many Junker sons, while also functioning as a formidable tool of domestic repression. Virginian Thomas R. Dew maintained in 1836 that Prussia, with a population smaller than that of the United States, maintained a peacetime military twenty-one times the size of the U.S. Army: 126,000 versus 6000 men.[21] Dew's figures seem to have exaggerated the divergence, since at mid-century Prussia's regular army numbered about 30,000 men, almost one-third of them commissioned.[22] Even so, on the eve of the 1848–49 revolution the Prussian officer corps was nearly nine times larger than the U.S. officer corps on the eve of the Civil War: 9,434 officers in Prussia, of whom 77 percent had noble titles, versus 1,080 officers in the United States, of whom some 300 left with the seceding slave states.[23] Regardless of how one defines the term "militarism"— whether one sees it as an imbalance between civil and military authorities in the favor of the latter, or as a function of symbiotic relationships between the military establishment and certain socio-economic structures[24]—East Elbia was clearly a more militaristic society than the South. Prussian militarism could serve as an authoritarian cement between Hohenzollern monarchy and landed Junkerdom that could have no counterpart in the relations between planters and their republican federal government. King Friedrich Wilhelm IV repeatedly emphasized the importance of the military in the history of the Hohenzollern dominions. "It has been God's providence," he told the United Diet in April of 1847, "to make Prussia great through the sword, through the sword of war externally, through the sword of the spirit internally . . . the spirit of order and discipline."[25] Two years later, after Prussian troops had played a major role in breaking the back of liberal-democratic revolutions in several states of the German Confederation, the king declared that "My army is the foundation of the existence of my throne and the preservation of the Fatherland . . . ; the solid pillar on which the monarchy rests."[26] Monarch and Junkers alike believed that the military should remain under absolute royal control. Count Adolph Heinrich von Arnim-Boitzenburg of Brandenburg summarized the feelings of his Junker peers when he wrote in 1849 that "The Prussian army is more accustomed than any other to see in its king the one and only commander, its personal leader and highest lord." Requiring the officer corps to pledge abstract allegiance to a constitutional document rather than personal loyalty to their king, as liberals desired, would sap "the spirit of the army," insisted Arnim-Boitzenburg; and this spirit was necessary to protect Prussia's relatively small population against the other great powers of Europe.[27]

Granted that the plantation regime and the need to keep a large slave population in subordination imbued some of the planter elite with a martial spirit.[28] The Old South's gentry acquired a widespread and in part deserved reputation for militant violence from such concrete historical realities as extra-legal duelling, occasional nighttime slave patrols, and the attendance of many planter sons at either the West Point on the Hudson or the lesser "West Points of the South" such as the Virginia Military Institute.[29] Slavery apologists sometimes embellished this reputation by boasting about the instinctive and salutary "habit of command" bred in planter scions by their plantation upbringings. However, the geographical isolation of the American colonies and states, somewhat like the separation of England from the European continent, obviated the need for a powerful standing army. And the absence of such an army precluded the development (prior to the emergence of modern industrial-urban society) of the sort of centralized and expansive bureaucracy that military absolutism fostered in Prussia.

— II —

The origins of Prussia's military establishment can be traced back to the horrific destruction of the Thirty Years' War (1618–48) and the ongoing wars with Sweden and Poland during the subsequent two decades. These wars enabled Friedrich Wilhelm, the "Great Elector," to extract from the provincial assemblies of Brandenburg, Pomerania, and East Prussia—dominated by fiercely independent landed nobles who tended to view their prince as merely "first among equals"—formal permission to finance a standing army with taxes, to be levied on the peasantry and towns only. The Junkers, in acceding to the Great Elector's demands "to give the state political prestige and greater military weight,"[30] made possible the evolution of both a more powerful monarchy and an expansive royal bureaucracy. The army grew from approximately 4500 men when the Great Elector took the throne in 1640, to 80,000 in 1740, when Friedrich II (Frederick the Great) inherited the throne from "Soldier King" Friedrich Wilhelm I, to 200,000 at Friedrich II's death in 1786. Maintenance of this army required ever increasing state revenues. In turn, the collection of taxes, management of the monarchy's own extensive landholdings, and the provisioning of the army fostered the growth of a professional civil service. This bureaucracy became the monarchy's principle weapon in its struggle, says Reinhart Koselleck, "to prop up its supra-provincial power and authority over against the provincial assemblies."[31] The authority of these assemblies, in which titled *Rittergut* owners predominated as the foremost corporatist group *(Stand),* steadily waned as the bureaucracy's power and initative waxed. Under the Prussian Civil Code *(Allgemeines Landrecht)* promulgated in 1791–94, the civil service even obtained its own legally privileged status in Prussian society as a corporatist group, which meant in practice the exemption of civil servants from the payment of most taxes and from the jurisdiction of the lower, provincial courts.[32]

"Throughout the history of the Prussian state, from the cradle to the grave" in 1945, explains Hans Rosenberg, "the armed forces, not the civil bureaucracy, were the primary mode of the Junkers' active participation in professionalized government."[33] It was during the eighteenth-century reigns of the "Soldier King" and Frederick the Great that the officer corps became a virtual Junker preserve, thereby serving the interests of both less affluent Junker families and Hohenzollern monarchs anxious to secure the dynastic loyalty of their provincial landed aristocracy. In 1806 all but 695 of the more than 7000 officers belonged to the nobility.[34] Most eighteenth-century Junkers, accustomed to rustic life-styles and not partial to higher education, found service as army officers more congenial than bureaucratic desk work. It also made eminently good military logic to use the autocratic relationship between lord and serf as the basis for the even more authoritarian relationship between officer and foot-soldier. Under the canton system of recruitment instituted in 1733, all members of a regiment had to come from the peasantry of the same geographical district; and it frequently happened that a soldier's commanding officer was also his manorial lord. Thus the structure of the Prussian military served to reinforce the local political authority of *Rittergut* owners and the corporatist distinction between aristocracy and peasantry. As Otto Büsch has shown, "This interweaving and social identification transformed the civil life of the rural nobles and peasants into a concurrent military regimen. The consequence was the militarization of rural society."[35]

Even as the Prussian Civil Code of 1791–94 granted the civil service privileged corporatist status, it also affirmed the position of the landed nobility as the premier *Stand* in the kingdom. The Civil Code charged Junkerdom with primary responsibility for "the defense of the state," which entailed "the support of both its external dignity and its inner fabric."[36] Only when the army and its Junker officer corps failed to maintain Prussia's "external dignity" against the military might of Napoleonic France in 1806 would the monarchy and royal bureaucracy act decisively to reduce the privileges of the nobility and reform the structure of rural society. During the eighteenth century the monarchy did not disturb the "inner fabric" of the Junkers' control over the enserfed peasantry, and the Civil Code confirmed the estate owner's right to use whips and rods in punishing "lazy, disorderly and refractory menials."[37] In other words, in return for their concessions to a stronger central government, *Rittergut* owners retained unchallenged dominance in the countryside, in their manorial autocracies, and also in the county assemblies *(Kreistage)*. The Junkers of each *Kreistag* submitted to the monarchy a list of three nominees for the county's crucial administrative link with Berlin, the semi-bureaucratic *Landrat*, or county commissioner. From the sympathetic perspective of Georg-Christoph von Unruh, the structure of county government in East Elbia "prevented the absolutism of the royal government from reaching down to the lowest level of administration."[38] Otto von Bismarck explained that the *Landrat* "carries a Janus head, which has one face to the bureaucracy, one to the countryside."[39] Nevertheless, most county commissioners seem to have shown more solicitude for their Junker peers than for the higher civil authorities.[40]

The upper levels of administration came to include increasing numbers of untitled "commoners" during the eighteenth and early nineteenth centuries. As the royal bureaucracy grew in size and complexity, and the value and status of university training in the law grew accordingly, the number of middle-class *Bürger* entering the civil service grew apace. After the death in 1786 of Frederick the Great, who had been very stingy with patents of nobility, commoners who achieved high bureaucratic positions often received noble titles as well. From 1786 to 1806 patents of nobility were conferred on 68 government officials *(Beamten)*.[41] The employment of commoners by the royal bureaucracy, and the co-opting of some of their number into ranks of the nobility, may have contributed somewhat to the slow development in Prussia of an aggressively self-conscious middle class. Yet the influx of educated burghers encouraged the bureaucracy's development of an identity and outlook quite distinct from, and even antagonistic to, those of landed Junkerdom. Especially after the promulgation of the Civil Code in the early 1790s, the civil service came to view itself as a select group in which membership depended on merit, and whose members shared a disinterested commitment to the welfare of the Prussian state. Consequently, many bureaucrats tended to see their "universal" *Beamtenstand* as superior to the parochial landed nobility *(Ritterstand)*, a caste based on birth, lacking in education and initiative, and preoccupied with its own selfish and narrow interests.[42] Conversely, during the Stein-Hardenberg era "Old Prussian" Junkers looked upon reform-minded bureaucrats as irreverent rationalists and impractical scribblers who had insufficient respect for the provincial aristocracy's record of distinguished service to the Hohenzollern monarchy, and who seemed infatuated with some of the new-fangled libertarian notions current in western Europe during the eras of the American and French revolutions. "Oh how unfortunate that God's omnipotence, wisdom and goodness, but especially his omniscience, does not reside in these improvers of the world," lamented Ludwig von der Marwitz.[43] To be sure, there were tensions within the civil service itself between what Barbara Vogel terms "liberal reformers" and "conservative bureaucrats." Although the liberal bureaucrats were more interested in promoting representative government and elected assemblies than were the conservatives, the latter still challenged the provincial particularism of most Junkers by supporting measures that would increase the centralized "unity and power" of the royal administration.[44]

— III —

The growing tension and rivalry between civil service and landed Junkerdom exploded into open conflict during the "revolution from above" that the monarchy and bureaucracy attempted during the Stein-Hardenberg Reform Era of

1807–19. Napoleon provided the catalyst by inflicting crushing military defeats on Prussia in 1806, and then imposing heavy financial indemnities on a Hohenzollern monarchy whose territorial possessions he reduced by almost half in the Franco-Russian Treaty of Tilsit (1807). These disasters persuaded Friedrich Wilhelm III of the necessity for quick and substantive changes in Prussia's governmental apparatus, tax system, military organization, and social and economic structures. In seeking to effect such changes the king relied on untitled officials such as Johann Gottfried Frey, Karl Ferdinand Friese, Barthold Georg Niebuhr, Johann August Sack, and Christian Friedrich Scharnweber. In addition, just as the French nobility at the time of the 1789 Revolution had included an influential clique of liberal aristocrats like the Marquis de Lafayette and the Comte de Mirabeau, so also Prussia's civil service and officers corps during the Stein-Hardenberg Reform Era included a determined coterie of reformist Junkers, prominent among them Theodor von Schön of East Prussia, the Pomeranian Hermann von Boyen, and Wilhelm von Humboldt of Brandenburg.[45] Friedrich Wilhelm III also relied heavily on the advice and leadership of non-Junker German aristocrats, in particular Stein (Minister-President, 1807–8) and Hardenberg (Chancellor, 1810–22). Baron Karl vom Stein (1757–1831), born into a family of German imperial knights in Nassau prior to Napoleon's abolition of the Holy Roman Empire, had become "a determined 'Anglophile' " during his student days at the University of Göttingen, in the Electorate of Hanover.[46] As such he disliked bureaucratic rigidity and advocated representative institutions for all propertied groups on both the local and national levels. Baron Karl August von Hardenberg (1750–1822) also studied at Göttingen, and came from a noble family in Hanover. Yet when he entered Prussian employ in 1790 he seems to have been less of an Anglophile and more of a bureaucratic authoritarian than Stein.[47]

Two of the Stein-Hardenberg reformers' most pressing concerns were the "boundness" of East Elbia's enserfed peasantry and the landed nobility's traditional corporatist privileges, especially their legal monopoly on the ownership of *Rittergüter*, their tax exemptions, and their autocratic control over local government. These appeared to the reformers as antiquated obstacles to three necessary developments: first, the continued growth in power and influence of Prussia's central government and its "enlightened" civil service, which might agree to extend a limited measure of self-government to Prussia's propertied populace; second, the evolution of a healthy social order founded on the "classical liberal" principle of "careers open to talents," which required that the ranks of landed Junkerdom and the army officer corps be opened wide to capable commoners;[48] and third, the increased vitality of Prussia's economic life, which necessitated a "peasant emancipation" *(Bauernbefreiung)* that would liberate the agrarian sector from the inefficient fetters of serfdom. As the Minister of the Interior would explain to Friedrich Wilhelm IV in an 1844 memorandum, the post-1806 reforms constituted an effort to "muster all the material and intellectual resources of the state in order to rebuild from within the strength that the French had broken from without." Since Prussia at that time consisted of "nothing but purely agricultural provinces" (with the exception of mountainous Upper Silesia), the process of "rebirth and renewal" was based primarily on "the emancipation of ground and soil."[49] Nonetheless, two of the reformers' "classical liberal" principles—their respect for formal property rights and their distrust of political democracy—precluded their even attempting a radical reconstruction of the Prussian polity. It is interesting to note that an analogous concern for private property in real estate helped prevent the victorious North and the federal government from attempting a thoroughgoing economic and social reconstruction of the defeated South during the post-1865 "Era of Reconstruction." The New York *Nation* and the *New York Times* seem to have spoken for most Northerners in their responses to "radical" proposals for the confiscation of plantation land and its distribution among ex-slaves. "A division of rich men's lands amongst the landless . . . ," argued the *Nation*, "would give a shock to our whole social and political system from which it would hardly recover without the loss of liberty." According to the *Times*, "any attempt to justify the confiscation of southern land under the pretense of doing justice to the freedmen strikes at the root of all property rights in all sections. It concerns Massachusetts quite as much as Mississippi."[50] To be sure, the failures of both the Stein-Hardenberg reforms and the South's postbellum Reconstruction owed much to the talents of planters and Junkers for determined and organized resistance.

Baron vom Stein desired "more than anything else," says Holborn, "a state that was healthy because of its citizens' devotion to the moral betterment of mankind."[51] Such genuine devotion has always been a rare commodity. Stein knew that most *Rittergut* owners anticipated an increase in the value of their estates due to the additional land they would gain from peasants as compensation for the abolition of personal servitude and feudal dues. While visiting Königsberg in February of 1808, he bluntly informed representatives of the East Prussian nobility that "so unjust and distasteful" an outlook was a major reason for the stagnation of Prussian culture.[52] But Stein held the reigns of government only fourteen months, due to the discovery by agents of Napoleon that Stein was secretly plotting against the French. His successors, the Junkers Baron Karl von Altenstein and Count Alexander von Dohna, displayed considerably less capacity for bold initiative than Stein during their joint ministry of eighteen months (1808–10). After Altenstein, as Minister of Finance, recommended that the province of Silesia be ceded to Napoleon in lieu of the dictated financial "contributions," the king called Hardenberg to office as State Chancellor.[53]

It was during Hardenberg's chancellorship (1810–22) that the reform movement attenuated and eventually fizzled. "The moral objectives so prominent in Stein were heavily outweighed with Hardenberg by practical considerations," concludes Walter Simon; "his chief concerns were power and efficiency."[54] In his famous Riga Memorandum of 1807 Hardenberg had advised Friedrich Wilhelm III that "We must do from above what the French have done from below," that the Prussian monarchy should seek to follow "democratic principles in monarchical government: this seems to me the mixture appropriate to the present *Zeitgeist*." As Chancellor, however, Hardenberg was more concerned about the truncated and threatened monarchy's financial condition and international stature than about the degree to which domestic developments accorded with "democratic principles." Understandably, his overriding concern upon taking office in 1810 was to pay the French indemnities, lest Napoleon decide to do what Czar Alexander had dissuaded the French Emperor from doing in 1807; that is, do away with the Kingdom of Prussia altogether. Yet Hardenberg even reneged on his promise to implement a uniform land tax after his proposal in the fall of 1810 to tax all *Rittergüter* provoked a storm of Junker protests. The nobility in the East Prussian county of Schesten submitted a formal declaration of their refusal to pay the new taxes without additional explanations from the king; and the first two signatories to the declaration, *Rittergut* owners von Collrepp and von Sierakowski, were eventually imprisoned during the winter of 1810–11. Another, weightier protest against the government's imperiousness came from the Brandenburg counties of Lebus, Beeskow, and Storkow. Again the first two signatories—the famous duo Count Friedrich Ludwig von Finckenstein and Friedrich August Ludwig von der Marwitz, whom Ursula Wiese calls "the purest and most important prototype of the Brandenburg Junker *Frondeur*"—went to prison, spending six weeks in Spandau during the summer of 1811.[55] Hardenberg attempted without success to mobilize support for both his tax and agrarian proposals by summoning to Berlin in 1811 a consultative "Assembly of Notables," which was supposed to represent Prussia's chief "occupational groups" *(Berufstände)*. The fact that half of the summoned "notables" were titled noblemen helped make for an obstreporous assembly that the Chancellor quickly adjourned; but at the same time he backed down from his original intention to tax Junker estates.[56] It is interesting to consider the parallels between the financial nationalism of Hardenberg in 1811 and that of U.S. Treasury Secretary Alexander Hamilton twenty years earlier, each confronting strong opposition from spokesmen for provincial or state's rights who feared the growth of centralizing and self-serving monied oligarchies.

It would be excessively cynical to argue that the Chancellor's backing down from tax reform in 1811 had anything to do with his ownership of the Brandenburg *Rittergut* Tempelberg, which he had acquired no later than 1806.[57] At the same time, his acquisition of a knight's estate probably reinforced his elitist judgment, as expressed in the Riga Memorandum, that "the landowner must retain the means of compelling his peasants, laborers, and servants, swiftly and without cost, to fulfill their obligations; and though these people must not be denied a hearing, neither must the landlord be made dependent in these matters on the arbitrary decisions of a judge who may be far away."[58] According to Theodor von Schön, the Chancellor told him in 1810, during a conversation about the Junkers' local police authority, that "He could not and would not give up his manorial right *(gutsherrliches Recht),* and all references to civilized lands could not bring him to another opinion."[59] Hardenberg's original Regulation Edict of 1811, which set guidelines for allowing peasants to become independent proprietors over part of the land they had farmed under serfdom, left the *Rittergut* owner's local judicial and police powers untouched. Moreover, his retrogressive Declaration of 1816 met the Junkers more than half way by excluding the majority of peasants from the possibility of establishing independent farms, thereby assuring their manorial lords an ongoing supply of relatively inexpensive manual laborers. As Ernst Klein has emphasized, the historical record allows no other conclusion "than that the estate owner was first and foremost the benefactor of these agrarian reforms."[60]

The Junkers of Hardenberg's day, like those of the 1840s, did not object to representative assemblies so long as they could dominate them, in traditional corporatist fashion, and use them as weapons in the fight against what they considered expropriatory or radical reforms. Indeed, the compromising of bureaucratic efforts on behalf of an independent peasantry and a uniform land tax owed much to the persistent counterproposals and obstructionist tactics of Junker assemblies on the county and provincial levels.[61] Despite the skepticism of many Junkers about Hardenberg's consultative and provisional National Assembly, which met from 1812 to 1815 and in which noble delegates held a plurality of seats (18, versus 22 for the cities and peasantry), even this assembly behaved "as a tool of the nobility rather than as an arm of the administration," observes Robert Berdahl.[62] Friedrich Wilhelm III's royal decree of May 1815 on "developing representation of the people *(Volk)"* offered the prospect of even greater political influence for Junkerdom. It stipulated that an "assembly of national deputies" was to be elected from among the membership of the corporatist provincial assemblies, and that this assembly would provide "consultation on all matters of legislation which concern the personal and property rights of citizens, including taxation."[63] Yet Hardenberg still hoped to restrict the Junkers' political clout. He and Wilhelm von Humboldt, who served briefly in 1819 as special minister for constitutional affairs, envisioned national, provincial, and local assemblies that, although not empowered to challenge monarchical and bureaucratic authority, would allow substantial representation to the urban middle classes and the peasantry as well as to the owners of knight's estates. Their failure to realize this vision can be ascribed to a number of factors in addition to Junker resistance, including the vehement opposition to any form of political liberalism on the part of Austria's reactionary Prince von Metternich, who wielded great influence over the Prussian king and the newly formed Germanic Confederation. As

James J. Sheehan points out, "The Prussian reformers' defeat on the issue of a state parliament was part of a broad reactionary wave which engulfed central Europe after 1815. Once Napoleon's defeat had removed the main impetus for change, conservative forces in almost every state returned to power and tried to set tighter limits on political activity."[64]

Some of the responsibility for the failure must be attributed to Hardenberg himself, who subordinated the goal of constitutional assemblies to the business of revamping Prussia's bureaucratic structures, partly so as to incorporate the new western provinces acquired at the Congress of Vienna. Furthermore, contrary to Humboldt's demand for equality and independence among cabinet ministers, the Chancellor insisted on retaining his own prerogatives as a "superminister" empowered to interfere directly in all departments and enjoying exclusive access to the king. Hardenberg, apparently believing that he alone was capable of controlling both king and Junkers, soon dismissed the proud and intractable Humboldt. This dismissal followed quickly upon the resignation of war minister Hermann von Boyen, who refused to accede in the king's wish to subordinate the national guard *(Landwehr)*, with its predominantly middle-class officers, to the Junker-dominated regular army. Boyen, who had overseen the creation of the *Landwehr* in 1813–14 as part of Prussia's "War of Liberation" from Napoleon, viewed the continued independence of the national guard as an essential corollary to the reformist goal of creating a citizenry whose loyalty to the state would justify a gradual extension of political rights. With the departures from office of Humboldt and Boyen disappeared any real chance of fostering even a limited measure of constitutional electoral government in Prussia, and the evolution of bureaucratic and military authoritarianism at Berlin and Potsdam continued apace.[65]

But the formal demise of Hardenberg's constitutional plans did not come until 1821, when Friedrich Wilhelm III accepted the recommendations of a royal commission that Prussia had no need for a national constitution, and that the only representative assemblies appropriate to the Prussian polity were the traditional "provincial estates in the spirit of the ancient Germanic constitutions," that is, organized by estates and with noble predominance.[66] In 1823, after Hardenberg's death, the monarchy promulgated a general directive concerning the provincial assemblies, according to which the seats in each *Landtag* were to be divided among the three traditional *Stände* of the realm: landed Junkerdom *(Ritterschaft)*, the towns, and the peasantry. "The provincial estates are the lawful mouthpiece of the various estates of Our loyal subjects in each province," read the royal decree.[67] *Rittergut* owners received the lion's share of the representation. Out of 432 seats in the assemblies of the six eastern provinces, the *Ritterschaft* held 200; and in four of these provinces (Brandenburg, Pomerania, Prussia, and Posen) Junkerdom enjoyed an absolute majority of seats. In order to be elected a provincial representative of the *Ritterschaft,* a Junker had to have owned his estate for at least a decade, a requirement that helped to maintain the predominance of the old nobility in the *Landtage,* although the Crown could grant exceptions to the rule.[68] Nevertheless, the provincial assemblies were in reality more cosmetic concessions to an anachronistic tradition of provincial autonomy than organs of real political influence, for the preponderance of political power on the provincial as well as national level lay with the royal bureaucracy.

Much more important than the *Landtage* to the survival of Junkerdom's traditional corporatist privileges were the ordinances concerning county govenment *(Kreisordnungen)* promulgated for Brandenburg and Pomerania in 1825, and for the other provinces in 1827–28. In each of East Elbia's 237 county assemblies *(Kreistage),* which continued to nominate candidates for country commissioner, or *Landrat,* the proprietors of knight's estates had one vote apiece, each town had a single vote, and the entire peasant population had three votes. On the eve of the 1848–49 revolution all the county assemblies in Prussia numbered about 10,000 estate owners and fewer than 2000 delegates representing both the towns and the peasants (970 and 975 respectively).[69] At the United Diet of 1847 a non-noble delegate from the Brandenburg town of Prenzlau bemoaned the unbalanced make-up of his county's assembly, which included 50 *Rittergut* owners, three representatives from three towns with a combined population of 18,000, and three representatives for the 30,000 people living in peasant villages. Yet the *Rittergut* owners paid only 18,000 *Thaler* in taxes, whereas the towns paid 42,000 *Thaler* and the peasant villages 55,000 *Thaler.*[70] To the mind of an Old Prussian ideologue, however, the *Kreistage* constituted "the most interesting and significant part of the corporatist organization of our Fatherland."[71] Although the 1848–49 revolution spurred a temporary restructuring of local government (in 1850–52) that was as much bureaucratic as democratic, a royal decree of 1853 re-established the corporatist assemblies on both the county and provincial levels. In 1863 the *Kreistage* of East Elbia included 11,764 Junkers, 1,069 town delegates, and 1,315 delegates from the villages.[72]

— IV —

The royal commission of 1821 which endorsed the corporatist provincial assemblies was chaired by the Crown Prince, the future Friedrich Wilhelm IV (ruled 1840–58). Without this invaluable ally at court, Old Prussian Junkers simply would not have exerted anywhere near the political clout they wielded from the 1820s to the 1850s. The Crown Prince's tutor during the Napoleonic Wars, the cleric Johann Peter Friedrich Ancillon, had encouraged in him a passionate distrust of eighteenth-century rationalism and the principles of the French Revolution, in conjunction with a respect for traditional corporatist representation as an institutional check on monarchical despotism.[73] Old Prussian ideologue Friedrich Julius Stahl, in his 1861 eulogy to the king, declared that Friedrich Wilhelm IV had recognized his royal calling as that of defending "the eternal truths of faith and justice" against the " 'negative spirit of the age' ": that is, "revolution, materialistically oriented civilization, nationalism, 'liberalism,' 'the ideas of 1789,' " all products of the philosophical and political teachings of the seventeenth and eighteenth centuries, which preached "emancipation from God's revelation and divine order."[74]

During the early 1820s the future king became the center of a "romantic-conservative," "Christian-Germanic" clique of ideological Junkers in Berlin, the "Club on *Wilhelmstrasse*," also known as the "Crown Prince's Circle." Here, wrote Gerhard Ritter in 1913, "were the political and social class interests of the old Prussian aristocracy dogmatized into a consistent system,"[75] that is, into Old Prussian ideology. The *Wilhelmstrasse* Club comprised mainly "Neo-Pietist" noble zealots from Brandenburg and Pomerania who were closely involved in the religiously fundamentalist and politically reactionary "Awakening" then current in northern, Protestant Germany. Many of the Club's members—prominent among them the brothers Ludwig and Leopold von Gerlach and their brothers-in-law Adolf von Thadden-Trieglaff and Ernst Senfft von Pilsach—remained a tightly knit and influential clique for several decades. They helped to provide organizers and sponsors for two important publications that propagandized Old Prussian ideology: the *Berlin Political Weekly (Berliner Politische Wochenblatt*, 1831–41), founded in response to the French Revolution of 1830; and the *New Prussian Gazette (Neue Preussische Zeitung)*, founded in Berlin during the summer of 1848, and better known as the *Kreuzzeitung*, or "Newpaper of the Cross."[76] These men and their publications sought to protect landed Junkerdom's privileges, power, and probity against the "leveling" impact of both bureaucratic authority from above and liberal democracy from below. Most important, Friedrich Wilhelm IV shared their aim of reasserting Junkerdom's political independence and respon-sibilities, and wished with them to re-establish something of the collegial loyalty that they believed had existed between monarchy and nobility prior to the devel-opment of bureaucratic absolutism. From 1848 to 1858, via their input in the king's "kitchen cabinet," or so-called *Kamarilla*, Old Prussian corporatists played an important part in breaking the force of liberal and democratic movements in Prussia and the German Confederation. The most impressive step toward the realization of their corporatist vision came in 1853–1854 with the transformation of the plutocratically elected upper chamber of Prussia's new legislature into a House of Lords *(Herrenhaus)* in which the landed nobility predominated. This House of Lords, "an agency for the interests of Junkerdom" in the words of Thomas Nipperdey, enjoyed veto power over legislation passed by the lower chamber, and survived until the demise of the Hohenzollern monarchy in 1918.[77]

During the *Vormärz* years (1815–48) Old Prussian corporatists often found literary support for their position in those "romantic" writers of the late eigh-teenth and early nineteenth century who idealized the pre-absolutist Middle Ages as an era of Christian virtue and aristocratic honor. Yet Old Prussian ideologues also relished the unromantic and naturalistic tendentiousnes of the massive *Restoration of Political Science* (6 vols., 1816–22), the principal work of Swiss-German patrician Karl Ludwig von Haller (1768–1854).[78] In Haller, says Sigmund Neumann, Junker spokesmen discovered "a powerful and manageable theory of corporatist monarchy."[79] It is significant, however, that the "Christian-Germanic" pietists were never comfortable with Haller's naturalistic, materialistic premises, and found his conception of the patrimonial state objectionable for what Ludwig von Gerlach termed its "defective theology" *(mangelhefte Gotteslehre)*.[80] For Haller the feudal authority of the prince over his aristocratic vassals, and the feudal authority of these vassals over their dependents, derived solely from the patrimonial, hereditary powers that both prince and aristocracy enjoyed as large landholders, even though this hierarchical system was indirectly sanctioned by God the Creator as author of the "natural law" that the majority of weak and powerless men must seek protection with the few strong and powerful ones. But the self-styled "Christian-Germanic" pietists around Crown Prince Friedrich Wilhelm insisted that the legitimacy of both monarchical authority and Junkerdom's corporatist privileges derived directly and immediately from God. As Wolfgang Scheel explains, "the idea of the theocratic corporatist state *(Ständestaat)* founded firmly in God separated the circle associated with the *Berlin Political Weekly* from Haller, who had dissolved the state into pure power relationships."[81]

During the 1840s Haller was supplanted as Old Prussian corporatism's ideological kingpin by Friedrich Julius Stahl (1802–61), who had first won academic renown for *The Philosophy of Law* (2 vols., 1830–37). Stahl was a Bavarian Jew (born Julius Jolson) who had made an apparently devout conversion to Lutheranism in his late teens, had been educated at the Protestant University of Erlangen, and was a law professor at the University of Würzburg before the newly crowned Friedrich Wilhelm IV invited him to join the faculty at the University of Berlin in 1840. During the 1840s Stahl became an associate of the Gerlach brothers, a regular contributor to the *Kreuzzeitung,* and the leading Old Prussian spokesman in the upper house of the Prussian legislature in 1849–50.[82] Stahl rejected "the private law-feudal doctrine of Haller," insisting that the monarch's authority derived not from his position as the most powerful landholder in the kingdom, nor from reciprocal agreements with the landed aristocracy, but from "the essence of the institution" as a divinely ordained agent upholding God's laws on earth. "The patriarchal condition must become an institutional one, the monarchy merely as a private landholder must become the monarchy which is through and through the representative of God and a public office. . . ."[83] Stahl's thought thus completed the union of throne and altar that had been evolving in the thinking of "Christian-Germanic" corporatists since the 1820s. In doing so he seems to have confirmed the truth of historical sociologist Alfred von Martin's observation that immediate historical circumstances dictated whether Prussian conservatives put greater ideological emphasis on aristocratic freedoms and corporatist privileges *("gutes altes Recht")*, or on royal authority and the "monarchical principle." Against Stein, Hardenberg, and their bureaucratic cohorts, Junker spokesmen emphasized the former. However, the overthrow of Bourbon Charles X in 1830 raised once again the specter of popular revolution, thereby shattering the illusory hope that the defeat of Napoleon, the Congress of Vienna, and the post-1815 Restoration orchestrated by Metternich had exorcized this more fearsome demon from Europe. After the Crown Prince's coronation in 1840, and especially after the outbreak of popular revolution in 1848, Old Prussian ideologues talked more and more about the sanctity of monarchical authority. In von Martin's words, "only where the danger of a revolution from below appears threatening, can conservatism opt for absolutism as the lesser evil."[84]

Yet Stahl did not endorse traditional monarchical absolutism on the model of Louis XIV or Frederick the Great. In *The Monarchical Principle* (1845) Stahl anticipated and provided an ideological solution to the pressing problem that would confront the Hohenzollern monarchy and landed Junkerdom after 1848: that is, how to reconcile divine-right monarchy and aristocratic privilege with a formal constitution and popularly elected assembly. Although the Western, specifically English model of constitutionalism upheld "the parliamentary principle" that the king's authority be subordinate to that of parliament, wrote Stahl, German constitutionalism must endorse "the monarchical principle," whereby ultimate sovereignty resides not with the citizenry and its delegates, but with the king, who functions as "the positively shaping power in the state." "The monarchical principle demands finally and primarily, and consists first and foremost of the fact, that the prince has the right and power to rule himself." At the same time, the prince should seek the advice and assistance of a corporately structured representative assembly, to which the constitution guarantees regular meetings, the right of petition, and perhaps the prerogative to alter the level of taxation and expenditure for "optional" versus "necessary" items in the royal budget. The assembly should include delegates not simply from the three traditional estates of landowners, town residents, and peasants, but from all important occupational groups *(Berufstände)*. "Every healthy representation in our time must represent the national unity *and* the corporate structure, it must represent the essential strata *(Lagen)* and occupations, 'the country' *(Land)*, *and* the essence of 'the people' *(Volk)*."[85] This system he would later term "the constitutional estates monarchy," as opposed to both "the old estates monarchy" and "absolute monarchy."[86] To be sure, the dominant occupational estate was to be the large landowners.[87] As Stahl wrote in *The Philosophy of Law*, at the beginning of a chapter entitled "The Governmental Rights of the Landowner," "It is the natural condition, that social position is the foundation for political position, that is, that those who through extensive property have in reality a power over others, are also legally the bearers of governmental authority over them."[88]

— V —

Despite Stahl's growing importance during the 1840s, the most authoritative explication of Old Prussian corporatist thought published prior to the 1848 revolution was *Concerning Monarchy and Representative Bodies in Prussia* (1846). The author, Karl von Lancizolle, was a royal adviser and law professor at the University of Berlin who had been one of the original "Crown Prince's Circle" in the 1820s. According to Lancizolle, Prussia could not really be termed a "nation," since the kingdom's population encompassed not only Slavic peoples but elements from both great stems of the German race: the Franks *(Franken)* on the Rhine and the Saxons *(Sachsen)* of Westphalia and the Elbe region. Moreover, each Prussian province had a "strongly pronounced individuality *(Eigentumlichkeit)*" that was often the product of centuries of historical development, and each provincial assembly served to protect "the peculiar institutions of the province." The principal internal threat to the provincial assemblies, suggested Lancizolle, sprang from a veritable "political religion" among those urbanites with even a smattering of education, a religion based on "the entirely abstract concept of the state in modern political doctrine, as the Civil Code (of the 1790s) has implanted it in the current style of thinking of our bureaucratic civil servants, along with everything that has to do with centralization, codification, the passion for levelling and uniformity, the despotism of laws, the mechanization of the entire legal order."[89] In other words, since Prussia had not yet experienced a popular revolution from below, corporatist Junkerdom's major domestic enemy was the civil bureaucracy. Although proslavery ideologues in the Old South did not confront a formidable federal bureaucracy in the United States, there is a striking parallel between the provincial particularism of Old Prussian thought and the emphasis on states' rights in Southern political thought. Much like Old Prussian ideologues, Jeffersonian "Old Republicans" of the early national era, and then anti-tariff and proslavery sectionalists during the antebellum decades, often railed against centralized or consolidated political power as a threat to liberty, while glorifying the diffusion of power among the states as the surest guarantee of local self-government.[90] Of course, just as Southern planters had nothing but disdain for the sort of monarchical corporatism favored by most Junkers, so Junkers scorned the American brand of republican constitutionalism. At the United Diet of 1847 Adolph von Werdeck of Brandenburg insisted that Prussia must hold fast to "the principle of estatist organization," and cited both France and the United States as negative examples. France had been governed under eight different constitutions in sixty years, he declared, and as of 1847 only 250,000 eligible voters governed a nation of 34 million. As for the North American Republic, whose 17 million residents included 2.5 million slaves, Werdeck saw it as no model of freedom. "The estatist component, I repeat, is the only foundation of political freedom."[91]

Given Old Prussian fears of bureaucratic despotism, it is ironic that when a revolution from below erupted during the spring of 1848 and established the first popularly elected parliament in Prussia's history, "a good part" of the royal bureaucracy reacted with as much hostility as did the Junkers.[92] During *Vormärz* increasing numbers of civil servants, especially in the higher ranks of the administrative (versus judicial) bureaucracy, had begun to fear that Europe's mounting movement for civil equality and democratic politics posed a threat to both responsible government and the bureaucracy's privileged corporatist status under the Prussian Civil Code. At the same time, as more and more knight's estates fell into the hands of commoners, more and more sons and grandsons of noble *Rittergut* owners became dependent on the bureaucracy for secure and genteel employment. According to John R. Gillis, by 1839 some 46 percent of Prussia's higher bureaucracy (that is, above the county commissioners in the chain of command) came from the landed nobility.[93] During the first half of the nineteenth century, while commoners were acquiring greater numbers of knight's estates, the number of noble households rose dramatically, due to East Elbia's rapid population growth and the fact that in Prussia the law of primogeniture applied only to the family estate and not, as in England, to the noble title as well. Circa 1800, when 85 to 90 percent of Prussia's *Rittergüter* belonged to noblemen, the estimated number of titled families (20,000) was already nearly double the number of knight's estates. By the mid-1850s, when less than 60 percent of *Rittergüter* remained in noble hands, the number of titled families had risen to at least 30,000.[94] Since the army officer corps could not absorb all of these "surplus" noblemen, more and more aristocratic offspring joined the ranks of the bureaucracy. In the words of Walter Görlitz, "The influx of impoverished lesser nobility into middle and upper bureaucratic positions also strengthened the bureaucracy's feudal perceptions."[95] Although a university diploma did not become a formal prerequisite for admission to the civil service until 1846, the number of young noblemen pursuing university studies, the law in particular, began to rise substantially during the 1830s.[96] Legal training and expertise were becoming in bureaucratic East Elbia the sort of genteel high road to public office and elite status that they had been in the parliamentary South since the late colonial era.

Although Old Prussian corporatists always denounced the dangers of bureaucratic absolutism, they saw a potentially greater evil in the liberal movement for constitutional, representative government and the concomitant democratic principle of popular sovereignty. Liberalism and democracy often seemed like a virulent disease spreading to Germany from France, which compounded her sin of 1789 by experiencing another anti-legitimist revolution in 1830. Adolf von Thadden-Trieglaff complained in an 1842 address that the common people of the day expected their princes to "make them happy and prosperous"; and if a monarch failed, his subjects would protest through "a babbling and scheming chamber of deputies." Such was the result of a liberal constitution like "the botched piece of work by the French on the far side of the Rhine," as opposed to the constructive "corporatist constitutions" east of the Rhine.[97] In similar fashion did Lancizolle condemn the "modern system of representation" advocated by the liberal "men of 'progress,' of 'light' " whose writings appeared in the daily papers. This system of representation was foreign to "the Christian-Germanic nature of our state," which had not yet dissolved into a society of "atoms." Constitutionalism and popular sovereignty (*Volks-Souverainetät*) would inevitably lead to the sort of harsh absolutism that had emerged in post-1789 France under Napoleon, and could even result in "the most extreme phantasy of an un-Christian and unGermanic communism." Lancizolle noted that Friedrich Wilhelm IV was interested in summoning a united Prussian *Landtag* which would represent "a restoration of authentic corporatist life" in Prussia. Such a national assembly would serve as a dam against "vulgar liberalism and constitutionalism," with their attendant scheme of representation according to pure numbers or amount of taxes paid.[98]

— VI —

Lancizolle himself took part in the several years of deliberations that resulted in the king's decision to convene a "United Diet" (*Vereinigte Landtag*) in Berlin in 1847. This Diet—a composite of all the provincial assemblies, with 458 of the 613 delegates coming from the eastern provinces—was intended both to quell the swelling movement for a Prussian constitution and parliament and to provide a compliant assembly that would sanction the monarchy's request for new taxes and loans, in accord with an 1820 law on Prussia's state debt. However, a great many *Ritterschaft* delegates, particularly among those from Silesia and provincial Prussia, proved to be "conservative opportunists."[99] Contrary to the king's wishes, these Junkers joined with constitutional liberals from the western provinces (prominent among them the Rhenish businessmen Ludolf Camphausen and David Hansemann) in refusing by a 360–179 vote to approve two major state loans without royal assurances that the Diet would henceforth be summoned on a regular basis. As in the 1810s, many Junkers could endorse a national assembly in which their class would be pre-eminent. Friedrich Wilhelm IV dissolved the Diet, says Gordon Craig, "in a general atmosphere of recrimination and disgust."[100]

Popular unrest soon took control of events from the hands of the Junkers as well as the king, and played temporarily into the hands of the liberals. The principal short-term cause of this popular unrest, as it manifested itself in Berlin during the "March Days" of 1848 and in the East Elbian countryside during the spring and summer months, was an economic crisis that had begun in 1845. This crisis resulted from a combination of many factors: rapid population growth in the rural districts; potato blight, poor harvests, and the resultant high food prices; and high unemployment among urban artisans, badly hurt by declining local demand and competition from English and Rhenish factories. The "March Days" in Berlin, explains William Langer, resulted from "an insurrection of the workers, by which must be understood artisans and journeymen in the traditional trades, since the number of factory workers was still insignificant." Although there were some radical democrats and even a few socialists active among the Berlin insurrectionaries, says Langer, the rebellious workers were in fact "less interested in revolutionary theory than in securing better wages and shorter hours."[101] Sparks from the cities helped to ignite the fires of rural discontent that had been smoldering for decades, ever since Hardenberg's program of "peasant emancipation" had not only limited the number of former serfs who could establish independent farms and free themselves from traditional feudal dues to their manorial lords but also allowed *Rittergut* owners to incorporate much peasant and common land into their estates as compensation for the abolition of feudal obligations. A five-member legislative committee (including three noblemen) would conclude in the spring of 1849 that the survival of servile dues in labor and in kind for "unregulated" peasants constituted "the most important source of discontent and dissatisfaction in all classes of the rural population."[102] After the revolution the new Prussian parliament finally provided in 1850 for the extension of "regulation" to all peasants and for the commutation of all remaining feudal obligations.

In 1848 there was also considerable "discontent and dissatisfaction" among the cottagers *(Insten)* and other day-laborers *(Gutstagelöhner)* who lived and labored on Junker estates. Recall that these workers were still subject to the Junkers' control over local government, and that their ranks included some "unregulated" peasants who had been compelled to give up their land to *Rittergut* owners. The desire to acquire land and become independent farmers seems to have been as strong among the day-laborers as it was among the South's newly freed slaves at the end of the Civil War. Just as many freedmen expected emancipation to include "forty acres and a mule," so did the expectation spread "like wildfire" in Pomerania that "every *Tagelöhner* should have three *Morgen* of crop land, a *Morgen* of meadow, lodging and pasturage for a cow, three sheep and geese."[103] This is not to suggest that most day-laborers, or most ex-slaves, cast off habits of dependence and deference by becoming violently self-assertive; for they could crave land and independence and still have no desire or inclination to inflict punishment or humiliation on the persons of their lords and masters. "When the owner of an estate in eastern Pomerania returned home from Berlin," reports Erich Jordan, "his people explained to him that they had divided things up. To him they had awarded the manor house." Jordan also recounts the story of a Baron von Hoverbeck in provincial Prussia whose day-laborers, out of appreciation for their lord's "constant helpfulness," were willing to take only half of the estate for themselves. Perhaps the Baron was as bewildered by their behavior as was a Southern master by the behavior of his enslaved body servant on a Civil War battlefield. The slave "risked his life to carry his wounded master to safety," reports Leon Litwack, "and then remounted the master's horse and fled to the Yankee lines."[104] The relations between Southern planters and slaves, like those between East Elbian lords and dependent laborers, often manifested a myriad of tensions, ambiguities, and contradictions.

Junkers should not have been too surprised in 1848 by the extent of discontent and unrest among the rural population, because during the 1840s East Elbia's agricultural journals offered a number of perspicacious warnings. For example, in 1844 Pomerania's *General Agricultural Monthly* published an essay whose author, a Captain von Versen (probably Eduard von Versen, owner of two estates in the Pomeranian county of Belgard), expressed great concern about the ongoing concentration of wealth in Prussia in the hands of the "lords of agriculture," the "lords of industry," and the "lords of commerce" (*Grundherren, Fabrikherren,* and *Handelsherren*). This concentration of wealth was accompanied by the growing "impoverishment" (*Pauperismus*) of the propertyless "fourth estate." Versen's analysis of the situation in East Elbia anticipated many of the conclusions reached by recent historians: the prices of land and its products were rising due to increasing demand from abroad as well as from a growing population at home; and since the number of rural workers was rising more quickly than the number of available jobs, the wages of day-laborers remained at a subsistence level. The common man, insisted von Versen, wanted first and foremost property and independence. It would redound to everyone's benefit if steps were taken to enlarge the class of self-sufficient smallholders owning 12 to 19 acres (20 to 30 *Morgen*) of medium-quality land. Otherwise, "Communism," "Fourierism," and "St. Simonism" would win more and more popular appeal. "Necessity makes thieves, and if the manorial lord (*Grundherr*) creates want through excessive demands (on his workers), then it is not a reprehensible act if they take the first recourse against him."[105] Labor unrest and employer anxiety were especially acute in mountainous Upper Silesia, where some Junkers had developed mines, foundaries, and linen textile factories on their estates, and where handloom workers had staged a large-scale insurrection in 1844.[106] Silesian *Rittergut* owner and government adviser (*Geh. Rath*) Alexander von Bally-Chutow made it clear during the mid-1840s that rural *Pauperismus* was breeding unrest and discontent among the laboring classes. A local business society like the one in the county Rybnick should strive, he argued, "not only to keep itself distant from *Communismus,* which the present-day preaches, but to step openly and relentlessly against it, to battle it everywhere it wants to take root."[107]

However, it was principally urban street fighting and barricades during mid-March of 1848 that drove the shaken Friedrich Wilhelm IV to call the old United Diet back into session. He then promised that a new constituent assembly would be elected for the purpose of drafting a national constitution, and appointed a liberal ministry led by the moderates Camphausen and Hansemann. After a special deputation from Breslau warned the king on 22 March that the Silesian city would follow the riotous example of Berlin unless the future National Assembly were elected by universal manhood suffrage, the king and then Minister-President Adolf Heinrich Count von Arnim-Boitzenburg reluctantly agreed. The old United Diet, during its brief convocation in early April, endorsed extending the suffrage to all males twenty-four and older by a vote of 271–232.[108] The 1 May election constituted an overwhelming victory for the constitutional liberals and testified to the disastrous impact of political democracy on landed Junkerdom's power and influence. Whereas 73 of the 291 delegates from the six East Elbian provinces (that is, 25 percent) were peasants, shopkeepers, artisans, and laborers, large landowners numbered only 22, 12 nobles and 10 commoners (that is, 7.5 percent)[109] 16 of the 22 came from the anomalous provinces of Posen and Prussia. In Posen, which sent 11 large landowners to the National Assembly, aristocrats were often leaders of the Polish nationalist movement against Prussian rule; and the five large landowners from provincial Prussia reflected a long tradition of aristocratic "liberalism" in East Prussia, dating back to the *Ritterschaft*'s maneuvers during the sixteenth and seventeenth centuries to play off Poland against the Hohenzollerns in order to win a high degree of autonomy for the provincial estates.[110] In contrast, Brandenburg and Pomerania, "the core regions of Prussian conservatism,"[111] elected between them only three large landowners as delegates to the National Asembly. The Assembly was dominated by moderate liberals from what James Sheehan terms Prussia's "educated elites"—that is, state administrators, state judges, and free professionals, who together accounted for 60 percent of all the delegates.[112] The election results served to debunk the expectations of those Junkers, including Otto von Bismarck, who believed that the rural masses would instinctively rally behind the Junkers as leaders of a monarchical counter-revolution. Although deep-seated loyalty to the crown and distrust of urban society does seem to have characterized rural East Elbia, "the Junkers' calculation of a counter-stroke emerging in the countryside under their leadership included a serious error," explains Richard Schult. That error was the assumption that "an identity of interests" existed between most estate owners and those working in the fields, and that therefore the rural populace looked upon manorial lords as their natural leaders.[113]

A quick and firm "Old Prussian" denunciation of the March Days came from the prolific pen of Ludwig von Gerlach (1795–1877), who had served as president of the Magdeburg Court of Appeals since 1844. To the minds of Ludwig and his brother Leopold, God himself had ordained for Prussia a system of monarchical authority and aristocratic privilege. What Ludwig wrote in his memoirs about himself and his brother during the late 1810s, during Hardenberg's chancellorship, was actually better applicable to their activities during the revolutionary crisis of 1848–49: "We fought with passion and enthusiasm against Rousseau's revolutionary state from below, and we fought for the state that comes from God."[114] After Berlin had exploded with escalating confrontations between 13 and 18 March 1848, leading to the withdrawal of troops from the city and the king's decision to behave in public like a constitutional monarch, Ludwig issued an "Appeal to My Comrades *(Standesgenossen)*" on 26 March.[115] This document proclaimed that the revolution ignited in Paris in February had spread to Prussia, and threatened to reduce the country to the degraded status of France—that is, "suffering under the capricious whimsies of the rabble *(Pöbel)* in the capital city." Although the riots and barricades had caught supporters of the status quo "scattered and unprepared," said Gerlach, the army remained loyal to King and Fatherland, and had managed to contain the violence to Berlin. (This was a self-serving or self-deluding observation. Gordon Craig explains that "It was the confused, and not entirely intentional, withdrawal of the troops from the city on 19 March which placed the party of constitutional reform in effective control of events"; and it was this temporary liberal victory that restored order to the streets of Berlin.[116]) It was high time, insisted Gerlach, for all estates and classes loyal to the monarchy to take the debates over Prussia's future out of the hands of the "raging vulgar masses *(tobenden Pöbelmassen),*" and to do battle for a cause "whose honor and worth is independent of every earthly success." The accommodationist stance taken by the United Diet in early April disgusted Ludwig von Gerlach. Only during the summer months would significant numbers of less doctrinaire Junkers begin to recover from the immobilizing sense of confused despair that had gripped them during the spring. Gerlach's "Newspaper of the Cross" (whose first issue appeared on 30 June), the proliferation of Junker-dominated agitational associations like the "Union for King and Fatherland" (founded in July) and Bülow-Cummerow's Junker Parliament of August together signified the birth of an expansive conservative political movement, a fledgling "organized conservatism" working to promote "a radical counterrevolutionary politics."[117]

Although Gerlach's self-described *Junkerpartei* denounced the National Assembly as a *Tagelöhnerparlament* and called for its dissolution, the initiative for a successful counter-revolution in Prussia had to come from the king and the army which he commanded. Friedrich Wilhelm IV remained deeply hostile to parliamentary government, and relied less for advice on his cabinet ministers than on the Old Prussian members of his *Kamarilla,* or "kitchen cabinet," whose pre-eminent figures in 1848 were the generals Leopold von Gerlach and Friedrich Wilhelm von Rauch.[118] During August and September conflict between monarchy and assembly centered on who had authority over the military. In October the king and his advisers became indignant when the Prussian Assembly adopted a draft constitution whose provisions included abolishing noble titles and deleting the phrase "by the grace of God" from the royal title. On 2 November the king appointed a new government under Minister-President Count Friedrich Wilhelm Brandenburg, a relative of the monarch, owner of several *Rittergüter,* and the military commandant in Breslau, whom Ludwig von Gerlach had recommended for the post as early as July.[119] The new ministry, emboldened by the Hapsburg army's reconquest of Vienna from the forces of revolution at the end of October, announced on 9 November that renewed violence in the streets of Berlin necessitated both the imposition of martial law and the adjournment of the Assembly until 27 November, when it would reconvene in a small provincial town near Berlin. Within a week of the adjournment, notes William James Orr, "the entire capital had been subjected to a military 'state of siege' which soon brought to an effective end most activities and publications of the Berlin radical movement."[120] This outcome brings to mind what Bismarck later considered "the old motto of 1848 . . . *'Gegen Demokraten helfen nur Soldaten.'* ("Against democrats only soldiers are of use.")[121]

On 5 December the king ordered the National Assembly formally dissolved, and at the same time bestowed upon his subjects what became known as the "imposed constitution" *(oktroyierte Verfassung).* This constitution emphasized the divine-right character of the Hohenzollern monarchy, and made both the appointment of cabinet ministers and the oversight of the army solely royal prerogatives. Yet because the Brandenburg ministry recognized the necessity of calming the storm of revolution by stealing some of its thunder, the new constitution also contained many concessions to the Assembly's draft document, notably a bicameral legislature whose second chamber was to be elected, at least provisionally, by universal manhood suffrage. When elections for this lower house were held in January and February of 1849, the increasing sophistication and growing effectiveness of the electoral strategies employed by conservative associations helped large landowners to win a few more seats than they had garnered in the previous spring's elections to the National Assembly: 39 seats (11 percent of the delegates), up from 27 seats (less than 7 percent of the delegates).[122] Yet the Junkers and their anti-revolutionary allies in the upper bureaucracy and officer corps were hardly satisfied with such modest successes. Ludwig von Gerlach spoke for much of Junkerdom when he wrote in the *Kreuzzeitung* that continuation of the democratic suffrage endangered the "organic body of the people" and menaced "everything and all freedom with wild anarchy and tyranny."[123]

The Second Chamber chosen in early 1849 was itself dissolved by royal decree on 27 April, after it had voted in favor of lifting martial law and approving the liberal constitution for a unified Germany proposed by the Frankfurt Parliament. On 30 May the Ministry of the Interior promulgated a new electoral law that constituted "a kind of coup d'état" against the democrats and that survived until the end of World War I.[124] (The Interior Minister was Baron Otto von Manteuffel, an experienced bureaucrat, owner of several Brandenburg *Rittergüter,* and, in Holborn's words, "the chief political brain of the cabinet";[125]

he would become Minister-President in November of 1850.) Manteuffel's electoral law established the infamous three-class suffrage, which insured a lower house more affluent and less radical than one elected under universal manhood suffrage. Although all adult males could still vote under the new arrangement, they were divided into three voting classes, each of which paid in the aggregate one-third of the direct taxes collected by the monarchy, and each of which elected one-third of the lower chamber's deputies. Consequently, the first and second voting classes, comprising less than one-fifth of the citizenry in 1849, together chose twice as many members of the lower house as did the third voting class, comprising over four-fifths of the electorate.[126] Instead of a parliament organized along traditional corporatist lines, Prussia now had a plutocratic assembly, one that privileged commercial and industrial wealth as well as *Rittergut* ownership. The three-class system had antecedents in local government voting ordinances instituted in the southwest German state of Baden in 1837 and in the Prussian Rhineland in 1845, areas where the urban bourgeoisie and landed aristocracy shared political power on the local level. Although the three-class suffrage "derived from the plutocratic-capitalist spirit, and not from the corporate-feudal," observes Heinrich Heffter, "the result was that while it favored the upper middle class in the cities, in the rural districts it favored the aristocratic landed estate."[127] Consequently, when we compare the outcome of the plutocratic elections in July of 1849 with the results of democratic elections earlier in the year, we find that the number of large landowners winning seats doubled, from 39 to 78 (22 percent of the delegates).[128] As we would expect, the overall political tone of the Second Chamber elected in July was decidedly more rightist than that of the lower house elected earlier in the year, although "conservative" and "ministerial" delegates still did not constitute a majority.

Thanks to the combined influence of the three-class suffrage, voter mobilization by conservative associations, and government interference in elections (especially via the *Landräte*), subsequent lower houses elected in 1852 and 1855 contained "conservative" monarchical majorities. That is, these majorities included some doctrinaire "Old Prussian" adherents to the *Kreuzzeitung* faction of Ludwig von Gerlach and Stahl, but consisted primarily of "ministerial" loyalists who followed the lead of the royal cabinet. Although the Old Prussian emphasis on corporatist anti-centralism led to recurring conflicts with the bureaucratic-ministerial conservatives during the 1850s, both factions agreed on the necessity for a common front against constitutional liberals and radical democrats.[129] To borrow a phrase from liberal parliamentarian Karl Twesten, the conservatives were "hermetically closed toward the outside, torn by strife and animosities within."[130] Heinrich Heffter observes that "The instinct for power, which for most Junkers weighed more heavily than all ideologies—most actively in Bismarck, although he rose (politically) as a follower of the extreme right—drew them after as before (the revolutionary crisis of 1848–49) to the closest attachment to the monarchy, which still appeared as the most secure and reliable prop of aristocratic privilege; the Prussian monarchy was, however, essentially a bureaucratic state *(Beamtenstaat),* and the nobility was represented in the administrative bureaucracy in great numbers."[131]

To be sure, Old Prussian Junkers continued for years to advocate a lower chamber organized along corporatist lines, because the three-class suffrage did not award sufficient political weight and prestige to landed property.[132] Even the iconoclastic Otto von Bismarck paid homage to the corporatist vision when he claimed in the 1890s that his political "ideal" had always been a monarchy sharing authority with "an independent national representation organized by estates or occupational groups." Because he saw "in the decline of agriculture one of the greatest dangers for our national stability," Bismarck clearly believed that landowners should constitute the pre-eminent group in the ideal national assembly.[133] It is worth emphasizing that the three-class suffrage based an individual's voting power on the amount of direct taxes he paid, and that most *Rittergut* land was exempt from taxes on land until 1861. Hence, the three-class suffrage law served during the post-1849 "Era of Reaction" under Manteuffel to reduce somewhat Junkerdom's electoral strength vis-à-vis affluent bourgeoisie.[134] Yet a good many "liberal" merchants, industrialists, professionals, and bureaucrats apparently would have preferred an outright propertied restriction of the vote to those deemed economically "independent."[135] Rhenish businessman David Hansemann, writing in 1850, maintained that it would have been better "to establish the right to vote everywhere in Germany so that the ballot is exercised only by those possessing property and by those who, through position, occupation, or cultivation *(Bildung),* have as a rule a certain independence."[136] Nonetheless, the abolition of equal manhood suffrage brought immense relief both to Junkers and urban patricians, and helped make possible a "right liberal-conservative compromise" in 1849.[137] After the July 1849 elections, Count Friedrich zu Dohna-Lauck of provincial Prussia expressed his hope that the three-class suffrage was only the first step toward establishing a corporatist scheme of representative government under which large landowners would enjoy their traditional predominance. Nonetheless, he saw the three-class system as decidedly superior to a democratic suffrage, which led to class conflict between the propertied and the propertyless by promoting a concentration of parliamentary power "in the hands of those working, propertyless, and possessing very little, classes which do not possess the cultivation necessary for such responsibility."[138] Also after the elections of July 1849, the liberal Rhenish newspaper *Cologne Gazette* declared that the three-class suffrage meant security from the "terrorism of the extreme left."[139] Many Junker conservatives and bourgeois liberals alike could agree on the necessity of excluding unpropertied rural and urban workers from political participation in order to secure government in the interests of the propertied. Thus, the plutocratic electoral system established by the forces of counter-revolution in 1849 played an important role (along with the continuing influx of commoners into the ranks of landed Junkerdom and of noblemen into the bureaucracy) in setting the stage for collaboration between older agrarian and newer industrial-financial elites in Bismarck's Prusso-German Empire.

— VII —

Henry Dwight, a Connecticut school teacher who visited Berlin in 1826, observed that "The Prussians are almost idolaters of royalty. To them nothing is so pure, so holy, so elevated above the world, so worthy of reverence, as the monarch and his family."[140] Antebellum Americans, North and South, fervently believed in the superiority of their form of republican and constitutional government. It is hard to imagine a Junker diplomat to Brazil reacting to his reception at the imperial court with the sorts of feelings expressed by Virginia planter Henry A. Wise in 1847. His "Republican heart," Wise wrote to the U.S. Secretary of State, bridled at having to wait three hours in a hot uniform to make three bows forward and three backward, after which he had to "bob out of (the) Imp[erial] presence."[141] Yet seventeenth-century English colonists had brought with them to the South a tradition of strong monarchical authority tempered by a legislative assembly representing the upper classes. During the first two-thirds of the eighteenth century the distance of the American colonies from the Mother Country, together with the willingness of Britain's imperial authorities to grant a relatively inexpensive and pacifying measure of colonial self-government, allowed the elected lower houses (versus the appointed upper houses, or governors' councils) of the colonial assemblies to embark on what Jack Greene terms a "quest for power." Greene notes "a marked correlation between the appearance of economic and social elites produced by the growth in colonial wealth and population on the one hand and the lower houses' demand for increased authority, dignity, and prestige on the other." By the end of the Seven Years' War in 1763, the lower houses had succeeded in "raising themselves from dependent lawmaking bodies to the center of political authority in their respective colonies."[142] From these lower houses emerged leaders of the post-1763 movement first for resistance to, and then for republican independence from, the British Empire and monarchy.

To the minds of more and more free residents of British North America during the decade prior to 1776, the English government's determination to ignore the colonial legislatures in its efforts to increase tax revenues made it seem intent on violating the colonists' trumpeted "rights of Englishmen," thereby undermining the foundations of their political liberties and subjecting them to tyranny. And those who submitted to tyranny became slaves, whose legal presence in every colony served to accentuate the dichotomy between freedom and slavery. As wealthy slaveholder Thomas Jefferson argued in 1774, the British government had implemented "a series of oppressions" that "too plainly prove a deliberate and systematical plan of reducing us to slavery."[143] Many, perhaps most planters still hesitated in 1774 to endorse Jefferson's platform of bold resistance to parliamentary authority. The planter elite was internally divided over the most appropriate response to the English Parliament and monarchy, just as plantation owners would be of a divided mind in 1860–61 over the most efficacious response to the prospect of an avowedly antislavery presidency. Some endorsed revolutionary separatism, while others favored conservative loyalty to the existing imperial or national framework. Even so, during the secession crisis advocates of disunion invoked much of 1776's revolutionary rhetoric about the threat of tyranny and enslavement, this time emanating from the Republican North rather than monarchical England. As Alabama Congressman David Clopton wrote to Senator C. C. Clay on 18 December 1860, he would "rather die a freeman than live like a slave to Black Republicanism."[144] Moreover, the British authorities prior to 1776, by promulgating regulations restricting the colonists' geographic expansion beyond the Appalachians, also alienated wealthy planters and merchants with speculative investments in western territory, as well as less affluent farmers who hoped for a new and inexpensive start on fresh lands. In the words of Clement Eaton, "the British government on the eve of the Revolution frustrated one of the strongest urges in American history, westward expansion."[145] In 1860–61, when a newly elected Republican administration promised to prohibit the further westward expansion of slavery, the response from most white Southerners was another revolution for political autonomy.

There is, of course, a fascinating incongruity to the "spirit of 1776," that is, the execution of a libertarian revolution, and the propagandizing of an anti-authoritarian, natural-rights political ideology, at the hands of slaveholding planters like Thomas Jefferson and George Mason of Virginia. After reading the Declaration of Independence, the acerbic Dr. Samuel Johnson queried, "How is it that we hear the loudest *yelps* for liberty from the drivers of Negroes?"[146] Decades later this same incongruity impressed itself upon the Prussian historian Friedrich von Raumer. After his visit to the United States in the 1840s, Raumer portrayed Southern politicians in Washington as proclaiming, in effect, "On our estates we are patriarchs, in Congress the champions of unbounded freedoms."[147] Such suggestions that Negro slavery and America's libertarian republicanism were fundamentally at odds usually provoked only righteous indignation from antebellum planter politicians and proslavery spokesmen, especially those from the Cotton Kingdom of the Deep South.

— VIII —

During the 1819–21 Missouri debates in Congress, Northern critics of slavery and its geographic extension disparaged the republican legitimacy of Missouri's proposed state constitution for its recognition of slavery and its exclusion of free blacks from the state.[148] In response, South Carolina congressman and lowcountry planter Charles Pinckney (1757–1824) insisted that Missouri's constitution was "the very best republican constitution that I have ever seen; one not only superior to that of the other States, but even to the boasted one of the United States."[149] Pinckney represented a slave state that had adopted white manhood suffrage in 1810, whereas several Northern free states still maintained property requirements for voting in 1820—including New York, home of prominent antislavery Congressman James Tallmadge and Senator Rufus King. Pinckney also spoke with the authority of a Founding Father who had sat in the Philadelphia convention of 1787, which incorporated into the U.S. Constitution a number of provisions protecting the peculiar interests of slaveholders.[150] "Our ancestors, with those gone, and a few, very few of our Revolutionary heroes and statesmen still left," Pinckney told the House of Representatives in 1820, "by the noblest effort which ever adorned the page of history, have erected such a monument of rational liberty as the world has never before seen." The American monument to "rational liberty" rested on the bedrock assumption that each state would decide for itself whether to establish or disestablish black slavery. Consequently, said the South Carolinian, "the majority of this House," in seeking to regulate Missouri's internal affairs, acted "either from a wish to dissolve the Union, and separate themselves from the slaveholding States, or from a total want of knowledge of the distinction which has, from time immemorial, existed in the civilized world, between the black and white race, and the strong and immovable line which has separated, and will continue forever to separate, them in the Southern and Western states of this Union." Indeed, "all the most enlightened nations of Europe" had decided "instantly" to import African slaves to their new American colonies, for the reason "that they found no other part of the human race so inferior in intelligence to the whites as the Africans, or none which it can be so fairly presumed were created for the purpose of serving them."

Pinckney's was clearly a racially delimited republicanism. Yet, off to the side of the deep-seated racism that characterized Pinckney and the other Founding Fathers from the slave states, there usually lurked a discomforting recognition that American slavery did in fact contradict the nation's libertarian and republican principles as set forth in the Declaration of Independence. This was indubitably the case with the document's principal author. Although Thomas Jefferson (1748–1826) was in France when the Constitution was written and ratified, he serves to represent what William Wiecek calls the "apologetic resignation of the Virginians" among the Founding Fathers, as opposed to the "determined, defiant pro-slavery of the Carolinians."[151] Discomfort at the discrepancy between the ideals of the American Revolution and the persistent reality of black slavery seems to have been more acute among slaveholders in the Chesapeake region (Virginia and Maryland) than in the Deep South (South Carolina and Georgia), where rice plantations yielded grander profits and promoted a higher ratio of slave to free population than did tobacco and grain plantations farther north. As William Freehling has suggested, even before the birth of the Cotton Kingdom "South Carolina leaders never much doubted that the institution (of slavery), whether good or bad, was permanently necessary," whereas a number of prominent Virginians were open to the idea of government-sponsored gradual emancipation in conjunction with the forced deportation of freed blacks outside the United States.[152]

Thomas Jefferson, like Pinckney the Carolinian, lived to witness the political storm raised by Missouri's application to become the first slave state located entirely west of the Mississippi River, which meant that the Ohio River could no longer function as the long-accepted geographical line of division between free and slave states. The "Missouri question" sparked fierce congressional debate that, "like a firebell in the night, awakened and filled me with terror," wrote Jefferson in 1820 from retirement at Monticello. The controversy seemed to signify "the death knell of the Union"; for the often heated exchanges between Northern critics and Southern defenders of black bondage indicated that for the first time a "geographical line, coinciding with a marked principle, moral and political," was being drawn across the United States. Jefferson feared that "once conceived, and held up to the angry passions of men, it will never be obliterated; and every new irritation will make it deeper and deeper." Like Pinckney, he believed that Congress had no business regulating "the condition of the different conditions of men composing a State. This certainly is the exclusive right of every State, which nothing in the Constitution has taken from them and given to the General Government."[153]

Also like Pinckney, Jefferson believed that blacks were innately inferior to whites, and that this inferiority, along with white prejudice against Negroes, meant that the South's slave population could not be permitted to live free in Southern society. Although Jefferson insisted "that there is not a man on earth who would sacrifice more than I would to relieve us from this heavy reproach (of slavery), in any practicable way," his concept of practicability dictated that "a general emancipation" had to be accompanied by *"expatriation"* of the freed Negroes. Even as he penned these words in 1820, the rapid westward expansion of cotton plantations and slavery since Whitney's invention of the cotton gin in 1793 was assuring that Jefferson's "practicable way" had become virtually impracticable. "As it is," he wrote, "we have the wolf by the ears, and we can neither hold him, or safely let him go. Justice is in one scale, and self-preservation in the other."[154]

Jefferson's legacy on the subject of slavery is full of ambiguity and inconsistency. Antebellum abolitionists could and did cite the dramatically egalitarian passages in the Declaration of Independence, as well as the severe criticisms of slavery's impact on white values and behavior expressed in Jefferson's *Notes on the State of Virginia,* written and published in France in the 1780s, the high tide of Jeffersonian antislavery.[155] During this decade before the birth of the Cotton Kingdom, Jefferson's efforts to have his state adopt a plan of gradual emancipation and deportation, and also to have the Confederation Congress prohibit slavery in all of the Mississippi Valley then owned by the new Republic, encountered determined resistance. In the 1790s, as he strove to climb the political ladder from the State Department to the Presidency, he maintained a circumspect silence on the topic of slavery. In 1803, when President Jefferson effected the Louisiana Purchase from Napoleon, and thereby acquired the western half of the Mississippi Valley for the United States (including the future slave state of Missouri), he made no effort whatsoever to have slavery excluded from the new territory. When news of the Missouri debates disturbed the political tranquility of his retirement, the Sage of Monticello surmised that the entire controversy was a smokescreen behind which diehard and vengeful Federalists like Rufus King plotted to resurrect their political power. They were exploiting the slavery issue, Jefferson alleged, in order to create a sectional party in the North devoted to expanding the powers of the federal government in the service of his old Hamiltonian enemies, the urban stock-jobbers and manufacturers. Because Jefferson saw the South as the true bastion of decentralized and agrarian republicanism in the United States, he endorsed the further spread of slavery west of the Mississippi as essential to both Southern power and republican permanency. In the process, observes John Chester Miller, the septuagenarian Jefferson "assumed the accoutrements of an ardent and an uncompromising champion of Southern rights."[156] Nonetheless, in 1820 he raised the oft-repeated but illusory hope that greater geographical diffusion of slavery and Negroes would in the long run facilate the goal of emancipation and expatriation "by dividing the burden among a greater number of coadjutors." Still professing antislavery principles, he insisted that "The cession of that kind of property, for so it is misnamed, is a bagatelle which would not cause me a second thought"—provided that the freed blacks were deported, of course, and expelled from American society.[157] Yet, as David Brion Davis has suggested, Jefferson was more committed than he realized or could admit to "the preservation of a social order based on slavery."[158] He could not have built and maintained his genteel Shangri-la at Monticello without slave labor; and despite selling some fifty human chattel between 1783 and 1794 to meet debts, he saw his own slave property increase from about 150 in the 1770s (after his marriage to heiress Martha Wayles Skelton) to nearly 270 at his death in 1826.[159]

Jefferson was clearly a racist republican, thought less virulently prejudiced, and more palpably uncomfortable with the anti-libertarian character of slavery, than were most antebellum planters. The compunction which Southern politicians on the eve of the Civil War often felt to refute Jefferson's queasiness about human bondage is exemplified in the so-called "Cornerstone Speech" that Alexander Stephens of Georgia, the vice president of the new Confederate States of

America, delivered in Savannah on 21 March 1861. After declaring that "our peculiar institution, African slavery . . . was the immediate cause of the late rupture and present revolution" that culminated in the formation of the Southern Confederacy, Stephens noted that "Jefferson, in his forecast, had anticipated this as the 'rock upon which the old Union would split.' " Although his prediction had clearly come to pass, "whether he fully comprehended the great truth upon which that rock *stood* and *stands* may be doubted. The prevailing ideas entertained by him and most of the leading statesmen at the time of the formation of the old (U.S.) constitution, were that the enslavement of the African was in violation of the laws of nature; and that it was wrong in principle, socially, morally, and politically." The new Confederate government, proclaimed Stephens, "is founded upon exactly the opposite idea; its foundations are laid, its corner-stone rests upon the great truth, that the negro is not equal to the white man; that slavery— subordination to the superior race—is his natural and normal condition." [160] Stephens showed far less reluctance to utter this self-evident truth than had Jefferson Davis at the time of his augural address a month earlier. Indeed, the Confederate president was "dismayed" by Stephens's speech, reports Thomas Schott. The vice president's bold remarks had "seriously compromised the Con-federacy's public political stance," designed in large part for foreign govern-ments, that the crucial issue in the ongoing secession crisis was not slavery, but "state versus national sovereignty." [161]

— IX —

The issues of state sovereignty, black bondage, and republican government are inseparably intertwined in the history of the Old South, from the plantation states' permanent separation from England to their temporary separation from the United States. Although the roles played by state sovereignty and anti-monarchical republicanism in the American Revolution of 1776 seem obvious, slavery's part in the Southern colonies' commitment to republican independence is cloudier. According to a provocative thesis framed by Edmund Morgan, eighteenth-century Virginia developed Caucasian republicanism and produced Jeffersonian democratic theory because Negro slavery virtually eliminated the troublesome problem of a free working class whose poverty and exclusion from political power inspired social and political agitation. This was precisely the problem that confronted the Junkers in 1848, in the cities as well as the countryside. Since the labor force in eighteenth-century Virginia, says Morgan, "was com-posed mainly of slaves, who had been isolated by race and removed from the political equation," anti-Negro racism could absorb "the fear and contempt" which European upper classes (like the Junkers) "felt for the inarticulate lower classes." Furthermore, because slaves were not likely to become "levelling mobs," Virginia's gentleman-planters "could more safely preach equality in a slave society than a free one." While disclaiming the conclusion "that a belief in republican equality had to rest on slavery," Morgan asserts that "in Virginia (and probably the other southern colonies) it did." [162] Although this argument goes far toward explaining the planters' racist republicanism, it does not account for the fact that while some planter politicians of the early Republic may have preached the doctrine of "republican equality" for whites, the planter elites in the Tidewater and Lowcountry sections of Virginia and the Carolinas did not grant it willingly in political practice. Indeed, they resisted white manhood suffrage until it was forced upon them by the non-slaveholding majority of white freemen, who also desired legislative apportionment according to free population. By and large, planter spokesmen in the Old Dominion and the Palmetto State seem to have waved the flag of white equality most vigorously, to have promoted most actively "the illusion of equality as citizens that informed the political culture of white men," [163] when confronted by a serious external threat whose repulsion required internal unity—that is, during the American Revolution and again on the eve of the Civil War.

Edmund Morgan's analysis of the connection between white freedom and black slavery was anticipated long ago by a number of slavery apologists in the Old South, who argued in essence that republican liberty required public order and political stability, and that in the South these required the enslavement of Negro laborers. Consider the arguments of South Carolina's John C. Calhoun (1782–1850) and Virginia's Thomas R. Dew (1802–46), probably the most influential proslavery ideologues in the antebellum South's political and academic circles respectively. Southerners, Calhoun told the Senate in the 1830s, looked upon slavery "as the most safe and the most stable basis of free institutions in the world"; for it enabled the South to enjoy "an entire exemption from those dangers originating in a conflict between labor and capital, which at this time threatens so much danger to constitutional governments." [164] After Calhoun's death these ideas were reiterated by the Charleston periodical *Southern Quarterly Review* in an essay whose author was probably lawyer-planter James Chesnut, Jr., famous as the husband of diarist Mary Boykin Chesnut and a secessionist U.S. Senator from South Carolina on the eve of the Civil War. Chesnut wrote in 1853 that "the mass of mankind constitute the laboring class, and are, perforce, required to live by the sweat of the brow." Given this inescapable fact of life, the South was fortunate to have a working class composed of those "who are not pampered with false notions of their own claims to liberty and unnatural elevation." [165]

Thomas R. Dew, William and Mary College professor and president (from 1836), has received less attention from historians of the South than has Calhoun. Yet Dew was, in the words of Michael O'Brien, "the most influential social philosopher, certainly of Virginia, possibly of the South" during the antebellum era.[166] Dew pursued a line of argument analogous to Calhoun's in an address composed for delivery to the new Virginia Historical and Philosophical Society, and published in the Richmond periodical *Southern Literary Messenger* in 1836. "One of the most fatal evils with which the republican system of government is likely to be assailed is the diffusion of a spirit of agrarianism (that is, socialism) among the indigent classes of society"—a spirit which excites "that most blighting and deadly hostility of all, the hostility of the poor against the rich." (This was the sort of hostility that so frightened Junkerdom and the affluent bourgeoisie in the late 1840s.) The French Revolution of 1789 had already provided a frightful example of what could happen, said Dew, "if the spirit of agrarianism shall ever get abroad in our land." "First comes disorganization and legislative plunder, then the struggles of faction and civil war, and lastly a military dictatorship (like that of Napoleon—and the one imposed by the Prussian monarchy when it declared martial law in November of 1848), into whose arms all will be driven by the intolerable evils of anarchy and rapine." Dew thought he saw in "the lawless mobs of the north" the "premonitory symptoms of the approaching calamity" of agrarianism in America; for this calamity was the inevitable result of "the almost unlimited extension of suffrage in the most populous states." However, the professor was confident that the slave South had little to fear. "Domestic slavery, such as ours, is the only institution which I know of, that can secure the spirit of equality among freemen, so necessary to the true and genuine spirit of republicanism, without propelling the body politic at the same time into the dangerous devices of agrarianism, and legislative intermedling between the laborer and capitalist."[167]

Dew's 1836 address enlarged upon a thesis set forth in his oft-cited *Review of the Debate in the Virginia Legislature of 1831 and 1832* (1832).[168] The professor had composed this treatise in response to proposals introduced in the Virginia General Assembly for the gradual emancipation and removal of the state's slave population; these proposals, in turn, had been triggered by the Nat Turner slave revolt in Southampton County in August of 1831. In one section of his *Review* Dew responded to the charge that "slavery is unfavourable to a republican spirit." On the contrary, slavery was responsible "for the perfect spirit of equality so prevalent among the whites of all the slaveholding States." How so? "The menial and low offices being all performed by the blacks, there is at once taken away the greatest cause of distinction and separation of the ranks of society." Thanks to black bondage, "Color alone is here the badge of distinction, the true mark of aristocracy, and all who are white are equal in spite of the variety of occupation."[169]

Yet Virginia's own political system belied Dew's 1832 insistence on Caucasian egalitarianism. The state convention of 1829–30, dominated by representatives from the slaveholding counties of the eastern Tidewater and Piedmont regions (who held 60 of 96 seats), had refused to adopt either white manhood suffrage or apportionment of seats in the state legislature on the basis of current white population, reforms whose support came primarily from the more rapidly growing and predominantly non-slaveholding western counties of the Valley and Trans-Allegheny regions. Eastern planters, especially those from the old Tidewater counties, had opposed these reforms primarily, in the words of Charles Henry Ambler, out of "fear that the west would use its political power thus gained to impose (heavier) taxes on slave property to be used in the construction of works of internal improvement." [170] Like Junkers, planters could be decidedly anti-democratic, for whites as well as blacks, when they saw the security of their property at risk. Yet the political culture of the Old South, unlike that of monarchical East Elbia, prescribed that Virginia planters defend a propertied franchise and unequal representation for white citizens as compatible with the fundamental tenets of republicanism.

During Virginia's 1829–30 convention debates the most outspoken and influential planter spokesman—apart, perhaps, from the irascible and idiosyncratic John Randolph of Roanoke—were the lawyer-planters Abel Parker Upshur of Northampton County (on the Eastern Shore) and Benjamin Watkins Leigh of Chesterfield County (on the border between the southern Tidewater and Piedmont regions). Upshur set out to discredit those reformers who insisted "that there is in the majority, an a priori, inherent and indestructible right to rule a minority." The reformers' logic, he maintained, even required that they "admit women to the polls." [171] Benjamin Watkins Leigh encapsulated the anti-democratic stance of most eastern planters when he declared that "No government can be just, or wise, or safe for Virginia, which shall place the property of the East in the power and at the disposal of the West." According to Leigh, loyalty to the principles of 1776 did not require full-fledged democracy: "It does not follow that, because all men are born equal, and have equal rights to life, liberty, and property that they can acquire by honest industry, therefore, all men may rightly claim, in an established society, equal political powers—especially, equal power to dispose of the property of others." [172] Thomas R. Dew would take a similar stance two years later, despite his argument that black slavery made for Caucasian egalitarianism. "It may be with truth affirmed," stated Dew's *Review*, "that the exclusive owners of property ever have been, ever will, and perhaps ever ought to be, the virtual rulers of mankind." In fact, "The great object of government is the protection of property;—from the days of the patriarchs down to the present time." [173]

Virginia's Constitution of 1830 substituted for the old freehold voting requirement a complex suffrage law ("as complicated as any in American suffrage history" [174]) that left almost one-third of the Old Dominion's adult male taxpayers, and almost half of all adult white males, without the franchise. Instead of the longstanding system of representation in the General Assembly by counties, without regard to population, another compromise incorporated into the Constitution of 1830 provided that apportionment of legislative seats would be based on white population according to the 1820 census, a compromise which under-represented the more rapidly growing western counties. As Alison Goodyear Freehling concludes, "Virginia, in 1830, held back white-basis democracy and opted instead for slaveholders' political ascendancy."[175] Yet the reformist impulse waxed rather than waned over the next two decades, as the white population of the western counties came to surpass that of the eastern counties by over 90,000. At the "Reform Convention of 1850–1851" the eastern delegates, although still holding a majority of 76 to the west's 59, confronted a Trans-Allegheny region so recalcitrant as to threaten secession and independent statehood as "Appalachia" if its political demands were not met.[176] The 1850–51 convention voted to enfranchise all adult white males save paupers, and also agreed upon another compromise plan of apportionment that gave the western regions their first majority in the House of Delegates. Eastern lawyer-planter Henry Wise supported western demands with the argument that white manhood suffrage, and a more democratic apportionment of seats in the General Assembly, might help to unite the state's population in support of slavery and against the growing antislavery movement in the North.[177] Nonetheless, many eastern planters agreed, at least privately, with the views expressed anonymously in an open letter "To the Conservatives of Virginia," published on the eve of the convention in the Richmond *Whig:* if the franchise should be further liberalized, so as to "invest with power the ignorant, besotted and depraved, and give to them an ascendancy over the good and the wise," then "whatever other merits the (political) system may possess, it cannot fail to engender incalculable mischief."[178] Richmond attorney James Lyons stated publicly in 1850 that "All dignity of sentiment, all purity of principle, all delicacy of honor, must perish in the coarse and savage conflicts of the new democracy."[179] Lyons, who became a prominent secessionist and won election to the Confederate House of Representatives in 1861, was one of "Virginia's genuine conservatives," notes Craig M. Simpson; these men "waited until the Civil War began before launching a reactionary counteroffensive against the constitution (of 1851)."[180]

Nonetheless, many Virginia planters seem to have accepted the Dewian counterargument that slavery protected the slave states from the worst consequences of democracy. While the 1850–51 convention was in session, Tidewater lawyer-planter George Fitzhugh noted that "A fair opportunity will be afforded to draw a wider line of distinction between freemen and slaves, to elevate higher the condition of the citizen, to inspire every man with pride of rank and position."[181] Fitzhugh, like Dew before him, was making the oft-repeated proslavery argument that, in the words of William Sumner Jenkins, "slavery caused an identity of interests among all whites to the extent that they approached singleness of class."[182] After Lincoln's election, when the level of support for slavery among nonslaveholders was a special cause of concern among advocates of secession, Fitzhugh invoked the "singleness of class" argument once again. Southerners, he wrote, "are the most aristocratic people in the world. Pride of caste, and color, and privilege, makes every white man an aristocrat in feeling." [183] Another Tidewater planter who carried a version of this argument into the secession crisis was Dr. Richard Eppes of Prince George County. Eppes was familiar with the writings of both Calhoun and Dew, although the latter's influence was no doubt greater, since Eppes, while a student at William and Mary College in 1843–44, had taken Dew's "Senior Political Course, embracing Political Economy, Government, and Philosophy of the Human Mind." [184] Dew's influence on Eppes's thinking was evident in November of 1860, a few days after Lincoln's election, when Eppes wrote in his diary about having told a neighbor that "a Republic could not endure where the law of universal suffrage existed without a slave basis." He cited the "Athenian & Roman Republics" as examples—even though these republics had failed to endure with slavery. A month later Eppes explained to a visiting relative that "A strong monarchical government was the only one adapted to the free states where every office is ruled by universal suffrage or mob law legalized." The recent political victories of the Republican party demonstrated that the free states were much more susceptible to radical fanaticism than were the slave states, and were therefore quite likely to succumb to military despotism under Lincoln, as had post-revolutionary France under Napoleons I and III. "I believe," wrote Eppes, "that with a slave basis such as we have in the South, the slaves occupying the place of northern free laborers, we can still retain our republican institutions and be a permanent government." [185] His optimism was no doubt reinforced by the response of the nonslaveholding citizens in his community to the Confederate bombardment of Fort Sumter in April of 1861. After news of the bombardment had reached Virginia, Eppes signed a circular letter instructing his county's delegate to the Virginia State Convention of 1861 to vote for secession. Eppes expressed satisfaction that "almost all the male inhabitants" of the town of City Point had signed the letter, as "most of the inhabitants are non-slaveholders and it was striking to see the unanimity of opinion on this most important move." [186]

The fundamental proslavery argument of Calhoun, Dew, and their many disciples can be reduced to the following statement: a stable and enduring form of Caucasian republicanism required that the working class be political eunuchs and enslaved members an inferior race. A recent historian of antebellum Georgia, J. William Harris, has suggested that this vision of republicanism became the "dominant public ideology" in the slave South. [187] Evidence for this assertion is not limited to the older seaboard and coastal regions of the South. For example, the *Memphis Weekly Avalanche* for 18 June 1859 insisted that slavery was not only "a blessing to the negro. It is more than that. By affording a barrier against the old and vicious Democracy which has settled onto our country from Europe in so irresistable a flood (that is, of recent immigration), and is infusing itself so rapidly into the popular mind of the North, Southern slavery is destined to prove a lasting blessing to the Union, rendering these Southern States the nurseries of the only sound republican tenets, and the only safe and steadfast political philosophy."[188] What percentage of Southern planters endorsed this judgment is indeterminable,[189] as is the number of planters so consistently anti-democratic that they would have much preferred restricting the suffrage to white adult males with substantial property or incomes. Nonetheless, if we could determine the number of planters who held one of these two outlooks, I suspect that the total figure would support James L. Roark's statement that on the eve of the Civil War, "most members of the planting class supported strongly anti-democratic values."[190] To be sure, any such evaluation of the planter class and its values can be neither proved nor disproved; for it must be based largely on the historian's reading of extant collections of private letters and diaries that are not necessarily representative of the plantation gentry as a whole. Moreover, as Roark recognizes, the "public pronouncements" of most planters during the 1850s "loudly proclaimed the equality of all white Southerners."[191] What we know for certain is that at the time of the American Revolution none of the Southern state constitutions extended the right to vote to all white adult males, and that for decades to come many planters in the older, more "aristocratic" parts of the South—from eastern Virginia to the "Old Natchez District" of Mississippi—remained publicly as well as privately hostile to white manhood suffrage.[192] Nonetheless, as Fletcher Green has emphasized, "The history of the southern state constitutions and governments from 1776 to 1860 reveals a progressive expansion in the application of the doctrine of political equality."[193] Due to the egalitarian ethos fostered by the American Revolution, the more fluid economic and social structures in the newer states west of the Appalachians, and the development of competitive two-party politics during the era of the second party system (the "Age of Jackson"), by 1850 all the slave states save Virginia and North Carolina had adopted white manhood suffrage for elections to both houses of their state legislatures. The Old Dominion and the Tar Heel State followed suit during the 1850s, in 1851 and 1857 respectively.

Regardless of how many planters continued to adhere in private to "strongly anti-democratic values," in the public arena the planter elite as a whole adapted quite successfully to the democratization of both style and structure that transformed American politics during the antebellum decades. From the 1830s to the mid-1850s planters participated enthusiastically and adeptly in the competition between Whigs and Democrats that flourished in all the slave states except the politically monolithic South Carolina of John Calhoun. Even in South Carolina, notes Lacy K. Ford, Jr., "Any action or utterance which even faintly suggested elitism or hauteur usually meant political death."[194] To be sure, Whig and Democratic politicians in the South—regardless of their disagreements on issues like the national bank, the protective tariff, federal funds for internal improvements, immigration, or the efficacy of rapid westward expansion—were anxious to present their respective parties as especially "sound" on the slavery question.[195]

Some statistics will serve to illustrate the plantation gentry's success in adapting to political democratization. In Virginia about 3 percent of white families owned 20 or more slaves in 1860, and in that year over 24 percent of the state legislators owned at least 20 slaves. Of the 152 members of Virginia's secession convention, elected in February of 1861, 35, or 23 percent, were owners of 20 or more slaves. In Mississippi, which had adopted both white manhood suffrage and legislative apportionment according to white population in 1832, planters wielded even more power in the legislature, primarily because Mississippi had many fewer backcountry counties with low slave populations than did the Old Dominion. In 1860, when about 9.5 percent of the Magnolia State's free population belonged to families possessing 20 or more slaves, almost half the state legislators owned a minimum of 20 human chattel. In Mississippi's secession convention, elected in December of 1860, at least 44 of the 100 delegates owned 20 or more slaves.[196] Moreover, of the state's seven U.S. Senators and Representatives for 1859–61, only one owned fewer than 15 slaves, and the average slaveholding was 43.5.[197]

One careful and judicious scholar, Ralph Wooster, while saying that "The role of the plantation aristocracy in southern government is impossible to measure in precise terms," nonetheless concludes that "the number of property holders and slaveholders among southern officeholders was increasing during the 1850–60 decade." His figures show a disproportionately large number of planters among state officeholders in all the slave states.[198] Moreover, in seven Southern states (Maryland, Virginia, North Carolina, South Carolina, Georgia, and Louisiana), planter and proslavery interests succeeded up to the Civil War in defeating proposals to apportion representation in both houses of their state legislatures according to the number of voters or total white population. Instead, they continued to allot legislative seats in one of two ways that awarded greater representation to areas with large slave populations: that is, according to a "mixed basis" that took account of both taxes paid and white population, or according to the federal three-fifths ratio used in the House of Representatives.[199]

— X —

But the planter elite could not adapt so successfully to the declining demographic and political weight of the slave states in Washington. While East Elbia remained the preponderant heartland of the Kingdom of Prussia, the South increasingly became a minority section within the United States, especially so after 1845, when Florida and Texas became the last slave states to enter the Union. During the forties and fifties the growing influx of European immigrants (especially from Ireland and the states of German Confederation) settled overwhelmingly in the more rapidly industrializing and urbanizing free states, where many voted for the Republican presidential ticket in 1860.[200] When Lincoln won the presidential election of that year, the U.S. Republic included 15 slave states with 39.4 percent of the national population (12.3 million inhabitants, black and white), versus 18 free states with 60.6 percent of the nation's populace (18.8 million).[201] By way of contrast, when Prussian regular troops in 1849 helped to suppress the vestiges of revolutionary protest in the monarchy's western provinces,[202] the six provinces of East Elbia contained a population of 12 million, and Prussia's two western provinces had less than 4.5 million inhabitants.

The Compromise of 1850 provided a temporary resolution to the nagging conflict over slavery's westward expansion into the vast new territories won during the Mexican War of 1846–48, although enforcement of the new Fugitive Slave Law quickly stirred sectional animosities. The Kansas-Nebraska Act of 1854, by explicitly substituting the fuzzy concept of "popular sovereignty" for the distinct latitudinal line of the Missouri Compromise, reopened the question of slavery's status in the northern part of the Louisiana Purchase. During the mid-1850s increasingly rancorous sectional disputes over "Bleeding Kansas" (the site of armed conflict between proslavery and free soil settlers) and "Bleeding Sumner" (the caning of Massachusetts Senator Charles Sumner by South Carolina Congressman Preston Brooks) assured destruction of the Jacksonian party system and produced the meteoric political ascent of the antislavery Republican Party.[203] When the Republicans entered the presidential race in 1856, the *Richmond Dispatch* expressed dismay at the prospect of a Republican administration "whose avowed object is to abolish slavery, to rob six millions of Southerners of two thousand millions of property (the estimated dollar value of 3.2 million slaves—according to the 1850 census—valued at $600 apiece), and the incalculable amount of other property which would be rendered valueless by emancipation; to say nothing of all the horrors of civil and servile war which would necessarily accompany the attempt to accomplish this stupendous and unparalleled wrong."[204]

With the disappearance of the Whigs' national organization during the mid-fifties, the Democratic party emerged as the South's only practical hope of protecting slavery within the Union,[205] although vigorous two-party politics on the state level survived in the more heterogeneous Upper South until the Civil War. Even the national "Democracy" was torn apart during the spring and summer of 1860 by fierce quarreling between the party's Northern and Southern wings over the status of slavery in the territories. In addition, abolitionist John Brown's effort to incite a slave insurrection in October of 1859 at Harper's Ferry, Virginia, did much to raise the anxiety level of white Southerners on the eve of the presidential campaign. It became increasingly difficult for them to reconcile the proslavery argument that "slaves were well treated and cheerful in their bondage" with their intensified dread of slave rebellion, observes James McPherson; and few could see any meaningful distinction between the violent abolitionism of a John Brown and Lincoln's moderate antislavery policy of constitutional containment.[206] The *Report of the Joint Committee of the General Assembly of Virginia on the Harper's Ferry Outrages* evaluated Brown's actions as "neither more nor less than practical illustrations of the doctrines of the leaders of the Republican party." In response, the Old Dominion had to evince "a proper sense of self-respect and the instinct of self-preservation" by taking measures against the possibility that "the knife of the assassin and the torch of the incendiary" might strike again.[207]

Southern Democrats nominated John Breckinridge of Kentucky in 1860 and insisted that the U.S. government should actively protect slavery in all federal territories, while Northern Democrats put forward Stephen Douglas of Illinois and advocated removing the issue from the purview of Congress via the localized solution of "popular sovereignty." The new Constitutional Union party (composed of remnants from the Whig and nativist American parties) wished to push the divisive issue of slavery into the background in the interests of preserving the Union, and chose John Bell of Tennessee as its candidate. Among the eleven states that would eventually join the Confederacy, the Breckinridge Democrats carried all seven Deep South states plus Arkansas and North Carolina, and Bell won the electoral votes of Virginia and Tennessee. Although the supporters of Breckinridge included some fire-eaters determined to break up the Union, until Lincoln's election most of the planter elite remained loyal to the Union. They abjured secession and believed that the federal Constitution, properly interpreted and enforced, offered a secure defense of both their property rights in slaves (ensured by the fugitive slave clause and the Fifth Amendment) and their political power in Washington (enhanced by the three-fifths rule and Southern strength in the Senate). North Carolina Democrat and judge Thomas Ruffin of Alamance County represented the pro-Union views of most planters in the 1850s when he maintained that "one of the conservative effects of slavery" was to impress upon Southerners "a deep conviction of the inestimable value of the Union, and a profound reverence for the Constitution which created it"; for this document "clearly recognizes our slavery, sustains the rights of ownership, and enforces the duty of service."[208]

But in 1860 the Republicans not only supplanted the Democrats as the majority party in the Senate but captured the White House without receiving a single electoral vote in the slave states. As Daniel Crofts has emphasized, "That stunning demonstration of apparent southern political powerlessness in the Union probably fueled the secession movement as much as any other single factor."[209] The Republican victory seemed to portend the long-term abolition of slavery via its geographical containment—the "ultimate extinction" envisioned by Lincoln in 1858—and perhaps via congressional restrictions on the interstate trade in slaves.

In the short run, a Republican administration and Congress seemed to presage more frequent slave insurrections and the prospect that some nonslaveholding whites, particularly those in the mountainous backcountry areas of the South, might gravitate to the party in power. These ominous prospects would encourage a decline in both the stability of slave society and the monetary value of slaves. When Lincoln was inaugurated in March of 1861, seven cotton states in the Lower South, led by South Carolina, had already seceded and met in Montgomery to organize an independent Confederate States of America. "Conservative" Unionist sentiments held greater sway in the Upper South, where substantial internal divisions (geographic, economic, and social) had promoted the persistence of two-party political competition. This competition inspired greater voter confidence in 1861 "that the normal workings of the political process would absorb and deflect the Republican challenge," explains William Barney.[210] Nevertheless, after the Confederacy's decision to bombard Fort Sumter into submission in April led President Lincoln to call for 75,000 volunteer troops (including militia contingents from the slave states still in the Union) in order to subdue the secessionist "rebellion," four states in the Upper South, led by the Old Dominion, voted to secede rather than submit to federal "coercion." Virginia's secession ordinance, passed by a convention vote of 89–55 that reflected the continuing importance of intrastate sectional differences, declared that the federal government had "perverted" its constitutional powers "not only to the injury of the people of Virginia, but to the oppression of the Southern slaveholding States."[211]

— XI —

During the 1860 election and subsequent secession crisis, members of the planter elite took a variety of political stands that reflected divergent outlooks on how best to protect the interests of slavery and slaveholders. In other words, they supported different tactical means to the same strategic end. Whereas Junkers disagreed during the revolutionary crisis of 1848–49 about how much of their *Rittergut* autocracies could and should be preserved, there was no disagreement among planters during the secession crisis of 1860–61 about the need to preserve intact their plantation autocracies based on black slavery, although they did quarrel among themselves over what political stance would best serve that common resolve. This point can be illustrated by examining some political thoughts that three affluent cotton planters in the Mississippi River valley confided to their diaries. In the Natchez District of Mississippi, planter-physician Dr. Walter Wade, owner of 126 slaves in Jefferson County, voted for Breckinridge in the presidential election and then supported cooperationist steps among the slave states to assure "Southern safety, since the Election of Abram. Lincoln, the Abolition candidate for President in the U.S." On 19 November, Wade attended "a political meeting of the people" at the county seat, where "Resolutions were passed Unanimously Recommending the legislature to call a Convention of the State, to confer with other Conventions of Southern States, to take Council to secure their Equality in the Union, or Independence out of it. It all looks to a dissolution of the Union as inevitable: as the Abolitionists of the North will never cease to war on slavery, until it is abolished finally in all the States." Mississippi's decision to follow the immediatist lead of South Carolina and to secede solo apparently did not distress Wade, who rejoiced on 15 January that five states had already separated from the Union. "The South says her constitutional rights in Slavery are totally disregarded and nullified by the North"— the term "nullified" referring to the "Personal Freedom Laws" passed by nine free state legislatures during the 1850s in protest against the Fugitive Slave Law of 1850. The South's response, explained Wade, was to claim "the right of secession under the doctrine of State sovereignty as her remedy."[212]

In northern Mississippi's Panola County, Everard Green Baker owned 57 slaves and supported the Constitutional Union ticket of Bell and Edward Everett of Massachusetts, "because I think they are able statesmen—& honest men— and belong to the only national party in the Union." In response to Lincoln's election and the subequent string of state secession ordinances, his commitment to the Confederate cause was restrained by anxieties about commercial disruptions and the possibility of military conflict. In late April of 1861, a week after learning "that Virginia had seceded—joyful news to us all," Baker expressed his prescient fear of "the bloodiest civil war that has ever darkened the pages of history." Nonetheless, he found "consolation" in the libertarian conviction "that we will be fighting for our homes (and) our lives—the honor and safety of ourselves, our families, & our property."[213]

West Tennessee planter John Houston Bills, owner of 80 slaves in Hardeman and Fayette counties, disliked the "sectional candidate" Breckinridge and considered himself one of the "old line Democrats" supporting the candidacy of "Judge Douglas." On 15 November, Bills recorded in his diary news of "cecession (*sic*) in the ascendant" in South Carolina, "without shadow of Cause except that Lincoln (anti-Slavery) is elected by a Majority of the people of the U.S." Two weeks later he noted ruefully that "The general impression is that several of the Southern states will secede from the Union & thus break up & destroy the Verry best government on Earth for some good reason it is true, but not enough yet to justify so great a sacrifice of good." Nonetheless, in January of 1861 Bills complained that the South could win "no recognition of our rights by the North. I go with my section come what will—but give up the (U.S.) government as I would an old friend, in sorrow." After the Confederacy's bombardment of Fort Sumter and Lincoln's call for troops in April, Bills concluded that "Now the south will be a unit. However wrong the leaders may have acted, no one will see the south Coerced into submission to such a Motley Abolition Crew as is headed by Lincoln."[214] Bills's own state of Tennessee seceded on 7 May, the last of the Confederacy's eleven states to abandon the Union.

As the examples of Wade, Baker, and Bills indicate, the planter elite, like the Southern electorate at large, was split before the presidential election of 1860 among supporters of Breckinridge, Bell, and Douglas, and after the election did not agree about the proper response to Lincoln's victory. Some voters, concentrated in but hardly limited to the mountainous and predominantly non-slaveholding regions of Appalachia and the Ozarks, insisted on unconditional loyalty to the Union. Many more, especially in the high-slaveholding areas of the Lower South, called for immediate, separate-state secession. Finally, there were several varieties of "cooperationists," most durable in the Upper South, who wanted the slave states to consult among themselves. The states could work together in order to extract greater concessions to "Southern rights" from the federal government, or could agree to withdraw together from the Union once the Lincoln administration had shown itself actively hostile to slavery.[215]

It is important to emphasize that, with a very few exceptions among those staunch Unionists who gave Lincoln 3 percent of the total popular vote in the states of the Upper South, these splits before and after the 1860 election reflected disagreement among white Southerners over what political strategy would serve best to preserve slavery, not disagreement over the fundamental necessity of maintaining blacks in bondage. As Dwight Lowell Dumond demonstrated decades ago, "At the South, the members of all political parties (in 1860) were dedicated to the preservation of the institution of slavery."[216] But what of the Upper South, where elections to state conventions in Virginia, North Carolina, and Tennessee in February of 1861 showed a "Unionist groundswell" among nonslaveholding voters? Daniel Crofts, the most thorough and astute scholar of Upper South Unionism, has determined that the "emerging Union parties" had "a base of support in which slaveholders were incidental and irrelevant," a constituency which "came closer to being nonplanter, if not yet antiplanter, than any political coalition ever to hold power in a slaveowning state." Nonetheless, advises Crofts, this "pro-Union mobilization of nonslaveholders in the upper South certainly did not, by itself, signal an overt challenge to planter hegemony, let alone opposition to slavery."[217] To be sure, in Upper and Lower South alike, there existed tensions between plantation owners and nonslaveholding farmers that reflected a complex blend of class and intra-state regional divisions. And these tensions intensified during the Civil War as the Confederate government imposed military conscription and heavier taxes on its citizenry. By 1864, concludes William Barney, "The basic dividing line in white society, the one between those who had slave labor and those dependent solely upon family labor, was threatening to split into a chasm."[218] Yet this potential chasm was but a small crack during the secession crisis. J. D. B. DeBow, editor of the New Orleans periodical *DeBow's Review*, was essentially correct when he wrote shortly after Lincoln's election that "a class conscientiously objecting to the ownership of slave property does not exist at the South."[219]

During the winter and spring of 1860–61 Southern opposition to secession seldom meant hostility to slavery per se. The distinction is made clear in a 21 April 1861 letter written to former Tennessee Whig governor William B. Campbell from F. H. Gordon, a fellow resident of middle Tennessee. Gordon declared himself "opposed to Republicanism and to secession," and in favor of "armed neutrality of the Border States." "I will say to you in confidence," wrote Gordon, "that whenever Tennessee shall go out, there will be a strong force of non-slaveholders in our State, who will rebel. . . . They are not many of them Abolitionists; they do not want the negroes set free; (but) they are not willing to fight for slavery; and they say they will not do it."[220] In mid-March former governor Campbell had himself expressed well the Unionism that still gripped numerous planters in the Upper South. "The great upheaving of the Southern States has been avowedly for the protection of negro slavery, while I regard the whole (secessionist) movement as the most unfortunate and injurious to that institution," wrote Campbell to a cousin in Alabama. "As a pro-slavery man I repudiate the Southern move as unwise and impolitic, and tending to the ruin and overthrow of negro slavery. The rights of the slaveholder cannot be maintained out of the Union so well as in it, and I fear cannot be maintained at all outside of it."[221] The Civil War would prove Campbell a prophet. Indeed, as Roger Ransom has noted, the U.S. polity "probably offered the most secure haven for a slave society in the world of the nineteenth century."[222]

— XII —

The foregoing sketches of the political histories of planters and Junkers have, I trust, indicated why the planter elite, unlike Junkerdom, proved so compatible with democratic republicanism in its own region. However, in order to explain this crucial contrast clearly and concisely, it is necessary to return to more systematic comparative analysis, and to focus on some geographical, demographic, and racial differences between the South and East Elbia.

The geography and demography of the Old South provided many more opportunities for upward social mobility into the landed upper class than could exist in contemporaneous East Elbia, which did not have an expansive frontier, and which contained much less uncultivated land than did the South. With a total land area smaller than that of Mississippi and Louisiana combined, East Elbia in 1858 supported a population larger than that of all fifteen slave states in 1860.[223] The continuing availability of unsettled land in the antebellum South, together with the substantial profits that raising cotton could bring to enterprising farmers, gave humble but ambitious whites opportunities for social as well as geographical mobility that were impossible in the Prussian East. Granted, the percentage of Southern families who owned slaves dipped slightly between 1790 and 1850 (from 35.3% to 30.9%), and then fell precipitously to 26.1% by 1860.[224] This relative decline in the number of slaveholders encouraged a minority of proslavery spokesmen during the 1850s to agitate unsuccessfully for a reopening of the African slave trade in order to make available a greater number of slaves at lower prices.[225] Nonetheless, the absolute number of planters and lesser slaveholders continued to rise substantially until the Civil War. According to U.S. census figures, between 1850 and 1860 (the only antebellum decade in which a new slave state did not enter the Union) the number of planters increased by almost 23 percent, from 37,662 to 46,282; and the number of slaveholders in toto grew by more than 10 percent, from 347,525 to 384,884.[226] In eastern Texas—part of the cotton frontier on the eve of the Civil War—the percentage of Harrison County farmers owning at least 20 slaves increased from 12 percent in 1850 to 17.9 percent in 1860.[227] On the eastern seaboard, in central Georgia's Houston County, the number of those owning 20 or more slaves rose from 41 in 1825, to 81 in 1844, to 168 in 1859, despite the county's loss of land to Macon County in 1837–40.[228] These figures indicate that, just as ambitious yeoman farmers could realistically hope to acquire a few slaves, so could ambitious lesser slaveholders strive for and attain membership in the plantation gentry.[229] While the antebellum planter elite expanded both geographically and numerically, East Elbia's perforce limited number of increasingly expensive *Rittergüter* could only change hands among the wealthy upper-crust.[230] Therefore, the number of East Elbian Prussians who could hope to join the ranks of landed Junkerdom was far smaller than the number of white Southerners who could aspire to the status of gentlemen planters. If only for this reason, the planters enjoyed a much higher degree of popular legitimacy in the South than did the Junkers in East Elbia. In 1833 Alexis de Tocqueville made an incisive observation about the English aristocracy (gentry and peerage) that is even more apropos of the planter elite. The English aristocracy, wrote Tocqueville, was "not in the least founded on birth, but on the wealth that everyone can acquire." Since "everyone had the hope of being among the privileged, the privileges made the aristocracy not more hated, but more valued."[231]

A perspicacious planter in antebellum Virginia, even if he or his relations had no plans to establish a new plantation west of the Appalachians, had at least a threefold interest in seeing that new territory was always available for the expansion of slavery and the plantation system: first, to augment the South's representation in Congress through the creation of new slave states; second, to guarantee a steady market for surplus slaves, which would maintain and even increase the market value of slaves kept in the Old Dominion, and at the same time, by holding down the size of the intrastate black population, reduce the possibility of a successful slave revolt; and third, to assure the continued availability of cheap, fresh land for generations of aspiring planters, whose aspirations were instrumental in legitimating plantation society.[232] All these considerations help to explain the reaction of Virginia's premier newspaper to the Missouri Compromise of 1820, the first federal restriction on the spread of slavery west of the Mississippi River. Since Texas was outside the territory of the Louisiana Purchase affected by the Compromise, the Richmond *Enquirer* declared in early 1821 that the slave states "owe it to themselves, to keep their eye firmly on Texas. If we are cooped up on the north (by the 36°30′ line of latitude), we must have elbow room to the west."[233] It is a remarkable coincidence that later this same year, 1821, the first slaveholding settlers from the United States arrived in the new Austin colony on the Brazos and Colorado rivers of Mexican Texas, and that this migration was orchestrated by a native of Virginia, Stephen F. Austin.[234] Thanks largely to Presidents John Tyler of Virginia and James Polk of Tennessee, along with Secretaries of State Abel P. Upshur of Virginia and South Carolina's John C. Calhoun, Texas became one of the United States at the end of 1845—the last slave state to enter the Union.

Another crucial difference between the regional environments of planters and Junkers was racial. Whereas the South was a racially bifurcated society in which the enslavement of Negroes and anti-Negro prejudice had fed on each other since the seventeenth century, Junkerdom never presided over a labor force whose dramatic racial differences from the population at large could be used to justify excision from the body politic. Consequently, as the revolutionary crisis of 1848–49 made clear, *Rittergut* owners had much more to fear than did plantation owners from an indigenous popular movement for democratic politics. Thus Count Friedrich zu Dohna-Lauck wrote disparagingly in 1849 about "the lack of political judgment and the gullibility of the lower classes," and insisted upon "the necessity for the complete exclusion of the working class and those not economically self-sustaining from any participation in the election of representatives of the country."[235] For antebellum planters, as Calhoun and Dew pointed out, black slavery practically eliminated the Junkers' troublesome problem of a free agricultural proletariat whose poverty and exclusion from political participation inspired social and political agitation. "If it be true that the African is an inferior variety of the human race, of less elevated character, and more limited intellect," wrote South Carolinian William Harper in the 1830s, "is it not desirable that the inferior laboring class should be made up of such, who will conform to their condition without painful aspirations and vain struggles?"[236] Harper, like most slavery apologists, wanted to believe that blacks accepted bondage without widespread discontent and frustration, rather than acknowledge that the foundation of Southern slavery was Caucasian coercion and the slaves' recognition that whites had at their disposal vastly superior armed force. As slaves themselves understood, the preponderance of Southern whites, slaveholders and non-slaveholders alike, believed in the innate inferiority of African-Americans.[237] Because the South's Caucasian majority had a Negrophobic fear that emancipation without deportation would lead to either genocidal racial warfare or black-white amalgamation, the link between white freedom and black bondage endured until broken by the military might of Union armies.

In short, antebellum planters could preach and even practice democratic republicanism among whites first and foremost because their labor force was excluded by racial enslavement from the political process, and because non-slaveholding whites could and did share in the planters' racist contempt for the deprived and depraved Negro. While the Junkers believed that only representative assemblies organized along traditional corporatist lines would preserve their status and influence as a landed elite, and depended upon military monarchism to turn back the tide of constitutional and parliamentary government, the planters could participate in and even preside over a *Herrenvolk* democracy for Southern whites. Thus, Alabama governor and Black Belt planter John A. Winston could argue in 1855, during his second inaugural address, that "the existence of a race among us—inferior by nature to ourselves, in a state of servitude—necessarily adds to the tone of manliness and character of the superior race." According to Winston, the non-slaveholding white was "higher in the scale of intelligence" than lower-class whites in the free states, and "above those menial acts of servitude" which the latter performed. Furthermore, the non-slaveholding white was distinguished by his high degree of patriotism, by his high regard for duty, and by "his polite bearing to, and his chivalrous defense of the fairer and better portion of creation." Such admirable sentiments, insisted Governor Winston, were "not peculiar to the educated and accomplished gentleman only. They belong to the Southern man without regard to his rank or position in life." Thus it could be claimed that chivalry and gentility, the traditional accoutrements of an aristocratic class in monarchical Europe, had become the democratized prerogatives of a superior race in the republican South.[238]

5

Patriarchy and Paternalism

ONE CAN NOT study the historical literature on either planters or Junkers without encountering questions about the degree to which each landed elite and its regional society were characterized by "patriarchy" and "paternalism." It is hardly surprising that scholars have provided different answers to these questions, and that the differences sometimes reflect disagreement about the precise meanings and proper usage of the key terms. This chapter has two interrelated goals: to investigate the etymological roots and historical usages of the terms patriarchy and paternalism, and to explore questions about the patriarchal and paternalistic characteristics of the planter and Junker elites in a comparative context.

— I —

Whereas the terms patriarchy and patriarchal were widely used in Europe and America during the early and middle decades of the nineteenth century, paternalism and paternalistic (as distinct from paternal or *väterlich*) are of more recent vintage.[1] Because patriarchy and paternalism both derive from Greek and Latin roots signifying the adult male holder of authority in a familial household, they can and have been used in interchangeable or overlapping fashion by a variety of scholars. Two historians of the family in Europe, Michael Mitterauer and Reinhard Sieder, posit "the model of the patriarchal family structure, with its emphasis on the 'natural authority' of husband over wife and children," and also refer to "the paternalistic structure of the large family, which favored the domination of the male."[2] According to feminist historian Gerda Lerner, "If patriarchy describes the institutionalized system of male dominance, paternalism describes a particular mode, a subset of patriarchal relations." This subset, "best described as paternalistic dominance," involves "the relationship of a dominant group, considered superior, to a subordinate group, considered inferior, in which the dominance is mitigated by mutual obligations and reciprocal rights."[3] Many scholars agree with Lerner in positing "dominance . . . mitigated by mutual obligations and reciprocal rights" as the crux of a paternalistic relationship. The nature of those obligations and rights seems to derive from the ideal-typical model of a family within which the father provides sustenance and protection in return for childlike (or wifely) obedience and loyalty.[4] Hence there seem to be analogies between the models of paternalistic-patriarchal governance and feudal-seigniorial authority (the term "seignior" referring to "a man of rank; specifically, a feudal lord"[5]). These analogies are highlighted in Charles Morazé's statement that population growth in early nineteenth-century Germany created a "surplus population" whose numbers "were no longer protected by the old paternal feudal traditions."[6] Dietrich Gerhard suggests that "the basic concept of feudalism" was "mutual fidelity" between noble lords and their free vassals. Although relations between seigniorial lords and unfree peasants existed "outside and below the feudal ladder," the lord-peasant relationship still manifested "distinct parallels to the mutual obligations of protection and fidelity in the emerging feudal system."[7] To be sure, the degree to which the reality of lord-peasant relations in feudal Europe approximated this model of mutuality and reciprocity remains open to debate.[8]

Consider how the linkages between feudal-seigniorial and patriarchal-paternalistic authority have impressed two prominent yet very dissimilar historians of the Old South, Eugene Genovese and James Oakes. For Genovese the slaveholders "grew into the closest thing to feudal lords imaginable in a nineteenth-century bourgeois republic." Long before the development of slave societies in the New World, medieval Europe had given birth to "a seigneurial world in which lords and serfs (not slaves) faced each other with reciprocal demands and expectations. This land-oriented world of medieval Europe slowly forged the traditional paternalistic ideology to which southern slaveholders fell heir." This ideology's vibrancy in the Old South reflected "the patriarchalism of the plantation community," which nurtured in both masters and slaves a paternalistic "insistence upon mutual obligations—duties, responsibilities, and ultimately even rights."[9] Whereas Genovese sees the Old South as an essentially precapitalist and paternalistic society rooted in the master-slave relationship, Oakes insists that slaveholders lived in a decidedly capitalist and liberal world. For Oakes the preponderance of antebellum masters, living as they did in a market-oriented, mobile, and increasingly democratic society, could not embrace "paternalism"— that is, "the ideological legacy of a feudal political system with no fully developed market economy." Nor could the Old South incarnate the "patriarchalism" that had grown "slowly but logically out of the medieval understanding of society as a hierarchy of orders so thoroughly interdependent as to be 'organically' unified, like the various parts of the human body itself." Oakes's capitalist slaveholders embraced a liberal ideology of individual rights and self-interest which "repudiated the patriarchal premise of organic unity and the natural subordination of the child to the father as the model for political life." [10]

Although scholars have frequently employed the adjectives patriarchal and paternalistic in overlapping and even interchangeable fashion, in late twentieth-century usage the latter, as an ideological -ism word, seems to allow substantially greater leeway for ambiguous and subjective connotations than does the more structural term patriarchy. Whereas patriarchy denotes societal dominance and governance by males, paternalism signifies a practice or policy of governing and treating people in a fatherly fashion. [11] What does it mean to govern and treat people in a "fatherly fashion"? The answer can reflect the respondent's own experience of paternal authority, which may have run the gamut from affectionate and nurturing to coercive and repressive. The answer can also depend on whether the paternalism in question is directed toward children or adults. For late twentieth-century Western culture, with its emphasis on the inherent dignity and freedom of every individual, a caring and nurturing "paternalism" that seeks to bridge the gap between dependent childhood and independent adulthood deserves to be commended, while an oppressive and exploitative "paternalism" that presumes to regulate adults like irresponsible children deserves only contempt. One might well wonder whether use of the word to signify condescending and repressive behavior on the part of upper-class adults toward lower-class adults does not have the indirect and unintended effect of disparaging the importance of the nurturing and affectionate "paternalism" that most children desperately need from male parents or caregivers. On the other hand, one can insist that the actual behavior of fathers throughout history has run the gamut from loving tenderness to brutal exploitation, from selfless altruism to selfish egoism. Accordingly, in order to reflect accurately these extremes of fatherly behavior, the concept of paternalism must necessarily encompass, to quote an English scholar, "autocracy and obligation, cruelty and kindness, oppression and benevolence, exploitation and protection." [12] Anthropologist John W. Bennett has sought to systematize these ambiguities and contradictions by distinguishing between the "benevolent mode of paternalistic action," whereby "the superior person's actions are dominantly supportive of the inferior," and "exploitative paternalism," whereby the "child" is treated in such a way as to serve the interests of the "adult." [13]

This ambivalent constuction of paternalism as involving both benevolence and exploitation informs the sophisticated perspective of Eugene Genovese on planters as well as that of Robert M. Berdahl on Junkers. Southern paternalism "had little to do with Ole Massa's ostensible benevolence, kindness, and good cheer," explains Genovese. Not only did it encourage "cruelty and hatred" as well as "kindness and affection," [14] but masters and slaves could attach different interpretations and expectations to the paternalism that mediated their relationship. Similarly, Berdahl emphasizes that Junker paternalism had in practice a

"Janus face," with "its brutality and its beneficence."[15] Both historians clearly want their readers to distinguish between the self-serving ideologies of benevolent paternalism often propounded by planter and Junker apologists, and the pronounced presence of exploitative paternalism on actual plantations and knight's estates. At the same time, Genovese and Berdahl alike emphasize that reciprocity of duties and obligations is the heart of paternalism, and argue that paternalistic reciprocity is fundamentally incompatible with the free wage labor that they see as part and parcel of capitalist development. Genovese sees in the plantation South, from the closing of the African slave trade in 1808 until the Civil War, a marked growth in the power and reality of paternalism, as slaves subtly exploited their increasing market value to extract greater concessions from their owners.[16] In contrast, Berdahl sees a marked decline in the efficacy of paternalism in East Elbia during the *Vormärz* era (1815–48) that followed the abolition of hereditary servitude, as the personalistic lord-serf relationship based on reciprocal obligations and duties was supplanted by the more impersonal market relationship between employers and contractual laborers.[17]

Whereas Genovese and Berdahl view paternalistic social relations as fundamentally incompatible with free-labor capitalism, more than a few recent studies in both U.S. and Prusso-German history have argued that a type of "paternalism" proved quite compatible with capitalist industrialization and wage labor in the nineteenth century. However, it is not always clear in these studies whether the term paternalism signifies first and foremost an upper-class ideology and mode of behavior or, in addition, a species of employer-employee relations that actually reflected the ideal of reciprocal duties and obligations. In *Proprietary Capitalism: The Textile Manufacture at Philadelphia, 1800–1885* (1983), Philip Scranton discovers among owners of the relatively small, proprietary firms of mid-century Philadelphia (as opposed to the larger, corporate firms of Lowell, Massachusetts) a "factory paternalism" analogous to that in early industrial England. Scranton applies the label "paternalist actions" to mill-owner efforts on behalf of education, churches, and (after their retirement) "public service in politics and associational activities," all of which the owners perceived to be "duties as much as opportunities to extend the networks of dominion."[18] According to Gerald David Jaynes's *Branches Without Roots: Genesis of the Black Working Class in the American South, 1862–1882* (1986), "The paternalism of industrializing capitalism" involved efforts by employers "to remold the workers into inferior images of themselves," that is, into "laborers with a work discipline compatible with the demands of continuous and efficient production." Employers sought to effect this remolding by buying "both the laborer's services and loyalty through material incentives that exceed(ed) the going market rate."[19] Ironically, it may be that scholarly emphasis on paternalism as a potential link between management and labor has served to obscure the degree to which employees developed a form of familial solidarity over against their employers. In *Like a*

Family (1987), a study of Southern cotton mill workers during the late nineteenth and early twentieth century, Jacquelyn Dowd Hall and her coauthors rely heavily on oral history interviews. They note that former mill workers often "chose a family metaphor" to describe mill village life, a metaphor which historians have usually interpreted as "evidence of a paternalistic management style that provided for workers' needs while depriving them of independence and responsibility." Yet mill workers did not invoke family imagery "to describe their dependence on a fatherly employer so much as they were emphasizing their relationships to one another."[20]

Germanist Lawrence Schofer, in *The Formation of a Modern Labor Force: Upper Silesia, 1865–1914* (1975), sees the term paternalism as "referring to the attempt by management to control the daily life of employees by supervising many of their extramural activities through measures like company owned housing, leisure time organizations, company stores, and the like, all intended to guide workers in the 'correct' way of life." Ironically, although most industrialists in Upper Silesia were or became titled Junkers, they proved far less inclined to implement such paternalist programs than did the the non-noble proprietors of the Krupp and Stumm enterprises in the Ruhr district of Westphalia.[21] Because "company paternalism" could serve the purpose of "controlling labor costs by preventing workers from organizing and striking," concludes David Crew in *Town in the Ruhr: A Social History of Bochum, 1860–1914* (1979), efforts by heavy industry in the Ruhr to effect "the 'paternalistic' control of their workforce" appear to have been "a specific form of capitalist rationality appropriate to the development of heavy industry in the German context."[22] Geoff Eley, writing in 1984, reiterated Crew's argument that scholars should not simply attribute the frequency of company paternalism in German heavy industry to the anachronistic persistence of "some 'pre-industrial' or 'traditional' mentality." The prominence of "a particularly ruthless variety of company paternalism" in the American as well as the German process of "capitalist industrial development," insists Eley, is prima facie evidence against the persistence of traditionalism thesis, since "anything remotely resembling the 'feudal' traditions so avidly invoked by German historians was patently absent from American society."[23]

An ethos of employer paternalism does in fact seem to have been part and parcel of what one Americanist terms "the values and ideology of industrial capitalism."[24] From my perspective, the label paternalism should be limited to a type of upper-class ideology, one that persists into the late twentieth century and was widespread in the nineteenth-century Western world, urban as well as rural, free as well as slave. As Lacy K. Ford, Jr., has observed, "In both slave and free societies, paternalism was an idiom of social responsibility and moral uplift adopted with more or less sincerity by those who enjoyed economic and social power."[25] Just as we tend to see a father as responsible for the discipline and upbringing of his children, so elite groups have often tended to see themselves as responsible for the control and uplift of subordinate groups. To the extent that members of a subordinate group seem to have accepted or endorsed an elite's paternalistic aspirations, their acceptance or endorsement can be evaluated as a form of loyalty or submission (often calculated) or some mixture of the two, without using familial language that suggests children's relations with father figures. Thus we can avoid the semantic risks and analytical pitfalls involved in applying the label paternalistic, with its seemingly inescapable connotations of beneficent fatherly concern and filial affection,[26] to a class relationship between subordinate and superordinate groups. When we think about the way in which dependent laborers have generally responded to the paternalistic poses of their masters, lords, or employers, we would do well to keep in mind I. A. Newby's explanation for the failure of the industrial paternalist's vision for the cotton mills of the "New South." "The paternalists encountered obstacles they never overcame, and the reasons for their failure seem apparent," concludes Newby. "Their relationship with the mill folk was exploitative, and that plus the arbitary exercise of power it permitted compromised their pose as selflessly benevolent men."[27]

— II —

In Europe the development of sophisticated upper-class ideologies of benevolent paternalism accelerated during the early nineteenth-century era of literary romanticism and political reaction. For England, David Roberts describes early Victorian writings about "patriarchal principles" and "paternal government" as primarily "a response to social upheavals" like the Chartist movement and the Irish famines. English paternalist theory, with its glorification of rural life, personal relations, and "reciprocal bonds of authority and deference," incorporated "some of the most powerful intellectual developments of the age: romanticism, religious seriousness, historical scholarship, the cult of the medieval, and other idealistic reactions to the latitudinarianism of the eighteenth century and the mechanistic calculations of nineteenth-century political economy and utilitarianism." Despite these idealistic influences on paternalist ideology, Roberts concludes from his study of contemporary testimony on rural life that in reality "the average landowner expressed a greater interest in the cash nexus than in the duties of landed property."[28]

From his extensive study of the Prussian aristocracy, Robert Berdahl has concluded that "Paternalism appears as the center of the conceptual universe *(Begriffswelt)* of conservative political ideology during *Vormärz*."[29] To be sure, as Berdahl recognizes, the distorted mirror of paternalistic ideology hardly gave an accurate reflection of life on East Elbian Junker estates, either before or after the abolition of hereditary bondage.[30] Junker scholar Baron Theodor von der Goltz insisted in 1896 that the familial image of relationships between manorial lords *(Gutsherren)* and their serfs was primarily a product of the half-century following Stein's emancipation decree of 1807. Prussian landowners and bureaucrats circa 1800, far from celebrating "the so-called patriarchal relationship," constantly complained that peasants did not perform their manorial services willingly. "To patriarchal conditions belong," wrote Goltz, "on the one hand 'the mild government of a father' and on the other 'the genuine affection of a child.'" Applying this model to pre-1807 *Rittergüter* reflected "a complete misunderstanding of conditions at that time," when "reciprocal trust" was the exception, and the rule was "harsh treatment and oppression on the one hand," and "on the other hate, recalcitrance, ignorance, brutality."[31]

Von der Goltz suggested that conditions actually improved for *Rittergut* workers after the abolition of serfdom. This judgment finds confirmation in the work of the Baron's younger and more famous contemporary, historical sociologist Max Weber. At mid-century, when Junkers depended for most of their field labor on cottagers and lodgers *(Insten)* who received a small fraction of the grain crop as part of their compensation, there existed a palpable "community of interest" *(Interessengemeinschaft)* between the Junker and his field hands, wrote Weber in the early 1890s. Although the *Inst* relationship involved "complete subjection to the will of the lord," it also bound the Junker and cottager together in the estate's "community of economic interest," since both stood to gain from high yields and a successful harvest.[32] Weber described the mid-nineteenth-century *Rittergut* as "predominantly a form of communal economy managed and ruled patriarchally," and emphasized the contrast between such patriarchal social relations and capitalist relations. The latter, marked by "the proletarianization of the rural working class" and the replacement of "personal authority relationships" with "impersonal class authority," became increasingly widespread on East Elbian estates during the last quarter of the century, as Junkers phased out the cottager arrangement and instead hired local or migrant wage laborers.[33] Although Weber stressed the differences between patriarchal and capitalist labor relations, he also emphasized that exploitation pervaded the former. To speak of the traditional *Inst* relationship as "patriarchal," noted Weber, and to characterize it as a "community of interest" between worker and lord, was not to say that "some relationship of personal trust" existed beween worker and lord. Indeed, "the unmodern patriarchal organization of labor, with which the well hated Junker of the East operates, leads to conditions, compared with which the situation of the most wretchedly placed industrial worker is a pleasant one."[34] This last judgment probably infuriated the contemporary Junker Elard von Oldenburg-Januschau, who inherited the West Prussian estate Januschau in 1883. East Elbian agricultural workers have long enjoyed "one of the most secure of human existences," he wrote in his 1936 *Reminiscences*. "According to old custom . . . the rural laborer of the German East is provided for in old age. He is not deprived of house and farmland, but continues to live on the manorial estate and receives his old-age allowances."[35] Oldenburg-Januschau reads here remarkably like a Southern defender of antebellum slavery.

Indeed, when evaluating both the antebellum and postbellum Souths, one might invoke Weber's distinction between an economic community of interest and a relationship based on mutual trust, and find something of the former on plantations worked by black labor. Before the Civil War many slaves seem to have recognized that much of their well-being depended on the economic prosperity of their masters.[36] The decentralized cotton plantation system that evolved after the Civil War, based largely on sharecropping, created a different dynamic between freedmen and planters; for a profitable harvest redounded to the direct financial benefit of sharecropper and landowner alike.[37] Nonetheless, several recent scholars of the postbellum South have concluded that there was less "paternalism" on plantations after than before the Civil War.[38] Since black sharecroppers were uncapitalized "free" laborers rather than enslaved capital assets, this is not surprising. It is important to emphasize, here and again later in this chapter, that the abolition of chattel slavery in 1863–65 brought about what economic historian Gerald Jaynes has called "the severing of the connection between economic incentives and acts of benevolence" toward black labor.[39]

— III —

I have argued that an unambiguous and value-neutral definition of paternalism seems more problematic than such a definition of patriarchy. This is not to say that the more structural term patriarchy has been altogether free from definitional latitude and variegated usage. Biblical scholar Phyllis Byrd, after describing the Old Testament as "a collection of writings by males from a society dominated by males," carefully explains in an endnote her decision not to use the terms patriarchy and patriarchal in the text: "The term 'patriarchy' is appropriate to designate such a society, but is avoided here because of the fact that widespread indiscriminate use of the term has led to the blurring of significant social and cultural distinctions among various 'patriarchal' societies."[40] Nonetheless, as the Old South and contemporaneous East Elbia were clearly societies "dominated by males," it seems "appropriate" to label them patriarchal. Formal participation in the political arena of both regions was, of course, limited to adult males. Although the ranks of both landed elites included some women, generally widows, female proprietors of knight's estates and plantations were decidedly anomalous. The legal authority of a male planter or Junker encompassed not only the wife and dependent children in his immediate family but also the slaves or servants and day-laborers who worked the estate and constituted members of an extended household economy, albeit one that also functioned as a highly commercial enterprise.

Such a patriarchal structuring of political and familial relations seems to have been part and parcel of most pre-industrial and pre-democratic (that is, pre-modern) Western societies.[41] Throughout Europe and colonial America for most of the eighteenth century, the extended household, or *familia,* was governed by the master of the household, or *pater familias.* During the first half of the nineteenth century most of the South and East Elbia experienced little of the separation of home and workplace that we associate with industrialization, urbanization, and economic modernization. Since plantation and *Rittergut* owners retained much of the pre-industrial patriarch's authority over his relations and minions, planter and Junker spokesmen could plausibly portray the plantation or knight's estate as an extended household governed by a pater familias. According to Berlin law professor and Old Prussian ideologue Friedrich Julius Stahl, "the property relationship *(Besitzverhältniß)*" attached to aristocratic estates required that the estate owner exercise "governmental rights" over his laborers; for the relationship constituted "in reality an unbroken union, from whose head the state authority naturally requires the administration of order, much as it does from the master of the household *(Hausvater)* over his family and servants, or from the master of a guild over his journeymen and apprentices."[42] Georgia planter-physician John S. Wilson wrote that "Plantation government should be eminently patriarchal, simple, and efficient. The pater-familias, or head of the family, should, in one sense, be the father of the whole concern, negroes and all."[43] Wilson's argument held even greater etymological weight than he may have realized. As medievalist David Herlihy has explained, the classical Latin word *familia* "originally meant a band of slaves" and "thus implied an authoritarian structure and hierarchical order, founded on but not limited to relations of marriage and parenthood."[44]

Some planters and Junkers also compared the governance of plantations and knight's estates with the patriarchal authority wielded by the Old Testament fathers of Israel, an apologia that reflected the powerful impact of pietistic and evangelical Protestantism on both the antebellum South and contemporaneous East Elbia (a topic to be discussed further in Chapter 6).[45] Even the aged Jeffersonian John Hartwell Cocke, resident at Bremo Bluff plantation in Virginia's Piedmont county of Fluvanna, resorted to invocations of Biblical patriarchy during the desperate years of the Civil War. Although his personal journal acknowledged that slavery had become "one of the most prolific sources of crime & wickedness" in the world, he nevertheless insisted that divine Providence, largely in order to bring the Christian gospel to benighted blacks, had blessed the South with the establishment of "patriarchal institutions" modeled after Biblical Abraham's "patriarchal government" over his relations, dependents, and slaves.[46] Yet Cocke's own patriarchal power, like that of most planters and Junkers, was hardly as absolute and extensive as he would have liked. The general's concerted antebellum efforts to Christianize his own slaves seem to have brought only a minority to professions of faith.[47]

In her study of plantation mistresses, Catherine Clinton acknowledges that a "patriarchal structure" of male-female relations was "not in the least unique to southern society." Yet she also insists that "Patriarchy was the bedrock upon which slave society was founded, and slavery exaggerated the pattern of subjugation that patriarchy had established," because the power and authority of planters, sexual and racial as well as political and economic, required the simultaneous subordination of both white women and black slaves.[48] Of course, most plantation and *Rittergut* mistresses did not have to endure the kind of physical brutality and coercion often experienced by slaves or servants, despite the often burdensome responsibilities of household management carried by many planter and Junker wives,[49] and despite the resentment some of them felt at their husbands' adultery with slave or servant girls. Moreover, we should not assume that the prevalence of black bondage necessarily made the antebellum South a more intensely patriarchal society than contemporaneous East Elbia, where a form of contractual labor was fast becoming the norm. In fact, according to the patriarchal model that had taken shape in seventeenth-century Europe, monarchical East Elbia was a more thoroughly and consistently "patriarchal" society than the republican South. Cissie Fairchilds offers an admirable summary of patriarchal theory (which can be termed patriarchalism) in Old Regime France that is equally applicable to the "absolutist patriarchalism" of Prussia: "The authority of the father of the family was the model for all authority: a king was the father of his people, God was the Father of all mankind."[50] During the 1840s Friedrich Wilhelm IV repeatedly insisted that it was "the natural duty of a German prince" to preserve "a patriarchal regime" unencumbered by parliamentary constitutionalism.[51] In the Old South patriarchy inevitably swam against the republican and increasingly democratic, egalitarian currents of American political culture, producing a tension that was absent from monarchical and aristocratic Prussia even after the abolition of serfdom in 1807–10. Well before Britain's North American colonies effected their republican revolution from monarchical Britain in the late eighteenth century, concludes Allan Kulikoff, some planters in the Chesapeake colonies "rejected the connection between male supremacy in the family and royal absolutism in government that lay at the heart of European patriarchal theory." Kulikoff uses the term "domestic patriarchalism" to distinguish these planters' belief in male authority within the family from the monarchical argument for a patriarchal politics.[52] In analogous fashion would many antebellum proslavery writers use the term "domestic servitude" to distinguish the allegedly benevolent autocracy of patriarchal plantations from the democratic republicanism of Southern white politics.[53]

During the eighteenth century most of the Western world began to experience a marked shift in cultural emphasis away from the extended household or *familia* in favor of the more intimate and sentimental nuclear family as the foundation stone of society.[54] On both sides of the Atlantic the "traditional patriarchal family"—in which, says Fairchild, "husband and wife, parents and children were bound together by ties of duty and obedience rather than love"—began to recede in cultural importance before the more private and sentimental "modern affectionate family." The new family model no longer included the household's domestic servants, but was limited to "the nuclear unit of parents and children," and was "more affectionate, more egalitarian, and more child-centered."[55] Indeed, the German language did not employ the word *Familie* to signify the private nuclear family of parents and children before the second half of the eighteenth century. Until then German writers had used the awkward phrase "with wife and child" to identify such intimate family relations, which existed within the larger circle of a household economy that encompassed servants as well as blood relations.[56]

As the ideal of the private and affectionate family achieved cultural sway among affluent and literate groups during the late eighteenth and early nineteenth century, the words patriarchy and patriarchal became associated more and more with sentimental images of "caring father and submissive child."[57] These affectionate and beneficent connotations clearly informed the ways in which some spokesmen for the planter and Junker elites invoked familial imagery and paternal language when seeking to paint flattering verbal portraits of relations between masters and slaves or lords and their pre-1807 enserfed laborers. That is, they might romanticize and idealize the proprietor's interaction with his minions as a relationship between "benevolent fathers" and "obedient sons,"[58] akin to John W. Bennett's anthropological model of benevolent paternalism. For example, in 1818 the East Prussian Count Alexander von Dohna argued that if the royal bureaucracy became involved in settling disputes over real estate between former serfs and their manorial lords, this interference would serve only to disturb the "happy patriarchal relationship" that pervaded the countryside.[59] Friedrich August Ludwig von der Marwitz of Brandenburg had written in 1811, in response to Baron vom Stein's condemnation of serfdom as "the last vestige of slavery," that "serfdom was rather a patriarchal bond that joined the peasants to the noblemen," and that the *Rittergut* constituted a "small patriarchal state" governed by "a member of the family."[60] Proslavery writers in the South would hardly have appreciated Marwitz's implied rebuke that the master-slave relationship, unlike relations between lord and serf, did not involve such a familial and paternal bond. "We are well convinced," declared Thomas R. Dew of Virginia's William and Mary College in 1832, "that there is nothing but the mere relations of husband and wife, parent and child, brother and sister, which provide a closer tie, than the relations between master and servant."[61] On the eve of the Civil War another Virginian, lawyer-planter George Fitzhugh, claimed that "domestic affection and self-interest shield the patriarchal subjects from oppression, and secure to them kind treatment, protection, and support," despite the fact that the patriarchal form of government was "seemingly the most despotic form." [62] Here Fitzhugh brings to mind the Swiss thinker Karl Ludwig von Haller, the intellectual guru of Old Prussian ideologues during the 1820s and 1830s. [63] Although Haller tended to use the term "patrimonial" rather than "patriarchal," he maintained that the relationship between father and child constituted the archetypal model for all social relations. "What our imperfect language calls authority and servitude, is nothing more than beneficial superiority on the one hand, and grateful assistance on the other, an exchange of favors, a continual reciprocity of service." [64]

Despite Haller's popularity among Old Prussian ideologues during the pre-1848 era, and despite similarities between his paternal imagery and that of George Fitzhugh, we must remember that hereditary servitude was a flourishing and expansive institution in the antebellum South, while contemporaneous East Elbia contained only its waning vestiges. Consequently, Old Prussian ideologues tended to employ patriarchal language most frequently when casting nostalgic looks back to the eighteenth-century days of serfdom. As pauperism and social unrest mounted in East Elbia during the late 1840s, most Junker spokesmen took great care to appear in the public arena like flexible moderates rather than doctrinaire reactionaries; and such moderation required tempering patriarchal paeans. Writing in February of 1848, a Silesian member of Prussia's Board of Rural Economy *(Landes-Ökonomie-Collegium)* presented an ambiguous view of serfdom as at the same time a benevolent and an exploitative institution: "there existed between lord and servants a type of patriarchal relationship; happily for both was the lord the loving father and protector of his subjects, but he was oppressive and degrading the rights of men, having only his own advantage in view, an exploiter of the servants bound to him." [65] In the Prussian National Assembly of 1848 a leading spokesman for the Junker-dominated agricultural associations was Eduard Baumstark, director of the Eldena Royal Academy for Political and Agricultural Sciences. On 16 August, during a debate on the living conditions of rural day-laborers and urban wage earners, Baumstark stated that little importance should be attached to such reactionary arguments as, "for example, it would be better if bondage, serfdom *(Leibeigenschaft, Erbuntertänigkeit)* still existed, for then the workers would be cared for when they reached old age." Nonetheless, noted Baumstark, a thorough investigation would be necessary to disprove this argument. [66]

Baumstark's remarks point to an important aspect of the familial analogies invoked by both planter and Junker spokesmen at mid-century. Paternal imagery, even when employed nostalgically, could serve as a weapon in the arsenal of proslavery and Old Prussian ideologues engaged in mounting counterattacks against planterdom's or Junkerdom's social and political critics, especially among philanthropic patricians in Prussia's western provinces or the Northern free states. Planter and Junker apologists could contrast the allegedly familial and personal character of social relations on plantation or *Rittergut* with what they saw as the more impersonal and exploitative relations prevailing in cities and industrial factories. In other words, they could cast a more flattering light on plantations and knight's estates by attacking free-labor, "liberal" capitalism at what German historian Theodore Hamerow calls "its most vulnerable point, its indifference to the social consequences of unrestrained individualism."[67]

In East Elbia some relatively cosmopolitan intellectuals argued that the Junker elite should take the lead in attempting to elevate the condition of industrial labor. Consider the case of Victor Aimé Huber, a renegade ideologue who wanted Junkerdom to accept the inevitability of "the gigantic development of modern large-scale industry," and to take some initiative in improving the material and cultural level of the working classes. Huber wrote in 1852 that the landed aristocracy *(Ritterschaft)* should ideally serve as a societal counterweight to "the temperament of the middle classes," with their selfishness and inclination "predominantly towards profit." In order for Junkerdom to assume this exalted role, wrote Huber, the political "Right" and the conservative press first had to stop painting the conditions of rural workers "in white and rosey colors" while painting factory life "in all black colors." Then Junker spokesmen could open their eyes to the evidence that "factory workers can also lead a Christian and moral life."[68] From Huber's perspective Junkerdom had to get beyond the myopic defensiveness shown at the United Diet of 1847 by *Rittergut*-owner and bureaucrat Adolph von Werdeck of Brandenburg. In responding to the charge that "an agricultural proletariat *(Ackerbau-Proletariat)*" existed in Prussia, Werdeck insisted that "So far as I am familiar with Brandenburg, it does not exist. I know many communities, where there is no systematic poor relief. Why? because there are no poor. A proletariat and calls for poor relief always go hand in hand." He insisted that an impoverished proletariat came only with industrial development, in conjunction with the construction of canals, highways, and railroads.[69]

The challenge of incorporating industrial labor into a corporatist-conservative vision of Prussian society was taken up in the 1850s by perhaps the most important Junker manifesto of the decade. *Foundations of Conservative Politics* (1856) presented arguments that had been anticipated in the pages of the *Berlin Political Weekly* during the 1830s. The principal author, the Brandenburg Baron Karl Adolph Alexander von Hertefeld, condemned "the modern masterless slavery" and "the atomization of society" promoted by economic and political liberalism. The foremost task of "conservative agrarian policy" was the "feudalization of landed property" against the vagaries of the market; and in the industrial sector conservatives must effect "the feudalization of the attitude of the factory master toward his workers."[70] Hertefeld would probably have concurred, at least privately, with the assertion by migrant Southern academic George Frederick Holmes that "the serf of the feudal ages was more happily situated than the labouring freeman of today." Holmes made this statement in an 1856 review of George Fitzhugh's *Sociology for the South; or the Failure of Free Society* (1854). Although Holmes, like the vast majority of proslavery writers, refused "to go so far as Mr. Fitzhugh and maintain that nothing but slavery can be right," he praised Fitzhugh's efforts "to refute the arrogant pretensions, and neutralize the vain malignity of those who introduce the presumption of the exclusive righteousness of the free labor system as a ground for the denunciation of slave communities."[71] Southern proslavery writers often insisted that the benevolent treatment of workers under their region's patriarchal system of "domestic servitude" was decidedly superior to the treatment that legally free workers received under the Northern and European system of "wage slavery."[72] In an 1837 address to the U.S. Senate, South Carolinian John C. Calhoun contrasted "the subtle and artful fiscal contrivances" by which "modern" free laborers were kept in subjection to "the more direct, simple, and patriarchal mode by which the labor of the African race is, among us, commanded by the European."[73] When a subsequent South Carolina senator, James Henry Hammond, delivered his famous "mud-sill" speech in 1858, he told his colleagues from the free states that "your whole hireling class of manual laborers and 'operatives,' as you call them, are essentially slaves. The difference between us (in the South and North) is, that our slaves are hired for life and well compensated; . . . Yours are hired by the day, not cared for, and scantily compensated. . . ."[74] An unidentified essayist in Richmond's *Southern Literary Messenger* went so far as to claim in 1857 that U.S. slaves were "in social, moral, and material well being, superior to the labouring class in every country on earth."[75] Although it is hard to imagine an Old Prussian ideologue taking this claim seriously, it is instructive to read what the son of Carl von Rosenberg, the renegade-Junker-become-Texas-slaveholder-and-secessionist whom we met in Chapter 1, had to say about the material condition of slaves. Wilhelm von Rosenberg, working a farm in southeast Texas, wrote to German friends in April of 1850 that the "Negroes have it better here than the entire servant class with you." Why? "The Negro is capital to the owner. The latter doesn't let it deteriorate nor does he strike it dead if he himself wants to prosper."[76]

— IV —

A few inconoclastic planters and Junkers spoke out vigorously against the claim that slave plantations or pre-1807 *Rittergüter* could be adjudged familial or patriarchal in nature. Cassius M. Clay (1810–1903) grew up on his father's White Hall plantation in Madison County, Kentucky, but attended New England's Yale College before inheriting the family estate. Clay emancipated the slaves in 1844, when they were worth some $40,000, and began to agitate in Kentucky for a state-sponsored system of gradual emancipation. He argued that slavery was responsible for "wrongs to the blacks," the impoverishment of the nonslaveholding white majority, and the corruption of white republicanism. A decade later, when the Republican party was born north of the Ohio River, he still resided in Kentucky; but Clay joined the new antislavery organization and during the summer of 1854 crossed the Ohio River into Illinois to deliver a series of lectures entitled "The Despotism of Slavery."[77] That the South's republican planters distinguished between despotic tyranny and familial patriarchy is illustrated by one who portrayed himself in Georgia's *Southern Cultivator* as "the patriarch (not tyrant)" of his plantation family.[78]

In East Elbia the Silesian Count Hermann zu Dohna-Kotzenau (1809–72) gained the title of "red count" for his strictures against the status quo. In 1847, as another poor harvest raised sparks that would help to fan the fires of revolution the following year, Dohna-Kotzenau published a short book whose purpose was to focus public concern on the deplorable plight of the Prussian working classes. He penned an arresting response to traditionalists who continued to extoll the pre-1807 master-serf relationship: "It is ironic that this relationship has been labelled patriarchal. Its participants were not united into a family by indissoluble bonds; the dependents were chained indissolubly only to the authority of the *Rittergut,* whose owner could sell the estate to a new lord without hindrance and, with it, the dependents. The children awaken one morning and discover that their father has sold them, that they have a new father. Is this the subject for a family portrait?" Then Dohna-Kotzenau showed that a monarchist could also distinguish between tyranny and patriarchy. "Nor have I spoken here of a lord who was tyrannical toward his dependents, but of a kind, considerate lord who lightened the labor obligations of his subordinates when possible and who maintained them in misfortune; but I believe I have shown that he could only be a kind lord and that he stood in too high and isolated a position to be called the father of a family."[79] No doubt Dohna-Kotzenau would have responded even more negatively to patriarchal apologists for bondage in the U.S. South. There slaves constituted the personal property of their masters, who could and did sell slaves not only separately from the landed estate but away from family relations, as a means of both profit-taking and labor discipline. As Dohna-Kotzenau's analysis suggests, to evaluate life on plantations with familial language that recalls the proslavery appraisal of Southern bondage as "an institution patriarchal in its nature and tendencies" is to compound the difficulties inherent in the historian's obligation to distinguish as clearly as possible between the flattering images historical actors created for themselves and the more sullied realities of their historical situation.[80] The need to discredit the proslavery argument's patriarchal propaganda was evident to former slave Harriet Jacobs, who wrote disparagingly of apologists proclaiming that slavery "is a beautiful 'patriarchal institution'; that slaves don't want their freedom. . . ."[81]

To be sure, many a planter, like many a Junker, viewed himself as a stern but generous pater familias tending to the welfare of his faithful "people."[82] Indeed, the historical record offers numerous examples of a planter's expressing sincere feelings of familial affection for, and patriarchal benevolence toward, a particular slave who had worked long years in the master's home as a domestic servant. As Charles Flynn, Jr., notes, "Evidence of antebellum paternalism comes largely from the friendships between masters and personal servants that many whites upheld as the ideal against which to judge the treatment of slaves as a group."[83] Since friendships between planters and their field-hands were exceedingly rare, Kenneth Stampp concludes that "Plantation paternalism was . . . in most cases merely a kind of leisure-class family indulgence of its domestics."[84] Regardless of how much benevolent paternalism could be found in the Big House, it was much attenuated in the fields where most slaves spent their working hours.

"Planters sometimes called their bondsmen their 'black family,' " writes Jane Turner Censer about North Carolina's landed gentlemen, "but historians should not allow that term to mask the stark contrast that existed between the treatment of slaves and of children. Despite the demands elite Carolinians sometimes made of their offspring and the concern they sometimes manifested toward slaves, their treatment of slaves was far harsher." In other words, planters expended far greater benevolent paternalism on their biological white children—who were, after all, being reared with the goal of mature independence in mind—than on their perpetually enslaved black minions. Censer notes that North Carolina planters "erected a barrier between themselves and their servants by focusing upon blacks as property," and always "stressed the profit motive" in their handling of slaves.[85] This tendency to view slaves first and foremost as profitable property could characterize marginal planters as well as the more affluent families studied by Censer, even though the lesser planter probably had more regular personal contact with all his slaves. Consider the case of upcountry South Carolina's David G. Harris, owner of ten slaves in 1860. His journal for 1858 reports that he had experienced "a difficulty" with twenty-five-year-old Matt. After administering "a gentle admonition in the shape of a good whipping," Harris considered selling the troublemaker. "I think it a great piece of folly for any person to keep a negro that will not behave himself, particularly when they can (get) more for them than they are worth." The entreaties of Matt and "the other negroes" persuaded Harris "to try him once more." Nonetheless, two months later Harris reported selling Matt for the good price of $1,050, the bondsman having allegedly "said that he was willing to be sold."[86]

Throughout Western history slavery and its defenders were always beset by a tension rooted in the slave's dual status as person and property.[87] This tension was evident in Southern proslavery efforts to reconcile the goals of familial patriarchy and monetary profit. In the Republic of Texas a Houston newspaper editor defended an 1841 law exempting slave property from forced sales to pay debts on the grounds that the master-slave relationship was akin to family ties. "Is it not only right that this 'property' not be sold?" Yet the Texas legislature repealed the law within a year, leading one recent historian to quip that "Texans revered slave property, but the majority stopped short of placing it on a level with their homesteads," which remained exempt from forced sales.[88] That the financial constraints of chattel slavery could compromise the benevolent intentions of even an unusually benign slaveholder is clearly demonstrated in the will that Mississippian Cornelius Vanhauten composed in 1850. "4th. I direct and empower my Executors to sell all my Negro Slaves with the exception of Joe hereafter to be disposed of at private sale to humane masters *provided it can be done to advantage near the valuation fixed by my appraisers* (my emphasis) but in no event to separate families."[89]

Nathan Bass of Floyd County, Georgia, who wrote the prize-winning 1851 "Essay on the Treatment and Management of Slaves," declared it the "imperative duty" of masters to govern their slaves "as property, conducive to our pecuniary interest." At the same time, Bass offered guidelines for governing slaves that he might have followed in the upbringing of his own children: to "exercise our power and authority over them in such a manner as to inspire them with respect for that authority," and to "regard them as frail, erring humanity, subject to temptations and passions as ourselves."[90] Such declarations lend support to those scholars who see in antebellum slavery a pronounced patriarchal-paternalistic character. This interpretation is bolstered by the fact that proslavery spokesmen, unlike apologists for Junkerdom before or after the end of serfdom, could also attach a racist dimension to the familial analogy, maintaining that blacks should be viewed as "perpetual children, placed in servitude by a merciful Providence."[91] For such reasons, insists Bertram Wyatt-Brown, "To ignore the familial character of slavery is to miscontrue the institution itself. When masters referred to slaves as children, as they did with growing regularity throughout the pre-civil war era, they were not altogether deceiving themselves."[92]

If the planters' patriarchal-paternalistic posing was not really self-deception, then it seems to follow that a large number of slaves must have responded positively to their masters' fatherly posture and assumed the corresponding role of filial dependents, entitled to receive from their masters both concern for the slaves' physical well-being and respect for their humanity. Here we touch upon one of the most controversial and sensitive questions in the historical literature on the peculiar institution, one that I would not presume to answer definitively. Eugene Genovese has made a subtle and eloquent argument that slaves did endorse the planters' paternalistic ethos, and thereby "developed their most powerful defense against the dehumanization implicit in slavery," even though the endorsement reduced the possibilities for group resistance.[93] In sharp contrast to Genovese stands Paul Escott, who vigorously debunks the idea that the slaves themselves recognized obligations owed to their masters. He does so after a systematic examination of the interviews with elderly ex-slaves collected in the 1920s and 1930s by researchers at Fisk University and with the Federal Writers' Project. According to Escott, "The evil of enslavement and the strength of cultural differences set these two groups (masters and slaves) apart from each other and gave the slaves a fundamental sense of themselves as an oppressed group." [94] My own reading of the sources leads me to endorse Michael Wayne's conclusion that the great majority of slaves obeyed their masters "out of pragmatism, not acquiescence or, as their owners liked to think, gratitude." They "made at best a troubled peace" with their situation. [95] Though a good many slaves were adept at playing the role of loyal Sambos or docile Cuffees in order to curry their masters' favor and perhaps avoid punishment, only a few seem to have "capitulated to masters' power," in the words of William Freehling; and only these few capitulators became "grateful worshipers of overbearing paternalists." [96] The slaves' expertise at dissimulation serves to explain why so many antebellum planters failed to recognize the intensity of their minions' longing for freedom, their desire to escape from the childhood of bondage to adult independence. As Solomon Northup explained in his 1853 slave narrative, ninety-nine out of a hundred slaves "cherish in their bosoms the love of freedom," though such thoughts they "dare not utter in the hearing of the white man." [97]

Despite the frequent appearance of familial and patriarchal-paternalistic imagery in some proslavery treatises authored by clergymen and academics, most planter spokesmen in the political arena placed far less emphasis on slavery as a familial institution than on the slaves' dual character as personal property and a potentially rebellious underclass—I suspect because this mode of argument was likely to carry more weight among the predominantly nonslaveholding white electorate. To be sure, on the eve of the Civil War proslavery politicians did occasionally talk or write about the "beneficent and patriarchal system of African slavery," to quote the Texas secession convention. [98] Nonetheless, the emphasis on slaves as valuable property and possible insurgents emerges clearly from the many speeches and memorials about slavery and the Union offered by delegates to the Virginia State Convention of 1861, which met in Richmond for two months before adopting a secession ordinance on 17 April. [99] So far as I can determine, only one secessionist delegate offered an explicitly patriarchal defense of slavery—George Richardson, an attorney from Hanover County, where he owned eleven slaves in 1860. In a long address delivered on 3 and 4 April, Richardson declared that all natives of the Old Dominion had "a thousand pleasant memories of the patriarchal institution of the State—of the good will between the servants and the families of their masters . . . ." The Negro, as "a happy part of a patriarchal institution," benefited from his master's infusion "into his savage and gloomy mind" of "the kindlier sympathies and feelings leading to contentment and happiness." The master was also "unsealing the word of God" to the "degraded African," who, "when he has faithfully performed his duties here," would become eligible for "a world of eternal happiness" in the hereafter.[100]

Richardson repeated all the important arguments of evangelical apologists for slavery, including the notion that the African race comprised the descendants of Ham's son Canaan—upon whom, as reported in the ninth chapter of Genesis, Noah had placed the curse of servitude—and that the Negro's racial inferiority sprang from this curse. Indeed, said Richardson, God had commissioned "the free men of our Southern states" to be "the honored instruments of good to a fallen race in the very act of developing the resources of their own beautiful and blooming land." The Hanover attorney also felt a compulsion to vindicate the moral dignity of Southern slaveholders. The opening of all federal territories to slavery, as required by the Supreme Court's *Dred Scott* ruling of 1857, should be a sine qua non of Southern adherence to the Union, because only thereby could slaveholders free themselves from the "moral degradation" which Northerners heaped upon the slave states. "They must cease to insult us by telling us that our property in slaves is a claim so infamous, so polluting, as to be put under the ban of Northern morality and excluded from the constitutional right to protection in the Territories, or there can be no peace between us, and the sooner the better." According to Richardson, Virginia's reluctance to secede was leading a number of the Commonwealth's slaveowners to prepare for emigration to the new Southern Confederacy, an exodus which "would weaken our strength by the withdrawal not only of their energy, virtue and ability, but of millions of property from our soil." His explanation of the two motives behind this prospective exodus implies that Virginia slaveholders looked upon their bondsmen as something both more capitalist and more sinister than patriarchal dependents. First, "by an unsettled policy they fear the reduction in the value of their slaves." Second, "they know that of all institutions on earth slavery is the most sensitive, and the most dangerous to be meddled with by any but its friends and owners. They well know that the history of every outside interference with the institution is written in blood—hence they desire to place themselves and the institution in the keeping of its friends."[101] Thus, although Richardson invoked the patriarchal defense of slavery, he devoted even more attention to slaves as private property and latent rebels.

Anxiety over slaves as a potentially rebellious underclass manifested itself most clearly in the long address delivered on 20 March by James Philemon Holcombe of Jefferson's own Albemarle County. Already a prominent defender of slavery, and one of the most ardently secessionist fire-eaters in the convention, he had resigned his position as professor of law at the University of Virginia in order to serve as a delegate.[102] Holcombe pointed out "that we own our slave property by a different tenure, from that which secures to us our land and chattels," for "the slave is a man as well as his master." It was this dual character of the bondsman, as both property and person, which made it exceedingly risky for the South to remain in the Union under a government administered by the antislavery Republican party. "The slave is an ignorant man," said Holcombe, "and liable, therefore, like all ignorant men, to be misled by extravagant expectations—by false hopes held out to him; and with the voice of a mighty movement for his emancipation sounding always in his ears, can you expect aught else than that, from time to time, there should be outbursts of violence in your society, which will fill the master with continual apprehensions, and render it necessary for him to provide safeguards so costly and burdensome, as that the institution itself will become intolerable?" Holcombe identified the revolt of St. Domingue's slaves against French rule in the 1790s, and the "tragedy at Southampton" led by Nat Turner in 1831, as harbingers of the South's fate under Lincoln's government. Holcombe argued that the continued geographic expansion of Southern slavery into new territory was essential not only to preserve the economic vitality of the institution in Virginia and elsewhere but to promote the geographic diffusion of the black race, so as to reduce the risk of successful slave revolts. "Notwithstanding the immense superiority of the white over the black man, there is a numerical equilibrium which is essential to preserve in peace, the requisite subordination and control."[103]

One 1861 convention delegate from whom one might well have expected a decidedly paternalistic portrait of slavery was fifty-four-year-old James Coles Bruce of Halifax County, in the southern Piedmont. The college-educated son of a successful merchant-planter, between 1835 and 1840 he had built an impressive mansion in the Greek revival style at his Berry Hill plantation. He was the only member of the 1861 secession convention who, according to the 1860 census, owned more than a hundred slaves (134 to be exact) in a single county. As a member of the 1831–32 General Assembly, he had voted against proposals for the gradual abolition of slavery; and during the Nullification Controversy of 1832–33 he had supported South Carolina's extremist stance against the federal government. At the 1861 convention, in a lengthy speech delivered on 23 and 25 March, and sparkling with urbane witticisms and well-placed allusions to classical and Biblical literature, Bruce declared that "this question of slavery is not a question of dollars and cents," that slaves "are now so inter-twined with our social habits and interests, and laws, that to sever the connection must be political death even if done with the tenderest hand." Because "the hatred of our Southern institutions and our system of slavery, is deeply, irradically ingrafted into the minds of the Northern people," the Southern people must perforce resort to "the assumption of our own nationality." Yet Bruce's principal concern in this speech was not to preserve the peculiar character of the master-slave relationship, but to protect the "honor" and good repute of slaveholders from the degrading criticism and debilitating "contempt" being showered upon them by Northerners and foreigners alike. "I want to have our honor protected, which is far more precious than that of person or property." At the same time,

Bruce's speech included strong evidence that during his own career as a planter he had tended to view his own bondsmen as first and foremost a source of commercial profit. After returning to Virginia from a visit to New Orleans in 1844, he recalled, "I advised my friends who were also large planters to carry a portion of their negroes South, where their profits were great, and not keep them here where our profits were small. To show my sincerity in this belief, I went to Louisiana, and became a cotton and sugar planter."[104]

— V —

Although I do not consider it advisable or appropriate to characterize the generality of relations between plantation or *Rittergut* owners and their laboring minions as "patriarchal" or "paternalistic," I do think it important to emphasize that mid-century planters and Junkers most certainly did not extract productive labor from their slaves or cottagers solely through fear and compulsion. The mere fact that enslaved field-hands and contractual cottagers were sentient human beings capable of resisting brute discipline and exploiting opportunities for self-advancement, combined with the ethical scruples that most planters and Junkers felt as professing Christians, led sensible and sensitive proprietors of plantations and *Rittergüter* to realize that positive incentives and even considerate treatment could yield substantial dividends in the form of worker efficiency and loyalty. Judge John Belton O'Neall of the South Carolina upcountry distinguished himself during the 1830s for both his Unionist opposition to nullification and his principled insistence that slaves should be permitted to read in order to study the Bible. Yet in 1842, speaking before a meeting of the Palmetto State's agricultural society, O'Neall sounded almost opportunistic: "You cannot succeed with negroes, as operatives, as you desire to do, *unless you feed and clothe well* (emphasis in the original). Make them contented, and then 'Massa' will be, as he ought to be, the whole world to them."[105] In 1839 wealthy Natchez magnate John A. Quitman, who would in the 1850s become a prominent proponent of the South's geographic expansion into the Caribbean basin and governor of Mississippi, made a comparable argument in a letter to his younger sibling Albert, manager of John's sugar plantation in Louisiana: "Clothe them well, make them be clean and neat in their persons and dwellings, encourage them to have gardens and fruit-trees and vines, regulate their little domestic dissensions, and grant them every indulgence consistent with discipline. Harshness makes the negro stubborn; praise, even flattery, and, more than all, kindness makes them pliable and obedient."[106] Analagous advice came from the East Elbian owner of an estate near Königsberg, who wrote in 1849 that "In general, the cottagers, if they are well treated and also supervised, are capable and not incompetent workers who perform more work on their poor diet than one ought to expect; one must seek merely to maintain their good will and fresh spirit. Without supervision and with bad treatment they accomplish little and do not take adequate care of property." [107] A similar evaluation of day-laborers and servants *(Arbeitsleute* and *Knechte)* came in 1847 from the owner of an estate in Posen: "I have found that one gets on best with them by calm, affable treatment, although one must also adhere strongly to principles of right and obligation *(Recht und Pflicht).* The Polish servant *(Dienstbote)* is generally tractable, fairly industrious and quite competent; it is only necessary that the superior employ reasonable means to awaken the mental powers slumbering in the servants, that he seek to improve them and guide them on the right path. He who handles his inferiors in this manner will always have good and hardworking people; with improper treatment, however, one has to struggle with working people who are stubborn and gloat over the misfortunes of others." [108] To be sure, the threat of corporal punishment always lurked in the background, as it did with young children. Most thoughtful Junkers and planters alike would have endorsed the observations on the "Management of Servants" composed by W. W. Gilmer of Virginia's Albemarle County in 1852. "A great deal of whipping is not necessary; *some is* (emphasis in the original). If they know that they will be corrected when orders are disobeyed, in a proper manner, it is sufficient." [109]

Southern planters had yet another and even more compelling reason to treat their slaves with at least a modicum of humane consideration—the huge capital investment embodied in plantation laborers, unlike *Rittergut* laborers. As we saw in Chapter 2, an astute slaveholder could expect to reap substantial capital gains from the increase in both the market value and the number of his slaves. Andrew Flynn of northern Mississippi went so far as to advise his overseer in 1840 that "the children must be very particularly attended to, for rearing them is not only a duty, but also the most profitable part of plantation business." [110] Hence, there was some truth in the arresting argument, made in 1853 by Dr. William C. Daniell of Georgia, that planters were "the only capitalists whose system embraces humanity to the laborer consistently with economy of investment." [111] Daniell's argument for a congruence between humane treatment of slaves and their yield as capital investments has been reformulated by historian William Scarborough. He insists on "the paternalistic character of southern slavery" and yet sees planters as "tough-minded businessmen—capitalists in every sense of the word." [112] Although slavery manifested some paternalistic features, positing "the paternalistic character" of the peculiar institution seems more problematical than portraying planters as "capitalists in every sense of the word." Even plantation labor itself was capital, in the literal sense of a productive asset used to create more wealth.

6

Planter and Junker Conservatism

In 1902 ULRICH Bonnell Phillips, a Georgia native who was among the first genuine scholars to study the history of the Old South, pointed out that "the institution of domestic servitude had naturally a conservative influence upon those who were interested in its maintenance." His cogent explanation of this "conservative influence" deserves to be quoted in full: "Slaves were capital, and capital is always conservative in its tendency. Moreover, slavery was generally on the defensive against attack, and thus in a conservative position. It was a long-established institution, and for that reason its maintenance was conservative. Secession was advocated by its supporters as a means to the more certain preservation of slavery, and in that light the policy seems to have been conservative."[1] The deductive simplicity and penetrating straightforwardness of this analysis are especially remarkable in that Phillips was, in the words of Eugene Genovese, "a racist, however benign and paternalistic,"[2] and lived at a time when the prevailing Southern view of antebellum planters seems to have been been the maudlin and romantic image painted by such popular writers as Thomas Nelson Page of Virginia. The "Old Virginia" plantation owner, wrote Page, "believed in a democracy, but understood that the absence of a titled aristocracy had to be supplied by a class more virtuous than he believed them to be. This class was, of course, that to which he belonged."[3]

Almost half a century later, in 1947, Illinois-born historian Allan Nevins reiterated the essence of U. B. Phillips's analysis of planter conservatism. Nevins noted that "the fate of some sixteen hundred million dollars in slave property was directly involved in the controversy" between North and South circa 1850. "Conservative slaveholders (and nearly all propertied men were conservative) loved the Union so long as it promised to cherish order and prosperity. But as soon as planters became convinced that the Northern attack would lead gradually to abolition, they turned about and regarded the Union not as a bulwark but as a chain binding them with the destroyer."[4] Accordingly, we find the following rather materialistic statement in the "Declaration of the Immediate Causes Which Induce and Justify the Secession of the State of Mississippi from the Federal Union," adopted on 26 January 1861 by the state's secession convention, forty-four of whose one hundred members owned twenty or more slaves. "We must either submit to degradation (that is, Abraham Lincoln's election without a single electoral vote from the slave states, and on a Republican party platform that pledged to prevent any further spread of slavery in the federal territories), and to the loss of property worth four billions of money, or we must secede from the Union framed by our fathers, to secure this as well as every other species of property."[5] In the eleven slave states that, like Mississippi, joined the Confederate States of America, almost all planters and lesser slaveholders came to endorse withdrawal from the Union, albeit many with great reluctance and anxiety, as a radical means to a conservative end. The reluctant secessionists included many "conservative Unionists," whose attachment to the United States could reflect both their distrust of what one considered the insurrectionary and revolutionary "Demon of Secession" and their belief that the peculiar institution would be safer within than without the old Union.[6]

Allan Nevins also emphasized that planters were concerned about more than simply the financial security of their huge investments in slave property; for the Northern antislavery movement represented a powerful threat to "their social forms and institutions, their peace and safety."[7] The crux of those "social forms and institutions" was the hierarchical and authoritarian plantation community, whose "peace and safety" seemed to depend first and foremost upon the continued enslavement of the planter's Negro minions. As planter-lawyer John C. Rutherfoord told the Virginia House of Delegates in 1853, "the due subordination of our slave population is not only of vast pecuniary importance to us: it is also essential to the peace and happiness alike of the master and the slave. The security of our firesides, as well as the value of our property, is dependent upon it." To Rutherfoord this subordination was threatened by the presence of free Negroes in the Old Dominion; for "too often" the free Negro "has imbibed the doctrines of abolitionism," which Rutherfoord lumped with such "Utopian and impracticable systems" as "socialism" and "communism."[8] "The theory of universal human freedom is the mad offspring of delusion and passion," insisted Richard K. Call of Florida in February of 1861, after Florida's decision to secede the month before. Call, a former territorial governor and Whig leader who supported moderate, conditional Unionism during the secession crisis, condemned "the idolatous worshippers of *negro freedom*" who seemed so numerous in New England, although he continued to hope that "a conservative power of wisdom and virtue" slumbering in New England would "come forth in dignified authority to rebuke fanaticism." In rebuttal to abolitionists who denounced the repressive character of slavery, Call insisted: "I sleep soundly with my doors unlocked, unbarred, unbolted, when my person is accessible to the midnight approach of more than two hundred African slaves." This idyllic condition would continue "if the white man will not corrupt the virtue, or seduce the fidelity, of the faithful African slave," insisted Call; for "the black man . . . will *ever remain a slave so long as there is a superior race willing to be his master*."[9]

Although mid-nineteenth-century Junkers did not harbor the sort of racial fears and fantasies that plagued planters, East Elbia's landed elite were comparably "conservative" in that they feared for the security of their property and sought to preserve their hierarchical *Rittergut* communities against "levelling" intrusions, whether from a reformist bureaucracy or a democratic parliament. As with planters, the two concerns were interrelated; for Junkers viewed their property rights as encompassing not only allodial titles to their knight's estates but also substantial indemnification for the loss of their "ancient" rights to compulsory dues and labor services from enserfed peasants. In November of 1811 Junkers in the eastern Pomeranian county of Stolp submitted a famous petition to King Friedrich Wilhelm III in which they denounced Hardenberg's September 1811 "Regulation Edict" as contrary to "the principles of justice." The edict required them to "give away to the managers *(Wirte)* of our peasant farms *(Bauernhöfe)*, gratis, as hereditary personal property, large parcels of farmland, which are our property." "If the peasant becomes a proprietor," the petition queried, "where are we manorial lords supposed to find workers in order to operate our farms?"[10] Some forty years later, in August of 1848, almost four hundred Junkers convened in Berlin as the so-called "Junker Parliament" to protest two bills, introduced to the Prussian National Assembly in June and July, which called for a speedy end to the servile obligations of heretofore "unregulated" peasants and for the imposition of a land tax on *Rittergüter*. It was not the final completion of "regulation" and "peasant emancipation" per se that disturbed the overwhelming majority of the "Junker Parliament," but the low level of monetary compensation to manorial lords proposed by the liberal ministry of Ludolf Camphausen. His Minister of Trade, Baron Erasmus von Patow, had drawn up legislation that called for each peasant affected to receive allodial title to his farm in return for paying to his manorial lord, with the help of new mortgage banks *(Rentenbanken)*, a sum equal to eighteen times the value of the peasant's annual manorial dues. Some Silesian estate owners supported the Patow Promemoria on the very pragmatic grounds that the large number of "unregulated" peasants in their province were so desparate and angry that they simply refused to render any labor dues. But the majority sentiment of the Junker Parliament insisted that compensation should be equal to twenty-five times the value of the peasant's yearly services, the rate of compensation that had been established in Hardenberg's agrarian legislation of the 1810s.[11]

Is it sufficient or accurate to say that antebellum planters and contemporaneous Junkers were comparably "conservative" landed elites by virtue of their concern for the protection of their established property rights as proprietors of slave plantations and legally privileged knight's estates? Were Old Prussian corporatist thought and Southern proslavery thought thereby comparably "conservative" ideologies, despite the substantial political differences between planters as libertarian though racist republicans and Junkers as militarist and corporatist monarchists? The answer to these questions obviously depends on what exactly is meant by the ubiquitous and slippery words "conservative" and "conservatism." According to the dependable good judgment of *The American Heritage Dictionary of the English Language* (1969), the words denote "the disposition in politics and culture to maintain the existing order and to resist or oppose change or innovation."[12] Although this definition clearly warrants evaluating both planters and Junkers as "conservative," the labels "comparably conservative landed elites" and "comparably conservative ideologies" raise more difficult and complex issues.

— I —

Let us establish a flexible conceptual touchstone, an historical ideal-type of conservatism that does not violate the *American Heritage Dictionary*'s common-sense, everyday definition. This ideal-type must recognize, first, that every historical manifestation of conservatism is the product of a particular, unique "existing order," and, second, that the conservative stance is one of defending the status quo before critics who demand "change or innovation," and who see themselves as forward-looking, progressive advocates of a more just and healthy society. Although individuals often exhibit a strongly conservative disposition to distrust and resist change in their own immediate lives, an historically significant conservative movement only emerges when the members of a substantial group or community confront sustained and threatening progressive attacks on established values and institutions—that is, "traditional" values and institutions that they have heretofore been able to take by and large for granted. As Karl Mannheim has emphasized, unreflective, passive "traditionalism" becomes conscious and active "conservatism" only when forced to defend and define itself.[13] The South's planter elite confronted no substantial and sustained attack on their interests and values as slaveholders until the Missouri controversy of 1819–21.[14] Junkers confronted no comparable domestic threat to their interests and status as *Rittergut* owners until Baron vom Stein took office in 1807.[15]

Reactionary, backward-looking ideas can often serve conservative purposes, in that the reactionary's romantic glorification of a bygone era can have the effect of discrediting forward-looking change in the present. Old Prussian thought included a much more pronounced reactionary strain than did Southern proslavery thought, because Junkers were responding to the actual abolition of bondage, while planters confronted only the threat of abolition. Yet it would be misleading to suggest that Junkers were more genuinely reactionary or more genuinely conservative because serfdom's historical roots extended back to the medieval era. Full-blown serfdom (that is, hereditary bondage to a particular estate) did not emerge in most of East Elbia before the sixteenth century. As for historical roots and precedents, Southern slavery apologists could and did point not only to classical, "republican" Greece and Rome, but also to the world of the ancient Hebrews as revealed in the Old Testament.[16]

An elitist type of conservatism appears when an economically affluent, socially prestigious, and politically influential minority group faces potent reformist challenges to those established institutions and values that seem essential to its favored or privileged position in society. Accordingly, planters and Junkers, the most propertied, prestigious, and influential classes in their respective regional societies, first became "conservative" landed elites when compelled to defend and justify themselves against rigorous and sustained attacks on the morality and security of their plantation- and *Rittergut*-centered worlds. For the planter elite, a formidable antislavery attack from the North, and a widespread proslavery response in Southern thought and politics, emerged during the decade and a half between the Missouri controversy and the debates of 1835–37 over abolitionists' use of the federal mails, the reception of abolitionist petitions by Congress, and the first request by the newly independent Republic of Texas for annexation by the U.S. as a slave state. During these years the planters' apprehensions that a free-state majority in Congress would restrict the expansion of slavery were augmented by their more intense fears that unrestrained antislavery agitation (from within as well as from without the South) would set free the vengeful demon of slave violence, both individual and collective. These threats received extensive treatment in a famous proslavery treatise published shortly after the Missouri controversy, *A Refutation of the Calumnies Circulated Against the Southern Western States, Respecting the Institution and Existence of Slavery Among Them* (1822), written by South Carolinian Edwin C. Holland. According to Holland, the Missouri debates made it clear that the free states of the East and North sought, "under the mask of religion and humanity, of liberty and philanthropy," "to wrest from the Southern and Western States the ascendancy that their wealth and talents have given them in the councils of the nation; and, by diminishing their (Southerners') representation, to secure to themselves the whole management of the affairs of Government." Also in Holland's thoughts was the connection between the Missouri debates and the slave revolt planned in Charleston by the literate free Negro carpenter Denmark Vesey but betrayed by two house servants in the spring of 1822; for Vesey was known to have seen the Missouri debates in print, and therefore to have read such blistering attacks on slavery as the speeches of New York Senator Rufus King. Holland insisted upon the "utter impracticality" of a successful slave revolt, especially since black slaves felt an "instinctive dread" before their white masters that was comparable to the "spell . . . latent in the magic rod of a Prussian or Austrian officer." Yet he conceded that the attempted rebellion of 1822 was "a subject of deep and breathless anxiety," and severely qualified his own contention that South Carolinians need not worry about a successful slave revolt: "We regard our negroes as the 'Jacobins' of the country, against whom we should always be on our guard, and who, although we fear no permanent effects from any insurrectionary movements on their part, should be watched with an eye of steady and unremitted observation." Why? "They are the *anarchists* and the *domestic enemy*; the *common enemy of civilized society*, and the barbarians who would, IF THEY COULD, become the DE-STROYERS *of our race*." [17]

Less than a decade after Vesey's ill-fated conspiracy, slave preacher Nat Turner actually commenced a bondsmen's rebellion in southeastern Virginia's Southampton County that took the lives of over sixty whites before being suppressed. Ironically, Turner was indirectly responsible for perhaps the most influential of all antebellum proslavery treatises, Thomas R. Dew's *Review of the Debate in the Virginia Legislature of 1831–1832* (1832). Herein Dew employed "Burkean" arguments in order to demonstrate "that the time for emancipation has not yet arrived, and perhaps it never will." [18] (By "Burkean" arguments I mean the line of conservative reasoning advanced by Edmund Burke during the early 1790s in response to the French Revolution, even though most of his particular ideas had been expressed earlier and were hardly original with Burke.) Specifically, Dew set out to discredit proposals introduced to the Virginia General Assembly for the gradual emancipation and removal of the state's slaves; and these proposals, which received most of their support from the low slaveholding counties west of the Blue Ridge, came as a direct result of the fear and consternation broadcast by Nat Turner's "fierce rebellion." [19] Although there is no evidence that nascent Northern abolitionism had anything to do with the South-ampton revolt, many Southerners sought to attribute any sign of slave unrest to the "*diabolic* intentions" of the abolitionists. This attitude was well illustrated in a letter which Alabama Whig William Lucas wrote to the editors of the Washington *National Intelligencer* in 1835. "The fact is that we of the South *detest slavery* as well as our Northern Brethren, but what are we to do?" exclaimed Lucas. Either the free states must put down their "misguided fanatics," or the slave states would call a sectional convention in the interests of "self-preservation." Although Southerners ardently loved the Union, "to suffer foreign interference with their domestic concerns, to go on until, they know not what moment they and their families may be massacred; this cannot, will not be suffered." [20]

For Junkerdom, the emergence of a potent and direct progressive challenge, and of an "Old Prussian" corporatist response, occurred during the reformist ministries of Stein and Hardenberg (1807–8, 1810–22). In the words of Hans Rosenberg, the bureaucracy's quasi-liberal revolution from above provoked an aristocratic "counterrevolution from below," which "transformed the landed Junker class into a self-conscious, ideologically fortified political group."[21] Sigmund Neumann points out that Berlin's "Christian-Germanic Supper Club" *(Christlich-germanische Tischgesellschaft)* of 1811—the year of Hardenberg's original "Regulation Edict" and his proposal to tax *Rittergut* land—was "the first club association" of conservatives in Prussia, and formulated "a first concentration of conservative demands." These demands included "Christianity (in contradistinction to the "atheism" encouraged by the French Revolution), loyalty to the monarchy (as distinct from the bureaucracy), freeing of the Fatherland from foreign domination (by Napoleon and the French Empire), protection of historically evolved rights (those of the nobility and *Rittergut* proprietors)." The Christian-Germanic Supper Club, says Neumann, "drew its members from the most distinguished circles in Berlin—nobility of birth, officers, artists, writers, scholars, bureaucrats."[22] The best-known today among the club's members was the ambitious intellectual Adam Heinrich Müller, whom we first met in Chapter 1. Like Dew of Virginia, Müller had great admiration for Edmund Burke's *Reflections on the Revolution in France* (1790) and relied extensively on Burkean arguments in his own political writings. Although Müller left Berlin in May of 1811, eventually taking a position in Vienna under Metternich and Friedrich von Gentz, while in Berlin he made notable contributions to the aristocratic Fronde of Brandenburg Junkerdom. Pre-eminent among the Fronde's leaders was Ludwig von der Marwitz-Friedersdorf, whom one historian has labeled "the most important and most self-willed representative of the Brandenburg *(Kurmark)* nobility" in their struggles against Hardenberg.[23]

An elitist conservative movement, like the progressive challenge that provokes it, is both a political and a philosophical phenomenon, giving rise to elaborate but diverse theoretical justifications of the status quo—in other words, a multifarious conservative ideology. The conservative ideologies propounded by Southern proslavery and Old Prussian intellectuals could and did serve as occasional weapons in political struggles to protect the concrete interests of the planter and Junker elites. This is obvious from the speeches, essays, and petitions of John Calhoun and Jefferson Davis, Ludwig von der Marwitz and Ludwig von der Gerlach—four atypical plantation or *Rittergut* owners, in that they were at the same time sophisticated ideologues and political leaders of national stature. However, it is important to realize that many of the arguments advanced by proslavery spokesmen and Old Prussian corporatists served to enhance the subjective self-esteem as well as the objective interests of planters and Junkers. Most proprietors of plantations and *Rittergüter* were prideful individuals who deeply resented the mounting attacks, often laced with a strong dose of strident hyperbole, on their personal values and behaviors, and desired public vindication at the podium or in the press. One form of "progressive" attack that seems to have caused much irritation and anger among planters and Junkers, largely because it could be supported by a good deal of irrefutable evidence, was the recurring argument that they often treated their estate laborers exploitatively, cruelly, or violently. Consequently, as was discussed in Chapter 5, planter and Junker apologists often advanced the conservative counterargument that social relations on plantations and *Rittergüter* were essentially patriarchal, familial, and beneficent.

Antebellum planters and slavery enjoyed a much higher level of popular legitimacy in the South than did Junkers and *Rittergüter* in East Elbia; and the South, unlike East Elbia, was fast becoming a minority section. Hence Southern proslavery thought was much less overtly elitist, and more overtly regional in tenor, than was Old Prussian thought. It was hardly accidental, however, that both conservative ideologies first unfolded in older states and provinces with relatively old and entrenched planter elites: South Carolina and Virginia, Brandenburg and Pomerania.[24] Of course, only a small number of planters and Junkers, even in these older states and provinces, had the temperaments of systematic ideologues. Some of the ideologues were bright, sensitive, and well-educated "outsiders"—what Alfred Weber called "socially unattached intelligentsia"[25]— who were driven by both social ambition and intellectual conviction to become defenders of the planters' or the Junkers' interests and stature. In East Elbia the foremost non-Junkers to become Old Prussian corporatists were Adam Müller, Karl Ernst Jarcke, Friedrich Julius Stahl, and Hermann Wagener. We have not yet met Jarcke and Wagner. Jarcke (1801–52), the son of a Lutheran merchant at Danzig, studied law at Bonn and Göttingen, and converted to Roman Catholicism in the process. He taught jurisprudence first at the University of Bonn and then, from 1825, at the University of Berlin. When the French Revolution of 1830 frightened the Berlin clique of Old Prussians around the Crown Prince into founding a conservative journal, the *Berlin Political Weekly (Berliner Politische Wochenblatt*, 1831–41), Jarcke became the first editor. Another member of the editorial staff, the Crown Prince's intimate friend General Joseph Maria von Radowitz, observed that "Jarcke possesses an unusual ability to interpret the thoughts of others, to develop them systematically and to present them in extremely precise and incisive form."[26] According to Frieda Peters, "Jarcke was a political journalist, and never wrote an all-encompassing, systematic work in constitutional law."[27] Jarcke did an exceptional job of writing forceful essays that summarized and interpreted the reactionary arguments of Karl Ludwig von Haller's *Restoration of Political Science* (6 vols., 1816–22). Jarcke evaluated this massive work as probably the best analysis ever written of "the spirit and character of Germanic freedom," a freedom that sprang from a "corporatist system of government *(ständische Verfassung)*," which was in turn "a product of the total legal and political life of the Christian-Germanic world."[28] However, Jarcke forsook the editorship of the *Berlin Political Weekly* after scarcely a year; and in 1832, like Adam Müller two decades before, he moved to Vienna as an adviser to the Hapsburg government. He remained a frequent contributor to the *Berlin Political Weekly* until 1837, when he broke with the Protestant-dominated Prussian government over its arrest and imprisonment of the Catholic Archbishop of Cologne, who had followed canon law and papal policy in refusing to permit the assistance and blessing of priests at some interdenominational marriages.[29]

Hermann Wagener (1815–89), the son of a pastor and a native of Pomerania, was another lawyer who associated himself with the Gerlachs' "Christian-Germanic" coterie during the *Vormärz* era, and proved himself an able journalist. From 1848 to 1853 he served as editor of the Old Prussian flagship *Kreuzzeitung* (Newspaper of the Iron Cross). During the subsequent two decades he contributed to the corporatist though anti-pietist journal *Berlin Review (Berliner Revue,* from 1855), and compiled the *Political and Social Encyclopedia (Staats- und Gesellschafts-Lexikon,* 23 vols., 1859–1867), a conservative answer to the liberal *Staatslexikon* of Rotteck and Welcker.[30] He won election to the lower house of the Prussian legislature in 1856, a few years after Junkers in Brandenburg and Pomerania had subscribed 100,000 *Taler* to purchase him a knight's estate, Dummerfitz, in eastern Pomerania.[31] Wagener was the only non-noble among the fourteen members of the original central election committee of the *Preussische Volksverein,* the conservative electoral machine created in September of 1861 as a counterweight to the liberal-democratic and nationalist *Nationalverein* founded in 1859.[32]

Across the Atlantic, South Carolina proslavery economist and journalist Jacob N. Cardozo (1786–1873) was originally an "outsider" in plantation society. His father was a mercantile Sephardic Jew who left England in the 1750s, settling first in New York and then in Charleston, home to the most important Jewish community in America during the first quarter of the nineteenth century. While a youth he worked as an apprentice and a lumber clerk, and had no formal education beyond the age of twelve. Yet he began a career in journalism in 1816, and soon became a newspaper editor in Charleston, editing first the *Southern Patriot* (1817–45) and then the *Evening News* (1845–61). Like Thomas R. Dew, Cardozo viewed slavery as necessary to the success of republican government in the South. The effect of black slavery, he wrote, is that "we have no mobs, . . . no popular uprisings, no agrarianism, no open contempt of law, no violence to those who administer it. . . ."[33] In *Reminiscences of Charleston* (1866), Cardozo mourned the passing of the genteel and refined planter elite that slavery had made possible in South Carolina's Lowcountry, and recalled slavery in paternalistic terms as based on a "reciprocity of protection and obedience" that had been beneficial to both parties.[34]

Proslavery essayist George Frederick Holmes (1820–97) was born to an English couple in British Guiana, where his father practiced law and owned slaves. After being educated in England, he came to the New World in 1837, moving steadily southward from Quebec to South Carolina, where he was admitted to the bar in 1842 and served as an associate editor of Charleston's *Southern Quarterly Review*. Holmes did not enjoy the practice of law, and in 1846, a year after his marriage to the daughter of former Virginia governor John Floyd, he became a professor of ancient languages at Virginia's Richmond College. In 1847 he succeeded Thomas R. Dew as president of William and Mary College, and in 1848 became the first president of the new University of Mississippi, only to be dismissed in 1849. Holmes "retired" to "Burke's Garden," the Floyd plantation home in Virginia, where he wrote many articles for a variety of Southern periodicals, until in 1857 he became a professor of history and literature at the University of Virginia. He had published his first serious defense of slavery in 1850, when he endorsed the rationale for bondage given by Aristotle in the *Politics:* "Nature has clearly designed some men for freedom and others for slavery,—and with respect to the latter, slavery is both just and beneficial."[35]

— II —

The fact that Southern proslavery and Old Prussian ideologues composed their arguments during the first two-thirds of the nineteenth century is crucial for understanding much of the ideational content of their thought. Europe and the United States were in the early throes of the modernization process which, as discussed in Chapter 3, took off in the late eighteenth century with England's industrial revolution and France's political revolution of 1789. Old Prussian and Southern proslavery ideologues often wrote as participants in the great philosophical debates of their era concerning the advantages and disadvantages of industrialism and democracy. Historical sociologist Robert Nisbet explains that modern "philosophical conservatism," with its emphasis on "the values of community, kinship, hierarchy, authority, and religion," was born in the intellectual reaction to the impact of modernization. "Modern conservatism, is, at least in its philosophical form, the child of the Industrial and French Revolutions: . . . What the two revolutions attacked, the conservatism of such men as Burke, Bonald, Haller, and Coleridge defended."[36] Furthermore, just as the humanists' rediscovery of classical thought and culture had shaped the intellectual character of the European Renaissance, so the romantics' rediscovery of the Middle Ages, and the medieval world of "localism, hierarchy, and religious constitution," gave "theme and atmosphere" to nineteenth-century conservative thought. (To be sure, twentieth-century scholarship has shown that both romantic conservatives and Marxian radicals had a simplistic and homogenizing view of the feudal Middle Ages.) Romantic medievalism, together with a distaste for the disruptive effects of urban growth and industrialization on the old order of rural localism and hierarchical deference, inspired Nisbet's philosophical conservatives to make land "the pillar of conservative ideology."[37]

Southern proslavery and Old Prussian writers often took part in the nineteenth-century West's philosophical denigration of industrialism and democracy, and frequently invoked romantic notions of medieval stability and rural wholesomeness in defending the plantation- and *Rittergut*-centered worlds of the South and East Elbia. Ironically, as we have seen, East Elbian serfdom and Southern slavery were hardly legacies of medieval feudalism; and planters and Junkers enjoyed great weath, prestige, and influence in the nineteenth century largely because of their entrepreneurial successes in producing agricultural commodities that were essential to the progress of industrialization outside their regions. Eckart Kehr observed in the early 1930s that "Prussian conservatism is usually defined as feudalism and brushed aside as obsolete, like the dinosaurs in the Field Museum." In reality, "the Prussian aristocracy," despite its "romantic and feudal" image, "has survived not on the strength of its feudalism but as modern agrarian capitalism."[38] Some of Kehr's logic can be transferred to the Old South, whose planter elite can be seen as the bearer of both agrarian capitalism and an authentic "Burkean" conservatism.

A very different perspective on Southern proslavery thought informs Louis Hartz's *The Liberal Tradition in America* (1955), among the most influential studies of American political thought to appear since the Second World War. Hartz acknowledges that defenders of slavery in the Old South, "when they began to break with their Jeffersonian past around 1830, duplicated in every essential aspect the argument of Europe's feudal reaction." (It is well to recall here, as was discussed in Chapter 4, that by the early 1820s septuagenerarian Thomas Jefferson had himself taken the stance of "an ardent and uncompromising champion of Southern rights."[39]) Southern proslavery thought involved far more than "the mere parroting of a few of Burke's phrases," acknowledges Hartz. Yet he insists that the South's invocation of Burke "was in large measure a simple fraud," for "beneath the feudal and reactionary surface of Southern thought we do not find feudalism: we find slavery."[40] A number of substantive objections can be raised against this line of argument. In the first place, Edmund Burke was not really a "reactionary" in the proper sense of desiring "to restore an earlier condition which history has passed by." Rather, he more nearly fits Klaus Epstein's description of a "Reform Conservative" who, in Burke's own words, has "a disposition to preserve and an ability to improve."[41] This combination, wrote Burke in *Reflections on the Revolution in France,* "would be my standard of a statesman. Everything else is vulgar in the conception, perilous in execution." Although Englishmen should and did take pride, said Burke, in "an inheritable crown, an inheritable peerage, and a House of Commons and a people inheriting privileges, franchises and liberties from a long line of ancestors," the English well understood "that the idea of inheritance furnishes a sure principle of conservation and sure principle of transmission, without at all excluding a principle of improvement."[42] Burke's principal motive in writing the *Reflections* was to defend England's existing political system and social order against the sort of

"Jacobinical" demands for reform that he saw disrupting France in 1789–90—demands based on "intellectual abstractions" and "untried speculations." In the process he sought to demonstrate that English history, contrary to that of France, was a story of gradual, evolutionary, constructive changes that had not violated the need for historical continuity between past, present, and future. J. G. A. Pocock has even concluded that "Burke to the last was a man of his modern age, with little nostalgia in his make-up."[43]

Second, it is at least problematical, if not misleading, to label Burke an apologist for "feudalism" per se—a word which "refers technically to the institutions of the medieval era," says Hartz, but which he employs "broadly" to identify "feudal institutions and feudal ideas as they persisted into the modern period amid the national states and economic movements which progressively undermined them."[44] Granted that Burke roundly condemned the French revolutionaries of 1789 for what he deemed their hasty, unwise, and injurious legislative assault on France's medieval legacy (for example, the legal privileges of the monarchy, nobility, and established Catholic Church). But the British society that Burke sought to defend and glorify in the *Reflections* was, with the possible exception of the Netherlands, the least "feudal" in eighteenth-century Europe. England had a parliamentary monarchy, the most fluid upper classes in Europe, no substantive remnants of manorial serfdom, and the most diversified, sophisticated economy of the century—all of which helped to make England the cradle of the Industrial Revolution. Of course, Edmund Burke, like almost all English "gentlemen" of his day, was a fervent opponent of political democratization, and believed that sovereignty in England lay not with the populace, but in the elitist institution of Parliament, dominated at that time by the landed aristocracy (peerage and gentry).[45] Yet Burke was no economic traditionalist, and often advocated the principle of a laissez-faire, "hands off" relationship between state and society.[46] In his essay "Thoughts on Scarcity" (1795), Burke described labor as "a commodity, and, as such, an article of trade," and spoke out against the government's stepping in to lower food prices during short harvests so as to "supply to the poor those necessaries which it has pleased the Divine Providence for a while to withhold from them."[47] Indeed, in his simultaneous admiration for Adam Smith and England's eighteenth-century "constitution," Burke seems to have exemplified the blend of "bourgeois" economic behavior with "aristocratic" political and social views that characterized the British upper classes—the gentry in particular, that most peculiarly English of social classes.

According to R. R. Palmer, "Burke's conservatism was really directed against the democratization of government even by peaceful means."[48] This hostility to democracy reflected Burke's fundamental conviction that an inegalitarian distribution of property and wealth, such as existed in eighteenth-century England, could not coexist with democratic government. "The characteristic essence of property, formed out of the combined principles of its acquisition and conservation, is to be unequal, " he wrote in the *Reflections*. But a democratic society breeds "envy against wealth and power." Burke's august principle of "rational liberty" required that private property, however unequally distributed, must be protected against the egalitarian, expropriatory envy of the masses. Liberty, therefore, constituted "a principle totally different from the equality of man, and utterly irreconcilable to it." Burke recognized that France's bourgeois revolutionaries of 1789 "were embarrassed by their contradictory ideas of the rights of men and the privileges of riches," a contradiction that also emerged during the American Revolution of 1776. This contradiction was especially obvious under a republican form of government, where no hereditary (monarchical and aristocratic) distinctions of rank and office existed to blunt the egalitarian implications of natural-rights philosophy. "I readily admit (indeed I should lay it down as a fundamental principle) that in a republican government which has a democratic basis the rich do require an additional security above what is necessary to them in monarchies. They are subject to envy, and through envy to oppression."[49]

On the eve of the Civil War the South had the advantage of "a republican government" with "a democratic basis" for whites and the "additional security" of enslavement for blacks, who happened to make up the great majority of the region's poor manual laborers. According to proslavery ideologues like Calhoun and Dew, the racial enslavement of the South's working class served to protect the South from the egalitarian envy against republican wealth that plagued the North with its free white laborers. Moreover, since slaves were property as well as persons, Burke's argument that the republican rich require special security for their property against democratic envy and oppression held great appeal for antebellum planter politicans such as Benjamin Watkins Leigh and Abel Parker Upshur of Virginia, who insisted at the Virginia Constiutional Convention of 1829–30 that slave property should not be taxed *ad valorem,* and that the apportionment of seats in their state legislatures should take into account amount of taxes paid as well as white population. Indeed, the three-fifths rule for slave representation in the U.S. House of Representatives was in accord with the Burkean principle that the interests of property deserved special protection in popularly elected legislatures. The *Reflections* could even be cited in support of the plutocratic three-class suffrage introduced to Prussia at mid-century. Burke had recommended to France's middle-class revolutionaries of 1789 that the potentially dangerous contradiction between "the rights of men" and "the privileges of riches" would be muted if, in their scheme of representation for the National Assembly, "the voices of the masses were rendered equal" and "the votes within each mass were proportioned to property."[50] This was precisely the scheme of representation that Otto von Manteuffel's Interior Ministry decreed for the lower house of the new Prussian legislature in May of 1849. Despite the enduring preferences of many Junkers for a more traditional scheme of corporatist representation, under the Second Empire (1871–1918) both the landed and the non-landed upper classes in Prussia proved quite happy to have this "additional security" against "envy" and "oppression," above and beyond the existence until 1918 of a Prusso-German monarchy whose powers were far more extensive than those of the contemporaneous British monarchy.

Like almost all English gentlemen of his day, Burke expressed a strong preference for the "noble ancient landed interest" over the "new monied interest," because mobile capital was "the kind of wealth which will be resorted to by all who wish for change."[51] Yet England's eighteenth-century gentlemen farmers, says G. E. Mingay, showed great interest in bringing profitable improvements and innovations to their estates, and were in general quite willing to join in both the creation and the benefits of non-landed wealth "in order to improve the level of rents, to keep the tenants prosperous and content, and to make the estate an efficient business organization."[52] Burke himself became a member of the landed gentry with his purchase of a 600–acre estate in the shire of Buckingham in 1768, less than two decades after coming to England from Ireland. There he lived during summers and between sessions of Parliament, and conducted agricultural experiments that attracted the attention of no less than Arthur Young and James Boswell. According to Carl Cone, "Burke was not a Townshend, a Tull, or a Blakewell, and his experiments did not produce results that appreciably changed English agriculture, but amidst all his cares and labors, he found time for farming, he knew much about it, and he made it pay."[53] In June of 1779, after two plentiful harvests had driven down the price of grain and made it difficult for most farmers to pay their rents, Burke wrote to his agent: "I cannot conceive why the tenants should be so very much behind-hand in their payments . . . if persons so poor as they are, should be suffered to run long in arrears, nothing will be got from them."[54] Hence Morton Auerbach has emphasized that Burke was "an enthusiastic advocate of Liberal capitalism" and at the same time a spirited spokesman for "the defense of existing traditions and institutions" (as they had evolved in England after the Glorious Revolution of 1688–89) in the name of an "ethic of social harmony and personal tranquility."[55]

Burkean conservatism, as presented in the *Reflections*, seems reducible to two fundamental principles. The first is the necessity for historical continuity, which entails respect for established property rights and regard for tradition and experience over "philosophical presumptions" and "untried speculations" as the source of "political wisdom."[56] This regard for tradition and experience is imperative because human nature is too sinful and human reason too flawed to be relied upon as the fonts of worldly wisdom. The second principle is the belief that the status quo's hierarchical structure and inegalitarian values are in accord with divine law; consequently, any natural-law doctrine of inherent, universal human rights is at the least misguided and perhaps even satanic.[57] It was no more fraudulent to invoke these Burkean principles in the ideological defense of plantation slavery than in the defense of the privileges enjoyed by *Rittergut* owners. Consider Thomas R. Dew's 1832 Burkean retort to antislavery spokesmen who insisted, in the name of "abstract truths" like the injustice or evil of chattel slavery, that Virginia's slaves should be emancipated. "No set of legislators ever have, or ever can, legislate upon purely abstract principles, entirely independent of circumstances, without the ruin of the body politic, which should have the misfortune to be under the guidance of such quackery. Well and philosophically has Burke remarked that circumstances give in reality to every political principle its distinguishing color and discriminating effect. The circumstances are what render every political scheme beneficial or noxious to mankind, and we cannot stand forward and give praise or blame to anything which relates to human actions and human concerns, on a simple view of the object as it stands, stript of every relation, in all the nakedness and solitude of metaphysical abstraction." The most important of the actual "circumstances" which Dew had in mind was the racial distinction between Virginia masters and their slaves. History had conclusively demonstrated, he argued, that "two races differing in manners, customs, language, and civilization, can never harmonize upon a footing of equality. One must rule the other, or exterminating wars must be waged," such as the wars which the European colonists and their descendants had waged, and were still waging, against the American Indians.[58]

Over two decades later a less well-known apologist for the plantation South, Georgia planter-physician Dr. William Coffee Daniell, again illustrated the suitablity of Burkean conservatism to the defense of slavery, though without citing the author of the *Reflections* by name. Daniell's lengthy evaluation of the worldwide antislavery movement, presented to the members of a group meeting in Montgomery, Alabama, in 1853 to organize an Agricultural Association of the Slaveholding States, deserves to be quoted in full. "On a suitable occasion, it might be instructive to investigate and trace back to their sources the abstract idealities which have so earnestly and so powerfully seized upon the public mind in the last 60 or 80 years, and from small beginnings have diffused themselves over large portions of the civilized world, in violation of principles long established, and regardless of past authority, sacred and profane. Idealities based upon assumed facts and defying all practical denials of their truthfulness and adaptation to the condition of society: One of these idealities involves the subject of African Slavery."[59] As Burke had emphasized in the *Reflections,* the most dangerous of all these idealities was "the monstrous fiction" of universal liberty and equality, "which, by inspiring false ideas and vain expectations into men destined to travel in the obscure walk of laborious life, serves only to aggravate and embitter that real inequality which it can never remove. . . ."[60] Obviously, planters did not want their slaves to be inspired with such "false ideas and vain expectations" any more than Junkers wanted their servants and cottagers so inspired. Any Junker would have sympathized with the deep apprehension that South Carolina planter Whitemarsh Seabrook expressed in 1834 about "those false notions

of liberty and equality which the modern philanthropist is struggling to dissemi-
nate." "If abstract notions on the rights of man are allowed in any instance to
modify the police system of a plantation," declared Seabrook, "the authority of
the master, and the value of his estate, will be as certainly impaired, as that the
peace of the blacks will be injuriously affected."[61]

— III —

William Gilmore Simms, a South Carolina planter by virtue of his wife's inheritance and editor of the *Southern Quarterly Review* from 1849 to 1854, was probably the Old South's leading literary figure. In 1854 he described Burke in the
Review as "the great man, par excellence, of his time, in the British Parliament."[62] According to the journal's principal historian, "Burke perhaps ranks
fourth on the *Southern Quarterly Review*'s honor role of heroes, just behind Jesus
Christ, John C. Calhoun, and Sir Walter Scott."[63] Indeed, Burke's writings and
ideas had more overall influence on intellectual and political life in the Old South
than in contemporaneous East Elbia. This was due in large part to the fact that
Britain, for obvious historical reasons, affected the development of American
society and culture far more directly and strongly than it affected Prussian society and culture. Add to this Burke's sympathy for the colonists' grievances
against England before and during the American Revolution, and especially the
rather flattering appraisal of Southern slaveholders in his famous March 1775
speech before Parliament, in which he sided with the Americans' protests against
"taxation without representation." While maintaining that "the fierce spirit of
liberty is stronger in the English colonies than in any other people on earth,"
Burke singled out the Southern colonies for a "circumstance" which "makes the
spirit of liberty still more high and haughty than in those to the northward." "It
is, that in Virginia and the Carolinas they have a multitude of slaves. Where this
is the case in any part of the world, those who are free are by far the most
proud and jealous of their freedom. Freedom is to them not only an enjoyment,
but a kind of rank and privilege. Not seeing there that freedom, as in countries
where it is a common blessing and as broad and as general as the air, may be
united with much abject toil, with great misery, with all the exterior of servitude
liberty looks amongst them like something that is more noble and liberal. I do
not mean Sir, to commend, the superior morality of this sentiment, which has at
least as much pride as virtue in it; but I cannot alter the nature of man. The
fact is so; and these people of the southern colonies are much more strongly,
and with a higher and more stubborn spirit, attached to liberty than those to the
northward." This excerpt from Burke's 1775 speech became almost holy writ to
many antebellum defenders of slavery. For example, in 1851 Christopher Gustavus Memminger of Charleston, later Confederate Secretary of the Treasury,
told the Young Men's Library Association of Augusta, Georgia, that the "great

master of Political Science, Mr. Burke," had well understood "the elevating and liberalizing influence of the Slave Institution upon the master." However, Memminger neglected to mention Burke's judgment that the slaveholders' spirit of liberty had "at least as much of pride as of virtue in it."[64]

Much of Burke's thinking on the delicate subject of emancipation and abolition was quite congenial to many Chesapeake planters of his generation. As a member of Parliament, Burke supported a cautious plan for the "gradual manumission of slaves" in Britain's West Indian colonies (for example, Jamaica, Barbados, Antigua, Grenada), and in 1780 he composed a "Sketch of the Negro Code" which outlined how the African slave trade would be terminated and how those Africans already enslaved would make a slow transition from servitude to "a fitness for freedom." These two goals, stated the Code's preamble in classic Burkean fashion, were "expedient, and conformable to the principles of true religion and morality, and to the rules of sound policy," only if they "may be effected without producing great inconveniences in the sudden change of practices of long standing."[65] Although many Virginia planters of Jefferson's generation would have endorsed Burke's insistence on a gradual and non-disruptive plan of manumission, they would not have accepted the provision that the freed slaves remain in the land of their former enslavement. Given the pervasive Anglo-Saxon prejudice against black Africans, British M.P.s in London could contemplate emancipation without deportation in the distant West Indies with far more equanimity than white Southerners could bring to the thought of emancipation without deportation in their own slave states. However, when the slaves in the French West Indian colony of St. Domingue (present-day Haiti) rose up in fierce rebellion in 1791, Burke denounced the rebellion as fervently as did American slaveholders. He declared in 1792 that "the cause of humanity would be far more benefited by the continuance of the (slave) trade and servitude, regulated and reformed, than by the total destruction of both or either."[66] Burke lay the blame for the St. Domingue rebellion at the feet of the intemperate revolutionaries in France, whose libertarian rhetoric he saw as having awakened "false ideas and vain expectations" of freedom among the slaves. In fact, Burke had seen the slave rebellion coming in 1790, and had chastised the French with words that rang in the ears of Southerners who read the *Reflections:* "As the colonists rise on you, the Negroes rise on them. Troops again—Massacre, torture, hanging! These are your rights of men! These are the fruits of metaphysic declarations wantonly made, and shamefully retracted!"[67]

In the spring of 1861 an unidentified Southerner then in Paris, upon receiving news that Fort Sumter had been bombarded, wrote a "Burkean" essay on slavery and the secession crisis that was published in the short-lived periodical *Southern Monthly,* published first at Memphis and then at Granada, Mississippi, in 1861–62. The American in Paris saw Burke as representing the "moderate party" of gradual emancipation, as opposed to the "party of fanaticism" and its demands for sudden emancipation. "Burke strove earnestly to convince England of the fallacy of sudden reform, predicting the horrors of the French revolution and the decay of Jamaica," which the Southerner believed had occurred after the abolition of slavery in the British West Indies in 1833. "[William] Fox (a prominent leader of the party of fanaticism, under the garb of philanthropy, so rife at the end of the eighteenth century,) was the eloquent pleader for Jamaica. The world is witness of his successful efforts in her behalf. Mirabeau and Lafayette were disciples of the same political creed in France, and for St. Domingo. Agonized memory and horror-stricken students of history are cognizant of their success in those devoted lands." The essayist, like most Southerners in 1860–61, mistakenly attributed radical demands for the immediate abolition of slavery to Abraham Lincoln and the leading spokesmen for the Republican party. "I grow heart-sick at the spectacle called up by the imagination, as the result of the realization of the reform measures held in prospect by the Black Republican party in America. Strange that nations do not profit by the examples of which history is so fruitful; and that the moderate party. . . (led by Burke) has so often been overwhelmed by fanaticism. . . . "[68] Implicit in this argument was the self-deluding belief, so common among white Southerners both before and after the Civil War, that the slave states were well on their way to adopting plans of gradual emancipation until abolitionist fanatics to the north voiced their irrational demands and made the South a stubborn and recalcitrant section. As late as the summer of 1862, after Lincoln had proposed to the border slave states still in the Union a voluntary plan for the gradual emancipation of slavery over a thirty-year period, with financial compensation provided by the federal government, the border-state members of Congress rejected Lincoln's proposal by a 20–9 vote. "Their intransigence was a sober lesson to Lincoln," explains Stephen B. Oates. "It was proof indeed that slaveowners—even loyal slaveowners—were too tied up in the slave system ever to free their own Negroes and voluntarily transform their way of life."[69]

Yet another factor in Burke's greater overall influence in the South than in East Elbia was the Irishman's career as a renowned parliamentary spokesman for the English Whigs in the House of Commons. This career had much more relevance to the two-party electoral politics of the antebellum United States than to the predominantly bureaucratic and authoritarian polity of contemporaneous Prussia. After Adam Müller's departure from East Elbia in 1811 and the folding of Heinrich von Kleist's *Berlin Evening Newpaper* in the same year, Burke's imprint on Old Prussian corporatism became less pronounced, and then quickly faded before the dramatic influence of Swiss-German patrician Karl Ludwig von Haller.[70] Haller became the ideological guru of the second "club association" in the history of Old Prussian conservatism (that is, after the 1810–11 "Christian-Germanic Supper Club")—the 1816–1819 *Maikäferei*, or "May Chafers," so named after the innkeeper May at whose establishment the group met. The brothers von Gerlach and Karl von Lancizolle were prominent May Chafers, and would carry their enthusiasm for Haller over into the "Crown Prince's Circle" formed during the 1820s.[71] Haller's reactionary vision of an aristocratic "patrimonial state," in which the prince was merely *primus inter pares,* rejected both absolute monarchies and parliamentary constitutions as the misguided and dangerous products of modern rationalism, and thus held great appeal for Old Prussian corporatists during the *Vormärz* era. However, once the 1848–49 revolution had introduced a formal constitution and electoral politics to Prussia, Haller's influence in East Elbia quickly faded before the resurgence of Burkean ideas. These found their principal advocate and interpreter in Friedrich Julius Stahl, the most visible and forceful parliamentary spokesman for Old Prussian conservatism during the decade 1848–58.[72] In *The Philosophy of Law* (1st edition, 1830–37), which led the newly crowned Friedrich Wilhelm IV to appoint its author professor of public law at the University of Berlin in 1840, Stahl had described Burke as "without peer the most powerful and profound writer of the contra-revolution, even one of the most distinguished political writers of all time."[73] In 1848 Stahl invoked Burke in order to deprecate the "Revolution of March" in Berlin and the establishment of popular sovereignty (universal manhood suffrage for elections to the Prussian National Assembly). He asked rhetorically to which of the two types of revolution the March Days belonged: "whether it is the type of revolution which, to use the words of Burke, is administered to the community like a bitter medicine at a time of such extraordinary disability, that there is no hope of recovery, or whether it is only the effect of that general appetite for revolution characteristic of the age." Of course, Stahl saw in 1848, as Burke had seen in 1789, "a revolution without basis, without purpose, without principle, and without spokesmen for a principle"; and he echoed the Irishman's judgment that such a revolution must bring "undisguised calamities."[74]

— IV —

Scholars on both sides of the Atlantic have suggested that the dominant characteristic of conservative thought in the nineteenth-century West was its opposition to the Enlightenment doctrine that all men had an inherent and inalienable right to civil and political rights.[75] Given the autocratic authority that plantation and *Rittergut* owners wished to maintain over their laboring minions, it seems only logical that both Southern proslavery and Old Prussian spokesmen should have railed against what Ludwig von der Marwitz called "demagogic and egotistical ideas of equality," what George Frederick Holmes termed "the cant maxim, 'All men are created equal.' "[76] Many Southern and East Elbian ideologues understood that, in the words of Edmund Ruffin, "the abstract right of all mankind to personal liberty, and the right to equal participation in the government, . . . stand upon precisely equal and like grounds."[77] And they were absolutely right. During the 1848–49 revolution, some forty years after Baron vom Stein's October Edict of 1807 had proclaimed personal freedom for all Prussians, the children and grandchildren of former serfs were among those demanding representative democracy from the Hohenzollern monarchy. Only a few years after Lincoln's Emancipation Proclamation of 1863 first proclaimed the abolition of bondage in the Confederate South, ex-slaves helped elect black delegates to state constitutional conventions and state legislatures in the Reconstruction South.

"Civil and political privileges," insisted South Carolinian William Harper, "are no matter of natural right, but to be settled by convention, as the good and safety of society may require."[78] Obviously the "good and safety" of plantation society required first and foremost that slave laborers remain divested of all "civil and political privileges." Those who denounced slavery on the basis of natural-rights philosophy, opined Thomas R. Dew, lacked "a clear perception of the varying rights of man amid all the changing circumstances by which he may be surrounded."[79] In other words, such critics needed a relativistic and elitist rather than an absolutist and democratic perspective on human freedom—what an Old Prussian intellectual might have termed a "qualitative conception of freedom" rather than an "equalitarian conception of freedom."[80] Junker apologists argued for a qualitative, corporatist conception of freedom, whereby each *Stand* or estate had its own peculiar set of privileges or liberties. In the antebellum South, as it became clear that white manhood suffrage was inevitable and irresistable in all the slave states, and that the white South needed to be internally united against an increasingly influential antislavery movement in the North, proslavery spokesmen tended to emphasize a more simple, bifurcated conception of freedom—that is, a caste distinction between enslavement for blacks and equal civil and political rights for whites. Consequently, by the 1850s almost all Southern proslavery writers were denying the validity of natural-rights political philosophy *only* with respect to Negroes.

Although the caste distinction between black slavery and white freedom had the effect of making the proslavery attack on natural-rights theory more simple and straightforward than the Old Prussian attack, another circumstance made it more difficult and convoluted. Where the Junkers had a long history of militarist monarchism, the planters had their own forefathers' Declaration of Independence from England. For Junkers sovereignty resided in their Hohenzollern monarch, even though they wished him to rule in many matters (tax and agrarian policy in particular) with the advice and cooperation of corporatist assemblies in which *Rittergut* owners constituted the dominant estate. Without a viable democratic or even parliamentary tradition in Prussia prior to 1848, Old Prussian ideologues tended to identify dangerous, libertarian political ideas—like the natural rights of man, and the belief that governments derived their legitimacy from "social contracts" and the consent of the governed—with the subversive foreign influences of Jean-Jacques Rousseau and his "Jacobinical" disciples among the French revolutionaries of 1789 and 1830.[81] Even after the 1848–49 revolution demonstrated that there was considerable support for parliamentary government in Prussia, and pushed Friedrich Wilhelm IV to accept a constitutional monarchy (albeit a pseudo-parliamentary and plutocratic one), Junkers often sought to discredit theories about individual rights and popular sovereignty as French bourgeois notions that were essentially foreign to Prussia's monarchical and corporatist traditions. According to Baron Karl Adolf Alexander von Hertefeld in 1856, Prussian conservatives must continue to fight "the power of evil" emanating from France, which was "swaying to and fro between anarchy and despotism," having moved from Orleanist monarchy to revolutionary Third Republic to Second Empire in less than five years. The French evil derived from the French bourgeois concept of the individual, "the doctrine which, denying both the grace and providence of God, treads underfoot history and law and seeks to build state and society upon the virtue *(Tugend)* of sinful men."[82] The economically diversified Rhineland, infected by the French political virus since the province's occupation by France's revolutionary armies in the 1790s, had obviously played an important role in spreading the disease to Prussia.[83] Southern proslavery ideologues confronted the much more uncomfortable and ticklish task of discrediting, or at least qualifying, the natural-rights principles enunciated in their own country's Declaration of Independence. This document, written well over a decade before the French Declaration of the Rights of Man and Citizen, had been composed by a Virginia planter who decried the injustice and cruelty inherent in human slavery, and who hoped that both slavery and Negroes might someday be expunged from America. As Virginia fire-eater Edmund Ruffin wrote in his dairy in October of 1858, Jefferson "has done great harm, by the countenance which his opinions on this subject, & even the words of the Declaration of Independence, have afforded to the anti-slavery fanatics of the present times."[84]

Some proslavery ideologues insisted that the slaveholding Sage of Monticello had simply neglected to make the obvious distinction between the unbounded rights and freedoms possible in a pre-political state of nature and the practical restraints and obligations incumbent upon any individual living in an organized polity. To Jefferson, wrote an unidentified "Southron" (perhaps William Gilmore Simms) in the Richmond periodical *Southern Literary Messenger* in 1838, "the distinction was clear between the conventional or political and the natural rights of man."[85] Since Jefferson owned nearly 270 slaves at his death, and emancipated only five of them in his will, the argument was eminently plausible.[86] Thus Virginia lawyer-planter Abel P. Upshur could say of "Mr. Jefferson" that "his principles were perfectly safe when entrusted to himself or to others who understood them, with their necessary limitations and qualifications, but they were too philosophical and speculative for the mass of mankind."[87] According to the anonymous writer in the 1862 *Southern Monthly* cited above, Lincoln and the

Republican party mistakenly interpreted the Jeffersonian phrase "All men are born free and equal" in "the literal sense." In contrast, "the Southern or secession party" viewed it "in the practical sense, viz: a reservation of the rights of citizenship with reference to the negro population."[88] Not only did this tactic have the manifest advantage of avoiding a direct assault on such a distinguished Southerner and Founding Father; but it was logically compatible with the belief that the Negro slave was inherently, racially inferior to his Caucasian master, a belief that Jefferson seems to have shared.[89] Since blacks were permanently inferior, they could never intermingle with whites on the basis of civil, political, or social equality without causing great harm to both races. Consequently, severe restraints and obligations— slavery—had to be imposed on blacks so that they could live in white society.[90]

Another proslavery tack around Jefferson and the Declaration, a different course to the same end, reconstituted the concept of natural law inherited from the Enlightenment so as to make white enslavement of blacks compatible with the "law of Nature." According to University of Virginia law professor James Philemon Holcombe, speaking in Richmond in 1858, "African Slavery in the United States is consistent with Natural Law, because if all the bonds of public authority were suddenly dissolved, and the community called upon to reconstruct its social and political system, the relations of the two races remaining in other respects unaltered (that is, the whites remaining superior to the blacks), it would be our right and duty to reduce the negro to subjection."[91] The "right" of whites to enslave blacks derived from the "natural" prerogative of a superior group to extract labor and service from an inferior group; the correlative "duty" sprang from the obligation of whites to protect blacks and introduce them gradually to a higher level of civilization. This proslavery reformulation of "natural law," so as to justify the reduction of a portion of the community to "subjection," found striking correspondence in the political thought of Karl Ludwig von Haller, who rejected the faulty suppositions of those Enlightenment political philosophers who viewed government as a contractual creation of free and independent men seeking to impose order and security on the state of nature. Haller insisted that men had never left the state of nature, "the eternal, unchanging order of God" by which "the more powerful rules, must rule, and will always rule." Hence all societal relations, from the family to the state, were reciprocal relationships of authority and dependence. "Authority and freedom" belonged only to the strong and the independent, whom Haller identified with the large landowners; to the weak and the needy inhered "a greater or a lesser degree of dependence and servitude."[92] However, Haller and his Old Prussian disciples, unlike Southern proslavery spokesmen, had no cause to translate the distinction between the strong and the weak, the estate proprietor and his laborers, into a caste dichotomy of race and color.

— V —

As was suggested in Chapter 3, the historical development and character of proslavery conservatism in the Old South and its Old Prussian counterpart in East Elbia cannot be properly understood apart from a fluctuating, often muted tension between what can be termed doctrinaire (romantic and idealistic) and pragmatic (realistic and interest-oriented) defenses of the status quo. To some extent, of course, this tension reflected an apparently universal characteristic of human character, in that the same individual is frequently torn between princi-pled and opportunistic motives. At the same time, human beings seem to insist over time upon some sort of conscious reconciliation between ideals and behav-ior, either in the interests of a peaceful conscience or out of what Paul Gaston calls "the universal need to make experience intelligible and agreeable."[93] Many planters and Junkers achieved this kind of reconciliation through religious faith and organized churches in the Protestant Christian tradition. (Whereas the United States had a variety of voluntaristic Protestant denominations to which the ma-jority of Americans belonged, Prussia had a Protestant state church established by a royal union of the Lutheran and Reformed faiths in 1817.) The idea that the hierarchical and authoritarian relations on plantation and *Rittergut* were a divinely sanctioned arrangement, ordained by God to regulate and uplift the affairs of flawed and sinful men, was fundamental to the conservative arguments advanced by many defenders of Southern and East Elbian society. In 1844 Meth-odist pastor W. T. Hamilton of Mobile, Alabama, preached that "there ever has been, and there must be, great inequality in the condition of men," contrary to the views of the few "rabid advocates of universal equality and immediate eman-cipation" in America. Slavery, like poverty and pain, said Hamilton, "may, in the view of Infinite Wisdom, be indispensable to the attainment of the greatest good," which he identified as the development of personal character. "Forbear-ance, self-control, justice and benevolence in owners; and patience, humility, fidelity, and deference to God's will, in servants, may be the fruits of this insti-tution."[94] A comparable theological and pastoral argument came from C. W. Hoffman, in the Upper Silesian county *(Kreis)* of Gross-Strehlitz, in March of 1849, a year after the outbreak of revolution in Berlin. Pastor Hoffman recalled the "lamentable events" and "fearful acts of violence" of the previous year, and urged upon his parishioners **"scrupulous attention to the law, constant loy-alty to authority, sincere brotherly love, and pure, genuine fear of the Lord"** (bold-face emphasis in the original). For a long time, said Hoffmann, "a false enlightenment and haughty arrogance" had battled the truth that those in positions of authority act in the name of God. People seemed to misunderstand, or to have forgotten, the importance of "the right to authority, resting on divine investiture, of the King himself and all those who conduct public affairs with and under him to a greater or lesser degree, and who are entrusted with the heavy responsibility of exercising executive power."[95] As these excerpts from Hoffman's sermon suggest, the monarchical, militaristic, and bureaucratic traditions in Prussia, along with the absence of a frontier, imbued East Elbian Protestantism with with a more pronounced authoritarian strain that was present in Southern Protestantism.

The argument for divine approval of relations on plantations and *Rittergüter* struck a responsive chord in many a planter and Junker psyche, and not merely because the gentleman farmer thought that it could be an effective tool when preached to his laborers. It also fit logically and comfortably into the regional styles of pietistic and quietistic Protestantism that won so many converts within the two landed elites during the first third of the century. John Randolph of Roanoke's conversion in 1816 from religious skepticism to Christian fervor coincided with a steady decline among the Virginia gentry of the dignified if occasionally free-thinking deism which had reigned during the second half of the eighteenth century, and the concurrent emergence of a more theocratic, evangelical, and emotional brand of religiosity under the impact of the "Second Great Awakening," whose revivalist camp meetings had hit the South full force during the first decade of the nineteenth century.[96] "Congratulate me, my dear Frank— wish me joy you need not; give it you cannot—" Randolph wrote to Francis Scott Key in 1818; "I am at last reconciled to my God, and have assurance of his pardon, through faith in Christ, against which the gates of hell cannot prevail."[97] The impact of such conversions was summarized by an eastern delegate to the Virginia Constitutional Convention of 1829–30, Lucas Thompson, who observed that "in these days, you will find no atheists and few professed deists."[98] Junker Adolf von Thadden, who became "the patriarch of the Pomeranian pietists," seems to have had a conversion experience similar to John Randolph's, and also in 1816, while visiting Bavaria during a Roman Catholic revival. In 1820 he married Henriette von Oertzen, assumed control of the Oertzen estate Trieglaff in Pomerania, and played a leading role in promoting the "Pomeranian Awakening" of the 1820s.[99] During the 1850s clergyman Carl Büchsel (1803– 89)—the Prussian state church's General-Superintendant for Brandenburg, who had served in rural parishes in East Elbia from the late 1820s to the 1840s— recalled attending a pietist conference at the Trieglaff estate of Adolf von Thadden, "with his knightly bearing sanctified by the gospel." Thanks to such men, wrote Büchsel, religion was taken much more seriously than it had been during his student days, when "A nobleman who attended public worship, or an officer who read his Bible was hardly to be found."[100]

Where the Lutheran neo-Pietism of contemporaneous East Elbia originated among Junker landowners and military officers, the evangelical pietism of the antebellum South seems to have begun among predominantly lower-class whites and then gradually infiltrated the ranks of the plantation gentry. Yet Southern evangelical pietism and Lutheran neo-Pietism alike stressed the doctrine of original sin, thereby accentuating the inherent imperfection and inadequacy of the human condition, both individual and collective. In so doing, these faiths denigrated the optimistic, Enlightenment notion that humankind could achieve self-fulfillment through the rational, purposeful manipulation of their social and physical environment.[101] While prominent spokesmen for pietistic Protestantism in the South and East Elbia strongly counseled benevolent, familial treatment of slaves and estate laborers, its theological focus was on transforming the individual's personal relation to God in heaven, not on restructuring human society in order to promote the Kingdom of God on earth. The Lord worked his greatest wonders not in the chambers of elected assemblies or in the offices of bureaucrats, but in individual human hearts. In short, pietistic Protestantism in the South and East Elbia usually served to foster a passive, quietistic outlook on social and political affairs that did not openly challenge the regional status quo.[102]

Nonetheless, religion did not completely resolve the tension in planter and Junker ranks between pragmatic and doctrinaire modes of conservatism. This tension also indicated that the visionary designs of many conservative intellectuals often diverged from the more mundane concerns of most planters and Junkers.[103] In fact, only a minority of these landed entrepreneurs had much interest in the formulation of systematic philosophical defenses of their own positions. The largely rural or military experiences of most plantation and *Rittergut* owners did not dispose or equip them to evaluate their interests and values in abstract, theoretical categories; and as proprietors of large estates with sizable work forces, they did not find ideological refinement to be a necessary virtue or systematic ethics a pressing concern. The small but vocal contingent of doctrinaire ideologues comprised men of ideas, often deeply devout, whose temperaments and educations inclined them to attach great significance to a degree of metaphysical sophistication and ethical consistency that, as their own lives often testified, is far more easily attained on the printed page than in personal or public affairs. Their ideological perceptions of the world were molded more by ideals and principles (and sometimes by the ambitious self-righteousness that can consume the true believer) than by the considerations of economic and political feasibility that impelled most planters and Junkers.[104]

Relations between doctrinaire intellectuals and the pragmatic majority of planters and Junkers were, as might be expected, ambiguous and problematic. The intellectuals vacillated between what Drew Faust has called "transcendence and partisanship."[105] As partisan ideologues, they tended to "romanticize" and "idealize" the established, traditional institutions of the South and East Elbia. They would depict life on the plantation or *Rittergut* in rosy colors of mutual obligation and reciprocal affection, usually obscuring or minimizing the intrinsic cruelty and oppression. In so doing they elevated social relations on the estates to a noncommercial, familial, even spiritual level of meaning and quality that pragmatic, nonspeculative planters and Junkers sometimes found flattering or appealing. Yet, as transcendent intellectuals, the doctrinaires sometimes reproached mundane planters and Junkers for their failure to live up to the ideal standards of altruism and patriarchal *noblesse oblige* set for them. The intellectuals, in defending plantation slavery or the Junkers' *Rittergut*-based privileges, were also waging an ideological crusade to purge the economic, cultural, and political life of the South or East Elbia of selfish expediency, intellectual vapidness, and moral corruption. And in the process they hoped to win greater respect and esteem for themselves and their calling. As Edward Shils has observed, "It is practically given by the nature of the intellectuals' orientation that there should be some tension between the intellectuals and the value-orientations embodied in the actual institutions of any society." For intellectuals are driven by the simultaneous urges "to submit to authority as the bearer of the highest good . . . and to resist or condemn authority as betrayer of the highest values."[106]

Consider William Gilmore Simms (1806–70), the son of an immigrant Irish merchant who became the antebellum South's most prolific and widely read native author. His fictional and critical writings generally portrayed the South's plantation-based society as "the best possible way of life," and under his editorship Charleston's *Southern Quarterly Review* consistently propounded a "romantic view of Southern civilization."[107] Yet, as Drew Faust emphasizes, "Simms had an introspective and moral streak and felt . . . alienated and isolated from the society around him," even after marriage in 1836 to a wealthy planter's daughter brought him a plantation home, Woodlands, in the South Carolina Lowcountry.[108] This sense of alienation, in conjunction with his immodest sense of intellectual superiority, fueled his inclination to chastise the planter class for their short-sighted "lust for immediate gain" as well as their undisciplined profligateness.[109] In evaluating Harriet Martineau's critical account of the South in *Society in America* (London, 1837), Simms criticized the Englishwoman's view of slavery and slaveholders as largely inaccurate and unfair, but acknowledged that a chapter on the "Morals of Slavery" made for "painful" reading "because it is full of truth. It is devoted to the abuses among slaveholders of the institution of slavery; and it gives a collection of statements, which, I fear, are in too many cases founded upon fact, of the illicit and foul conduct of many among us, who make their slaves the victims and the instruments alike, of the most licentious passions."[110] Nonetheless, when an expanded version of this essay review was included in the 1852 compendium *The Pro-slavery Argument*, Simms's new preface portrayed slavery in highly idealistic terms, as "a domestic institution, which we hold to be not simply within the sanctions of justice and propriety, but as constituting one of the most essential agencies, for promoting the general progress of civilization, and for elevating, to a condition of humanity, a people otherwise barbarous, easily depraved, and needing the help of a superior condition—a power from without—to rescue them from a hopeless savage state."[111]

An approximate East Elbian analogue to Simms was Theodor Fontane (1819–

1898), even though his first important books date from the 1860s.[112] Born in Pomerania to a pharmacist of French ancestry, after the 1848–49 revolution he spent three years in England as a correspondent for the press bureau established by Manteuffel's Interior Ministry. During the 1860s he worked in Berlin for the Old Prussian newspaper *Kreuzzeitung* as an editor, responsible for coverage of English politics and culture.[113] Ernst K. Bramsted reports that after the publication of his *Travels through Brandenburg* (*Wanderungen durch die Mark Brandenburg*, 4 vols., 1862–82), "the middle-class liberals accused him of having written the book to the order of the (Prusso-German) Conservative Party and denounced his servile pandering to the aristocracy."[114] Yet in this work's "Concluding Remarks" of 1881, Fontane wrote that "there lives on in our aristocracy as much as ever a naive conviction of their right and capacity to rule." He belittled "the pseudo-conservatism of our aristocracy, which in the long run desires nothing but its own interests and what serves them. . . ."[115] Fontane's "mixed feelings" toward Junkerdom, says Bramsted, "found their best expression" in a sentence from *Travels:* "These fellows are intolerable and charming at the same time."[116] In 1884 he wrote to his wife Emilie that "in spite of their enormous failings, Brandenburg *(märkisch)* Junkers and rural clergymen remain my ideals, my unavowed love." Fontane claimed that Carl Büchel's *My Ministerial Experiences* represented them properly, although Büchsel "had a strong admixture of the narrowness and small-mindedness typical of the *Uckermark* (a part of Brandenburg)."[117]

Yet the distinction between doctrinaire intellectuals and pragmatic landowners was more blurred in the Old South than in contemporaneous East Elbia. The planter elite included a higher percentage of men in the learned professions—attorneys, medical doctors, and ministers[118]—than did landed Junkerdom. The planters' familiarity with competitive electoral politics, unlike the Junkers' long experience with monarchical, military, and bureaucratic absolutism, meant that planters were by and large more articulate and persuasive public spokesmen for their own values and interests. At the same time, antebellum party politics was less conducive to maintaining ideological purity and consistency than was the non-parliamentary, absolutist political environment that prevailed in Prussia until the revolution of 1848–1849.[119] The emergence of electoral politics and propagandizing associations in the late forties brought to the fore a younger generation of Junker leaders born circa 1815, men such as Mortiz von Blankenburg, Hermann Wagener, Hans-Hugo von Kleist-Retzow, and Otto von Bismarck. These younger leaders proved to be more flexible, pragmatic, and materialistic than the older generation of doctrinaire and principled Junker spokesmen born in the 1790s, men such as Ludwig and Leopold von Gerlach, Adolf von Thadden-Trieglaff, and Ernst von Senfft-Pilsach.[120] In other words, at mid-century the mounting tensions between doctrinaire and pragmatic conservatism in East Elbia reflected a generational conflict within Junker leadership, despite exceptions to the rule such as Ernst von Bülow-Cummerow, a pragmatic materialist born in 1775. Among Southern planters and their political leaders there also appears to have been some generational differences on the eve of the Civil War between, on the one hand, younger men on the make, receptive to the "radical" idea of secession, and, on the other hand, older, more established "conservatives" with stronger attachments to the Union.[121] Yet the number of exceptions to the generational rule within the planter elite seem to have been much greater than within Junkerdom, as indicated by the examples of older secessionists such as Virginian Edmund Ruffin (1794–1865), Mississippian John Quitman (1799–1858), and South Carolinian Robert Barnwell Rhett (1800–1876). Furthermore, although many doctrinaire proslavery ideologues endorsed secession and Southern nationalism, there were also idealistic apologists for slavery among the moderate and conditional Unionists on the eve of the Civil War, for example, John Hartwell Cocke of Virginia, James Henry Hammond of South Carolina, and Jefferson Davis of Mississippi.[122]

— VI —

I have not yet specified the most important reason for the more imprecise boundaries between doctrinaire and pragmatic conservatism in the South than in East Elbia. In defending Negro slavery before the Southern electorate, planters and proslavery spokesmen could assume a simpler and more popular conservative stance than could Junkers in defending their more complex and less popular network of aristocratic privileges. For this reason first and foremost, the pragmatic-doctrinaire tension had negligible influence on the plantation gentry during the secession crisis of 1860–61, but a dramatic impact on Junkerdom during the revolutionary crisis of 1848–49.

During the spring and summer of 1848, as Friedrich Wilhelm IV attempted to conciliate the forces of revolution in both Prussia and throughout the German Confederation, the Junkers were temporarily shorn of absolutist protection; and at the same time they confronted radical demands from the first democratically elected national assembly in Prussian history. The doctrinaire, idealistic impulse in Junker conservatism was represented by some pietist and legitimist "Christian-Germanic" members and associates of the Old Prussian court clique *(Kamarilla)* serving as the king's kitchen cabinet. The *Kamarilla's* two most memorable members were the brothers Leopold and Ludwig von Gerlach, the king's personal adjutant and a Magdeburg jurist respectively, and joint owners of the 2900–acre *Rittergut* Rohrbeck (inherited from their father) in eastern Brandenburg.[123] Ludwig von Gerlach took a leading role in establishing the newspaper *Kreuzzeitung* during the spring and summer of 1848, and in its pages he and his Old Prussian associates insisted that landed Junkerdom must retain its traditional, legally privileged position in state and society as the divinely ordained intermediary power between the monarch and his people. This doctrinaire position did not correspond to the outlook of the pragmatic Junkers who predominated at the "General Assembly of the Union for the Protection of the Interests of Landed Property and for the Promotion of the Welfare of All Classes of People." This so-called "Junker Parliament" met in Berlin in August to protest the agrarian and tax legislation proposed by the liberal ministries of Camphausen-Hansemann (to 20 June) and Auerswald-Hansemann (to 22 September).[124] Ludwig von Gerlach attended the meetings, and was finally persuaded by his brother-in-law Adolf von Thadden to speak out against the assembly's spirit of "gross materialism." When von Gerlach rose to speak on 19 August, he was greeted with exclamations like "Pietist!" and "Now we'll hear a pretty sermon!" Then he delivered what William Orr terms "probably the most effective speech of his entire career."[125] He argued eloquently that the assembly's membership should not consider property rights apart from political responsibilities, and that *Rittergut* owners should insist on retaining their control over local government, because their corporatist privileges were in fact obligations imposed on Prussia's landed aristocracy by God. "Let us not forget," he concluded, "that the true calling of the aristocracy is to ennoble the entire nation."[126]

Despite Gerlach's eloquence, the great majority of the nearly 400 members of the Junker Parliament were ready and willing to sacrifice aristocratic privileges like local judicial and police power, and to commute the remaining manorial obligations owed by lesser peasants into long-term monetary payments, if such concessions would help to defuse popular unrest and radicalism. These men, concerned primarily about the security of their property rights, were prepared to accept a moderate political revolution if a radical social revolution could be averted.[127] And during the late 1840s Junker spokesmen often made subtle appeals to the anxieties of other property owners (that is, well-to-do peasants and the urban business and professional classes) about the threat of socialist encroachments on property rights. At the United Diet of 1847, Woldemar von Heyden-Kartelow of Pomerania had emphasized his concern for "the freedom of trade and of property rights" when arguing against a proposed prohibition on the export of potatoes and wheat as a way of lowering food prices. "The right to property is the most sacred of rights, and it should not be encroached upon in such ways."[128] When the septuagenarian pragmatist Ernst von Bülow-Cummerow composed his opening address to the Junker Parliament of 1848 (an address delivered by Hans Hugo von Kleist-Retzow on 18 August because of Bülow-Cummerow's illness), he included a dramatic appeal to pragmatic materialism. "Material interests have an importance that outweighs all others; insofar as we follow them, we will always have firm ground under our feet. Let us call foward all our powers to further them, and, if we succeed, we can count on the concurrence of the great mass of people and of all propertied classes."[129] The slippery Friedrich Julius Stahl, in a September 1849 parliamentary speech denigrating universal manhood suffrage and defending the recently decreed three-class voting arrangement, declared it "an unbearable tyranny that the educated and propertied classes should be handed over to the majority of the propertyless."[130]

The success of such appeals was well illustrated during the debates at the 1848 National Assembly on the question of abolishing the manorial tithe levied on livestock born or raised on land subject to the lord's manorial authority (*Fleischzehnt* or *Blutzehnt*). On 27 October Privy Counselor Kette, who called himself an "agriculturist" (*Landwirt*), declared that the historical origins of this tithe "goes so far back into remote antiquity that we can no longer determine from whence it derives." In response to a motion to abolish it without compensation, Kette stated: "I see in the entire proposal an attack on property, to which I cannot give my vote." A middle-class delegate, the factory owner Bothmer, acknowledged the well-made argument "that feudal rights (*Feudalrechte*) are civil rights (*Privatrechte*) just as soundly established as any others." Should the Assembly's members vote to seize property from estate owners, they risked "making all property owners (*Besitzstand*) reactionary by arraying the propertyless against the propertied."[131] Historian James Oakes has argued that insistence on "the primacy of rights" is the essence of liberalism, and that "the right of property" is "the simplest of all liberal assumptions."[132] If so, then Junkers in 1848–49 had no more difficulty in adapting liberal principles to the conservative defense of their interests as a landed elite than did planters in 1860–61.

During the revolutionary crisis of 1848–49 in East Elbia, pragmatic and doctrinaire Junkers disagreed fundamentally over whether to concede their aristocratic privileges and their formal control over local government, which included the autocratic authority of the *Rittergut* owner over his work force. During the secession crisis of 1860–61 in the South, the pragmatic-doctrinaire tension within the proslavery movement was subsumed under a common determination to protect the institution of slavery against outside interference. Although planters, like white Southerners of all classes, disagreed among themselves over how the slave states could and should respond most effectively to the federal government after the Republican electoral victory of 1860, these disagreements had to do with tactical means to the same strategic end, the security of slavery. Doctrinaire and pragmatic defenders of slavery had no disagreement whatsoever about the fundamental need to maintain slavery as a rigid system of social and labor control. In other words, whereas the pragmatic majority of Junkers were prepared to compromise the long-standing character of the knight's estate as a "private law state," pragmatic planters were resolutely determined to preserve the plantation as a petty autocracy founded on chattel slavery. What conditions and circumstances present in the South and absent from East Elbia prevented the pragmatic majority of planters from considering any substantive change in their peculiar institution prior to the Civil War?

One such condition was demographic. In the Prussian East the population had been growing since the mid-eighteenth century, especially after 1815; and during the 1830s and 1840s the region had a labor surplus. Although that surplus was drained away in subsequent decades both by migration to the industrial cities west of the Elbe and by emigration overseas, at the time of the 1848 revolution Junkerdom enjoyed a temporary abundance of cheap labor.[133] In the more sparsely settled South, with its much higher land/labor ratio, the demand for plantation labor usually outstripped the supply (in other words, there were more buyers than sellers, which drove slave prices upward), especially on the southwestern frontier.[134] Without the autocratic control over labor provided by the institution of slavery, planters could not be sure of a sufficient supply of suitable gang workers. Slaves also constituted, in addition to a labor force, a huge capital investment that Junkers never had to make. As Gavin Wright has emphasized, slaveholders who merely kept their chattel alive during the decade before the Civil War made a respectable profit from capital gains alone. Planters were understandably concerned, therefore, about the threat to confidence in the future of slavery posed by the prospect of congressional interference from a federal government dominated by the antislavery North.[135] Finally, antebellum planters refused to consider seriously even a gradual modification of slavery because of their deep-seated racist fears about the general societal consequences of losing their thoroughly autocratic control over several million Negroes.

In short, pragmatic planters and doctrinaire intellectuals were united by their apprehensions for the security of slave property and by their profound racist fears about the consequences of abolition and emancipation—fears that magnified their terror at the thought of retributive slave violence. And these concerns were those most likely to unite the white South in support of withdrawal from the federal Union. As David Potter has emphasized, "the determination to keep blacks in subordination took priority over the other goals of southern society"; hence "the entire socio-economic system had to be conducted in a way that would maximize the effectiveness of racial control."[136] In 1860–61, when planter and proslavery interests in eleven states concluded that the election, inauguration, and subsequent conduct of a "Black Republican" President posed a real and present danger to both the short-term stability and the long-range survival of slavery, pragmatic and idealistic conservatives could agree that constitutional secession from the United States, or revolutionary separation from it, was the necessary, if regrettable, step to be taken. The white South had to effect a political revolution in order to avoid the threat of a social one. In March of 1860 North Carolina planter-pragmatist Henry King Burgwyn, of Thornburg plantation in Northampton County, declared that "No Southern man, nor any man well informed as to the situation of the South and of the negro character, will deny that to preserve our property, even more our very lives and the honor of our wives and families, the four millions of negroes among us, must be kept in their present state of subjection."[137] Shortly after Lincoln's election William

Henry Holcombe—a well-educated, reflective, and literary slaveholding physician living in Tensas Parish, Louisiana—wrote that "Opposition to slavery, to its existence, its extension and its perpetuation, is the sole cohesive element of the triumphant faction." Consequently, "The only alternative left with us is this: *a separate nationality or the Africanization of the South.*" In explaining "the fearful import" of the latter choice, Holcombe maintained that "According to the present rate of increase, in fifty years the negroes of these states will amount to twenty millions. Suppose them to be restricted to their present arena. Suppose them in addition to be free. Imagine the crime, the poverty, the barbarism, the desolation of the country!" "In opposition to the prevailing sentiment of the North, we believe that men are created neither free nor equal," stated Holcombe. "That government is the best, and the people the happiest, not in which all men are free and equal, but in which equal races are free, and the inferior race is wisely and humanely subordinated to the superior, whilst both are controlled by the sacred bonds of reciprocal duty."[138]

— VII —

The comparability of Southern proslavery and Old Prussian thought as "conservative" ideologies, and of antebellum planters and contemporaneous Junkers as "conservative" landed elites, derives primarily from the analogies between the two established, "traditional" institutions that, in the final analysis, planters and Junkers were most concerned to protect and defend: the plantation with its enslaved work force, and the *Rittergut* with its dependent laborers. The continuing economic vitality of these two institutions and their owners, until the 1860s and 1870s respectively, served to make the plantation gentry and landed Junkerdom especially formidable landed elites, and also served to prolong the exclusion of large segments of the American and Prussian populations from civil and political equality.

If, following Burke, we posit a respect for established property rights and a regard for existing civil, political, and social equalities as archetypal conservative qualities, then perhaps planters and proslavery ideology should be adjudged even more conservative than Junkers and Old Prussian ideology. But this overly simplistic perspective has two major shortcomings. First, it risks falling into the trap of an inflexible, homogenizing mode of social-class analysis that is insensitive to the tension within both planter and Junker ranks between doctrinaire and pragmatic manifestations of conservatism. Even though, for a variety of historical reasons, the pragmatic-doctrinaire tension had less impact on antebellum planters than on contemporaneous Junkers, the historian of the Old South should nonetheless be cognizant of a divergence between the transcendent, idealistic values and perspectives that inspired a good many proslavery ideologues and the more interest-oriented, mundane concerns and attitudes that characterized the majority of planters.

Second, reliance on Burkean principles as the touchstone of nineteenth-century conservatism in the West serves to reinforce the traditional emphasis in both American and German historiography on the structure and content of proslavery or Old Prussian thought as the measure of authentic conservatism among the planter and Junker elites. Historically, conservatism has been a political as well as a philosophical phenomenon; and to study intellectual conservatism apart from its complex interaction with political conservatism is to present a partial, even distorted view of the past. Political scientist Hans-Gerd Schumann has persuasively argued that "the real criterion of conservatism" is "the conscious political action taken by socially privileged classes, strata, or groups to safeguard the institutions in which their social position is embedded against attempts to alter the norms prevailing in the political domain, or polis." [139] Accordingly, a crucial measure of planter or Junker conservatism is to be found in the assiduousness with which each landed elite fought in the political arena to preserve its plantation- or *Rittergut*-centered world. Perhaps planters should again be adjudged more conservative than Junkers, because they felt a far greater compulsion in 1860–61 to preserve the character of the plantation as a hierarchical and authoritarian private law state than did Junkerdom in 1848–49 with regard to their *Rittergüter*. Yet the Junkers could afford to sacrifice some of the traditional character of the knight's estate as a private law state, since, unlike planters, they were privileged members of a larger hierarchical, authoritarian, and "illiberal" political order. These linkages, together with East Elbia's regional preponderance within the Prussian monarchy, gave Junkerdom a high degree of political flexibility at mid-century. The planter elite's flexibility waned with their region's declining influence over the federal government, until most planters determined in 1861 to wager their survival on state secession, regional independence, and civil war. Not only did the planters face stronger and more intractable political and ideological opposition than did the Junkers, but the crucial financial and racist aspects of Southern slavery engendered in planters far greater fears about the economic and social consequences of losing personal autocratic control over their labor force.

Epilogue

AFTER DEFEAT IN the Civil War the eleven states of the Confederate South experienced a period of congressionally mandated Reconstruction that achieved a temporary extension of civil and political rights to ex-slaves. During the 1870s this so-called "Radical Reconstuction" foundered, at different times in different states, due to a combination of mounting white resistance (including violence and fraud) and waning Northern interest in guaranteeing the new rights of black Southerners. Yet the white South and its planter elite, despite the success of their "Redeemer counterrevolution,"[1] did not regain the high level of national political clout in the U.S. Republic that they had enjoyed at mid-century. The Junkers of East Elbia, in contrast, retained their strong links with and influence upon Prussia's authoritarian monarchy.[2]

Indeed, the man who created a unified German Empire under Prussian leadership in 1871 came from the ranks of landed Junkerdom, although the diplomatic and domestic pragmatism that characterized Otto von Bismarck's solution to the "German problem" infuriated a few diehard Old Prussian idealists such as Ludwig von Gerlach. They could not abide such anti-legitimist *Realpolitik* as his war against the Austrian Hapburgs and destruction of the German Confederation in 1866, nor such political demagoguery as his sponsoring of a democratic suffrage for elections to the new Reichstag in order to win popular support for the Prussianized North German Confederation in 1867. Nonetheless, it was Bismarck's genius to realize that despite Junker fears after 1848 of an inseparable link between nationalism and revolution, the overwhelming majority of Junkers would at least acquiesce in the creation of a German national state if two conditions were met: if the process of national unification appeared as an extension of Prussian "Great Power" politics in the tradition of Frederick the Great, and if that process presented no substantive challenge to "the social and economic interests of the Prussian landed aristocracy."[3] Bismarck did not really damage those interests even when some of his fellow Junkers thought him most traitorous to his class—as when he cooperated with the coalition of constitutional liberals in the Prussian legislature to approve the County Reorganization Act, or *Kreisordnung*, of 1872. This legislation, which reduced the Junkers' traditional control over political and administrative organization in the counties through "a mixture of self-government from below and bureaucratic control from above," passed the House of Lords only after King Wilhelm appointed twenty-four new and pliable peers. Old Prussian spokesmen denounced the law for destroying the corporatist foundations of local government. To eliminate the traditional estates *(Stände)*, insisted one right-wing member of the Conservative party, "is a further step toward a republic." By planter standards the *Kreisordnung* created precious little republicanism, and it hardly destroyed the Junkers' power in the countryside. "It reflected Bismarck's genius for granting concessions (to liberalism) in form but not in substance," concludes Robert Berdahl. Junkers retained half the seats in the county assemblies, which continued to nominate candidates for county commissioner *(Landrat)* to the Prussian king. Although the new law deprived the *Rittergut* owner of personal police power over his estate, it provided that the officials charged with supervising the newly created police districts should be chosen by the provincial chairmen *(Ober-Präsidenten)*, who usually selected these officials from among the resident Junkers.[4]

Wilhelm I had appointed Bismarck minister president in 1862 during a deadlocked clash over the army budget between aspirations of constitutional liberals to parliamentary government on the one hand and Prussia's militarist and autocratic traditions on the other. The shrewd Junker sought to preserve the latter by circumventing rather than resolving the deadlock. He determined that the nationalist carrot of a united Germany could be used to distract the Prussian liberals from constitutional issues and to undermine the nascent vitality of their parliamentary opposition to monarchical government. The wars of 1864, 1866, and 1870 (against Denmark, Austria, and France respectively) were necessary not only to accomplish national unification under Prussian leadership but also to sabotage the liberal goal of a truly constitutional and parliamentary monarchy. Due in part to Bismarck's domestic and diplomatic maneuverings between 1862 and 1871, Prussia's "preindustrial authoritarian state," and "a preindustrial conservative hierarchy of power and values," retained substantial sway even as Prusso-German industrialization accelerated during the second half of the nineteenth century.[5] Nonetheless, the introduction of universal and equal manhood suffrage for elections to the German Reichstag, in conjunction with the onset of two decades of agrarian depression in the 1870s (as Prusso-Germany underwent its rapid transformation from an agrarian into an industrial society), compelled Junker leaders to begin in earnest what Hans Rosenberg calls "the recasting of 'aristocratic' into 'plebiscitary' conservatism."[6] The necessity for a conservative politics with mass appeal became increasingly evident as industrial workers undergirded the growing national strength of the Social Democratic party, which also sought to mobilize support in the countryside. In the national elections of 1912 the Social Democrats won a plurality of seats in the Reichstag. As a retired county commissioner *(Landrat)* in Posen declared that same year, a fundamental question in the minds of most Junkers and their conservative allies within the ranks of Germany's industrial and professional elites was "whether we shall succeed in the long run in maintaining the monarchy against the democratic assault."[7] Their short-run success was due in part to the Agrarian League *(Bund der Landwirte)*, founded in 1893. From the mid-1890s to the First World War the Agrarian League took the lead in transforming the German Conservative party of 1876 into a dynamic political organization that employed "grassroots democratic techniques" and a blend of corporatist, agrarian-populist, racist (anti-Polish and anti-Semitic), and imperialist appeals to garner electoral support for agricultural protectionism and German nationalism from rural smallholders and other lower-middle-class groups hostile to urban industrialism and leftist cosmopolitanism.[8] Although the interests of the Junker elite had been tied for three centuries to the fate of the Prussian state as a militarist and authoritarian monarchy, many Junker leaders came to understand that the maintenance of their power and influence in the new German Empire also required the creation of an independent electoral base.

The First World War and its aftermath in Germany, the revolution of 1918–19, brought an end to such aristocratic props in Prussia as the three-class suffrage, the House of Lords, and the right to establish entailed estates *(Fideikommisse)*.[9] Most important, the Hohenzollern monarchy collapsed and was succeeded by the Weimar Republic, which the majority of Junkers repudiated for its democratic principles and Social Democratic input. The government of the Weimar Republic extended to agricultural workers a civil and political status equal to that of industrial workers and abolished the remnants of the *Rittergut* owner's formal authority within his manorial district. Yet the revolution of 1918–19 had wrought no land reform in East Elbia, just as the post–Civil War era of Reconstruction had wrought no major redistribution of landownership in the South. Junker landowners remained a power to be reckoned during the Weimar years, partly because of ongoing ties to the army and bureaucracy. Moreover, although the Social Democratic party attracted the votes of many day-laborers on knight's estates, Junkers and the National Rural League *(Reichslandbund,* the Weimar successor to the imperial Agrarian League) retained substantial electoral and ecclesiastical clout in the East Elbian countryside.[10] The frequency of anti-democratic and anti-Semitic pronouncements by Junker spokesmen support Shelly Baranowski's argument that a significant degree of ideological and political "symbiosis" existed between the "traditional right" and the "right radicalism" of Hitler's National Socialism circa 1930.[11] Although some Junkers were critical of the National Socialist personnel and program, the East Elbian elite must certainly bear some responsibility for both governmental instability and Nazi electoral gains during the late Weimar period. Indeed, as Larry Jones notes, "no one would seriously dispute the central role which the east Elbian Junkers played in the destruction of the Weimar Republic or in Hitler's appointment as Chancellor" by President Paul von Hindenburg in 1933.[12] Nonetheless, Junker power and influence clearly suffered from the Third Reich's policy of "totalitarian integration" *(Gleichschaltung)*, which involved elimination of all potential centers of political opposition;[13] and a number of them were executed after the failure of the 20 July 1944 plot against Hitler. It was the Soviet military conquest and occupation of East Elbia at the end of World War II that abruptly terminated the Junkers' history as a landed elite. The victorious Allies reached agreement in 1947 that "The Prussian state, which from its earliest days has been the bearer of militarism and reaction in German, has de facto ceased to exist."[14] Two years earlier a scholarly study published in New York had strongly recommended just this step. "Prussia ought to be eliminated as a single unit within Germany," wrote Arnold Brecht, on the grounds that the country's history demonstrated its unsuitability as a political entity within the federal state envisioned for postwar Germany, "least of all within a democratic republic."[15]

The liberal-democratic national state, whether in the form of a limited, constitutional monarchy or a constitutional republic, seems to have encountered far more consistent and persistent opposition in Junkerdom than in the planter elite. Yet we must not forget that the South's caste distinction between black African-Americans and white European-Americans, and the pervasive prejudice of whites against blacks, was the key to the door of liberal republicanism for eighteenth-century plantation owners.[16] With a labor force of enslaved blacks in a society whose "ruling race" was white,[17] the planter elite could survive and even flourish in the political arena as white manhood suffrage and competitive party politics emerged in the South during the first half of the nineteenth century. The Confederacy's defeat in the Civil War, and victorious Union's abolition of slavery, drastically altered the South's economic and political landscape, but did not spell the end of planterdom in the same way that the defeat of Nazi Germany would mark the demise of Junkerdom eight decades later. To be sure, uncompensated emancipation abolished the bulk of most planters' capital assets and wealth, leaving the postbellum Southern economy starved for credit even as the growth of international demand for cotton slackened. Yet the planters' real estate was not expropriated or confiscated, and it appears that in 1880, after the end of Reconstruction, half of all plantations still belonged to the same families that had owned them two decades earlier, on the eve of the Civil War.[18]

Antebellum laborlords became postbellum landlords,[19] who learned how to work plantations and maintain white supremacy without chattel slavery. In the tobacco and especially the cotton regions of the South, white landowners with little cash and former slaves with no land usually settled on sharecropping as a compromise organization of production, whereby plantations became decentralized (or fragmented) farming operations and the freedmen gained a measure of autonomy from white supervision. Although sharecropping can be a form of tenancy, new laws adopted by Redeemer governments after the end of Reconstruction defined the sharecropper not as a tenant, but as a hired laborer paid in shares of the crop rather than in cash wages. The Redeemer legislatures of the 1870s in effect launched "a counteroffensive on the part of the landholders and planters" by passing laws that restricted the mobility and rights of labor, and also gave first priority to the landlord's lien on his tenants' crops (tenancy in its various forms being a rung above sharecropping on the ladder to landowner-ship).[20] The decentralized plantation system based on sharecropping and tenancy prevailed from the 1870s until the mid-twentieth century. "The prerogatives all rested with the landlord," explains George Tindall, "the choice of crop, its cultivation and marketing, the conditions of credit, the bookkeeping, the final settlement. On the other side the system bred dependence and servility; on both sides insecurity and distrust."[21] Between 1880 and 1930 the percentage of Southern farms operated by sharecroppers and tenants rose from just over 36 percent to over 55 percent. Because an increasing percentage of tenants and sharecroppers were white farmers (two-thirds by the mid-1930s), Southern landlords had to manage a more complex system of race relations than had confronted antebellum "laborlords."[22] Most planters and Southern Democrats had known how to deal politically with this state of affairs at least since the 1890s, when some third-party Populists had sought to unite debt-ridden black and white farmers against the exploitative hegemony of the Democratic party.[23] In response Democratic leaders determined to keep the poor divided along racial lines by beating the drum of Negrophobia. This counterattack, which coopted some of the Populists' white leadership, succeeded between 1890 and 1910 in intensifying Jim Crow segregation and formally disfranchising the opposition through suffrage restrictions like poll taxes and literacy tests. Such disfranchisement devices not only deprived blacks of the right to vote but also reduced the Euro-American electorate by one-third to one-half, as poor and uneducated whites also lost access to the ballot box. In the Solid South of the early twentienth century, concludes J. Morgan Kousser, "the electorate was tiny and party competition was almost nonexistent."[24]

Consider Virginia, where blacks seem to have had more influence within the Populist rank and file than elsewhere. After the Populists won over 40 percent of the votes in the 1893 elections, the legislature adopted a new ballot law (the Walton Act of 1894) which served to keep the majority of Afro-Americans from voting and also promoted white voter apathy.[25] Nonetheless, the Republican party remained a potential threat to the Democrats, many of whom wanted to incorporate suffrage restrictions into the state constitution. In 1901 a convention met in Richmond to revise the Reconstruction constitution of 1869, which the Richmond *Dispatch* castigated as "forced upon Virginians by carpetbaggers, scalawags, (and) Negroes, supported by federal bayonets."[26] The new constitution of 1902 established as voting requirements the advance payment of a poll tax, a handwriting requirement, and satisfactory oral answers to "any and all questions" concerning a would-be registrant's "qualifications as an elector." In a state where African-Americans composed less than 36 percent of the population, these suffrage provisions served to cut the electorate at least in half. Many of the disfranchised whites were Republican voters in the mountainous counties of southwestern Virginia. The suffrage restrictions seem to have had the indirect effect of keeping even qualified white voters away from the polls. "Apathy was a by-product of the new constitution and of the one-party system it helped to make secure," explains Allen Moger. "The Negro had been removed and the state was safely in the hands of the Democrats, so why bother to register, to pay the poll tax, or even to vote?"[27]

In the absence of slavery, therefore, the postbellum landed elite eventually abandoned white male democracy in order to preserve both the subordination of plantation labor and the planter-landlord's position atop the rural social structure. Concurrently, the planter class became integrated into a "multifarious establishment" composed of landowners, manufacturers, merchants, bankers, and professionals that, says George Mowry, "might be described as, for want of a better term, the southern power elite."[28] During the first half of the twentieth century this reconstituted elite presided over a regional economy characterized by a highly unequal distribution of income between the rich and poor ends of the spectrum, and manifested as much hostility toward labor unions as did Junkers of the late nineteenth and early twentieth century. As Mowry suggests, perhaps Ulrich Bonnell Phillips's "central theme of Southern history" should be amended. For Phillips the "white folk" of the nineteenth-century South shared "a common resolve indomitably maintained" that their region "shall be and remain a white man's country." Mowry views the South for most of the twentieth century as "an upper-class white man's country."[29]

Ironically, during the Great Depression of the 1930s the Southern elite supported federal agricultural policies (especially New Deal crop reduction and subsidy programs for cotton) that helped to undermine the decentralized plantation system by promoting something of an "'American enclosure movement.'"[30] "Even as many planters complained of federal intrusion," notes Pete Daniel, "they greedily took government money, invested it in machinery, rationalized their farm operations in a more businesslike way, and looked to the end of the rainbow, at the pot of federal money, at a host of farm machines, and at chemicals."[31] The process of reducing acres under cultivation, evicting sharecroppers and tenants, consolidating farmland, adopting new capital-intensive equipment (like mechanical cotton pickers) operated by hired labor, and even shifting to new commodities like soybeans, accelerated during and after the Second World War.[32] The massive displacement of sharecroppers and tenant farmers encouraged a great African-American emigration from the South, primarily to Northern and Western cities, where blacks could vote and lend electoral support to the postwar civil rights movement. The reconsolidation and mechanization of plantation agriculture also set the stage for a dramatic shift from individual ownership to corporate agribusiness during the sixties and seventies.[33]

Thus, when Soviet troops occupied Prusso-German East Elbia in 1945 and quickly destroyed Junkerdom as a landed elite, Southern plantations were already embarked on a economic and social transformation that would drastically reduce the size and power of the planter class. This transformation ended the symbiosis of labor-intensive agriculture and anti-Negro racism that had sustained the regional clout of the planter elite for over two centuries.

Notes

Introduction

1. The term elite, or "the most influential and prestigious stratum in a society," is preferable here to the term aristocracy, "a hereditary upper class." For Southern planters did not enjoy the kind of hereditary, group-specific legal privileges that distinguished Junkers from the mass of East Elbia's population. George A. and Achilles G. Theodorson, *A Modern Dictionary of Sociology* (New York: Thomas Y. Crowell, 1969; Apollo paperback, 1970), 129, 16. As Gerhard Lenski points out in *Power and Privilege: A Theory of Social Stratification* (New York: McGraw-Hill, 1966), 78–79, an elite is "the highest ranking segment of any social unit, whether a class or total society, ranked by whatever criteria one chooses." For a helpful discussion of how the term elite has been used and defined since its earliest known use in English in 1823, see T. B. Bottomore, *Elites and Society* (London: C. A. Watts, 1964; Penguin paperback, 1966), chs. 1 and 2.

2. Max Weber, "National Character and the Junkers" (1917), in H. H. Gerth and C. Wright Mills, eds. and trans., *From Max Weber: Essays in Sociology* (New York: Oxford Univ. Press, 1946), 386.

3. Here I am paraphrasing Lawrence Stone, *The Crisis of the* (English) *Aristocracy, 1558–1641* (abridged ed.; London: Oxford Univ. Press, 1967), 4.

4. Karl Marx, *The Eighteenth Brumaire of Louis Bonaparte. With Explanatory Notes* (New York: International Publishers, 1963), 15.

5. Irving Kristol, *On the Democratic Idea in America* (New York: Harper & Row, 1972), 108. Ironically, Kristol makes this judgment with reference to my own professional group, American college and university professors.

6. Marc Bloch, "Toward a Comparative History of European Societies," trans. Jelle C. Riemersma, in Frederick C. Lane and Riemersma, eds., *Enterprise and Secular Change: Readings in Economic History* (Homewood, Ill.: R. D. Irwin, 1953), 496. A subsequent English translation of this classic and invaluable essay is Bloch, "A Contribution Towards a Comparative History of European Societies," in *Land and Work in Medieval Europe: Selected Papers by Marc Bloch*, trans. J. E. Anderson (Berkeley: Univ. of California Press,

1969). Bloch was a French medievalist advocating comparative studies of different European societies; but his observations are germane to all comparativists. William H. Sewell provides a sophisticated analysis of Bloch's views in "Marc Bloch and the Logic of Comparative History," *History and Theory* 6 (1967), 208–18.

7. "The failure to link emancipation of the peasantry with a new system of police and justice left the agrarian reforms compromised from the outset." Robert M. Berdahl, *The Politics of the Prussian Nobility: The Development of a Conservative Ideology, 1770–1848* (Princeton: Princeton Univ. Press, 1988), 122–23.

8. Robert Brentano, *Two Churches: England and Italy in the Thirteenth Century* (Princeton: Princeton Univ. Press, 1968), v.

9. Philip Morgan, "Three Planters and Their Slaves: Perspectives on Slavery in Virginia, South Carolina, and Jamaica, 1750–1790," in Winthrop D. Jordan and Sheila Skemp, eds., *Race and Family in the Colonial South* (Jackson & London: Univ. Press of Mississippi, 1987), 42.

10. Also worthy of mention is an unpublished essay by Maura McDowell Kealey, "The Response of the Prussian and Virginia Landed Elites to the Extension of Political Participation at Mid-19th Century: The Interrelation of Ideology and Practice" (seminar paper, University of California at Berkeley, 1969). Kealey focuses on debates in the Prussian *Landtag* of 1849–50 and the Virginia Constitutional Convention of 1850–51 and concludes that both Prussian aristocrats and Virginia planters "jettisoned" ideological rigidity in the interests of practical politics. In addition, I should mention two essays dealing with "populism" in the U.S. and Germany which do not compare planters and Junkers. Kenneth Barkin, "A Case Study in Comparative History: Populism in Germany and America," in Herbert J. Bass, ed., *The State of American History* (Chicago: Quadrangle Books, 1970), 373–404, argues for important parallels between the late-nineteenth century agrarian movements led in Germany by the Farmers' League *(Bund der Landwirte)* and in the United States by the Farmers' Alliances. Barkin notes that "the estate-owning Junkers took the lead in the agrarian movement" but states that "There were no American counterparts of the Prussian Junkers." Although Barkin cites historians who have pointed to "the surprising number of socially prominent Southerners who left the Democratic party for the farmers movement," he never refers explicitly to planters. A rather different analysis is offered by David Peal in "The Politics of Populism: Germany and the American South in the 1890s," *Comparative Studies in Society and History* 31 (April 1989), 340–62, whose German focus is on the state of Kurhessen, west of the Elbe and annexed by Prussia in 1866. Peel concludes that "racism was too pervasive not to infuse populist movements in both countries," in the form of American Negrophobia and German anti-Semitism. Whereas in the South the leftist Southern Farmers Alliance and the Populists provoked a successful racist counterattack from the Democratic party, the German *Bund der Landwirte,* "situated on the far Right," constituted "a belated attempt to articulate elite agrarian interests with one voice and to counteract populist politics."

11. In his 1935 intellectual biography of John C. Calhoun, German historian Dietrich Zwicker sought to establish some important parallels between "the philosophy of the cotton planter" and contemporaneous Prussian conservatism, between "Old Prussian 'Junkers' and the American 'slave barons.'" Zwicker, *Der amerikanische Staatsmann John C. Calhoun, Ein Kämpfer gegen die "Ideen von 1789": Studien zur Vorgeschichte des ameri-*

kanischen Bürgerkrieges, Historische Studien, no. 280 (Berlin: Emil Ebering, 1935), 92–93, 110–12.

12. In 1966 comparative historical sociologist Barrington Moore, Jr., briefly compared planters and Junkers as "labor-repressive" capitalists who constituted conservative roadblocks on the democratic-capitalist path from "the preindustrial to the modern world," although the Junkers proved to be a more formidable roadblock in Germany than did the planters in the United States. Moore, *Social Origins of Dictatorship and Democracy: Lord and Peasant in the Making of the Modern World* (Boston: Beacon Press, 1966), 115, xiv-xv.

13. In 1968 Southern historian Eugene Genovese challenged Barrington Moore's portrayal of the two elites as comparably capitalist, insisting that *Social Origins* "exaggerates the prebourgeois character of the post-Napoleonic Junkers and underestimates the prebourgeois quality of the slaveholders." Eugene D. Genovese, "Marxian Interpretations of the Slave South," in Barton Bernstein, ed., *Towards a New Past: Dissenting Essays in American History* (New York: Knopf, 1968; Vintage paperback, 1969), 118–19. Genovese essentially reiterated this criticism of Moore in 1969, when he also wrote of "the Prussian road to capitalism" not followed by the United States—"that is, the road of authoritarianism based on a coalition of industrialists and great aristocratic landowners." Genovese, *The World the Slaveholders Made: Two Essays in Interpretation* (New York: Pantheon Books, 1969; Vintage paperback, 1971), 228–30. The concept of the Prussian road will be discussed toward the end of Chapter 3.

14. In 1978 Richard Rubinson, a sociologist and disciple of Immanuel Wallerstein, portrayed planters and Junkers as agrarian capitalists simply because they produced marketable commodities for the "capitalist world-system" dominated by England, and as essentially conservative because they resisted the transformation of the United States and Germany into industrial nation-states capable of competing with England. Rubinson, "Political Transformations in Germany and the United States," in Barbara Hockey Kaplan, ed., *Social Change in the Capitalist World Economy,* Political Economy of World-System Annuals, vol. 1 (Beverly Hills and London: Sage Publications, 1978), 39–73.

15. In 1985 Southern historian Barbara Jeanne Fields rejected the Wallersteinian perspective on capitalist development with regard to both the eastern Europe of the Junkers and the plantation South. Fields also pointed out that Lenin coined the phrase "Prussian road" to describe the country's post-serfdom route to "capitalist agriculture," and argues that there was "a world of difference" between the "authentic Prussian way" and the experience of the postbellum South. Fields, "The Advent of Capitalist Agriculture: The New South in a Bourgeois World," in Thavolia Glymph and John J. Kushma, eds., *Essays on the Postbellum Southern Economy* (College Station, Texas: Texas A & M Univ. Press for the University of Texas at Arlington, 1985), 73–94; quotations from 85–86.

16. In 1990 Southern historian Steven Hahn pointed to similarities between the defensive conservatism of Continental European aristocracies like the Junkers and "the conservative and anti-democratic trajectory of the slave regime as a whole" in the antebellum South. Nonetheless, what Hahn found most significant in the planter-Junker comparison is "the swift and dramatic decline in the fortunes of the Southern planter class" after the Civil War, versus the enduring power of Prussia's Junkers in the wake

of emancipation and German national unification. Hahn, "Class and Status in Postemancipation Societies: Southern Planters in Comparative Perspective," *American Historical Review* 95 (February 1990), 75–98; quotations from 83 and 98. In "Emancipation and the Development of Capitalist Agriculture: The South in Comparative Perspective," in Kees Gispen, ed., *What Made the South Different?* (Jackson & London: Univ. Press of Mississippi, 1990), 71–88, Hahn argues that "while the abolition of slavery and servile labor ended up accelerating the development of capitalist agriculture most everywhere abolition took place, it propelled the South most quickly and fully down that road." This quotation is from p. 74.

17. Edward L. Ayers observed in 1990 that "in both the South and in Prussia honor was not some naive holdover from a 'traditional' culture. Instead, it was something that had to be self-consciously constructed and maintained" during the nineteenth century. "Neither the planters nor the Junkers were simple preindustrial classes," observed Ayers, "but constantly negotiated among contradictory demands, modern and archaic. . . ." Ayers, "Commentary" on Shearer Davis Bowman, "Honor and Martialism in the U.S. South and Prussian East Elbia during the Mid-Nineteenth Century," in Gispen, ed., *What Made the South Different?*, 45–46, 48.

18. See Wolfgang Pfeifer, ed., *Etymologisches Wörterbuch des Deutschen, H-P* (Berlin: Akademie Verlag, 1989), 768.

19. Steven Hahn and Jonathan Prude, emphasizing the need for historians of the United States to pursue carefully constructed foreign comparisons, state: "There is no reason historians of the American South would not profit from looking at Eastern Europe—especially Prussia—where a 'second serfdom' took hold at roughly the same time slavery was established in the Western Hemisphere." "Introduction" to Hahn and Prude, eds., *The Countryside in the Age of Capitalist Transformation: Essays on the Social History of Rural America* (Chapel Hill & London: Univ. of North Carolina Press, 1985), 14.

20. Rudolf von Thadden, *Prussia: The History of a Lost State,* trans. from the 1981 German ed. by Angi Rutter (Cambridge & Paris: Cambridge Univ. Press and Editions de la Maison des Sciences de l'Homme, 1987), 84–85. For a useful introduction to the complex territorial history and fluctuating provincial boundaries of the Prussia state, see Manfred Schlenke, ed., *Preußen-Ploetz: Eine historische Bilanz in Daten und Deutungen* (Freiburg & Würzburg: Verlag Ploetz, 1983), 24–40.

21. Don E. Fehrenbacher, *The South and Three Sectional Crises* (Baton Rouge: Louisiana State Univ. Press, 1980), 13–14.

22. The quotations are the titles of Chapters 7 and 8 in James M. McPherson, *Battle Cry of Freedom: The Civil War Era* (New York & Oxford: Oxford Univ. Press, 1988).

23. "Hindsight allows us to see the growth and consolidation of a new dominant class made up of some elements of the older planter aristocracy and some newcomers who were able to capitalize on the new conditions." Harold D. Woodman, "The Reconstruction of the Cotton Plantation in the New South," in Glymph and Kushma, eds., *Essays on the Postbellum Southern Economy,* 111.

24. William W. Freehling points out that in 1850 slaves made up 17% of the Border South's population, 30% of the population in the Middle South, and 43% of the Lower South's population. Of those slaveholders who owned 20 or more slaves in 1850, the

Border South contained 6%, the Middle South 32%, and the Lower South 62%. "The farther north the southern state, the cooler the clime, the fewer the slaves, and the lower the relative commitment to perpetuating slavery." Freehling, *The Road to Disunion, Volume I: Secessionists at Bay, 1776–1854* (New York & Oxford: Oxford Univ. Press, 1990), 17–18.

25. As Barbara Jeanne Fields observes of Maryland on the eve of the Civil War, "however independent of slave society Baltimore and the northern counties might be in terms of their economic pursuits, they remained subaltern where political power was concerned." Fields, *Slavery and Freedom on the Middle Ground: Maryland during the Nineteenth Century* (New Haven & London: Yale Univ. Press, 1985), 20.

26. "The relative absence of slavery," reports one monograph on western North Carolina, "did not make the mountain people abolitionists. . . . Like many northerners, Unionist highlanders disliked Negroes as well as slavery. . . . Their Unionism was not founded on racial egalitarianism but a resentment of slaveholders, a resentment that in many cases took on class lines." Phillip Shaw Paludan, *Victims, a True Story of the Civil War* (Knoxville: Univ. of Tennessee Press, 1981), 59.

27. I was fortunate to locate extensive collections of Prussian agricultural periodicals in the *Niedersächsische Staats- und Universitäts-Bibliothek* at Göttingen, West Germany, and in the United States Department of Agriculture's National Agricultural Library at Beltsville, Maryland.

28. C. Vann Woodward, "The Comparability of American History," in Woodward, ed., *The Comparative Approach to American History* (New York & London: Basic Books, 1968), 3.

29. Thus the venerable Vann Woodward observed in 1986: "I believe it is fair to say that the greatest number and probably the most successful and stimulating experiments in comparative history of recent years have stemmed from, or been suggested by, questions arising from the history of the South." C. Vann Woodward, *Thinking Back: The Perils of Writing History* (Baton Rouge & London: Louisiana State Univ. Press, 1986), 133. See the review of this comparative literature in Peter J. Parish, *Slavery: History and Historians* (New York: Harper & Row, 1989), 112–21. George Fredrickson, one of the authors discussed by Parish, wrote in 1980 that "the dominant impression . . . bound to arise from any recent survey of recent comparative work by American historians is not how much has been done but how little." Fredrickson, "Comparative History," in Michael Kammen, ed., *The Past Before Us: Contemporary Historical Writing in the United States* (Ithaca, N.Y.: Cornell Univ. Press, 1980), 472. Fredrickson's principal comparative work appeared the following year: *White Supremacy: A Comparative Study in American and South African History* (New York & Oxford: Oxford Univ. Press, 1981). Fredrickson's negativism was countered in 1982 by Peter Kolchin, another of the authors discussed by Parish, on the grounds that the former's "excessively narrow definition" of comparative history includes only international comparisons and excludes "significant comparative work done over space and time within the United States," such as comparisons of the Southern and Northern economies before the Civil War. Peter Kolchin, "Comparing American History," in Stanley I. Kutler and Stanley N. Katz, eds., *The Promise of American History: Progress and Prospects* (Baltimore: Johns Hopkins Univ. Press, 1982; also published as *Reviews in American History* 10, no. 4 (December 1982)),

78, 74, and 80–81, n. 28, where Kolchin samples "the vast literature" comparing North and South. Kolchin's comparative work on Southern slavery and Russian serfdom will be discussed briefly later in this chapter.

30. See John Higham, with Leonard Krieger and Felix Gilbert, *History* (Englewood Cliffs, N.J.: Prentice-Hall, 1965), Part I, ch. 1, and Part IV, ch. 1.

31. One astute historian of the United States has recently concluded that "amid the technical brilliance and narrow specialization of so much of the recent work" in American history, "a sense of the overall picture has been lost" for the study of U.S. history alone. William L. Barney, *The Passage of the Republic: An Interdisciplinary History of Nineteenth-Century America* (Lexington, Mass.: D. C. Heath, 1987), viii.

32. Robert R. Palmer, *The Age of Democratic Revolution: A Political History of Europe and America, 1760–1800* (2 vols.; Princeton: Princeton Univ. Press, 1959–64), and Eric Hobsbawm, *The Age of Revolution, 1789–1848* (London: Weidenfeld and Nicolson, 1962).

33. Louis Hartz, *The Liberal Tradition in America: An Interpretation of American Political Thought Since the Revolution* (New York: Harcourt, Brace & World and Harvest Books, 1955), 3–4. Hartz's analysis of the Old South will be discussed further in Chapter 6.

34. According to Hajo Holborn, while "feudalism was all played out" in western Europe by the early nineteenth century, "the economic and social aspects of feudalism ruled Germany until well into the nineteenth century." Holborn, "German Idealism in the Light of Social History," in his *Germany and Europe: Historical Essays* (New York: Anchor Books, 1970), 7–8. My own perspective on the term "feudalism" will be discussed in Chapter 3.

35. It is somewhat surprising that Louis Hartz and his work are not mentioned in James Oakes, *Slavery and Freedom: An Interpretation of the Old South* (New York: Knopf, 1990), for Oakes's book is a sophisticated and wide-ranging effort to grapple with the complex tension between chattel slavery and "liberalism" in Southern history. For Oakes, however, the significant historical predecessor and counterpoint to liberalism was "patriarchalism" rather than feudalism.

36. "Needless to say," observes Hartz, "I have not tried in this book to explore in special detail the European pattern." Hartz, *Liberal Tradition in America*, 26. Most Europeanists would deny that there was a single "European pattern."

37. Allan Nevins, *Ordeal of the Union, Vol. II: A House Dividing, 1852–1857* (New York: Charles Scribner's Sons, 1947), 541.

38. Edgar T. Thompson, "The Plantation: Background and Definition," in his *Plantation Societies, Race Relations, and the South: The Regimentation of Societies. Selected Papers of Edgar T. Thompson* (Durham, N.C.: Duke Univ. Press, 1975), 23.

39. Eugene D. Genovese, *The Political Economy of Slavery: Studies in the Economy and Society of the Old South* (New York: Pantheon, 1965; Vintage paperback, 1967), 31; and Genovese, *Roll, Jordan, Roll: The World the Slaves Made* (New York: Pantheon, 1974; Vintage paperback, 1976), 5.

40. F. N. Boney, *Southerners All* (Macon, Georgia: Mercer Univ. Press, 1984), 3, 29.

41. John Peyton Little, "History of Richmond," *Southern Literary Messenger* 18 (1851), 608.

42. Daniel R. Hundley, *Social Relations in Our Southern States* (New York, 1860), ed. William J. Cooper, Jr. (Baton Rouge: Louisiana State Univ. Press, 1979), 27. For a perceptive study of the way in which the Cavalier gentleman planter and the entrepreneurial Yankee businessman became important literary and cultural symbols among antebellum writers North and South, see William R. Taylor, *Cavalier and Yankee: The Old South and American National Character* (1961; Cambridge, Mass.: Harvard Univ. Press, 1979).

43. Thomas Jefferson Wertenbaker, *Patrician and Plebeian in Virginia: The Origin and Development of the Social Classes of the Old Dominion* (1910; rpt. ed., New York: Russell & Russell, 1959), 3, 28; Louis Wright, *The First Gentlemen of Virginia: Intellectual Qualities of the Early Colonial Ruling Class* (1940; rpt. ed., Charlottesville, Va.: Univ. Press, of Virginia and Dominion Books, 1964), 41–43; and Bernard Bailyn, "Politics and Social Structure in Virginia" (1959), in Stanley N. Katz, ed., *Colonial America: Essays in Politics and Social Development* (Boston: Little, Brown, 1971), 143–44. Edmund S. Morgan, *American Slavery, American Freedom: The Ordeal of Colonial Virginia* (New York: Norton, 1975), 166, 303–5, relies heavily on Bailyn's essay.

44. Clement Eaton, *The Growth of Southern Civilization, 1790–1860* (New York: Harper & Row, 1961; Harper Torchbooks, 1963), 1–2, 318–19. According to Avery Craven, "a rural way of life capped by an English gentleman ideal" was one of the "three great forces" that shaped the Old South, along with a "mellow" climate and "the presence of the Negro race in quantity." Craven, *The Coming of the Civil War*, 2nd ed. (Chicago: Univ. of Chicago Press, 1957), 33.

45. George Fitzhugh, "Southern Thought," *DeBow's Review* 23 (1857), 343. In addition to Kolchin's *Unfree Labor: American Slavery and Russian Serfdom* (Cambridge & London: Belknap Press of Harvard Univ. Press, 1987), see his "The Process of Confrontation: Patterns of Resistance to Bondage in Nineteenth-Century Russia and the United States," *Journal of Social History* 11 (1978), 457–90; and his "In Defense of Servitude: American Proslavery and Russian Proserfdom Arguments, 1760–1860," *American Historical Review* 85 (1980), 809–27.

46. For some suggestive comparative comments on the Prussian and Russian aristocracies during the eighteenth century, see Reinhard Bendix, *Kings or People: Power and the Mandate to Rule* (Berkeley: Univ. of California Press, 1978), 163.

47. Bloch, "Towards a Comparative History of European Societies," 496.

48. Henri Pirenne, "What Are Historians Trying to Do?," in Stuart A. Rice, ed., *Methods in Social Science: A Case Book* (Chicago: Univ. of Chicago Press, 1931), 435, 445.

49. Bloch, "Towards a Comparative History of European Societies," 507.

50. Woodward, "The Comparability of American History," 16.

Chapter 1. Landed Autocrats, Gentlemen Farmers, and British Influences

1. Friedrich von Raumer, *America and the American People*, trans. William W. Turner (New York: J. & H.G. Langley and Astor House, 1846), 113, 136. An analogous if self-serving observation came decades later from South Carolina planter William Henry Trescott in an 1889 oration before the alumni of the College of Charleston: "I am sure

no one would deny that if the slave had been of the same race as his master, slavery would have been long ago extinguished and forgotten." Trescott quoted in Lacy K. Ford, Jr., *Origins of Southern Radicalism: The South Carolina Upcountry, 1800–1860* (New York & Oxford: Oxford Univ. Press, 1988), 359.

2. August Meitzen and Friedrich Grossman, *Der Boden und die landwirtschaftlichen Verhältnisse des preussischen Staates* (8 vols.; Berlin: Paul Parey, 1868–1908), vol. 3, p. 438. *Insten*, about whom more in Chapter 2, constituted a relatively favored sub-group within the general category of *Tagelöhner*, or day-laborers.

3. Ibid., vol. 6, pp. 286–87. Cf. Erich Jordan, *Die Entstehung der konservativen Partei und die preussischen Agrarverhältnisse von 1848* (München & Leipzig: Duncker & Humblot, 1914), 28–29; and Friedrich Lütge, *Deutsche Sozial- und Wirtschaftsgeschichte: Ein Überblick*, 3rd ed. (Berlin: Springer-Verlag, 1966), 60. The estate owner's patrimonial judicial authority remained in effect until 1849; his police powers were suspended in the same year but re-established in 1856, surviving until 1872. Until the local government regulations of 1891 (*Landgemeindeordnung*), according to Heinrich Heffter, manorial authority constituted "the real bulwark of Junker authority in East Elbia, the most powerful obstacle to all broad reform efforts to create a comprehensive and unified system of self-government." Heffter, *Die deutsche Selbstverwaltung im 19. Jahrhundert: Geschichte der Ideen und Institutionen* (Stuttgart: K. F. Koehler, 1950), 132. Cf. Gerhard Schultz, "Deutschland und die preussischen Osten: Heterologie und Hegemonie," in Hans-Ulrich Wehler, ed., *Sozialgeschichte Heute: Festschrift für Hans Rosenberg zum 70. Geburtstag* (Göttingen: Vandenhoeck & Ruprecht, 1974), 90–93, who sees *Rittergüter* as the foundation of Junker power until German unification and the onset of agricultural depression in the 1870s.

4. William A. Smith, president of Randolph-Macon College (a Methodist college), *Lectures on the Philosophy and Practice of Slavery* (Nashville, Tenn.: Stevenson and Evans, 1856), 154. Cf. Frederick Douglas's 1855 observation that the Maryland plantation of his former master "is a little nation of its own, having its own language, its own rules, regulations and customs. The laws and institutions of the state, apparently touch it nowhere." Douglas, *My Bondage and My Freedom*, ed. William L. Andrews (Urbana & Chicago: Univ. of Illinois Press, 1987), 45. Edgar T. Thompson points out that "Both lord and planter exercised judicial functions and both tended eventually to become officials of the larger state. Both manor and plantations are political institutions, that is, institutions based upon the principle of authority, which in both cases implies the existence of an aristocracy." Thompson, "The Plantation: Background and Definition," in *Plantation Societies, Race Relations, and the South: The Regimentation of Societies/Selected Papers of Edgar T. Thompson* (Durham, N.C.: Duke Univ. Press, 1975), 23.

5. On the Junkers' right to inflict physical punishment, see Max Weber, *Die Verhältnisse der Landarbeiter im ostelbischen Deutschland*, Schriften des Vereins für Sozialpolitik, vol. 55 (Leipzig: Duncker & Humblot, 1892), 17–18, and Reinhart Koselleck, *Preussen zwischen Reform und Revolution: Allgemeines Landrecht, Verwaltung, und soziale Bewegung von 1791 bis 1848*, 2nd corrected ed. (Stuttgart: Ernst Klett Verlag, 1975), 549.

6. Elizabeth Fox-Genovese and Eugene D. Genovese, *Fruits of Merchant Capital: Slavery and Bourgeois Property in the Rise and Expansion of Capitalism* (Oxford: Oxford Univ. Press, 1983), 127.

7. "Beiträge zur Gesinde-Pädagogik," *Allgemeine Landwirtschaftliche Monatschrift* (1845),

168. There is nothing in the historical literature on East Elbia and the Junkers comparable to James O. Breeden, ed., *Advice Among Masters: The Ideal in Slave Management in the Old South* (Westport, Conn.: Greenwood Press, 1980).

8. Whitemarsh B. Seabrook, *An Essay on the Management of Slaves, and Especially on their Religious Instruction, Read Before the Agricultural Society of St. John's Colleton* (Charleston: A. E. Miller, 1834), 4.

9. On the ways in which state or provincial authorities served at the same time to undergird and circumscribe the rural autocracies of planters or Junkers, see especially Edward L. Ayers, *Vengeance and Justice: Crime and Punishment in the 19th-Century American South* (New York & Oxford: Oxford Univ. Press, 1984), 134–36, and Koselleck, *Preussen zwischen Reform und Revolution*, 540–52.

10. Weber, "Entwicklungstendenzen in der Lage der ostelbischen Landarbeiter" (slightly revised version of an article first published in 1894), in *Gesammelte Aufsätze zur Sozial- und Wirtschaftsgeschichte von Max Weber* (Tübingen: J. C. B. Mohr (Paul Siebeck), 1924), 471, 473–74. This important essay is available in English translation: "Developmental Tendencies in the Situation of East Elbian Rural Laborers," trans. Keith Tribe, *Economy and Society* 8 (1979), 177–206.

11. Koselleck, *Preussen zwischen Reform und Revolution*, 674, and Manfred Kliem, "Die Rolle der feudaljunkerlichen Reaktion in der Revolution von 1848/49," *Zeitschrift für Geschichtswissenschaft* 17 (1969), 311.

12. Kenneth M. Stampp, *The Peculiar Institution: Slavery in the Ante-bellum South* (New York: Knopf, 1956), 30–31.

13. Ernst Rudolf Huber, *Deutsche Verfassungsgeschichte seit 1789, I: Reform und Restauration, 1789–1830* (Stuttgart: W. Kohlhammer, 1957), 184.

14. *Gesinde* were "drafted" each year, from children age 10 or 11, who were to work for at least 3 to 5 years in return for room, board, and a small wage, and who were usually housed in stalls or barns without beds, boys and girls together. Gerhard Czybulka, *Die Lage der ländliche Klassen Ostdeutschlands in 18. Jahrhundert* (Braunschweig: Albert Limbach, 1949), 81.

15. Koselleck, *Preussen zwischen Reform und Revolution*, 544–49.

16. It seems obvious that enslaved African-Americans in the South had greater cultural distinctiveness vis-à-vis their Euro-American masters than did servants and cottagers vis-à-vis their manorial lords in East Elbia, where upper and lower classes alike included persons of both Germanic and Slavic ancestry; and I suspect that this greater cultural distinctiveness often translated into a higher degree of communal cohesion. The historian who would compare the lives and outlooks of laborers on plantations and knight's estates will find far less published source material for East Elbian cottagers and servants than for Southern slaves. Peter Kolchin's observation about Russian sources also applies to East Elbia: "There is no Russian equivalent to the Federal Writers' Project Interviews, and only a handful of autobiographies were written by ex-serfs." Kolchin, *Unfree Labor: American Slavery and Russian Serfdom* (Cambridge, Mass.: Belknap Press of Harvard Univ. Press, 1987), 379. Hence there are no substantial and well-edited collections of testimony from *Rittergut* laborers comparable to such compendiums for Southern slaves as John W. Blassingame, ed., *Slave Testimony: Two Centuries of Letters, Speeches, Interviews, and Autobiographies* (Baton Rouge: Louisiana State Univ. Press, 1977), and Charles L.

Perdue, Jr., Thomas E. Barden, and Robert K. Phillips, eds., *Weevils in the Wheat: Interviews with Virginia Ex-Slaves* (Charlottesville: Univ. Press of Virginia, 1976). Among the few examples of autobiographical testimony from East Elbian day-laborers, the best known by far is Franz Rehbein (1867–1909), *Das Leben eines Landarbeiter,* ed. Paul Göhre (Jena: Eugen Diederichs Verlag, 1911; rpt. ed. Darmstadt/Neuwied: Hermann Leuchterhand Verlag, 1973); a newer edition with photographs has been prepared by Urs J. Diederichs & Holger Rudel (Hamburg: Christians Verlag, 1985). Several excerpts from Rehbein are included in Gerhard A. Ritter and Jürgen Kocka, eds., *Deutsche Sozialgeschichte. Dokumente und Skizzen, Band II: 1870–1914* (München: C. H. Beck, 1974), ch. 7, "Agriculture and Rural Life." A translated excerpt from Rehbein's autobiography is available in Alfred Kelly, ed., *The German Worker: Working-Class Autobiographies from the Age of Industrialization* (Berkeley & Los Angeles Univ. of California Press, 1987), 188–203.

17. "This *Gesindeordnung* regulated relations between lord and servant in any household and was not abolished until 1918. Under it no laborer or maid could resign prematurely, striking was punishable by imprisonment, 'paternal discipline' could be applied, and obedience enjoined, in an absolute manner." Hajo Holborn, *A History of Modern Germany, 1648–1840* (Princeton: Princeton Univ. Press, 1964), 409. See also Koselleck, *Preussen zwischen Reform und Revolution,* 65–66, 550; and Hanna Schissler, *Preussische Agrargesellschaft im Wandel: Wirtschaftliche, gesellschaftliche, und politische Transformationsprozesse von 1763 bis 1847* (Göttingen: Vandenhoeck & Ruprecht, 1978), 129, 131, 177.

18. Cited in Jordan, *Die Entstehung der konservativen Partei,* 78.

19. The term "private law state" is taken from Hans Rosenberg, *Bureaucracy, Aristocracy, and Autocracy: The Prussian Experience, 1660–1815* (Boston: Beacon Press, 1958), 43.

20. On the incompatibility of the planter's or Junker's private autocratic authority with the democratic nation-state, see esp. William H. McNeill, *The Rise of the West* (Chicago: Univ. of Chicago Press, 1963; NAL/Mentor paperback, 1965), 815–16, and Reinhard Bendix, *Nation-Building and Citizenship: Studies in Our Changing Social Order,* new enlarged ed. (Berkeley, Los Angeles, & London: Univ. of California Press, 1977), 122, 128.

21. My usage of the terms civil, political, and social equality follows that of T. H. Marshall, "Citizenship and Social Class" (1949), in *Class, Citizenship, and Social Development: Essays by T. H. Marshall* (Garden City, N.Y.: Anchor Books, 1965), 78.

22. As Eric Foner has argued, during the postwar era of Reconstruction the new "activist state" and its "vastly expanded authority" became temporarily wedded to the Radical Republican "ideal of a national citizenship whose equal rights belonged to all Americans regardless of race." Foner, *A Short History of Reconstruction* (New York: Harper & Row, 1990), xvi; see also p. 105.

23. Karl Ludwig von Haller, *Restauration der Staats-Wissenschaft oder Theorie des natürlichgeselligen Zustands,* 2nd ed. (6 vols.; Winterthur: Steiner, 1820–34), vol. 1, p. 382. For Haller's influence on Old Prussian intellectuals, see Friedrich Meinecke, *Cosmopolitanism and the National State,* trans. from the 1907 German ed. by Robert B. Kimber (Princeton: Princeton Univ. Press, 1970), Book I, ch. 10: "Haller and the Circle of Friedrich Wilhelm IV"; and Wolfgang Scheel, *Das "Berliner Politisches Wochenblatt" und die poli-*

tische und soziale Revolution in Frankreich und England. Ein Beitrag zur konservativen Zeitkritik in Deutschland, Göttinger Bausteine zur Geschichtswissenschaft, vol. 36 (Göttingen: Vandenhoeck & Ruprecht, 1964), 45–54.

24. A. P. Upshur, "Domestic Slavery," in *Southern Literary Messenger* 5 (1839), 681.

25. Haller, *Restauration*, vol. 1, pp. 369, 375–76; vol. 6, pp. 561–62.

26. William Harper, "Slavery in the Light of Social Ethics" (originally published as *Memoir on Slavery* (Charleston, 1838)), in E. N. Elliott, ed., *Cotton Is King, and Pro-Slavery Arguments* (Augusta, Ga.: Abbott & Loomis, 1860; rpt. ed., New York: Negro Universities Press, 1969), 559–60.

27. (David J. McCord), "Africans at Home," *Southern Quarterly Review* (July 1854), 91. McCord is identified as the author in Frank Winkler Ryan, Jr., "*The Southern Quarterly Review*, 1842–1857. A Study in Thought and Opinion in the Old South" (Ph.D. diss., University of North Carolina at Chapel Hill, 1956), 527.

28. Heros von Borcke, *Memoirs of the Confederate War for Independence* (Philadelphia: J. R. Lippincott, 1867; rpt. ed. Gaithersburg, Md.: Butternut Press, 1985), 4. Von Borcke makes numerous appearances in C. Vann Woodward, ed., *Mary Chesnut's Civil War* (New Haven & London: Yale Univ. Press, 1981).

29. Borcke quoted in Major Edgar Erskine Hume, U.S. Army, "Colonel Heros von Borcke: A Famous Prussian Volunteer in the Confederate States Army," in J. D. Eggleston, ed., *Southern Sketches*, First Series, No. 2 (Charlottesville, Va.: Historical Publishing Co., 1935), 20.

30. Murhard and Krug cited in Rainer Koch, "Liberalismus, Konservatismus, und das Problem der Negersklaverei: Ein Beitrag zur Geschichte des politischen Denkens in Deutschland in der ersten Hälfte des 19. Jahrhunderts," *Historische Zeitschrift* 222 (1976), 540–52, 567–68, 561.

31. Leo cited in ibid., 568.

32. Gerlach cited in Eugene N. Anderson, *The Social and Political Conflict in Prussia, 1858–1864* (Lincoln: Univ. of Nebraska Press, 1954), 376. Cf. Gerlach's sympathetic comments on slavery in an essay that appeared in the newspaper *Kreuzzeitung* in 1857, as reported in William James Orr, Jr., "The Foundation of the Kreuzzeitung Party in Prussia, 1848–1850" (Ph.D. diss., University of Wisconsin, 1971), 303–4.

33. Adolf von Thadden-Trieglaff, "Der Schacher mit Rittergüter," an address delivered 10 May 1842 before the General Assembly of the Pomeranian Economic Society at Cöslin, in Eleonore Fürstin Reuss, ed., *Adolf von Thadden Trieglaff. Ein Lebensbild Gezeichnet nach Errinerung seiner Kinder und Freude*, 2nd ed. (Berlin: W. Herz, 1894), 246–48.

34. Huber, "Die nordamerikanische Sclaverei" (dated Nov. 1863), No. 2 in *Soziale Fragen* (Nordhausen: Ferd. Förstemanns Verlag, 1864), 19. On Huber, see Hans-Joachim Schoeps, "Victor Aimé Huber," in Historische Kommission bei der Bayerischen Akademie der Wissenschaften, ed., *Neue Deutsche Biographie*, vol. 9 (Berlin: Duncker & Humblot, 1971), 688–89, and Rudolf Vierhaus, "Konservativ, Konservatismus," in Otto Brunner, Werner Conze, & Reinhart Koselleck, eds., *Geschichtliche Grundbegriffe: Historisches Lexikon zur politisch-sozialen Sprache in Deutschland, Band 3, H–Me* (Stuttgart: Klett-Cotta, 1982), 547–49.

35. Carl Schurz, *Lebenserinnerungen* (3 vols.; Berlin: G. Reimer, 1906–12), vol. 2,

pp. 205–6. Von Borcke's *Memoirs,* cited above, do not discuss attitudes in Prussia toward the South.

36. Otto zu Stolberg-Wernigerode, *Germany and the United States of America during the Era of Bismarck,* trans. Otto E. Lessing (Reading, Pa.: Henry Janssen Foundation, 1937), 2, 51, 61, 110–11.

37. "Einige Nachrichten über die landwirthschaftlichen Zustände der Vereinigten Staaten von Nordamerika," *Allgemeine Landwirtschaftliche Monatschrift* (1848), 214.

38. James H. Kettner, *The Development of American Citizenship, 1608–1870* (Chapel Hill: Univ. of North Carolina Press, 1978), 300.

39. Two studies that emphasize the crucial role played by racism in slaveholders' efforts to reconcile black bondage and white liberty are Duncan J. MacLeon, *Slavery, Race and the American Revolution* (Cambridge, Eng.: Cambridge Univ. Press, 1974), and James Oakes, *The Ruling Race: A History of American Slaveholders* (New York: Knopf, 1982). Anne C. Loveland has demonstrated that evangelical ministers in the South, of all denominations, forcefully defended the morality and Biblical legitimacy of slavery without endorsing the "positive good" argument "that slavery was an ideal state that should be perpetual." Loveland, *Southern Evangelicals and the Social Order, 1800–1860* (Baton Rouge: Louisiana State Univ. Press, 1980), ch. 7, "Slavery"; the quotation is from p. 207.

40. William Cooper, Jr., has emphasized the impossibility of determining how many Southerners "accepted or believed" the argument that slavery was a positive good instead of the necessary evil argument. "In practical terms," however, "it mattered little whether or not a southerner accepted or rejected the argument that slavery was a positive good," since those who favored the argument from necessity also insisted that the South must deal with its peculiar institution free from outside influence. Cooper, *The South and the Politics of Slavery, 1828–1856* (Baton Rouge: Louisiana State Univ. Press, 1978), 60–63. As William W. Freehling has noted, apologetic "conditional terminators" who advocated geographic diffusion of slavery, like more bombastic spokesmen for "unconditional perpetualism," firmly agreed on the necessity for slavery's ongoing westward and/or southward extension. Freehling, *The Road to Disunion, Volume I: Secessionists at Bay, 1776–1854* (New York & Oxford: Oxford Univ. Press, 1990), 150–56 and passim. Although there were many more planters with moral misgivings about slavery than there were Junkers with qualms about their aristocratic privileges, I am not convinced that moral anxiety or guilt feelings over slavery played a major role either in prodding slaveholders to precipitate the Civil War or in causing the Confederacy's defeat. For challenging arguments to the contrary, see Charles B. Sellers, "The Travail of Slavery," in Sellers, ed., *The Southerner as American* (Chapel Hill: Univ. of North Carolina Press, 1960), 40–71; Kenneth M. Stampp, "The Southern Road to Appomattox," in Stampp, *The Imperiled Union: Essays on the Background of the Civil War* (New York & Oxford: Oxford Univ. Press, 1980), 246–69; and Richard E. Beringer, Hermann Hattaway, Archer Jones, and William N. Still, Jr., *Why the South Lost the Civil War* (Athens & London: Univ. of Georgia Press, 1986), chs. 14 and 15.

41. Mary B. McGehee to brother John Wm. Burruss, 17 March 1836, in John C. Burruss and Family Papers, Southern Historical Manuscripts (microfiche) from Louisiana State University, Baton Rouge.

42. Mississippi Slave Schedules for 1860, National Archives Microfilm Publication, Microcopy No. 653 (Washington, D.C., 1967).

43. Francis Terry Leak Diary, 1859–62 (typescript), in Southern Historical Collection of the University of North Carolina at Chapel Hill. Eloquent post–Civil War testimony to the compatibility of slavery and freedom in the minds of many white Southerners comes from Lillian Smith's *Killers of the Dream,* originally published in 1949. Smith (1897–1966) was born and raised during the era of segregation and disenfranchisement in a small Florida town just south of the Georgia line; and in recalling the subtle conditioning of her racial consciousness during her childhood, she describes a process that pervaded the antebellum South as well: "From the day I was born, I began to learn my lessons . . . I learned it is possible to be a Christian and a white southerner simultaneously; . . . I learned to believe in freedom, to glow when the word *democracy* was used, and to practice slavery from morning to night. I learned it the way all of my southern people learn it: by closing door after door until one's mind and heart and conscience are blocked off from each other and from reality." Smith, *Killers of the Dream,* rev. ed. (New York: Norton, 1961; Norton Library paperback, 1978), 29. On Lillian Smith, see Martin Sosna, *In Search of the Silent South: Southern Liberals and the Race Issue* (New York: Columbia Univ. Press, 1977), ch. 9, "Lillian Smith: The Southern Liberal as Evangelist."

44. Frederick Law Olmsted, *A Journey in the Back Country, 1853–1854* (New York: Mason Brothers, 1860; rpt. ed., New York: Schocken Books, 1970), 135, 138.

45. Hauptmann von Versen, "Der Ruchaldo," *Allgemeine Landwirtschaftliche Monatschrift* (1840), 163.

46. Karl Theodor Griesinger, *Land und Leute in Amerika. Skizzen aus dem amerikanischen Leben,* 2nd ed. (Stuttgart: A. Kroner, 1863), 71. Chapter 3, from which the quotation is taken, is entitled "The Southern Plantation Owner or the Cotton Baron of the New World."

47. David Castronovo, *The English Gentleman: Images and Ideals in Literature and Society* (New York: Ungar, 1987), 16. Another useful study, even more focused on literature, is Philip Mason, *The English Gentleman: The Rise and Fall of an Ideal* (New York: William Morrow, 1982).

48. Peter Laslett, *The World We Have Lost: England Before the Industrial Age,* 2nd ed. (New York: Charles Scribner's Sons, 1971), 30.

49. According to James Oakes, "Slaveholding professionals were probably the single most influential class in the antebellum South." He points to "their control of much of the southern press" and their election to political office "in staggeringly unrepresentative numbers." Oakes, *The Ruling Race,* 61. I would emphasize that the "most influential" professional slaveholders belonged to the planter elite as defined here. One could argue that Junker professionals were "probably the single most influential class" in nineteenth-century East Elbia by pointing to the predominance of *Rittergut* owners and their sons in the higher ranks of the officer corps and civil bureaucracy. To wit, a study of the Marienwerder administrative area *(Regierungsbezirk,* a governmental district between the level of county and province) in provincial Prussia for the years 1830–70 informs us that most district counsellors *(Landäte)* came from the ranks of bureaucrats whose fathers owned knight's estates, and whose fathers transferred estate titles to their sons so that

the sons could meet the formal criteria for the position of *Landrat*. Horst Mies, *Die Preußische Verwaltung des Regierungsbezirks Marienwerder 1830–1870* (Köln & Berlin: Grote, 1973), 50. Another study for the years 1815–66 of Prussia's highest civil officials on the provincial level—the *Oberpräsidenten*, or Lord Lieutenants, who were the closest equivalent in royalist Prussia to U.S. governors—reveals that 31 of the 45 men who served as Lord-Lieutenants were sons of estate owners; and of these 31 estate-owning fathers 13 had served in the higher administration (including the position of *Landrat*), two had served as judges, and seven had served in the military with the rank of captain or above. For the six East Elbian provinces, we find that seven of the eight Lord Lieutenants in Brandenburg from 1815 to 1866 were sons of estate owners, four of the five in Pomerania, five of the eight in Silesia, three of the five in Saxony, five of the nine in Posen, and only two of the seven in Prussia (West and East). Rüdiger Schütz, "Die Preußischen Oberpräsidenten von 1815 bis 1866," in Klaus Schwabe, ed., *Die preußischen Oberpräsidenten 1815–1945, Deutsche Führungsschichten in der Neuzeit,* vol. 15 (Boppard am Rhein: Harald Boldt Verlag, 1985), 34–35, 77–81.

50. Bertram Wyatt-Brown begins his analysis of Southern "gentility" with the statement that it "was a more specialized, refined form of honor, in which moral uprightness was coupled with high social position." "Difficult though it was to tell the genuine article from the fake, three components appeared to be necessary for public recognition of gentility in the Old South: sociability, learning, and piety." Wyatt-Brown, *Southern Honor: Ethics and Behavior in the Old South* (New York & Oxford: Oxford Univ. Press, 1982), 88–89. His focus is on the cultural ideal of the gentleman, the ethos of gentility, rather than on the basic economic and social foundations of gentlemanly status in the Old South. Compare Wyatt-Brown's approach with a definition proposed by the editor of an antebellum agricultural journal: "A Gentleman. — It takes four things to make a thorough gentleman. You must be a gentleman in your principles, a gentleman in your tastes, a gentleman in your manners, a gentleman in your person." *American Cotton Planter and Soil of the South* (Feb. 1857), 46.

51. On the continuing cultural importance of the distinction between manual and nonmanual occupations in industrial societies, see Seymour Martin Lipset and Reinhard Bendix, *Social Mobility in Industrial Societies* (Berkeley: Univ. of California Press, 1959), 165–67.

52. Poultney Bigelow, an Englishman who lived in Prussia as a boy in the 1860s and attended boarding school in Bonn, reported that "Some of my German friends have shown irritation when I pointed out sympathetically that the conception of a gentleman was not at home in Prussia and had to be imported in a mutilated form. Here again I am at a loss to analyse so subtle a matter. . . ." Bigelow, *Prussian Memories, 1864–1914* (New York & London: G.P. Putnam's Sons, 1915), 10.

53. In 1843 legal scholar and minister of justice Karl von Savigny reported that a royal Commission for Noble Affairs recommended the development in Prussia of a gentry along the English model. Robert M. Berdahl, *The Politics of the Prussian Nobility: The Development of a Conservative Ideology, 1770–1848* (Princeton: Princeton Univ. Press, 1988), 328.

54. Tocqueville, *The Old Regime and the French Revolution* (1856), trans. Stuart Gil-

bert (Garden City, N.Y.: Anchor Books, 1955), 81–82. In "Journey to England" (1833), Tocqueville noted that the difference between the English and French aristocracies "turns on the examination of a single world in each language. 'Gentleman' and 'gentilhomme' evidently have the same derivation, but 'gentleman' in England is applied to every well-educated man whatever his birth, while in France *gentilhomme* applies only to a noble by birth. . . . This grammatical illustration is more illuminating than many long arguments." Tocqueville, *Journeys to England and Ireland*, ed. J. P. Mayer and trans. George Lawrence (New Haven: Yale Univ. Press, 1958), 67. An introduction to contrasts between "The English Aristocracy and the Continental Nobility" is provided by J. V. Beckett, *The Aristocracy in England 1660–1914* (Oxford & New York: Basil Blackwell, 1986), 22–26.

55. Werner Sombart noted the assumption among members of the *"parti feodal"* in Wilhelmine Prusso-Germany—that is, the "feudal agrarian" Junkers—that "one could not willingly engage in commerce or in retailing and at the same time be a genteel, distinguished man *(ein vornehmer Mann).*" Sombart, *Die Deutsche Volkswirtschaft in neunzehnten Jahrhundert,* 3rd ed. (Berlin: G. Bondi, 1913), 465.

56. F. M. L. Thompson, *English Landed Society in the Nineteenth Century* (Toronto & London: Univ. of Toronto Press, 1963), 22. The steady flow of wealthy commoners into the landed gentry "must be accounted a prime reason for the failure of the cleavage between capitalists and landowners ever to become so deep as to be unbridgeable." Ibid.

57. Sherman M. Kuhn, ed., *Middle English Dictionary* (Ann Arbor: Univ. of Michigan Press, 1963), vol. G-H, pp. 71–72. See also Ruth Kelso, "The Institution of the Gentleman in English Literature of the Sixteenth Century: A Study in Renaissance Ideals" (Abstract of a Ph.D. diss., University of Illinois, 1923); and Esmé Wingfield-Stratford, *The Making of a Gentleman* (London: Williams and Norgate, 1938), esp. 26–27.

58. John Stuart Mill, *A System of Logic, Ratiocinative and Inductive,* 10th ed. (2 vols.; London: Longmans, Green, 1879), vol. 2, p. 240. Cf. George P. Marsh, *Lectures on the English Language,* 4th ed. (New York & London: Charles Scribner and Sampson, Low, Son, 1859), 257.

59. "The Anglo-Saxon conventions," wrote Weber, "mold behavior down into the lowest strata. They stem from the social habits of the gentry stratum, which has set the tone in England since the seventeenth century," and whose conventions "could be easily and universally imitated and hence could be democratized." But "there is no social form of German gentility," argued Weber, because the "conventions and gestures" of Junkerdom "are simply not suited to serve as a model for the whole nation down to its lowest strata." Max Weber, "National Character and the Junkers," in H. H. Gerth and C. Wright Mills, eds., *From Max Weber: Essays in Sociology* (New York: Oxford Univ. Press, 1946; Oxford paperback, 1958), 390–92. What I call the social democratization of gentility has been investigated in the context of American history by Stow Persons: "During the course of the nineteenth century the theory and practice of gentility in America underwent a continuous process of diffusion and attenuation, so that after the First World War it served no useful purpose to make the older distinction between gentleman and common man." Although Persons focuses almost entirely on New Eng-

land, he makes a passing reference to the Old South's "old gentry class" as having been an important exception to gentility's "diffusion and attentuation." Persons, *The Decline of American Gentility* (New York: Columbia Univ. Press, 1973), v, 82.

60. Carl Brinkmann, "Die Aristokratie im kapitalistischen Zeitalter," in his *Wirtschaftsformen und Lebensformen: Gesammelte Schriften zur Wirtschaftswissenschaft und Wirtschaftspolitik*, 2nd ed. (Tübingen: J. C. B. Mohr (Paul Siebeck), 1950), 39–40.

61. Harold Perkin, *The Origins of Modern English Society, 1780–1880* (Toronto: Univ. of Toronto Press, 1969; Toronto paperback, 1972), 24. "For the leisured gentleman was the ideal at which the whole society aimed, and by which it measured its happiness and ambitions." Ibid., 55.

62. Ibid., 61.

63. Hans Rosenberg writes of "the process of *'Neufeudalisierung,'*" or "the gradual *Aristokratisierung*" of commoner Junkers; parvenu *Rittergut* owners in the nineteenth century tended to become "stock-conservative haters of democracy, who often behaved more like Junkers *(junkerlicher)* than did the old landed nobility." Rosenberg, "Die Pseudodemocratisierung der Rittergutsbesitzerklasse," in his *Probleme der deutschen Sozialgeschichte* (Frankfurt am Main: Suhrkamp Verlag, 1969), 26–27. According to G. F. Knapp, "Already at the beginning of our (19th) century the landed nobility conceded to the commoner estate owners the most ample space alongside it, but at the same time inspired this part of the middle class *(Bürgerstand)* with its spirit." Knapp, "Landarbeiter und innere Kolonization" (1897), in his *Die Landarbeiter in Knechtschaft und Freiheit. Gesammelte Vorträge von Georg Friedrich Knapp*, 2nd ed. (Leipzig: Duncker & Humblot, 1909), 24.

64. Thorstein Veblen, *The Theory of the Leisure Class* (1899), in Max Lerner, ed., *The Portable Veblen* (New York: Viking, 1948), 88, 95.

65. A memorable sketch of a decidedly ungentlemanly though extremely wealthy Texas planter—John C. Clark of Wharton County, who owned 137 slaves and 8,739 acres of land when he died in 1862—was included in a statement of evidence put before the state supreme court after his death: "Clark was a man of little or no education, unsocial temperament, and apparently engrossed by a desire to accumulate property." Richard G. Lowe and Randolph B. Campbell, *Planters and Plain Folk: Agriculture in Antebellum Texas* (Dallas: Southern Methodist Univ. Press, 1987), 103–4.

66. J. R. Pole, "Introduction" to Pole, ed., *The American Constitution, For and Against: The Federalist and Anti-Federalist Papers* (New York: Hill and Wang, 1987), 16.

67. According to a scholar of slavery in Florida, "The owner of a small plantation, though hardly in the planter class (which she identifies as those owning at least 30 slaves), deserves to be classified as one since he directed the labor of others and played the role of planter as defined here. He did not engage in field work." Julia F. Smith, *Slavery and Plantation Growth in Antebellum Florida, 1821–1860* (Gainesville: Univ. of Florida Press, 1973), 3. In one of the best state studies of antebellum Southern agriculture, John Hebron Moore makes a helpful distinction between the plantation and the farm in Mississippi. "On units large enough to be designated correctly as cotton plantations, there were always enough Negro slaves to require a special system of labor and social control." On yeoman farms, "most of the work was done by white members of the owner's family," and if there were any slaves they worked alongside the whites. "In

brief, the distinguishing characteristic of a true cotton farm was the employment of free white labor—with or without additional help from an occasional Negro slave. On true cotton plantations, however, no white labor was employed except highly skilled workmen and overseers, or perhaps an occasional person in a special capacity." Moore, *Agriculture in Antebellum Mississippi* (New York: Bookman Associates, 1958), 65. Moore has also written a more recent monograph on Mississippi agriculture: *The Emergence of the Cotton Kingdom in the Old Southwest: Mississippi, 1770–1860* (Baton Rouge & London: Louisiana State Univ. Press, 1988).

68. Randolph B. Campbell, in his analysis of 1850 census information on public leaders in Harrison County, in eastern Texas on the Louisiana border, has identified a number of professional men with fewer than 20 bondsmen who would nevertheless have to be accounted "planters": e.g., Dr. W. F. Baldwin, with 115 improved acres and 11 slaves; attorney M.J. Hall, with 200 improved acres and 14 slaves; and lawyer John F. William, with 100 improved acres and 18 slaves. According to the 1860 census, lawyer G. W. Whitmore owned 125 improved acres and 7 slaves, and Dr. A. H. Willie owned 30 improved acres and 16 slaves. Campbell, "Planters and Plainfolk: Harrison County, Texas, as a Test Case, 1850–1860," *Journal of Southern History* 40 (1974), 393–97. Frederick Law Olmsted wrote as follows about the South's Appalachian Highlands: "Of the people who get their living entirely from agriculture, few own negroes; the slave-holders being chiefly professional men, shop-keepers, and men in office, who are also land owners, and give a divided attention to farming." Olmsted, *A Journey in the Back Country, 1853–1854,* 226.

69. John J. Clendinen Diary, 1836–60, Arkansas History Commission, Little Rock; and Arkansas Slave Schedules for 1860, National Archives Microfilm Publications, Microcopy No. 653 (Washington, D.C., 1967).

70. A planter's male and female field-hands usually amounted to about half the total number of slaves on his plantation. "Masters who had at their command as few as a half-dozen field hands were tempted to improve their status by withdrawing from the fields and devoting most of their time to managerial functions." Stampp, *The Peculiar Institution,* 35. Stampp emphasizes that planters with more than 30 slaves tended to have the most efficient and complex operations and generally had both overseers and drivers, while planters who owned fewer than 30 bondsmen tended to rely on their sons or slave foremen. Ibid., 35–38.

71. Robert Partin, ed., "A Connecticut Yankee's Letters from Concecuh, County, Alabama, 1847–1866," *Alabama Review* 4 (1951), 55–56.

72. Stephen B. Oates, *The Fires of Jubilee: Nat Turner's Fierce Rebellion* (New York: Harper and Row, 1975), 65. F. N. Boney reports that in 1830 Francis owned 15 slaves (six of them under the age of 10) and only 567 acres. By the time of his death in 1849, Francis owned 37 slaves (among them just five aged 12 or younger) and had accumulated about 3,500 acres of land through inheritance and purchase. Boney, "Nathaniel Francis, Representative Antebellum Southerner," *Proceedings of the American Philosophical Society* 118 (1974), 452, 455.

73. James Monette Day Book and Diary, 1848–63 (typescript), Library of Congress, Washington, D.C.; and Louisiana Slave Schedules for 1860, National Archives Microfilm Publications, Microcopy No. 653 (Washington, 1967).

74. Philip N. Racine, ed., *Piedmont Farmer: The Journals of David Golightly Harris, 1855–1870* (Knoxville: Univ. of Tennessee Press, 1990), 3, 18.

75. Olmsted, *Journey in the Back Country, 1853–1854,* 160. Of course, there were planters throughout the South who owned more than 20 slaves and employed no overseer. In 1838–39 John Blackford raised corn, wheat, barley, oats, rye, clover, hay, potatoes, apples, cattle, horse, sheep, and hogs on 700-plus acres located on the north side of the Potomac River in western Maryland. His 25 slaves, together with a good many hired laborers, worked "individually with little or no supervision." "Blackford, like most Southern planters, was a busy and hard working man. He did not of course do manual labor but he chose to manage his plantation and supervise his various business interests without the help of an overseer." Fletcher M. Green, "Introduction" to Green, ed., *Ferry Hill Plantation Journal, January 4, 1838 - January 15, 1839,* James Sprunt Studies in History and Political Science, vol. 43 (Chapel Hill: Univ. of North Carolina Press, 1961).

76. The percentages are based on figures in U.S. Census Office, *Eighth Census: Statistics of the U.S.* (District of Columbia: Government Printing Office, 1866), 247, and J. G. Randall and David Herbert Donald, *The Civil War and Reconstruction,* 2nd ed. (Lexington, Mass.: D. C. Heath, 1969), 68, as amended by Orville W. Taylor, *Negro Slavery in Arkansas* (Durham, N.C.: Duke Univ. Press, 1958), 58. Taylor corrects the grossly inaccurate published census figures for the number of Arkansas slaveholders in 1860. Where the 1860 census reported 66 planters among 1,149 slaveholders, Taylor reports 1,363 planters among 11,481 slaveholders. The inaccurate figures have misled many historians, including Randall and Donald. Lewis Cecil Gray, the most thorough student of agriculture in the Old South, has distinguished between upper-class planters who owned 50 or more slaves and the much larger group of middle-class planters who owned 10 to 50 slaves. Thus, according to Gray, there were nearly 110,000 planters in 1860. Gray, *History of Agriculture in the Southern United States to 1860* (2 vols.; Washington, D.C.: Carnegie Institution, 1933; rpt. ed., Gloucester, Mass.: Peter Smith, 1958), vol. 1, pp. 481–83. My own statistically imprecise definition of planters would place the figure somewhere between Gray's total of 110,000 and the census takers' total of 47,500, but probably closer to the later.

77. Robert S. Starobin, *Industrial Slavery in the Old South* (New York & Oxford: Oxford Univ. Press, 1970), vii, 9; and Richard C. Wade, *Slavery in the Cities: The South, 1820–1860* (New York & Oxford: Oxford Univ. Press, 1964), 243. In Richmond, the South's leading industrial city, the number of statistical planters was 93 in 1860, including a large number of corporations. Ibid., 22–23.

78. According to Ralph A. Wooster's examination of the 1860 census, Philip St. George Cocke's total wealth came to $1.5 million, which ranks him number 19 on Wooster's list of 49 Southern millionaires. Wooster, "Wealthy Southerners on the Eve of the Civil War," in Gary W. Gallagher, ed., *Essays on Southern History, Written in Honor of Barnes F. Lathrop* (Austin: General Libraries of the University of Texas at Austin, 1980), 139–40.

79. My essay "Conditional Unionism and Slavery in Virginia, 1860–1861: The Case of Dr. Richard Eppes," *Virginia Magazine of History and Biography,* 96 (1988), 37, n. 14, reports that the younger Cocke owned three Virginia plantations, totaling 224 slaves and

6,562 acres, and eight Mississippi plantations, totaling 435 slaves and 11,796 acres. I computed these totals using notes taken years ago from "Summary of Property, Estate of Philip St. George Cocke, February 1860," in Philip St. George Cocke Papers, Alderman Library, University of Virginia, Charlottesville. In response to my journal article, Professor William K. Scarborough at the University of Southern Mississippi, who is at work on a study of large slaveholders, wrote on 29 March 1988 to say that according to his records, Cocke owned a total of 658 rather than 659 slaves and six rather than eight Mississippi plantations. Since I have great respect for Professor Scarborough's meticulous scholarship, I am using his set of figures.

80. Clement Eaton, *A History of the Old South,* 3rd ed. (New York: Macmillan, 1975), 390.

81. Robert Henderson Allen Diary, 1858–63, pp. 198, 216–18, 221, in Virginia Historical Society Library, Richmond; and Virginia Slave Schedules for 1860, National Archives Microfilm Publications, Microcopy No. 653 (Washington, D.C., 1967).

82. James M. Clifton, "Introduction" to Clifton, ed., *Life and Labor on Argyle Island: Letters and Documents of a Savannah River Rice Plantation, 1833–1867* (Savannah, Ga.: Beehive Press, 1978), xix-xx.

83. Mack B. Swearingen, "Thirty Years of a Mississippi Plantation: Charles Whitmore of 'Montpelier,' " *Journal of Southern History* 1 (1935), 201. This essay is reprinted in Elinor Miller and Eugene D. Genovese, eds., *Plantation, Town, and County: Essays on the Local History of Slave Society* (Urbana, Chicago, & London: Univ. of Illinois Press, 1974), 270–83. Robert Christian's Fair Oaks cotton plantation, in Perry County in the Alabama Black Belt, seems to have had 25 slaves and 400 acres in 1857. Robert Christian Diary, 1854–57, Alabama Department of Archives and History, Montgomery. In the South Carolina Upcountry during the 1820s and 1830s Mary Moragne's father, descended from Huguenot colonists who settled along the upper Savannah River in 1764, owned about 300 acres and 25 to 30 slaves. He provided "a comfortable but unpretentious style of living" for 11 children; they were accepted socially by the "first families" of the district, like the Calhouns and Nobles. George Patrick Germany, "The South Carolina Governing Elite, 1820–1860" (Ph.D. diss., University of California at Berkeley, 1972), 121–24.

84. "(T)he class of knight's estates encompasses such great estates as have attached to them certain political privileges and rights in the county and provincial diets." Georg von Viebahn, *Statistik des zollvereinten und nördlichen Deutschlands* (3 vols.; Berlin: Georg Reimer, 1858–68), vol. 2, p. 553.

85. Charles S. Sydnor, *American Revolutionaries in the Making: Political Practices in Washington's Virginia* (New York: Free Press, 1965), ch. 6, "County Oligarchies."

86. Albert Ogden Porter, *County Government in Virginia: A Legislative History, 1607–1905* (New York: Columbia Univ. Press, 1947), 89. Until mid-century "the county court was still the main spring of county administration and was still organized on the theory of gentleman justices giving their unpaid services from a sense of class duty and privileges." Ibid., 225.

87. Koselleck, *Preussen zwischen Reform und Revolution,* 525–26, 549.

88. See Eaton, *History of the Old South,* 328–329; Charles Henry Ambler, *Sectionalism in Virginia from 1776–1861* (Chicago: Univ. of Chicago Press, 1910), 267–68; J.

Mills Thornton III, *Politics and Power in a Slave Society: Alabama, 1800–1860* (Baton Rouge: Louisiana State Univ. Press, 1978), 100–101; Ford, *Origins of Southern Radicalism,* 312; and Randolph B. Campbell, *An Empire for Slavery: The Peculiar Institution in Texas, 1821–1865* (Baton Rouge & London: Louisiana State Univ. Press, 1989), 94–95. Campbell suggests that the Texas tax rate on slave property was low partly because in many counties the upkeep of public roads was delegated to slaveholders.

89. Computed from figures in Viebahn, *Statistik,* vol. 2, pp. 43, 309. Viebahn estimated that in all the states of the German *Zollverein* (Customs Union), the families of *Rittergut* owners and all noble families totaled 250,000 persons. Ibid., 311. According to East German scholar Manfried Kliem, in 1848 "the feudal and Junker class" made up 1 percent of the total population of Prussia. Kliem, "Die Rolle der feudaljunkerlichen Reaktion in der Revolution von 1848/49," 311.

90. Carl Wilhelm von Lancizolle, *Über Königtum und Landstände in Preussen* (Berlin: Ferdinand Dümmler, 1846), 492–93; Viebahn, *Statistik,* vol. 2, pp. 309–10; and F. W. Schmidt, "Gutsbezirke (selbstständige)," in Max Fleischmann, ed., *Wörterbuch des Deutschen Staats- und Verwaltungsrechts,* 2nd ed. (Tübingen: J. C. B. Mohr (Paul Siebeck), 1913), vol. 2, p. 300.

91. Karl Friedrich von Rauer, *Alphabetischer Nachweis (Addressbuch) des in den Preussischen Staaten mit Rittergütern angesessenen Adels* (Berlin: Durch die Herausgeber, 1857), 9–11.

92. To be sure, the 45% figure disguises significant provincial variations, from a high of 66% non-noble in the province of Prussia to a low of 34% in Posen. The figure for Brandenburg was 38% non-noble, for Pomerania 40%, for Silesia 41%, and for Saxony 45%. Computed from figures in Karl Friedrich Rauer, *Hand-Matrikel der in sämtlichen Kreisen des preussischen Staats auf Kreis- und Landtagen vertretenen Rittergüter* (Berlin: Durch die Herausgeber, 1857), 451. Cf. Viebahn, *Statistik,* vol. 2, pp. 309–10. Manfred Kliem says that of 14,700 noble families owning Prussian *Rittergüter* in 1816, only 8000 of these retained ownership in 1848. Kliem, "Die Rolle der feudaljunkerlichen Reaktion," 311.

93. Koselleck, *Preussen zwischen Reform und Revolution,* 507.

94. Computed from *Morgen* figures in C. F. W. Dieterici, *Handbuch der Statistik des preussischen Staats* (Berlin: E. S. Mittler und Sohn, 1861), 318–21. Not all "large landed estates" qualified as knight's estates. In 1856 there were 1,742 *Rittergüter* in Pomerania, and as of 1855 the province contained 2,516 owners of estates with a minimum of 600 *Morgen.* Rauer, *Hand-Matrikel,* 134; and Bureau des Königl. Ober-Präsidiums, *Jahrbuch der Provinz Pommern,* 10th ed. (Stettin: Th. von der Nahmer, 1857), 44. Robert Berdahl notes that "Old noble estates remained noble as long as they were not subdivided, regardless of their size or annual profit; new estates could be designated as noble only if they were of a certain size and income." Berdahl, *Politics of the Prussian Nobility,* 279.

95. Wilhelm Adolf Lette cited in Johannes Ziekursch, *Hundert Jahre schlesischer Agrargeschichte. Vom hubertusburger Frieden bis zum Abschluss der Bauernbefreiung* (Breslau: Ferdinand Hirt, 1915), 66. A Silesian Junker reported in 1846 that knight's estates in Upper Silesia ranged from debt-free estates of 200,000 *Morgen* to heavily indebted estates of 200 *Morgen.* Von Bally, "Oberschlesische Zustände," *Annalen der Landwirtschaft* 7 (1846), 86.

96. Erich Marcks, *Bismarck: Eine Biographie, 1815–1851* (Stuttgart and Berlin: Cotta, 1915), 175–77, and Ernst Engelberg, *Bismarck, Urpreuße und Reichsgründer* (Berlin: Siedler, 1985), 155, 215–16. According to Engelberg, the community of Schönhausen included a total of roughly 10,710 acres (17,000 *Morgen*) and 2000 residents. Over half of these acres were owned by village smallholders, the remainder being divided between Bismarck's estate and a much larger *Rittergut* belonging to a non-noble bureaucrat *(Staatsrat)* named Gärtner.

97. Jordan, *Die Entstehung der konservativen Partei,* 64.

98. "Specialle Ertragsnachweisung einer Vorpommerschen Wirthschaft in den Jahren 1843–1846," *Allgemeine Landwirtschaftliche Monatschrift* (published in Coslin till 1844; then published in Berlin) (1846), 88–97.

99. Max Weber, *General Economic History,* intro. by Ira J. Cohen (New Brunswick, N.J.: Transaction Books, 1981), 110. For evidence that the preponderance of *Rittergut* owners managed their own estates, see August von Miaskowski, *Das Erbrecht und die Grundeigentumsvertheilung im Deutschen Reiche. Eine socialwirtschaftlicher Beitrag zur Kritik und Reform des deutschen Erbrechts. Teil I: Die Verhältnisse des landwirtschaftlich benutzten Grundeigenthums und das gemeine Erbrecht,* Schriften des Vereins für Sozialpolitik, Vol. 20 (Leipzig: Duncker & Humblot, 1882), 6: as of 1867 there were a total of 12,150 *Rittergüter* in the eight old provinces of Prussia, including the Rhineland and Westphalia; and of 10,786 estates with a minimum taxable net income of 1000 *Taler,* only about 1800 were leased. The management of one's own estate was the rule except among the larger estates of the upper nobility *(Standesherren),* which were often bound in family trust entail *(Fideikommiß).*

100. Beckett, *The Aristocracy in England 1660–1914,* 156.

101. David Spring, *The English Landed Estate in the Nineteenth Century: Its Administration* (Baltimore: Johns Hopkins Univ. Press, 1963), 181.

102. Planters in the "sugar bowl" of south-central Louisiana were a notable exception. There "the short growing season, as compared with more southerly climes, was an obstacle to sugar culture, but a protective tariff compensated for this handicap." Joe Gray Taylor, *Negro Slavery in Louisiana* (Baton Rouge: Louisiana State Univ. Press, 1963), ix.

103. E. J. Hobsbawm, *Industry and Empire. The Making of Modern English Society, Vol. II: 1750 to the Present Day* (New York: Pantheon, 1968), 2. Hobsbawm explains that the term world economy "must be understood to mean only that the European economy was the center of a world-wide network, but *not* that all parts of the world were involved in this network." It "developed as a single system of free flows, in which the international transfers of capital and commodities passed largely through British hands and institutions, in British ships between the continents, and were calculated in terms of the pound sterling."

104. Francois Belarida, *A Social History of England, 1851–1975,* trans. A. S. Forster (London & New York: Methuen, 1979), 41.

105. Larry Edward Tise argues that Burke's influence on most of the first generation of antebellum proslavery intellectuals came by way of Southerners trained in Federalist thought during their education at schools in New England and the coastal Northeast. Tise, "Proslavery Ideology: A Social and Intellectual History of the Defense of Slavery

in America, 1790–1840" (Ph. D. diss., University of North Carolina at Chapel Hill, 1975), esp. 672–75. Tise has published a much revised version of this dissertation as *Proslavery: A History of the Defense of Slavery in America, 1701–1840* (Athens, Ga., & London: Univ. of Georgia Press, 1988), see 340–44.

106. Reinhold Aris, *History of Political Thought in Germany from 1789 to 1815* (London: Frank Cass, 1936; rpt. ed., New York: Russell & Russell, 1965), 394. Cf. Kenneth A. Lockridge's arresting explanation of what it means to be "conservative" in U.S. history: "In the depths of the American experience lies a craving for peace, unity, and order within the confines of a simple society." Lockridge, *A New England Town, the First Hundred Years: Dedham, Massachusetts, 1636–1736* (New York: Norton, 1970), 169.

107. Isaac Kramnick, *The Rage of Edmund Burke: Portrait of an Ambivalent Conservative* (New York: Basic Books, 1977), 27.

108. Edgar Johnson, *Sir Walter Scott: The Great Unknown* (2 vols.; New York: Macmillan, 1970), vol. 1, p. 522.

109. Thomas Carlyle, *The French Revolution: A History* (1837) (New York: Modern Library, no date), 408.

110. George Fitzhugh, "Southern Thought," *DeBow's Review* (1857), 349. This essay is reprinted in Drew Gilpin Faust, ed., *The Ideology of Slavery: Proslavery Thought in the Antebellum South, 1830–1860* (Baton Rouge: Louisiana State Univ. Press, 1981); the quotation is on p. 287.

111. Richard Current, *John C. Calhoun* (New York: Washington Square Press & Twayne Publishers, 1963), 43.

112. Charles M. Wiltse, *John C. Calhoun* (3 vols.; Indianapolis: Bobbs-Merrill, 1944–51), vol. 3, p. 420.

113. Friedrich Meusel, ed., *Friedrich August Ludwig von der Marwitz: Ein märkischer Edelmann im Zeitalter der Befreiungskriege* (2 vols.; Berlin: Ernst Siegfried Mittler und Sohn, 1908–13), vol. 1, pp. 59–60.

114. The quotation is from Current, *Calhoun*, 44.

115. Freehling, *Prelude to Civil War*, 168.

116. See Faust, ed., *The Ideology of Slavery*, 78–79. Harper's *Memoir* was republished on the eve of the Civil War as "Slavery in the Light of Social Ethics," in E. N. Elliott, *Cotton Is King, and Pro-Slavery Arguments* (Augusta, Ga., 1860; rpt. ed., New York, 1969), 547–626. Although Harper does not cite Burke by name in this essay, he repeatedly cites Thomas R. Dew's even more influential proslavery treatise *Review of the Debate in the Virginia Legislature of 1831–1832* (1832), which cites Burke by name on several occasions, and which will be discussed at length in Chapter 6.

117. Harper quoted in Tise, "Proslavery Ideology," 622.

118. Gentz, from the Silesian city of Breslau, worked in Berlin from 1792 to 1802 as a member of Friedrich Wilhelm III's Council of War *(Kriegsrat);* then he became a confidante of Prince Klemens von Metternich and an advisor to the Hapsburgs in Vienna. See Paul R. Sweet, *Friedrich von Gentz, Defender of the Old Order* (Madison: Univ. of Wisconsin Press, 1941), 20–28.

119. Adam Müller, "Studium der positiven Wissenschaften. 1808," in Jakob Baxa, ed., *Adam Müller, Ausgewählte Abhandlungen* (Jena: Gustave Fischer, 1931), 25–26.

120. Müller quoted in Hans Barth, *The Idea of Order: Contributions to a Philosophy*

of Politics (1958), trans. Ernst W. Hankamer & William W. Newell (Dordrecht-Holland: Reidel, 1960), 30–31.

121. See "Marwitz an Hardenberg" (11 Feb. 1811), "Bemerkungen von Marwitz am Rande des Konzepts von Adam Müllers Eingabe" (11 Feb. 1811), and "Müller an Marwitz" (21 Feb. 1811), in Jakob Baxa, ed., *Adam Müller's Lebenszeugnisse* (2 vols.; München, Paderborn, & Wien: Ferdinand Schöningh, 1966), vol. 1, pp. 608–21.

122. Sigmund Neumann, *Die Stufen des preussischen Konservatismus: Ein Beitrag zum Staats- und Gesellschaftsbild Deutschlands im 19. Jahrhundert,* Historische Studien, no. 190 (Berlin: Emil Ebering, 1930), 77–79, and Berdahl, *Politics of the Prussian Nobility,* 168.

123. Georg Friedrich Knapp, "Die Erbuntertänigkeit und die kapitalistische Wirtschaft" (1891), in his *Die Landarbeiter in Knechtschaft und Freiheit,* 2nd ed. (Leipzig: Duncker & Humblot, 1909), 57. The process of creating bound labor forces in East Elbia and the South will be discussed further in Chapter 2.

124. Geoffrey Barraclough, *The Origins of Modern Germany* (1946; rpt. ed., New York: Capricorn Books, 1963), 251.

125. James Westphall Thompson, "East German Colonization in the Middle Ages," *Annual Report of the American Historical Association for the Year 1915* (Washington, D.C.: Government Printing Office, 1917), 149–50.

126. Kleist-Retzow quoted in Herman von Petersdorff, *Kleist-Retzow, Ein Lebensbild* (Stuttgart & Berlin: J.G. Cotta'sche Buchhandlung Nachfolger, 1907), 3–4, and Wolfgang Schröder, "Hans Hugo von Kleist-Retzow: Ein Junker von Schrot und Korn," in Gustav Seeber, ed., *Gestalten von Bismarckzeit* (East Berlin: Akademie-Verlag, 1978), 218–19. On the von Dziembowski family, see Rauer, *Alphabetischer Nachweis,* 56, and *Allgemeine Landwirtschaftliche Monatschrift,* (1841), 219.

127. After the insurrection of 1830–31 in Russian Poland, Prussian officials began to pursue a policy of enforced "Germanization" in Prussian Poland that peaked under Bismarck in the 1880s. See William W. Hagen, *Germans, Poles, and Jews: The Nationality Conflict in the Prussian East, 1772–1914* (Chicago: Univ. of Chicago Press, 1980), chs. 3 and 4.

128. Durnford (1800–1859), the son of a white slaveholder and a free woman of color, owned 27 slaves in 1834 and purchased 25 more the following year during a visit to Virginia. At his death he owned 77 slaves. David O. Whitten, "Slave Buying in 1835 in Virginia as Revealed by Letters of a Louisiana Negro Sugar Planter," *Louisiana History* 11 (1970), 231–44, and David C. Rankin, "Black Slaveholders: The Case of Andrew Durnford," *Southern Studies* 21 (1982), 343–47. On Louisiana's Creole culture and mulatto planters in the state's southern parishes—"where a long history of miscegenation left a legacy of 'black' slaveholders with French and Spanish names like Ciprien Ricard, Marie Metoyer, Charles Roques, and Martin Donato"—see Oakes, *The Ruling Race* 44–45, 49. Oakes also points out that almost four thousand free black slaveholders lived in the South in 1830, of whom the "vast majority" had "purchased members of their families" or "acted out of benevolence." Ibid., 47–48.

129. On Ellison (1790–1861), who owned 63 slaves in 1860, see Michael P. Johnson and James L. Roark, *Black Masters: A Free Family of Color in the Old South* (New York & London: Norton, 1984), a remarkable work of scholarship.

130. Horst Dippel, *Germany and the American Revolution, 1770–1800: A Sociohistor-*

ical Investigation of Late Eighteenth-Century Political Thinking, trans. Bernard A. Uhlendorf (Chapel Hill: Univ. of North Carolina Press for the Institute of Early American History and Culture, Williamsburg, 1977), 201.

131. Charles W. von Rosenberg, ed., "Ancestral Voices: The Letters of the Von Rosenberg and Meerscheidt Families, 1844–1897" (bound photocopy of typescript dated 1978 and published by the Reunion Association Publication Committee), in the Barker Texas History Center, University of Texas at Austin; and Leonie Rummel Weyland and Houston Wade, *An Early History of Fayette County* (LaGrange, Texas: LaGrange Journal, 1936), 107–113. The more than 4000 acres of Nassau Farm had been part of the original 1822 Austin Colony, centered on the lower Brazos River. On the Texas settlements orchestrated by the so-called *Adelsverein*, or *Verein zum Schutze deutscher Einwanderer in Texas*, a helpful overview is William C. Pool, *A Historical Atlas of Texas* (Austin: Encino Press, 1975), 93–95.

132. *The Prussian Primary School System as Seen by a Virginia Traveler a Century Ago, With Suggestions as to Its Application to the State of Virginia: A Report Submitted to the Governor of Virginia on January 15, 1839, by the Rev. Benjamin Mosby Smith of Danville, Virginia, Reprinted from a Photostat of House Document 26, Virginia*, Foreword by Charles William Dabney (n.p., n.d.), 31.

133. Randolph was chair of the 1861 Virginia constitutional convention's military committee. George Green Shackelford, *George Wythe Randolph and the Confederate Elite* (Athens & London: Univ. of Georgia Press, 1989), 62.

134. For the lack of evidence, see Stephen Mansfield, "Thomas Roderick Dew at William and Mary: 'A Main Prop of That Venerable Institution,'" *Virginia Magazine of History and Biography* 75 (1967), 429–30; this essay is based on Mansfield, "Thomas Roderick Dew: Defender of the Southern Faith" (Ph.D. diss., University of Virginia, 1968). For the older notion, see William E. Dodd, *The Cotton Kingdom: A Chronicle of the Old South* (New Haven: Yale Univ. Press, 1919), 49; Carl L. Becker, *The Declaration of Independence: A Study in the History of Political Ideas* (1922; rpt. ed., New York: Vintage Books, 1942), 247, 255; and Lowell Harrison, "Thomas Roderick Dew, Philosopher of the Old South," *Virginia Magazine of History and Biography* 57 (1949), 390–91.

135. The quotation is taken from Stanley K. Schultz, "Lieber, Francis," in John A. Garraty, ed., *Encyclopedia of American Biography* (New York: Harper & Row, 1974), 662–64. Lieber received his doctorate from the University of Jena in Saxony in 1820. See also Frank Friedel, *Francis Lieber, Nineteenth-Century Liberal* (Baton Rouge: Louisiana State Univ. Press, 1947; rpt. ed., Gloucester, Mass.: Peter Smith, 1968).

136. See J. D. B. DeBow, *Encyclopaedia of Trade and Commerce of the United States, More Particularly of the Southern and Western States*, 2nd ed. (London: Trübner & Co., 1854), 325, 557, 565, 580.

137. *Annalen der Landwirtschaft* (1852), 218. In 1850–51 the city of Berlin imported via railroad from Hamburg 105,000 hundredweight (*Zentner*, or fifty kilograms) of raw cotton. Friedrich Wilhelm von Reden, *Erwerbs- und Verkehrs-Statistik Königsstaats Preussen* (3 vols; Darmstadt: G. Jonghaus, 1853–54), vol. 1, p. 432. The first mechanized cotton-spinning mill east of the Elbe was set up in 1825 at Breslau, on the Oder River in Silesia. During the decade 1841–50 the German Customs (*Zollverein*), founded under Prussian leadership in 1828–33, imported an annual average of 490,000 tons of raw

cotton. W. O. Henderson, *The Rise of German Industrial Power, 1834–1914* (Berkeley & Los Angeles: Univ. of California Press, 1975), 68–69.

138. See Sister Mary Anthonita Hess, *American Tobacco and Central European Policy, Early Nineteenth Century* (Washington, D.C.: Catholic Univ. of America Press, 1948), 105–6; Günther Franz, "Landwirtschaft, 1800–1850," in Hermann Aubin and Wolfgang Zorn, eds., *Handbuch der deutschen Wirtschafts- und Sozialgeschichte, II: Das 19. und 20. Jahrhundert* (Stuttgart: Ernst Klett, 1976), 288; and Rosser Howard Taylor, *Slaveholding in North Carolina: An Economic View,* James Sprunt Historical Publications, vol. 18 (Chapel Hill: Univ. of North Carolina Press, 1926), 34–35; and Joseph Clark Robert, *The Tobacco Kingdom: Plantation, Market, and Factory in Virginia and North Carolina, 1800– 1860* (Durham, N.C.: Duke Univ. Press, 1938), 29–30.

139. Hess, *American Tobacco and Central European Policy,* 94, 105–6. From 1835 to 1838 the German Customs Union imported, primarily through Bremen, an annual average of 25,753 hogsheads of American tobacco, second only to Great Britain's 28,773 hogsheads. John Ramsey McCulloch, *A Dictionary, Practical, Theoretical, and History, of Commerce and Commercial Navigation,* ed. Henry Vethake, vol. 2 (Philadelphia: A. Hart, 1852), 650.

140. Maldwyn Allen Jones, *American Immigration* (Chicago: Univ. of Chicago Press, 1960), 110. Cf. Günter Moltmann, "The Pattern of German Emigration to the United States in the Nineteenth Century," in Frank Trommler and Joseph McVeigh, eds., *America and the Germans, Volume One: Immigration, Language, Ethnicity* (Philadelphia: Univ. of Pennsylvania Press, 1985), 19–21.

141. Otto W. Tretzlaff says that homelands of the New Braunfels settlers "may have been somewhere in the Duchy of Oldenburg, the Münsterland (in Prussian Westphalia), or Württemberg." Tretzlaff, ed. and trans., "Translator's Notes," *The Emigrant to Texas: A Handbook and Guide* (1846; Burnet, Texas (?), 1979), 4. Nonetheless, Lauren Ann Kattner has found evidence that some natives of the Prussian Northeast were living in at least two Texas towns by the 1850s: Yorktown in southeast Texas and Fredericksburg in the hill country west of Austin. Kattner, "Land and Marriage: German Regional Reflections in Four Texas Towns, 1845–1860" (Paper presented at the German-American Conference in New Harmony, Indiana, 28 Sept.–1 Oct. 1989).

142. Terry G. Jordan, "Germans and Blacks in Texas," in Randall M. Miller, ed., *States of Progress: Germans and Blacks in America over 300 Years. Lectures from the Tricentennial of the Germantown Protest Against Slavery* (Philadelphia: German Society of Pennsylvania, 1989), 95–96.

143. Jordan, "Germans and Blacks in Texas," 92.

144. Eric Foner, *Reconstruction: America's Unfinished Revolution, 1863–1877* (New York: Harper & Row, 1988), 299, and Foner, *A Short History of Reconstruction* (New York: Harper & Row, 1990), 131.

145. Jordan, "Germans and Blacks in Texas," 95; and Campbell, *An Empire for Slavery,* 215. See also James Marten, *Texas Divided: Loyalty and Dissent in the Lone Star State, 1856–1874* (Lexington: Univ. Press of Kentucky, 1990), 26–29.

146. Most of these German slaveholders had come to Texas in the 1830s and had accumulated enough capital to buy slaves. "Germans had to buy whatever slaves they had, unlike Anglo-Americans, many of whom inherited slaves or acquired at no cost the

offspring of Negroes already owned. Had slavery survived long enough for the Germans to acquire the needed capital, it is quite likely that more of them would have bought Negroes." Terry G. Jordan, *German Seed in Texas Soil: Immigrant Farmers in Nineteenth-Century Texas* (Austin: Univ. of Texas Press, 1966), 109–10.

147. Rosenberg, ed., "Ancestral Voices," quotations from 42–44 and 68, and "Solms-Braunfels Archiv Index, Abteilung I, Personenverzeichnis N–Z," 830–832 (bound carbon copies of 1930s typescript, in Barker Texas History Center, University of Texas at Austin). Wilhelm, or William, had moved to Austin in 1856, worked as a draughtsman in the general land office, and in 1863 became "topographical engineer" under Confederate General John Magruder in Texas. See the sketch of "William von Rosenberg" in *Confederate Military History*, Vol. XI (Atlanta: Confederate Publishing, 1899), 604–5.

Chapter 2. Agrarian Entrepreneurs

1. C. Joseph Pusateri, *A History of American Business* (Arlington Heights, Ill.: Harlan Davidson, 1984), 5–9. Cole's definition is taken from "Entrepreneurship and Entrepreneurial History," in Harvard University Research Center in Entrepreneurial History, *Change and the Entrepreneur* (Cambridge: Harvard Univ. Press, 1949), 88.

2. Gavin Wright, *The Political Economy of the Cotton South: Households, Markets, and Wealth in the Nineteenth Century* (New York: Norton, 1978), 114, following Heywood Fleisig, "Slavery, the Supply of Agricultural Labor, and the Industrialization of the South," *Journal of Economic History* 36 (1976), 581.

3. The quotation is taken from James J. Sheehan, *German Liberalism in the Nineteenth Century* (Chicago & London: Univ. of Chicago Press, 1978), 80: "it was not until after 1871 that Unternehmer in Berlin began to use the term in a way that captures its modern connotation of technical and organizational innovation." According to Pusateri, *A History of American Business*, 6, "the modern theory of entrepreneurship," with its emphasis on creative innovations, is most closely associated with the influential Harvard economist Joseph Schumpeter (1883–1950), a native of Austria.

4. That bound labor increased productive efficiency in East Elbia has been persuasively argued by Edgar Melton, "*Gutsherrschaft* in East Elbian Germany and Livonia, 1500–1800: A Critique of the Model," *Central European History* 21 (1988), esp. 342–45, where Melton concludes that *Gutsherrschaft* compelled seigniorial peasants to be more productive than freeholders. An analogous argument is made for the plantation South by Robert William Fogel, *Without Consent or Contract: The Rise and Fall of American Slavery* (New York & London: W. W. Norton, 1989), passim, esp. 410–11, where Fogel emphasizes that "efficiency is not a synonym for good and it is a disservice to the struggle for a moral society to make it a synonym."

5. See the discussion in Pusateri, *A History of American Business*, 7.

6. J. V. Beckett, *The Aristocracy in England, 1660–1914* (Oxford & New York: Basil Blackwell, 1986), 155.

7. "Reports from Her Majesty's Representatives Respecting Tenure of Land in the Several Countries of Europe" (J. P. Harriss-Gastrell in Berlin and Consul Herslet in Königsberg), in *British Sessional Papers, House of Commons*, vol. 67 (1870), part 1, p. 309. (microprint ed., ed. Edgar J. Erickson). "By 1800 Germany possessed 490 kilome-

ters of canals and approximately 670 kilometers of rivers had been made navigable with locks and other improvements. Eighty per cent of these routes were situated in Prussia's north German lowlands." Knut Borchardt, "Germany 1700–1914," trans. George Hammersley, in Carlo M. Cipolla, ed. *The Fontana Economic History of Europe: The Emergence of Industrial Societies, Part One* (London & Glasgow: Collins/Fontana Books, 1973), 109. In 1898 Carl Johannes Fuchs cited W. H. Riehl to the effect that Germany had three basic physical divisions: lowland Northern Germany (including most of East Elbia), mountainous Central Germany, and the plateau of Upper Germany. "The first is predominantly maritime, particularly suited for navigation and commerce, with its navigable rivers leading to the sea; but the rivers have little fall, hence scant development of industries dependent on water power." Fuchs, "The Epochs of German Agrarian History" (Inaugural Address at the University of Freiburg in 1898), trans. Francis Kingsley Ball, in Thomas Nixon Carver, ed., *Selected Readings in Rural Economics* (Boston: Ginn and Co., 1916), 242.

8. See Steven Hahn, "The 'Unmaking' of the Southern Yeomanry: The Transformation of the Georgia Upcountry, 1860–1890," in Hahn and Jonathan Prude, eds., *The Countryside in the Age of Capitalist Transformation: Essays in the Social History of Rural America* (Chapel Hill & London: Univ. of North Carolina Press, 1985), 180–85, and Allen Tullos, *Habits of Industry: White Culture and the Transformation of the Carolina Piedmont* (Chapel Hill & London: Univ. of North Carolina Press, 1989), 77–84.

9. On early American steamboats, see George Rogers Taylor, *The Transportation Revolution, 1815–1860* (1951; New York: Harper Torchbooks, 1968), 63, where Taylor identifies the Pennsylvania-built *Enterprise* as the first steamboat to sail from Pittsburgh to New Orleans and back again, in 1815; and Malcolm Rohrbough, *The Trans-Appalachian Frontier: People, Societies, and Institutions, 1775–1850* (New York: Oxford Univ. Press, 1978), 175–76. On early Prussian steamboats, see Oskar Eggert, *Geschichte Pommerns* (Glückstadt/Elbe: Gerhard Rautenberg, 1961), 79, where Eggert states that first steamboat to ply the Oder, the *Crown Princess Elizabeth,* made its maiden voyage in 1826; and Thomas Nipperdey, *Deutsche Geschichte 1800–1866: Bürgerwelt und Starker Staat* (München: C. H. Beck, 1983), 190.

10. Charles S. Sydnor, *The Development of Southern Sectionalism, 1819–1848* (1948; rpt. ed., Baton Rouge: Louisiana State Univ. Press, 1968), 268; and C. F. W. Dieterici, *Handbuch der Statistik des preussischen Staats* (Berlin: E. S. Mittler und Sohn, 1961), 611.

11. Lewis Cecil Gray, *History of Agriculture in the Southern United States to 1860* (2 vols., 1933; rpt. ed., Gloucester, Mass.: Peter Smith, 1958), vol. 2, pp. 905, 696; and Charles S. Davis, *The Cotton Kingdom in Alabama* (Montgomery: Alabama State Dept. of Archives and History, 1939), 1. In 1859–60 (year ending 31 August) the Mobile and Ohio Railroad delivered about 180,000 of the 840,000 bales shipped from Mobile. This railroad had been chartered in 1848, and the entire 483–mile road was finished between Mobile and Columbus, Kentucky, in April of 1861, when it was the South's longest railroad. Only 63 miles were located in the state of Alabama, while more than 250 ran through Mississippi to the west. Davis, *Cotton Kingdom in Alabama,* 132, and John F. Stover, *Iron Road to the West: American Railroads in the 1850s* (New York: Columbia Univ. Press, 1978), 80–81. During the 1850s, writes J. Mills Thornton III, this railroad "became a sort of obsession" for Mobilians, who "dreamed that with this

railway they could cancel the advantage of New Orleans' river and replace their Louisiana adversary as the great entrepot of the South." Thornton, *Power and Politics in a Slave Society, 1800–1860* (Baton Rouge & London: Louisiana State Univ. Press, 1978), 278.

12. Conrad-Maulen, "Acker- und Wiesenbau der Provinz Preussen," in *Der Provinz Preussen. Geschichte ihrer Cultur und Beschreibung ihrer land- und forst-wirthschaftlichen Verhältnisse. Festgabe für die Mitglieder der XXIV Versammlung deutscher Land- und Forstwirthe zu Königsberg* (Königsberg, 1863), 34.

13. H. E. Landsberg, H. Lippmann, K. H. Paffen, and C. Troll, *World Maps of Climatology*, eds. E. Rodenwaldt and H. J. Jusatz, 3rd ed. (Berlin, Heidelberg, & New York: Springer-Verlag, 1966), 26–28 (Map 5: "The Seasonal Climates of the Earth"); Sam Bowers Hilliard, *Atlas of Antebellum Southern Agriculture* (Baton Rouge & London: Louisiana State Univ. Press, 1984), 17; and A. E. Parkins, *The South: Its Economic-Geographic Development* (New York: John Wiley & Sons, and London: Chapman & Hall, 1938), 41; and August Meitzen and Friedrich Grossman, *Der Boden und die landwirtschaftlichen Verhältnisse des preussischen Staates* (8 vols.; Berlin: Paul Parey, 1868–1908), vol. 1, pp. 141–42; and Heinrich Niehaus, "Agricultural Conditions and Regions in Germany," *Geographical Review* 23 (1933), 25–31.

14. Lorin Bladget, *Climatology of the United States and of the Temperate Latitudes of the North American Continent* (Philadelphia, 1857), 42–45.

15. Computed from degrees Reaumyr in Meitzen, *Der Boden*, vol. 1, p. 134.

16. Quoted in ibid., 126. Hans Gatzke summarizes the differences between northwest and northeast German weather patterns as follows: "While the North German Plain west of the Elbe River has cool summers, mild winters, medium rainfall, and much cloudiness, the Plain east of the Elbe has warm summers, cold winters that become more severe as one moves eastward, little rain, and few clouds." Gatzke, *Germany and the United States: "A Special Relationship?"* (Cambridge, Mass., & London: Harvard Univ. Press, 1980), 14.

17. David Landes, "Introduction" to Landes, ed., *The Rise of Capitalism* (New York: Macmillan, 1966), 9.

18. The quotation is from Sidney Ratner, James H. Soltow, and Richard Sylla, *The Evolution of the American Economy: Growth, Welfare, and Decision Making* (New York: Basic Books, 1979), 13.

19. A precedent for the profitable export of grain from the eastern Baltic to western Europe had been set during the fourteenth century in East Prussia by the Teutonic Knights *(Deutschordensritter)*, which marketed grain raised on their demesne farms as well as grain received from peasants as rents-in-kind. After the Knights had defeated the native Prussians in the thirteenth century, "The settlement which ensued was carried out frequently by consortia of wealthy knights or urban capitalists, with the aim of maximizing profits." Alan Mayhew, *Rural Settlement and Farming in Germany* (New York: Barnes and Noble/Harper and Row, 1973), 54.

20. Sidney W. Mintz, "The So-Called World System: Local Initative and Local Response," *Dialectical Anthropology* 2 (1977), 265.

21. Jan De Vries, *The Dutch Rural Economy in the Golden Age, 1500–1700* (New Haven: Yale Univ. Press, 1974), 74, 166; Wilhelm Abel, *Agrarkrisen und Agrarkonjunktur.*

Eine Geschichte der Land- und Ernährungswirtschaft Mitteleuropas seit dem hohen Mittelalter, 2nd ed. (Hamburg & Berlin: Paul Parey, 1966), 106 (Note: the third German edition of Abel's book, published in 1978, is available in English as *Agricultural Fluctuations in Europe from the Thirteenth to the Twentieth Centuries,* trans. Olive Ordish (New York: St. Martin's Press, and London: Methuen, 1980)); Jerome Blum, "The Rise of Serfdom in Eastern Europe," *American Historical Review* 62 (1957), 826–30; Henry Kamen, "Seigneur and Soil in Eastern Europe," in his *The Iron Century: Social Change in Europe, 1550–1660* (London: Weidenfeld and Nicolson, 1971), 211–14; and Marion Malowist, "Poland, Russia, and the Western Trade in the 15th and 16th Centuries," *Past and Present,* no. 13 (April 1958), 27–29.

22. Peter-Michael Hahn, *Struktur und Funktion des brandenburgischen Adels im 16. Jahrhundert,* Historische und Pädagogische Studien, Band 9 (Berlin: Colloquium-Verlag, 1979), 70.

23. Hartmut Harnisch, "Die Gutsherrschaft in Brandenburg. Ergebnisse und Probleme," *Jahrbuch für Wirtschaftsgeschichte,* 1969, Teil IV, pp. 120–31.

24. Thomas Kantzow, *Pomerania, oder Ursprung, Altheit und Geschichte der Völcker und Lande Pomern, Cassuben, Wenden, Stettin, Rhügen* (circa 1538), ed. Hans G. L. Kosegarten (2 vols.; Greifswald: Ernst Mauritius, 1816–17), vol. 2, pp. 404–5.

25. Brandenburg estate owners could expect to harvest only three kernels of rye for every kernel sown, and at least a third of the harvest was needed to cover local consumption. See William W. Hagen, "How Mighty the Junkers? Peasant Rents and Seigneurial Profits in Sixteenth-Century Brandenburg," *Past and Present,* no. 108 (Aug. 1985), 112–13.

26. Ralph Davis, *The Rise of the Atlantic Economies* (Ithaca, N.Y.: Cornell Univ. Press, 1973), 208.

27. Ibid., 264–65; Jacob M. Price, "The Economic Growth of the Chesapeake and the European Market, 1697–1775," *Journal of Economic History* 24 (1964), 505, emphasizes "the permanent emergence of the French as large-scale buyers in 1723–1724."

28. Henry Hartwell, James Blair, and Edward Chilton, *The Present State of Virginia, and the College* (London, 1727), 6–14, reprinted in Aubrey Land, ed., *Bases of Plantation Society* (Columbia: Univ. of South Carolina Press, 1969), 24–28; the quotation is from p. 25.

29. Gregory A. Stiverson and Patrick H. Butler, eds., "Virginia in 1732: The Travel Journal of William Hugh Grove," *Virginia Magazine of History and Biography* 85 (1977), 35.

30. "The advent of plantation self-sufficiency (in the Upper South) was partly the result of efforts to reduce the risk of dependence on a single crop, but it resulted as well from the need to keep servants and slaves employed during slack times in the tobacco cycle." John J. McCusker and Russell R. Menard, *The Economy of British America, 1607–1789* (Chapel Hill & London: Univ. of North Carolina Press, 1985), 127.

31. Davis, *Rise of the Atlantic Economies,* 264–65; Ratner et al., *Evolution of the American Economy,* 47; and Allan Kulikoff, *Tobacco and Slaves: The Development of Southern Cultures in the Chesapeake, 1680–1800* (Chapel Hill & London: Univ. of North Carolina Press, 1986), 120.

32. Joyce E. Chaplin, "Creating a Cotton South in Georgia and South Carolina,

1760–1815," *Journal of Southern History* 57 (1991), 186–94, and John Hebron Moore, *The Emergence of the Cotton Kingdom in the Old Southwest: Mississippi, 1770–1860* (Baton Rouge & London: Louisiana State Univ. Press, 1988), 2–5.

33. Gray, *History of Southern Agriculture*, vol. 1, pp. 288–92; James M. Clifton, "Rice," in Randall M. Miller and John David Smith, eds., *Dictionary of Afro-American Slavery* (New York: Greenwood Press, 1988), 644; John J. Winberry, "Reputation of Carolina Indigo," *South Carolina Historical Magazine* 80 (1979), 246–49; and Jack P. Greene, *Pursuits of Happiness: The Social Development of Early Modern British Colonies and the Formation of American Culture* (Chapel Hill and London: Univ. of North Carolina Press, 1988), 144.

34. Long-staple, black-seed, Sea Island cotton was introduced to the Georgia and South Carolina Sea Islands during the years 1786–90, but climatic requirements limited its cultivation to the coastal districts. It was the short-staple, green-seed, upland variety whose cultivation was made profitable by the new cotton gins of the 1790s. On Sea Island versus upland cotton, see Theodore Rosengarten, *Tombee, Portrait of a Cotton Planter; With the Journal of Thomas B. Chaplin (1822–1890)* (New York: William Morrow, 1986), 50–54. The simultaneity of the cotton gin and sugar mill as "technological breakthroughs at both ends of the South" during the 1790s is emphasized by John B. Boles, *Black Southerners, 1619–1869* (Lexington, Ky.: Univ. Press of Kentucky, 1984), 62.

35. Chirot, "The Growth of the Market and Service Labor Systems in Agriculture," *Journal of Social History* (1975), 75–76. Economist Robert Millward has recently sought to demonstrate with reference to East Elbia that "serfdom can be profitable to the lords independent of any exogenous increase in market demand," while conceding that "It is analytically possible that the profitability of enserfment was determined in some places or periods by the profitability of exports." Millward, "An Economic Analysis of the Organization of Serfdom in Eastern Europe," *Journal of Economic History* 42 (1982), 544, 546.

36. F. L. Carsten explains that "the principle income of the noblemen consisted of peasant dues—whether they were the successors of Slav lords, or were granted land by a prince or some other feudal lord, or acquired it in the course of time. The peasants, whether of Slav or German origin, depended on a landlord, a knight, a monastery or the burgher of a town, to whom they owed annual dues in kind or money." Carsten, *A History of the Prussian Junkers* (Aldershot, Eng., & Brookfield, Vt.: Scolar Press, 1989), 3.

37. That Virginia tobacco planters also enslaved Native Americans in the late seventeenth century is emphasized by James H. Merrell, *The Indians' New World: Catawbas and Their Neighbors from European Contact through the Era of Removal* (Chapel Hill & London: Univ. of North Carolina Press, 1989; Norton paperback, 1991), 36–37. "The attention focused upon South Carolina's trade in slaves has obscured Virginia's version." A 1682 law permitted enslavement of Indians imported into the colony, and Indian slaves seem to have been brought from as far south as the Savannah River Valley. Although the Amerindians had no status or practice equivalent to what Europeans considered slavery (that is, use of human chattel as forced labor on plantations), "Virginia's demand for slaves built upon an existing framework of conflict and capture" among Indian peo-

ples. A similar statement could be made about the impact of European demand for slaves on West African peoples, although Africans imported to English North America certainly did not experience the "demographic disaster" that afflicted Native Americans when exposed to Old World diseases. On "slavery" in Africa, see T. A. Osae, S. N. Nwabara, and A. T. O. Odunsi, *A Short History of West Africa, A. D. 1000 to the Present* (New York: Hill and Wang, 1973), 162–63; and Igor Kopytoff and Suzanne Miers, "Introduction: African 'Slavery' as an Institution of Marginality," in Miers and Kopytoff, eds., *Slavery in Africa: Historical and Anthropological Perspectives* (Madison: Univ. of Wisconsin Press, 1977), 3–81. On the "demographic disaster" among Amerindian peoples, see James A. Rawley, *The Transatlantic Slave Trade: A History* (New York & London: W. W. Norton, 1981), 13–14.

38. The terms *Gutswirtschaft* (literally "estate economy") and *Gutsherrschaft* ("estate authority"), despite their subtle differences, can be used interchangeably. *Gutswirtschaft*, explains William W. Hagen, refers to "large-scale demesne farms employing servile labor." Hagen, "How Mighty the Junkers?," 82. The "system of *Gutsherrschaft*," writes F. L. Carsten, consisted of "demesne farming and serf labor." Carsten, *A History of the Prussian Junkers*, 19. Edgar Melton emphasizes that enserfed peasants were less often bound personally to their lords than to their manorial farmsteads, and that the serfs employed hired hands to perform the labor services owed to their manorial lords. Melton, "Gutsherrschaft in East Elbian Germany and Livonia," 332–36.

39. Peter Brandt, with Thomas Hofmann and Reiner Zilkenat, eds., "Die ständische Agrargesellschaft," in *Preussen. Zur Sozialgeschichte eines Staates: Eine Darstellung in Quellen* (Reinbeck bei Hamburg: Rowohlt Taschenbuch, 1981), 23. Max Weber explained the "difference between east and west" as simply "that the western landlord used the peasants as taxpayers, while the eastern landlord, by becoming a cultivator, began to use the peasants as a laboring force." Weber, "Capitalism and Rural Society in Germany" (1904), in H. H. Gerth and C. Wright Mills, eds. and trans., *From Max Weber. Essays in Sociology* (New York: Oxford Univ. Press, 1946), 376. More recently East German scholar Hartmut Harnisch brought greater precision to this distinction: "Feudal rents, here meaning labor services first and foremost, adhered east of the Elbe simultaneously and inseparably to the land and the human producers subject to feudal authority, while west of the Elbe they adhered only to the land." Harnisch, "Die Gutsherrschaft. Forschungsgeschichte, Entwicklungszusammenhänge and Strukturelemente," *Jahrbuch für Geschichte des Feudalismus* 9 (1985), 237.

40. On resistance among colonial slaves, see Gerald W. Mullin, *Flight and Rebellion: Slave Resistance in Eighteenth-Century Virginia* (New York & London: Oxford Univ. Press, 1972); and Peter H. Wood, *Black Majority: Negroes in Colonial South Carolina from 1670 Through the Stono Rebellion* (New York: Norton, 1974). On peasant resistance in early modern East Elbia, see Heidi Wunder, "The Mentality of Rebellious Peasants—The Samland Rebellion of 1525," in Bob Scribner and Gerlard Benecke, eds., *The German Peasant War of 1525, New Viewpoints* (London: George Allen and Unwin, 1979), 148–59; Robert M. Berdahl, *The Politics of the Prussian Nobility: The Development of a Conservative Ideology, 1770–1848* (Princeton: Princeton Univ. Press, 1988), 37–40; and the following three essays by American scholar William W. Hagen, which focus on Brandenburg in the sixteenth, seventeenth, and eighteenth centuries respectively: "How Mighty

the Junkers? Peasant Rents and Seigneurial Profits in Sixteenth-Century Brandenburg," *Past and Present,* no. 108 (Aug. 1985), 80–116, and "Seventeenth-Century Crisis in Brandenburg: The Thirty Years' War, The Destabilization of Serfdom, and the Rise of Absolutism," *American Historical Review* 94 (1989), 302–35, and "The Junkers' Faithless Servants: Peasant Insubordination and the Breakdown of Serfdom in Brandenburg-Prussia," in Richard J. Evans and W. R. Lee, eds., *The German Peasantry: Conflict and Community in Rural Society from the Eighteenth to the Twentieth Centuries* (London & Sydney: Croom Helm, 1986), 71–101. Hagen's work is a wonderful complement to that of East German scholar Hartmut Harnisch, whom Hagen calls "the most knowledgeable present-day historian of the east Elbian manorial-serf system." Hagen, "How Mighty the Junkers?," 84.

41. Heidi Wunder summarizes the historical background to the peasantry's communal cohesion and powers of resistance: "It is now well established that from the twelfth century independent peasant communities were founded in east Elbia in which interference by either landlord or territorial lord in the jurisdiction and economic affairs of the village was very limited." Responsibility for day-to-day supervision of the village, including the compulsory services owed by the peasants, lay with the *Schulz,* whose hereditary position "enabled him to resist becoming a mere agent of the lord" and in fact to act as "the spokesman of peasant interests and the leader of peasant protest" against encroachments by the lord. Wunder, "Peasant Organization and Class Conflict in East and West Germany," *Past and Present,* no. 78 (Feb. 1978), 48–49.

42. William W. Hagen notes that "many village communes" in sixteenth-century Brandenburg carried suits for fixed labor dues to the high court in Berlin, and stresses the peasants' "communal solidarity" and "hereditary tenures." Hagen, "How Mighty the Junkers?," 103, 114. See also Carsten, *A History of the Prussian Junkers,* 11–12, which does not cite Hagen's article.

43. The importance of manorial servants to Junkerdom has been well summarized in the following statement: "Without peasants *(Bauern)* no servants *(Gesinde)* and without servants no farming of the lord's own land *(Gutseigenbetrieb)!*" Hans and Gertrud Mortensen, "Über die Entstehung des ostdeutschen Grossgrundbesitzes," *Nachrichten der Akademie der Wissenschaften in Göttingen aus dem Jahre 1955. Philologisch-Historische Klasse* (Göttingen: Vandenhoeck & Ruprecht, 1955), 30

44. Harnisch, "Die Gutsherrschaft. Forschungsgeschichte, Entwicklungszusammenhänge and Strukturelemente," 238–40 (quotation from p. 240), and F. L. Carsten, *The Origins of Prussia* (Oxford: Oxford Univ. Press, 1954), ch. 11, "The Decline of the Peasantry and the Imposition of Serfdom," esp. 157.

45. "1616. Pommerische Leibeigenschaft. Aus der Bauern- und Schäfordnung," in Günther Franz, ed., *Quellen zur Geschichte des Deutschen Bauernstandes in der Neuzeit* (München & Wien: R. Oldenbourg, 1963), 109. See also Eggert, *Geschichte Pommerns,* 49; Carsten, *Origins of Prussia,* 149–64. Hartmut Harnisch emphasizes that peasants without a hereditary claim on their land were compelled to perform unlimited services, while those with right of ownership in their farms continued to perform limited services, that is, no more than two or three days per week per peasant. Harnisch, "Die Gutsherrschaft. Forschungsgeschichte, Entwicklungszusammenhänge and Strukturelemente," 233.

46. Carsten, "The Origins of the Junkers," *English Historical Review* 62 (1947),

164–65. For Carsten's most recent statements on this subject, see his *A History of the Prussian Junkers,* esp. 9–13. Cf. Marian Malowist, "The Economic and Social Development of the Baltic Countries from the Fifteenth to the Seventeenth Centuries," *Economic History Review,* 2nd series, vol. 12 (1959), esp. 188: "what is called the second period of serfdom developed only gradually, especially during periods of good market conditions for corn"; and Josef Petran, "Die Mitteleuropäische Landwirtschaft und der Handel im 16. and am Anfang des 17. Jahrhunderts. Abhandlungen über Probleme und Methoden," *Historica* 18 (1973), esp. 113–21; and Hartmut Harnisch, "Peasants and Their Markets: The Background to the Agrarian Reforms in Feudal Prussia East of the Elbe, 1760–1807," in Richard J. Evans and W. R. Lee, eds., *The German Peasantry: Conflict and Community in Rural Society from the Eighteenth to the Twentieth Centuries* (London & Sydney: Croom Helm, 1986), esp. 40: "For a long time the main features of the estate system and the reasons for its emergence in the sixteenth century were matters of controversy in German research. Today, partly under the additional influence of the results of research in Poland, it seems to be commonly accepted that the decisive impulses for the enlargement of the feudal estates and the increase of the peasants' enforced labor were provided by the market."

47. See Otto Hintze, "The Hohenzollern and the Nobility" (1914), in Felix Gilbert, with Robert M. Berdahl, eds., *The Historical Essays of Otto Hintze* (New York: Oxford Univ. Press, 1975), 46; Hans Rosenberg, "The Rise of the Junkers in Brandenburg-Prussia, 1410–1653. Part Two," *American Historical Review* 49 (1944), 239–40 ("the great compromise of 1653"); and Carsten, *The Origins of Prussia,* ch. 13, "The Great Elector's Victory Over the Estates of Brandenburg," esp. 187. Recently William W. Hagen, "The Seventeenth-Century Crisis in Brandenburg," has argued that Rosenberg and Carsten exaggerate the strength of the Brandenburg nobility's position vis-à-vis both peasantry and absolutist state after the 1653 Recess; but I do not think his revisionism invalidates the significance of "the great compromise of 1653."

48. See Otto-Ernst Schüddekopf, *Die deutsche Innenpolitik im letzten Jahrhundert und der konservative Gedanke: Die Zusammenhänge zwischen Aussenpolitik, innerer Staatsführung und Parteigeschichte, dargestellt an der Geschichte der Konservativen Partei von 1807 bis 1918* (Braunschweig: Albert Limbach, 1951), 8; Walter Görlitz, *Die Junker: Adel und Bauer im deutschen Osten,* 3rd ed. (Limburg a. d. Lahn: C. A. Starke, 1964), 195; Carsten, *A History of the Prussian Junkers,* 82–83; and Berdahl, *Politics of the Prussian Nobility,* 194.

49. Clement Eaton, *A History of the Old South: The Emergence of a Reluctant Nation,* 3rd ed. (New York: Macmillan, 1975), 13. The somewhat different system of headrights operative in late seventeenth-century South Carolina is described in Rosengarten, *Tombee,* 47. For Georgia, see Allan Gallay, *The Formation of a Planter Elite: Jonathan Bryan and the Southern Colonial Frontier* (Athens & London: Univ. of Georgia Press, 1989), 90.

50. A. E. Smith, *Colonists in Bondage: White Servitude and Convict Labor in America, 1607–1776* (Chapel Hill: Univ. of North Carolina Press, 1947), 306. A good discussion of indentured servitude as an "English system of modified serfdom" is provided by Boles, *Black Southerners,* 8–9.

51. Edmund S. Morgan, *American Slavery, American Freedom: The Ordeal of Colonial Virginia* (New York: Norton, 1975), 308.

52. "There are no early Virginia or Maryland laws creating slavery per se. Rather,

there are laws acknowleging that slavery exists." Paul Finkelman, "Introduction" to his *Slavery in the Courtroom: An Annotated Bibliography of American Cases* (Washington: Library of Congress, 1985), 4. See also Winthrop D. Jordan, *White Over Black: American Attitudes Toward the Negro, 1550–1812* (1968; Baltimore, Md.: Penguin Books,1969), 73–74. T. H. Breen and Stephen Innes have asserted that "it was not until the slave codes of 1705 that the tragic fate of Virginia's black population was finally sealed." Breen and Innes, *"Myne Owne Ground": Race and Freedom on Virginia's Eastern Shore, 1640–1676* (New York: Oxford Univ. Press, 1980), 5.

53. Morgan, *American Slavery, American Freedom*, 331–32. On racial attitudes, see Jordan, *White Over Black*, esp. 80–81 and 91–98.

54. Morgan, *American Slavery, American Freedom*, 299–304.

55. Fitzhugh quoted in ibid., 303–4. Since slaves and servants constituted long-term and short-term investments respectively in the late 1600s, "Slavery in a word was a strategy best suited to those at least reasonably well-to-do and preferably wealthy." Darrett B. and Anita H. Rutman, *A Place in Time: Middlesex County, Virginia, 1650–1750* (New York & London: Norton, 1984), 180–83.

56. McCusker and Menard, *Economy of British America*, 137.

57. Allan Kulikoff states that planters began to purchase "substantial numbers" of slaves only between 1695 and 1700, when they bought "about 3000 Africans, as many as had arrived in the previous twenty years." Kulikoff, *Tobacco and Slaves*, 40. Jack P. Greene writes of "the slow displacement of white servitude by black slavery as the predominant form of labor after 1675" and locates "the beginning of massive importations in the 1680s." Greene, *Pursuits of Happiness*, 82, 96. Although there were doubtless local variations in the timing of the first "massive importations," a recent study of Tidewater Virginia's Middlesex County tends to support Greene's timetable: "Blacks began arriving in significant numbers in the 1680s, concomitant with the decline in the number of new white servants"; and "black slaves came to exceed white servants in the labor force sometime between 1687 (when blacks constituted just 8 percent of the total population) and 1699 (by which time blacks constituted 22 percent)." Rutman & Rutman, *A Place in Time*, 165–66.

58. Jordan, *White Over Black*, 103. Between 1700 and 1750 Virginia imported roughly 45,000 slaves, and during this same period the number of blacks increased from approximately 10,000 (perhaps 15% of the colony's population) to about 100,000 (circa 40% of the population). Morgan, *American Slavery, American Freedom*, 301, 422–23.

59. Boles, *Black Southerners*, 22.

60. See Wood, *Black Majority*, 3–91, and Charles Joyner, *Down by the Riverside: A South Carolina Slave Community* (Urbana & Chicago: Univ. of Illinois Press, 1984), 13–14, where Joyner states "there could hardly have been successful rice culture in South Carolina without the strength and skills of enslaved Africans."

61. William Gerard De Brahm (appointed Surveyor General for the Southern Colonies by the British Crown in 1763–64), *Report of the General Survey in the Southern District of North America* (completed in 1773), ed. Louis De Vorsey, Jr. (Columbia: Univ. of South Carolina Press, 1971), 94. On p. 28 De Brahm says that he himself owned four slaves in 1758, when he contracted to buy four more. See also Gallay, *Formation of a Planter Elite*, 97.

62. Higgins, "The Ambivalence of Freedom: Whites, Blacks, and the Coming of the American Revolution in the South," in Higgins, ed., *The Revolutionary War in the South: Power, Conflict, and Leadership* (Durham, N.C.: Duke Univ. Press, 1979), 47. Cf. Boles, *Black Southerners*, 25: "By the final decade of the founding (seventeenth) century, planters in the Chesapeake and in South Carolina had accepted slavery with few philosophical reservations."

63. Greene, *Pursuits of Happiness*, 96–98. See also Daniel Blake Smith, *Inside the Great House: Planter Family Life in Eighteenth-Century Chesapeake Society* (Ithaca & London: Cornell Univ. Press, 1980), 28–29. For a different perspective on the patriarchal "complacency" of eighteenth-century planters, see Rhys Isaac, *The Transformation of Virginia, 1740–1790* (Chapel Hill: Univ. of North Carolina Press, 1982), 308–9.

64. Hans Rosenberg, "Die Ausprägung der Junkerherrschaft in Brandenburg-Preussen 1410–1618," in his *Machteliten und Wirtschaftskonjunkturen: Studien zur neureren deutschen Sozial- und Wirtschaftsgeschichte* (Göttingen: Vandenhoeck & Ruprecht, 1978), 78. He writes of the Junkers' "transformation into progressive, expansive economic entrepreneurs with very pronounced interest in commercial profit." Ibid., 66–67.

65. On Hartwig von Bredow II and his family background, see Hartmut Harnisch, "Die Gutsherrschaft in Brandenburg. Ergebnisse und Probleme," *Jahrbuch für Wirtschaftsgeschichte*, 1969, Teil IV, pp. 131–35; Herbert Helbig, *Gesellschaft und Wirtschaft der Mark Brandenburg im Mittelalter* (Berlin & New York: Walter de Gruyter, 1973), 5–6; and Hahn, *Struktur und Funktion des Brandenburgischen Adels*, 64, 105–8, 164–65. On William Fitzhugh, see Ulrich Bonnell Phillips, *Life and Labor in the Old South* (1929; Boston: Little Brown, 1963), 37–38; Richard B. Davis, ed., *William Fitzhugh and his Chesapeake World, 1676–1701: The Fitzhugh Letters and Other Documents* (Chapel Hill: Univ. of North Carolina Press, 1963); and Warren M. Billings, John E. Selby, and Thad W. Tate, *Colonial Virginia: A History* (White Plains, N.Y.: KtO Press, 1986), 130–31, where the authors state that "Fitzhugh and his class were newly self-made men."

66. Reinhard Bendix, *Max Weber: An Intellectual Portrait* (1960; Garden City, N.Y.: Anchor Books, 1962), 68–69. Cf. William H. McNeill's comments on the "comparatively radical rationality" introduced to European economic life by the expanding markets and inflationary price movements of the sixteenth and seventeenth centuries. McNeill, *The Rise of the West: A History of the Human Community* (1963; New York: Mentor, 1965), 639–40.

67. The term is taken from Phyllis Deane, *The First Industrial Revolution*, 2nd ed. (Cambridge: Cambridge Univ. Press, 1979).

68. David Landes, "Introduction" to *The Rise of Capitalism*, 10–11.

69. Ralph Davis, *The Industrial Revolution and British Overseas Trade* (Atlantic Highlands, N.J.: Humanities Press, 1979), 36.

70. J. D. B. DeBow, *Encyclopaedia of the Trade and Commerce of the United States, More Particularly of the Southern and Western States*, 2nd ed. (London: Trübner and Co., 1854), 325.

71. See Rolf Engelsing, "Die Häfen an der Südküste der Ostsee und der Ostwestverkehr in der ersten Hälfte des 19. Jahrhunderts," *Vierteljahrschrift für Sozial- und Wirtschaftsgeschichte* 58 (1971), 50–64; Rolf H. Dumke, "Anglo-deutscher Handel und Frühindustrialisierung in Deutschland, 1822–1865," *Geschichte und Gesellschaft: Zeitschrift für*

Historische Sozialwissenschaft 5 (1979), 190–91; Robert G. Albion, *The Rise of New York Port* (1815–1860) (1939; rpt. ed., Hamden, Conn.: Archon Books, 1961), 98–117; and Douglass C. North, *The Economic Growth of the United States, 1790–1860* (New York: Norton, 1966), 126–28.

72. Engelsing, "Die Häfen," 59, and Albion, *Rise of New York Port,* 103–4.

73. Davis, *The Industrial Revolution,* 39.

74. Davis, *Rise of the Atlantic Economies,* 108–24, 190. Despite the decline in Baltic grain exports during the seventeenth century, these exports (via Dutch ships) apparently became crucial for a number of Mediterranean cities by the end of the century. Harry A. Miskimin, *Economy of Later Renaissance Europe,* 1460–1600 (Cambridge: Cambridge Univ. Press, 1977), 142. On "intensification of agricultural production" in England and the Netherlands versus the rest of Europe, see Peter Kriedte, *Peasants, Landlords and Merchant Captitalists. Europe and the World Economy, 1500–1800,* trans. V. R. Berghahn (German ed.,1980; Cambridge: Cambridge Univ. Press, 1983), 68, 109.

75. See Jan De Vries, *Economy of Europe in an Age of Crisis, 1600–1750* (Cambridge: Cambridge Univ. Press, 1976), 35–37, and Kriedte, *Peasants, Landlords and Merchant Capitalists,* 61–70.

76. Hagen, "Seventeenth-Century Crisis in Brandenburg," 320–34; Hartmut Harnisch, "Peasants and Markets: The Background to the Agrarian Reforms in Feudal Prussia East of the Elbe, 1760–1807," in Evans and Lee, eds., *The German Peasantry,* 44, 50; Otto Büsch, *Militärsystem und Sozialleben im Alten Preussen, 1713–1807: Die Anfänge der sozialen Militisierung der preussisch-deutschen Gesellschaft* (Berlin: Walter de Gruyter, 1962), 110–13, 96; and Gustavo Corni, "Absolutische Agrarpolitik und Agrargesellschaft in Preussen," *Zeitschrift für Historische Forschung* 13 (1986), 298–310.

77. Harnisch, "Peasants and Markets," 50; Bruno Schumacher, *Geschichte Ost- und Westpreussens,* 4th ed., ed. Göttingen Arbeitskreis (Würzburg: Holzner, 1959), 235–36; and Berdahl, *Politics of the Prussian Nobility,* 95.

78. McCluskey and Menard, *Economy of British America,* 130. "The first serious shipment of wheat from Virginia and Pennsylvania" to England, says Ralph Davis, came "a few years before the Revolution." Davis, *Rise of the Atlantic Economies,* 285.

79. See Gray, *History of Southern Agriculture,* vol. 1, pp. 164–67, and vol. 2, pp. 606–8; Paul G. E. Clemens, "The Operation of an Eighteenth-Century Chesapeake Tobacco Plantation," *Agricultural History* 49 (1975), 521–22; and Davis, *Rise of Atlantic Economies,* 267; and Kulikoff, *Tobacco and Slaves,* 99–101.

80. Louis Morton, *Robert Carter of Nomini Hall: A Virginia Tobacco Planter of the Eighteenth Century* (Williamsburg, Va.: Colonial Williamsburg, 1941), 141–46; Robert McColley, *Slavery and Jeffersonian Virginia,* 2nd ed. (Urbana: Univ. of Illinois Press, 1973), 28; James Thomas Flexner, *Washington: The Indispensable Man* (1974; New York: Mentor, 1979), 47–48; and Bruce A. Ragsdale, "George Washinton, the British Tobacco Trade, and Economic Opportunity in Prerevolutionary Virginia," *Virginia Magazine of History and Biography* 97 (1989), 156–58; and Kulikoff, *Tobacco and Slaves,* 120.

81. Cornelius O. Cathey, *Agricultural Developments in North Carolina, 1783–1860* (Chapel Hill: Univ. of North Carolina Press, 1956), 116–18, explains that even though England remained the best foreign market for American tobacco to 1860, "When the colonies became free they gained the privilege of selling their tobacco wherever they

chose, but lost the exclusive right of supplying the British market." All European countries levied high duties on imported tobacco in the 1790s. Western competition progressively lowered the price of tobacco from 10 to 15 cents per pound for the years 1816–19 to 4 cents for the years 1842–50. See also Fogel, *Without Consent or Contract*, 63–64.

82. Wilhelm Abel has determined that between the 1730s and the first decade of the nineteenth century "the price of the chief bread grains, taken in 10–year averages," went up by 250% in England and 210% in Germany, with the price increases accelerating after 1790. Abel, *Agricultural Fluctuations in Europe*, 197–98. According to Thomas Nipperdey, however, from 1730–40 to 1800–10 grain prices in "northern Germany" rose 110%, although he also reports that the rise was especially steep after 1790. Nipperdey, *Deutsche Geschichte 1800–1860*, 146.

83. Abel, *Agrarkrisen und Agrarkonjunktur*, 196, 207; Ernst Klein, *Geschichte der deutschen Landwirtschaft im Industriezeitalter* (Wiesbaden: Franz Steiner, 1973), 50; and Hanna Schissler, *Preussische Agrargesellschaft im Wandel: Wirtschaftliche, gesellschaftliche, und politische Transformationsprozesse von 1763 bis 1847* (Göttingen: Vandenhoeck & Ruprecht, 1978), 59.

84. Gunther Ipsen, "Die preussische Bauernbefreiung als Landesausbau," *Zeitschrift für Agrargeschichte und Agrargesellschaft* 2 (1954), reprinted in Ernst-Wolfgang Böckenförde and Rainer Wall, eds., *Moderne Deutsche Verfassungsgeschichte (1815–1918)*, Neue Wissenschaftliche Bibliothek, No. 51 (Köln & Berlin: Kiepenheuer & Witsch, 1972), 358.

85. The Liverpool Cotton Association Limited, *Liverpool Raw Cotton Annual, 1957* (Liverpool: Turner, Routledge, 1957), 205, 224.

86. Eckert Kehr, "The Genesis of the Prussian Bureaucracy and the Rechtstaat," in his *Economic Interest, Militarism, and Foreign Policy: Essays on German History*, ed. Gordon A. Craig and trans. Grete Heinz (Berkeley, Los Angeles, & London: Univ. of California Press, 1977), 144; and M. Tcherkinsky, *The Landschaften and Their Mortgage Credit Operation in Germany, 1770–1920* (Rome: International Institute of Agriculture, 1922), 9–43; Friedrich Wilhelm Henning, *Landwirtschaft und ländliche Gesellschaft in Deutschland, Band 2: 1750 bis 1976* (Paderborn: Ferdinand Schöningh, 1978), 89–90; and Berdahl, *Politics of the Prussian Nobility*, 108.

87. Quoted in Abel, *Agrarkrisen und Agrarkonjunktur*, 203.

88. Fritz Martiny, *Die Adelsfrage in Preussen vor 1806 als politisches und soziales Problem. Erläutert am Beispiele des kurmärkischen Adels*, Beiheft 35 zur *Vierteljahrschrift für Sozial- und Wirtschaftsgeschichte* (Stuttgart & Berlin: W. Kohlhammer, 1938), 33. Speculative Junkers seldom farmed knight's estates themselves, but instead leased them to innovative commoners. See Hans-Heinrich Müller, "Bauern, Pächter und Adel im alten Preussen," *Jahrbuch für Wirtschaftsgeschichte*, 1966: Teil I, esp. 276.

89. On the growing interest of nobles in innovative agricultural methods at the end of the eighteenth century, see Martiny, *Die Adelsfrage in Preussen*, 11–13, and Wilhelm Abel, *Geschichte der deutschen Landwirtschaft vom frühen Mittelalter bis zum 19. Jahrhundert*, 3rd ed. (Stuttgart: Verlag Eugen Ulmer, 1978), esp. 330–31.

90. Abel, *Agrarkrisen und Agrarkonjunktur*, 187.

91. See in particular Harnisch, "Peasants and Markets," 45–59, and Hagen, "The Junkers' Faithless Servants," esp. 90–94.

92. H. A. Graf von Borcke, *Beschreibung der Stargordtischen Wirtschaft in Hinterpommern (dated 16 Oct. 1777), nebst G. M. L. von Wedells, Königl. Preuss. Oberforstmeisters in Schlesien, Vorlesungen in der patriotischen Gesellschaft in Breslau über diesen Gegenstand, auf Verlangen des Gesellschaft herausgegeben, nebst einigen Anmerkungen des Grafen von Borcke über dieselbe; and von Eckstädts Beschreibung der Hohenholtzischen Wirtschaft in Vorpommern* (estate Hohenholtz near Stettin*), nebst beigefügten Plans* (1779, Auf Kosten des Verfassers), 11, 13. On Borcke, see Graf zu Lippe, "A. H. Graf von Borcke," in *Allgemeine Deutsche Biographie* 3 (Leipzig, 1876), 157–58; Hans Saring, Helmut Dahm, and Hans Banig, "Borcke," in *Neue Deutsche Biographie* 2 (Berlin, 1955), 459–61; and C. B. A. Behrens, *Society, Government, and the Enlightenment: The Experiences of Eighteenth-Century France and Prussia* (New York: Harper & Row, 1985), 149–50. Stargord offers dramatic testimony to the enlargement of many knight's estates in the nineteenth century during the course of dissolving the lord-serf relationship; for in the mid-1850s the estate was reported to encompass nearly 3100 acres. Karl Friedrich Rauer, *Hand-Matrikel in sämmtlichen Kreisen des Preussischen Staats auf Kreis- und Landtagen vertretenen Rittergüter* (Berlin: Durch die Herausgeber, 1857), 157. Siegfried Korth has calculated that in two parts of Brandenburg (the *Uckermark* and *Mittelmark*) the percentage of *Rittergut* land in 1860 that dated back to noble ownership in 1375 (versus peasant and common land) was 29% and 36%. Korth, "Die Entstehung und Entwicklung des ostdeutschen Grossgrundbesitzes. Eine Untersuchung auf siedlungsstatistischer Grundlage in sieben Kreisen der Ucker- und Mittelmark von Jahre 1375 bis 1860," *Jahrbuch des Albertus-Universität zu Königsberg/Preussen* 3 (1953), esp. 158–62

93. Albrecht Thaer, "Begriff der rationellen Landwirtschaft," in Günther Franz, ed., *Quellen zur Geschichte des Deutschen Bauernstandes in der Neuzeit* (München & Wien: R. Oldenbourg, 1963), 348. According to Thomas Nipperdey, Thaer exemplified "the modern capitalist way of economic thinking." Nipperdey, *Deutsche Geschichte 1800–1866*, 146.

94. Borcke, *Beschreibung der Stargordtischen Wirtschaft*, 32, 4–6, 19–20, 27–28. In 1783 the Count claimed that since 1770 his net profit at Stargord had more than quadrupled, from 700 to 3000 *Taler*. Abel, *Agrarkrisen und Agrarkonjunktur*, 193, and Abel, *Geschichte der deutschen Landwirtschaft*, 330.

95. Jack P. Greene, ed., *The Diary of Colonel Landon Carter of Sabine Hall, 1752–1778* (2 vols.; Charlottesville: Univ. Press of Virginia, 1965), vol. 1, pp. 498–501. The introduction to this diary has been separately published in paperback: Greene, *Landon Carter: An Inquiry into the Personal Values and Social Imperatives of the Eighteenth-Century Virginia Gentry* (Charlottesville: Dominion Books of the Univ. Press of Virginia, 1967).

96. Borcke, *Beschreibung der Stargordtischen Wirtschaft*, 22–32; the quotations are from p. 32.

97. Ibid., 30–32.

98. See esp. Kenneth M. Stampp, *The Peculiar Institution: Slavery in the Ante-bellum South* (New York: Vintage, 1956), 125–27.

99. Greene, ed., *The Diary of Colonel Landon Carter*, vol. 1, p. 147, and vol. 2, p. 1149. See also Gerald W. Mullin, *Flight and Rebellion: Slave Resistance in Eighteenth-Century Virginia* (New York: Oxford Univ. Press, 1972), 53–56.

100. Ralph B. Flanders, *Plantation Slavery in Georgia* (Chapel Hill: Univ. of North Carolina Press, 1933), 292. This Howell Cobb is not to be confused with the more famous Democratic politician from Clarke County of the same name.

101. Howell Cobb, *A Scriptural Examination of the Institution of Slavery in the United States, With Its Objects and Purposes* ((Perry), Ga.: Printed for the author, 1856), 121.

102. See, for example, the condescension in Landes-Oeconomie-Rathe Koppe zu Wollup, "Bericht über eine Reise durch die Provinz Posen, behufs Untersuchung des Zustandes der dortigen Landwirtschaft," *Annalen der Landwirtschaft* 6 (1845), esp.163–64, 182–83; and an unsigned report on the Posen county of Bromberg, "Schilderungen landwirtschaftlicher Züstande in der Provinz Posen. 3. Bromberg, Nach bei dem Königlichen L.O.C. eingegangenen Vereins-Berichten," ibid., vol. 11 (1847), 419–27. On Prussian/Polish tensions in the mid-nineteenth century, see William W. Hagen, *Germans, Poles, and Jews: The Nationality Conflict in the Prussian East, 1772–1914* (Chicago & London: Univ. of Chicago Press, 1980), chs. 3 and 4.

103. See Schissler, *Preussische Agrargesellchaft im Wandel*, 75, for the oft-repeated figure of 10%. Christof Dipper, *Die Bauernbefreiung in Deutschland, 1790–1850* (Stuttgart & Berlin: W. Kohlhammer, 1980), 100, estimates that circa 1800 about 15% of knight's estates already belonged to commoners, and that 75% of noble families were no longer landed. Alexander von Harnier, *Beitrag zur Geschichte des deutschen Grossgrundbesitz im Lande der Netze and Warthe* (Essen: Selbstverl., 1971), 48, points to Frederick the Great's 27 June 1780 cabinet order allowing the purchase of *Rittergüter* in the Netz district (recently acquired via the first partition of Poland) by good, propertied Prussian *Bürger*, but only from Poles. Harnier says that 25 such purchases were approved in 1780 alone. Wolfgang Treue, "Die land-wirtschaftliche Unternehmer in Ostdeutschland," *Tradition*, vol. 3 (1958), 37, tells the story of a peasant's son in Silesia, Jeremias Förster, who purchased seven *Rittergüter* during the last years of Frederick the Great's reign, and soon after the monarch's death in 1786 received a noble title from the newly crowned king. At this time, reports Gustavo Corni, 13% of all Brandenburg *Gutsherrschaftern* belonged to commoners. Corni, "Absolutische Agrarpolitik und Agrargesellschaft in Preussen," 313.

104. Erich Jordan, *Die Entstehung der konservativen Partei und die preussischen Agrarverhältnisse von 1848* (München & Leipzig: Duncker and Humblot, 1914), 30. Robert Berdahl says about sales of *Rittergüter* to commoners that "The data are very incomplete, but of 59 cases of land transfers in East Prussia between 1806 and 1829 in which the occupation of the commoner buying a noble estate can be ascertained, 12 were military officers, 20 were former managers of royal estates, 18 were civil servants, 1 had been the owner of a smaller, non-noble estate, and 2 had formerly leased smaller non-noble estates. Only 3 of the 59 were businessmen." Berdahl, *Politics of the Prussian Nobility*, 278.

105. Hugo Rachel and Paul Wallich, *Berliner Grosskaufleute und Kapitalisten, Vol. III: Übergangseit zur Hochkapitalismus, 1806–1856* (Berlin: Als Handschrift Gedruckt, 1939), 191, and Heinrich Berghaus, *Landbuch der Mark Brandenburg und des Markgrafthums Niederlausitz in der Mitte des 19. Jahrhunderts* (3 vols.; Berlin: Adolph Müller, 1854–56), vol. 3, p. 618.

106. Rittergutsbesitzer Eben, "Bericht über die Ackererträge des Gutes Schlagenthin bei Arnswalde," *Annalen der Landwirtschaft* (1847), 393–401; Berghaus, *Landbuch*, vol. 3, pp. 504–7; and Görlitz, *Die Junker*, 211–12.

107. Berghaus, *Landbuch*, vol. 3, pp. 302–3.

108. Leisewitz, "Johann Gottlieb Koppe," *Allgemeine Deutsche Biographie* 16 (Leipzig, 1882), 693–97; Eberhard Gerhardt, "Johann Gottlieb Koppe zur 100. Wiederkehr seines Todestages," *Zeitschrift für Agrargeschichte und Agrarsoziologie* 12 (1964), 49–53; and Klein, *Geschichte der deutschen Landwirtschaft*, 64–67.

109. L-O-C Rat J. G. Koppe zu Beesdau, "Über die Vertheilung des productiven Bodens," *Annalen der Landwirtschaft* 13 (1849), 335–48; the quotation is from p. 346.

110. On Nathusius and his sons, see Leisewitz, "J. G. Nathusius" and "Hermann Engelhard von Nathusius," in *Allgemeine Deutsche Biographie* 23 (Leipzig, 1886), 271–83; and Görlitz, *Die Junker*, 167, 220.

111. Abel, *Agrarkrisen und Agrarkonjunktur*, 211–21.

112. Klein, *Geschichte der deutschen Landwirtschaft*, 52, and Berdahl, *Politics of the Prussian Nobility*, 274–75. Christof Dipper has estimated that "Between 1815 and 1830 eighty percent of estates in the eastern provinces changed owners because of indebtedness." Dipper, *Die Bauernbefreiung in Deutschland*, 125.

113. Even prior to the Panic of 1819, the shortage of good tobacco land east of the Blue Ridge had inspired many Chesapeake yeomen and slaveholders alike to move west. "When new frontier areas opened in the Southwest between 1790 and 1820, a quarter of a million whites migrated, taking 175,000 slaves with them, and leaving the worn-out land to those who stayed." Kulikoff, *Tobacco and Slaves*, 429.

114. *Proceedings and Debates of the Virginia State Convention of 1829–30* (Richmond: Thomas Ritchie, 1830), 178. Mercer also stated that the market value of slaves had plunged 50%.

115. William W. Freehling, *Prelude to Civil War: The Nullification Controversy in South Carolina, 1816–1836* (1966; New York: Harper Torchbooks, 1968), 36.

116. See Alfred Glaze Smith, *Economic Readjustment of an Old Cotton State, South Carolina, 1820–1860* (Columbia: Univ. of South Carolina Press, 1958), 8–11.

117. Ulrich B. Phillips, ed., *Plantation and Frontier Documents: 1649–1863, Illustrative of Industrial History in the Colonial and Antebellum South, collected from MSS and Other Rare Sources* (2 vols.; Cleveland, Ohio: A. H. Clark, 1909), vol. 1, p. 284.

118. Perhaps the most celebrated case is that of Thomas Smith Gregory Dabney, born in 1788 in Virginia at Bellevue, his father's plantation. In 1835 he moved to Mississippi, where he had bought 4000 acres from half a dozen small farmers. See Susan Dabney Smedes, *Memorials of a Southern Planter* (Baltimore, 1887), excerpted in Stuart Bruchey, ed., *Cotton and the Growth of the American Economy: 1790–1860. Sources and Readings* (New York: Harcourt, Brace & World, 1967), 211–17; introductory notes on p. 170.

119. "In fact, most of the South's impressive economic growth between 1840 and 1860 can be attributed to the massive shift of population to the more productive lands of the old Southwest. . . . Fresh land on the frontier provided cotton growers with a place to go; slavery provided Southern slaveholders with a mobile base of social and economic power unavailable to European landlords." Lacy K. Ford, Jr., *Origins of South-*

ern Radicalism: The South Carolina Upcountry 1800–1860 (New York & Oxford: Oxford Univ. Press, 1988), 40–41.

120. Herbert A. Kellar, ed., "A Journey Through the South in 1836: Diary of James D. Davidson," *Journal of Southern History* 1 (1935), 355–57. Cf. the observations for Arkansas by Albert Pike, who became proprietor and editor of the *Arkansas Advocate* in Little Rock in 1835, just prior to Arkansas's admission to the Union: if "a poor man" should settle in the rich bottom lands with nothing other than an axe and rifle, and proceed to clear land for cotton, "In four or five years that man will raise some twenty bales of cotton and a thousand bushels of corn, and be steadily enlarging his crop and increasing his income." Pike, "Letters from Arkansas" (1835–36), in Eugene L. Schwaab, ed., *Travels in the Old South, Selected from Periodicals of the Times* (2 vols.; Lexington: Univ. Press of Kentucky, 1973), vol. 1, pp. 212–13.

121. Martha von Briesen, ed., *The Letters of Elijah Fletcher* (Charlottesville: Univ. Press of Virginia, 1965), 226, 207.

122. Edmund Ruffin, "Agricultural Review," *Farmers' Register* 1 (June, 1833), 39.

123. Herbert Gutman and Richard Sutch, "Victorians All? The Sexual Mores and Conduct of Slaves and Their Masters," in Paul A. David et al., *Reckoning With Slavery: A Critical Study in the Quantitative History of American Negro Slavery* (New York: Oxford Univ. Press, 1976), 160.

124. The members of the *Vereine* were predominantly large estate owners, as is clear from repeated comments in the *Annals of Agriculture* about the dearth of participation by peasants and urban landowners. See, for example, editor Alexander von Lengerke, "Kritische Blick in die landwirtschaftliche Journal-Literartur," *Annalen der Landwirtschaft* 13 (1849), 198–99. The Board of Rural Economy reported in 1848 that there were 318 *Vereine* in all of Prussia, 233 of them in the six eastern provinces. The East Elbian societies included 16,489 of all 28,081 members in Prussia. "Vierter Rechenschaftsbericht des Königlichen L.-O.-C. an ein hohes Ministerium des Innern" (dated 31 March 1848), *Annalen der Landwirtschaft* 12 (1848), 6–7. Only 39 of the 318 *Vereine* had been founded before 1830. "Die landwirtschaftiche Vereine in den Preussichen Staaten," *Annalen der Landwirtschaft* 3 (1844), 1. See also D. J. Brown, "Encouragement of Agriculture in Prussia," in *Report of the Commissioner of Patents for the Year 1857: Agriculture* (Washington, D.C.: Government Printing Office, 1858), 7–13.

125. Erich Marcks, *Bismarck: Eine Biographie, 1815–1851* (Stuttgart & Berlin: Cotta, 1915), 179–80, and Ernst Engelberg, *Bismarck: Urpreusse und Reichsgründer* (Berlin: Siedler, 1985), 149, 166–69, 180–81. Bismarck also made it clear in the 1844 letter that he was restless, that he could "no longer endure the solitary life of a Landjunker" and was debating "whether I should involve myself again in government service or go on long trips." By the 1870s Bismarck's political successes in engineering German unification under Prussian leadership had made him a wealthy man via monetary dotations and the financial expertise of his ambitious Jewish banker Bleichröder. As the owner of several dispersed estates, Bismarck found that agriculture pure and simple did not yield a profit, and "attacked his financial problem by becoming a petty rural industrialist," establishing potato distilleries and and paper factories. Otto Pflanze, *Bismarck and the Development of Germany, Volume II: The Period of Consolidation, 1871–1880* (Princeton: Princeton Univ. Press, 1990), 67–77; quotation from p. 74.

126. Hauptmann von Wulffen-Pietzpuhl, "Gutachten betreffend die von Herrn Franz zu Eggenstadt bei Seehausen . . . mitgetheilte Denkschrift: Über die Notwendigkeit eigenthümlich gestellter Musterwirtschaften behufs der Förderung der praktischen Landwirtschaft Preussens," *Annalen der Landwirtschaft* 5 (1845), 60. On Wulffen-Pietzpuhl, see Klein, *Geschichte der deutschen Landwirtschaft*, 67–68.

127. "Die Methodik zur Berechnung der Feldsystem, von C. von Wulffen-Pietzpuhl," *Allgemeine Landwirtschaftliche Monatschrift* 22 (1847), 273–317; the quotation is from p. 274. This article also appeared in *Zeitschrift des Landwirtschaftlichen Provinzial-Vereins für die Mark Brandenburg und Niederlausitz* 4 (1846), 179–223.

128. Theodor Freiherr von der Goltz, *Geschichte der Deutschen Landwirtschaft, Vol. II: Das neunzehnten Jahrhundert* (Stuttgart & Berlin: J. G. Cotta'sche Buchhandlung Nachfolger, 1903), 172. Cf. Otto-Ernst Schüddekopf, *Die deutsche Innenpolitik im letzten Jahrhundert und der konservative Gedanke* (Braunschweig: Albert Limbach, 1951), 22; Hans Rosenberg, "Die Pseudodemocratisierung der Rittergutsbesitzerklasse" (1958), in his *Probleme der deutschen Sozialgeschichte* (Frankfurt am Main: Suhrkamp Verlag, 1969), 21–22; and Reinhart Koselleck, *Preussen zwischen Reform und Revolution: Allgemeines Landrecht, Verwaltung, und soziale Bewegung von 1791 bis 1848*, 2nd corrected ed. (Stuttgart: Ernst Klett, 1975), 507–14; and Schissler, *Preussische Agrargesellschaft im Wandel*, 165–67; and, from the Marxist-Leninist perspective of DDR scholars, a good example is Georg Moll, "Bürgerlich Umwalzung und kapitalistische Agrarentwicklung. Zur Diskussion um die Wege der bürgerlichen Umgestaltung," *Zeitschrift für Geschichtswissenschaft* 27 (1979), 140–44.

129. Davis, *The Industrial Revolution and British Overseas Trade*, 50–51.

130. See Klaus Klatte, "Die Anfänge des Agrarkapitalismus und der preussische Konservatismus" (D.Phil. diss., Hamburg University, 1974), 123–24; and Schissler, *Preussische Agrargsellschaft im Wandel*, 149–53, 169–70; and Harnisch, *Kapitalistische Agrarreform und Industrielle Revolution*, 249–51.

131. Schissler, *Preussische Agrargesellschaft im Wandel*, 169–70.

132. "Aufklärungen des Herrn Grafen von Harrach über die Bewirthschaftung seiner Romochauer Güter," *Annalen der Landwirtschaft* 4 (1844), 129–32. The author mentions on p. 124 that he also owns estates near Breslau; and as of 1856 Count Karl von Harrach owned four knight's estates in the Breslau district *(Kreis)*. See Karl Friedrich Rauer, *Alphabetische Nachweis (Addressbuch) des in den Preussischen Staaten mit Rittergütern angessessen Adels* (Berlin: Durch die Herausgeber, 1857), 85.

133. F. W. Schubert, "Über die Schafzucht im Preussischen Staate," *Zeitschrift des Landwirtschaftlichen Provinzial-Vereins für die Mark Brandenburg und Niederlausitz* 6 (1847), 180. In 1841 von Beckedorff told the General Assembly of the Pomeranian Economic Society that 70% of the value of Prussia's net exports (estimated at 30 million *Taler* for the year) came from, in descending order, wool and woolen goods, flax thread and linen, and grain; another 13% came from lumber, metals, coal, glass, and liquor *(Branntwein)*. Opening Address of President von Beckedorff, 19 Nov. 1841, *Allgemeine Landwirtschaftliche Monatschrift* 5 (1841), 130.

134. Friedrich Wilhelm Henning, *Landwirtschaft und ländliche Gesellschaft in Deutschland, Band 2: 1750 bis 1976* (Paderborn: Ferdinand Schöningh, 1978), 95; Schissler,

Preussische Agrargesellschaft im Wandel, 244, n. 26; and Schubert, "Über die Schafzucht im Preussischen Staate," 177.

135. Ernst Engel, "Die Viehhaltung im preussischen Staate," *Landwirtschaftliche Centralblatt für Deutschland* 9 (1861), 142.

136. Philip Schwab, "Zur landwirtschaftlichen Statistik," *Annalen der Landwirtschaft* 17 (1851), 174–75; and Schubert, "Über die Schafzucht im Preussischen Staate," 167.

137. Adolf von Thadden-Trieglaff, "Ueber Menschenschau unter Landwirthen" (an 1837 address at Regenwalde), reprinted in Eleonore Furstin Reuss, *Adolf von Thadden Trieglaff: Ein Lebensbild,* 2nd ed. (Berlin: Wilhelm Hertz, 1894), 220. "In Pomerania (during the 1820s) one talked about the 'Era of the Golden Fleece.'" Görlitz, *Die Junker,* 209. See also Wilhelm Treue, *Wirtschafts- und Technik-Geschichte Preussens,* Veröffentlichungen der Historischen Kommission zu Berlin, vol. 56 (Berlin & New York: Walter de Gruyter, 1984), 259.

138. *Liverpool Raw Cotton Annual, 1957,* 311, and Douglass North, *The Economic Growth of the United States, 1790–1860* (1961; New York: Norton, 1966), 233, where a table gives the value of total U.S. exports in 1860 as $333,576,000 and the value of cotton exports as $191,806,000. *DeBow's Review* (Dec. 1860), 789, reports that the 1859–60 cotton crop totaled 4.68 million bales, of which 2.67 million were shipped to Great Britain.

139. Editorial comment in *American Cotton Planter* (Oct. 1856), 305. The previous month's issue carried "Cotton Is King," W. N. Reeves's June valedictorian address at Howard College, in Marion, Ala.; see *American Cotton Planter* (Sept. 1856), 257–60.

140. Hammond, "Speech on the Admission of Kansas, Under the Lecompton Constitution, Delivered in the Senate of the United States, March 4th, 1858," in *Selections from the Letters and Speeches of the Hon. James H. Hammond of South Carolina* (New York: John F. Tow, 1866), 316–17.

141. "The Cotton Supply of England," *De Bow's Review* (April 1860), 472. Cf. *Considerations Relative to a Southern Confederacy, With Letters to the North, on the Preservation of the Union, and a Note from the Secret History of the Emancipation in the English West Indies. By a Citizen of North Carolina* (Raleigh: "Standard Office," 1860), 6: "Lord Stanley, the son of the present Premier of England, and himself one of the first statesman of the country, declared in a speech to his constituents, only a few years since, on occasion of the difficulties between the United States and Great Britain, . . . that the deprivation of the supplies of Cotton would, in six months, produce almost universal bankruptcy, and in twelve months an insurrection of the working classes." The author was wheat planter Henry King Burgwyn of Northampton County, and the essay originally appeared in the 28 March 1860 *North Carolina Standard.*

142. Gavin Wright, "Prosperity, Progress, and American Slavery," in David et al., *Reckoning with Slavery,* 306.

143. *Liverpool Raw Cotton Annual, 1957,* 277–95.

144. *Allgemeine Landwirtschaftliche Monatschrift* 4 (1841), 342.

145. Davis, *Industrial Revolution and British Overseas Trade,* 50; and Schwab, "Zur landwirtschaftlichen Statistik," 174–75; and Robert A. Dickler, "Organization and Change in Productivity in Eastern Prussia," in William N. Parker and Eric L. Jones, eds.,

European Peasants and Their Markets: Essays in Agrarian Economic History (Princeton: Princeton Univ. Press, 1975), 287.

146. E. L. Jones, *The Development of English Agriculture, 1815–1873* (London: Macmillan, 1968), 13; and F. M. L. Thompson, *English Landed Society in the Nineteenth Century* (Toronto & London: Univ. of Toronto Press,1963), 232–33; and Davis, *Industrial Revolution and British Overseas Trade*, 40–42.

147. "Landwirtschaftliche Berichte. IV. Aus dem Halberstädtischen und Anhältischen (Den 1sten Mai 1840)," *Allgemeine Landwirtschaftliche Monatschrift* 1 (1840), 273. Halberstadt was a town in provincial Saxony, and Anhalt (to the east) was a small, politically independent state surrounded by Prussian territory.

148. Klatte, "Die Anfänge des Agrarkapitalismus und der preussische Konservatismus," 117–19.

149. "Über Arbeitslohne in England," in Editor's "Miscellen," *Annalen der Landwirtschaft* 9 (1847), 402. An agricultural reporter in provincial Saxony told readers of the *General Agricultural Monthly* that "the free import (of wheat) into England assures that that country will determine the price on the Continent." Report dated beginning of November 1847, *Allgemeine Landwirtschaftliche Monatschrift* 25 (1847), 219.

150. C. F. W. Dieterici, *Statistische Uebersicht der wichtigen Gegenstände des Verkehrs und Verbrauchs im deutschen Zollvereine. Vierte Fortsetzung. Zeitraum von 1846 bis 1848* (Berlin, 1851), 306–8. During the three non-crisis years 1844–46, wheat averaged twenty *Silbergroschen* more per hundredweight than did rye: three *Taler* for a hundredweight of wheat versus two *Taler* and ten *Sgr.* for the same amount of rye. Th. Henning, "Die Ein- und Ausfuhr landwirtschaftlicher Producte im Zoll-verein," *Annalen der Landwirtschaft* 13 (1849), 416–21.

151. Henning, "Die Ein- und Ausfuhr landwirtschaftlicher Producte im Zoll-verein," 416–21.

152. Eduard Bleich, ed., *Der Erste Vereinigte Landtag in Berlin, 1847* (4 vols.; Berlin, 1847; rpt. ed., Vaduz, Lichtenstein: Topos Verlag, 1977), Teil 2, pp. 101, 107–8. One *Wispel* = 24 Berlin bushels. See also Jordan, *Die Entstehung der konservativen Partei and die Preussischen Agrarverhältnisse von 1848*, 113–14.

153. Klatte, "Die Anfänge der Agrarkapitalismus und der preussische Konservatismus,"117–19, and J. Potter, "Atlantic Economy, 1815–1860: the U.S.A. and the Industrial Revolution in Britain" (1960), in A. W. Coats and Ross M. Robertson, eds., *Essays in American Economic History* (London: Edward Arnold, 1969), 21.

154. See Frank B. Tipton, Jr., *Regional Variations in the Economic Development of Germany During the Nineteenth Century* (Middletown, Conn.: Wesleyan Univ. Press, 1976), 25–26.

155. Ernst Engel, "Die Getreidepreise, die Ernteerträge und die Getreidehandel im preussischen Staate," *Landwirtschaftliche Centralblatt für Deutschland* 9 (1861), 403–4. Cf. the comparison of Prussian, English, and French grain prices for the years 1816–68 in August Meitzen and Friedrich Grossman, *Der Boden und der landwirtschaftlichen Verhältnisse des preussischen Staates* (8 vols.; Berlin: Paul Parey, 1868–1908), vol. 3, 424–25. I have computed the rough *Taler*/dollar equivalence from figures in Georg Friedrich Kolb, *Handbuch der vergleichenden Statistik der Völkerzustands- und Staatenkunde*, 4th ed. (Leipzig: Arthur Felix, 1865), 445. According to Sister Mary Anthonita Hess, *American Tobacco*

and Central European Policy, Early Nineteenth Century (Washington, D.C.: Georgetown Univ. Press, 1948), 90, circa 1837 one *Taler* equalled 67 cents.

156. Kenneth D. Barkin, *The Controversy over German Industrialization, 1890–1902* (Chicago: Univ. of Chicago Press, 1970), 28.

157. Tipton, *Regional Variations in the Economic Development of Germany* 54; Ivo Lambi, *Free Trade and Protectionism in Germany, 1868–1879*, Vierteljahrschrift für Sozial- und Wirtschaftsgeschichte, Beiheft 44 (Wiesbaden: Franz Steiner, 1963), 19–20. Lambi says that Germany remained "the granary of Britain" until the Schleswig-Holstein war of 1864 encouraged English imports of American grain.

158. Schissler, *Preussische Agrargesellschaft im Wandel*, 199.

159. The quotation comes from Eckart Kehr, "The Genesis of the Prussian Bureaucracy and the Rechtstaat," in his *Economic Interest, Militarism, and Foreign Policy: Essays on German History*, ed. Gordon A. Craig, trans. Grete Heinz (Berkeley & Los Angeles: Univ. of California Press, 1977), 149. On *Bauernlegen* versus *Bauernschutz* in the early nineteenth century, see Treue, *Wirtschafts- und Tecknik-Geschichte Preussens*, esp. 252–53.

160. Günther Franz, "Landwirtschaft 1800–1850," in Hermann Aubin and Wolfgang Zorn, eds., *Handbuch der deutschen Wirtschafts- und Sozialgeschichte, II: Das 19. und 20. Jahrhundert* (Stuttgart: Ernst Klett, 1976), 304–5. Cf. Schumacher, *Geshichte Ost- und Westpreussens*, 263.

161. On the ex-slaves' desire for land, see Leon Litwack, *Been in the Storm So Long: The Aftermath of Slavery* (New York: Knopf, 1979; Vintage paperback, 1980), 398–404, and Eric Foner, *Reconstruction: America's Unfinished Revolution* (New York: Harper & Row, 1988), 103–6, 374–77.

162. Quoted in Eggert, *Geschichte Pommerns*, 71.

163. See Ursula Wiese, *Zur Opposition des ostelbischen Grundadels gegen die agraren Reformmassnahmen 1807–1811* (Berlin: Triltsch & Huther, 1935), 34–48; and Klaus Vetter, *Kurmärkischer Adel und Preussiche Reformen*, Veröffentlichungen des Staatsarchiv Potsdam, Vol. 15 (Weimar: Hermann Böhlaus Nachfolger, 1979), 124, 131–32.

164. "Aus einer Eingabe der Gutsbesitzer der Kreises Stolp an König Friedrich Wilhelm III, vom 2. 11. 1811," in Werner Conze, ed., *Quellen zur Geschichte der deutschen Bauernbefreiung* (Göttingen: Musterschmidt, 1957), 126–27.

165. Ernst Rudolf Huber, *Deutsche Verfassungsgeschichte seit 1789, Vol. I: Reform und Restauration, 1789 bis 1830* (Stuttgart: W. Kohlhammer, 1957), 197–98, and Dipper, *Die Bauernbefreiung in Deutschland*, 118.

166. See Tipton, *Regional Variations in the Economic Development of Germany*, 24–25.

167. Dipper, *Die Bauernbefreiung in Deutschland*, 117–18. The Ministry for Agricultural Affairs' official statistics are in "Die Ablösungen in Preussen im Jahre 1859," *Landwirtschaftliche Centralblatt für Deutschland* 9 (1861).

168. See Franz, "Landwirtschaft 1800–1850," 298–99; Dipper, *Die Bauernbefreiung in Deutschland*, 120–21; and Treue, *Wirtschafts- und Technik-Geschichte Preussens*, 256–57. Hartmut Harnisch, *Die Herrschaft Boitzenburg. Untersuchungen zur Entwicklung der sozialökonomischen Struktur landwirtschaftlicher Gebiete in der Mark Brandenburg von 14. bis 19. Jahrhundert*, Veröffentlichungen des Staatsarchiv Potsdam, vol. 6 (Weimar: Hermann Böhlaus Nachfolger, 1968), 243, says that compensatory payments in cash were of greater

importance than land cessions at Boitzenburg, where the Arnims received 7,910 *Taler* in 1847 alone.

169. August von Miakowski, *Das Erbrecht und die Grundeigenthumsvertheilung in Deutschen Reiche. Ein sozialwirtschaftlicher Beitrag zur Kritik und Reform des deutschen Erbrechts. Teil I: Die Vertheilung des landwirtschaftliche benutzten Grundeigenthums und das gemeine Erbrecht,* Schriften des Vereins für Sozialpolitik, vol. 20 (Leipzig: Duncker & Humblot, 1882), 142–43.

170. Neumann, *Die Stufen des preussischen Konservatismus: Ein Beitrag zum Staats- und Gesellschaftsbild Deutschlands im 19. Jahrhundert,* Historische Studien, No. 190 (Berlin: Emil Ebering, 1930), 34. Cf. Treue, *Wirtschafts- und Technik-Geschichte Preussens,* 307.

171. Konigl. Landes-Oekonomie-Rat L. Hering in Stendal, "Allgemeine historische Entwickelung der agrarische Gesetzgebung in Preussen," *Möglin'sche Jahrbücher der Land-wirthschaft* (formerly *Möglinsche Annalen der Landwirthschaft,* 27 vols., 1817–31), ed. Franz Körte (Thaer's son-in-law), vol. 2 (1837), 129, 112–13.

172. Computed from figures in Rudolf Berthold, "Zur Herausbildung der kapitalist-ischen Klassenschichtung des Dorfes in Preussen," *Zeitschrift für Geschichtswissenschaft* 25 (1977), 569–71.

173. Franz, "Landwirtschaft 1800–1850," 297.

174. Computed from *Morgen* figures in Harnisch, *Die Herrschaft Boitzenburg,* 258.

175. Dipper, *Die Bauernbefreiung in Deutschland,* 131–33: "From 1805 to 1840 yields-per-hectare for grain only rose from 9.1 to 11.6 *Doppelzenter* (one *Doppelzentner* = 200 Prussian pounds = 206.226 English pounds), that is 12.7%." But the increase from 9.1 to 11.6 translates to a jump of 27.47%! According to Dipper, cultivated land *(Ackerland)* increased by 70% in all of Prussia and by 130% in the Prussian Northeast (that is, East Elbia minus provincial Saxony). In this instance the percentages accord with Dipper's absolute numbers (from 7.3 million to 12.46 million hectares for all of Prussia, and from 3.2 million to 7.38 million hectares in the Prussian Northeast). According to Nipperdey, *Deutsche Geschichte 1800–1866,* 152, arable land in all of Prussia increased by 94% between 1815 and 1864.

176. Franz, "Landwirtschaft 1800–1850," 292.

177. See Dickler, "Organization and Change in Productivity in Eastern Prussia," 288–91.

178. "*Spiritusbrennerei* of potatoes" was "the most important *technische Gewerbe*" in provincial Prussia; it had begun in earnest during the 1820s. Conrad-Maulen, "Acker-und Wiesenbau der Provinz Preussen" (1863), 37. According to Erich Jordan, "No where had Schnaps become so widespread as in Upper Silesia." Jordan, *Die Entstehung der konservativen Partei und die preussischen Agrarverhältnisse von 1848,* 104. On Branden-burg, see Harnisch, *Kapitalistische Agrarreform und Industrielle Revolution,* 218–20.

179. See J. A. Perkins, "The Agricultural Revolution in Germany, 1850–1914," *Journal of European Economic History* 10 (1981), 83–84.

180. "Die Runkelrübernzucker-Fabrikation im Zollverein," *Annalen der Landwirtschaft* 13 (1849), 167; Klein, *Geschichte der deutschen Landwirtschaft,* 100–101; and Treue, *Wirtschaft-und Technik-Geschichte Preussens,* 167.

181. Sprengel, "Hinterpommern," *Allgemeine Landwirtschafliche Monatschrift* 1 (1840), 71–72.

182. "Betrachtungen über den gegenwärtigen Standpunkt des Landwirtschaftlichen Betriebes in der Provinz Neumark," *Allgemeine Landwirtschaftliche Monatschrift* 4 (1841), 14–23.

183. Rittergutsbesitzer Paalzow, auf Kützkow, "Schlempefütterung und Lungenseuche des Rindviehes," *Annalen der Landwirtschaft* 1 (1843), 494–96. He wrote that his brother, Friedrich Wilhelm Paalzow, had done much the same thing at the estate Mesendorf, in Kreis Ost-Prignitz, which he had owned since 1814. See Berghaus, *Landbuch*, vol. 2, p. 616.

184. These comments come from a discussion of distilleries during the second annual meeting of the Brandenburg-Niederlausitz Central Agricultural Association, May 1845, in *Zeitschrift des Landwirtschaftlichen Provinzial-Vereins für die Mark Brandenburg and Niederlausitz* 2 (1845), 277–85.

185. "Betrachtungen über den gegenwärtigen Standpunkt des Landwirtschaftlichen Betriebes in der Provinz Neumark," 20.

186. Klatte, "Die Anfänge des Agrarkapitalismus and der preusssische Konservatismus," p. 122, and Bleich, ed., *Der Erste Vereinigte Landtag in Berlin, 1847*, Teil II, pp. 121–25.

187. On the smallholders, see Berthold, "Zur Herausbildung der kapitalistischen Klassenschichtung des Dorfes in Preussen," 561–65; Schissler, *Preussische Agrargesellschaft im Wandel*, 159–60, 179–80; and Nipperdey, *Deutsche Geschichte 1800–1866*, 161.

188. On Irish laborers in the South, see Ulrich B. Phillips, *American Negro Slavery* (1918; rpt. ed., Baton Rouge: Louisiana State Univ. Press, 1966), 301–2. Everard G. Baker, who owned 57 slaves in Mississippi's Panola County in 1860, hired two Irishmen to work on his cisterns in February of 1857. Everard G. Baker Diary (1848–76), typescript, in Southern Historical Collection at the University of North Carolina at Chapel Hill; Mississippi Slave Schedules for 1860, National Archives Microfilm Publications, Microcopy No. 653 (Washington, D.C., 1967). On the hiring of additional slaves, see Stampp, *The Peculiar Institution*, 70–71. Robert Henderson Allen of Southside Virginia owned 27 slaves in Lunenburg County in 1860. In June of 1856 he hired four male hands at $1.50 per day each from Gee and Co. to cut wheat. On 12 November 1860 at the courthouse he hired until Christmas "a negro fellow, Ned, of A J J Brown" for $15.50. Robert Henderson Allen Account Book (1850–61) and Diary (1858–63), in Virginia Historical Society, Richmond; and Virginia Slave Schedules for 1860, National Archives Microfilm Publications, Microcopy No. 653 (Washington, D.C., 1967).

189. See Alan Richards, "The Political Economy of *Gutswirtschaft*: A Comparative Analysis of East Elbian Germany, Egypt, and Chile," *Comparative Studies in Society and History* 21 (1979), 487–88.

190. On the *Insten*, see esp. Oberamtmann Proseleger, "Über den Zustand der landwirtschaftlichen Verhältnisse in Graudenzer Kreis (in provincial Prussia), 1843," *Annalen der Landwirtschaft* 8 (1846), 74–78, reprinted in Georg Friedrich Knapp, *Die Bauernbefreiung und die Usprung der Landarbeiter in den älteren Theilen Preussens*, 2nd ed. (2 vols.; München & Leipzig: Duncker & Humblot, 1927), vol. 1, 337–40; Knapp, "Landarbeiter und innere Kolonization" (1893), in his *Grundherrschaft und Rittergut. Vorträge, nebst biographischer Beilage* (Leipzig: Duncker & Humblot, 1897), 12–13; and Max Weber, *Die Verhältnisse der Landarbeiter im ostelbischen Deutschland*, Schriften des Vereins für

Sozialpolitik, vol. 55 (Leipzig: Duncker & Humblot, 1892), 11–19. See also Jordan, *Die Entstehung der konservativen Partei,* 60–73; Franz, "Landwirtschaft 1800–1850," 302–4; Richards, "Political Economy of *Gutswirtschaft*," passim; and Nipperdey, *Deutsche Geschichte 1800–1866,* 165.

191. Hauptmann von Versen, "Die Kartoffelbau für die besitloze Arbeiter-Klasse," *Allgemeine Landwirtschaftliche Monatsschrift* 5 (1841), 229.

192. Taylor, "A Premium Essay on the Practical, Economical and Profitable Arrangement of a Farm of 300 Acres Devoted to the Cultivation of Corn and Wheat as Staple Crops" (premium awarded by the Virginia State and Central Agricultural Societies, October, 1860), *Southern Planter* 21 (1861), 131. On cash payments and gifts to slaves, see Stampp, *The Peculiar Institution,* 166–67; and Eugene Genovese, *Roll, Jordan, Roll: The World the Slaves Made* (New York: Pantheon Books, 1974; Vintage paperback, 1976), 313–14. On slave garden plots and the selling of slave produce, see Stampp, *The Peculiar Institution,* 163–66, and Genovese, *Roll, Jordan, Roll,* 535–40.

193. J. A. Perkins, "The German Agricultural Worker, 1815–1914," *Journal of Peasant Studies* 11 (1984), 8. Hanna Schissler describes the *Inst* arrangement as "a kind of semifeudal sharecropping system." Schissler, "The Junkers: Notes on the Social and Historical Significance of the Agrarian Elite in Prussia," in Robert G. Moeller, ed., *Peasants and Lords in Modern Germany: Recent Studies in Agricultural History* (Boston: Allen & Unwin, 1986), 48, n. 66.

194. Kenneth Stampp points out that in the South "A few masters stimulated their laborers by making profit-sharing agreements with them"; Stampp, *The Peculiar Institution,* 167. Virginia in the 1830s was the site of a variation on this theme. In the Tidewater J. H. Barnard owned 2000 acres divided into two farms. At one of these farms he replaced his overseer with a slave foreman and divided his 20 "effective hands" into three competing groups, to which he gave annual payments (in the form of credits at a local merchant's store) "according to service and merit," all the payments totaling the former overseer's salary. Members of the top group received a full share of credit, members of the second a half-share, and members of the third a quarter-share. A slave could be promoted to a higher group, or demoted to a lower group, according to "delinquency or desert." Bernard considered the venture a resounding success. Although his neighbors were skeptical, fearing that the arrangement "will tend to foster discontent, and that spirit of insubordination which had its origins in abolitionism," Bernard felt that the arrangement had served to improve his relations with the slaves, and "they could scarcely be persuaded to change it by Arthur Tappan and his minions." He concluded that "avarice, combined with pride and vanity," were "stong principles even in the breast of a negro." Barnard, of Port Royal Virginia, "The Importance of Grass Crops— Unsuccessful Experiments," *Farmers' Register* 5 (1837), 171–73; and his "Statements of Practice in Tillage and Improvement of Rappahannock Lands," *Farmers' Register* 4 (1836), 61–63.

195. Mechanical threshers were in use in parts of provincial Prussia (for example, Litauen) even before the 1848 revolution, and were already having an adverse effect on the *Insten.* See Wilhelm Adolf Lette's report on provincial Prussia in *Annalen der Landwirtschaft* (1847), 27–28. For mechanical threshers in Pomerania by the late 1840s, see

Agricola, "Handdrusch und Maschinendrusch," *Allgemeine Landwirtschaftliche Monatschrift* (1848), 314–16.

196. Max Weber, "Die Entwicklungstendenzen in der Lage der ostelbischen Landarbeiter" (1894), in his *Gesammelte Aufzätze zur Sozial- und Wirtschaftsgeschichte* (Tübingen: J. C. B. Mohr (Paul Siebeck), 1924), 477–88. Keith Tribe provides a wide-ranging discussion of Weber's thoughts on this transformation in "Prussian Agriculture—German Politics: Max Weber 1892–1897," *Economy and Society* 12 (1983), 181–226.

197. To be sure, a modest though illicit trans-Atlantic slave trade continued throughout the antebellum era, despite an 1820 federal law that made engaging in the trade a form of piracy and punishable by death. Yet "probably fewer that 60,000 slaves were illegally brought into the country" between 1810 and 1860. James E. Crisp, "Closing of the African Slave Trade," in Miller and Smith, eds., *Dictionary of Afro-American Slavery*, 117.

198. Heywood Fleisig, "Slavery, the Supply of Agricultural Labor, and the Industrialization of the South," *Journal of Economic History* 36 (1976), 581–83. Cf. Gavin Wright's analysis of slavery as "providing an elastic labor supply at the farm level" in "Prosperity, Progress, and American Slavery," 302–36 (quotation from p. 303), and in his *Political Economy of the Cotton South*, esp. 155.

199. Clement Eaton, *The Growth of Southern Civilization, 1790–1860* (1961; New York: Harper Torchbooks, 1963), 28.

200. "As compared with serfdom, however, slavery possessed the manifest advantage that the laborer could be moved to the point of greatest productive advantage, while the serf was bound to a particular manor." Gray, *History of Agriculture in the Southern United States to 1860*, vol. 1, p. 471. Cf. Phillips, *American Negro Slavery*, 346: "slavery and indentured servitude . . . have this difference (from serfdom), immense for American purposes, that they permit labor to be territorially shifted, while serfdom keeps it locally fixed."

201. See Eaton, *A History of the Old South*, 218–21. The very limited impact of Ruffin's crusade is stressed in William M. Mathew, *Edmund Ruffin and the Crisis of Slavery in the Old South: The Failure of Agricultural Reform* (Athens & London: Univ. of Georgia Press, 1988). To be sure, there were also outspoken proponents of agricultural reform in the Old Southwest; the best-known was probably Dr. Martin W. Philips, editor of the short-lived *South-western Farmer* (1842–43) of Raymond, Mississippi, who had migrated from South Carolina to Hinds County in 1831, and moved in 1836 to a small plantation that he named "Log Hall." On Philips, see Albert L. Demaree, *The American Agricultural Press, 1819–1869* (New York: Columbia Univ. Press, 1941), 103–4; and John Hebron Moore, *Agriculture in Ante-bellum Mississippi* (New York: Bookman Associates, 1958), 97–98 and passim. The impetus toward agricultural reform, like the impetus toward greater investment in industrial enterprises, gained strength from relatively low cotton prices in the 1840s. But cotton prices rose steadily during the 1850s, and Southwestern agriculture may have been less diversified at the end of the decade than at its beginning. See William Barney, *The Secessionist Impulse: Alabama and Mississippi in 1860* (Princeton: Princeton Univ. Press, 1974), 159–60.

202. "Cotton," reprinted in *American Cotton Planter and Soil of the South* (April 1860), 163–64.

203. William McKinley Book, Georgia, 1842–63, microfilm of original manuscript in the Southern Historical Collection at the University of North Carolina at Chapel Hill.

204. A. C. Morton, Petersburg, Va., 1 May 1855, "Agriculture in North Carolina," *Carolina Cultivator* 1 (June 1855), 131–32, and Cathey, *Agricultural Developments in North Carolina, 1783–1860,* 88–89, 190–91. Cathey says that Burgwyn was "one of North Carolina's most successful planters and heaviest purchasers of farm implements and machinery." Ibid., 69. On Burgwyn and his older brother Tom, see also Solon Robinson, "Mr. Robinson's Tour—No. 12," in Herbert A. Kellar, ed., *Solon Robinson, Pioneer and Agriculturist. Selected Writings* (2 vols.; Indianapolis: Indiana Historical Bureau, 1936; rpt. ed., New York: Da Capo Press, 1968), vol. 2, pp. 223–31; and Archie K. Davis, *Boy Colonel of the Confederacy: The Life and Times of Henry King Burgwyn, Jr.* (Chapel Hill & London: Univ. of North Carolina Press, 1985), 16–26.

205. Gray, *History of Southern Agriculture,* vol. 1, p. 483; Stampp, *The Peculiar Institution,* 30; and James Oakes, *The Ruling Race: A History of American Slaveholders* (New York: Knopf, 1982), 65. In 1860 McKinley employed two overseers, and seems to have owned about 100 slaves. William McKinley Book, Georgia, 1842–63. Burgwyn owned two different plantations and employed two overseers as early as 1843. H. K. Burgwyn, in Boston, 25 Sept. 1843, to overseer Arthur Souter, at Hillside plantation, in Burgwyn Family Papers, Southern Historical Collection of the University of North Carolina at Chapel Hill; in this letter he mentions overseer "Mr. Taylor," at Thornburg plantation. For an improving and extremely entrepreneurial large planter in Tidewater Virgina, see Solon Robinson, "Farm of Mr. Bolling in Virginia" (originally in *American Agriculturist* for 1849), in Kellar, ed. *Solon Robinson,* vol. 2, pp. 231–35, dealing with Robert P. Bolling at Sandy Point (the confluence of the James and Chickahominy rivers), who owned 180 slaves, 4000 acres of timberland, and planted 2700 acres in wheat, corn, oats, and clover.

206. Richardson, "Management of a Farm in Prince Edward" (dated 2 Feb. 1852), *Southern Planter* 12 (1852), 114–17, and 1850 Census, Slave Schedule for Prince Edward County, microfilm in Virginia State Library, Richmond.

207. Solon Robinson made an especially interesting observation in 1851, after mentioning lawyer-planter William C. Dawson of Greene County, Georgia: "Speaking of lawyers, reminds me that some of the most improving cultivators of the soil, are gentlemen of this profession. Why? Because they are reading men. They are disposed to look to every source of information by which they can gain knowledge in the profession of farming, as well as law." "The Traveler—No. 7" (originally in *American Agriculturist* for 1851), in Kellar, ed., *Solon Robinson,* vol. 2, 472–73.

208. Julius Rubin, "The Limits of Agricultural Reform in the Nineteenth-Century South," *Agricultural History* 49 (1975), 362–73; the quotation is from p. 364. Two recent local studies that lend support to Rubin's argument are J. William Harris, *Plain Folk and Gentry in a Slave Society: White Liberty and Black Slavery in Augusta's Hinterlands* (Middletown, Conn.: Wesleyan Univ. Press, 1985), 28–29, which deals with a cotton-growing area in the Lower South; and, for the Upper South, Frederick F. Siegel, *The Roots of Southern Distinctiveness: Tobacco and Society in Danville, Virginia, 1780–1865* (Chapel Hill and London: Univ. of North Carolina Press, 1987), 68–75. Siegel's additional

emphasis on "the underlying sandy infertility of the soil" in Southside Virginia's Pittsylvania County is not relevant to a comparison of the South and East Elbia, where much of the soil was also very sandy. Siegel also suggests that a truly progressive capitalist agriculture circa 1850 involved the dairy herds that characterized farming in the Valley of Virginia and the Middle Atlantic states. But this rather arbitrary standard discounts the very influences of climate and soil fertility that Siegel is at such pains to stress. For example, J. A. Perkins explains that "The majority of farmers in the eastern territories (of Prusso-Germany) were not in a position to fatten cattle or establish dairies on permanent pasture in consequence of the infertility of their land, and in central Germany the rainfall was too small for such activities to be remunerative. Sheep rather than cattle were the typical livestock of extensive farming systems under German conditions." Perkins, "Agricultural Revolution in Germany," 78.

209. In beet-growing areas of central Germany, "even the best of soils had begun to 'tire' of the crop (by the 1860s) through the build-up of nematodes or eelworms in the soil." Perkins, "Agricultural Revolution in Germany," 83.

210. U.S. Census Office, *Preliminary Report of the Eighth Census* (Washington, D.C.: Government Printing Office, 1862), 8.

211. Computed from statistics in Georg von Viebahn, *Statistik,* vol. 2, p. 164.

212. Prussia's six eastern provinces encompassed 90,283 square miles in the 1850s and had a total population of just under 13 million in 1858. Mississippi and Louisiana encompassed 47,146 and 46,431 square miles respectively, for a total of 93,577; and the 15 slave states had a total population of 12.3 million (white and black) in 1860.

213. Henry Marie Brackenridge, "The Southern States" (originally published in the *New York Mirror,* 24 Dec. 1831), in Schwaab, *Travels,* vol. 1, p. 247. Brackenridge (1786–1871) moved from his native Pittsburgh to Louisiana at age seven, and served as a judge in Florida until 1832.

214. P. L. Ford, ed., *Writings of Thomas Jefferson,* vol. 3, p. 190, cited in William C. Bagley, *Soil Exhaustion and the Civil War* (Washington, D.C.: American Council on Public Affairs, 1942), 17.

215. Southron, "The Policy of the Southern Planter," *American Cotton Planter and Soil of the South* (Oct. 1857), 293. Cf. Edmund Ruffin, "Sketch of the Progress of Agriculture in Virginia, and the Causes of Its Decline, and Present Depression. An Address to the Historical and Philosophical Society of Virginia, by Edmund Ruffin," in *Farmers' Register* (1836), 748: "In a new country, where land is cheap and labor dear, it is good economy so to direct tillage that each laborer might be able to yield the greatest product (without much regard to the land) and also, in such manner that as little intellect as possible may be necessary in the operative class."

216. "Editor," *American Cotton Planter and Soil of the South* (Jan. 1858), 39.

217. (Jacob Cardozo), "The Cotton Region of the United States," *DeBow's Review* (April 1848), 370. This essay appeared earlier as "The Growth and Consumption of Cotton," *Southern Quarterly Review* (Jan. 1848), the quotations on pp. 122–23. On Cardozo as the probable author, see Melvin M. Leiman, *Jacob N. Cardozo: Economic Thought in the Antebellum South* (New York and London: Columbia Univ. Press, 1966), 248.

218. "Address of Hon. J. M. Gallant before the Agricultural Society of Amite County," *Mississippi Planter & Mechanic* (published at Jackson), vol. 1 (Dec. 1857), 282–92. Amite

Country, located in southwestern Mississippi, was definitely plantation country; in 1860 slaves made up over half of its population.

219. Wright, *The Political Economy of the Cotton South,* pp. 132–33; and Randolph B. Campbell, *An Empire for Slavery: The Peculiar Institution in Texas, 1821–1865* (Baton Rouge & London: Louisiana State Univ. Press, 1989), 64–65.

220. I am paraphrasing Edgar T. Thompson, "The Plantation: The Physical Basis of Traditional Race Relations" (1939), in *Plantation Societies, Race Relations, and the South. The Regimentation of Populations: Selected Papers of Edgar T. Thompson* (Durham, N.C.: Duke Univ. Press, 1975), 89–90.

221. Michael Tadman, "Slave Trading in the Ante-bellum South: An Estimate of the Extent of the Inter-Regional Slave Trade," *Journal of American Studies* 13 (1979), 195–220. However, according to Campbell, *An Empire for Slavery,* 51, of "the thousands of new bondsmen" who came to Texas each year from 1836 to 1860, "the majority migrated with their owners," although Campbell concedes that "the quantitative evidence necessary for conclusive proof does not exist." According to Laurence J. Kotlikoff and Sebastian Pinera, between 1850 and 1860 alone—the only antebellum decade in which a new slave state did not enter the Union—the Carolinas, Georgia, Virginia, Tennessee, Kentucky, Maryland, and the District of Columbia showed a net export of almost 270,000 slaves south or west to Texas, Louisiana, Mississippi, Alabama, Florida, and Arkansas, a number which they estimate to be 32% of all slave movements for 1790–1860. Nonetheless, the authors argue that the older slave states had "no economic stake" in westward expansion, since the income from slave sales was offset by concurrent reductions in land product prices. Kotlikoff and Pinera, "The Old South's Stake in the Inter-Regional Movement of Slaves, 1850–1860," *Journal of Economic History* 27 (1977), 434–47. Regardless of whether this trade-off in fact occurred, I do not think that many planters had a clear understanding of it.

222. "Professor Dew on Slavery," in *The Pro-slavery Argument; As Maintained by the Most Distinguished Writers of the Southern States* (Charleston, S.C.: Walker Richards, 1852; rpt. ed., New York: Negro Universities Press, 1968), 359, and Ruffin, "Agricultural Review," in *The Farmers' Register* 1 (June 1833), 39. On slave exports from the border and middle slave states, Virginia in particular, see Stampp, *The Peculiar Institution,* 238; and Freehling, *The Road to Disunion,* 24.

223. Thomas Affleck, "The Duties of an Overseer," reprinted in *American Cotton Planter* (1854), 356; also reprinted in *De Bow's Review* (1855), 345. Affleck's manual had gone through seven editions by 1857. Affleck, a native of Scotland, moved from Mississippi to Texas in 1858. See *William Kauffman Scarborough, The Overseer: Plantation Management in the Old South* (Baton Rouge: Louisiana State Univ. Press, 1966), 70–71; and Campbell, *An Empire for Slavery,* 199–200.

224. "An Address, Delivered by James L. Gaines, Esq., before the Moore County Agricultural Society, at Carthage, Moore County," *Carolina Cultivator* (July 1856), 131–32.

225. Gray, *History of Southern Agriculture,* vol. 2, pp. 898–900.

226. Hubard, resident at Saratoga plantation in Buckingham County, had owned the Nelson County farm since the 1830s. The advertisement ran in the Lynchburg *Virginian* from 11 November to 7 December 1859. Hubard Family Papers, Southern Historical

Collection, University of North Carolina at Chapel Hill. On Edmund Wilcox Hubard's entrepreneurial outlook, see his "On the Manner and Time of Employing Overseers," *Farmers' Register* 3 (April 1836), 713–15.

227. Tuscaloosa *Flag of the Union*, 20 Sept. 1843, cited in James Benson Sellers, *Slavery in Alabama* (University: Univ. of Alabama Press, 1950), 23.

228. Klein, *Geschichte der deutschen Landwirtschaft*, 30.

229. Sprengel, "Landwirtschaftliche Bericht aus Hinterpommern. Anfang April 1840," *Allgemeine Landwirtschaftliche Monatschrift* 1 (1840), 144.

230. Gutsbesitzer Lüdersdorf auf Christoplack, "Die landwirtschaftlichen Verhältnisse des Labiauer Kreises, in Reg.-Bezirk Königsberg," *Annalen der Landwirtschaft* 13 (1849), 116

231. Abel, *Agrarkrisen und Agrarkonjunktur*, 256.

232. *Landwirtschaftliche Centralblatt für Deutschland* 4 (1856), 140. The editor believed, however, that "Even the growing encumbering of estates with mortgages does not reduce their real security," because the ongoing growth of agricultural knowledge was bringing higher yields, and the growth of population and consumption assured "strong market demand."

Chapter 3. Contentious Concepts

1. Theda Skocpol and Margaret Somers, "The Uses of Comparative History in Macrosocial Inquiry," *Comparative Studies in Society and History* 22 (1980), 178. On history versus social science, see T. B. Bottomore, *Sociology: A Guide to Problems and Literature*, 2nd ed. (New York: Pantheon Books, 1971; Vintage paperback, 1972), 77, and Reinhard Bendix, *Nation-Building and Citizenship: Studies in Our Changing Social Order*, new enlarged ed. (Berkeley: Univ. of California Press, 1977), 170.

2. William McNeill's review of Skocpol's *States and Revolutions*, in *American Historical Review* 85 (1980), 86.

3. A persuasive argument for the interconnectedness between history and sociology is presented by Philip Abrams, *Historical Sociology* (Ithaca, N.Y.: Cornell Univ. Press, 1982), esp. ch. 1, "Introduction: Sociology as History," 3–17.

4. Skocpol and Summers, "The Uses of Comparative History," 178.

5. H. Stuart Hughes, *History as Art and as Science: Twin Vistas on the Past* (New York: Harper & Row, 1964), 6. Cf. the caveat issued by anthropologist Igor Kopytoff and historian Suzanne Miers in discussing the term slavery: "In scholarship, few pursuits are more sterile than the pursuit of 'correct' terminology and few declarations are more impotent than those proclaiming new obligatory definitions." Kopytoff and Miers, "Introduction to African 'Slavery' as an Institution of Marginality," in Miers and Kopytoff, eds., *Slavery in Africa: Historical and Anthropological Perspectives* (Madison: Univ. of Wisconsin Press, 1977), 76. However, for a cross-cultural approach to the phenomenon of slavery that grapples in stimulating fashion with the word's meaning, see sociologist Orlando Patterson, *Slavery and Social Death: A Comparative Study* (Cambridge, Mass., and London: Harvard Univ. Press, 1982).

6. Max Weber, "Religious Rejections of the World and Their Directions" (1915),

in H. H. Gerth & C. Wright Mills, eds. and trans., *From Max Weber: Essays in Sociology* (New York: Oxford Univ. Press, 1946), 324.

7. David S. Landes, *The Unbound Prometheus: Technological Change and Industrial Development in Western Europe from 1750 to the Present* (Cambridge: Cambridge Univ. Press, 1969), 540.

8. Marc Bloch, "Towards A Comparative History of European Societies" (1928), trans. J. S. Riemersma, in Frederick C. Lane and Riemersma, eds., *Enterprise and Secular Change: Readings in Economic History* (Homewood, Ill.: R. D. Irwin, 1953), 495.

9. C. E. Black, *The Dynamics of Modernization: A Study in Comparative History* (New York: Harper Torchbooks, 1966), 45.

10. Jürgen Kocka, "Theoretical Approaches to the Social and Economic History of Modern Germany: Some Recent Trends, Concepts, and Problems in Western and Eastern Germany," *Journal of Modern History* 47 (1975), 117.

11. Walter Hugins, "American History in Comparative Perspective," *Journal of American Studies* 11 (1977), 42–43.

12. Hughes, *History as Art and as Science*, 3.

13. Tipps, "Modernization Theory and the Comparative Study of Societies: A Critical Perspective," *Comparative Studies in Society and History* 15 (1973), 199. U.S. historian Richard D. Brown reported in the late 1970s that most historians reacted in comparable fashion, viewing modernization as "too broad and vague to be useful," or "as merely a new fad, a packaging gimmick that mixes the old wine of industrialization, urbanization, the Enlightenment, and the rise of the nation-state together in a new bottle." Brown, *Modernization: The Transformation of American Life, 1600–1865* (New York: Hill and Wang, 1976), 18–19. I suspect that these historians would also object to the recent formulations by Theodore H. Von Laue, *The World Revolution of Westernization: The Twentieth Century in Global Perspective* (New York: Oxford Univ. Press, 1987), esp. 301–16, and by Jean Baechler, "The Origins of Modernity: Caste and Feudality (Europe, India and Japan)," in Baechler et al., *Europe and the Rise of Capitalism* (Oxford & New York: Basil Blackwell, 1988), esp. 40. A recent brief for the concept's usefulness to historians of the South is Winfred B. Moore and Joseph F. Tripp, "Modernization and the South: An Introductory Essay," in Moore, Tripp, and Lyon G. Tyler, Jr., eds., *Developing Dixie: Modernization in a Traditional Society* (New York: Greenwood Press, 1988), xvii-xxiii.

14. See esp. Reinhard Bendix, "Tradition and Modernity Reconsidered," first published in *Comparative Studies in Society and History* 9 (1967); and republished with revisions in Bendix, *Nation-Building and Citizenship*, 361–434.

15. Hans-Ulrich Wehler, *Modernisierungstheorie und Geschichte* (Göttingen: Vandenhoeck & Ruprecht, 1975), 41–42, 47–50, 58.

16. Eric Hobsbawm, *The Age of Revolution: Europe, 1789–1848* (London: Weidenfeld and Nicolson, 1962), xv. Of course, the American Revolution of 1776 contributed mightily to the rising tide of revolution that engulfed France in 1789. See R. R. Palmer, *The Age of the Democratic Revolution: A Political History of Europe and America, 1760–1800* (2 vols.; Princeton: Princeton Univ. Press, 1959–64), vol. 1, ch. 9, "Europe and the American Revolution." And the roots of English industrialization can be traced all the way back to the uniqueness of English rural society during the medieval centuries;

see esp. Alan Macfarlane, *The Origins of English Individualism: The Family, Property and Social Transition* (1978; rpt. ed. Cambridge and New York: Cambridge Univ. Press, 1979).

17. Bendix, *Nation-Building and Citizenship*, 361, 122.

18. Bendix, *Kings or People: Power and the Mandate to Rule* (Berkeley, Los Angeles, & London: Univ. of California Press, 1978), esp. ch. 1, "Introduction."

19. Ibid., 12.

20. Bendix, *Nation-Building and Citizenship*, 96–97, cites T. H. Marshall to demonstrate the connection between equality before the law and economic individualism: "Civil rights are essential to a competitive market economy in that 'they give to each man, as part of his individual status, the power to engage as an independent unit in the economic struggle.'" The quotation is taken from Marshall, *Class, Citizenship and Social Development* (Garden City, N.Y.: Doubleday, 1964), 87.

21. Michael Kammen, "The Historian's Vocation and the State of the Discipline in the United States," in Kammen, ed., *The Past Before Us: Contemporary Historical Writing in the United States* (Ithaca, N.Y.: Cornell Univ. Press, 1980), 38–39. Similar comments are in Heidi Wunder, "The Mentality of Rebellious Peasants—The Samland Peasant Rebellion of 1525" (1975), in Bob Scribner and Gerhard Benecke, eds., *The German Peasant War of 1525—New Viewpoints* (London: George Allen and Unwin, 1979), 144–45.

22. Edward Pessen, *Riches, Class, and Power Before the Civil War* (Lexington, Mass.: Heath, 1973), 165.

23. William P. Reddy, *Money and Liberty in Modern Europe: A Critique of Historical Understanding* (Cambridge: Cambridge Univ. Press, 1987), 105. Reddy's hearty critique of class analysis seems to focus on a rigid Marxian definition of class, and does not take sufficient account of the refinements and subtleties advocated by Weber. For Marx's and Weber's differing approaches to social classes and stratification, see the concise comments in T. B. Bottomore, *Classes in Modern Society* (London: George Allen and Unwin, 1965; Vintage paperback, 1966), 24–26; and in Adam Przeworski, *Capitalism and Social Democracy* (Cambridge & Paris: Cambridge Univ. Press and Editions de la Maison des Sciences de l'Homme, 1985), 64.

24. Joseph Schumpeter, "Social Classes in an Ethnically Homogenous Environment" (1927), in *Imperialism (&) Social Classes: Two Essays by Joseph Schumpeter*, trans. Heinz Norden (New York: Meridien Books, 1955), 105.

25. Przeworski, *Capitalism and Social Democracy*, 92–97: "Postscript (to Chapter 2): Methodological Individualism and the Concept of Class."

26. Great influence in this direction has been exerted by anthropologist Clifford Geertz, "Ideology as a Cultural System," in David E. Apter, ed., *Ideology and Discontent* (New York & London: Free Press and Collier Macmillan, 1964), 47–76. See, for example, Eric Foner, *Free Soil, Free Labor, Free Men: The Ideology of the Republican Party before the Civil War* (New York and London: Oxford Univ. Press, 1970), 4–5; and David Brion Davis, *The Problem of Slavery in the Age of Revolution, 1770–1823* (Ithaca, N.Y., & London: Cornell Univ. Press, 1975), 14; and Larry E. Tise, *Proslavery: A History of the Defense of Slavery in America* (Athens & London: Univ. of Georgia Press, 1987), xvi; and James J. Sheehan, *German History, 1770–1866* (Oxford: Clarendon Press,

1989), 589–90. The Theodorsons's *Modern Dictionary of Sociology* defines ideology as "a system of interdependent ideas (beliefs, traditions, principles, and myths) held by a particular group or society, which reflects, rationalizes, and defends its particular social, moral, religious, political, and economic institutional interests and commitments." George A. and Achilles G. Theodorson, *A Modern Dictionary of Sociology* (New York: Thomas Y. Crowell, 1969), 195. This formulation suggests that all members of a particular group or society endorse the same set of ideas, a suggestion that runs counter to what I have learned about planters and Junkers.

27. Peter Kolchin, *Unfree Labor: American Slavery and Russian Serfdom* (Cambridge, Mass.: Belknap Press of Harvard Univ. Press, 1987), 240.

28. The term "Old Prussian," a translation of the adjective *altpreußisch,* is used in Hans Rosenberg, *Bureaucracy, Aristocracy, and Autocracy: The Prussian: The Prussian Experience, 1660–1815* (Boston: Beacon Press, 1958), 221–28. During and after the so-called Stein-Hardenberg Reform Era, 1807–19, *altpreußisch* became a historical synonym for the adjectives *hochkonservativ* ("high conservative") and *ständisch-konservativ* ("corporatist-conservative"). Ernst Rudolf Huber has used these two terms exclusively in discussing conservatives in the 1840s, those whom I call Old Prussian. Huber, *Deutsche Verfassungsgeschichte seit 1789, II, Der Kampf um Einheit und Freiheit, 1830 bis 1850* (Stuttgart: W. Kohlhammer, 1960), 331–39.

29. E. P. Thompson, *The Making of the English Working Class* (New York: Pantheon and Vintage Books 1963), 9–10. Cf. Peter Laslett's distinction between a status group, "a number of people enjoying the same social status," and a class, "a number of people banded together in the exercise of collective power, political and economic." Laslett, *The World We Have Lost: England before the Industrial Age,* 2nd ed. (New York: Charles Scribner's Sons, 1971), 23–24.

30. See the discussion in Seymour Martin Lipset and Reinhard Bendix, "Karl Marx's Theory of Social Classes," in Lipset and Bendix, eds., *Class, Status, and Power: Social Stratification in Comparative Perspective,* 2nd ed. (New York: Free Press, 1966), 6–11.

31. Karl Marx and Friedrich Engels, *The German Ideology, Part I, with Selections from Parts Two and Three, Together With Marx's "Introduction to a Critique of Political Economy,"* ed. C. J. Arthur (New York: International Publishers, 1970), 82.

32. Jon Elster, *An Introduction to Karl Marx* (Cambridge: Cambridge Univ. Press, 1986), 129. This is an abridgement of Elster's *Making Sense of Marx* (Cambridge: Cambridge Univ. Press, 1985).

33. The quotations are from Marx and Engels, *German Ideology,* 64–65.

34. H. H. Gerth and C. Wright Mills, "Introduction: The Man and His Work," to Gerth and Mills, eds., *From Max Weber,* 62.

35. Otto Hintze, "Calvinism and Raison d'Etat in Early Seventeenth-Century Brandenburg," in Felix Gilbert, ed. and trans., with the assistance of Robert M. Berdahl, *The Historical Essays of Otto Hintze* (New York: Oxford Univ. Press, 1975), 95. Cf. Barbara J. Fields, "Ideology and Race in American History," in J. Morgan Kousser and James M. McPherson, eds., *Region, Race and Reconstruction: Essays in Honor of C. Vann Woodward* (New York & Oxford: Oxford Univ. Press, 1982), 152.

36. Marx and Engels, *German Ideology,* 64–65.

37. Thorstein Veblen, *Theory of the Leisure Class* (1899), in Max Lerner, ed., *The Portable Veblen* (New York: Viking, 1948), 86–90.

38. (Cardozo), "The Growth and Consumption of Cotton," *Southern Quarterly Review* (1848), 109–10. On Cardozo as the probable author, see Melvin M. Leiman, *Jacob N. Cardozo: Economic Thought in the Antebellum South* (New York and London: Columbia Univ. Press, 1966), 248.

39. Joseph G. Baldwin, *The Flush Times of Alabama and Mississippi: A Series of Sketches* (New York: Hill and Wang, 1957), quote on p. 72; and Gustav Freytag, *Debit and Credit*, trans. L.C.C. (New York: Harper and Brothers, 1858). On Freytag's novel, see Ernst K. Bramsted, *Aristocracy and the Middle Classes in Germany: Social Types in German Literature, 1830–1900*, rev. ed. (Chicago: Univ. of Chicago Press, 1964), 113–24.

40. Paul David and Peter Temin, "Capitalist Masters, Bourgeois Slaves," in Paul David et al, *Reckoning with Slavery: A Critical Study in the Quantitative History of American Slavery* (New York: Oxford Univ. Press, 1976), 40–44.

41. Alfred Huger to R. Bunch, 20 Oct. 1857; to William Porcher Miles, 23 Jan. 1858; to John Vanderhorst, 1 Aug. 1856; Alfred Huger Letterpress Books, 1853–63, Perkins Library, Duke University, Durham, N.C.

42. Director Geh. Ober-Regierungsrat von Beckedorff, "Die landwirtschafliche Vereine, ihre Zwecke, ihre Bestimmung und ihre Nutzen," *Annalen der Landwirtschaft* (1843), 222–23; and von Beckedorff, Grünhof, remarks made 28 Feb. 1841 as president of the directors of the Pomeranian Economic Society, *Allgemeine Landwirtschaftliche Monatschrift* (1841), 77–78. See Fritz Fischer, "Georg Philipp von Beckedorff," in Historische Kommission bei der Bayerischen Akademie der Wissenschaften, ed., *Neue Deutsche Biographie*, vol. 1 (Berlin: Duncker & Humblot, 1953), 709. Beckedorff's father was a clerk for the Lutheran Church Council of Hanover.

43. David Potter wrote in 1968 that "the landed proprietors of the South who opposed American nationalism were not unlike the landed proprietors in central Europe who opposed German or Polish or Italian or Hungarian or Bohemian nationalism. All of them were traditionalists. All feared to release from the bottle the genii of manhood suffrage, of democratic equality, of social mobility, of universal education—and in the South, of emancipation for almost four million slaves." Potter, "The Civil War in the History of the Modern World: A Comparative View," in his *The South and the Sectional Conflict* (Baton Rouge: Louisiana Sate Univ. Press, 1968), 292–93. Although mid-century Junkers certainly feared that German national unification would entail democracy, Polish and Hungarian landed aristocrats were often in the vanguard of nationalist leaders calling for the independence of Poland from Russia and Prussia or of Hungary from Austrian domination.

44. On this general subject of interaction between aristocracy and bourgeoisie, see the differing perspectives of Arno J. Mayer, *The Persistence of the Old Regime: Europe to the Great War* ((New York: Pantheon Books, 1981), esp. ch. 2, "The Ruling Classes: The Bourgeoisie Defers"; and David Blackbourn, "The Discreet Charm of the Bourgeoisie: Reappraising German History in the Nineteenth Century," in Blackbourn and Geoff Eley, *The Peculiarities of German History: Bourgeois Society and Politics in Nineteenth-Century Germany* (Oxford & New York: Oxford Univ. Press, 1984), esp. 228–37. As

Blackbourn emphasizes (p. 233), "The new élite which was formed in Germany in the nineteenth century, especially in the last decades, continued to have a powerful aristocratic component, as in England and elsewhere. But the bourgeoisie which constituted the growing part of this élite did not simply succumb to the aristocratic embrace. The nature of the symbiosis of old and new wealth, the terms on which the new men intermarried, bought estates, and received titles, is a subject that deserves closer attention. What seems too easy, even when we consider the classic examples of 'feudalization,' is to regard them as evidence of a simple one-way process. The process in question, like the growing bourgeois conservatism of which it formed a part, was altogether more ambiguous." For a perceptive summary and critique of Blackbourn's and Eley's often iconoclastic judgments on modern German history and historiography, see Robert G. Moeller, "Die Besonderheiten der Deutschen? Neue Beiträge zur Sonderwegsdiscussion" (text in English), *Internationale Schulbuchforschung. Zeitschrift des Georg-Eckert-Instituts* 4 (1982), 71–74.

45. Otto Pflanze, *Bismarck and the Development of Germany, Volume II: The Period of Consolidation, 1871–1880* (Princeton: Princeton Univ. Press, 1990), 92. Gerald D. Feldman points out that "The Junker-industrialist alliance, which Bismarck had cemented, lived on to dominate Prussian politics, promote high tariffs, support the imperialistic naval building program of the Wilhelmine era, and fight for the suppression of the labor movement. It corrupted the conservatives and split the bourgeois liberals." Feldman, *Army, Industry and Labor in Germany, 1914–1918* (Princeton: Princeton Univ. Press, 1966), 15. In the years after 1866, concludes James J. Sheehan in his study of German liberals, "Politically, a reevalution of the aristocracy was nourished by desires for an alliance with the conservatives against the left; socially by the ambitions of propertied and educated elites for aristocratic status; economically, by a growing communality of interests between protectionists in industry and agriculture." Sheehan, *German Liberalism in the Nineteenth Century,* 177.

46. Northern soldiers certainly did not think they were fighting Southerners to further "the growth of large-scale industry, large cities, and the leviathan state." Eric Foner, "The Causes of the American Civil War: Recent Interpretations and New Directions," *Civil War History* 20 (1974), 213–14.; this essay is reprinted in Foner, *Politics and Ideology in the Age of the Civil War* (Oxford & New York: Oxford Univ. Press, 1980), ch. 2.

47. The North as a whole gave Lincoln 55% percent of its votes, but "in seven of the eleven cities with populations of 50,000 or more, he failed to get a majority." David M. Potter, *The Impending Crisis, 1848–1861,* ed. Don E. Fehrenbacher (New York: Harper and Row, 1976), 443. On business interests in Massachusetts and New York City, see Thomas H. O'Connor, *The Lords of the Loom: The Cotton Whigs and the Coming of the Civil War* (New York: Scribners, 1968), and Philip S. Foner, *Business and Slavery: The New York Merchants and the Irrepressible Conflict* (Chapel Hill: Univ. of North Carolina Press, 1941). On racism as a powerful contributor to Northern opposition to slavery expansion, see esp. George M. Fredrickson, *The Black Image in the White Mind: The Debate on Afro-American Character and Destiny, 1817–1914* (New York: Harper and Row, 1971; Harper Torchbook, 1972), ch. 5, "White Nationalism: 'Free Soil' and the Ideal of Racial Homogeneity."

48. Barrington Moore, Jr., *Social Origins of Dictatorship and Democracy: Lord and Peasant in the Making of the Modern World* (Boston: Beacon Press, 1966), 428.

49. Abrams, *Historical Sociology,* 155.

50. Moore, *Social Origins of Dictatorship and Democracy,* xiv-xv.

51. Ibid., 115, 434.

52. Ibid., 152.

53. Ibid., xv, 112.

54. Ibid., 153–54.

55. Eugene D. Genovese, "Marxian Interpretations of the Slave South," in Barton Bernstein, ed., *Towards a New Past: Dissenting Essays in American History* (New York: Random House, 1968; Vintage paperback, 1969), 118–19. Genovese expanded his criticism of Moore a bit in *The World the Slaveholders Made: Two Essays in Interpretation* (New York: Pantheon Books, 1969; Vintage paperback, 1971), 228–30.

56. The quotation "planter capitalism" is taken from Albert V. House, "Introduction" to House, ed., *Planter Management and Capitalism in Ante-bellum Georgia: The Journal of Hugh Frazer Grant, Rice Grower* (New York: Columbia Univ. Press, 1954), 38–39. Although the monograph on slavery which Genovese was most concerned to discredit, Kenneth M. Stampp, *The Peculiar Institution: Slavery in the Ante-bellum South* (New York: Knopf, 1956), does not engage in a theoretical discussion of capitalism, the neoclassical approach is clearly implicit in Stampp's analysis, especially ch. 9, "Profit and Loss."

57. Lewis Cecil Gray, *History of Agriculture in the Southern United States to 1860* (2 vols., Washington, D.C.: Carnegie Institution, 1933; rpt. ed. Gloucester, Mass.: Peter Smith, 1958), vol. 1, p. 302.

58. Eugene D. Genovese, *Roll, Jordan, Roll: The World the Slaves Made* (New York: Pantheon Books,1974; Vintage paperback, 1976), 122.

59. Eugene D. Genovese and Elizabeth Fox-Genovese, "The Slave Economies in Political Perspective," *Journal of American History* 66 (1979), 22, 12; this essay is reprinted in their *Fruits of Merchant Capital: Slavery and Bourgeois Property in the Rise and Expansion of Capitalism* (Oxford: Oxford Univ. Press, 1983), ch. 2.

60. Genovese first made this argument in "The Significance of the Slave Plantation for Southern Economic Development," *Journal of Southern History* 28 (1962), 422–37; this essay is reprinted in Genovese, *The Political Economy of Slavery: Studies in the Econmy and Society of the Slave South* (New York: Pantheon Books, 1965; Vintage paperback, 1967), ch. 7, and in Hugh G. J. Aitken, ed., *Did Slavery Pay? Readings in the Economics of Black Slavery in the United States* (Boston: Houghton Mifflin, 1971), 251–70.

61. Barbara Jeanne Fields, "The Advent of Capitalist Agriculture: The New South in a Bourgeois World," in Thavolia Glymph and John J. Kushma, eds., *Essays on the Postbellum Southern Economy* (College Station, Texas: Texas A & M Univ. Press for the University of Texas at Arlington, 1985), 74, 76, 88, 75. The same emphasis on "capitalist social relations" informs Fields's monograph *Slavery and Freedom on the Middle Ground: Maryland during the Nineteenth Century* (New Haven & London: Yale Univ. Press, 1985).

62. Fields, "Advent of Capitalist Agriculture," 74–75, 84–86.

63. Steven Hahn, "Emancipation and the Development of Capitalist Agriculture:

The South in Comparative Perspective," in Kees Gispen, ed., *What Made the South Different?* (Jackson: Univ. Press of Mississippi, 1990), 74. This essay is complementary to Hahn's "Class and State in Postemancipation Societies: Southern Planters in Comparative Perspective," *American Historical Review* 95 (1990), 75–98.

64. Hahn, "Emancipation and the Development of Capitalist Agriculture," 83–86. Cf. William N. Parker, "Capitalism: Southern Style," in his *Europe, America, and the Wider World: Essays on the Economic History of Western Capitalism, Volume 2: America and the Wider World* (Cambridge: Cambridge Univ. Press, 1991), 89: "The pre-capitalist form in the North and in the non-plantation areas in the South was the semi-self-sufficient family farm."

65. Richard Rubinson, "Political Transformations in Germany and the United States," in Barbara Hockey Kaplan, ed., *Social Change in the Capitalist World Economy*, Political Economy of World-System Annals, vol. 1 (Beverly Hills & London: Sage Publications, 1978), 39–73.

66. Immanuel Wallerstein, "The Rural Economy in Modern World Society," in his *The Capitalist World Economy* (Cambridge: Cambridge Univ. Press, 1979), 120. The best brief introduction to Wallerstein's outlook is his "The Rise and Future Demise of the World Capitalist System: Concepts for Comparative Analysis," *Comparative Studies in Society and History* 16 (1974), 387–415; reprinted in *The Capitalist World Economy*, 1–36. See also Wallerstein, *Historical Capitalism* (London: Verso, 1983).

67. Immanuel Wallerstein, *The Modern World-System: Capitalist Agriculture and the Origins of the European World Economy in the Sixteenth Century* (New York: Academic Press, 1974), esp. 88–91, 99–100.

68. Rubinson, "Political Transformations in Germany and the United States"; the quotations are on pp. 53 and 68.

69. Genovese, "Marxian Interpretations of the Slave South," 112. Jay Mandle has amplified this argument that the plantation was neither feudal nor capitalist. Because he, like Genovese, has a decidedly free-labor view of capitalism, Mandle argues that the postbellum plantation was not capitalist because planters still made use of "nonmarket" mechanisms of labor coercion. The plantation was a "market-oriented but archaic social organization." Mandle, *The Roots of Black Poverty: The Southern Plantation Economy After the Civil War* (Durham, N.C.: Duke Univ. Press, 1978), 10–14.

70. Dietrich Zwicker, *Der amerikanische Staatsmann John C. Calhoun, Ein Kämpfer gegen die 'Ideen von 1789': Studien zur Vorgeschichte des amerikanischen Bürgerkrieges*, Historische Studien, no. 280 (Berlin: Emil Ebering, 1935), 111–12.

71. Elizabeth A. R. Brown, "The Tyranny of a Construct: Feudalism and Historians of Medieval Europe," *American Historical Review* 79 (1974), 1086. She seems to favor restricting use of the word "feudal" to its narrow meaning, "relating to fiefs." Ibid., 1084. Marx and his disciples are partly to blame for the vague and indiscriminate uses to which the terms feudalism and feudal are often put. As Otto Brunner explains, for Marx feudalism existed "anywhere in the world where there are large estates with dependent people on them." Otto Brunner, "Feudalism—The History of a Concept" (1958), trans. Miriam Samburscky & Frederic L. Cheyette, in Cheyette, ed., *Lordship and Community in Medieval Europe: Selected Readings* (New York: Holt, Rinehart and Winston 1968), 45–46. J. S. Critchley points up the influence of the Marxist legacy: "Land re-

form' has a long history, and in this context feudalism, as something to be abolished, can refer both to the political and economic dependence of the landless upon the landowners, and to the disproportionate power enjoyed by the latter, because of their wealth within the society as a whole." Critchley, *Feudalism* (London: Allen Unwin, 1978), 127.

72. See Marc Bloch, *Feudal Society, vol. 2: Social Classes and Political Authority*, trans. L. A. Manyon (Chicago: Univ. of Chicago Press, 1961), esp. 446, and Dietrich Gerhard, *Old Europe: A Study of Continuity, 1000–1800* (New York: Academic Press, 1981), 15–16.

73. See Francis James West, "On the Ruins of Feudalism—Capitalism?," in Eugene Kamenka and R. S. Neale, eds., *Feudalism, Capitalism and Beyond* (London: Edward Arnold, 1977), 51–60, and Georg Friedrich Knapp, "Die Erbuntertänigkeit und die kapitalistische Wirtschaft" (1891), in his *Die Landarbeiter in Knechtschaft und Freiheit*, 2nd ed. (Leipzig: Duncker & Humblot, 1909), 62–63.

74. See Raymond de Roover, "Capitalism," in Joseph Dunner, ed., *Handbook of World History: Concepts and Issues* (New York: Philosophical Library, 1967), 149–50, and Nathan Rosenberg and L. E. Birdzell, Jr., *How the West Grew Rich: The Economic Transformation of the Industrial World* (New York: Basic Books, 1986), 12.

75. Thus, Hans-Ulrich Wehler sees in modernization theory the potential "to provide foundations for an analysis of total social change." He devotes considerable discussion toward demonstrating that the Marxist framework is inadequate to account for the variegated developmental patterns of modern societies, and concludes that "historical-comparative modernization theory" offers a multi-variable and hence more viable theory of social change. Noting that "one who shares the historical philosophy of Marx, wants to possess certainty about what are the essential motive powers of history," Wehler correctly maintains that the historian need not possess such absolute certainty in order to embrace the general aim of Marxist historiography: that is, "to grasp the working connections between economic development, social change, and political authority, ideas and ideologies, and out of their reciprocal action to derive the dynamic of the developmental process." Wehler, *Moderniserungstheorie und Geschichte*, 39, 56, 7.

76. Jean Baechler, *The Origins of Capitalism*, trans. from the 1971 French ed. by Barry Cooper (New York: St. Martin's Press, 1975), 144.

77. Jürgen Kocka, *Klassengesellschaft im Krieg. Deutsche Sozialgeschichte, 1914–1918* (Göttingen: Vandenhoeck and Ruprecht, 1973), 149, n. 14. This book has been translated into English by Barbara Weinberger as *Facing Total War: German Society, 1914–1918* (Leamington Spa, Engl.: Berg Publishers, 1984), and Weinberger's rendition of Kocka's definition goes as follows: "Capitalism is to be understood as an economic system that is predominantly based on private ownership and private control of capital for the production and exchange of goods for profit. Modern industrial capitalism, with which we are exclusively concerned here, is additionally determined by industrial enterprise based on capital accounting and formally free, contractually regulated wage labour." Ibid., 181, n. 15. That nineteenth-century Junkers clearly qualified as "agrarian capitalists" by this definition, see Robert G. Moeller, "Introduction" to Moeller, ed., *Peasants and Lords in Modern Germany: Recent Studies in Agricultural History* (Boston: Allen & Unwin, 1986), 11.

78. Susan Archer Mann, *Agrarian Capitalism in Theory and Practice* (Chapel Hill &

London: Univ. of North Carolina Press, 1990), 127, 139. Mann is a specialist in the history of Southern agriculture who endorses the Marxian perspective on capitalism as a social organization of production based on free wage labor. While she evaluates both antebellum slavery and postbellum sharecropping as "noncapitalist" forms of production, she also feels that "historians have ignored the impact the peculiar natural features of agricultural production had on limiting the capitalist development of the South" (pp. 75, 79). Her book 'emphasizes that "the labor processes that characterize agriculture continue to be significantly different from those in modern industry" due to "the problematic of agriculture as a natural production system"; hence "the persistence of the family farm" (pp. 26–27).

79. Raymond de Roover, after pointing to the distinction between private and state capialism, notes that "In the minds of most people, however, the concept of capitalism is associated with private ownership of the instruments of production." De Roover, "Capitalism," 150.

80. See Baechler, *Origins of Capitalism*, esp. 41, 79–82, and Rosenberg and Birdzell, *How the West Grew Rich*, esp. 24, 61–62, 87–88, 136–39.

81. E. J. Hobsbawm, *Industry and Empire. The Making of Modern English Society, Vol. II: 1750 to the Present Day* (New York: Pantheon Books, 1968), 33–34.

82. The greater governmental support for railroad construction provided by various levels of government in the U.S. than in Prussia, and hence the need to make a clear distinction between economic and political liberalism, are demonstrated by Colleen A. Dunlavy, "Political Structure and Early Railroad Development: The United States and Prussia" (paper presented in Reno, Nevada, at the 1988 annual meeting of the Organization of American Historians). Dunlavy's paper is based on her "Politics and Industrialization: Early Railroads in the United States and Prussia" (Ph.D. diss., MIT, 1988).

83. M. Boyd Coyner, "John Hartwell Cocke of Bremo. Agriculture and Slavery in the Antebellum South" (Ph.D. diss., University of Virginia, 1961), 22–23, 266–87; and Charles S. Sydnor, *The Development of Southern Sectionalism, 1819–1848* (1948; rpt. ed., Baton Rouge: Louisiana State Univ. Press, 1968), 260–61, 271; and Gray, *History of Agriculture in the Southern United States to 1860*, vol. 2, p. 899; Lacy K. Ford, *Origins of Southern Radicalism: The South Carolina Upcountry, 1800–1860* ((New York & Oxford: Oxford Univ. Press, 1988), 18, 219–43; Milton Sydney Heath, *Constructive Liberalism: The Role of the State in the Economic Development of Georgia to 1860* (Cambridge, Mass.: Harvard Univ. Press, 1954), 254–92; and Peter Wallenstein, *From Slave South to New South: Public Policy in Nineteenth-Century Georgia* (Chapel Hill & London: Univ. of North Carolina Press, 1987), 35–39; Wallenstein uses the term "planter-capitalists" on p. 38.

84. M. Tcherkinsky, *The Landschaften and Their Mortgage Credit Operations in Germany, 1770–1920* (Rome: International Institute of Agriculture, 1922), 9–16; Walter Görlitz, *Die Junker: Adel und Bauer im deutschen Osten*, 3rd ed. (Limburg a. d. Lahn: C. A. Starke, 1964), 131–32, 213; and Frank B. Tipton, Jr., *Regional Variations in the Economic Development of Germany During the Nineteenth Century* (Middletown, Conn.: Wesleyan Univ. Press, 1976), 53–54; W. O. Henderson, *The State and the Industrial Revolution in Prussia, 1740–1870* (Liverpool: Liverpool Univ. Press, 1958), 163–68; Martin Kitchen, *The Political Economy of Germany, 1815–1914* (London & Montreal: Croom Helm and McGill-Queen's Univ. Press, 1978), 49–51; Norman J. G. Pounds, *The Upper Silesian*

Industrial Region, Slavic and East European Series, vol. 11 (Bloomington: Indiana Univ. Publications, 1958), 62, 71–72, 97–98; and Eduard Bleich, ed., *Der Erste Vereinigte Landtag in Berlin, 1847* (4 vols.; Berlin, 1847; rpt. ed., Vaduz, Lichtenstein: Topos Verlag, 1977), vol. 4, pp. 1448–49, 1476–77, 1481–82 (7 June 1847 speeches of Pomeranian delegate von Heyden and Prussian delegates von Brünneck and Graf von Finkenstein). Dietrich Eichholtz, *Junker und Bourgeoisie vor 1848 in der Preussischen Eisenbahngeschichte* (Berlin: Akademie-Verlag, 1962), tends to exaggerate Junker opposition to and fear of railroads.

85. Rosenberg and Birdzell, *How the West Grew Rich,* 71–72.

86. William N. Parker, *Europe, America, and the Wider World. Essays on the Economic History of Western Capitalism. Volume 1: Europe and the World Economy* (Cambridge: Cambridge Univ. Press, 1984), 144–46.

87. Györky Ranki, "Probleme der komparativen Geschichtsschreibung," *Jahrbuch für Geschichtswissenschaft,* 1978, Part II, p. 141.

88. On the United States, see Douglass C. North, *The Economic Growth of the United States, 1790–1860* (Englewood Cliffs, N.J.: Prentice Hall, 1961; Norton paperback, 1966), esp. 66–74; and Stuart Bruchey, *The Roots of American Economic Growth, 1607–1861* (New York: Harper Torchbooks, 1968), esp. 159–60; and Stanley Lebergott, *The Americans: An Economic Record* (New York & London: Norton, 1984), 198–209; and Sydney Ratner, James H. Soltow, and Richard Sylla, *The Evolution of the American Economy: Growth, Welfare, and Decision Making* (New York: Basic Books, 1979), 222–26, which emphasizes the importance of intrasectional as well as intersectional trade. On Prusso-Germany see Walther G. Hoffman, "The Take-Off in Germany," in W. H. Rostow, ed., *The Economics of Take-Off into Sustained Growth* (New York: St. Martin's Press, 1965), 100–101; Knut Borchardt, "Germany 1700–1914," trans. George Hammersley, in Carlo M. Cipolla, ed., *The Fontana Economic History of Europe. The Emergence of Industrial Societies, Part One* (London & Glasgow: Collins/Fontana Books 1973), 101, Tipton, *Regional Variations in the Economic Development of Germany During the Nineteenth Century,* 13–38; and Hans-Ulrich Wehler, *The German Empire, 1871–1918,* trans. from the 1973 German edition by Kim Traynor (Leamington Spa, Eng., & Dover, N.H: Berg Publishers, 1985), 11–12. East German historians tended to emphasize that in Prusso-Germany during the early nineteenth century, as earlier in England, the expropriation and dispossession of a great portion of the peasantry, and the concurrent destruction of rural household industry, created both a pool of labor for the new industrial proletariat and the inner market necessary for the development of capitalist industry. Perhaps the most authoritative exposition of this argument is Hartmut Harnisch, *Kapitalistische Agrarreform und Industrielle Revolution: Agrarhistorische Untersuchungen über das ostelbische Preussen zwischen Spatfeudalismus und bürgerlich-demokratischer Revolution von 1848/49 unter besonderer Berücksichtigung der Provinz Brandenburg,* Veröffentlichungen des Staatsarchivs Potsdam, vol. 19 (Weimar: Hermann Böhlaus Nachfolger, 1984), esp. 14. As the title indicates, Harnisch's focus is on the province of Brandenburg, which contained the Berlin-Potsdam district, one of two significant industrial areas in nineteenth-century East Elbian Prussia. For a comparable analysis of the other significant industrial area, Upper Silesia, see Michael R. Haines, "Agriculture and Development in Prussian Upper Silesia, 1846–1913," *Journal of Economic History* 42 (1982), 355–84.

89. Weber emphasized rational calculation *and* free labor as essential to modern capitalism. "Capitalism is identical with the pursuit of profit, and forever renewed profit, by means of continuous, rational, capitalistic enterprise." Because "exact calculation" was "only possible on a basis of free labor," Weber equated "the modern form of capitalism" with "the rational capitalistic organization of (formally) free labor." Weber, *The Protestant Ethic and the Spirit of Capitalism* (1904–5), trans. Talcott Parsons (New York: Scribner, 1958), 17–22. Anthropologist Eric R. Wolf, *Europe and the People Without Memory* (Berkeley, Los Angeles, & London: Univ. of California Press, 1982), 297–98, argues that Weber defined capitalism as simply pursuit of profit in the marketplace.

90. The quotation is from Wolf, *Europe and the People Without Memory*, 23. According to Wolf, there is "no such thing as mercantile or merchant capitalism," since "the capitalist mode of production did not come into being until the latter part of the eighteenth century" (pp. 79, 298).

91. See MacFarlane, *The Origins of English Individualism*, ch. 2, "When England Ceased to be a Peasant Society: Marx, Weber and the Historians," and ch. 6, "English Economy and Society in the Thirteenth to Fifteenth Centuries."

92. Marx's correspondence did refer to "capitalism" in 1877. Rosenberg and Birdzell, *How the West Grew Rich*, xi.

93. See R. Stephen Warner, "The Methodology of Marx's Comparative Analysis of Modes of Production," in Ivan Vallier, ed., *Comparative Methods in Sociology. Essays on Trends and Applications* (Berkeley: Univ. of California Press, 1971), 51–60, and G. A. Cohen, *Karl Marx's Theory of History: A Defense* (Oxford: Clarendon Press, 1978), 180–93.

94. Karl Marx, *The Grundrisse: Foundations of the Critique of Political Economy*, trans. Martin Nicolaus (Harmondsworth, Eng.: Penguin Books, 1973), 513.

95. Marx, "Colonial Land, Farming, and Capitalism," from *Theories of Surplus Value*, in Marx, *On America and the Civil War*, ed. Saul K. Padover (New York: McGraw-Hill, 1972), 29.

96. Marx, *Capital, A Critique of Political Economy, Vol. I: The Process of Capitalist Production*, ed. Frederick Engels (New York: International Publishers, 1967), 759–60.

97. Marx, *Poverty of Philosophy* (New York: International Publishers, 1963), 111.

98. Friedrich Engels, *Socialism Utopian and Scientific, With the Essay on "The Mark,"* trans. Edward Aveling (New York: International Publishers, 1935), 90.

99. Baechler, *Origins of Capitalism*, 57.

100. Fernand Braudel, *Civilization and Capitalism, 15th–18th Century, Volume II: The Wheels of Commerce*, trans. from the 1979 French ed. by Sian Reynolds (New York: Harper & Row, 1982), 251.

101. Braudel, *Afterthoughts on Material Civilization and Capitalism*, trans. Patricia Ranum (Baltimore: Johns Hopkins Univ. Press, 1977), 45, 112–13.

102. Braudel, *Wheels of Commerce*, 265, 271–72. Similarly tortuous distinctions seem to inform Peter Kriedte's valuable study *Peasants, Landlords and Merchant Capitalists. Europe and the World Economy, 1500–1800*, trans. from the 1980 German ed. by V. R. Berghahn (Cambridge: Cambridge Univ. Press, 1983). Kriedte evaluates the post-medieval enserfment of East Elbia's peasantry as a "refeudalization of agriculture," even though "the world market rather than the seigneurial estate provided the central reference point."

During the sixteenth century the "European market widened to form the world market," and in response both the *Rittergüter* of East Elbia and the new slave plantations in the Americas participated in an "enforced commercialization'" of agriculture. Kriedte even concludes that "the world market which was slowly coming into existence acted as the engine of proto-industrial growth" in western Europe, and thereby helped effect the transition from "merchant capitalism" to industrial capitalism (pp. 21–22, 30, 40, 16–17, 13–14). The phrase "enforced commercialization" is taken from the influential Polish scholar and orthodox Marxist Withold Kula, on whom Kriedte relies heavily. See Kula, *An Economic Theory of the Feudal System: Towards a Model of the Polish Economy, 1500–1800*, trans. from the 1962 Polish ed. by Lawrence Garner (London: NLB, 1976).

103. Kocka, *Klassengesellschaft im Krieg*, 149, n. 14. Cf. Richard Graham, "Economics or Culture? The Development of the U.S. South and Brazil in the Days of Slavery," in Kees Gispen, ed., *What Made the South Different?* (Jackson & London: Univ. Press of Mississippi, 1990), 98: "Making labor-power into a commodity to be traded in a market is a valid definition of industrial capitalism." However, Graham also describes debates over the "proper definition" of capitalism as "futile."

104. Sidney W. Mintz, "The So-Called World System: Local Initiative and Response," *Dialectical Anthropology* 2 (1977), 263.

105. This caveat is inspired by my reading of Steven J. Stern's critique of Wallerstein in "Feudalism, Capitalism, and the World-System in the Perspective of Latin America and the Caribbean," *American Historical Review* 93 (1988), 829–72.

106. Morton Rothstein, "The Cotton Frontier of the Antebellum United States: A Methodological Battleground," in *Agricultural History* 44 (1970), 151–52. Rothstein's essay appears in the special January 1970 issue of *Agricultural History* edited by William N. Parker and entitled *The Structure of the Cotton Economy of the Antebellum South.* Cf. Harold D. Woodman, "The Profitability of Slavery: A Historical Perennial" (1963), in Aitken, ed., *Did Slavery Pay?*, 3, and Robert William Fogel, *Without Consent or Contract: The Rise and Fall of American Slavery* (New York & London: W. W. Norton, 1989), 108–9.

107. Fleisig, "Slavery, the Supply of Agricultural Labor, and the Industrialization of the South," *Journal of Economic History* 36 (1976), 581–83.

108. Schissler, *Preussische Agrargesellschaft im Wandel: Wirtschaftliche, gesellschaftliche, und politische Transformationzprozesse von 1763 bis 1847*, Kritische Studien zur Geschichtswissenschaft, vol. 33 (Göttingen: Vandenhoeck & Ruprecht, 1978), 187.

109. The words "bourgeoisie" and "bourgeois" seem to be among the most overworked and underdefined terms in recent historical and sociological scholarship. Derived from the French word for a medieval fortified town, the term originally referred to the urban business and artisan classes of the Middle Ages, as distinct from the nobility, peasantry, and clergy. Marx and his late nineteenth-century followers made the terms synonymous with the class of property-owning capitalists who exploit the proletariat and who are preoccupied with material gain and social respectability, and in the process assured, ironically, that the word bourgeois would retain "the residual aristocratic and philosophical contempt" carried over from the eighteenth century. (The quotation is from Raymond Williams, *Keywords: A Vocabulary of Culture and Society*, rev. ed. (New York: Oxford Univ. Press, 1985), 47.) Werner Sombart equated bourgeois values and

the bourgeois spirit with "calculation, careful policy, reasonableness, and economy." Sombart, *The Quintessence of Capitalism* (London, 1915), quoted by Donald M. Barnes, "Bourgeoisie," in Dunner, ed., *Handbook of World History*, 130. It is interesting that Sombart, in an article on "Capitalism" for the *Encyclopedia of the Social Sciences*, vol. 3 (New York, 1937), 195–208, does not even use the adjective bourgeois when discussing "the spirit or the economic outlook of capitalism"—that is, "acquisition, competition, and rationality."

110. Moore, *Social Origins of Dictatorship and Democracy*, 121.

111. See Harnisch, *Kapitalistische Agrarreform und Industrielle Revolution*, 218–20, 234–35, and Haines, "Agriculture and Development in Prussian Upper Silesia, 1846–1913," 378–79.

112. On planters as diversified investors, see Frederick F. Siegel, *The Roots of Southern Distinctiveness: Tobacco and Society in Danville, Virginia, 1780–1865* (Chapel Hill & London: Univ. of North Carolina Press, 1987), esp. 37; Ford, *Origins of Southern Radicalism*, esp. 63–64; and Rothstein, "The Cotton Frontier of the Antebellum United States," 160–61. That the South (where slaves made up 32% of the population in 1860) far outstripped Brazil (where 15% of the population was enslaved in 1872) in transportation, agricultural technology, and industrial manufacturing is demonstrated in two remarkable essays by Richard Graham: "Slavery and Economic Development: Brazil and the United States South in the Nineteenth Century," *Comparative Studies in Society and History* 23 (1981), 620–55, and "Economics or Culture?," 97–124. Graham seeks to explain the disparity between Southern and Brazilian economic development by pointing to significant differences in social structures, the roles played by the two major export crops (cotton and coffee) in the growth of industrial capitalism, and cultural legacies from England and Portugal.

113. William N. Parker, "The Slave Plantation in American Agriculture" [1960], in A. W. Coats and R. M. Robertson, eds., *Essays in American Economic History* (London: Edward Arnold, 1969), 132–33. Parker portrays antebellum planters as "capitalists," while also emphasizing "differences in business capitalism between the North and the South," in "Capitalism: Southern Style," 89. Adam Smith, whose *Wealth of Nations* (1776) glorified the economic efficiency promoted by of the free market and individual freedom, recognized that "The pride of man makes him love to domineer. . . . Wherever the law allows it, and the nature of the work can afford it, therefore, he will generally prefer the service of slaves to that of freemen." Smith, *An Enquiry into the Nature and Causes of the Wealth of Nations*, ed. Edwin Cannan (New York: Modern Library, 1937), 365. For a provocative analysis of the Southern economy that attributes the slow pace of industrialization largely to a "planter ethos" which emphasized land and slaves as sources of status and caused "the region's comparative advantage" in large-scale agriculture to be "overindulged," see Fred Bateman and Thomas Weiss, *A Deplorable Scarcity: The Failure of Industrialization in the Slave Economy* (Chapel Hill: Univ. of North Carolina Press, 1981), esp. ch. 8: "Summary and Conclusions"; the quotations are from pp.162–63. John Majewski reviews the Bateman/Weiss argument in "Manufacturing and Agricultural Reform in the Old South" (B.A. Honors Thesis, University of Texas at Austin, 1988), ch. 3, esp. 10: "In the words of economic historian Joseph Reid, the profitability figures (for Southern manufactures) of Bateman and Weiss suggest either

'a real opportunity waiting to be exploited or a risky opportunity with scant chance of payoff.' "

114. Cooper describes the English landowner as "a risk-bearing entrepreneur using capital." J. P. Cooper, "In Search of Agrarian Capitalism," *Past and Present*, no. 80 (Aug., 1978), 64, 26.

115. Thorstein Veblen's *Theory of the Leisure Class* is a forceful though unempirical demonstration of this truth.

116. See, for example, Carl Degler, "Rethinking Post-Civil War History," *Virginia Quarterly Review* 57 (1981), esp. 263; Harold Woodman, "Economic Reconstruction and the Rise of the New South," in John B. Boles and Evelyn Thomas Nolen, eds., *Interpreting Southern History: Historiographical Essays in Honor of Sanford W. Higginbotham* (Baton Rouge & London: Louisiana State Univ. Press, 1987), 271; Lawrence Powell, "Review Essay: The Prussians Are Coming," *Georgia Historical Quarterly* 71 (1987), 641; and James C. Cobb, "Beyond Planters and Industrialists: A New Perspective on the New South," *Journal of Southern History* 54 (1988), 48–54.

117. Two historians of the South who have correctly attributed the term to Nicolai Lenin are Fields, "Advent of Capitalist Agriculture," 84–86, and Hahn, "Class and State in Postemancipation Societies," 76–77. The Leninist model of the Prussian road will be discussed at length below.

118. Genovese, *The World the Slaveholders Made*, 228–29. A few years earlier, in *Political Economy of Slavery*, p. 207, Genovese posited "a Prussian road to industrial capitalism, paved with authoritarianism, benevolent despotism, and aristocratic pretension."

119. Jonathan Wiener, *Social Origins of the New South: Alabama, 1860–1885* (Baton Rouge: Louisiana State Univ. Press, 1978), esp. 71–72, 201–2; and Lewis Nicholas Wynne, *The Continuity of Cotton: Planter Politics in Georgia, 1865–1892* (Mercer, Ga.: Mercer Univ. Press, 1986), esp. 66, 183. The phrase "Prussian road to modernity" appears only once in Dwight B. Billings, Jr., *Planters and the Making of a "New South": Class, Politics, and Development in North Carolina, 1865–1900* (Chapel Hill: Univ. of North Carolina Press, 1979), 128–29. Billings, who makes extensive use of Barrington Moore, Jr.'s thinking on the process of "conservative modernization," seems to equate "the Prussian road to modernity" with "State encouragement of industry and state sponsorship of transportation and educational improvements."

120. In 1974 Genovese wrote that "Those modern states which have most directly attempted to play the role of collective padrone fall roughly into the category which Marx referred to as having taken the 'second' or 'Prussian' road to capitalism." Genovese, *Roll, Jordan, Roll: The World the Slaves Made* (New York: Pantheon Books, 1974; Vintage Books, 1976), 663. No citation from Marx's writings is provided.

121. For helpful discussions which, however, do not refer to the work of either East German scholars or historians of the U.S. South, see Athar Hussain and Keith Tribe, *Marxism and the Agrarian Question, Volume 1: German Social Democracy and the Peasantry 1890–1907* (London: Macmillan, 1981), 40–51, entitled "The Prussian Road," and Anthony Winson, "The 'Prussian Road' of Agrarian Development: A Reconsideration," *Economy and Society* 11 (1982), 381–408.

122. V. I. Lenin, "The Agrarian Programme of Social Democracy in the First

Russian Revolution, 1905–1907" (1907), in his *Selected Works*, vol. 3 (London: Lawrence Wishart, 1936); the quotations that appear in my summary of Lenin's argument are from 180–84, 217, 234, 278–86. In his "Preface to the Second Edition" of *The Development of Capitalism in Russia* (1908), Lenin contrasts "the internal metamorphosis of feudalist landlord economy" into "purely capitalist, 'Junker' economy" with a revolutionary transformation of "the old landlord economy" that makes possible "the free development of small peasant farming," which is also "capitalist." V. I. Lenin, *The Development of Capitalism in Russia: The Process of the Formation of a Home Market for Large-Scale Industry* (Moscow: Foreign Languages Publishing House, 1956), 8.

123. Harold D. Woodman, "The Reconstruction of the Cotton Plantation in the New South," in Glymph & Kushma, eds., *Essays on the Postbellum Southern Economy*, 113. See also Carl Degler, *Place over Time: The Continuity of Southern Distinctiveness* (Baton Rouge: Louisiana State Univ. Press, 1977), 119.

124. Alfred G. Meyer, *Leninism* (Cambridge, Mass.: Harvard Univ. Press, 1957), 131–32.

125. A very helpful survey of the importance of "the Prussian path of capitalist agricultural development" in East German historiography from the 1950s to the early 1980s is provided by Hartmut Harnisch, "Zum Stand der Diskussion um Probleme des 'preußischen Weges' kapitalistischer Agrarentwicklung in der deutschen Geschichte," in Gustave Seeber and Karl-Heinz Hoack, eds., *Preußen in der deutschen Geschichte nach 1789*, Studienbibliothek DDR-Geschichtswissenschaft, vol. 3 (Berlin: Akademie-Verlag, 1983), 116–44. There is a brief discussion of the Prussian way in Andreas Dorpalen, *German History in Marxist Perspective: The East German Approach* (Detroit, Mich.: Wayne State Univ. Press, 1984), 177–78. Dorpalen's book, published posthumously, is a valuable critical survey of DDR scholarship. Yet Hartmut Harnisch, who has been publishing extraordinary work in German agricultural history for two decades, is not listed in Dorpalen's Index or Biographical Appendix.

126. Jürgen Kuczynski, *Darstellung der Lage der Arbeiter in Deutschland von 1789 bis 1849* (Berlin: Akademie-Verlag, 1961), 62–63. Gerhard Heitz, "Varianten des preussischen Weges," *Jahrbuch für Wirtschaftsgeschichte* (1969), Part 3, pp. 99–109, is an essay review of important books by three of Kuczynski's students (Georg Moll on Mecklenburg, Reiner Groß on Saxony, and Hartmut Harnisch on Brandenburg.) A biographical sketch of Kuczynski, who joined the German Communist Party in 1930, is provided by Dorpalen, *German History in Marxist Perspective*, 524–25, Cf. the use of the term by Martin Kitchen, a Canadian historian of Germany, in his discussion of German economic development during the 1840s: the " 'Prussian way' to modernization, with the great estates of the land-owning aristocracy still showing remnants of the feudal order, the feudal estates gradually becoming capitalist Junker estates. . . ." Kitchen, *Political Economy of Germany*, 61.

127. See the positive comments by non-DDR historians Klaus Klatte, "Die Anfänge des Agrarkapitalismus und der preussische Konservatismus" (D.Phil. diss., University of Hamburg, 1974), 14; and Wilhelm Treue, *Wirtschafts- und Technik-Geschichte Preussens*, Veröffentlichungen der Historischen Kommission zu Berlin, vol. 56 (Berlin & New York: Walter de Gruyter, 1984), 308; and Ian Farr, " 'Tradition' and the Peasantry: On the Modern Historiography of Rural Germany," in Richard J. Evans and W. R. Lee, eds.,

The German Peasantry: Conflict and Community in Rural Society from the Eighteenth to the Twentieth Centuries (London & Sydney: Croom Helm, 1986), 7–8.

128. Georg Moll, "Agrarfrage und bürgerliche Umwälzung in Deutschland," *Zeitschrift für Geschichtswissenschaft* 30 (1982), 945–46.

129. Georg Moll, "Bürgerliche Umwälzung und kapitalistische Agrarentwicklung," *Zeitschrift für Geschichtswissenschaft* 27 (1979), 143.

130. Walter Schmidt et al., *Deutsche Geschichte, Band 4: Die bürgerliche Umwälzung von 1789 bis 1871* (Köln, 1984), 400–401, which states that as of 1861 in all of Prussia there were 2.1 million servants and day-laborers (*Knechte*, *Mägde*, and *Tagelöhner*), as opposed to 792,000 landowners and renters. On p. 520, n. 15, the authors note that Hartmut Harnisch sees the Prussian road transformation as essentially completed by 1848.

131. Hans Mottek, *Wirtschaftsgeschichte Deutschlands, Ein Grundriss, II: Von der Zeit der französischen Revolution bis zur Zeit der Bismarckischen Reichsgründung* (Berlin: VEB Deutscher Verlag der Wissenschaften, 1964), 39–40.

132. See Harnisch, "Zum Stand der Diskussion um Probleme des 'preußischen Weges' kapitalistischer Agrarentwicklung in der deutschen Geschichte," 139–44, and Helmut Bleiber, "Staat und bürgerliche Unwälzung in Deutschland. Zum Charakter des preußischen Staates in der ersten Hälfte des 19. Jahrhunderts," also in Seeber and Noack, eds., *Preußen in der deutschen Geschichte nach 1789*, 94, 111.

133. E. J. Hobsbawm, *The Age of Capital, 1848–1875* (New York: Charles Scribner's Sons, 1975), 186–87. I cannot find any mention of the Prussian road in Hobsbawm's earlier and better known *The Age of Revolution, 1789–1848* (London: Weidenfeld and Nicolson, 1962).

134. Hobsbawm, *Age of Capital*, 150–51.

135. Genovese, *The World the Slaveholders Made*, 228–29.

136. Moore, *Social Origins of Dictatorship and Democracy*, xiv–xv.

137. Karl Dietrich Bracher, *The German Dictatorship: The Origins, Structure, and Effects of National Socialism*, trans. from the 1969 German ed. by Jean Sternberg (New York: Praeger, 1970), 19.

138. See Bleiber, "Staat und bürgerliche Unwälzung in Deutschland," 112, and Dorpalen, *German History in Marxist Perspective*, 230–31.

139. Harnisch, "Zum Stand der Diskussion um Probleme des 'preußischen Weges' kapitalistischer Agrarentwicklung in der deutschen Geschichte," 123, 140.

140. Wiener, *Social Origins of the New South*, 71–72. Cf. Wiener, "Class Structure and Economic Development in the American South, 1865–1955," *American Historical Review* 81 (1979), 985.

141. See David F. Crew, *Town in the Ruhr: A Social History of Bochum, 1860–1914* (New York: Columbia Univ. Press, 1979), 156–57.

142. Wiener, *Social Origins of the New South*, 201–2.

143. See W. O. Henderson, *The Rise of German Industrial Power, 1834–1914* (Berkeley & Los Angeles: Univ. of California Press, 1975), 173–77.

144. Wynne, *The Continuity of Cotton*, 66, 183.

145. The quotation is from Helmut Böhme, *An Introduction to the Social and Economic History of Germany: Politics and Economic Change in the Nineteenth and Twentieth Centuries*,

trans. from the 1972 German ed. by W. R. Lee (New York: St. Martin's Press, 1978), 64. The population statistics for Berlin are from Treue, *Wirtschafts- und Technik-Geschichte Preussens,* 516, and Gordon A. Craig, *Germany, 1866–1945* (New York: Oxford Univ. Press, 1978), 216, n. 76.

146. Fields, "The Advent of Capitalist Agriculture," 86.

147. For an arresting argument that after the Civil War and abolition "capitalism had not evolved but merely changed forms," see Crandall A. Shifflett, *Patronage and Poverty in the Tobacco South: Louisa County, Virginia, 1860–1900* (Knoxville: Univ. of Tennessee Press, 1982); the quotation is from p. 65. A provocative analysis of the ideological changes involved in the shift from a slave-based to a free-labor capitalism is presented in Laurence Shore, *Southern Capitalists: The Ideological Leadership of an Elite, 1832–1885* (Chapel Hill & London: Univ. of North Carolina Press, 1986).

148. See esp. Fogel, *Without Consent or Contract,* 64.

149. For a helpful discussion of this issue by a scholar whose theoretical perspective on capitalism is more like Fields's than my own, see Steven Hahn, "Emancipation and the Development of Capitalist Agriculture," in Gispen, ed., *What Made the South Different?,* 83–84.

150. Peter Kolchin, "Commentary" on Hahn, in ibid, 95.

151. We will return in the Epilogue to the twentieth-century transformation of the South. For a good overview of the region's history from the 1930s to the 1960s, see William J. Cooper, Jr., and Thomas E. Terrill, *The American South: A History* (New York: McGraw-Hill, 1991), chs. 25 and 62.

152. Hanna Schissler, "The Junkers: Some Notes on the Social and Historical Significance of the Agrarian Elite in Prussia," in Moeller, ed., *Peasants and Lords in Modern Germany,* 48, n. 6.

153. Max Weber, "Entwicklungstendenzen in der Lage der ostelbischen Landarbeiter" (1894), in his *Gesammelte Aufsätze zur Sozial- und Wirtschaftsgeschichte* (Tübingen: J.C.B. Mohr/Paul Siebeck, 1924), 484. In the South, "a share hand received as pay a portionof all he grew; he shared the profits, or in a bad year, the losses." Charles L. Flynn, Jr., *White Land, Black Labor: Caste and Class in Late Nineteenth-Century Georgia* (Baton Rouge: Louisiana State Univ. Press, 1983), 77.

154. Frieda Wunderlich, *Farm Labor in Germany, 1810–1945* (Princeton: Princeton Univ. Press, 1961), 24.

155. See Ulrich Herbert, *A History of Foreign Labor in Germany, 1880–1980: Seasonal Workers/ Forced Laborers/Guest Workers,* trans. from the 1986 German ed. by William Templar (Ann Arbor: Univ. of Michigan Press, 1990), 32–45, 16.

156. Woodman, "Economic Reconstruction and the Rise of the New South," in Boles and Nolen, eds., *Intepreting Southern History,* 290.

Chapter 4. Planter Republicanism versus Junker Monarchism

1. Gerhard Lenski, *Power and Privilege: A Theory of Social Stratification* (New York: McGraw-Hill, 1966), 77. For a contemporaneous definition of *Stand,* see *Dr. Johann Georg Krünitz's ökonomisch-technologisch Encyklopädie,* continued by Johann Wilhelm David

Notes to pages 112–114

Korth, vol. 169 (Berlin: J. Pauli, 1838), 604–5. Also see Robert M. Berdahl, "The Stände and the Origins of Conservatism in Prussia," *Eighteenth-Century Studies* 6 (1973), 298–321.

2. Sigmund Neumann, *Die Stufen des preussischen Konservatismus: Ein Beitrag zum Staats- und Gesellschaftsbild Deutschlands im 19. Jahrhundert*, Historische Studien, vol. 190 (Berlin: Emil Ebering, 1930), 108–9, and Erich Angermann, "Ernst Gottfried von Bülow-Cummerow," *Neue Deutsche Biographie* 2 (Berlin: Duncker & Humblot, 1955), 737–38.

3. After his father's death in 1796, his father's three estates passed to another line of von Bülows. Erich Krauß, *Ernst von Bülow-Cummerow, ein konservativer Landwirt und Politiker des 19. Jahrhundert*, Historische Studien, vol. 313 (Berlin: Emil Ebering, 1937), 25–26.

4. Hans-Jürgen Puhle calls the Junker Parliament "the first interest group for large estate owners, composed of people of rank." It appears much more like a forerunner of the later Conservative party than "the shadowy groups around the *Kreuzzeitung* (counter-revolutionary newspaper founded in Berlin in June of 1848) and the Gerlachs." Puhle, "Radikalisierung und Wandel des deutschen Konservatismus vor dem ersten Weltkrieg," in Gerhard A. Ritter, ed., *Deutsche Parteien vor 1918*, Neue Wissenschaftliche Bibliothek, Vol. 61 (Köln & Berlin: Kiepenhauer & Witsch, 1973), 183, n. 31. On the crucial roles played by members of the Junker Parliament as leading activists on behalf of the conservative *Junkerpartei* for several years after the 1848–49 revolution, see Hubertus Fischer, "Konservatismus von unten. Wahlen im ländlichen Preußen 1849/52—Organization, Agitation, Manipulation," in Dirk Stegmann, Bernd-Jurgen Wendt, and Peter-Christian Witt, eds., *Deutscher Konservatismus im 19. und 20. Jahrhundert: Festschrift für Fritz Fischer zum 75. Geburtstag und zum 50. Doktorjubiläum* (Bonn: Verlag Neue Gesellschaft, 1983), 71ff.

5. Ernst von Bülow-Cummerow, *Preussen, Seine Verfassung, Seine Verwaltung, Sein Verhältnis zu Deutschland* (2 vols.; Berlin: Weit und Comp, 1842), vol. 1, 37, 43, vol. 2, 4–5, 9.

6. Bulow-Cummerow, *Die Wahlen nach der oktroyierten Verfassung* (Berlin: J. Sittenfeld, 1848), as discussed in Günther Grünthal, "Das Preussische Dreiklassenwahlrecht: Ein Beitrag zur Genesis und Funktion des Wahlrechtsoktrois," in *Historische Zeitschrift* 226 (1978), 30–34. See also Gerhard Schilfert, *Sieg und Niederlage der demokratischen Wahlrechts in der deutschen Revolution, 1848/49* (East Berlin: Rütten & Loening, 1952), 155.

7. Bülow-Cummerow, *Die Reaction und ihre Fortschritte* (Berlin: Wilhelm Hertz, 1850), 5, 7, 17–18, and his *Die Revolution, ihre Früchte, die Politik, die Reform* (Berlin: Wilhelm Hertz, 1850), 5, 31.

8. The fascinating story of Joseph Davis, including his extraordinary relationship with slave and freedman Ben Montgomery, is recounted in two books by Janet Sharp Hermann: *The Pursuit of a Dream* (New York: Oxford Univ. Press, 1981; Vintage paperback, 1983), and *Joseph Davis: Pioneer Patriarch* (Jackson & London: Univ. Press of Mississippi, 1990).

9. John Jenkins, editor of the *Vicksburg Sentinel*, cited in William C. Davis, *Jefferson Davis, The Man and His Hour* (New York: Harper Collins, 1991), 114.

10. Paul D. Escott, "Jefferson Davis and Slavery in the Territories," *Journal of Mississippi History* 39 (1977), 114.

11. Davis to a friend in Mississippi, cited in Davis, *Jefferson Davis,* 251.

12. On Davis's antebellum attitudes toward African-Americans, see Clement Eaton, *Jefferson Davis* (New York: Free Press, 1977), 95–98, and Davis, *Jefferson Davis,* esp. 80–81, 181–82, 273.

13. Jefferson Davis, *Inaugural Address of President Davis* (Montgomery, Ala.: Shorter and Reid Printers, Advertiser Office, 1861), 4. See also "Inaugural Address of the President of the Provisional Government," in Dunbar Rowland, ed., *Jefferson Davis, Constitutionalist: His Letters, Papers and Speeches,* vol. 5 (Jackson: Mississippi Department of Archives and History, 1923), 50, and James D. Richardson and Allan Nevins, eds., *The Messages and Papers of Jefferson Davis and the Confederacy, Including Diplomatic Correspondence, 1861–1865* (1966; New York: Chelsea House, 1983), vol. 1, p. 33.

14. Jefferson Davis, in his 21 January 1861 farewell speech before the U.S. Senate, had declared that the principles of Jefferson's Declaration of Independence had no reference to slaves. According to Robert Durden, the Raleigh *Register* and the New Orleans *Picayune* represented most Confederates in claiming the Fourth of July for the South in 1861. Durden, "The American Revolution as Seen by Southerners in 1861," *Louisiana History* 19 (1978), 38–41.

15. Charles S. Sydnor sees the 1832 constitution as "the beginning of Mississippi's swing toward democracy," contrary to the control wielded by the Natchez-Vicksburg aristocracy under the 1817 constitution. Sydnor, *Slavery in Mississippi* (1933: Baton Rouge: Louisiana State Univ. Press, 1966), 247.

16. "Message of Jefferson Davis, April 29, 1861," in Frank Moore, ed., *The Record: A Diary of American Events,* vol. 1 (New York: G. P. Putnam, 1864), 166–69. See also "Jefferson Davis to the Confederate Congress," in Rowland, ed., *Jefferson Davis, Constitutionalist,* vol. 5, 67–85, and Richardson and Nevins, eds., *Messages and Papers of Jefferson Davis and the Confederacy,* vol. 1, pp. 63–82.

17. Pierre L. van den Berghe, *Race and Racism: A Comparative Perspective* (2nd ed.; New York: John Wiley & Sons, 1978), 18, 29, and George M. Fredrickson, *The Black Image in the White Mind: The Debate on Afro-American Character and Destiny, 1817–1914* (1971; New York, Harper Torchbooks,1972), 61–68.

18. Hans-Jürgen Puhle, "Aspekte der Agrarkapitalismus im 'Organisierten Kapitalismus,' " in Hans-Ulrich Wehler, ed., *Sozialgeschichte Heute: Festschrift für Hans Rosenberg zum 70. Geburtstag* (Göttingen: Vandenhoeck & Ruprecht, 1974), 547.

19. Although the militia were "a source of titles for Southern gentlemen, the meaning of a militia title had . . . very little to do with martial spirit." Dickson D. Bruce, Jr., *Violence and Culture in the Antebellum South* (Austin: Univ. of Texas Press, 1979), 167–68. Cf. the evaluation of Virginia's eighteenth-century colonial planters as county militia officers in A. G. Roeber, *Faithful Magistrates and Republican Lawyers: Creators of Virginia Legal Culture, 1680–1810* (Chapel Hill: Univ. of North Carolina Press, 1981), 30.

20. "The Virginia Bill of Rights, June 12, 1776," in J. R. Pole, ed., *The Revolution in America, 1754–1788: Documents and Commentaries* (Stanford, Calif.: Stanford Univ. Press, 1970), 520. See the lively and informed discussion in Christopher Collier and

James Lincoln Collier, *Decision in Philadelphia: The Constitutional Convention of 1787* (New York: Ballantine Books, 1986), 315–17.

21. Thomas R. Dew, "On the Influence of the Federative Republican System of Government upon Literature and the Development of Character," *Southern Literary Messenger* 2 (Dec. 1836), 279. This essay has recently been reprinted in Michael O'Brien, ed., *All Clever Men Who Make Their Way: Critical Discourse in the Old South* (Fayetteville: Univ. of Arkansas Press, 1982), 125–76.

22. See Richard Schult, "Partie wider Willen. Kalküle und Potentiale konservativer Parteigründer in Preußen zwischen Erstem Vereinigtem Landtag und Nationalversammlung (1847/48)," in Stegmann, Wendt, and Witt, eds., *Deutscher Konservatismus im 19. und 20. Jahrhundert,* 56.

23. Otto-Ernst Schüddekopf, *Die deutschen Innenpolitik im letzten Jahrhundert und der konservative Gedanke: Die Zusammenhänge zwischen Aussenpolitik, innerer Staatsführung und Parteigeschichte, dargestellt an der Geschichte der Konservativen Partei von 1807 bis 1918* (Braunschweig: Albert Limbach, 1951), 23, and Edward M. Coffman, *The Old Army: A Portrait of the American Army in Peacetime* (New York: Oxford Univ. Press, 1986), 92.

24. See the helpful discussion in V. R. Berghahn, *Militarism: The History of an International Debate, 1861–1979* (Cambridge: Cambridge Univ. Press, 1981), esp. 123.

25. Eduard Bleich, ed., *Der Erste Vereinigte Landtag in Berlin, 1847, Erster Teil* (Vaduz/Liechtenstein: Topos Verlag, 1977), 22.

26. Friedrich Wilhelm IV quoted in Huburtus Fischer, "Der 'Treubund mit Gott Für König und Vaterland,' " *Jahrbuch für die Geschichte Mittel- und Ostdeutschlands* 24 (1975), 78.

27. Graf (Adolph Heinrich) von Arnim-Boytzenburg, *Ueber die Vereidigung des Heeres auf die Verfassung. Geschrieben im August 1849* (Berlin: Verlag der Deckerschen Geheimen Ober-Hofdruckerie, 1849), 11–12.

28. "A spirit approaching the martial pervaded the entire plantation atmosphere." John Hope Franklin, *The Militant South, 1800–1861* (1956; Boston: Beacon Press, 1964), 70. I have discussed this and related topics in "Honor and Martialism in the U.S. South and Prussian East Elbia during the Mid-Nineteenth Century," in Kees Gispen, ed., *What Made the South Different?* (Jackson & London: Univ. Press of Mississippi, 1990), 19–40.

29. The phrase "West Points of the South" is taken from Franklin, *The Militant South,* 146.

30. Rudolf Vierhaus, *Germany in the Age of Absolutism,* trans. Jonathan B. Knudsen (Cambridge: Cambridge Univ. Press, 1988), 101.

31. Reinhart Koselleck, *Preussen zwischen Reform und Revolution: Allgemeines Landrecht, Verwaltung und soziale Bewegung von 1791 bis 1848,* 2nd corrected ed. (Stuttgart: Ernst Klett, 1975), 103.

32. John R. Gillis, "Aristocracy and Bureaucracy in Nineteenth-Century Prussia," *Past and Present,* no. 41 (1968), 106.

33. Hans Rosenberg, *Bureaucracy, Aristocracy, and Autocracy: The Prussian Experience, 1660–1815* (1958; Boston: Beacon Press, 1966), 138–39.

34. Gordon A. Craig, *The Politics of the Prussian Army, 1640–1945* (New York and Oxford: Oxford Univ. Press, 1955), 17. "The sons of the nobility typically came to be

educated in special schools for cadets; these boarding schools educated them to their future military calling and prepared them to serve the military-monarchical state." Vierhaus, *Germany in the Age of Absolutism,* 102.

35. Otto Büsch, *Militärsystem und Sozialleben im Alten Preussen,* Veröffentlichungen der Berliner Historischen Kommission beim Friedrich-Meinecke-Institut der Freien Universität Berlin, vol. 7 (Berlin: Walter de Gruyter, 1962), 167.

36. Koselleck, *Preussen zwischen Reform und Revolution,* 80. As Robert M. Berdahl emphasizes, "the entire outline of civil society offered by the ALR is build on the ständisch scheme." Berdahl, *The Politics of the Prussian Nobility: The Development of a Conservative Ideology, 1770–1848* (Princeton: Princeton Univ. Press, 1988), 102.

37. Prussian Civil Code of 1794, quoted in F. L. Carsten, *A History of the Prussian Junkers* (Aldershot, Eng., & Brookfield, Vt.: Scolar Press and Gower Publishing, 1989), 51.

38. Georg-Christoph von Unruh, *Der Kreis: Ursprung und Ordnung einer communalen Körperschaft* (Köln & Berlin: G. Grote'sche, 1964), 49.

39. Otto Fürst von Bismarck, *Gedanken und Erinnerungen* (2 vols., Stuttgart: Verlag der J. G. Cotta'schen Buchhandlung Nachfolger, 1898), vol. 1, p. 10.

40. See Rosenberg, *Bureaucracy, Aristocracy, and Autocracy,* 167, and Fischer, "Konservatismus von unten," in Stegmann, Wendt, and Witt, eds., *Deutscher Konservatismus im 19. und 20. Jahrhundert,* 126–27. C. B. A. Behrens, *Society, Government, and the Enlightenment: The Experiences of Eighteenth-Century France and Prussia* (New York: Harper & Row, 1985), 145, insists that the monarchy "could reward or punish him (the *Landrat*) according to his success or failure in furthering its policies."

41. Between 1786 and 1840 the monarchy bestowed noble titles on 453 commoners, of whom 34%, reports John R. Gillis, "had distinguished themselves in government service." Gillis, "Aristocracy and the Bureaucracy in Nineteenth-Century Prussia," 111n.

42. See ibid., 109–11; and Heinrich Heffter, *Die deutsche Selbstverwaltung im 19. Jahrhundert: Geschichte der Ideen und Institutionen* (Stuttgart: K. F. Koehler, 1950), 68ff; and Barbara Vogel, "Beamtenkonservatism: Sozial- und verfassungsgeschichtliche Voraussetzungen der Parteien in Preußen im frühen 19. Jahrhundert," in Stegmann, Wendt, and Witt, eds., *Deutscher Konservatismus im 19. und 20. Jahrhundert,* 22.

43. Marwitz quoted in Friedrich Lütge, "Friedrich August Ludwig von der Marwitz, der grosse Gegner Stein-Hardenbergs," *Jahrbücher für Nationalökonomie und Statistik* 139 (1933), 484–85. Cf. Berdahl, *Politics of the Prussian Nobility,* 151.

44. Vogel, "Beamtenkonservatism," in Stegmann, Wendt, and Witt, eds., *Deutscher Konservatismus,* esp. 121. On the desires of liberal reformers like Stein and Schön to establish representative assemblies elected by property owners in place of traditional corporatist diets dominated by the hereditary nobility, see Marion W. Gray, "Government by Property Owners: Prussian Plans for Constitutional Reform on the County, Provincial, and National Levels in 1808," On-Demand Supplement to the *Journal of Modern History* 48 (1976), 51.

45. Concise biographical sketches of many important noble and non-noble bureaucratic reformers are presented in Wilhelm Treue, *Wirtschafts- und Technik-Geschichte Preussens,* Veröffentlichungen der Historischen Kommission zu Berlin, vol. 56 (Berlin & New York: Walter de Gruyter, 1984), 267–73.

46. Hajo Holborn, *A History of Modern Germany, 1648–1840* (1964; Princeton: Princeton Univ. Press, 1982), 396. This institution, which Holborn calls "the freest and most flourishing German university after 1750," had been founded three years after the Elector of Hanover had also become George I of England in 1734. Ibid., 296.

47. See Berdahl, *Politics of the Prussian Nobility*, 110–13.

48. George Lefebvre's evaluation of France's bourgeoisie in 1789 seems applicable to the Stein-Hardenberg bureaucracy as well: "The abolition of legal hierarchy and of privilege of birth seemed to be by no means incompatible with the maintenance of a hierarchy based on wealth, function, or calling." Lefebvre, *The Coming of the French Revolution*, trans. R. R. Palmer (1947; Princeton: Princeton Univ. Press, 1967), 47.

49. "Denkschrift betreffend die landwirtschaftliche Zustände und Bedürfnisse der Monarchie im Allgemeinen," *Annalen der Landwirtschaft* (1844), 212–15.

50. *Nation* cited in Kenneth M. Stampp, *The Era of Reconstruction, 1865–1877* (New York: Knopf, 1965; Vintage paperback, 1967), 130; and *Times* cited in Shearer Davis Bowman, "Abolition and Its Aftermath in the U.S. South, 1860–1900," *Itinerario* 12 (1988), 49.

51. Holborn, *History of Modern Germany, 1648–1840*, 398. As Marion Gray emphasizes, Stein tended to associate political virtue with property ownership, as did most contemporaneous U.S. leaders. Gray, "Government by Property Owners," passim; the comparative reference to U.S. history is on p. 18.

52. Baron vom Stein, "Aus seinem Schreiben an das Comité der ostpreussischen Stände, die sich gegen die Verordnung von 14. 2. 1808 ausgesprochen hatten," in Werner Conze, ed., *Quellen zur Geschichte der deutschen Bauernbefreiung* (Göttingen: Musterschmidt, 1957), 111–13.

53. Walter M. Simon, *The Failure of the Prussian Reform Movement, 1807–1819* (Ithaca, N.Y.: Cornell Univ. Press, 1955), 49–50.

54. Ibid., 52.

55. Ursula Wiese, *Zur Opposition des ostelbischen Grundadels gegen die agraren Reformmassnahmen 1807–1811* (Berlin: Triltsch & Huther, 1935), 38, 24, and Friedrich Meusel, "Einleitung," to Meusel, ed., *Friedrich August Ludwig von der Marwitz: Ein märkischer Edelmann im Zeitalter der Befreiungskriege* (2 vols.; Berlin: Siegfried Mittler und Sohn, 1908–13), vol. 1, xxxvi-xxxviii.

56. Simon, *Failure of the Prussian Reform Movement*, 62–66; Peter Gerrit Thielen, *Karl August von Hardenberg, 1750–1822: Eine Biographie* (Köln & Berlin: G. Grote'sche, 1967), 262–64; and Berdahl, *Politics of the Prussian Nobility*, 125–27.

57. Thielen, *Hardenberg*, 263–66.

58. Hardenberg quoted in Simon, *Failure of the Prussian Reform Movement*, 54.

59. Schön quoted in Ernst Klein, *Von der Reform zur Restauration: Finanzpolitik und Reformgesetzgebung des preussischen Staatskanzlers K. A. von Hardenberg* (Berlin: de Gruyter, 1965), 37–38.

60. Ibid., 163. Cf. James J. Sheehan, *German History, 1770–1866* (Oxford: Clarendon Press, 1989), 474–75.

61. For example, in 1814 the king received a petition from East Prussian *Rittergut* owners protesting the radical "French coloring" of the agrarian legislation. When Friedrich Wilhelm III demanded a review of the laws on peasant regulation, Hardenberg,

then preoccupied with foreign and diplomatic affairs, proceeded to solicit new recommendations from corporatist provincial assemblies, and even suggested that estate owners might demand a higher level of compensation for the end of the peasants' manorial obligations. Wiese, *Zur Opposition des ostelbischen Grundadels,* 38–40, 24–25.

62. Berdahl, *Politics of the Prussian Nobility,* 132–33.

63. An English translation of this short "Verordnung über die zu bildende Repräsentation des Volks," 22 May 1815, is printed in Simon, *Failure of the Prussian Reform Movement,* 109.

64. James J. Sheehan, *German Liberalism in the Nineteenth Century* (Chicago: Univ. of Chicago Press, 1978), 9.

65. I have relied heavily here on Simon, *Failure of the Prussian Reform Movement,* chs. 9–11.

66. *Gesetz-Sammlung für die Königlichen Preußischen Staaten* (1823), 120f, cited in Schult, "Partei wider Willen," in Stegmann, Wendt, and Witt, eds., *Deutscher Konservatismus,* 35–36. See also Leonard Krieger, *The German Idea of Freedom: History of a Political Tradition, from the Reformation to 1871* (Chicago: Univ. of Chicago Press, 1957), 226, and Heffter, *Die deutsche Selbstverwaltung,* 129–30.

67. Quoted in Carl Wilhelm von Lancizolle, *Ueber Königtum und Landstände in Preussen* (Berlin: Ferdinance Dümmler, 1846), 433.

68. Ibid., 585, 399, and Georg von Viebahn, *Statistik des zollvereinten und nördlichen Deutschlands* (3 vols.; Berlin: Georg Reimer, 1858–68), vol. 2, 311.

69. Conrad Bornhak, "The Local Government of County Communities in Prussia," in *Annals of the American Academy of Political and Social Science* 3 (1893), 395. As James Sheehan emphasizes, the "thinness of its bureaucratic apparatus" on the county level left the Prussian state no option but "to cooperate with traditional elites and institutions in order to maintain order, keep records, and regulate trade and commerce." Sheehan, *German History, 1770–1866,* 439–40.

70. The 50 *Rittergut* owners, who collectively owned 70 estates, included two towns, Prenzlau and Straßburg. Remarks by Ober-Burgermeister Grabow, representing the town of Prenzlau in the country of Prenzlau, in Bleich, *Der Erste Vereinigte Landtag, Erster Teil,* 655–66. Heinrich Heffter tells of another county assembly in which *Rittergut* owners claimed 163 votes, the remaining rural population of 62,000 held three votes, and a town of 10,500 had one vote. Heffter, *Die deutsche Selbsverwaltung,* 131–32

71. Lancizolle, *Ueber Königtum und Landstände,* 383.

72. August Meitzen and Friedrich Grossman, *Der Boden und der landwirtschaftlichen Verhältnisse des preussischen Staates* (8 vols.; Berlin: Paul Parey, 1868–1908), vol. 1, 539.

73. Robert M. Bigler, *The Politics of German Protestantism: The Rise of the Protestant Church Elite in Prussia, 1815–1848* (Berkeley: Univ. of California Press, 1972), 54, and Berdahl, *Politics of the Prussian Nobility,* 204–7.

74. Friedrich Julius Stahl, "Zum Gedächtniss seiner Majestät des hochseligen Königs Friedrich Wilhelm IV. und seiner Regierung. Vortrag gehalten im evangelischen Verein zu Berlin am 18. März 1861," in his *Siebzehn parlamentarische Reden und drei Vorträge von Stahl. Nach letzwilligen Bestimung geordnet und herausgeben* (Berlin: Wilhelm Hertz, 1862), 264.

75. Gerhard Ritter, *Die preussischen Konservativen und Bismarcks deutsche Politik, 1858–*

1876 (Heidelberg: C. Winter, 1913), 4. The Crown Prince's Circle was a successor to the less pietistic *Maikäferei* of 1816–19, which had "discovered" Karl Ludwig von Haller.

76. See Erich Jordan, *Die Entstehung der konservativen Partei und die preussischen Agrarverhaltnisse von 1848* (München & Leipzig: Duncker & Humblot, 1914), 135–42, and Bigler, *Politics of German Protestantism*, ch. 4, "The Pietist Aristocrats." On the difference between these "new" pietists and "old" pietists of the seventeenth and eighteenth centuries, see Berdahl, *Politics of the Prussian Nobility*, 247.

77. Thomas Nipperdey, *Deutsche Geschichte 1800–1866: Bürgerwelt und starker Staat* (München: Verlag C. H. Beck, 1983), 680–81; and Heffter, *Die Deutsche Selbstverwaltung*, 335–37.

78. Karl Ludwig von Haller, *Restauration der Staats-Wissenschaft oder Theorie des natürlich-geselligen Zustands*, 2nd ed. (6 vols.; Winterthur: Steiner, 1820–34). Nipperdey, *Deutsche Geschichte*, 317–18, juxtaposes the romantic and unromantic strains in *Vormärz* conservatism.

79. Neumann, *Die Stufen des preussischen Konservatismus*, 79–80. For a prime example of the way in which Old Prussian ideologues used Haller's political philosophy in defense of corporatist monarchy, see Carl Ernst Jarcke, "Revolution und Absolutismus" (originally published in the *Berliner Politisches Wochenblatt* in 1833), in Jarcke, *Vermischte Schriften* (3 vols.; München: Verlag der Literarisch-Artistischen Anstalt, 1839), vol. 1, 180–85.

80. Cited in Wolfgang Scheel, *Die "Berliner Politische Wochenblatt" und die politische und soziale Revolution in Frankreich und England. Ein Beitrag zur konservativen Zeitkritik in Deutschland*, Göttinger Bausteine zur Geschichtswissenschaft, vol. 36 (Göttingen: Vandenhoeck & Ruprecht, 1964), 47.

81. Ibid., 54–55.

82. See esp. William James Orr, Jr., "The Foundation of the *Kreuzzeitung* Party in Prussia, 1848–1850" (Ph.D. diss., University of Wisconsin, 1971), 282–99.

83. Cited in Neumann, *Die Stufen des preussischen Konservatismus*, 94, 98, and also in Alfred von Martin, "Weltanschauliche Motive im altkonservativen Denken," in his *Deutscher Staat und Deutsche Parteien* (München & Berlin: R. Oldenberg, 1922), 371. Martin's valuable essay is reprinted in Gerhard A. Ritter, ed., *Deutsche Parteien vor 1918*, Neue Wissenschaftliche Bibliothek, vol. 61 (Köln: Kiepenhauer & Witsch, 1973).

84. Von Martin, "Weltanschauliche Motive im altkonservativen Denken," 345–46.

85. Friedrich Julius Stahl, *Das Monarchische Prinzip: Eine staatsrechtliche-politische Abhandlung* (1845), ed. Mario Krammer (Berlin: Weltgeist-Bücher, 1926), 5–57. Helpful recent discussions of Stahl's ideas are presented in Berdahl, *Politics of the Prussian Nobility*, ch. 10; and Sheehan, *German History, 1770–1866*, 593–96.

86. Stahl, *The Present-Day Parties in the State and Church. Twenty-nine Academic Lectures* (1863), trans. Timothy David Taylor (State College, Pa.: Blenheim Publishing, 1976), 405–28. Ernst Rudolf Huber credits Stahl with turning Prussian conservatism away from "Haller's old corporatist-patrimonial view of the state" and steering it toward "conservative constitutionalism." Huber, "Der Deutsche Konservatismus," in his *Deutsche Verfassungsgeschichte seit 1789* (4 vols.; Stuttgart: W. Kohlhammer, 1957–69), vol. 2: *Der Kampf um Einheit und Freiheit*, 336.

87. During the heat of revolution in 1848, Stahl, like the Gerlach brothers, was ready to bestow the dignity of a lesser *Berufstand* on the unpropertied working classes;

but within a few years he was insisting that only the "higher classes"—landowners and industrialists—were entitled to representation in the legislature. See Otto Pflanze, *Bismarck and the Development of Germany. The Period of Unification, 1815–1871* (Princeton: Princeton Univ. Press, 1963), 32.

88. Stahl, *Die Philosophie des Rechts*, 6th ed. (text unchanged from the 5th ed. of 1878) (2 vols., Hildesheim: Georg Olms, 1963), vol. 2, p. 119.

89. Lancizolle, *Ueber Königtum und Landstände in Preussen*, 526–27, 240–41, 525. Another important ideological exposition of Old Prussian corporatism was (Carl Ernst Wilhelm Freiherr von Canitz), *Die Frage: Wohin? In Bezug auf die landständischen Verhältnisse der Preußischen Monarchie, vom Geschichtspunkt praktischer Ausführbarkeit betractet* (Berlin: Ferdinand Dümmler, 1843), which contrasts Prussian traditions of organic corporatism to the unrealistic "French model" of popular sovereignty.

90. See Norman K. Risjord, *The Old Republicans: Southern Conservatism in the Age of Jefferson* (New York: Columbia Univ. Press, 1965), esp. 176 and 281, where Risjord discusses the connections between the Old Republicans and Southern sectionalists. See also Jesse T. Carpenter, *The South as a Conscious Minority, 1789–1861* (New York: New York Univ. Press, 1930), esp. ch. 3, "The Principle of Local Self-Government."

91. Eduard Bleich, ed., *Der Erste Vereinigte Landtag in Berlin, 1847, Dritter Teil* (Vaduz/Liechtenstein: Topos Verlag, 1977), 945–46.

92. The phrase "a good part" is taken from Jordan, *Die Entstehung der konservativen Partei*, 205–6. See also John R. Gillis, *The Prussian Bureaucracy in Crisis, 1840–1860: Origins of an Administrative Ethos* (Stanford, Calif.: Stanford Univ. Press, 1971), Part II, "Revolution," and Schult, "Partei wider Willen," in Stegmann, Wendt, and Witt, eds., *Deutscher Konservatismus*, esp. 57.

93. Gillis, *Prussian Bureaucracy in Crisis*, 110.

94. Koselleck, *Preussen zwischen Reform und Revolution*, 80–82, 672; Viebahn, *Statistik*, vol. 2, pp. 309–11.

95. Walter Görlitz, *Die Junker*, 3rd ed. (Limburg a. d. Lahn: C. A. Starke, 1964), 229.

96. Gillis, *Prussian Bureaucracy in Crisis*, 34, and Gillis, "Aristocracy and Bureaucracy," 113.

97. Adolf von Thadden-Trieglaff, "Der Schacher mit Rittergütern. Vorgetragen in der General-Versammlung der Pommerschen ökonomischen Gesellschaft, am 10. Mai 1842 zu Cöslin," reprinted in Eleonore Fürstin Reuss, ed., *Adolf von Thadden Trieglaff. Ein Lebensbild*, 2nd ed. (Berlin: W. Hertz, 1894), 250–51.

98. Lancizolle, *Über Königtum und Landstände in Preussen*, 204, 264, 519–21.

99. Reinhard Koser, in a 1908 study of the Diet, applies the phrase "conservative opportunists" to the majority of "conservatives"—about 130 out of 200—who belonged to a faction known as the "English House." Koser as cited in Schult, "Partei wider Willen," in Stegmann, Wendt, and Witt, eds., *Deutscher Konservatismus*, 41–42.

100. Craig, *Politics of the Prussian Army*, 89.

101. William L. Langer, *Political and Social Upheaval, 1832–1852* (New York: Harper & Row, 1969), 394–97. See also P. H. Noyes, *Organization and Revolution: Working-Class Associations in German Revolution of 1848–1849* (Princeton: Princeton Univ. Press, 1966), esp. 69–70.

102. *Stenographische Berichte der Preussischen Zweiten Kammer* (26 Feb.–27 April 1849), 20th Sitting (31 March 1849), 340–41.

103. Leon Litwack, *Been in the Storm So Long: The Aftermath of Slavery* (1979; New York: Vintage Books, 1980), 401, and Jordan, *Entstehung der konservativen Partei*, 121. On the land hunger of many day-laborers and their expectations that Junker land would be divided among them, see also Treue, *Wirtschafts- und Technik-Geschichte Preussens*, 451–52, and Günter Vogler and Klaus Vetter, *Preußen: Von der Anfängen bis zur Reichsgründung* (East Berlin: VEB Deutscher Verlag der Wissenschaften, 1970), 242.

104. Jordan, *Entstehung der konservativen Partei*, 122–23, and Litwack, *Been in the Storm So Long*, 41.

105. Von Versen, "Welchen Einfluss übt das Parzellieren auf die allgemeine Verarmung?," in *Allgemeine Landwirtschaftliche Monatschrift* 2 (1844), 289–300. An "Eduard von Versen, Hauptmann a. D." is listed in Karl Freidrich von Rauer, *Alphabetischer Nachweis (Addressbuch) des in den Preussischen Staaten mit Rittergütern angesessenen Adels* (Berlin: Durch die Herausgeber, 1857), 240.

106. After the Silesian weavers' revolt of 1844, concludes P. H. Noyes, "the threat of working class violence was one of the realities of Germany in the mid-1840s." Noyes, *Organization and Revolution*, 34.

107. Von Bally, "Oberschlesische Züstande," *Annalen der Landwirtschaft* 7 (1846), 119–21, and von Bally-Chutow, "Entwurf einer Geschäftsordnung für den land- und forstwirthschaftlichen, Industrie-, Gewerb- und Arbeiter-Verein, Rybnicker Kreises, zur Erhebung der untern Volks- und Arbeiter-Klasses," *Annalen der Landwirtschaft* 6 (1845), 402–5. On von Bally, see J. G. Knie, *Alphabetisch-statistisch-typographische Uebersicht der Dörfer, Flecken, Städte und andern Orte der Königl. Preuss. Provinz Schlesien*, 2nd ed. (Breslau: von Bratz, Barth und Comp, 1845), 79.

108. Orr, "Foundation of the Kreuzzeitung Party," 58, 67.

109. Computed from figures in Gerhard Schilfert, *Sieg und Niederlage des demokratischen Wahlrechts in der deutschen Revolution 1848/49* (East Berlin: Rütten & Loening, 1952), 401. See also Manfred Botzenhart, *Deutscher Parlamentarismus in der Revolutionszeit von 1848–1850* (Düsseldorf: Droste Verlag, 1977), 516–17. Nipperdey, *Deutsche Geschichte*, 647, mistakenly reports that peasants and artisans *(Handwerker)* together numbered 46, which is the number of peasant delegates alone. Working with different statistics, Erich Jordan reports that the assembly as a whole included "49 delegates from the ranks of the little people and 24 members of the ruling class"; among the latter were 21 *Rittergut*-owners. Jordan, *Die Entstehung der konservativen Partei*, 126.

110. On the roots of East Prussian "liberalism," see Sidney B. Fay and Klaus Epstein, *The Rise of Brandenburg-Prussia to 1786*, rev. ed. (Hinsdale, Ill.: Dryden Press, 1964), 58.

111. Fischer, "Konservatismus von unten," in Stegmann, Wendt, and Witt, eds., *Deutscher Konservatismus*, 70.

112. Sheehan, *German Liberalism*, 56, and Gillis, *Prussian Bureaucracy in Crisis*, 242.

113. The petitions which peasants and day-laborers later submitted to the National Assembly suggest that "an identity of interests" between estate owners and those working the land existed "only in the rarest instances." Schult, "Partei wider Willen," in Stegmann, Wendt, and Witt, eds., *Deutscher Konservatismus*, 45–46 (where the footnotes

include references to the literature on this topic and suggest that more study is needed) and 51–52. Donald J. Mattheison notes that "there *was* a well-developed radical political movement in the countryside," which meant that "few genuine conservatives" managed to get elected. Mattheison, "Voters and Parliaments in the German Revolution of 1848: An Analysis of the Prussian Constitutent Assembly," *Central European History* 5 (1972), 14–18.

114. Ludwig von Gerlach quoted in Meinecke, *Cosmopolitanism and the National State,* 170.

115. Ernst Ludwig von Gerlach, "Aufruf an meine Standesgenossen, 26 März 1848," in Hans Fenske, ed., *Vormärz und Revolution, 1840–1849* (Darmstadt: Wissenschaftliche Buchgesellschaft, 1976), 274–75.

116. Craig, *Politics of the Prussian Army,* 82.

117. Schult, "Partei wider Willen," in Stegmann, Wendt, and Witt, eds., *Deutscher Konservatismus,* 68.

118. Manfred Kliem , "Die Rolle der feudaljunkerlichen Reaktion in der Revolution von 1848/49," *Zeitschrift für Geschichtswissenschaft* 17 (1969), 230, and Orr, "Foundation of the *Kreuzzeitung* Party," 131–32.

119. Rauer, *Alphabetischer Nachweis,* 32, which identifies Brandenburg as the owner of five estates in 1856; and Orr, "Foundation of the *Kreuzzeitung* Party," 152. The Auerswald-Hansemann minstry had been replaced in September by a new government under Minister-President General Ernst von Pfuel, "who continued to search for a way of accommodating both court and parliament." Sheehan, *German History, 1770–1866,* 704.

120. Orr, "Foundation of the *Kreuzzeitung* Party," 160.

121. Bismarck cited in Gordon A. Craig, *Germany 1866–1945* (New York: Oxford Univ. Press, 1978), 172.

122. See Botzenhart, *Deutscher Parlamentarismus in der Revolutionszeit,* 517 and 608. These figures are for all of the Prussian monarchy.

123. Ludwig von Gerlach quoted in Schilfert, *Sieg und Niederlage des demokratischen Wahlrechts,* 154.

124. Ludwig Bergsträsser, *Geschichte der politischen Parteien in Deutschland,* 9th ed. (München & Vienna: R. Oldenbourg, 1965), 88–89, and Günther Grünthal, "Das Preussische Dreiklassenwahlrecht: Ein Beitrag zur Genesis und Funktion des Wahlrechtsoktrois vom Mai 1849," *Historische Zeitschrift* 226 (1978), 56.

125. Rauer, *Alphabetischer Nachweis,* 141, and Holborn, *A History of Modern Germany, 1840–1945,* 76.

126. The percentages for 1849 come from Botzenhart, *Deutscher Parlamentarismus in der Revolutionszeit,* 748. Cf. Nipperdey, *Deutsche Geschichte,* 680.

127. Heffter, *Die Deutsche Selbstverwaltung,* 314. Cf. Schilfert, *Sieg und Niederlage,* 283–84. Grünthal, "Das Preussische Dreiklassenwahlrecht," 52–53, emphasizes that voting under the three-class system was public and oral, which allowed the ruling elites to intimidate voters and thus served as "a means of stabilizing conservative authority."

128. Botzenhart, *Deutscher Parlamentarismus in der Revolutionszeit,* 517 and 749. Of the 78 large landowners, 65 came from East Elbia; and these 65 composed almost 28%

of all East Elbian delegates. Computed from figures in Schilfert, *Sieg und Niederlage,* 408.

129. Fischer, "Konservatismus von unten," in Stegmann, Wendt, and Witt, eds., *Deutscher Konservatismus,* 118–19.

130. The phrase "*Festgeschlossen nach außen, innerlich Streit und Widerwille*" is from Karl Twesten's *Was uns noch retten kann: Ein Wort ohne Umschweife* (Berlin, 1861); the translation is from Eckart Kehr, "The Genesis of the Prussian Bureaucracy and the *Rechsstaat,*" in his *Economic Interest, Militarism, and Foreign Policy: Essays on German History,* ed. Gordon A. Craig and trans. Grete Heinz (Berkeley: Univ. of California Press, 1977), 148. Although Twesten and Kehr applied the phrase to bureaucrats, Fischer, "Konservatismus von unten," in Stegmann, Wendt, and Witt, eds., *Deutscher Konservatismus,* 120, argues that it is equally applicable to conservatives of the 1850s.

131. Heffter, *Die Deutsche Selbstverwaltung,* 328–29. As Nikolaus von Preradovich concluded from his examination of Prussia's leadership groups between 1804 and 1918, "The decisive element, not only in the Prussian army, but also in administration and diplomacy, was the nobility." Preradovich, *Die Führungsschichten in Osterreich und Preussen (1804–1918) mit einem Ausblick bis zum Jahre 1945* (Wiesbaden: Franz Steiner, 1955), 160.

132. See, for example, the summaries of pamphlets by Alexander von Schmeling-Diringshofen (1862), Max von Wittenburg (1862), and Ludwig Graf von Pfeil (1863), in Hans Rosenberg, *Die nationalpolitische Publizistik Deutschlands: Vom Eintritt der neuen Ära in Preussen bis zum Ausbruch des deutschen Krieges* (2 vols.; Berlin & München: R. Oldenbourg, 1935), vol. 2, pp. 512, 493–94, 518–19.

133. Bismarck, *Gedanken und Erinnerungen,* vol. 1, p. 15.

134. According to Gerhard Schilfert and Wilhelm Treue, the most important direct tax in the Prussian state at this time was not the land tax, but the class tax *(Klassensteuer),* a sort of progressive tax levied from 1820 until 1873 on all persons over 14 years of age. Those subject to the levy were grouped into tax brackets—the six brackets of 1820 expanding to a dozen by 1848—according to their estimated ability to make an annual payment ranging from a minimum of one-half *Taler* to a maximum of 144 *Taler.* Schilfert, *Sieg und Niderlage,* 263–64, and Treue, *Wirtschafts- und Technik-Geschichte Preussens,* 298. Yet Günther Grünthal has determined that the class tax yielded 13% of Prussia's total tax receipts in 1849, whereas taxes on land yielded 20%. Grünthal, "Das Preussische Dreiklassenwahlrecht," 40.

135. Schilfert, *Sieg und Niederlage,* 258–59, 283–86, and Sheehan, *German History, 1770–1866,* 596–603, point up well the fear and distrust of democracy and universal suffrage that characterized most "liberals."

136. Hansemann quoted in Schilfert, *Sieg und Niederlage,* 284. On Hansemann's reservations about the "democratic principle", see also Rudolf Vierhaus, "Konservativ, Konservatismus," in Otto Brunner, Werner Conze, and Reinhart Koselleck, eds., *Geschichtliche Grundbegriffe: Historisches Lexikon zur politisch-sozialen Sprache in Deutschland,* vol. 3: H-Me (Stuttgart: Klett-Cotta, 1982), 546.

137. Nipperdey, *Deutsche Geschichte,* 680. As Eugene A. Anderson explains, the three-class suffrage "widened the group of the powerful without destroying the old ruling

group and supplied a neutral foundation for a merger" between rural and urban elites. Anderson, *The Social and Political Conflict in Prussia, 1858–1864* (Lincoln: Univ. of Nebraska Press, 1954), 274.

138. Friedrich Graf zu Dohna-Lauck, *Ueber die nothwendige Abänderung der beiden Wahlgesetze für die erstse und die zweite Kammer. Eine Petition an die hohen Kammern* (Königsberg: E. I. Dalkowski, 1849), 37–38, 5–6.

139. *Cologne Gazette* cited in Schilfert, *Sieg und Niederlage*, 284.

140. Henry E. Dwight, *Travels in the North of Germany, in the Years 1825 and 1826* (New York: C. & G. & H. Carvill, 1829), 117. This book is a collection of letters which Dwight, an astute observer, wrote to friends in the United States.

141. Henry A. Wise to James Buchanan, 27 Feb. 1847 (photocopy), in Henry Wise Papers, Virginia Historical Society, Richmond.

142. Jack P. Greene, "The Role of the Lower Houses of Assembly in Eighteenth-Century Politics" (1961), in Paul Goodman, ed., *Essays in American Colonial History* (New York: Holt, Rinehart & Winston, 1967), 433, 439. See also Greene's *The Quest for Power: The Lower Houses of Assembly in the Southern Royal Colonies, 1689–1776* (Chapel Hill: Univ. of North Carolina Press, 1963).

143. Jefferson, *A Summary View of the Rights of British America* (1774), in Merrill D. Peterson, ed., *The Portable Thomas Jefferson* (New York: Penguin Books, 1975), 9. The resolutions adopted by the Continental Congress in October of 1774 echoed Jefferson's sentiments, concluding that "such acts and measures" as Parliament had adopted since the French and Indian War "demonstrate a system formed to enslave America." Pole, ed., *The Revolution in America*, 22. On "slavery" and political discourse in revolutionary America, see Bernard Bailyn, *The Ideological Origins of the American Revolution* (Cambridge, Mass.: Belknap Press of Harvard Univ. Press, 1966), 232–46.

144. Clopton cited in Allan Nevins, *The Emergence of Lincoln, Volume II: Prologue to Civil War, 1859–1861* (New York: Charles Scribner's Sons, 1950), 386. For perceptive elaborations of this point, see J. Mills Thorton III, *Politics and Power in a Slave Society: Alabama, 1800–1860* (Baton Rouge & London: Louisiana State Univ. Press, 1978), 442–61; Michael F. Holt, *The Political Crisis of the 1850s* (New York: John Wiley & Sons, 1978; Norton paperback, 1983), 242–43; and William J. Cooper, Jr., *Liberty and Slavery: Southern Politics to 1860* (New York: Knopf, 1983), 267–28.

145. Clement Eaton, *A History of the Old South*, 3rd ed. (New York: Macmillan, 1975), 101.

146. Johnson quoted in Betty Fladeland, *Men and Brothers: Anglo-American Antislavery Cooperation* (Urbana: Univ. of Illinois Press, 1972), 25.

147. Friedrich von Raumer, *America and the American People*, trans. William W. Turner (New York: J. & H. G. Langley, and Astor House, 1846), 145.

148. "One of the most hotly debated topics in the Missouri debates was the charge made by Northerners that Southern society and government were aristocratic, undemocratic, and antirepublican." Glover Moore, *The Missouri Controversy, 1819–1821* (Lexington: Univ. Press of Kentucky, 1953), 310–11.

149. Pinckney's speech is reprinted in Peter M. Bergman and Jean McCarroll, eds., *The Negro in the Congressional Record, Vol. VII: The Negro in the Congressional Record, 1819–1821,* (New York: Bergman Publishers, 1970), 733–40 (speech dated 13 Feb.

1821). Frances Leigh Williams, *A Founding Family: The Pinckneys of South Carolina* (New York & London: Harcourt Brace Jovanovich, 1978), 282–83, 338, 352, tells us that Charles Pinckney (III) owned a plantation near Columbia, but that his principal estate was across the Cooper River from Charleston in Christ Church parish; that he married a daughter of merchant prince Henry Laurens; that he switched from the Federalists to the Jeffersonian Republicans in the 1790s; and that he served several terms as state governor and a term as U.S. Senator before being elected to the House in 1819. According to Glover Moore, during the Missouri debates Pinckney and his fellow South Carolinian William Smith offered "the most spirited defense of Negro servitude." Moore, *The Missouri Controversy*, 125.

150. See Collier and Collier, *Decision at Philadelphia*, esp. ch. 14, and William M. Wiecek, "The Witch at the Christening: Slavery and the Constitution's Origins," in Leonard W. Levy and Dennis J. Mahoney, eds., *The Framing and Ratification of the Constitution* (New York: Macmillan, 1987), 167–84.

151. Wiecek, "The Witch at the Christening," 178–79.

152. William W. Freehling, *The Road to Disunion, Volume I: Secessionists at Bay, 1776–1854* (New York & Oxford: Oxford Univ. Press, 1990), 134–35, and Gary B. Nash, *Race and Revolution* (Madison: Wisconsin House, 1990), esp. 11–19.

153. Jefferson's letter to John Holmes (Congressman from the Maine District of Massachusetts), 22 April 1820, in Adrienne Koch and William Peden, eds., *The Life and Selected Writings of Thomas Jefferson* (New York: Modern Library, 1944), 698–99; and also in Peterson, ed., *The Portable Thomas Jefferson*, 567–69.

154. Ibid. For a clear and concise discussion of the close connections between slavery and American economic development during the early decades of the Republic, see Donald Robinson, *Slavery and the Structure of American Politics, 1765–1820* (New York: Norton, 1979), 430–34

155. On *Notes on Virginia*, see John Chester Miller, *The Wolf by the Ears: Thomas Jefferson and Slavery* (New York: Free Press, 1977), ch. 6. "Had Jefferson had his way, the only book he ever wrote would not have been published and his opinions on slavery would not have become public knowledge during his lifetime." Ibid., 39.

156. Ibid., 228. "Jefferson began his career as a Virginian; he became an American; and in his old age he was in the process of becoming a Southern nationalist." Ibid., 259.

157. Jefferson's letter to John Holmes, 22 April 1820, in Koch and Peden, *Life and Selected Writings*, 698–99. Duncan J. MacLeod, after suggesting that Jefferson shared "an almost universal dread that abolition would inevitably be followed by large-scale miscegenation," concludes that "Jefferson and others may have been prepared to sacrifice the economic benefits of slavery: they were not willing to sacrifice the benefits arising from its use as an instrument of racial and social control." MacLeod, *Slavery, Race and the American Revolution* (Cambridge: Cambridge Univ. Press, 1974), 82.

158. David Brion Davis, *The Problem of Slavery in the Age of Revolution, 1770–1823* (Ithaca & London: Cornell Univ. Press, 1975), 183.

159. Contrary to a widespread popular misconception, Jefferson's will freed only five of his slaves. On the still sensitive and controversial issue of the Sage of Monticello and black slavery, see especially Winthrop Jordan, *White over Black: American Attitudes Toward the Negro, 1550–1812* (1968; Baltimore: Penguin Books, 1969), ch. 12, "Thomas Jef-

ferson: Self and Society"; and William Cohen, "Thomas Jefferson and the Problem of Slavery," *Journal of American History* 56 (1969), 503–26; Davis, *The Problem of Slavery in the Age of Revolution*, 164–84; Miller, *The Wolf by the Ears*; and Freehling, *Road to Disunion*, 121–31.

160. Henry Cleveland, ed., *Alexander H. Stephens in Public and Private, With Letters and Speeches, Before, During, and Since the War* (Philadelphia: National Publishing, 1866), 721. According to James A. Rawley, "Historians have sometimes misconstrued this speech as saying slavery was the Confederate cornerstone, whereas a close reading shows Stephens saying racial inequality—from which slavery flowed—was the cornerstone." Rawley, ed., *Secession: The Disruption of the American Republic, 1844–1861* (Malabar, Fla.: Robert E. Krieger, 1990), 248.

161. Thomas E. Schott, *Alexander H. Stephens of Georgia. A Biography* (Baton Rouge & London: Louisiana State Univ. Press, 1988), 334.

162. Edmund S. Morgan, *American Slavery, American Freedom: The Ordeal of Colonial Virginia* (New York: Norton, 1975), 380–81, 386. See also Morgan's *Inventing the People: The Rise of Popular Sovereignty in England and America* (New York & London: Norton, 1988), 207–8, 293. Cf. William B. Hesseltine, "Some New Aspects of the Proslavery Argument," in Richard N. Current, ed., *Sections and Politics: Selected Essays by William B. Hesseltine* (Madison: Univ. of Wisconsin Press, 1968), 72–73.

163. The quotation is from Elizabeth Fox-Genovese, *Within the Plantation Household: Black and White Women of the Old South* (Chapel Hill & London: Univ. of North Carolina Press, 1988), 99.

164. Calhoun, "Remarks . . . in Respect to the Rights of the States and the Abolition of Slavery—December 27th, 1837," in Richard K. Crallé, ed., *The Works of John C. Calhoun*, (6 vols., New York: D. Appleton, 1851–55; rpt. ed., New York: Russell & Russell, 1968), vol. 3, p. 180; and "Speech on the Abolition Petitions . . . March 9th, 1836," in Crallé, ed., *Works*, vol. 2, p. 489. This aspect of Calhoun's thought receives thoughtful attention in Richard N. Current, *John C. Calhoun* (New York: Twayne Publishers, 1963).

165. (Chesnut), "The Destinies of the South," *Southern Quarterly Review* (Jan. 1853), 196–97. On James Chesnut, Jr., as the probable author of the unsigned essay, see, Frank Winkler Ryan, Jr., "*The Southern Quarterly Review*, 1842–1857. A Study of Thought and Opinion in the Old South" (Ph.D. diss., Univ. of North Carolina at Chapel Hill, 1956), 521, 538.

166. Michael O'Brien, introductory remarks to Thomas R. Dew, "Republicanism and Literature" (1836), in O'Brien, ed., *All Clever Men Who Make Their Way: Critical Discourse in the Old South* (Fayetteville: Univ. of Arkansas Press, 1982), 125.

167. Thomas R. Dew, "On the Influence of the Federative Republican System of Government upon the Literature and the Development of Character," *Southern Literary Messenger* 2 (March 1836), 276–77. This essay is reprinted as Dew, "Republicanism and Literature" (1836), in O'Brien, ed., *All Clever Men Who Make Their Way*. For a perceptive analysis of the link between slavery and republican liberty in Dew's thinking, see Eugene D. Genovese, *The Slaveholders' Dilemma: Freedom and Progress in Southern Conservative Thought 1820–1860* (Columbia: Univ. of South Carolina Press, 1991), 13–20, esp. 18.

168. Joseph Clark Robert calls Dew's *Review* "the bible of the proslavery cause" in the Old Dominion. Robert, *The Road from Monticello: A Study of the Virginia Slavery Debate of 1832* (Durham, N.C.: Duke Univ. Press, 1941), v. "Never has any work, of mere reasoning on previously known facts, had such effect," recalled secessionist Edmund Ruffin in 1857. Ruffin, *The Political Economy of Slavery* (Washington, D.C.: Lemuel Towers, 1857(?)), 14.

169. "Professor Dew on Slavery," in *The Pro-Slavery Argument; as Maintained by the Most Distinguished Writers of the Southern States* (Charleston, S.C.: Walker, Richards, 1852; rpt. ed., New York: Negro Universities Press, 1968), 461–62. Cf. Thomas R. Dew, "Review of the Debate in the Virginia Legislature, 1831–'32," in *The Political Register* 2 (1833), 822–23. Dew, "Abolition of Negro Slavery," in Drew Gilpin Faust, ed., *The Ideology of Slavery: Proslavery Thought in the Antebellum South, 1830–1860* (Baton Rouge & London: Louisiana State Univ. Press, 1981), 66–67, omits the sentence that begins "Color alone. . . ."

170. Charles Henry Ambler, *Sectionalism in Virginia from 1776 to 1861* (Chicago: Univ. of Chicago Press, 1910), 266. I do not think the truth of this statement is contradicted by Alison Goodyear Freehling's revisionist argument that "The struggle for equal political representation was not a rigidly east-west confrontation, as traditional studies . . . suggest. Rather, it was an effort by progressive, under-represented counties in all sections of Virginia to end the disproportionate legislative influence of the conservative Tidewater." As Freehling emphasizes, six out of the 60 eastern delegates did vote against the compromise Constitution of 1830; these six delegates represented some reformist districts in the northern and western Piedmont plus the towns of Lynchburg and Fredericksburg. Freehling, *Drift Toward Dissolution: The Virginia Slavery Debate of 1831–1832* (Baton Rouge & London: Louisiana State Univ. Press, 1982), 39, 77.

171. "Upshur on Majorities and Minorities," in Merrill D. Peterson, ed., *Democracy, Liberty, and Property: The State Constitutional Conventions of the 1820's* (Indianapolis: Bobbs-Merrill, 1966), 315.

172. "Leigh on Power and Property," in ibid., 347–50.

173. "Professor Dew on Slavery," in *The Pro-Slavery Argument*, 312, 387.

174. Chilton Williamson, *American Suffrage from Property to Democracy, 1760–1860* (Princeton: Princeton Univ. Press, 1960), 233. Virginia had instituted a freehold suffrage in 1705, in accord with the traditional English principle " 'that the right to vote should be granted only to such as by their estates real or personal have interest enough to tie them to the endeavor of the public good.' " Quoted in Robert E. and B. Katherine Brown, *Virginia, 1705–1786: Democracy or Aristocracy?* (East Lansing: Michigan State Univ. Press, 1964), 126.

175. Freehling, *Drift Toward Dissolution*, 80.

176. Richmond *Examiner*, 4 Feb. 1851; and Ambler, *Sectionalism in Virginia*, 252, 260.

177. Wise was the only eastern delegate to the convention who supported apportionment of seats in the General Assembly according to white population alone. He was elected governor in 1855 with a majority of 10,180 votes in the western counties, as opposed to a majority of only 955 votes in the East. Ambler, *Sectionalism in Virginia*, 261, 305–6.

178. Richmond *Whig*, 17 May 1850. Cf. the diatribe against political democracy which "fire-eater" Edmund Ruffin confided to his diary on the eve of the Civil War, in William Kauffman Scarborough, ed., *The Diary of Edmund Ruffin, Vol. I: Toward Independence, October, 1856–April, 1861* (Baton Rouge: Louisiana State Univ. Press, 1972), 543 (entry for 4 Feb. 1861).

179. Richmond *Examiner*, 17 Dec. 1850.

180. Craig M. Simpson, *A Good Southerner: The Life of Henry A. Wise of Virginia* (Chapel Hill & London: Univ. of North Carolina Press, 1985), 80.

181. George Fitzhugh, "Slavery Justified" (Fredricksburg, 1850), published as an appendix to *Sociology for the South, or the Failure of Free Society* (Richmond, Va.: A. Morris, 1854; rpt. ed., New York: Burt Franklin, 1964), 255.

182. William Sumner Jenkins, *Pro-slavery Thought in the Old South* (1935; rpt. ed., New York: Peter Smith, 1960), 288.

183. George Fitzhugh, "The Message, the Constitution, and the Times," *DeBow's Review* (Feb. 1861), 163–64.

184. *Catalogue of the Officers and Students of William and Mary College, Session of 1843–44* (Richmond, 1844), and William and Mary Matriculation Book, 1827–81 (manuscript), in the Special Collections Division of the Earl Gregg Swem Library at William and Mary College, Williamsburg, Va. Among the assigned readings in Dew's "Senior Political Course" was his own *Review*. That Richard Eppes owned and pondered some of Calhoun's political speeches is shown in the Richard Eppes Diary, 1859–62, entry for 20 Jan. 1861, in the Virginia Historical Society, Richmond.

185. Eppes Diary, 1859–62, entries for 11 Nov. and 8 Dec. 1860.

186. Richard Eppes Dairy, 1859–61, entry for 15 Feb. 1861. See my "Conditional Unionism and Slavery in Virginia, 1860–1861: The Case of Dr. Richard Eppes," *Virginia Magazine of History and Biography* 96 (1988), 31–54.

187. "The dominant public ideology held up the South as almost an ideal type of society in which black slavery allowed liberty for whites without the dangers of anarchy. This ideal, which white Southerners called republican, had as one important facet a strong commitment to an agrarian economy in which most white men were independent producers, and in which most menial labor was performed by a degraded and dependent race that was excluded from the political community." J. William Harris, *Plain Folk and Gentry in a Slave Society: White Liberty and Black Slavery in Augusta's Hinterlands* (Middletown, Conn.: Wesleyan Univ. Press, 1985), 6, 131–38. Cf. Laurence Shore, *Southern Capitalists: The Ideological Leadership of an Elite, 1832–1885* (Chapel Hill & London: Univ. of North Carolina Press, 1986), 20: "Southern leaders saw their own region, in contrast to the North, suffused with 'conservatism': slave labor prevented development of a huge, destitute laboring class." See also Jenkins, *Pro-slavery Thought in the Old South,* 192–99.

188. The town of Memphis was formally established in 1819; the *Avalanche* began publishing in early 1858.

189. Lacy K. Ford, Jr., notes simply that "many South Carolinians" endorsed the belief, as expressed by clergyman Iveson Brooks in *A Defense of Southern Slavery* (1850), that "no social state, without slavery as its basis, can permanently maintain a republican

form of government." Ford, *Origins of Southern Radicalism: The South Carolina Upcountry, 1800–1860* (New York: Oxford Univ. Press, 1988), 351–52.

190. James L. Roark, *Masters Without Slaves: Southern Planters in the Civil War and Reconstruction* (New York: Norton, 1977), 16. However, Roark does not seem to include among the "strongly anti-democratic" those planters who adhered to the Calhoun-Dew argument for slavery as essential to white republicanism. Nor does James Oakes, *The Ruling Race: A History of American Slaveholders* (New York: Knopf, 1982), ch. 7: "Masters of Tradition." Oakes limits what he calls a "conservative" hostility to democracy to a minority of "paternalist" slaveholders—"Masters of Tradition." Oakes's paternalist conservatism was to be found in the antebellum South pre-eminently "among three small groups of masters whose political and social traditions were, in significant ways, distinct from the typical patterns of slaveholding: those reared under the influence of the military; those born in the Northeast and influenced by federalism; and some of those in the oldest areas of the South around the South's perimeter." This perimeter is defined geographically as extending "down the Atlantic Coast, across the Gulf Coast and up the Mississippi River." Ibid., 196–97. It is worth noting that Oakes's "perimeter" included the vast majority of heavy slaveholding districts in the Old South, and therefore included the great majority of planters.

191. Roark, *Masters without Slaves*, 16.

192. On the lingering apprehensions of Mississippi "river planters" about democracy on the eve of the Civil War, see esp. William Banks Taylor, *King Cotton and Old Glory: Natchez, Mississippi in the Age of Sectional Controversy and Civil War* (Hattiesburg, Miss.: Fox, 1977), 18–34.

193. Fletcher M. Green, "Democracy in the Old South" (1945), in George Brown Tindall, ed., *The Pursuit of Southern History* (Baton Rouge: Louisiana State Univ. Press, 1964), 191.

194. Ford, *Origins of Southern Radicalism*, 111. Ralph Wooster writes that "South Carolina, in the late antebellum period, was the most aristocratic state in the lower South, if not in the entire nation. . . . Here, as perhaps nowhere else in America, with the possible exception of Virginia, political and social power remained in the hands of the rich and well born." Wooster, *The People in Power: Courthouse and Statehouse in the Lower South, 1850–1860* (Knoxville: Univ. of Tennessee Press, 1969), 4–5. The Lowcountry gentry had conceded white manhood suffrage in 1810, but managed throughout the antebellum era to maintain a "mixed" basis for representation in the legislature that weighed heavily in favor of the Lowcountry parishes. This odd combination of democracy and oligarchy was possible primarily because the mountainous portion of the Palmetto State's western backcountry was far smaller and much less geographically isolated from the lowlands than was the case in Virginia, and therefore slave agriculture and the plantation system could spread throughout most of the state. This in turn helps to explain why South Carolina experienced less internal political conflict during the antebellum decades than did the other slave states. On the emergence of intrastate political unity in South Carolina early in the nineteenth century, see Rachel N. Klein, *Unification of a Slave State: The Rise of the Planter Class in the South Carolina Backcountry, 1760–1808* (Chapel Hill & London: Univ. of North Carolina Press, 1990). On the eve of the

Civil War South Carolina's free population included the highest percentage of slaveholders among all the Southern states: 51.5% in 1850 and 48.7% in 1860. The comparable figures for Virginia were 33.1% in 1850 and 25.9% in 1860. The figures are taken from Lewis Cecil Gray, *History of Agriculture in the Southern United States to 1860* (2 vols., 1933; rpt. ed., New York: Peter Smith, 1958), vol. 1, p. 482.

195. On slavery and politics, see especially William J. Cooper, Jr., *The South and the Politics of Slavery, 1828–1856* (Baton Rouge: Louisiana State Univ. Press, 1978), 50–78, and Marc W. Kruman, *Parties and Politics in North Carolina, 1836–1865* (Baton Rouge: Louisiana State Univ. Press, 1983), ch. 5, "Parties, Slavery, and the Union, 1840–1854." For an overview of similarities as well as differences between Democatic and Whig ideologies, see Harry L. Watson, *Liberty and Power: The Politics of Jacksonian America* (New York: Noonday Press, 1990), ch. 8, "The Second American Party System."

196. Ralph A. Wooster, *The Secession Conventions of the South* (Princeton: Princeton Univ. Press, 1962), 32, 145; Wooster, *People in Power*, 41; Wooster, *Politicians, Planters, and Plain Folk: Courthouse and Statehouse in the Upper South, 1850–1860* (Knoxville: Univ. of Tennessee Press, 1975), 39–40; and J. G. Randall and David Herbert Donald, *The Civil War and Reconstruction*, 2nd ed. (Lexington, Mass.: D. C. Heath, 1969), 68; and U.S. Census Office, *Agriculture of the United States in 1860* (Washington, D.C.: Government Printing Office, 1864), 247.

197. Daniel P. Jordan, "Mississippi's Antebellum Congressmen: A Collective Biography," *Journal of Mississippi History* 38 (1976), 173. Jordan has calculated that the average slaveholding among members of Mississippi's congressional delegations was 21.95 for the years 1817–39 and 38.5 for the years 1839–61; he concludes that the Jacksonian era resulted in no withdrawal of the plantation gentry from politics. Ibid., 181.

198. Wooster, *Politicians, Planters and Plain Folk,* 127, 129. It is rather surprising that in North Carolina, which had a large mountainous backcountry, "In 1860 more than 85 percent of the members of the General Assembly were slaveholders (the highest percentage in the South), and more than 36 percent owned at least twenty slaves (one of the highest percentages in the South)." Paul D. Escott, *Many Excellent People: Power and Privilege in North Carolina, 1850–1900* (Chapel Hill & London: Univ. of North Carolina Press, 1985), 15.

199. Eaton, *A History of the Old South,* 328.

200. In 1850 "only 11 percent of the foreign population lived in the South," versus 59% in the Northeast and 29% in the West. By 1860 the South's fraction had fallen below 10%. Roger L. Ransom, *Conflict and Compromise: The Political Economy of Slavery, Emancipation, and the American Civil War* (Cambridge, Eng.: Cambridge Univ. Press, 1989), 132. Despite tensions and conflicts between Protestant "nativists" and Roman Catholic immigrants, "the nativists and immigrant groups in the North shared a deep seated antipathy toward the South" as an undemocratic region based on the unfree labor of degraded blacks, concludes Ransom; and "this antipathy was the foundation upon which a new political coalition—the Republican party—could be formed in the North." Ibid., 139. Even so, the Republican party had only partial success among immigrant voters in 1856. See William E. Gienapp, *The Origins of the Republican Party, 1852–1856* (New York & Oxford: Oxford Univ. Press, 1987), 423–28.

201. William L. Barney, *The Passage of the Republic: An Interdisciplinary History of Nineteenth-Century America* (Lexington, Mass.: D. C. Heath, 1987), 202. As Barney's table shows, the slave-state percentage of the national population declined from 46.4% in 1820 to 39.4 in 1860.

202. In 1849 the only "major uprising" in East Elbia took place in the Silesian city of Breslau. "Only in Prussia's western provinces, where regional loyalties joined with social discontent and political ambitions, were there pitched battles between regular troops and mutinous *Landwehr* units or rebellious workers." Sheehan, *German History, 1770–1866,* 707.

203. The best general accounts are David M. Potter, *The Impending Crisis, 1848–1861,* ed. Don E. Fehrenbacher (New York: Harper & Row, 1976), chs. 9–12, and James M. McPherson, *Battle Cry of Freedom: The Civil War Era* (New York: Oxford Univ. Press, 1988), chs. 3–6.

204. Richmond *Dispatch,* quoted in *American Cotton Planter* (published at Montgomery, Ala.) (Oct. 1856), 302

205. "The South, though increasingly a minority section, had continued to exercise enormous power in national politics. Southerners, at the beginning of the Buchanan administration (in 1857), dominated the Supreme Court, dominated presidential counsels, and, through the caucus system, controlled both houses of Congress. This had been possible because of a kind of holding-company arrangement, in which the South was the majority section within the Democratic party, and the Democrats were the majority party of the nation. Thus the critical task of southerners endeavoring to protect slavery within the confines of the Union was to maintain the majority status of the Democratic party." Don E. Fehrenbacher, *Slavery, Law, & Politics: The Dred Scott Case in Historical Perspective* (New York: Oxford Univ. Press, 1981), 267.

206. McPherson, *Battle Cry of Freedom,* 207–8, 212.

207. *Report of the Joint Committee of the General Assembly of Virginia on the Harper's Ferry Outrages* (dated 26 Jan. 1860), 23–24. (Document no. 31 in the A. H. H. Stuart Papers, in the Alderman Library at the University of Virginia.) Stuart, from Staunton, chaired the committee. For a forceful account of the way in which John Brown's raid fostered an already intense dread of slave rebellion in South Carolina, see Steven A. Channing, *Crisis of Fear: Secession in South Carolina* (New York: Norton, 1970), ch. 2, "Memories and Forebodings."

208. "Address of the Hon. Thomas Ruffin of Alamance. Delivered before the State Agricultural Society of North Carolina, Oct. 18, 1855," *Carolina Cultivator* (published at Raleigh) 1 (Dec. 1855), 309.

209. Daniel W. Crofts, *Reluctant Confederates: Upper South Unionists in the Secession Crisis* (Chapel Hill & London: Univ. of North Carolina Press, 1989), 193.

210. Barney, *The Passage of the Republic,* 210. See also Holt, *Political Crisis,* 244.

211. George H. Reese, ed., *Proceedings of the Virginia State Convention of 1861, February 13–May 1, in Four Volumes* (Richmond: Virginia State Library, 1965), vol. 4, pp. 144–46. The eastern counties supported the secession ordinance 56–10, the western counties opposed it 45–33.

212. Walter Wade Plantation Diary, 1854–65, entries for 19 Nov. 1860, 13 and 15 Jan. 1861. Microfilm in the Mississippi Department of Archives and History, Jackson.

213. Everard Green Baker Diaries, 1848–76, entries for 17 May 1860, 17 and 24 April 1861. Typescript in the Southern Historical Collection at the University of North Carolina at Chapel Hill. The number of slaves owned in 1860 is taken from the National Archives Microfilm Publications' Mississippi Slave Schedules from the Census of 1860.

214. John Houston Bills Diaries, 7 vols. (1847–71), vol. 4 (1860–62), entries for 1 Jan., 2 July, 23 Oct., 15, 29 Nov. 1860, 8 January 1861, 16 April 1861. Microfilm in Mississippi Valley Collection at Memphis State University, Memphis, Tennessee; the microfilm is of a typescript in the Southern Historical Collection at the University of North Carolina at Chapel Hill. Bills owned 87 slaves as of 1 Jan. 1860, of which at least seven lived in Mississippi on a farm near Tunica.

215. "Many upcountry districts with few slaves sent cooperationist delegates (to the secession conventions). In the conventions, delegates supporting delay or cooperation owned, on the average, less wealth and fewer slaves than immediate secessionists. The implications of these data should not be pushed too far. A good many low-slaveholding Democratic counties voted for immediate secession, while numerous high-slaveholding Whig counties backed cooperation. And, of course, cooperationism did not necessarily mean unionism." McPherson, *Battle Cry of Freedom*, 242.

216. Dwight Lowell Dumond, *The Secession Movement, 1860–1861* (1931; rpt. ed., New York: Octagon Books, 1963), 98.

217. Crofts, *Reluctant Confederates*, 193–94.

218. Barney, *The Passage of the Republic*, 225. "Only in the war's grim last two years did massive lower-class desertion somewhat justify longstanding upper-class distrust." Freehling, *Road to Disunion*, 45.

219. DeBow, "The Non-Slaveholders of the South: Their Interest in the Present Sectional Controversy Identical With That of the Slaveholders," in *DeBow's Review* 30 (1861), 69. This essay in included in his *The Interest in Slavery of the Southern Non-Slaveholder. The Right of Peaceful Secession. Slavery in the Bible* (Charleston, S.C.: Evans & Cogswell, 1860), 3–30, dated "Nashville, Dec. 5 1860." As Randolph B. Campbell has concluded, "there appears to be a problem in interpreting as class conflict sectional conflict between plantation areas and nonslaveholding backcountry regions in states such as Virginia and North Carolina. Even in these states, the great majority of plain folk in the backcountry showed no desire to abolish slavery or become Republicans." Campbell, "Planters and Plain Folks: The Social Structure of the Antebellum South," in John B. Boles and Evelyn Thomas Nolen, eds., *Interpreting Southern History: Historiographical Essays in Honor of Sanford W. Higginbotham* (Baton Rouge & London: Louisiana State Univ. Press, 1987), 74.

220. F. H. Gordon to W. B. Campbell, 21 April 1861, in Campbell Family Papers, in Perkins Library at Duke University, Durham, N.C.

221. William Bowen Campbell to cousin Arthur Campbell Beard, 15 March 1861, in Campbell Family Papers. W. B. Campbell (1807–67) was the nephew of former Virginia governor David Campbell (1779–1859), of Montcalm plantation near Abington, in southwest Virginia.

222. Ransom, *Conflict and Compromise*, 11.

223. In 1860 the 15 slave states plus the District of Columbia contained 12.3 million

people living on 878,000 square miles. In 1858 the six eastern provinces of Prussia contained nearly 13 million people living on 89,840 square miles—less than the area of Mississippi (46,362 square miles) plus Louisiana (45,409 square miles).

224. Gray, *History of Agriculture in the Southern United States to 1860,* vol. 1, p. 482.

225. According to Ronald T. Takaki, this agitation was "not only a response to Northern abolitionism, but also a response to the internal crisis of the Old South—a crisis based chiefly on the distressing awareness that slaveholding social mobility was tightening, and on the disturbing recognition that white Southerners themselves doubted the rightness of slavery." Takaki, *A Pro-slavery Crusade: The Agitation to Reopen the African Slave Trade* (New York: Free Press, 1971), x.

226. J. D. B. DeBow, *Statistical View of the United States . . . Being a Compendium of the Seventh Census* (Washington, D.C.: A. O. P. Nicholson, 1854), 95, and U.S. Census Office, *Agriculture of the United States in 1860,* 247–48. In 1860 some 31% of white families in the 11 states that joined the Confederacy owned slaves. Otto Olson has explained that "while 31 percent may not appear large as a voting or even isolated ownership statistic, it is enormous if . . . slavery is viewed as the economic foundation of an entire social system and the distribution of slaves is compared to analogous factors in a free society." In 1949 only 2% of U.S. families owned stock worth $5,000 or more, an investment comparable with the ownership of a single slave in 1860. Olson, "Historians and the Extent of Slave Ownership in the Southern United States," *Civil War History* 18 (1972), 111–12. In the words of James Oakes, "If the slaveholders were an aristocracy, they may well have been the most broadly based aristocracy in Western history." Oakes, *Ruling Race,* 39–40.

227. Moreover, the percentage of the farming population owning more than 500 improved acres—and such persons were definitely large planters in Harrison County—increased from 1.5% in 1850 to 7.3% in 1860. Randolph B. Campbell, "Planters and Plain Folk: Harrison County, Texas, as a Test Case, 1850–1860," *Journal of Southern History* 40 (1974), 374–79.

228. Ralph B. Flanders, *Plantation Slavery in Georgia* (Chapel Hill: Univ. of North Carolina Press, 1933), 74–75

229. "Well before the end of the colonial period, the American dream of upward mobility became implicitly linked to land and slavery in the minds of many white Southerners." Oakes, *Ruling Race,* 7. On the interests of many yeoman farmers and small slaveholders, especially the younger generation, in securing new land for the expansion of slavery, see also Gavin Wright, *The Political Economy of the Cotton South: Households, Markets, and Wealth in the Nineteenth Century* (New York: Norton, 1978), 33; and William R. Brock, *Parties and Political Conscience: American Dilemmas, 1840–1850* (Millwood, N.Y.: Kto Press, 1979), 236–37, 274; and Ransom, *Conflict and Compromise,* 59, 68. This is not to say that all Southern white males were driven by the ambition to become slaveholders. As Barbara J. Fields has emphasized, "The Southern backcountry was full of independent yeoman whites who had no use for slaves or their owners." Fields, "Ideology and Race in American History," in J. Morgan Kousser and James M. McPherson, eds., *Region, Race, and Reconstruction: Essays in Honor of C. Vann Woodward* (New York & Oxford: Oxford Univ. Press, 1982), 157.

230. Recall the discussion of rapidly rising *Rittergut* prices at the end of Chapter 2.

231. Tocqueville, "Journey to England," in his *Journeys to England and Ireland,* ed. J. P. Mayer (New Haven: Yale Univ. Press, 1958), 59.

232. To be sure, some indeterminable number of planters in antebellum Virginia continued to echo the Jeffersonian plea of 1820 that the continued extension and "diffusion" of slavery would ultimately make it possible to expunge both the institution and blacks from the Old Dominion. It should be emphasized that such "Jeffersonians," like Jefferson himself in 1820, still insisted on the necessity for as well as the right of slavery expansion.

233. Richmond *Enquirer,* 3 Feb. 1821, quoted in Moore, *The Missouri Controversy,* 344.

234. Randolph B. Campbell, *An Empire for Slavery: The Peculiar Institution in Texas, 1821–1865* (Baton Rouge & London: Louisiana State Univ. Press, 1989), 12–15. Campbell notes that the first Anglo-American slaveholders had begun to settle in Texas, on the south side of the Red River, as early as 1816.

235. Dohna-Lauck, *Ueber die nothwendige Abänderung der beiden Wahlgesetze,* 5–6, 15.

236. William Harper, "Slavery in the Light of Social Ethics," E. N. Elliot, ed., *Cotton Is King, and Pro-Slavery Arguments* (Augusta, Ga.: Pritchard, Abbott & Loomis, 1860; rpt. ed., New York: Negro Universities Press, 1969), 586. Harper's treatise was originally published as *Memoir on Slavery, Read Before the Society for the Advancement of Learning of South Carolina at Its Annual Meeting at Columbia, 1837* (Charleston: James S. Burges, 1838). It is reprinted in Faust, ed., *The Ideology of Slavery,* 78–135.

237. Some of the best evidence on the racist attitudes of non-slaveholders comes from Frederick Law Olmsted's records of his travels in the South during the 1850s. On the outlook of farming families in east Tennessee, see Olmsted, *A Journey in the Back Country, 1853–1854* (New York: Mason Brothers, 1860; rpt. ed., New York: Schocken Books, 1970), 270–72, 239–40. On the outlook of a young North Carolina native who was bound for Texas by way of Alabama, see Olmsted, *The Cotton Kingdom: A Traveller's Observations on Cotton and Slavery in the American Slave States* (1861), ed. Arthur M. Schlesinger (1953; New York: Modern Library, 1969), 222–24.

238. Winston reported in the Richmond *Enquirer,* 4 Jan. 1856, with an editorial note commending the governor's "just views" to the paper's readers. See also Bowman, "Honor and Martialism," 39–40.

Chapter 5. Patriarchy and Paternalism

1. The term "paternalism," as distinct from "patriarchy," seems to have entered popular usage in the United States long before it entered the German vernacular in central Europe. It is noteworthy that there is no listing for "paternalism" or "paternalistic" in the 1965 edition of *Cassell's German Dictionary,* edited by Harold T. Betteridge (New York: Funk & Wagnalls, 1965). The 1978 edition, also edited by Harold T. Betteridge (New York: Macmillan, 1978), lists *väterliche Fürsorge,* or fatherly care, as the German equivalent for paternalism, and *fürsorglich* or *väterlich sorgend* as the equivalent for paternalistic. In the United States "paternalism" seems to have entered common parlance toward the end of the nineteenth century. The earliest popular usage of the

term cited in the *Oxford English Dictionary,* vol. VII (Oxford: Clarendon Press, 1953), 551, comes from the 1881 *Chicago Times.* C. Vann Woodward, *Tom Watson, Agrarian Rebel* (1938; New York: Oxford Univ. Press, 1963), 167 and 178, reports that in Georgia Patrick Walsh's Augusta *Chronicle* attacked the platform of the Farmers' Alliance in 1890 for advocating "paternalism," "communism," and "downright socialism." Tom Watson replied: "Let me show you how communist and paternal it is. We are the people. We have created the corporations. They are our legal offspring. Shall it be said that the servant is above the master, or the child above the father?" The Augusta *Chronicle* seems to have used "paternalism" in the derogatory sense of treating adults like irresponsible children. The German language would probably use the word *Bevormundung* to designate such patronizing treatment of adults.

2. Michael Mitterauer and Reinhard Sieder, *The European Family: Patriarchy and Partnership from the Middle Ages to the Present,* trans. from the 1977 German ed. by Karla Oosterveen & Manfred Hörzinger (Oxford: Basil Blackwell, 1982; Univ. of Chicago Press paperback, 1983), 21 and 26.

3. Gerda Lerner, *The Creation of Patriarchy* (New York: Oxford Univ. Press, 1986), 239 and 217.

4. Elizabeth Fox-Genovese states that "paternalism invokes a specific metaphor of legitimate domination: the protective domination of the father over his family." Fox-Genovese, *Within the Plantation Household: Black and White Women of the Old South* (Chapel Hill & London: Univ. of North Carolina Press, 1988), 64.

5. William Morris, ed., *The American Heritage Dictionary of the English Language* (Boston & New York: Houghton Mifflin and American Heritage Publishing, 1969), 1175.

6. Charles Morazé, *The Triumph of the Middle Classes: A Political and Social History of Europe in the Nineteenth Century* (originally published in French in 1957 and in English in 1966) (Garden City, N.Y.: Anchor Books, 1968), 188.

7. Dietrich Gerhard, *Old Europe: A Study of Continuity, 1000–1800* (New York: Academic Press, 1981), 14–18.

8. Immanuel Wallerstein suggests that "What we usually think of as feudal values—the combination of the harsh exploitation of labor with paternalism—is in fact less a picture of Europe in the Middle Ages than of . . . 'plantation' zones in the capitalist world-economy." Wallerstein, "What Can We Mean by Southern Culture?," in Numan V. Bartley, ed., *The Evolution of Southern Culture* (Athens & London: Univ. of Georgia Press, 1988), 10.

9. Eugene D. Genovese, *The Political Economy of Slavery: Studies in the Economy and Society of the Slave South* (New York: Vintage Books, 1965), 31; and Genovese, *The World the Slaveholders Made: Two Essays in Interpretation* (New York: Vintage Books, 1969), 98; and Genovese, *Roll, Jordan, Roll: The World the Slaves Made* (New York: Vintage Books, 1974), 4–5.

10. James Oakes, *The Ruling Race: A History of American Slaveholders* (New York: Alfred Knopf, 1982), xii, and Oakes, *Slavery and Freedom: An Interpretation of the Old South* (New York: Alfred Knopf, 1990), 57, 60–61.

11. See, for example, the definitions presented in the *Oxford English Dictionary* (Oxford: Clarendon Press, 1953) and in William Morris, ed., *American Heritage Dictionary*

of the English Language (Boston: Houghton Mifflin and American Heritage Publishing, 1969). Alan Bullock and Stephen Trombley, eds., *The Harper Dictionary of Modern Thought, New and Revised Edition* (New York: Harper & Row, 1988), contains entries for "patriarchalism" and "patriarchy" but none for paternalism.

12. Howard Newby, "Paternalism and Capitalism," in Richard Scase, ed., *Industrial Society: Class, Cleavage and Control* (New York: St. Martin's Press, 1977), 58–73, explores "the dynamics of traditional, paternalist relationships under modern, capitalist conditions."

13. As Bennett explained, paternalism's etymology "suggests its root meaning: a type of behavior by a superior toward an inferior resembling that of a male parent to his child—in most cases, a son." John W. Bennett, "Paternalism," in *International Encyclopedia of the Social Sciences,* 2nd ed., vol. 11 (New York: Macmillan and Free Press, 1968), 472. The *International Encylcopedia* has no article on patriarchy, and the older *Encyclopaedia of the Social Sciences,* published in the 1930s, has no article on paternalism. Nor are there articles on paternalism or patriarchy in *Handwörterbuch der Sozialwissenschaften. Zugleich Neuauflage des Handwörterbuch der Staatswissenschaften,* vol. 8 (Stuttgart, 1964).

14. Genovese, *Roll, Jordan, Roll,* 4.

15. Robert M. Berdahl, "Preussischer Adel: Paternalismus als Herrschaftssystem," in Hans-Jürgen Puhle and Hans-Ulrich Wehler, eds., *Preussen im Ruckblick, Geschichte und Gesellschaft,* Sonderheft 6 (Göttingen: Vandenhoeck & Ruprecht, 1980), 125.

16. Genovese, *Roll, Jordan, Roll,* passim.

17. Robert M. Berdahl, *The Politics of the Prussian Nobility: The Development of a Conservative Ideology, 1770–1848* (Princeton: Princeton Univ. Press, 1988), passim.

18. Philip Scranton, *Proprietary Capitalism: The Textile Manufacture at Philadelphia, 1800–1885* (Cambridge: Cambridge Univ. Press, 1983), 247–51 (a section entitled "The Question of Paternalism").

19. Gerald David Jaynes, *Branches Without Roots: Genesis of the Black Working Class in the American South, 1862–1882* (New York: Oxford Univ. Press, 1988), 79, 93.

20. Jacquelyn Dowd Hall, James Leloudis, Robert Korstad, Mary Murphy, Lu Ann Jones, and Christopher B. Daly, *Like a Family: The Making of a Southern Cotton Mill World* (Chapel Hill & London: Univ. of North Carolina Press, 1987), xvii. On paternalism in postbellum Southern industry, see also C. Vann Woodward, *Origins of the New South, 1877–1913* (1951; rpt. ed. Baton Rouge: Louisiana State Univ. Press, 1971), esp. 223–25; Melton Alonzo McLaurin, *Paternalism and Protest: Southern Cotton Mill Workers and Organized Labor, 1875–1905* (Westport, Conn.: Greenwood Publishing, 1971), ch. 4; and Dwight B. Billings, Jr., *Planters and the Makings of a 'New South." Class, Politics, and Development in North Carolina, 1865–1900* (Chapel Hill: Univ. of North Carolina Press, 1979), chs. 6 and 7. Particularly helpful is I. A. Newby, *Plain Folk in the New South: Social Change and Cultural Persistence, 1880–1915* (Baton Rouge & London: Louisiana State Univ. Press, 1989), esp. 270.

21. Lawrence Schofer, *The Formation of a Modern Labor Force: Upper Silesia, 1865–1914* (Berkeley, Los Angeles, & London: Univ. of California Press, 1975), 78–80.

22. David F. Crew, *Town in the Ruhr: A Social History of Bochum, 1860–1914* (New York: Columbia Univ. Press, 1979), 156–57.

23. Geoff Eley, "The British Model and the German Road: Rethinking the Course of German History Before 1914," in Eley and David Blackbourn, *The Peculiarities of German History: Bourgeois Society and Politics in Nineteenth-Century Germany* (Oxford & New York: Oxford Univ. Press, 1984), 109–13, 122–23

24. Gary Kulik, "Pawtucket Village and the Strike of 1824: The Origins of Class Conflict in Rhode Island," in Robert Blair St. George, ed., *Material Life in America, 1600–1860* (Boston: Northeastern Univ. Press, 1988), 393. Although Kulik does not use the word "paternalism," the index identifies p. 393 as containing information relevant to the topic of "paternalism;" and Kulik does discuss the ways in which Pawtucket mill owners sought to achieve their goal of controlling the workers' behavior.

25. Lacy K. Ford, Jr., *Origins of Southern Radicalism: The South Carolina Upcountry 1800–1860* (New York & Oxford: Oxford Univ. Press, 1988), 358–59.

26. These connotations are exemplified in historian Adam Ulam's observation that "for American public opinion and government" after World War II, "the old relationship between East and West 'at their worst were exploitation . . . at their best paternalism.' " Ulam, *The Rivals: America and Russia since World War II* (New York: Viking Press, 1971), 168, quoting Secretary of State Dean Acheson.

27. Newby, *Plain Folk in the New South*, 270. Cf. Richard Sennett, *Authority* (New York: Knopf, 1980), 5, where Sennett argues that in the nineteenth-century world of "high capitalism" a new "paternalistic metaphor . . . pasted over the stark material fact that bosses were anything but supportive, protective, loving leaders of their employees. And what is interesting about this paternalism, apart from the frequency with which it appeared, is how those subjected to it learned to disbelieve in the pastiche they were offered to view."

28. David Roberts, *Paternalism in Early Victorian England* (New Brunswick, N.J.: Rutgers Univ. Press, 1979), 6, 270–71, 275–76. Harold Perkin sees "the resurgence of the language of paternalism" in England during the 1820s and again at mid-century. Perkin, *The Origins of Modern English Society, 1780–1880* (Toronto: Univ. of Toronto Press, 1969), 446. Of course, an aristocratic ethos of patriarchalism antedated the nineteenth century in England, as is demonstrated by the posthumous publication of Robert Filmer's *Patriarcha* in 1680. See H. T. Dickinson, *Liberty and Property: Political Ideology in Eighteenth-Century England* (London: Weidenfeld and Nicolson, 1977), ch. 5, "The Tories and the Ideology of Order."

29. Berdahl, "Preussischer Adel: Paternalismus als Herrschaftssystem," 145.

30. "Paternalism, however, should not be taken at face value, as an accurate description of social reality." Robert M. Berdahl, "Paternalism, Serfdom, and Emancipation in Prussia," in Erich Angermann and Marie-Luise Frings, eds., *Oceans Apart? Comparing Germany and the United States. Studies in Commemoration of the 150th Anniversary of the Birth of Carl Schurz* (Stuttgart: Klett-Cotta, 1981), 335.

31. Theodor Freiherr von der Goltz, *Die ländliche Arbeiterklasse und der preussische Staat* (Jena: Gustav Fischer, 1893), 189–91. Cf. Hartmut Harnisch's summary of 1847 testimony by Baron Magnus von Bassewitz of Brandenburg, according to whom "The much-talked of patriarchal relationship between lord and peasant had, he said, been an exception. The peasants did not feel they were looked after by the lords, they 'felt they were only used by them.' " Harnisch, "Peasants and Markets: The Background to the

Agrarian Reforms in Feudal Prussia East of the Elbe, 1760–1807," in Richard J. Evans and W. R. Lee, eds., *The German Peasantry: Conflict and Community in Rural Society from the Eighteenth to the Twentieth Centuries* (London & Sydney: Croom Helm, 1986), 63.

32. Weber, *Die Verhältnisse der Landarbeiter im ostelbischen Deutschland,* Schriften des Vereins für Sozialpolitik, vol. 55 (Leipzig: Duncker & Humblot, 1892), 18, and Weber, "Entwicklungstendenzen in der Lage der ostelbischen Landarbeiter (1894), in his *Gesammelte Aufsätze zur Sozial und Wirtschaftsgeschichte,* (Tübingen: J. C. B. Mohr (Paul Siebeck), 1924), 484.

33. Weber, "Entwicklungstendenzen," 473–74, 488–89, and Weber, *Die Verhältnisse,* 790.

34. Weber, "Entwicklungstendenzen," 488, and Weber, *Die Verhältnisse,* 775. "The psychological foundations of the traditional methods of management and of the traditional position of political authority of the landed aristocracy" were the workers' "dull resignation" and the lord's "lack of acquisitiveness in a specifically business sense." Weber, "Entwicklungstendenzen," 474, 488–89. As we have seen, both of these foundations crumbled during the nineteenth century.

35. Elard von Oldenburg-Januschau, "Der Gutsherr and seine Leute," in Gerhard A. Ritter and Jürgen Kocka, eds., *Deutsche Sozialgeschichte, Dokumente und Skizzen, Band II: 1870–1914* (München: C. H. Beck, 1974), 189.

36. Fox-Genovese notes that "most slaves recognized the importance of the master's prosperity to their own well-being, even if they did not accept his view of them as perpetual dependents." *Within the Plantation Household,* 96.

37. "A share hand received as pay a portion of all he grew; he shared the profits, or in a bad year, the losses." Flynn, *White Land, Black Labor,* 77.

38. See Crandall A. Shifflett, *Patronage and Poverty in the Tobacco South: Louisa County, Virginia, 1860–1900* (Knoxville: Univ. of Tennessee Press, 1982), xii–xiv, 25–26; Michael Wayne, *The Reshaping of Plantation Society: The Natchez District, 1860–1880* (Baton Rouge & London: Louisiana State Univ. Press, 1983), 140–48, 197–204; Flynn, *White Land, Black Labor,* 16–21; Eric Foner, *Reconstruction: America's Unfinished Revolution, 1863–1877* (New York: Harper & Row, 1988), 130; and Foner, *A Short History of Reconstruction, 1863–1877* (New York: Harper & Row, 1990), 59.

39. Jaynes, *Branches Without Roots,* 121. Cf. Flynn, *White Land, Black Labor,* 20.

40. Phyllis Byrd, "Images of Women in the Old Testament," in Rosemary Radford Ruether, ed., *Religion and Sexism: Images of Women in the Jewish and Christian Traditions* (New York: Simon and Schuster, 1974), 44, 77. Lerner, *Creation of Patriarchy,* chs. 8 and 9, does not hesitate to describe Hebrew society and religion as patriarchal.

41. Peter Laslett writes about "the traditional, patriarchal, pre-industrial society." Laslett, *The World We Have Lost: England Before the Industrial Age,* 2nd ed. (New York: Charles Scribner's Sons, 1971), 3–4. J. R. Pole sees eighteenth-century Virginia as shaped by a blend of cultural patterns that he terms patriarchy, personal independence, and deference. Pole, *The Foundations of America: Equality, Status, and Power in Thomas Jefferson's Virginia* (Williamsburg, Va.: Colonial Williamsburg Foundation, 1986), 3–13.

42. Friedrich Julius Stahl, *Die Philosophie des Rechts,* 6th ed. (2 vols. in 3; Hildesheim: Georg Olms Verlagsbuchhandlung, 1963), vol. 2, pt. 2, p. 127. This work, first published in the 1830s, had by the 1870s gone through five editions. The practical

management of the preindustrial extended household was the focus of concern in the *Hausväterliteratur* (literature for fathers of the household) that enjoyed such great popularity in central Europe from the late sixteenth to the mid-eighteenth century. See Berdahl, "Paternalism, Serfdom, and Emancipation in Prussia," 333.

43. John S. Wilson, M.D., in the *American Cotton Planter and Soil of the South* (1860), as excerpted in James O. Breeden, ed., *Advice to Masters: The Ideal in Slave Management in the Old South* (Westport, Conn.: Greenwood Press, 1980), 59. Cf. the comments of two prominent South Carolinians. George McDuffie stated that every planter "exercises in his own person, all the high functions of an unlimited monarch. The government of our slaves is strictly patriarchal." McDuffie's gubernatorial message of 1835, quoted in Orville Vernon Burton, *In My Father's House Are Many Mansions: Family and Community in Edgefield, South Carolina* (Chapel Hill & London: Univ. of North Carolina Press, 1985), 99. James Henry Hammond said of "our Patriarchal mode of administering justice": "Remember that on our estates we dispense with the whole machinery of public police and public Courts of Justice." James Henry Hammond, "Two Letters on the Subject of Slavery in the United States, Addressed to Thomas Clarkson, Esq.," in Hammond, *Selections from the Letters and Speeches of the Hon. James H. Hammond* (New York: John F. Trow, 1866), 149. These letters were originally published in the Columbia *South Carolinian* and in pamphlet form in 1845, and during the decade before the Civil War were included in the two major proslavery anthologies: "Hammond's Letters on Slavery," in *The Pro-slavery Argument as Maintained by the Most Distinguished Authors of the Southern States* . . . (Charleston: Walker, Richards, 1852; rpt. ed., New York: Negro Universities Press, 1968), 99–174, and Hammond, "Slavery in the Light of Political Science," in E. N. Elliott, ed., *Cotton Is King, and Pro-slavery Arguments* (Augusta, Ga.: Pritchard, Abbott & Loomis, 1860; rpt. ed., New York: Negro Universities Press, 1969), 629–88. The first of the two letters has recently been reprinted as James Henry Hammond, "Letter to an English Abolitionist," in Drew Gilpin Faust, ed., *The Ideology of Slavery: Proslavery Thought in the Old South, 1830–1860* (Baton Rouge: Louisiana State Univ. Press, 1981), 168–205. For a perspective that minimizes the importance of patriarchal apologetics for slavery, see Fox-Genovese, *Within the Plantation Household*, 63–64.

44. David Herlihy, "Family," *American Historical Review* 96 (Feb. 1991), 2. See also Philip Morgan, "Three Planters and Their Slaves: Perspectives on Slavery in Virginia, South Carolina, and Jamaica, 1750–1790," in Winthrop D. Jordan and Sheila L. Skemp, eds., *Race and Family in the Colonial South* (Jackson & London: Univ. Press of Mississippi, 1987), 38.

45. See esp. Robert M. Bigler, *The Politics of German Protestantism: The Rise of the Protestant Church Elite in Prussia, 1815–1848* (Berkeley & Los Angeles: Univ. of California Press, 1972), ch. 4, "The Pietist Aristocrats;" and H. Shelton Smith, *In His Image, But . . . Racism in Southern Religion, 1780–1910* (Durham, N.C.: Duke Univ. Press, 1972), ch. 3, "In Defense of Bondage." According to Lacy K. Ford, Jr., in the 1820s Baptist leader Richard Furman of South Carolina was "one of the very first Southerners to argue openly that slaves belonged to the master's extended family . . . with the master serving as benevolent patriarch." Ford, *Origins of Southern Radicalism*, 357. Eugene D. Genovese points out that Southern intellectuals "denounced early Roman

patriarchalism for giving the male head of household despotic power over woman, children, and slaves." Because of Christianity's impact, "the model invoked was that of the Abramic household, which made the patriarch subject to the laws of God and therefore recognized the human rights of wives, children, and dependents." Genovese, *The Slave-holders' Dilemma: Freedom and Progress in Southern Conservative Thought, 1820–1860* (Columbia: Univ. of South Carolina Press, 1991), 5 and 9, n. 3.

46. "To assume that domestic slavery is a positive moral, social & political blessing is the height of ultraism," noted Cocke; "but we have the assurance of God that it is compatible with the happiest state of human existence under certain conditions." Entries for August and September of 1863, in John Hartwell Cocke Journal, 1863–64, in Cocke Family Papers, Alderman Library, University of Virginia.

47. John C. Willis, "From the Dictates of Pride to the Paths of Righteousness: Slave Honor and Christianity in Antebellum Virginia," in Edward L. Ayers and John C. Willis, eds., *The Edge of the South: Life in Nineteenth-Century Virginia* (Charlottesville & London: Univ. Press of Virginia, 1991), 37–38.

48. Catherine Clinton, *The Plantation Mistress: Woman's World in the Old South* (New York: Pantheon Books, 1982), 6. Cf. Sara M. Evans, *Born for Liberty: A History of Women in America* (New York: Free Press, 1989), 89.

49. See Fox-Genovese, *Within the Plantation Household*, esp. 29, 96, and Ute Frevert, *Women in German History: From Bourgeois Emancipation to Sexual Liberation*, trans. from the 1986 German ed. by Stuart McKinnon-Evans (Oxford: Berg, 1988), 27–30.

50. Cissie Fairchilds, *Domestic Enemies: Servants and Their Masters in Old Regime France* (Baltimore & London: Johns Hopkins Univ. Press, 1984), 137. The phrase "absolutist patriarchalism" is taken from Rudolf Vierhaus, *Germany in the Age of Absolutism*, trans. Jonathan B. Knudsen, (Cambridge: Cambridge Univ. Press, 1988), 89. Sara Evans contrasts "a patriarchal view linking father, king, and God" with "a republican emphasis on contract, duty, and consent." Evans, *Born for Liberty*, 63.

51. See James J. Sheehan, *German History, 1770–1866* (Oxford: Clarendon Press, 1989), 623.

52. Allan Kulikoff, *Tobacco and Slaves: The Development of Southern Cultures in the Chesapeake* (Chapel Hill & London: Univ. of North Carolina Press, 1986), 166.

53. The tensions that beset the Old South as "a regime both democratic and despotic" are explored in William W. Freehling, *The Road to Disunion, Volume I: Secessionists at Bay, 1776–1854* (New York & Oxford: Oxford Univ. Press, 1990), Part II, "Social Control in a Despots' Democracy." Nonetheless, I am not convinced by Freehling's suggestions that slavery in the Upper South was less harsh and more familial than in the Lower South. Ibid, esp. 76.

54. Let me emphasize that this shift was relative rather than absolute. The idea that parents and children should be united by bonds of love and affection is hardly a "modern" innovation, as the writings of Cicero in classical Rome and Thomas Aquinas in medieval Europe demonstrate. See Herlihy, "Family," 5–8.

55. Fairchilds, *Domestic Enemies*, 17. Frevert, *Women in German History*, 14, and Daniel Blake Smith, *Inside the Great House: Planter Family Life in Eighteenth-Century Chesapeake Society* (Ithaca & London: Cornell Univ. Press, 1980), 21, both see the shift occurring after 1750. According to Carl N. Degler, the "modern American family emerged

first in the years between the American Revolution and about 1830" and included "a new and more favorable conception of children." Degler, *At Odds: Women and the Family in America from the Revolution to the Present* (New York & Oxford: Oxford Univ. Press, 1980), 8, 67. Jane Turner Censer writes of antebellum North Carolina: "Like well-to-do northerners, planters applauded the conjugal family held together by bonds of affection." Censer, *North Carolina Planters and Their Children, 1800–1860* (Baton Rouge & London: Louisiana State Univ. Press, 1984), 152. For an historiographical overview, see Tamara K. Haraven, "The History of the Family and the Complexity of Social Change," *American Historical Review* 96 (Feb. 1991), 119–20. See also David F. Allmendinger, *Ruffin: Family and Reform in the Old South* (New York & Oxford: Oxford Univ. Press, 1990), 21 and 197, n. 59.

56. Mitterauer and Sieder, *European Family*, 6, and Frevert, *Women in German History*, 13. Although German authors had used the noun *Patriarchat* and adjective *patriarchisch* since the sixteenth century, the modifier *patriarchalisch* dates from the 1700s; and in the nineteenth century it could be used in the sense of *väterrechtlich*. Wolfgang Pfeifer, ed., *Etymologisches Wörterbuch des Deutschen, H-P* (Berlin: Akademie-Verlag, 1989), 1242.

57. Fairchilds, *Domestic Enemies*, 5.

58. The quoted phrases are from Bigler, *Politics of German Protestantism*, 147. As Kenneth M. Stampp observed of slavery, "Ideally it was the relationship of parent and child." Stampp, *The Peculiar Institution: Slavery in the Ante-bellum South* (New York: Knopf, 1956), 327.

59. Dohna cited in Berdahl, *Politics of the Prussian Nobility*, 281. In the 1790s the East Prussian country commissioner von Ostau, writing in response to the natural-rights components of the new Prussian Civil Code *(Allgemeines Landrecht)* and the limits it placed on the right of a noble estate owner to inflict punishment on his peasants, had compared the relationship between manorial lords and their dependent subjects to that "between parents and children"; it was therefore characterized by "affection and mutual trust." Von Ostau cited in Günther Birtsch, "Gesetzgebung und Repräsentation im späten Absolutismus: Die Mitwirkung der preußischen Provinzialstände bei der Entstehung des Allgemeinen Landrechts," *Historische Zeitschrift* 208 (1969), 288.

60. Marwitz, "Kritik des Steinschen Testaments," in Friedrich Meusel, ed., *Friedrich August Ludwig von der Marwitz: Ein märkischer Edelmann im Zeitalter der Befreiungskreige* (2 vols.; Berlin: Ernst Siegfried Mittler und Sohn, 1908–13), vol. 2, pt. 1, pp. 240, 242.

61. "Professor Dew on Slavery," in *The Pro-slavery Argument*, 457. This influential essay was originally published as Thomas R. Dew, *Review of the Debate in the Virginia Legislature of 1831 and 1832* (Richmond: T. W. White, 1832). A large portion of the essay is reprinted as Dew, "Abolition of Negro Slavery," in Faust, ed., *The Ideology of Slavery*, 21–77.

62. George Fitzhugh, "Popular Institutions," *DeBow's Review* 28 (1860), 523.

63. On Haller's ideological influence, particularly on the Junker circle around Crown Prince Friedrich Wilhelm that founded the Old Prussian journal *Berlin Political Weekly* (1831–41), see Wolfgang Scheel, *Das "Berliner Politische Wochenblatt" und die politische und soziale Revolution in Frankreich und England. Ein Beitrag zur konservativen Zeitkritik in Deutschland*, Göttinger Bausteine zur Geschichtswissenschaft, vol. 36 (Göttingen: Vandenhoeck und Ruprecht, 1964), chs. 1 and 2. Berdahl, *Politics of the Prussian Nobility*,

242, terms Haller's thought "the most complete expression of the ideology of paternalism." Haller, who lived most of his life in towns and cities, seems to have believed that paternalism could even be extended to relations between owners of non-agricultural wealth and wage labor. Ibid., 244–45.

64. Karl Ludwig von Haller, *Restauration der Staats-Wissenschaft oder Theorie des natürlich-geselligen Zustands,* 2nd ed. (6 vols., Winterthur: Steiner, 1820–34), vol. 6, pp. 565–66.

65. A. Rother zu Schloss Reisen (owned by him for ten years), "Beitrag zu den Zeitfrage: über den Verfall der ländlichen Dienstboten, hier beleuchtet mit besonderer Berücksichtigen der auf den Fürstlich-Sulkowskischen Besitzungen bestehenden Verhältnisse" (dated 14 Feb. 1848), *Annalen der Landwirtschaft* (1849), 99.

66. *Stenographische Berichte über die Verhandlungen der zur Vereinbarung der preussischen Staats-Verfassung berufenen Versammlung, 22 Mai bis 1 Dezember 1848* (3 vols.; Berlin: Deckerschen Geheimen Ober-Hofdruckerei, 1848), vol. 2, p. 831. On Baumstark, see Klaus Klatte, "Die Anfänge des Agrarkapitalismus und der preussische Konservatismus" (D.Phil. diss., Hamburg University, 1974), 367, n. 142.

67. Theodore S. Hamerow, *Restoration, Revolution, and Reaction: Economics and Politics in Germany, 1815–1871* (Princeton: Princeton Univ. Press, 1958; Princeton paperback, 1966), 70. Cf. Ford, *Origins of Southern Radicalism,* 358.

68. (Victor Aimé Huber), *Bruch mit der Revolution und Ritterschaft* (Berlin: Wilhelm Hertz, 1852), 38–40, 54–55. In the preface to this pamphlet Huber claimed to have broken publicly with Old Prussian conservatives in 1849 for their short-sighted selfishness, in particular their rabid insistence on "the so-called doctrine of corporate monarchy and aristocratic co-government" *(ritterschaftlichen Mitregiments).* "The true and supreme calling of the *Ritterschaft"* lay in solving the social question. Ibid., vi–viii. A helpful discussion of Huber's significance is provided by Rudolf Vierhaus, "Konservativ, Konservatismus," in Otto Brunner, Werner Conze, and Reinhart Koselleck, eds., *Geschichtliche Grundbegriffe: Historisches Lexikon zur politisch-sozialen Sprache in Deutschland,* vol. 3: H-Me (Stuttgart: Klett-Cotta, 1982), 547–51.

69. Eduard Bleich, ed., *Der Erste Vereinigte Landtag in Berlin 1847. Dritter Teil* (Vaduz/Liechtenstein: Topos Verlag AG, 1977), 1027.

70. (Baron Karl Adolph Alexander von Hertefeld), *Grundzüge der conservativen Politik* (Berlin: Ludwig Rauh, 1856), 9, 17–18. Although journalist Hermann Wagener claimed authorship of the pamphlet in his *Die kleine aber mächtige Partei* (Berlin: R. Pohl , 1885), 5, historian Adalbert Hahn has demonstrated that it was originally composed by Hertefeld, though approved by Wagener, Graf Pinto, and von Lavergne-Peguilhen. Hahn, *Die Berliner Revue. Ein Beitrag zur Geschichte der konservativen Partei zwischen 1855 and 1875,* Historische Studien, vol. 241 (Berlin: Emil Ebering, 1934), 41, 264. On analogous arguments in the *Berlin Political Weekly,* see Berdahl, *Politics of the Prussian Nobility,* 262.

71. (George Frederick Holmes), "Slavery and Freedom," *Southern Quarterly Review* (published in Columbia, S.C. in 1856–57), (April 1856), 81–82, 71. Holmes gave a similar response to Fitzhugh, also emphasizing that Southern slavery was founded more on the racial inferiority of blacks rather than the merits of bondage per se, in "Failure of Free Societies," *Southern Literary Messenger* (published in Richmond, Va.) 21 (1855), esp. 132. Holmes is identified as the author of the two essay reviews in Neal C. Gillespie, *The Collapse of Orthodoxy: The Intellectual Ordeal of George Frederick Holmes* (Charlottes-

ville: Univ. Press of Virginia, 1972), 254–55. According to Eugene Genovese, however, "the notion that slavery was a proper system for all labor, not merely for black labor, . . . grew steadily as part of the growing self-awareness of the planter class," and George Fitzhugh provided "a more rigorous and mature presentation of a line of thought that had been gaining steadily for years." Genovese, *The World the Slaveholders Made: Two Essays in Interpretation* (New York: Pantheon, 1969: Vintage paperback, 1971), p. 130.

72. See Wilfred Carsel, "The Slaveholders' Indictment of Northern Wage Slavery," *The Journal of Southern History* 6 (1940), 504–20, and the comparative analysis in Marcus Cunliffe, *Chattel Slavery and Wage Slavery: The Anglo-American Context, 1830–1860* (Athens: Univ. of Georgia Press, 1979).

73. John C. Calhoun, "Remarks on Receiving Abolition Petitions (Revised Report) (In the Senate, 6 Feb. 1837)," in Clyde N. Wilson, ed., *The Papers of John C. Calhoun, Volume XIII, 1835–1837* (Columbia: Univ. of South Carolina Press, 1980), 396.

74. Hammond, "Speech on the Admission of Kansas, . . . March 4th, 1858," in his *Selections from the Letters and Speeches of the Hon. James H. Hammond*, 319.

75. "American Slavery in 1857," *Southern Literary Messenger* 24 (1857), 84.

76. Charles von Rosenberg, ed., "Ancestral Voices: The Letters of the Von Rosenberg and Meerscheidt Families, 1844–1897" (bound photocopy of typescript published in 1978 by the Reunion Association Publication Committee), 18, in the Barker Texas History Center at the University of Texas at Austin.

77. Clement Eaton, "The Emergence of the Radical," Ch. 6 in his *The Mind of the Old South,* rev. ed. (Baton Rouge: Louisiana State Univ. Press, 1967), 111, 115, 125, and Freehling, *Road to Disunion,* 462–74. Carl Degler points out that Clay "was especially unusual in that he never concealed his hatred of slavery even though he remained in the South." Degler, *The Other South: Southern Dissenters in the Nineteenth Century* (New York: Harper and Row, 1974), 56. Comparable to Clay was James Gillespie Birney (1792–1857), also a Kentucky-born planter-lawyer who freed his slaves and became a vocal abolitionist. Interestingly, both Birney and Clay attended Transylvania College in Kentucky before graduating from Northern schools: Birney from Princeton in 1810, Clay from Yale in 1832. Clement Eaton briefly compares and contrasts the two men in *The Mind of the Old South,* 168–69.

78. Foby, writing in the *Southern Cultivator* (1853), quoted in Breeden, ed., *Advice Among Masters,* 306.

79. Hermann Graf zu Dohna-Kotzenau, *Die freien Arbeiter im preussischen Staate* (Leipzig: Otto Wigand, 1847), 10–11. On Dohna-Kotzenau, see the entry in *Allgemeine Deutsche Biographie,* vol. 5 (Berlin: Duncker & Humblot, 1877), 303, and Lothar Graf zu Dohna, "Dohna, Burggrafen und Herren," in *Neue Deutsche Biographie,* vol. 4 (Berlin: Duncker & Humblot, 1955), 45.

80. The quotation "an institution patriarchal in its nature and tendencies" is taken from James L. Gaines, "An Address Delivered by James L. Gaines, Esq., Before the Moore County Agricultural Society, at Carthage, Moore County (North Carolina)," in *Carolina Cultivator* 2 (1856), 132. Charles Joyner, focusing on a rice-growing district in Lowcountry South Carolina, concludes that many planters liked to cast themselves in a "kindly, patriarchal role," and their "paternalism" had the effect of providing "standards of kindness and benevolence to aspire—or pretend—to." Joyner, *Down by the Riverside:*

A South Carolina Slave Community (Urbana & Chicago: Univ. of Illinois Press, 1984), 56.

81. Harriet A. Jacobs, *Incidents in the Life of a Slave Girl, Written by Herself* (1861), ed. Jean Fagan Yellin (Cambridge, Mass., and London: Harvard Univ. Press, 1987), 74, cf. 146 & 192.

82. Franz Rehbein (1867–1909) lived and worked with an *Instmann* on a Pomeranian *Rittergut* as a boy, and his autobiography, originally published in 1911, provides vivid testimony about the self-consciously patriarchal bearing of the estate owner, Herr Damerow, towards his " 'people' " *(Leute)* as late as the 1880s. Rehbein's autobiography also portrays instances of cruelty and oppression, as when the overseer *(Inspektor)* kicked a cottager's wife, yelled obscenities at her, beat her lame husband with a rod, and then docked their wages for a week. Rehbein, *Das Leben eines Landarbeiters,* ed. Karl Winfried Schafhausen (Darmstadt & Neuwied: Hermann Luchterhand, 1973), 52, 48–50. After losing one hand in a threshing machine accident in 1895, Rehbein became a socialist writer and trade union official. A different portion of the book, one recounting his stint during the early 1890s as a day laborer north of Hamburg, is available in English translation in Alfred Kelly, ed. and trans., *The German Worker: Working-Class Autobiographies from the Age of Industrialization* (Berkeley: Univ. of California Press, 1987), 188–203. According to Drew Gilpin Faust's wonderful biography of James Henry Hammond, the South Carolina planter "from the first cherished a conception of himself as a beneficent master whose guidance and control represented the best of all possible worlds for the uncivilized and backward people entrusted to him by God." Nonetheless, his efforts to mold his slaves "into a disciplined, productive, and expanding slave force would be thwarted at nearly every turn." Faust, *James Henry Hammond and the Old South: A Design for Mastery* (Baton Rouge & London: Louisiana State Univ. Press, 1982), 73, 72.

83. Charles L. Flynn, Jr., *White Land, Black Labor: Caste and Class in Late Nineteenth-Century Georgia* (Baton Rouge and London: Louisiana State Univ. Press, 1983), 19.

84. Stampp, *Peculiar Institution,* 326.

85. Censer, *North Carolina Planters and Their Children, 1800–1860* (Baton Rouge: Louisiana State Univ. Press, 1984), 135–37. "A man can act paternalistically toward his children," observes Michael Wayne, "but scarcely toward his property." Wayne, *The Reshaping of Plantation Society,* 23.

86. Philip N. Racine, ed., *Piedmont Farmer: The Journals of David Golightly Harris, 1855–1870* (Knoxville: Univ. of Tennessee Press, 1990), 46, 71. Cf. the 1859 sale of Bins by the wealthy and genteel Dr. Richard Eppes of Tidewater Virginia; see Shearer Davis Bowman, "Conditional Unionism and Slavery in Virginia: The Case of Dr. Richard Eppes," *Virginia Magazine of History and Biography* 96 (1988), 31–32, n. 2.

87. See especially David Brion Davis, *The Problem of Slavery in Western Culture* (Ithaca, N.Y.: Cornell Univ. Press, 1966). "Madison was right when he noted that the founding fathers defined slaves as both men and property," notes Roger L. Ransom; but "by the middle of the nineteenth century there was little doubt that property was the characteristic that dominated the lives of both slaves and their masters." Ransom, *Conflict and Compromise: The Political Economy of Slavery, Emancipation, and the American Civil War* (Cambridge: Cambridge Univ. Press, 1989), 44.

88. Randolph B. Campbell, *An Empire for Slavery: The Peculiar Institution in Texas,*

1821–1865 (Baton Rouge & London: Louisiana State Univ. Press, 1989), 98.

89. Vanhauten Manuscript Will (Draft), 9 Oct. 1850, in Richard Abbey Papers, Mississippi State Department of Archives and History, Jackson.

90. Nathan Bass, Esq., "Essay on the Treatment and Management of Slaves," in David W. Lewis, Secretary, *Transactions of the Southern Central Agricultural Society, from Its Organization in 1846 to 1851* (Macon, Ga.: Benjamin F. Griffin, 1852), 198. Bass won not only the silver pitcher at the Society's 1851 fair for the best essay on slave management, but the premiums for the best rice and corn as well.

91. The quotation is from Wayne, *The Reshaping of Plantation Society*, 25. Wayne concludes that legally a slaveholder's "relationship to his chattels took on an appearance that can legitimately, if roughly, be described as paternalistic. The planter, fatherlike, provided care and supervision; the slave, childlike, returned obedience." Ibid., 24.

92. Bertram Wyatt-Brown, "The Ideal Typology and Antebellum Southern History: A Testing of a New Approach," *Societas—A Review of Social History* 5 (1975), 15, 18. A similar argument is presented in Willie Lee Rose, "The Domestication of Domestic Slavery," in her *Slavery and Freedom*, expanded ed., ed. William W. Freehling (New York: Oxford Univ. Press, 1982), 18–36. An analogous perspective on the patriarchal self-image of *Rittergut* lords is presented in Wilhelm Treue, *Wirtschafts- und Technik-Geschichte Preussens*, Veröffentlichungen der Historischen Kommission zu Berlin, vol. 56 (Berlin & New York: Walter de Gruyter, 1984), 254.

93. Genovese, *Roll, Jordan, Roll,* esp. 6–7. Leon F. Litwack's masterful study of blacks and whites during the crucible decade of the 1860s carefully avoids applying ambiguous and argumentative terms like paternalism or patriarchy to the peculiar institution. Yet he not only notes that masters assumed "paternalistic roles" but also refers to "the mutual obligations implicit in the master-slave relationship." Litwack, *Been in the Storm So Long: The Aftermath of Slavery* (New York: Knopf, 1979; Vintage paperback, 1980), 215, 50.

94. Paul D. Escott, *Slavery Remembered: A Record of Twentieth-Century Slave Narratives* (Chapel Hill: Univ. of North Carolina Press, 1979), 18–20. Escott offers a remarkably evenhanded summary of the paternalism debate in "Paternalism," in Randall M. Miller and John David Smith, eds., *Dictionary of Afro-American Slavery* (New York: Greenwood Press, 1988), 589–62. It is worth noting here that the two best indexed collections of testimony from slaves and former slaves—John W. Blassingame, ed., *Slave Testimony: Two Centuries of Letters, Speeches, Interviews, and Autobiographies* (Baton Rouge: Louisiana State Univ. Press, 1977); and Charles L. Perdue, Jr., Thomas E. Barden, and Robert K. Phillips, eds., *Weevils in the Wheat: Interviews with Virginia Ex-Slaves* (1976; Bloomington & London: Indiana Univ. Press, 1980)—do not include the terms patriarchy or paternalism in their extensive indices.

95. Wayne, *The Reshaping of Plantation Society*, 22–23.

96. Freehling, *Road to Disunion: Secessionists at Bay*, 77. See also the discussion in Kenneth M. Stampp, "Rebels and Sambos: The Search for the Negro's Personality in Slavery," in his *The Imperiled Union: Essays on the Background of the Civil War* (New York & Oxford: Oxford Univ. Press, 1980), 39–71.

97. Solomon Northup, *Twelve Years a Slave*, ed. Sue Eakin and Joseph Logsdon, (Baton Rouge: Louisiana State Univ. Press, 1968), 158. Cf. Juliet E. K. Walker, *Free*

Frank: A Black Pioneer on the Antebellum Frontier (Lexington: Univ. Press of Kentucky, 1983), 48: "While for the owners of slaves the institution may have been viewed as resting on meaningful reciprocal obligations and a paternalistic accommodation, it lacked any meaningful recirpocal benefits for the slaves. Freedom was their ultimate goal, and its achievement found little encouragement from slaveholders."

98. "A Declaration of the Causes Which Impel the State of Texas to Secede from the Federal Union," adopted 2 Feb. 1861, in Ernest William Winkler, ed., *Journal of the Secession Convention of Texas, 1861* (Austin, Texas: Austin Printing, 1912), 63.

99. I have explored this question in "'The Great Question Which Is Uprooting This Government to Its Foundation': Slavery and the Virginia State Convention of 1861," a paper presented in November of 1988 at the Southern Historical Association's Annual Meeting in Norfolk, Virginia. This paper was inspired by Fred Siegel's comparable investigation of slaveholders' speeches during the Virginia State Convention of 1829–30 and the 1831–32 session of the Virginia General Assembly. Siegel, "The Paternalist Thesis: Virginia as a Test Case," *Civil War History* 25 (1979), 246–61.

100. George M. Reese, ed., *Proceedings of the Virginia State Convention of 1861, February 13–May 1, in Four Volumes* (Richmond: Virginia State Library, 1965), vol. 3, pp. 110, 81–82. On Richardson's slaves, see "Virginia Slave Schedules from the 1860 Census," National Archives Microfilm Publications, Microcopy 653 (Washington, D.C., 1967).

101. Reese, ed., *Proceedings*, vol. 3, pp. 81–82, 95–96, 91.

102. See Holcombe's *An Address on the Right of the State to Institute Slavery, Delivered Before the Seventh Annual Meeting of the Virginia State Agricultural Society, November 4th, 1858* (Richmond: McFarlane & Ferguson, 1858). A biographical sketch is available in William H. Gaines, Jr., *Biographical Register of Members, Virginia State Convention of 1861, First Session* (Richmond, 1961), 44–45. I could not find Holcombe's name among the slaveholders in the 1860 census slave schedule for Albemarle County.

103. Reese, *Proceedings*, vol. 2, pp. 86, 82–83.

104. Ibid., vol. 2, pp. 241–44, 261. On Bruce, see Ralph A. Wooster, *Secession Conventions of the South* (Princeton: Princeton Univ. Press, 1962), 144–45, and Gaines, *Biographical Register*, 21.

105. O'Neall, "Judge O'Neall's Address Delivered Before the South Carolina Agricultural Society, December 29, 1842," *Southern Cultivator* (published in Augusta, Ga.) 1 (1843), 109. On O'Neall, see William W. Freehling, *Prelude to Civil War: The Nullification Controversy in South Carolina, 1816–1836* (New York: Harper & Row, 1966; Harper Torchbook, 1968), esp. 261, 269, 317–18, 336–37.

106. J. F. H. Claiborne, *Life and Correspondence of John A. Quitman* (2 vols.; New York, 1860), vol. 1, p. 190, quoted in Clement Eaton, *Jefferson Davis* (New York: Free Press, 1977), 42. Robert E. May quotes part of this statement in his fine biography *John A. Quitman, Old South Crusader* (Baton Rouge & London: Louisiana State Univ. Press, 1985), 138. Noting that "In addition to showing restraint in disciplinary matters, Quitman permitted an incentive system to operate within his labor economy," May concludes that his subject "clearly approached more the paternalistic than the tyrannical model of southern planter." Ibid., 138–39. This paternalistic model was exemplified by Quitman's neighbor Joseph E. Davis at Hurricane plantation. See Janet Sharp Hermann, *The Pur-*

suit of a Dream (New York: Oxford Univ. Press, 1981; Vintage paperback, 1983), Part I.

107. Gutsbesitzer Lüdersdorf auf Christoplack, "Die landwirtschaftliche Verhältnisse des Labiauer Kreises, in Reg.-Bezirk Königsberg," *Annalen der Landwirtschaft* (published in Berlin) (1849), 129–30.

108. Friedrich at Piotrowo, "Die Provinz Posen. Eine landwirtschaftliche Skizze" (dated 8 Jan. 1847), *Allgemeine Landwirtschaftliche Monatschrift* (published in Berlin for the Pomeranian Agricultural Association) (1847), 196–97.

109. Gilmer also suggested that "Kindness when sick, and at all times when they deserve, or will *permit* it, is a great thing. The hope of reward and fear of punishment induce human action in master and servant. Never overtask your servant; feed and clothe him *well*, allow a reasonable time for sleep, and you will not be apt to injure him by work in the day." W. W. Gilmer, Ivy Creek, Albemarle, March 17 1852, "Management of Servants," *Southern Planter* (published in Richmond, Va.) 12 (1852), 106–7. Berdahl, *Politics of the Prussian Nobility*, 59, points out that prior to the abolition of serfdom in Prussia, "The primary function of corporal punishment was to induce fear, and therefore discipline, in the peasants; if it was administered too often, it lost its effect."

110. Andrew Flynn, 1840 Plantation Rules for Green River Plantation, in Andrew Flynn Plantation Book (Microfilm), in the Southern Historical Collection, University of North Carolina, Chapel Hill. Compare the advice, already quoted in Chapter 2, offered by Thomas Affleck in his widely used *Cotton Plantation Record and Account Book*'s section on "The Duties of an Overseer," which stipulated that the primary component of "*a fine crop*" was "an increase in the number and a marked increase in the condition and value of the negroes." Affleck, "The Duties of an Overseer," reprinted in *American Cotton Planter* 2 (1854), 356, and in *DeBow's Review* 18 (1855), 345.

111. Dr. William C. Daniell, "An Address" (to a convention called to organize an Agricultural Association of the Slaveholding States, held in Montgomery, Ala., 2 May 1853), *American Cotton Planter* (published in Montgomery) 2 (1854), 66. Daniell (1792–1868) was a planter-physician who resided in Savannah and owned Oglethorpe plantation (with 120 slaves in 1860) in South Carolina's Beaufort District. His active public career included tenures as mayor of Savannah, Georgia state representative, state senator, editor of the *Savannah Republican,* and chairman of the Executive Committee of the Southern Central Agricultural Society. See Chalmers Gaston Davidson, *The Last Foray: The South Carolina Planters of 1860: A Sociological Study* (Columbia: Univ. of South Carolina Press for the South Carolina Tricentennial Commission, 1971), 15, 188–89.

112. For Scarborough, as for Robert W. Fogel and Stanley Engerman in *Time on the Cross: The Economics of American Negro Slavery* (1974), "Paternalism is not intrinsically antagonistic to capitalist enterprise. Nor is it necessarily a barrier to profit maximization." Where Scarborough points to "the paternalistic mill villages of the New South" and "George Pullman's model town in Illinois" to demonstrate the compatibility of capitalism and paternalism, Fogel and Engerman point to the paternalism practiced by IBM and Eastman Kodak. "Their experience suggests that patriarchal commitments may actually raise profits by inducing labor to be more efficient than it would have been under a less benevolent management." William K. Scarborough, "Slavery—The White Man's Burden," in Harry P. Owens, ed., *Perspectives and Irony in American Slavery* (Jack-

son: Univ. Press of Mississippi, 1976), 105–8, and Robert William Fogel and Stanley L. Engerman, *Time on the Cross: The Economics of American Negro Slavery* (Boston & Toronto: Little, Brown, 1974), 73.

Chapter 6. Planter and Junker Conservatism

1. Phillips also noted that insofar as secession appeared to its opponents as a "drastic remedy" which should not be applied "without first taking milder measures which might render it unnecessary," "Secession appears from this point of view to have been radical." U. B. Phillips, *Georgia and States Rights* (1902; rpt. ed., Yellow Springs, Ohio: Antioch Press, 1968), 208–9. This monograph was Phillips's doctoral dissertation, completed in 1902 at Columbia University, when Phillips was not yet twenty-five.

2. Eugene D. Genovese, "Foreword: Ulrich Bonnell Phillips & His Critics," in Phillips, *American Negro Slavery* (1918; rpt. ed., Baton Rouge: Louisiana State Univ. Press, 1966), vii.

3. Thomas Nelson Page, "Social Life in Old Virginia Before the War," in his *The Old South: Essays Social and Political* (New York: Charles Scribner's Sons, 1892), 160. At the turn of the century Page was "settled prosperously in Washington, undisputed champion among the glorifiers of the Old South and the plantation legend." C. Vann Woodward, *Origins of the New South, 1877–1913* (1951; rpt. ed., Baton Rouge: Louisiana State Univ. Press, 1971), 429.

4. Allan Nevins, *Ordeal of the Union, Vol. I: Fruits of Manifest Destiny, 1847–1852* (New York: Charles Scribner's Sons, 1947), 256.

5. *An Address Setting Forth the Declaration of the Immediate Causes Which Induce and Justify the State of Mississippi from the Federal Union and the Ordinance of Secession* (Jackson: Mississippian Book and Job Printing Office, 1861), 5. The "Declaration" is reprinted in Herman V. Ames, ed., *State Documents on Federal Relations: The States and the United States* (Philadelphia: Univ. of Pennsylvania Department of History, 1906), 318–20. On the membership of the Mississippi convention, see Ralph A. Wooster, *The Secession Conventions of the South* (Princeton: Princeton Univ. Press, 1962), 32.

6. Arkansas lawyer-planter John W. Brown, who lived in Camden and owned seventeen slaves in Quachita Country in 1860, noted in his diary on 10 Jan. 1861: "The Demon of Secession is daily becoming more powerful and we are in fact in the midst of Revolution." On 20 he wrote that the Confederacy was engaged in an "insurrection." Yet on 3 May, three days before Arkansas adopted a secession ordinance, he declared that "The trouble is on us and we must make the best of it. Wicked men have brought it on us but it is too late now to look to that(.) we must make the best fight we can in defense with a full confidence that if we have the right a Just God will help us to defend it(.) if not we can only expect the fate of the unjust." John W. Brown Diary, 1852–65 (microfilm of typescript), Southern Historical Collection, University of North Carolina at Chapel Hill.

7. Nevins, *Ordeal of the Union*, vol. 1, p. 256.

8. *Speech of John C. Rutherfoord of Goochland in the House of Delegates of Virginia, on the Removal from the Commonwealth of the Free Colored Population. Delivered February 18, 1853* (Richmond: Ritchie & Dunnavant, 1853), 4–7.

9. *Letter of Governor R. K. Call of Florida to John S. Littell, of Germantown, Pennsylvania* (Philadelphia: C. Sherman & Son, 1861), 18, 12. See also "Letter of Gov. Call of Florida to J. S. Littell, of Pennsylvania, 12 February 1861," in Frank Moore, ed. *The Rebellion Record*, vol. 1 (New York: G. P. Putnam, 1864), 421, 419. On Call's life and career, see Herbert J. Doherty, *Richard Keith Call, Southern Unionist* (Gainesville: Univ. of Florida Press, 1961). Cf. Call's remarks with Jefferson Davis's testimony before the U.S. Senate in December of 1859, as reported in William W. Freehling, *The Road to Disunion, Volume I: Secessionists at Bay, 1776–1854* (New York & Oxford: Oxford Univ. Press, 1990), 81–82. Freehling argues that white Southerners were less fearful about the prospect of mass slave revolts than about the legion possibilities for a master's murder by a trusted household slave.

10. "1811, 2. November. Die Eingabe der Gustbesitzer des Kreises Stolp in Pommern an König Friedrich Wilhelm III. zum Regulierungsedikt," in Günther Franz, ed., *Quellen zur Geschichte der Deutschen Bauernstandes in der Neuzeit* (München & Vienna: R. Oldenbourg, 1963), 373–74.

11. See Klaus Klatte, "Die Angänge des Agrarkapitalismus und der preussischer Konservatismus" (D. Phil. diss., Hamburg University, 1974), 262–65. *Annalen der Landwirtschaft* (1849), 137 reports a *Rittergut* owner's 12 Aug. 1848 petition to the Prussian Board of Rural Economy arguing that the state should pay the estate owner, in the form of bonds paying no interest, an amount equal to 25 times the value of each peasant's remaining obligations, and that the peasant should pay off his obligations in monthly payments to the tax-collector's office in his county.

12. William Morris, ed., *The American Heritage Dictionary of the English Language* (New York & Boston: American Heritage Publishing and Houghton Mifflin, 1969), 284.

13. Karl Mannheim, "Conservative Thought" (1927), trans. Mannheim, Paul Kecskemeti, and Kurt Wolff, in Wolff, ed., *From Karl Mannheim* (New York: Oxford Univ. Press, 1971), esp. 173–74. In addition to Mannheim, the following authors have influenced my approach to the concept of conservatism: Sigmund Neumann, *Die Stufen des preussischen Konservatismus: Ein Beitrag zum Staats- und Gesellschaftsbild Deutschlands im 19. Jahrhundert*, Historische Studien, No. 190 (Berlin: Emil Ebering, 1930), esp. 7–12, which shows the strong influence of Mannheim; and Samuel Huntington, "Conservatism as an Ideology," *American Political Science Review* 51 (1957), 454–73; and Hans-Gerd Schumann, "The Problem of Conservatism: Some Notes on Methodology," *Journal of Contemporary History* 13 (1978), 803–17.

14. "Although the seeds of the sectional clash of 1860 were in the soil at the nation's founding, it was not until the Missouri controversy of 1820 that the conflict appeared at the surface of American politics. During this crisis, the South saw for the first time the possibility that it might one day be outnumbered in all branches of the federal government." Donald Robinson, *Slavery in the Structure of American Politics, 1765–1820* (New York: Norton, 1979), 444. John Richard Alden has demonstrated that white Southerners were conscious of their regional interests and "frequently behaved as a section before 1789;" yet he points out "that Northerners were not yet attacking the institution of slavery in the South, and that it was unnecessary for Southerners to defend it." Alden, *The First South* (Baton Rouge: Louisiana State Univ. Press, 1961), 7, 74.

15. "The aristocracy had to be and could be content with the recognition (under Friedrich II and Fiedrich Wilhelm II) of its unconditional manorial authority (*Gutsherrschaft*) and of its privileged position in state service. The crisis first came, when these two fundamentals of its power were attacked." Otto-Ernst Schüddekopf, *Die deutsche Innenpolitik im letzten Jahrhundert und der konservative Gedanke: Die Zusammenhänge zwischen Aussenpolitik, innerer Staatsführung und Parteigeschichte, dargestellt an der Geschichte der Konservativen Partie von 1807 bis 1918* (Braunschweig: Albert Limbach, 1951), 9. Even the bureaucracy's Prussian Civil Code of 1791–94, the brunt of so many Old Prussian tirades against codified (versus organic) law during the nineteenth century, did not evoke a substantial aristocratic opposition at the time of it promulgation. See Günther Birtsch, "Gesetzgebung und Repräsentation im späten Absolutismus. Die Mitwirkung der preussischen Provinzialstände bei der Entstehung des Allgemeinen Landrechts," *Historische Zeitschrift* 208 (1969), 265–94.

16. See William Sumner Jenkins, *Pro-slavery Thought in the Old South* (Chapel Hill, N.C., 1935; rpt. ed. New York: Peter Smith, 1960), passim. The most exhaustive Scriptural defense of slavery (over 600 pages!) was probably John Fletcher of Louisiana, *Studies on Slavery, in Easy Lessons. Compiled into Eight Studies and Subdivided into Short Lessons for the Convenience of Readers* (Natchez, Miss.: J. Warner, 1852). The proslavery writer who best understood and employed the Aristotelian defense of slavery was probably George Frederick Holmes, a classical scholar. See Neal C. Gillespie, *The Collapse of Orthodoxy: The Intellectual Ordeal of George Frederick Holmes* (Charlottesville: Univ. Press of Virginia, 1972), esp. 112–13, 188–89.

17. Edwin C. Holland, *A Refutation of the Calumnies Circulated Against the Southern and Western States, Respecting the Institution and Existence of Slavery Among Them* (Charleston: A. E. Miller, 1822), 36–37, 67, 77, 61, 86. On the Vesey rebellion and its aftermath, see Glover Moore, *The Missouri Controversy, 1819–1821* (Lexington: Univ. Press of Kentucky, 1953; Kentucky Paperbacks, 1966), 295, 348–49; William W. Freehling, *Prelude to Civil War: The Nullification Controversy in South Carolina, 1816–1836* (New York: Harper & Row, 1966; Harper Torchbooks, 1968), 53–65; and Michael P. Johnson and James L. Roark, *Black Masters: A Free Family of Color in the Old South* (New York: Norton, 1984), 36–50.

18. "Professor Dew on Slavery," in *The Pro-slavery Argument; As Maintained by the Most Distinguished Writers of the Southern States* (Charleston, S.C.: Walker, Richards, 1852; rpt. ed., New York: Negro Universities Press, 1968), 489.

19. On Nat Turner's rebellion and its aftermath, see Joseph Clark Robert, *The Road from Monticello: A Study of the Virginia Slavery Debate of 1832* (Durham, N.C.: Duke Univ. Press, 1941); and Irving Henry Tragle, ed., *The Southampton Slave Revolt of 1831: A Compilation of Source Material* (Amherst: Univ. of Massachusetts Press, 1971); Stephen B. Oates, *The Fires of Jubilee: Nat Turner's Fierce Rebellion* (New York: Harper & Row, 1975); and Alison Goodyear Freehling, *Drift Toward Dissolution: The Virginia Slavery Debate of 1831–1832* (Baton Rouge & London: Louisiana State Univ. Press, 1982).

20. William Lucas to Messrs. Joseph Gales Jr. & William W. Seaton, 2 Dec. 1835, in Gales and Seaton Papers, 1816–57, of the Harry L. Dalton and Mary K. Dalton Collection, Perkins Library, Duke University, Durham, N.C.

21. Hans Rosenberg, *Bureaucracy, Aristocracy, and Autocracy: The Prussian Experience,*

1660–1815 (1958; Boston: Beacon Press, 1966), 222. The bureaucracy's progressive challenge, says Mannheim, gave birth to a defensive alliance between "the social reaction of the nobility," or "feudalistic conservatism," and "the ideological reaction to the Enlightenment," that is, romanticism. Mannheim, "Conservative Thought," 157, 177–82. It was during the Reform era, says Robert M. Berdahl, that "self-concious conservatism first developed among the Prussian nobility." Berdahl, *The Politics of the Prussia. ᵀobility: The Development of a Conservative Ideology, 1770–1848* (Princeton: Princeton Univ. Press, 1988), 131.

22. Neumann, *Die Stufen des preussischen Konservatismus,* 77–79. See also Joachim Maass, *Kleist, A Biography,* trans. from the 1977 German ed. by Ralph Manheim (New York: Farrar, Straus, & Giroux, 1983), ch. 21, "Die Berliner Abendblätter," and Gerhard Ramlow, *Ludwig von der Marwitz und die Anfänge konservativer Politik und Staatsanschauung in Preussen,* Historische Studien, No. 195 (Berlin: Emil Ebering, 1930).

23. Peter Gerrit Thielen, *Karl August von Hardenberg, 1750–1822: Eine Biographie* (Köln & Berlin: G. Grote'sche, 1967), 261.

24. "The earliest systematic defenses of slavery were written by men in Virginia and South Carolina who resided in areas where the black population outnumbered the white." John McCardell, *The Idea of a Southern Nation: Southern Nationalists and Southern Nationalism, 1830–1860* (New York: Norton, 1979), 24. Huburtus Fischer describes mid-century Pomerania and Brandenburg as "the core regions of Prussian conservatism," in large part because Junkers in these provinces benefited most from the tax-exempt status of knight's estates. Fischer, "Konservatismus von unten. Wahlen in ländlichen Preußen 1849/52—Organisation, Agitation, Manipulation," in Dirk Stegmann, Bernd-Jürgen Wendt, and Peter-Christian Witt, eds., *Deutscher Konservatismus im 19. und 20. Jahrhundert: Festschrift für Fritz Fischer zum 75. Geburtstag und zum 50. Doktorjubiläum* (Bonn: Verlag Neue Gesellschaft, 1983), 70, 72.

25. Cited in Mannheim, "Conservative Thought," 183.

26. Radowitz quoted in Wolfgang Scheel, *Das "Berliner Politisches Wochenblatt" und die politische und soziale Revolution in Frankreich und England. Ein Beitrag zur konservativen Zeitkritik in Deutschland,* Göttinger Bausteine zur Geschichtswissenschaft, vol. 36 (Göttingen: Vandenhoeck & Ruprecht, 1964), 21–22.

27. Frieda Peters, *Carl Ernst Jarcke's Staatsanschauung und ihre Geistige Quellen* (Köln: Kölner Verlags-Anstalt und Druckerei, 1926), 8.

28. Carl Ernst Jarcke, "Der Absolutismus" (originally published in the *BPW* in 1832), in his *Vermischte Schriften* (3 vols; München: Verlag der Literarisch-Artistischen Anstalt, 1839), vol. 1, n. on 133–34; and "Revolution und Absolutismus" (*BPW,* 1833), in ibid., 189.

29. On Jarcke's life, see Peters, *Carl Ernst Jarcke's Staatsanschauung,* pp. 7–8, and Jakob Baxa, ed., *Adam Müllers Lebenszeugnisse* (2 vols.; München, Paderborn & Wien: Ferdinand Schöningh, 1966), vol. 2, p. 1023. On the "so-called Cologne troubles," see Hajo Holborn, *A History of Modern Germany, 1648–1840* (1964; rpt. ed., Princeton: Princeton Univ. Press, 1982), 504–6.

30. For example: "The collective concept '*Volk*' is an abstraction that first achieves reality in the organization of the *Stände;* only through his *Stand* does the individual belong to the nation; the *Stände* alone constitute the structure of the nation organized in the

state," as opposed to "the undifferentiated, disjointed mass of individuals with equal rights" posited by "the theoreticians of equality." "Stände, ständisches Repräsentativsystem," in Hermann Wagener, ed., *Staats- und Gesellschafts-Lexikon,* vol. 19 (Berlin: F. Heinicke, 1865), 669.

31. Fischer, "Konservatismus von unten," in Stegmann, Wendt, & Witt, *Deutscher Konservatismus,* 127.

32. "Hermann Wagener," in *Biographisches Wörterbuch zur Deutschen Geschichte,* vol. 3 (München, 1975), 3007–8; William O. Shanahan, *German Protestants Face the Social Question, Volume I: The Conservative Phase* (Notre Dame, Ind.: Univ. of Notre Dame Press, 1954), 303–5 and passim; Eugene N. Anderson, *The Social and Political Conflict in Prussia, 1858–1864* (Lincoln: Univ. of Nebraska Press, 1954), 356; and Adalbert Hahn, *Die Berliner Revue: Ein Beitrag zur Geschichte der konservativen Partei zwischen 1855 and 1875,* Historische Studien, vol. 241 (Berlin: Emil Ebering, 1934), passim; and Hans Rosenberg, *Die nationalpolitische Publizistik Deutschlands: Vom Eintritt der neuen Ära in Preussen bis zum Ausbruch des Deutschen Krieges* (2 vols.; Berlin & München: R. Oldenbourg, 1935), vol. 1, pp. 164–65.

33. Cardozo quoted in Melvin M. Leiman, *Jacob N. Cardozo: Economic Thought in the Antebellum South,* Columbia Studies in the Social Sciences, No. 608 (New York & London: Columbia Univ. Press, 1966), 215; and also in Allen Kaufman, *Capitalism, Slavery, and Republican Values: Antebellum Political Economists, 1819–1848* (Austin: Univ. of Texas Press, 1982), 133.

34. Cardozo quoted in Leiman, *Jacob N. Cardozo,* 202.

35. Holmes quoted in Neal C. Gillespie, *The Collapse of Orthodoxy: The Intellectual Ordeal of George Frederick Holmes* (Charlottesville: Univ. Press of Virginia, 1972), 188. This is an outstanding intellectual biography.

36. Robert A. Nisbet, *The Sociological Tradition* (New York: Basic Books, 1966), 11.

37. Ibid., 14–15, 27–28.

38. Eckart Kehr, "Modern German Historiography," in his *Economic Interest, Militarism, and Foreign Policy: Essays on German History,* ed. Gordon A. Craig, trans. Grete Heinz (Berkeley: Univ. of California Press, 1977), 178.

39. John Chester Miller, *The Wolf by the Ears: Thomas Jefferson and Slavery* (New York: Free Press, 1977), 228.

40. Louis Hartz, *The Liberal Tradition in America: An Interpretation of American Political Thought Since the Revolution* (New York: Harcourt, Brace & World and Harvest Books, 1955), 146–47, in pt. 4, "The Feudal Dream of the South."

41. Klaus Epstein, *The Genesis of German Conservatism* (Princeton: Princeton Univ. Press, 1966), 8–9; and Edmund Burke, *Reflections on the Revolution in France* (1790), ed. Thomas H. D. Mahoney (Indianapolis and New York: Bobbs Merrill and the Liberal Arts Press, 1955), 181.

42. Burke, *Reflections,* 181, 37–38.

43. J. G. A. Pocock, "The Political Economy of Burke's Analysis of the French Revolution," *Historical Journal* 25 (1982), 346.

44. Hartz, *Liberal Tradition in America,* 3–4.

45. Burke defended, says Frank O'Gorman, "the rule of a small, propertied class"

against the threat of "mob rule and anarchy." O'Gorman, *Edmund Burke: His Political Philosophy* (Bloomington: Indiana Univ. Press, 1973), 120.

46. See Isaac Kramnick, *The Rage of Edmund Burke: Portrait of an Ambivalent Conservative* (New York: Basic Books, 1977), 157–65; C. B. Macpherson, *Burke* (New York: Hill and Wang, 1980), ch. 5, "The Bourgeois Political Economist"; and M. Morton Auerbach, *The Conservative Illusion* (New York: Columbia Univ. Press, 1959), 36–37.

47. Burke, "Thoughts on Scarcity" (1795), in Louis I. Bredvold and Ralph G. Ross, eds., *The Philosophy of Edmund Burke: A Selection from His Speeches and Writings* (Ann Arbor: Univ. of Michigan Press, 1960; Ann Arbor Paperbacks, 1967), 28–30.

48. R. R. Palmer, *The Age of the Democratic Revolution: A Political History of Europe and America, 1760–1800* (2 vols.; Princeton: Princeton Univ. Press, 1959–64), vol. 1, p. 336.

49. Burke, *Reflections*, 58, 129, 205, 207.

50. Ibid., 207.

51. Ibid., 126, cf. 186, 228–29.

52. G. E. Mingay, *English Landed Society in the Eighteenth Century* (Toronto: Univ. of Toronto Press, 1953), 167–68, 105.

53. Carl B. Cone, "Edmund Burke, The Farmer," *Agricultural History* 19 (1945), 65–69; the quotation is from p. 69.

54. Letter to Garrett Nagle, June 1779, in John A. Woods, ed., The *Correspondence of Edmund Burke, Volume IV* (Cambridge: Cambridge Univ. Press, and Chicago: Univ. of Chicago Press, 1963), 93. In a footnote the editor writes, "Burke seems somewhat unfair to his tenants. It was generally agreed that because harvests in 1778 and 1779 were plentiful, the price of grain fell and farmers everywhere had genuine difficulties in paying their rents."

55. Auerbach, *Conservative Illusion*, 37.

56. Burke, *Reflections*, 182, 193,

57. Cf. Herbert Dinkel, "Die konservativ Bewegung in Deutschland," in Friedrich Schultes, ed., *Geschichte* (Frankfurt am Main: Fischer Taschenbuch, 1973), 125: ". . . belief in a divine world order, the imperfections and sinfulness of human nature, the inequality of man and consequently (the necessity for) a stratified social order, the necessary distinction between leaders and led, reverence for tradition as the expression of a collective reason, only cautious correction of what has evolved in history, mistrust of theories and abstractions, the importance of property."

58. "Professor Dew on Slavery," 354–55, 410.

59. Dr. William C. Daniell, Chairman, "An Address" to a convention for the organization of an Agricultural Association of the Slaveholding States, in Montgomery, 2 May 1853, in *American Cotton Planter* 2 (Feb. 1854), 33. According to Chalmers Gaston Davidson, Daniell (1792–1868) was one of the "Savannah–South Carolina planters" who "maintained a handsome Savannah residence from profits across the state line." He owned Oglethorpe plantation and 120 slaves in St. Peters' Parish, Beaufort District, and served as mayor of Savannah, a Georgia state representative, and a state senator. He attended Mt. Bethel School in South Carolina, and was taught by Elisha Hammond, Dartmouth graduate and father of James Henry Hammond. He received his M.D. degree from the University of Pennsylvania in 1815. Davidson, *The Last Foray; The South*

Carolina Planters of 1860: A Sociological Study (Columbia: Univ. of South Carolina Press 1971), 68, 188–89, 46.

60. Burke, *Reflections,* 42.

61. Whitemarsh B. Seabrook, *An Essay on the Management of Slaves. and Especially on Their Religious Instruction, Read Before the Agricultural Society of St. John's Colleton* (Charleston: A. E. Miller, 1834), 6.

62. William Gilmore Simms's comments on James Prior's *Life of Edmund Burke* (Boston, 1854), in "Critical Notices," *Southern Quarterly Review* (April 1854), 48.

63. Frank W. Ryan, "The *Southern Quarterly Review,* 1842–1857: A Study of Thought and Opinion in the Old South" (Ph.D. diss., Univ. of N.C. at Chapel Hill, 1956), 407. During Simms's tenure as editor, says Drew Gilpin Faust, the Charleston periodical became "the leading regional publication of the era." Faust, *A Sacred Circle: The Dilemma of the Intellectual in the Old South, 1840–1860* (Baltimore, Md.: Johns Hopkins Univ. Press, 1977), 90.

64. Burke, "Speech in Support of Resolutions for Conciliation with the American Colonies, March 22, 1775," in Elliott Robert Barkan, ed., *Edmund Burke on the American Revolution: Selected Speeches and Letters* (New York: Harper Torchbooks, 1966), 85, and Christopher Gustavus Memminger, *Lecture Delivered Before the Young Men's Library Association, of Augusta, April 10th, 1851, Showing African Slavery to Be Consistent With the Moral and Physical Progress of a Nation* (Augusta, Ga.: W. S. Jones, 1851), 25.

65. Burke, "A Letter to the Right Honourable Henry Dundas, One of His Majesty's Principle Secretaries of State. With the Sketch of a Negro Code" (letter dated "Easter-Monday night,1792"), in *The Works of the Right Honourable Edmund Burke. Vol. V* (London: George Bell and Sons, 1884), 525.

66. Ibid., 524. On Southern responses to the revolt in St. Domingue, see Duncan J. MacLeod, *Slavery, Race and the American Revolution* (Cambridge: Cambridge Univ. Press, 1974), 153–55; and Alfred N. Hunt, *Haiti's Influence on Antebellum America: Slumbering Volcano in the Caribbean* (Baton Rouge & London: Louisiana State Univ. Press, 1988), pp. 107–46.

67. Burke, *Reflections,* 260–61.

68. "Reverie on the Political Crisis of 1860 and 1861 in America," *Southern Monthly* 1 (May 1862), 38.

69. Stephen B. Oates, *Abraham Lincoln: The Man Behind the Myth* (New York: Harper & Row, 1984), 104. On the refusal of all but a few antebellum Southern leaders to consider federal involvement in compensated emancipation, see Betty L. Fladeland, "Compensated Emancipation: A Rejected Alternative," *Journal of Southern History* 42 (1976), 169–86.

70. Ludwig Bergsträsser, *Geschichte der politischen Parteien in Deutschland,* 9th ed. (München & Wien: R. Oldenbourg, 1965), 64 calls Haller "the characteristic theoretician of conservatism for Germany" during the early nineteenth century.

71. See Friedrich Meinecke, *Cosmopolitanism and the National State,* trans. from the 1907 German ed. by Robert B. Kimber (Princeton: Princeton Univ. Press, 1970), ch. 10: "Haller and the Circle of Friedrich Wilhelm IV," and Neumann, *Die Stufen des preussischen Konservatismus,* 79–88.

72. See Shanahan, *German Protestants Face the Social Question,* 241–54, and William

James Orr, Jr., "The Foundation of the *Kreuzzeitung* Party in Prussia, 1848–1850" (Ph. D. diss., University of Wisconsin, 1971), 282–99.

73. Friedrich Julius Stahl, *Die Philosophie des Rechts*, 6th ed., unchanged from the 5th ed. of 1878 (2 vols.; Hildesheim: Georg Ulms, 1965), vol. 1, pp. 553–54.

74. Dr. Julius Stahl, *Die Revolution und die constitutionelle Monarchie, eine Reihe ineinandergreifender Abhandlungen*, 2nd ed. (Berlin: Wilhelm Hertz, 1849), 3–4; the "Foreword to the First Edition" is dated 7 Dec. 1848. Cf. Burke, *Reflections*, 34–35, 42.

75. See Mannheim, "Conservative Thought," 174, and Carl L. Becker, The *Declaration of Independence: A Study in the History of Political Ideas* (1922; New York: Vintage Books, 1942), 255–88.

76. Marwitz quoted in Walter M. Simon, *The Failure of the Prussian Reform Movement, 1807–1819* (Ithaca, N.Y.: Cornell Univ. Press, 1955), 155, and Holmes, "Slavery and Freedom," *Southern Quarterly Review* (April 1856), 89.

77. Edmund Ruffin, *The Political Economy of Slavery; or, The Institution Considered in Regard to Its Influence on Public Wealth and General Welfare* (Washington, D.C.: Lemuel Towers, 1857(?)), 20.

78. William Harper, "Slavery in the Light of Social Ethics," in E. N. Elliott, ed., *Cotton Is King, and Pro-slavery Arguments* (Augusta, Ga.: Pritchard, Abbott & Loomis, 1860; rpt. ed., New York: Negro Universities Press, 1969), 554–55.

79. "Professor Dew on Slavery," 288.

80. Karl Mannheim, *Ideology and Utopia: An Introduction to the Sociology of Knowledge* (1929–31), trans. Louis Wirth and Edward Shils (New York: Harvest Books, 1936), 273.

81. Karl Ludwig von Haller called Rousseau "the most despicable of all the sophists." Haller, *Restauration der Staats-Wissenschaft oder Theorie des natürlich-geselligen Zustands*, 2nd ed. (6 vols.; Winterthur: Steiner, 1820–34), vol. 1, p. xxx.

82. (Baron von Hertefeld), *Grundzüge der conservativen Politik* (Berlin: Ludwig Rauh, 1856), 4–5. On Hertefeld rather than Hermann Wagener as the real author, see Adalbert Hahn, *Die Berliner Revue: Ein Beitrag zur Geschichte der konservativen Partei zwischen 1855 and 1875*, Historische Studien, No. 241 (Berlin: Emil Ebering, 1934), 41, 264.

83. See Carl Wilhelm von Lancizolle, *Ueber Königtum und Landstände in Preussen* (Berlin: Ferdinand Dümmler, 1846), 297.

84. Ruffin, *The Diary of Edmund Ruffin, Vol. I: Toward Independence, October, 1856–April, 1861*, ed. William Kauffman Scarborough (Baton Rouge: Louisiana State Univ. Press, 1972), 238.

85. "A Southron" (Simms?), "Thoughts on Slavery," *Southern Literary Messenger* 4 (Dec. 1838), 742. On Simms as perhaps the author, see David K. Jackson, *The Contributors and Contributions to the Southern Literary Messenger, 1834–1864* (Charlottesville, Va.: Historical Publishing, 1936), 32. See also the discussion of Simms's thought in Faust, *A Sacred Circle*, 119–20.

86. William Cohen, "Thomas Jefferson and the Problem of Slavery," *Journal of American History* 56 (1969), 519.

87. Abel P. Upshur, "Mr. Jefferson," *Southern Literary Messenger* (Sept. 1840), 649.

88. "Reverie on the Political Crisis of 1860 and 1861 in America," 35.

89. See esp. Winthrop D. Jordan, *White over Black: American Attitudes Toward the*

Negro, 1550–1812 (1968; Baltimore: Penguin Books, 1969), ch. 12, "Thomas Jefferson: Self and Society."

90. The most systematic presentation of this line of argument was probably Albert Taylor Bledsoe, LL.D., professor of mathematics in the University of Virginia, "Liberty and Slavery; or, Slavery in the Light of Moral and Political Philosophy" (1856), in Elliott, ed., *Cotton Is King*, esp. 278–310. For a perceptive and somewhat different evaluation of Bledsoe's "redefinition of natural rights," see Eugene D. Genovese, *The Slaveholders' Dilemma: Freedom and Progress in Southern Conservative Thought, 1820–1860* (Columbia: Univ. of South Carolina Press, 1991), 49–54.

91. James Philemon Holcombe, *An Address Delivered Before the Seventh Annual Meeting of the Virginia Agricultural Society, November 4th, 1858* (Richmond, Va.: McFarlane & Ferguson, 1858), 4. For a broad analysis of the rejection of Enlightenment natural-rights theory in proslavery thought, see Jenkins, *Pro-slavery Thought in the Old South*, 125–40.

92. Haller, *Restauration der Staats-Wissenschaften*, vol. 1, pp. 375, 340–41, 351, vol. 6, pp. 561–62, vol. 2, pp. 13–17, 57–60. Carl Ernst Jarcke's essay on the state of nature, originally published in the *Berliner Politisches Wochenblatt* in 1836, is a clear presentation of Haller's ideas. Jarcke, "Über die Entstehung des Staats durch die Natur," in his *Vermischte Schriften*, vol. 3, pp. 32–64.

93. Paul Gaston, *The New South Creed: A Study in Southern Mythmaking* (New York: Alfred A. Knopf, 1970), 213. As Kenneth Stampp emphasizes, "man's hypocrisy is not usually at the conscious level," and human beings have a remarkable "capacity for self-deception and self-justification." Stampp, *The Era of Reconstruction, 1865–1877* (New York: Knopf, 1965; Vintage paperback, 1967), 98.

94. Rev. W. T. Hamilton, D.D., *The Duties of Masters, and Slaves Respectively: or Domestic Servitude as Sanctioned by the Bible: A Discourse, Delivered in the Government-Street Church, Mobile, Alabama, . . . on Sunday Night, December 15th, 1844* (Mobile: F. H. Brooks, 1845), 8, 3–4, 16.

95. *Predigt über Jerm. 18. 7–14. am 18 März 1849 in der evangelische Kirche in Gross-Strehlitz gehalten und dem vaterländischen Vereine hiesigen Ortes auf Verlangen zum Druck überlassen von Pastor C. W. Hoffmann* (Gross-Strehlitz: (?), 1849), 5–6, 12.

96. See John B. Boles, *The Great Revival: The Origins of the Southern Evangelical Mind* (Lexington: Univ. Press of Kentucky, 1972); William G. McLoughlin, *Revivals, Awakenings, and Reform: An Essay on Religion and Social Change in America* (Chicago: Univ. of Chicago Press, 1978), 131–38, "Southern Camp Meetings and the Methodist Contribution to the Awakening."

97. Randolph quoted in Hugh A. Garland, *The Life of John Randolph of Roanoke*, 12th ed. (2 vols. bound in one.; New York: D. Appleton, 1850; rpt. ed., St. Clair Shores, Mich,: Scholarly Press, 1970), vol. 2, p. 99.

98. *Proceedings and Debates of the Virgina State Convention of 1829–1830* (Richmond: Thomas Ritchie, 1830), 411. Both Thompson, of Amherst County, and Randolph, of Charlotte County, lived in the tobacco-growing southern Piedmont. Another county in this area, Lunenburg, has been carefully studied by Richard R. Beeman, who notes that "The Second Great Awakening, rather than being a single explosion of religious piety, appears to have consisted of many ripples of enthusiasm, emanating not from a central source of inspiration, but rather from multitudinous local agencies of evangelism and

stimulated by competition among the growing number of religious sects in America." Beeman, *The Evolution of the Southern Backcountry: A Case Study of Lunenberg County, Virginia, 1746–1832* (Philadelphia: Univ. of Pennsylvania Press, 1984), 193.

99. See Ernst Engleberg, *Bismarck, Urpreuße und Reichsgründer* (Berlin: Siedler, 1985), 183–84; Berdahl, *Politics of the Prussian Nobility*, esp. 246–63; Robert M. Bigler, *The Politics of German Protestantism: The Rise of the Protestant Church Elite in Prussia, 1815–1848* (Berkeley: Univ. of California Press, 1972), 127–29, 140–41. As Bigler points out, the Pomeranian Awakening was part of a broader "Protestant North German 'Awakening.'" Bruno Schumacher, *Geschichte Ost- und Westpreussens*, 4th ed., ed. Göttingen Arbeitskreis (Würzburg: Holzner, 1959), 268–69, writes that during the 1820s "a strong mystical-pietist movement" spread from Königsberg out into old East Prussia.

100. Carl Büchsel, *My Ministerial Experiences* (London: Alexander Strahan, 1863), 63–64, 245. In the preface Büchsel says that the book first appeared in German, at the request of editor Ernst Wilhelm Hengstenberg, as a series of sketches in the religiously and politically conservative *Evangelischen Kirchen-Zeitung*, founded in 1827 by Hengstenberg, whom William O. Shanahan describes as symbolizing "the worst aspects of 'throne' and 'altar' politics." Shanahan, *German Protestants Face the Social Question*, 101–2. On Buchsel, see Hermann Strathmann's sketch in *Neue Deutsche Biographie*, vol. 2 (Berlin: Duncker & Humblot, 1955), 722–23. Ernst Schubert, *Die evangelische Predigt im Revolutionsjahre 1848: Ein Beitrag zur Geschichte der Predigt wie zum Problem der Zeitpredigt* (Giesen: Alfred Töpelman, 1913), 5, identifies Büchsel as the preacher of an antirevolutionary sermon on 19 March 1848 at the Berlin *Matthäikirche*, where he served as pastor from 1846 to 1853.

101. The optimistic, Enlightenment faith in mankind's secular future found its political corollary in the natural-law doctrine of inherent human rights, based on the beliefs that "reason is of divine origin," and that every person is endowed with "the rational ability to overcome his sensuous nature." Hajo Holborn, "German Idealism in the Light of Social History," trans. Robert Edwin Herzstein, in Holborn, *Germany and Europe: Historical Essays* (Garden City, N.Y.: Anchor Books, 1970), 20.

102. "The peculiarly nonabstract religious frame of mind that prevailed in the Old South," with its "personal, provincial, pietistic emphasis on the work of God in the hearts of individuals," promoted an unfriendly, critical attitude toward "societal worldliness." Boles, *The Great Revival*, 140–42. See also Donald G. Mathews, *Religion in the Old South* (Chicago: Univ. of Chicago Press, 1977), esp. 62–80. The neo-Pietist movement in Prussia "emphasized the traditional Lutheran and Pietist concept of man's sinful nature and his moral duty to subordinate himself to the God-given worldly order." Bigler, *The Politics of German Protestantism*, 46–47. See also Neumann, *Die Stufen des preussischen Konservatismus*, 87–88, 109–10.

103. My thinking on the distinction between doctrinaire proslavery ideologues and pragmatic planters has been strongly influenced by Faust, *A Sacred Circle*, esp. 59, 107–31, 147–48. Cf. Faust, *James Henry Hammond and the Old South: A Design for Mastery* (Baton Rouge & London: Louisiana State Univ. Press, 1982). See also John R. Welsh, "William Gilmore Simms, Critic of the Old South," *Journal of Southern History* 26 (1960), 201–14; Eugene D. Genovese, *The World the Slaveholders Made: Two Essays in Interpetation* (New York: Vintage Books, 1969), Part II, "The Logical Outcome of the Slave-

holders' Philosophy"; David Donald, "The Proslavery Argument Reconsidered," *Journal of Southern History* 38 (1971), 12–17; Donald G. Mathews, "Charles Colcock Jones and the Southern Evangelical Crusade to Form a Biracial Community," *Journal of Southern History* 3 (1975), 299–320; Robert J. Brugger, *Beverly Tucker: Heart over Head in the Old South* (Baltimore: Johns Hopkins Univ. Press, 1978), esp. 107–10, 198–209; and Bertram Wyatt-Brown, "Proslavery and Antislavery Intellectuals: Class Concepts and Polemical Struggle," in Lewis Perry and Michael Fellman, eds., *Antislavery Reconsidered: New Perspectives on the Abolitionists* (Baton Rouge: Louisiana State Univ. Press, 1979), 308–36. The distinction between principled and materialistic conservatives is long and well established in scholarship on the Junkers. See Erich Jordan, *Die Entstehung der konservativen Partei und die preussischen Agrarverhältnisse von 1848* (München and Leipzig: Duncker & Humblot, 1914), esp. 254–74; Mannheim, "Conservative Thought," 183–86; Neumann, *Die Stufen des preussischen Konservatismus*, esp. 54, 66, 111; Gerhard Ramlow, *Ludwig von der Marwitz und die Anfänge konservativer Politik und Staatsanschauung in Preussen*, Historische Studien, No. 195 (Berlin: Emil Ebering, 1930), esp. 78–80; Hans-Joachim Schoeps, *Das andere Preussen: Konservative Gestalten und Probleme im Zeitalter Friedrich Wilhelms IV*, 3rd ed. (Berlin: Haude und Spenersche Verlagsbuchhandlung, 1964), esp. 54–62; Marjorie Lamberti, "The Rise of the Prussian Conservative Party, 1840–1858" (Ph.D. diss., Yale University, 1966), esp. 157, 232–33, 284–85; Orr, "Foundation of the Kreuzzeitung Party," esp. 48, 94–97, 117–28; and Fischer, "Konservatismus von unten," in Stegmann, Wendt, and Witt, eds., *Deutscher Konservertismus*, 74–76.

104. There were, to be sure, doctrinaire planters and Junkers who were also "improving," even innovative owners of plantations and *Rittergüter*, men who tended to see economic progress as essential to cultural advance: for example, Edmund Ruffin and James Henry Hammond in the South, Ludwig von der Marwitz and Ernst von Senfft-Pilsach in East Elbia.

105. Faust, *A Sacred Circle*, 93.

106. Edward Shils, "The Intellectuals and the Powers: Some Perspectives for Comparative Analysis," *Comparative Studies in Society and History* 1 (1958), 9, 18.

107. Welsh, "William Gilmore Simms," 201, 208, and Jon L. Wakelyn, *The Politics of a Literary Man: William Gilmore Simms*, Contributions in American Studies, No. 5 (Westport, Conn.: Greenwood Press, 1973), 188.

108. Faust, *James Henry Hammond and the Old South*, 226, and Faust, *A Sacred Circle*, 30.

109. Welsh, "William Gilmore Simms," 205, 209.

110. Simms, "Miss Martineau on Slavery," *Southern Literary Messenger* 3 (Nov. 1837), 647.

111. Simms, "The Morals of Slavery," in *Pro-slavery Argument*, 177–78. Simms had the following to say about the slaveholders' gentility: "Their grace of manner, courteous bearing, gentleness of deportment, studious forbearance and unobtrusiveness—their social characteristics, in general—all assumed to spring from the peculiar institution of Negro Slavery as affording superior time, as well as leisure, to the controlling race—are usually admitted without question." Ibid., 185.

112. Fontane did not publish his first novel until 1878, and thereupon became "the

first German novelist since Goethe to enjoy a European reputation." Gordon A. Craig, *Germany, 1866–1945* (New York: Oxford Univ. Press, 1978), 217.

113. "Although a moderate liberal by conviction, his (Fontane's) feelings about the 1848 Revolution were ambiguous, and from 1850 onwards he moved mainly in conservative circles." Eda Sagarra, *Tradition and Revolution: German Literature and Society, 1830–1890* (London: Weidenfeld and Nicolson, 1971), 271.

114. Ernst K. Bramsted, *Aristocracy and the Middle Classes in Germany: Social Types in German Literature, 1840–1890*, rev. ed. (Chicago: Univ. of Chicago Press, 1964), 266.

115. Theodor Fontane, *Wanderungen durch die Mark Brandenburg, Vierter Teil. Spreeland: Beeskow-Storkow und Barnim-Teltow*, 15th-17th ed. (Stuttgart & Berlin: J. G. Cotta'sche Buchhandlung Nachfolger, 1920), "Schlusswort," 453. On this page Fontane gives credit to "my co-workers," "first of all the old families of the Mark."

116. Fontane quoted in Bramsted, *Aristocracy and the Middle Classes in Germany*, 265. On Fontane, see also Kurt Schreinert's biographical sketch in *Neue Deutsche Biographie*, vol. 5 (Berlin: Duncker & Humblot, 1961), 289–93.

117. Fontane, 10 June 1884 letter, in *Fontane Brief in Zwei Bänden*, ed. Gotthard Erler (2 vols., Berlin and Weimar: Aufbau-Verlag, 1968), vol. 2, pp. 128–29. In a 14 Aug. 1893 letter to writer Theodor Hermann Pontenius, Fontane said that he had been greatly influenced as a writer by Walter Scott, Ludwig von der Marwitz's *Memoirs*, Droysen's biography of York, Macaulay, Holberg's history of Denmark, and Büchsel's *Errinerungen*. Ibid., 309–10.

118. Perhaps the best-known pastor-planter was Baptist Thornton Stringfellow (1788–1869) of Virginia, author of *A Brief Examination of Scripture Testimony on the Institution of Slavery* (1841); he was the son of a well-to-do slaveholder, and himself owned 2000 acres near Fredericksburg when the Civil War began. See Drew Gilpin Faust, ed., *The Ideology of Slavery: Proslavery Thought in the Antebellum South, 1830–1860* (Baton Rouge: Louisiana State Univ. Press, 1981), 136–38. Another prime example of an outspokenly proslavery minister-planter was the North Carolina-born Baptist Basil Manly (1798–1868), who served as president of the University of Alabama from 1837 to 1855, and became pastor of the First Baptist Church in Montgomery, Ala., in December of 1860, just before being elected a delegate to Alabama's secession convention in January of 1861 and serving as chaplain at the inauguration of Jefferson Davis in February. At the time he owned cotton land in Tuscaloosa and Lowndes counties, and owned at least 20 slaves, some of which he had inherited from his father in 1824. See Harold Wilson, "Basil Manly, Apologist for Slaveocracy," *Alabama Review* 15 (Jan. 1962), 38–53, and W. Stanley Hoole, ed., "The Diary of Dr. Basil Manly, 1858–1867," in five parts, *Alabama Review* 4 and 5 (1951–52).

119. For suggestions to this effect, see David M. Potter, *The Impending Crisis, 1848–1861*, ed. Don E. Fehrenbacher (New York: Harper & Row, 1976), 226, and Mannheim, "Conservative Thought," 138–39: "As soon as parliamentary life begins, the definite contours of *Weltanschauung* and ideologies rapidly lose their sharpness."

120. See Richard Schult, "Partei wider Willen. Kalküle und Potentiale konservativer Parteigründer in Preußen zwischen Erstem Vereinigten Landtag und Nationalversammlung (1847/48)," in Stegmann, Wendt, and Witt, eds., *Deutscher Konservatismus*, 60–61; and Lothar Gall, *Bismarck: The White Revolutionary. Volume I, 1815–1871*, trans.

from the 1980 German ed. by J. A. Underwood (London: Allen and Unwin, 1986), xvi, 50–52.

121. According to Percy Rainwater, "professional men and small slaveholders, 'planters on the make,' " were the driving force behind secession in Mississippi's secession convention. Rainwater, *Storm Center of Secession, 1856–61* (1938; rpt. ed. New York: Da Capo Press, 1969), 203. Likewise, William L. Barney has concluded that "The young slaveholding planters, farmers, and lawyers of the Breckinridge Democrats, the most ambitious and dynamic elements in the South's political economy, were the first to perceive the crisis and they reacted most intensely to it." Barney, *The Secessionist Impulse: Alabama and Mississippi in 1860* (Princeton: Princeton Univ. Press, 1974), 313. Cf. Barney, *The Passage of the Republic: An Interdiscipinary History of Nineteenth-Century America* (Lexington, Mass.: D. C. Heath, 1987), 208–9. John McCardell suggests that these generational differences were anticipated during the South Carolina nullification controversy of 1828–33, in that the Southern nationalists among the Nullifiers were younger than either the Calhounite Nullifiers or the Unionists. McCardell, *The Idea of a Southern Nation*, 38–39.

122. Some fascinating insights into the idealistic defenses of slavery expressed by Jefferson Davis are provided by William C. Davis, *Jefferson Davis: The Man and His Hour* (New York: Harper Collins, 1991), esp. 180.

123. Heinrich Berghaus, *Landbuch der Mark Brandenburg und des Markgrafthums Nieder-Lausitz in der Mitte des 19. Jahrhunderts* (3 vols., Berlin: Adolph Müller, 1854–56), vol. 3, p. 409; K. Fr. Rauer, *Alphabetischer Nachweis (Adressbuch) des in den Preussischen Staaten mit Rittergütern angesessenen Adels* (Berlin: Durch die Herausgeber, 1857), 70. On the Gerlachs' lives and careers, see Hans-Joachim Schoeps, "von Gerlach," in *Neue Deutsche Biographie*, vol. 6 (Berlin: Duncker & Humblot, 1964), 294–99; and Helmut Diwald, "Einleitung" to Diwald, ed., *Von der Revolution zum Norddeutschen Bund. Politik und Ideengut der preussischen Hochkonservativen, 1848–1866. Aus dem Nachlass von Ernst Ludwig von Gerlach*, Deutsche Geschichtsquellen des 19. and 20. Jahrhundert, vol. 46 (2 vols.; Göttingen: Vandenhoeck & Ruprecht, 1970), vol. 1, pp. 9–70.

124. For an excellent account of the Junker Parliament, see Klatte, "Die Anfänge des Agrarkapitalismus und der preussische Konservatismus," 247–72. For a useful East German account that downplays the doctrinaire-pragmatic tension, see Gerhard Becker, "Die Beschlüsse des preussichen Junkerparlaments von 1848," *Zeitschrift für Geschichtswissenschaft* 24 (1976), 889–918.

125. Orr, "The Foundation of the Kreuzzeitung Party in Prussia," 124–26. The phrase "gross materialism" comes from a letter which von Thadden wrote to von Gerlach on 15 August; he applied the phrase to the organizers of the "assembly in Berlin announced by von Bülow-Cummerow" because of their willingness "to take away the manorial lord's civil rights *(die gutsherrlichen Ehrenrechte)*." Diwald, ed., *Von der Revolution zum Norddeutschen Bund*, vol. 2, p. 563.

126. Gerlach's short speech was originally published in the *Kreuzzeitung (Neue Preussische Zeitung)*, no. 44 (20 Aug. 1848), *Beilage*. It is reprinted in Gerlach, *Aufzeichnungen asu seinem Leben und Wirken, 1795–1877*, ed. Jakob von Gerlach (2 vols.; Schwerin: Verlag von Fr. Bahn, 1903), vol. 1, pp. 540–41; and in Diwald, ed., *Von der Revolution zum Nordeutschen Bund*, vol. 1, pp. 53–54.

127. Marjorie Lamberti concludes that during and after the 1848–49 revolution the "center of gravity" among conservatives "lay with those who made modest concessions to the demands for constitutional monarchy and libertarian reforms." Lamberti, "The Rise of the Prussian Conservative Party," 177.

128. Von Heyden's 27 April speech, in Eduard Bleich, ed., *Der Erste Vereinigte Landtag in Berlin 1847. Zweiter Teil* (Vaduz/Liechtenstein: Topos Verlag AG, 1977), 109.

129. Bülow-Cummerow's speech was originally published in the *Kreuzzeitung*, no. 45 (22 Aug. 1848), *Beilage;* and is reprinted in Hans Fenske, ed., *Vormärz und Revolution, 1840–1849* (Darmstadt: Wissenschaftliche Buchgesellschaft, 1976), 332–40.

130. The two "pet ideas *(Lieblings-Ideen)* of the year 1848," said Stahl, were "guaranteed employment and head-count voting." Friedrich Julius Stahl, "Rede wider die Wahlen nach Kopfzahl" (7 Sept. 1849), in his *Siebzehn parlamentarische Reden und drei Vorträge von Stahl. Nach letztwilliger Bestimmung geordnet und herauggegeben* (Berlin: Wilhelm Hertz, 1862), 166–67. On the success of such appeals in winning the cooperation of well-to-do peasants against propertyless agricultural laborers, see Hartmut Harnisch, "Probleme junkerlicher Agrarpolitik im 19. Jahrhundert," *Wissenschaftliche Zeitschrift der Universität Rostock* 21 (1972), 109–12.

131. *Stenographische Berichte über die Verhandlungen der zur Vereinbarung der preussischen Staats-Verfassung berufenen Versammlung* (3 vols.; Berlin: Deckerschen Geheimen Ober-Hofbuchdruckerei, 1848), vol. 3, pp. 1824–25. On the *Fleischzehnt* in Brandenburg from the fifteenth to seventeenth century, see Carl Brinkmann, *Wustrau, Wirtschafts- und Verfassungsgeschichte eines brandenburgischen Ritterguts*, Staats- und sozialwissenschaftliche Forschungen, No. 155 (Leipzig: Duncker & Humblot, 1911), 4, 32.

132. James Oakes, *Slavery and Freedom: An Interpretation of the Old South* (New York: Alfred Knopf, 1990), 60, 176. "(I)n the liberal-capitalist world the southern masters inhabited, proslavery thought focused most often on the primacy of rights—with particular fidelity to the rights of property." Ibid., 174.

133. See Hannah Schissler, *Preussische Agrargesellschaft im Wandel: Wirtschaftliche, gesellschaftliche und politische Transformationsprozesse von 1763 bis 1847*, Kritische Studien zur Geschichtswissenschaft, vol. 33 (Göttingen: Vandenhoeck & Ruprecht, 1978), 162–63, 198. Mack Walker has determined that from 1824 to 1848 the Kingdom of Prussia had a surplus net immigration of 769,215, but that the post-1850 emigration was greater from the eastern provinces than from the western provinces. During the years 1849–66 perhaps two-thirds of Prussian migrants went to the cities and the remainder to America. Walker, *Germany and the Emigration, 1816–1885* (Cambridge, Mass.: Harvard Univ. Press, 1964), 55–56, 165–67.

134. See especially Robert William Fogel, *Without Consent or Contract: The Rise and Fall of American Slavery* (New York & London: W. W. Norton, 1989), 63–64.

135. Gavin Wright, *The Political Economy of the Cotton South: Households, Markets, and Wealth in the Nineteenth Century* (New York: Norton, 1978), 141–50.

136. Potter, *The Impending Crisis*, 455.

137. (Burgwyn), *Considerations Relative to a Southern Confederacy, With Letters to the North, on the Preservation of the Union, and a Note from the Secret History of the Emancipation in the West Indies. By a Citizen of North Carolina* (Raleigh: Standard Office, 1860), 4. *Considerations* originally appeared in the Raleigh newspaper *North Carolina Standard*,

28 March 1860; see Joseph Carlyle Sitterson, *The Secession Movement in North Carolina,* James Sprunt Studies in History and Political Science, Vol. 23, No. 2 (Chapel Hill: Univ. of North Carolina Press, 1939), 160. This Burgwyn was the "improving" wheat planter whom we met in Chapter 2.

138. William Henry Holcombe, *The Alternative: A Separate Nationality, or the Africanization of the South* (n.p., 1860), soon reprinted in *Southern Literary Messenger* 32 (Feb. 1861), 81–88. See also his "Characteristics and Capabilities of the Negro Race," *Southern Literary Messenger* 33 (Dec. 1861), 401–10, and his "Sketches of Plantation Life," *The Knickerbocker* 57 (June 1861), 619–33. Holcombe (1825–93) was born in Lynchburg, Virginia, the son of Dr. William James Holcombe, an antislavery Methodist physician who, after freeing his slaves and helping them move to Liberia and Ohio, moved to Indiana in 1842. William Henry attended Washington College and graduated from the medical department of the University of Pennsylvania in 1847. After practicing medicine for a few years in Cincinnati, he married Rebecca Palmer in 1852, and moved to Natchez to practice in association with Dr. F. A. W. Davis. From 1855 to 1862 he lived at the river town of Waterproof, in Louisiana's Tensas Parish; and in 1860 he owned three slaves (ages 20 to 30, two females and one male). He returned to Natchez in 1862, and then moved to New Orleans two years later. His brother, James P. Holcombe, was the law professor at the University of Virginia whom we met in Chapter 5. William H.'s autobiography and diary notes are in the Southern Historical Collection of the University of North Carolina at Chapel Hill. For his ownership of three slaves in 1860, see Louisiana Slave Schedules for 1860, National Archives Microfilm Publications, Microcopy No. 653 (Washington, D.C., 1967).

139. Schumann, "The Problem of Conservatism," 807.

Epilogue

1. Eric Foner, *A Short History of Reconstruction, 1863–1877* (New York: Harper & Row, 1990), 254.

2. This contrast between planters and Junkers is emphasized by Stephen Hahn, "Class and State in Postemancipation Societies: Southern Planters in Comparative Perspective," *American Historical Review* 95 (1990), esp. 89–98.

3. Gerhard Ritter, *Die preussischen Konservativen und Bismarcks deutsche Politik, 1858–1876* (Heidelberg: C. Winter 1913), 7–8, 32–33, 35.

4. Robert M. Berdahl, "Conservative Politics and Aristocratic Landholders in Bismarckian Germany," *Journal of Modern History* 44 (1972), 7–14; Gordon A. Craig, *Germany, 1866–1945* (New York: Oxford Univ. Press, 1977), 66–67; and Otto Pflanze, *Bismarck and the Development of Germany, Volume II: The Period of Consolidation, 1871–1880* (Princeton: Princeton Univ. Press, 1990), 208–13.

5. Michael Stürmer, "Konservatismus und Revolution in Bismarcks Politik," in Stürmer, ed., *Das kaiserliche Deutschland: Politik und Gesellschaft, 1870–1918* (Düsseldorf: Droste Verlag, 1970), 143; and Stürmer, "Bismarck in Perspective," *Central European History* 4 (1971), 331. Otto Pflanze evaluates Bismarck's unification of Germany as "but the last of a long series of revolutionary acts by the Hohenzollern monarchy, its ministers and officials, stretching over a period of two centuries." Pflanze, *Bismarck and the Development*

of Germany, Volume III: The Period of Fortification (Princeton: Princeton Univ. Press, 1990), 431.

6. Hans Rosenberg, "Die Pseudodemocratisierung der Rittergutsbesitzerklasse," in his *Probleme der deutschen Sozialgeschichte* (Frankfurt am Main: Suhrkamp Verlag, 1969), 35.

7. Speech by retired *Landrat* Goßler in the *Posener Tageblatt*, 17 June 1912, cited in William W. Hagen, *German, Poles, and Jews: The Nationality Conflict in the Prussian East, 1772–1914* (Chicago & London: Univ. of Chicago Press, 1980), 280. On the emergence of "a new ruling class" which fused old agrarian and new industrial elites, see Pflanze, *Bismarck and the Development of Germany, Volume III*, 13.

8. See especially Hans-Jürgen Puhle, "Radikalisierung und Wandel der deutschen Konservatismus vor dem ersten Weltkrieg," in Gerhard A. Ritter, ed., *Deutsche Parteien vor 1918*, Neue Wissenschaftliche Bibliothek, vol. 61 (Köln & Berlin: Kiepenhauer & Witsch, 1973), 174–79, and Puhle, "Lords and Peasants in the Kaiserreich," in Robert G. Moeller, ed., *Peasants and Lords in Modern Germany: Recent Studies in Agricultural History* (Boston: Allen & Unwin, 1986), 81–109. "The Conservative Party and the Agrarian League stood for 'the agrarian interest'—not only that of the noble, but equally that of the bourgeois landlords who owned about half or more of the 12,000 knight's estates." F. L. Carsten, *A History of the Prussian Junkers* (Aldershot, Eng.: Scolar Press, 1989), 148.

9. Of 1,348 *Fideikommisse* in Prussia in 1918, almost 62% percent, or 829, had been established since 1850. As Max Weber argued in 1904, family trust entails had become for wealthy businessmen in Imperial Germany "a specifically modern-capitalistic form of income creation, serving much the same purpose as interest-bearing bonds." *Fideikommisse* preferred precisely those provinces where the "purely capitalistic character of agricultural estates" was most pronounced, and where a high degree of industrial development had served to drive up ground rents. Max Weber, "Agrarstatistische und sozialpolitische Betractungen zur Fideikommisse in Preussen," in his *Gesammelte Aufsätze zur Soziologie und Socialpolitik* (Tübingen: J. C. B. Mohr (Paul Siebeck), 1924), 329–31. Despite the decrees of 1919 calling for the end of family trust entails, their actual abolition and conversion into allodial property proceeded very slowly during the Weimar years. I have explored this topic in "Prussian *Fideikommisse* and the German Revolution of 1918/19" (unpublished seminar paper, University of California at Berkeley, 1975).

10. Shelly Baranowski, "Continuity and Contingency: Agrarian Elites, Conservative Institutions, and East Elbia in Modern German History," *Social History* 12 (1987), 290–97. F. L. Carsten notes that most peasants "left the representation of their interests to the big landowners." However, "The agricultural workers were no longer passive and willing to submit to the landlords, but the latter retained the upper hand with the help of the police, the army and the Freecorps; workmen who actively defended their interests could always be blacklisted." Carsten, *A History of the Prussian Junkers*, 155, 158.

11. Baranowski, "Continuity and Contingency," 306–8.

12. Larry Eugene Jones, "Crisis and Realignment: Agrarian Splinter Parties in the Late Weimar Republic," in Moeller, ed., *Peasants and Lords in Modern Germany*, 224. Carsten emphasizes that Hindenburg became much more sympathetic to Junker agrarians after receiving the estate Neudeck as a gift in 1927. Most of the money collected for

the purchase and renovation of the estate came from industrialists. Carsten, *A History of the Prussian Junkers,* 163–64.

13. See Karl Dietrich Bracher, "Stages of Totalitarian 'Integration' *(Gleichschaltung):* The Consolidation of National Socialist Rule in 1933 and 1934," in Hajo Holborn, ed. *Republic to Reich: The Making of the Nazi Revolution. Ten Essays,* trans. Ralph Manheim (New York: Vintage Books, 1972), 109–28.

14. Law No. 47, passed by the Allied Control Commission on 25 Feb. 1947, cited in Manfred Schlenke, "Vom Ende and vom Fortleben Preußens," in Schlenke, ed., *Preußsen-Ploetz: Eine historische Bilanz in Daten und Deutungen* (Freiburg/Würzburg: Verlag Ploetz, 1983), 268.

15. Arnold Brecht, *Federalism and Regionalism in Germany: The Division of Prussia* (New York: Oxford Univ. Press, 1945), 133.

16. "To the extent that American slavery had eliminated the need for a large, white, dependent, landless laboring class that would have made the espousal of republican beliefs much more dangerous (and perhaps impossible) for members of the revolutionary elite like Jefferson," emphasizes Drew McCoy, "it played an important, though unacknowleged, role in the formation of the Jeffersonian perspective." McCoy, *The Elusive Republic: Political Economy in Jeffersonian America* (1980; New York & London: W. W. Norton, 1982), 250–51, drawing upon the work of Edmund Morgan discussed in Chapter 4 of this book.

17. James Oakes, *The Ruling Race: A History of American Slaveholders* (New York: Knopf, 1982).

18. Jack Temple Kirby, "Plantations," in Charles Reagan Wilson and William Ferris, eds., *Encyclopedia of Southern Culture* (Chapel Hill & London: Univ. of North Carolina Press, 1989), 27, and Harold D. Woodman, "Economic Reconstruction and the Rise of the New South, 1865–1900," in John B. Boles and Evelyn Thomas Nolen, eds., *Interpreting Southern History: Historiographical Essays in Honor of Sanford W. Higginbotham* (Baton Rouge & London: Louisiana State Univ. Press, 1987), 277.

19. This terminology comes from Gavin Wright, *Old South, New South: Revolutions in the Southern Economy Since the Civil War* (New York: Basic Books, 1986), ch. 2.

20. The quotation is from Michael Perman, *The Road to Redemption: Southern Politics, 1869–1879* (Chapel Hill & London: Univ. of North Carolina Press, 1984), 242. On sharecropping and tenancy, see Gilbert C. Fite, *Cotton Fields No More: Southern Agriculture, 1865–1980* (Lexington: Univ. Press of Kentucky, 1984), 3–6.

21. George Brown Tindall, *The Emergence of the New South, 1913–1945,* A History of the South, Vol. X (Baton Rouge: Louisiana State Univ. Press, 1967), 410.

22. The percentages are from ibid., 409–10. As Ransom and Sutch have argued, anti-black racism "permeated the southern economy" and "distorted the economic institutions of the South" for whites as well as blacks. Roger L. Ransom and Richard Sutch, *One Kind of Freedom: The Economic Consequences of Emancipation* (Cambridge: Cambridge Univ. Press, 1977), 177. That racial prejudice constituted an economic impediment to black sharecroppers is well illustrated in Nate Shaw's first-hand experience in the early 1910s. "Colored man's cotton weren't worth as much as white man's cotton less'n it come to the buyer in white man's hands." Theodore Rosengarten, *All God's Dangers: The Life of Nate Shaw* (New York: Avon Books, 1974), 200.

23. For the rich and contentious literature on Populism, including the seminal work of C. Vann Woodward, see Richard L. Watson, Jr., "From Populism Through the New Deal: Southern Political History," in Boles and Nolen, eds., *Interpreting Southern History*, 310–29.

24. J. Morgan Kousser, *The Shaping of Southern Politics: Suffrage Restriction and the Establishment of the One-Party South, 1880–1910* (New Haven: Yale Univ. Press, 1974), 224.

25. Ibid., 173, and Beth Barton Schweiger, "Putting Politics Aside: Virginia Democrats and Voter Apathy in the Age of Disfranchisement," Edward L. Ayers and John C. Willis, eds., *The Edge of the South: Life in Nineteenth-Century Virginia* (Charlottesville & London: Univ. Press of Virginia, 1991), 204–5.

26. Richmond *Dispatch* cited in Virginius Dabney, *Virginia: The New Dominion* (Garden City, N.Y.: Doubleday, 1971), 430–31. Also at the turn of the century, the General Assembly voted to mandate racial segregation on railroads, streetcars, and steamboats.

27. Allen W. Moger, *Virginia from Bourbonism to Byrd, 1870–1925* (Charlottesville: Univ. Press of Virginia, 1968), 193. Schweiger, "Putting Politics Aside," in Ayers and Willis, eds., *The Edge of the South,* 211, emphasizes that the new restrictions of 1902 only "accelerated the trend of nonparticipation among state voters."

28. George E. Mowry, *Another Look at the Twentieth-Century South* (Baton Rouge: Louisiana State Univ. Press, 1973), 72. For other helpful evaluations of the evolving Southern elite, see Woodman, "Economic Reconstruction and the Rise of the New South, 1865–1900," in Boles and Nolen, eds., *Interpreting Southern History*, 279–81, and Foner, *Short History of Reconstruction*, esp. 176.

29. Mowry, *Another Look at the Twentieth-Century South*, 85, and Ulrich Bonnell Phillips, *The Course of the South to Secession*, ed. E. Merton Coulter (1939; New York: Hill and Wang, 1964), 152.

30. Russell R. Menard, "Plantation System," in Randall M. Miller and John David Smith, eds., *Dictionary of Afro-American Slavery* (New York: Greenwood Press, 1988), 582.

31. Pete Daniel, *Standing at the Crossroads: Southern Life Since 1900* (New York: Hill and Wang, 1986), 122.

32. See Jack Temple Kirby, *Rural Worlds Lost: The American South, 1920–1960* (Baton Rouge & London: Louisiana State Univ. Press, 1987), part I, "Transformations." Gavin Wright notes that "Mechanization of the tobacco harvest was also within technical reach as of the early 1950s, if not before. But mechanization was delayed until the 1970s by limitations on the size of farming operations, limitations that were institutionalized in the tobacco allotment system dating from 1938." Wright, *Old South, New South*, 248.

33. See Charles Reagan Wilson, "Agribusiness," in Reagan and Wilson, eds., *Encyclopedia of Southern Culture*, 14–15.

Index